LEADERSHIP FOR LAWYERS

ASPEN SELECT SERIES

LEADERSHIP FOR LAWYERS
Third Edition

Deborah L. Rhode
Ernest W. McFarland Professor of Law
Director, Center on the Legal Profession
Stanford Law School

Wolters Kluwer

Published by Wolters Kluwer in New York.

Wolters Kluwer Legal & Regulatory U.S. serves customers worldwide with CCH, Aspen Publishers, and Kluwer Law International products. (www.WKLegaledu.com)

Cover Image: iStock.com/oversnap

To contact Customer Service, e-mail customer.service@wolterskluwer.com, call 1-800-234-1660, fax 1-800-901-9075, or mail correspondence to:

Wolters Kluwer
Attn: Order Department
PO Box 990
Frederick, MD 21705

Printed in the United States of America.

2 3 4 5 6 7 8 9 0

ISBN 978-1-5438-2001-0

SUSTAINABLE FORESTRY INITIATIVE

Certified Chain of Custody
Promoting Sustainable Forestry

www.sfiprogram.org

Names: Rhode, Deborah L., author.
Title: Leadership for lawyers / Deborah L. Rhode, Ernest W. McFarland Professor of Law, Director, Center on the Legal Profession, Stanford Law School.
Description: Third edition. | New York : Wolters Kluwer, 2020. | Includes index. | Summary: "A course book for leadership classes in law school that includes excerpts from leadership publications, background material, practical problems and case histories, class exercises, and bibliographic and media references in areas of core leadership competencies"-- Provided by publisher.
Identifiers: LCCN 2019055407 (print) | LCCN 2019055408 (ebook) | ISBN 9781543820010 (paperback) | ISBN 9781543820966 (ebook)
Subjects: LCSH: Practice of law--United States. | Leadership--United States.
Classification: LCC KF300 .R46 2020 (print) | LCC KF300 (ebook) | DDC 340.068/4--dc23
LC record available at https://lccn.loc.gov/2019055407
LC ebook record available at https://lccn.loc.gov/2019055408

About Wolters Kluwer Legal & Regulatory U.S.

Wolters Kluwer Legal & Regulatory U.S. delivers expert content and solutions in the areas of law, corporate compliance, health compliance, reimbursement, and legal education. Its practical solutions help customers successfully navigate the demands of a changing environment to drive their daily activities, enhance decision quality and inspire confident outcomes.

Serving customers worldwide, its legal and regulatory portfolio includes products under the Aspen Publishers, CCH Incorporated, Kluwer Law International, ftwilliam.com and MediRegs names. They are regarded as exceptional and trusted resources for general legal and practice-specific knowledge, compliance and risk management, dynamic workflow solutions, and expert commentary.

For Christine Rhode

SUMMARY OF CONTENTS

TABLE OF CONTENTS

ACKNOWLEDGMENTS

This book grows out of research and teaching supported by Stanford Law School's Center on the Legal Profession. For assistance on this third edition, I am deeply indebted to the superb research and editorial assistance of Eun Sze and Alexandra Willingham, and also to the staff of the Stanford Law Library, particularly Shay Elbaum, Taryn Marks, Marion Miller, Sonia Moss, Katie Ott, Rich Porter, Kevin Rothenberg, Sergio Stone, Beth Williams, and George Wilson. I am also indebted to my Stanford Law School colleagues Diane Chin and Michael Callahan. The book is dedicated to my sister, Christine Rhode, who has taught me so much about the qualities necessary for leadership and so much else.

We gratefully acknowledge the permission granted by the authors, publishers, and organizations to reprint portions of the following copyrighted materials:

Adut, Ari, On Scandal: Moral Disturbances in Society, Politics, and Art (2008). Copyright © Ari Adut. Reprinted with the permission of Cambridge University Press.

Arendt, Hannah. From Eichmann in Jerusalem by Hannah Arendt, copyright © 1963, 1964 by Hannah Arendt, copyright renewed © 1991, 1992 by Lotte Kohler. Used by permission of Viking Penguin, a division of Penguin Group (USA) Inc.

Argyris, Chris. Reprinted by permission of *Harvard Business Review.* [Excerpt/Exhibit] From "Teaching Smart People How to Learn" by Chris Argyris, May 1991. Copyright © 1991 by the Harvard Business School Publishing Corporation; all rights reserved.

Bennis, Warren, On Becoming a Leader. Copyright © 2009 Warren Bennis. Reprinted by permission of Basic Books, a member of the Perseus Books Group.

Brest, Paul and Krieger, Linda Hamilton, Problem Solving, Decision Making, and Professional Judgment (2010). Copyright © by Oxford University Press, Inc. Reprinted with permission by Oxford University Press, Inc.

PART I

THE NATURE
OF LEADERSHIP

CHAPTER 1

DEFINING LEADERSHIP

A. INTRODUCTION: WHY STUDY LEADERSHIP?

The most crucial challenges of our times involve issues of leadership and, in the United States, no occupation is more responsible for producing leaders than law. The legal profession has supplied a majority of American presidents and, in recent decades, almost half the members of Congress.[1] Although they account for just 0.4 percent of the population, lawyers are well represented at all levels of leadership, as governors, state legislators, judges, prosecutors, general counsel, law firm managing partners, and heads of corporate, government, and nonprofit organizations.[2] Even when they are not occupying top positions in their workplaces, lawyers lead teams, committees, task forces, and charitable initiatives.

Lawyers' leadership capacities matter. Society faces problems of growing scale and complexity in areas such as civil rights, human rights, national security, environmental degradation, poverty, corporate governance, economic development, and inequality. Lawyers who lead in legal, policy, nonprofit, and business settings make decisions affecting thousands of individuals whose views are imperfectly registered in regulatory processes.

In this context, our need for leaders with vision, values, and technical competence has never been greater. Yet their ability to meet this need is in serious question. Over two thirds of Americans think that the nation has a leadership crisis.[3] Only 19 percent of the public rates the honesty and ethical standards of lawyers as high or very high, and only 8 percent feel similarly about members of Congress.[4] The percentage of Congressional members who are lawyers has declined from 80 percent in the mid-nineteenth century to 40 percent today.[5] Only 11 percent of the public has "a great deal of confidence . . . in people in charge of running law firms," and almost a third has "hardly any."[6] Less than a fifth of surveyed Americans trust the government in Washington to do what is right "just about always" (3 percent) or "most of the time" (15 percent), one of the lowest measures in the last 50 years.[7] The exceptional number of scandals involving top government officials under the Trump administration and the president's denunciations of "so called judges" and "witch hunts" by Department of Justice officials has compounded public distrust.[8]

In this context, leadership education takes on a new urgency. Although a traditional assumption was that leaders are "born, not made," contemporary research is to the contrary.[9] Genetic factors play a role, but environmental influences are greater, and leadership capabilities can be learned.[10] Indeed, as one expert notes, "It would be strange if leadership were the one skill that could not be enhanced through understanding and practice."[11]

It is, of course, true that for thousands of years, leaders have developed without formal education the qualities that made them effective. But informal methods of learning have been common, and many leaders have acquired knowledge from history, example, and experts in related fields. Civil rights leaders in many countries have borrowed techniques of non-violent resistance pioneered by Mahatma Gandhi in his campaign against British colonial rule in India. Barack Obama looked for guidance in Franklin D. Roosevelt's first 100 days in office.[12] Great political leaders have learned not only from their predecessors but also from masters in communication. John F. Kennedy famously worked hard on developing the personal magnetism that he observed among Hollywood actors.[13] And all of us have developed implicit theories about leadership from the innumerable examples we see around us in workplaces, politics, and in news and entertainment media.[14]

However, the value of formal leadership education is gaining increased recognition. Leadership development is roughly a $50 billion industry.[15] Courses in this area are now a staple in management and policy schools, and are attracting increased interest in law.[16] The Association of American Law Schools established a section on leadership in 2018. Attorneys who head law firms and nonprofit organizations are participating in a growing range of leadership development initiatives.

This book is a response to these trends, and it builds on three central premises. The first is that leadership involves core competencies that cut across traditional occupational and academic boundaries. Leaders in any context need skills involving vision, influence, innovation, decision-making, ethical reasoning, and conflict management. To develop necessary leadership skills, students can benefit from a wide range of disciplines including psychology, philosophy, management, economics, communication, organizational behavior, political science, and dispute resolution.

A second organizing premise is that effective leadership education requires an integration of theory and practice. To that end, this text situates foundational scholarship in the context of actual leadership problems and case histories. It draws not only on conventional sources but also on portraits from literature and the media that can broaden and deepen analysis. Each chapter includes references to short media clips that highlight particular leadership issues, and one chapter focuses on books and films that could be discussed in their entirety.

A third premise is that leadership education is not only about helping people become better leaders, but also about enhancing their understanding of leadership as a process. This understanding can help lawyers more effectively select and interact with leaders in a wide range of professional, political, and personal contexts.

This book proceeds in four parts. Part I focuses on defining and developing leadership. This introductory chapter explores the nature of leadership and the qualities most critical to its effectiveness. Chapter 2 focuses on the challenges and styles of leadership, and on how it can be learned. What can individuals do to prepare themselves for future challenges and enhance lifelong learning?

Part II of the book explores key leadership skills. Chapter 3 looks at what makes for effective decision-making and what cognitive biases and group dynamics can get in its way. Chapter 4 focuses on the exercise of influence: the relationship between leaders and followers, and the strategies necessary to promote change, resolve conflicts, and communicate persuasively.

Part III addresses ethical issues in leadership. Chapter 5 surveys the personal qualities and organizational structures that foster or undermine moral leadership. Chapter 6 looks more closely at the dynamics of authority and accountability that influence ethical conduct and help explain how the good go bad. Chapter 7 turns attention to scandals: financial, political, and sexual. At what point does "personal" conduct become a political or professional issue, and what strategies of crisis prevention and management are most effective?

Part IV of the book explores leadership in context. Chapter 8 examines diversity in leadership and how it can be achieved. Chapter 9 addresses leadership in law firms and in-house counsel offices. Chapter 10 focuses on leadership for social change. How can leaders motivate and mobilize followers in pursuit of social justice? How do they resolve competing views of what justice requires? Chapter 11 reviews literature and films that feature lawyers in leadership roles. Such fictional portrayals highlight the central themes of this book and provide models for dealing with recurrent leadership challenges. Chapter 12 concludes the discussion by reviewing core insights and their relationship to individuals' own leadership aspirations and values.

B. WHAT MAKES LEADERS: CHARACTERISTICS AND CIRCUMSTANCES

1. DEFINITIONS

A threshold question involves what exactly we mean by leadership. That issue has generated a cottage industry of commentary, and by some researchers' accounts, over 1500 definitions and 40 distinctive theories.[17] The term "lead" comes from the Old English word "leden," "laedan, or "loeden," which meant to make go, guide, or show the way, and the Latin word "ducere," which meant to draw, drag, pull, guide, or conduct. "Leader" dates to the thirteenth century, but "leadership" only appeared in the nineteenth century.[18]

Although popular usage sometimes equates leadership with power or position, most contemporary experts draw a distinction. They view leadership in terms of traits, processes, skills, and relationships. In many organizations, leadership is shared or distributed among multiple individuals.[19] John Gardner, founder of Common Cause, noted that heads of public and private organizations often mistakenly assume that their status "has given them a body of followers. And of course it has not. They have been given subordinates. Whether the subordinates become followers depends on whether the executives act like leaders."[20] At the heart of leadership is influence.[21] Just as many high officials are not leaders, many leaders do not hold formal offices. Mahatma Gandhi, Mother Teresa, Nelson Mandela, and Osama bin Laden led from the outside. In essence, "leadership requires a relationship, not simply a title. Leaders must be able to inspire, not just compel or direct their followers."[22] As former army chief of staff Eric Shinseki once noted, "You can certainly command" without commitment from followers, "but you cannot lead without it."[23]

2. EARLY THEORIES AND CONTEMPORARY CRITIQUES: TRAITS AND CHARISMA

The question then becomes, how do leaders forge such commitment? Do they share identifiable personal characteristics and styles that are effective across varying situations? Early Greek philosophers such as Plato, Aristotle, and Socrates all assumed that leadership required exceptional personal qualities, particularly intelligence. Abu Mohammad Al Farabi, a tenth-century Persian scholar, drew on Greek, Roman, and Chinese theorists to compile a list of leadership traits that are remarkably similar to those cited in contemporary accounts.[24] The importance of such traits gained currency during the Enlightenment, and Thomas Carlyle subsequently elaborated the view in *On Heroes, Hero Worship, and the Heroic in History* (1902). From his perspective, behind every great institution and social movement was the shadow of a "great man."

The noted social theorist Max Weber also stressed personal qualities and styles, most importantly "charisma." The term came from Catholic theologians, who borrowed it from St. Paul's concept of gifts manifesting God's grace.[25] Weber used the term in a secular sense to convey the magnetism and persuasiveness that enabled individuals to attract a wide following, particularly in times of turbulence.[26] Weber distinguished charismatic leadership from other forms of authority based on tradition (as with monarchies) or law and "technical rationality" (as with bureaucracies).

Building on Weber's insight, modern theorists have defined charisma in terms of qualities such as emotional expressiveness, empathy, competence, self-confidence, magnetism, enthusiasm, and control.[27] However, unlike Weber, contemporary theorists view these traits as acquired, rather than God-given or innate. Charismatic leaders make inspirational appeals that tap into followers' values and identity.[28] Some commentators also stress leaders' commitment and self-sacrifice.[29] Others focus on the needs of followers. When circumstances evoke feelings of uncertainty, powerlessness, and alienation, the stage is set for charismatic appeals.[30]

These "trait" theories of leadership have attracted widespread criticism, much of it summarized in the excerpt below from Heifetz's *Leadership Without Easy Answers*. The first systematic critique of the "great man" approach to leadership came from social theorist Herbert Spencer, who famously argued that the times produce great leaders rather than the converse.[31] A prominent case is Winston Churchill. In *The Power to Lead*, excerpted below, Joseph Nye argues that Churchill was widely viewed as inconsequential until Hitler invaded France in May of 1940. Then, Churchill became the "man of the moment."[32] His personal characteristics "did not change in 1940: the situation did."[33] Theodore Roosevelt similarly claimed that "if there is not a great occasion, you don't get the great statesmen. If Lincoln had lived in times of peace, no one would know his name now."[34] In short, as John Gardner notes, history makes leaders and leaders make history; no single pattern of styles and traits is appropriate for all contexts and characterstic of leaders as different as Franklin Roosevelt and Mahatma Gandhi. What produces leadership is "great opportunities greatly met."[35] Even in non-crisis situations, the same individual with the same traits may be a superb leader in some contexts but not in others. Franklin Roosevelt was an "indifferent student" at Columbia Law School and impressed none of the partners at the firm where he worked with his "intelligence, work ethic, or sense of purpose," but when family connections led to an offer to run for the New York assembly, he seized it and immediately distinguished himself as a politician.[36] Ralph Nader was extraordinarily effective during the activism of the 1960s and 1970s in galvanizing a progressive consumer movement. But he was far less successful decades later in running a presidential campaign on similar issues. The self-righteous iconoclasm that stood him well in one historical era worked against him as a third-party candidate in a different political climate.[37] President Lyndon Johnson was masterful in gaining civil rights legislation, but disastrous in handling the war in Vietnam.[38] Warren Burger had a skill set that gained him appointment as Chief Justice of the Supreme Court, but reportedly was not a good match for that role. His colleagues found him "pompous," "petty," "overbearing," and sometimes incompetent—incapable of recording votes accurately and unwilling to stop speaking long after he had run out of things to say.[39] Jimmy Carter failed to win reelection after a single frustrating term as president, but subsequently received a Nobel Peace Prize for his efforts to secure peace and international human rights. The commitment to principle that made him effective in some global contexts ill-suited him for the horse trading necessary to accomplish his domestic agenda.[40]

Systematic research confirms what those examples reflect. Over the last half-century, leadership scholars have conducted more than 1000 studies in an attempt to determine the definitive personal styles or traits of great leaders. Yet, as a *Harvard Business Review* summary notes, none of these studies has produced a clear profile of the ideal leader.[41] Nor has research identified consistent relationships between personality and leadership effectiveness.[42]

Even the much celebrated quality of charisma does not predict success. According to experts such as historian James MacGregor Burns, "charisma" is so ambiguously and inconsistently used that "it is impossible to restore the word to analytic duty."[43] Often it seems to function as a conclusory label that fails to specify what exactly accounts for the appeal described. Moreover, researchers do not find that leaders who score high in charisma score high in performance.[44] In one survey of some 4,300 leaders, as charisma scores increased above average, perceived effectiveness declined, as assessed by subordinates, peers, and supervisors. They saw charismatic leaders as often overconfident, narcissistic, and uninterested in day-to-day operational activities necessary to implement their ambitious strategic visions.[45] Some studies also suggest that charismatic leaders can impair performance because followers rely too heavily on such leaders' judgment and fail to challenge erroneous decisions.[46] These factors may help explain why research on the most continuously profitable corporations finds that their leaders have tended to be self-effacing and lacking in the qualities commonly considered charismatic.[47]

Management expert Peter Drucker put it bluntly. Denouncing efforts to find a "boardroom Elvis Presley," he argued that effective leadership has little to do with charismatic qualities. It is "mundane . . . and boring. Its essence is performance."[48] The most successful leaders that Drucker encountered had varied greatly in personality and styles, and the only thing they had in common "was something they did not have: They had little or no 'charisma' and little use either for the term or what it signifies."[49] For example, one of America's most distinguished secretaries of state, John Foster Dulles, was described by Winston Churchill as "Dull, Duller, Dulles."[50]

Yet even if charisma is not always predictive of performance, it does often explain the emergence of leaders, particularly politicians. Although leadership experts preach the virtue of humility, "narcissists are overrepresented in senior leadership positions."[51] As one overview of studies of American politics notes, "people vote for the candidate who elicits the right feelings, not the candidate who presents the best arguments."[52] Stanley McCrystal's recent overview of leadership points out that we are oddly capable of "selecting or tolerating immoral or incompetent leaders because they provide . . . [meaning] elsewhere, such as social identity or ideological affiliation."[53]

3. THE IMPORTANCE OF LEADERS

Focusing on the individual traits of leaders can also deflect attention from organizational factors and institutional structures that may be more consistent drivers of performance.[54] Contemporary experts caution against the "leader attribution error": the tendency to overvalue the contribution of leaders to organizational performance or political outcomes.[55] We are drawn to heroic accounts both because they make for compelling narratives, and because they make us feel more in control. As Gardner notes, "there is at least a chance that one can fire the leader; one cannot 'fire' historical forces."[56] But although biographies and memoirs are a better read than leadership research, they deflect attention from key issues about the conditions that enabled particular leaders to emerge and influenced their effectiveness.[57]

American politics, for example, presents a world of shared leadership in which institutional constraints interact with external conditions to influence individual effectiveness. Of course, presidential abilities and priorities matter. The nation's military and environmental policies would have been different if Al Gore had been president instead of George W. Bush.[58] And as Chapter 10 will note, Lyndon Johnson's skills in dealing with Congress were crucial in achieving landmark civil rights legislation in the 1960s. But on the whole, empirical research suggests that presidential legislative skills are not closely related to legislative outcomes; rather outcomes are more influenced by the composition of Congress.[59] And in foreign policy, results may often depend on factors beyond presidential control.[60] The most crucial skill for political leaders is often the ability to craft their policy ambitions to fit the opportunities of the day.[61]

Outside of politics, findings are somewhat mixed, but most research suggests that leadership makes only a modest impact on organizational performance. In the private sector, other factors such as the competitive circumstances within the industry and the organization's fixed assets and entrenched structures play a dominant role.[62] A school of thought labeled "critical leadership studies" warns against accounts that overemphasize elites and marginalize the role of workplace structures and relationships.[63] Some critical theorists focus instead on "leadership as practice," which emphasizes the processes of leading rather than the characteristics of leaders.[64]

However, most research also suggests that those characteristics inevitably affect leadership processes and often have some influence on organizational performance and public policy.[65] Similar leadership initiatives under similar circumstances can have quite different impacts depending on the competence of leaders.[66]

4. THE ROLE OF CONTEXT AND PROCESS: SITUATIONS AND CONTINGENCY IN LEADERSHIP

The inadequacies of trait-based theories of leadership have led to a wide variety of alternatives.[67] The most influential have been frameworks that acknowledge the importance of context and process, including their historical, cultural, psychological, and institutional dimensions.[68] Beginning in the 1960s, contingency theories began to explore what would make leadership effective under particular conditions.[69] The first and best known of these approaches focused on factors such as leaders' relationship to followers, the amount of power and resources conferred by their position, and the nature of the task at hand. Later models included additional considerations such as the importance of leaders' decisions, the availability of information, and the likelihood and importance of their acceptance by followers.[70] Some circumstances call for controlling behavior and others benefit from participatory styles. As a general matter, these approaches advocate more directive styles when subordinates have clearly defined tasks and low skills and motivation, but more supportive styles when well-educated employees have challenging assignments and significant intrinsic motivation.[71] Cultures also vary in the importance that they ascribe to particular leadership traits, such as aggressiveness and risk taking.[72]

Situational theories have similarly related leadership styles to followers' readiness. The ability and confidence that subordinates have in carrying out tasks dictates whether directive, consultative, participatory, or delegating strategies make the most sense.[73] Process models understand leadership as something that unfolds in stages. From this perspective, being a leader isn't "someone you are," but rather "something you do."[74] Contemporary policy experts have also emphasized timing as a key contextual factor. Successful reform efforts often require waiting until policy windows open—that is, until a need for action appears urgent, and effective political alliances and plausible proposals are available.[75]

Under these approaches, the key to effective leadership is a match between what the circumstances require or enable, and the strengths that an individual has to offer—what is sometimes labeled the "leadership sweet spot."[76] But, as Nye points out in the excerpt below, what is relevant in a situation and what is the appropriate way of handling it turn out to be "interpretative and contestable issues" that cannot be determined by objective criteria.[77] Nor does contingency theory explain exactly how leaders acquire and exercise power in light of the relevant considerations, and why some of them seem consistently effective in different situations.[78] Moreover, as Harvard Business School professors Nitin Nohria and Rakesh Khurana note, "It is hard to imagine what leadership is if there isn't a core set of leadership functions or behaviors that cut across different situations and persons."[79] One way to bridge these theoretical tensions is to think of leadership as involving certain core tasks, along with competencies that vary in effectiveness depending on the circumstances.

5. VALUES IN LEADERSHIP

One other limitation of both trait and contingency theories is the inattention to values. That is not to suggest that these approaches are value free. Rather, as Nye suggests, the value they privilege is impact; leaders are assessed in light of their effect on history, followers, and organizations. Yet missing or marginal in such frameworks is the morality of means and ends. Does an effective leader need to be an ethical leader? Ethical in what sense? Chapter 5 explores those issues in greater depth. The question here is simply what role values play in the definition of leadership.

For some commentators, good leadership depends on the ends being pursued. Theorists beginning with James MacGregor Burns have distinguished between transactional and transformational leadership. Transactional approaches focus on the relationship between leaders and subordinates and on what each gains or loses from the exchange. Such frameworks assume that people are motivated primarily by rewards and punishments and therefore need financial, psychological, and status-related incentives to comply with specified rules and goals.[80] Yet these approaches fail to capture the complexity of human motivation and the importance of values. Accordingly, transformational approaches stress the capacity of leaders not simply to influence followers' behaviors through rewards and sanctions, but also to reshape their objectives and, in the process, to elevate leaders' own sense of purpose. Transformational leadership inspires individuals to transcend their immediate self-interest in the service of the greater good of the organization or society. Such leadership is "moral in that it raises the level of human conduct and ethical aspiration of both leader and led."[81] Techniques include providing an inspirational vision and role model, and responding to followers' capacities for creativity and commitment.[82]

Other theorists have similarly argued for values-based leadership. "Servant leadership" frameworks focus on leaders' capacity to meet the needs of others, and to help them support the organizational mission.[83] "Strategic leadership" and "visionary leadership" approaches stress the ability to transform institutions in ways that better enable them to address change and pursue their mission.[84] Such approaches are considered superior to "laissez-faire leadership," in which those in positions of authority fail to take a stand on issues implicating fundamental values.[85]

Many contemporary theories of leadership have been subject to criticism on normative grounds. Some theories pay insufficient attention to the moral content of leaders' objectives, or to the methods of resolving conflicts among the values at issue. If influence is the only metric for leadership, without some focus on its moral purpose or effect, then Hitler and Osama bin Laden are in the same general category as Gandhi and Mother Teresa. Moreover, the transformational objectives that Burns identified for political leaders do not translate smoothly into contexts where the greater good is subject to dispute. In law firms, giving priority to profits per partner is a value choice, but not one that all lawyers accept as appropriate. Transformational leadership takes into account concerns other than the bottom line, but the theory says little about how to weigh competing goals.

Another concern with values-based approaches is that their focus on transformative ends can ignore the need for transactional strategies in ensuring compliance. So too, in political and policy contexts, theorists have noted the danger in relying on transformational or charismatic leadership at the expense of procedural values. Without institutional checks and balances, a majority led by a charismatic dictator may oppress the minority. Countries that have given too much authority to leaders such as Mao or Stalin have paid an enormous price in human life and liberty.[86]

For the most part, argues political scientist Nan Keohane, "good" and "bad" are terms more useful in judging specific acts than leaders themselves.[87] Even our most revered leaders often have some toxic qualities or blots on their records. Franklin D. Roosevelt's court-packing plan is one of Keohane's examples; his internment of Japanese Americans during World War II is another. Moreover, as

Chapter 5 notes, "dirty hands" are a common and, some believe, endemic aspect of political governance. Moral leadership may require moral tradeoffs that defy categorical judgments.

6. LEADING AND MANAGING

Values also play a role in the distinction many contemporary theorists draw between leading and managing. In a widely quoted phrase, Warren Bennis and Burt Nanus summarized the difference: "Managers are people who do things right; leaders are people who do the right things."[88] The term "management" comes from the Latin "manus," meaning hand. It originally referred to handling things and gained currency during the Industrial Revolution in the nineteenth century. Contemporary scholars often distinguish between leaders, who chart a destination, and managers, who enable individuals and institutions to get there. Managers reportedly administer and implement; leaders envision, inspire, innovate, and "look beyond the horizon."[89]

In his *Harvard Business Review* article "What Leaders Really Do," John Kotter claims that many American organizations are "overmanaged and underled" and that companies need to develop individuals who have both leadership and management skills.[90] According to Kotter, the fundamental difference is that management is about coping with complexity while leadership is about coping with change. The latter capability has become increasingly important because the private sector "has become more competitive and more volatile. Faster technological change, greater international competition, the deregulation of markets, . . . and the changing demographics of the work force are among the many factors that have contributed to this shift."[91]

Organizations manage complexity through planning, budgeting, organizing, staffing, and problem solving. Leading involves setting a direction and articulating a vision, which according to Kotter, is more strategic than mystical. It is a tough, sometimes exhausting process of gathering and analyzing information. People who articulate such visions are broad-based strategic thinkers who are willing to take risks.[92] Achieving the vision "requires *motivating and inspiring*—keeping people moving in the right direction, despite major obstacles to change, by appealing to basic but often untapped human needs, values, and emotions."[93]

Yet the distinction between leading and managing should not be overstated. Joanne Ciulla questions the normative assumption underlying Bennis and Nanus's formulation—that managers do things right and leaders do the right thing. If the implication is that leaders are virtuous and managers are "morally flabby," does that make Hitler a manager, not a leader?[94] Moreover, as many commentators have noted, managers need leadership skills to get things done, and leaders need management skills to ensure that systems are in place to realize organizational objectives. Although leaders' primary role is to formulate long-term goals, they also remain responsible for short-term performance.[95] And in John Gardner's experience, "first-class managers . . . turn out to have quite a lot of the leader in them."[96]

In law firms, managerial and leadership roles are typically combined and shared. Firm chairs work with management committees and chief financial officers to make key operational decisions, and with equity partners to set policy directions. So too, a growing trend in many other large corporate and public-sector organizations is toward diffused leadership and collaborative governance structures in which strategic and managerial authority is shared.[97]

7. THE LEADER'S LEGACY

One paradox of power is that leaders who are most effective in building a positive legacy that outlasts them are those least interested in exercising power for its own sake, or in establishing their own place in history. Lincoln, his biographers note, "liked to get on in the world . . . but the way he got on was by thinking about his job, not by thinking about himself."[98] Building on this insight, J. Patrick Dobel cautions leaders that "[i]nsisting on credit [for your achievements] invites disappointment and distortion of personal energy and aspirations."[99] He also advises aspiring leaders to be proactive "sooner rather than later[; a] person's legacy unfolds every day," and priorities and relationships formed early in a career create the foundations for later achievements. People cannot control how history will judge them, but they can be conscious of how their daily interactions and priorities affect followers and institutions.[100] Unless leaders' priorities include support for others' careers as well as their own, their legacy is likely to be limited. As one leadership development expert notes, "[T]he ultimate test of a leader is not whether he or she makes smart decisions . . . but whether he or she teaches others to be leaders and builds an organization that can sustain its success even when he or she is not around."[101]

The excerpts that follow explore the meaning of leadership and the qualities associated with its exercise. Based on these approaches, how would you define leadership?

JOSEPH S. NYE JR., THE POWERS TO LEAD

(New York: Oxford University Press, 2008), pp. 3-7, 10-11, 14-16, 18-22, 24, 53, and 56-64

Do Leaders Matter?

Skeptics deny that leaders matter all that much. People easily make the mistake of "leader attribution error." We see something going right or wrong with a group or organization and then attribute the result to the leader. He or she becomes a scapegoat, even while being more a symbol of failure than its cause. Sports teams fire coaches after a losing season whether or not they are blameworthy. Business executives lose their jobs after profits turn down; others get credit for success in bull markets. Voters reward and punish politicians for economic conditions that often were created before the leaders took office.

In the presence of multiple causes and random events, attributing blame or praise to a person can provide a sense of psychological comfort and reassurance about our ability to understand and control events in a complex and confusing world. . . . "Belief in a political leader's ability to alter affairs may generate a feeling of indirect control. The ability to reward or punish incumbents through the vote implies this influence." Various experiments have shown that the desire to make sense of confusing events leads to a romanticized, larger-than-life role for leaders, particularly in extreme cases of very good or very bad performance.

[Contexts matter in shaping that performance.] Social movement leaders like Gandhi and Martin Luther King, Jr. would not have made it to the top of GE, nor is it likely they would have done well if by some chance they had. Formal organizations are an important slice of life, but only a slice. Many leadership contexts are far more fluid, whether they are political groups, street gangs, universities, or online communities. Leading inside an institution is different from leading a movement without institutions. A prophetic style fits well with a loosely organized social movement, whereas managerial competence is important in an organization. In social movements, we might expect leaders to count for more (and in the case of online communities, less) than in corporate life. Conclusions drawn from studies of organizational behavior (which is the focus of the majority of academic and business studies) may not tell us much about these other dimensions of leadership.

History Lessons

This raises the age-old question of the role of leaders in history. For centuries, history was written as the record of the doings of great men. Thomas Carlyle wrote in 1840, "The history of what man has accomplished in this world, is at bottom the History of the Great Men who have worked here" (although a skeptical Herbert Spencer pointed out in 1873, "Before he can re-make his society, his society must make him"). Perhaps the best summary of this insoluble problem came from Karl Marx: "Men make their own history, but they do not make it as they please . . . but under circumstances existing already, given and transmitted from the past."

It seems obvious that Alexander the Great, Julius Caesar, Genghis Khan, Louis XIV, and Winston Churchill all made a difference in history, but it is much harder to say how much. History is an imperfect laboratory, and controlled experiments that hold other variables constant are impossible. Time and context have a huge impact. For example, President George W. Bush frequently refers to Churchill, whom many historians describe as one of the greatest leaders of the twentieth century. But at the beginning of 1940, Churchill was widely regarded as a washed-up backbench member of Parliament. As a conservative British prime minister said in 1936, "While we delight to listen to him in this House, we do not take his advice." Churchill would have been a minor figure in the history books if Hitler had not invaded France in May 1940. Then Churchill became the man who fit the moment. Churchill did not change; the context changed. Without Hitler's actions, Churchill would not be seen today as a great leader. . . .

The philosopher Sidney Hook once tried to sort out this question by distinguishing "eventful vs. event-making" leaders. An eventful leader influences the course of subsequent developments by his actions. In Hook's metaphor, the mythical little Dutch boy who stuck his finger in a leaking dike and saved his country was an eventful leader, but any little boy or any finger could have done the trick. An event-making leader, on the other hand, doesn't just find a fork in the historical road: he helps to create it. Such leaders are called *transformational* in the sense of changing what would otherwise be the course of history. They raise new issues and new questions. "Good politicians win the argument. Every now and then someone comes along and changes it." Margaret Thatcher and Tony Blair were not universally liked as prime ministers in Britain, but both were credited with changing the political weather. . . . Many opportunities for change go unfulfilled. Leaders matter when they have the intuition and skills to take advantage of those windows while they are open.

Heroic and Alpha Male Approaches to Leadership

The fact that history has been written in terms of heroes constrains our imagination and understanding of the enormous potential of human leadership that ranges from Attila the Hun to Mother Teresa. Most everyday leaders remain unheralded . . . . Humans seek heroes, but not all heroes are leaders, and not all leaders are heroic. . . .

Defining Leaders and Leadership

. . . I define a leader as someone who helps a group create and achieve shared goals. . . . Some leaders act with the formal authority of a position such as president or chair; others act without formal authority, as Rosa Parks did. . . . Holding a formal leadership position is like having a fishing license; it does not guarantee you will catch any fish.

Leadership is not just who you are but what you do. The functions that leaders perform for human groups are to create meaning and goals, reinforce group identity and cohesion, provide order, and mobilize collective work. In a careful study of work teams, Richard Hackman found that the functions of leaders are setting a compelling direction, fine-tuning a team's structure, and providing resource support and expert coaching: "Team leadership can be—and, at its best, often is— a *shared* activity. Anyone and everyone who clarifies a team's direction, or improves its structure, or secures organizational supports for it, or provides coaching that improves its performance processes is providing team leadership."

The test of a leader is whether a group is more effective in both defining and achieving its goals because of that person's participation. . . . We can think of leadership as a process with three key components: leaders, followers, and contexts. The context consists of both the external environment and the changing objectives that a group seeks in a particular situation. As we have seen, the traits that are most relevant to effective leadership depend on the context, and the situation creates followers' needs that lead them to search for particular leaders. A group of workers that wants someone to organize a weekend party may turn to a fun-loving member to take the lead. The same group will probably want a very different member to lead in negotiating a benefits package with management.

Rather than think of a leader as a particular type of heroic individual, we need to think of all three parts of the triangle together constituting the process of leadership. Leaders and followers learn roles and change roles as their perceptions of situations change. One of the key issues is for leaders and followers to understand how to expand and adapt their repertoires for different situations. They can learn to broaden their bandwidth and thus provide for a more effective leadership process in a wider range of situations. Because learning is possible, leadership studies, though not a science, is still a valid discipline. . . .

Charismatic Leadership

. . . Does charisma originate in the individual, in the followers, or in the situation? Some theorists say all three. . . . [One] study looked at seven major political spellbinders of the twentieth century: Hitler, Mussolini, and Roosevelt in industrialized countries; Gandhi, Sukarno, Castro, and Khomeini in less developed countries. The author concluded that in all cases "charisma is found not so much in the personality of the leader as in the perceptions of the people he leads." Ann Ruth Willner found that to locate the sources of charisma, she needed to look for the factors that called forth those perceptions and that they varied by culture and by time. She speculated that culture may explain why so few women charismatic leaders appear in political history; followers in most cultures have denied them the opportunity. Joan of Arc and Evita Peron are rare exceptions.

Social crises cause followers' distress, which leads them to turn to a leader and attribute charisma to him or her. But knowing that, leaders sometimes help to enlarge a crisis and exacerbate the distress that triggers the process of charisma creation. . . .

The power that charismatic leaders unleash among their followers can do great good or great harm. Some theorists categorize "negative charismatics" as those who are prone to grandiose projects, inattention to details, unwillingness to delegate, failure to create institutions that empower followers, and lack of planning for their succession. On the other hand, there have been historical moments when "positive" or "reparative" charismatic leaders like Gandhi, King, and Nelson Mandela have released energies among their followers that have transformed social and political situations for the better. . . .

Charismatic leaders are adept at communication, vision, confidence, being an exemplar, and managing the impressions they create. Some theorists distinguish between "close" charismatics, who work best in small groups or inner circles where the effects of their personality are felt directly, and "distant" charismatics, who rely on more remote theatrical performance to reach and move the broader imagined communities that they aspire to lead. In the first case, the personal charm is felt directly; in the latter case, it is projected and mediated. Other theorists distinguish "socialized" charismatics, who use their power to benefit others, and "personalized" charismatics, whose narcissistic personalities lead to self-serving behavior. . . .

Transformational and Transactional Leadership

Given the inadequate explanatory value of charisma alone, leadership theorists have incorporated it into a broader concept of transformational leadership. . . . Transformational leaders empower and elevate their followers; they use conflict and crisis to raise their followers' consciousness and transform them. Transformational leaders mobilize power for change by appealing to their followers' higher ideals and moral values rather than their baser emotions of fear, greed, and hatred.

Transformational leaders induce followers to transcend their self-interest for the sake of the higher purposes of the group that provides the context of the relationship. Followers are thus inspired to undertake what Ronald Heifetz has termed "adaptive work" and do more than they originally expected based on self-interest alone. Charisma in the sense of personal magnetism is only one part of transformational leadership. As defined and operationalized by the leadership theorist Bernard Bass, transformational leadership also includes an element of "intellectual stimulation" (broadening followers' awareness of situations and new perspectives) and "individualized consideration" (providing support, coaching, and developmental experiences to followers rather than treating them as mere means to an end). Thus a leader can be charismatic without being transformational, and vice versa. Transformational leaders who succeed may remain respected, but they may lose their aura of charisma as followers' needs change. Alternatively, charismatic leaders who come to believe they are truly exceptional may become autocratic and intolerant and no longer remain transformational.

Transformational leaders are contrasted with transactional leaders, who motivate followers by appealing to their self-interest. Transactional leaders use various approaches, but all rest on reward, punishment, and self-interest. Transformational leaders appeal to the collective interests of a group or organization, and transactional leaders rely on the various individual interests. The former depend more on the soft power of inspiration, the latter on the hard power of threat and reward. Transactional leaders create concrete incentives to influence followers' efforts and set out rules that relate work to rewards. . . .

Although the term transactional is clear, the concept of transformation is confusing because theorists use it to refer to leaders' objectives, the styles they use, and the outcomes they produce. Those three dimensions are not the same thing. Sometimes leaders transform the world but not their followers, or vice versa, and sometimes they use a transactional style to accomplish transformational objectives.

Consider the example of Lyndon Johnson. In the 1950s, Senator Johnson deeply wanted to transform racial injustice in the South, but he did not use soft power to preach to or inspire a new vision in other senators. Instead, he misled his fellow southerners about his intentions and used a transactional style of hard power bullying and bargaining to achieve progress toward his transformational objectives in passing a civil rights bill in 1957 that was anathema to many of the supporters who had made him majority leader. He did not change his followers, but he did begin to change the world of African Americans in the South.

─────

In the following excerpt, Ronald Heifetz similarly argues for viewing leadership as an activity, involving the interaction of ability, culture, and situation. He also recognizes the centrality of a leader's relationship with followers and the importance of adaptive work in advancing common goals.

RONALD A. HEIFETZ, LEADERSHIP WITHOUT EASY ANSWERS

(Cambridge, MA: Belknap Press of Harvard
University Press, 1994), pp. 16-23

Hidden Values in Theories of Leadership

Perhaps the first theory of leadership—and the one that continues to be entrenched in American culture—emerged from the nineteenth-century notion that history is the story of great men and their impact on society. (Women were not even considered candidates for greatness.) . . . Although various scientific studies discount the idea, this *trait approach* continues to set the terms of popular debate. Indeed, it saw a revival during the 1980s. Based on this view, trait theorists since Carlyle have examined the personality characteristics of "great men," positing that the rise to power is rooted in a "heroic" set of personal talents, skills, or physical characteristics. As Sidney Hook described in *The Hero in History* (1943), some men are eventful, while others are event-making.

In reaction to the great-man theory of history, *situationalists* argued that history is much more than the effects of these men on their time. Indeed, social theorists like Herbert Spencer (1884) suggested that the times produce the person and not the other way around. In a sense, situationalists were not interested in leadership per se. "Historymakers" were interesting because they stood at the vortex of powerful political and social forces, which themselves were of interest. Thus, the more or less contemporaneous emergence of the United States' first great leaders—Jefferson, Washington, Adams, Madison, Hamilton, Monroe, Benjamin Franklin—is attributed not to a demographic fluke but to the extraordinary times in which these men lived. Instead of asserting that all of them shared a common set of traits, situationalists suggest that the times called forth an assortment of men with various talents and leadership styles. Indeed, many of them performed marvelously in some jobs but quite poorly in others. Thus, "What an individual actually *does* when acting as a leader is in large part dependent upon characteristics of the situation in which he functions."

Beginning in the 1950s, theorists began (not surprisingly) to synthesize the trait approach with the situationalist view. Empirical studies had begun to show that no single constellation of traits was associated with leadership. Although this finding did not negate the idea that individuals "make" history, it did suggest that different situations demand different personalities and call for different behaviors.

Primary among these synthetic approaches is *contingency theory*, which posits that the appropriate style of leadership is contingent on the requirements of the particular situation. For example, some situations require controlling or autocratic behavior and others participative or democratic behavior. . . .

These four general approaches attempt to define leadership objectively, without making value judgments. When defining leadership in terms of prominence, authority, and influence, however, these theories introduce value-biases implicitly without declaring their introduction and without arguing for the necessity of the values introduced. . . . The problem emerges when we communicate and model these descriptions as "leadership" because "leadership" in many cultures is a normative idea—it represents a set of orienting values, as do words like "hero" and "champion." If we leave the value implications of our teaching and practice unaddressed, we encourage people, perhaps unwittingly, to aspire to great influence or high office, regardless of what they do there. We would be on safer ground were we to discard the loaded term leadership altogether and simply describe the dynamics of prominence, power, influence, and historical causation. . . .

Toward a Prescriptive Concept of Leadership

. . . Rather than define leadership either as a position of authority in a social structure or as a personal set of characteristics, we may find it a great deal more useful to define leadership as an *activity*. This allows for leadership from multiple positions in a social structure. A President and a clerk can both lead. It also allows for the use of a variety of abilities depending on the demands of the culture and situation. Personal abilities are resources for leadership applied differently in different contexts. As we know, at times they are not applied at all. Many people never exercise leadership, even though they have the personal qualities we might commonly associate with it. By unhinging leadership from personality traits, we permit observations of the many different ways in which people exercise plenty of leadership everyday without "being leaders."

The common personalistic orientation to the term leadership, with its assumption that "leaders are born and not made," is quite dangerous. It fosters both self-delusion and irresponsibility. For those who consider themselves "born leaders," free of an orienting philosophy and strategy of leadership, their grandiosity is a set-up for a rude awakening and for blindly doing damage. Minimally, they can waste the time and effort of a community on projects that go, if not over a cliff, then at least in circles. Conversely, those who consider themselves "not leaders" escape responsibility for taking action, or for learning how to take action, when they see the need. In the face of critical problems, they say, "I'm not a leader, what can I do?"

So, we ought to focus on leadership as an activity—the activity of a citizen from any walk of life mobilizing people to do something. But what is the socially useful something? What mode of leadership is likely to generate socially useful outcomes? Several approaches to these questions might work. We could imagine that a leader is more likely to produce socially useful outcomes by setting goals that meet the needs of both the leader and followers. This has the benefit of distinguishing leadership from merely "getting people to do what you want them to do." Leadership is more than influence.

Even so, setting a goal to meet the needs of the community may give no definition of what those needs are. If a leader personally wants to turn away from the difficulty of problems, and so do his constituents, does he exercise leadership by coming up with a fake remedy?

To address this problem, the leadership theorist James MacGregor Burns suggested that socially useful goals not only have to meet the needs of followers, they also should elevate followers to a higher moral level. Calling this *transformational leadership*, he posits that people begin with the need for survival and security, and once those needs are met, concern themselves with "higher" needs like affection, belonging, the common good, or serving others. This approach has the benefit of provoking discussion about how to construct a hierarchy of orienting values. However, a hierarchy that would apply across cultures and organizational settings risks either being so general as to be impractical or so specific as to be culturally imperialistic in its application.

We might also say that leadership has a higher probability of producing socially useful results when defined in terms of legitimate authority, with legitimacy based on a set of procedures by which power is conferred from the many to the few. This view is attractive because we might stop glorifying usurpations of power as leadership. But by restraining the exercise of leadership to legitimate authority, we also leave no room for leadership that challenges the legitimacy of authority or the system of authorization itself. No doubt, there are risks to freeing leadership from its moorings of legitimate authority. . . . Yet we also face an important possibility: social progress may require that someone push the system to its limit. . . . Hence, a person who leads may have to risk his moral state, and not just his health and job, to protect his moral state. Defining leadership in terms of legitimate authority excludes those who faced moral doubt and deep regret by defying authority. Vaclav Havel, Lech Walesa, Aung San Suu Kyi, Martin Luther King Jr., Margaret Sanger, and Mohandas Gandhi, to name a few, risked social disaster by unleashing uncontrollable social forces. . . .

Business schools and schools of management commonly define leadership and its usefulness with respect to organizational effectiveness. Effectiveness means reaching viable decisions that implement the goals of the organization. This definition has the benefit of being generally applicable, but it provides no real guide to determine the nature or formation of those goals. Which goals should we pursue? What constitutes effectiveness in addition to the ability to generate profits? From the perspective of a town official viewing a local corporation, effectiveness at implementation seems an insufficient criterion. A chemical plant may be quite effective at earning a profit while it dangerously pollutes the local water supply. We are left with the question: Effective at what?

This study examines the usefulness of viewing leadership in terms of adaptive work. Adaptive work consists of the learning required to address conflicts in the values people hold, or to diminish the gap between the values people stand for and the reality they face. Adaptive work requires a change in values, beliefs, or behavior. The exposure and orchestration of conflict—internal contradictions—within individuals and constituencies provide the leverage for mobilizing people to learn new ways.

In this view, getting people to clarify what matters most, in what balance, with what trade-offs, becomes a central task. In the case of a local industry that pollutes the river, people want clean water, but they also want jobs. Community and company interests frequently overlap and clash, with conflicts taking place not only among factions but also within the lives of individual citizens who themselves may have competing needs. Leadership requires orchestrating these conflicts among and within the interested parties, and not just between the members and formal shareholders of the organization. Who should play a part in the deliberations is not a given, but is itself a critical strategic question. Strategy begins with asking: Which stakeholders have to adjust their ways to make progress on this problem? How can one sequence the issues or strengthen the bonds that join the stakeholders together as a community of interests so that they withstand the stresses of problem-solving?

. . . The implication is important: *the inclusion of competing value perspectives may be essential to adaptive success.* In the long run, an industrial polluter will fail if it neglects the interests of its community. Given the spread of environmental values, it may not always be able to move across borders. Conversely, the community may lose its economic base if it neglects the interests of its industry.

The point here is to provide a guide to goal formation and strategy. In selecting adaptive work as a guide, one considers not only the values that the goal represents, but also the goal's ability to mobilize people to face, rather than avoid, tough realities and conflicts. The hardest and most valuable task of leadership may be advancing goals and designing strategy that promote adaptive work. . . .

Warren Bennis, one of America's first prominent scholars of leadership, offers his definition of its key characteristics in the following excerpt, and draws a commonly cited distinction between leaders and managers.

WARREN BENNIS, ON BECOMING A LEADER

(Cambridge, MA: Perseus Publishing, 2002), pp. 31-35,
39-40, 86, 89-91, and 108-109

. . . [Leaders] all seem to share some, if not all, of the following ingredients:

- The first basic ingredient of leadership is a *guiding vision*. The leader has a clear idea of what he or she wants to do—professionally and personally—and the strength to persist in the face of setbacks, even failures. Unless you know where you're going, and why, you cannot possibly get there. . . .
- The second basic ingredient of leadership is *passion*—the underlying passion for the promises of life, combined with a very particular passion for a vocation,

a profession, a course of action. The leader loves what he or she does and loves doing it. . . .

- The next basic ingredient of leadership is *integrity*. I think there are three essential parts of integrity: self-knowledge, candor, and maturity.

"Know thyself" was the inscription over the Oracle at Delphi. And it is still the most difficult task any of us faces. But until you truly know yourself, strengths and weaknesses, know what you want to do and why you want to do it, you cannot succeed in any but the most superficial sense of the word. Leaders never lie to themselves, especially about themselves, know their faults as well as their assets, and deal with them directly. You are your own raw material. When you know what you consist of and what you want to make of it, then you can invent yourself.

Candor is the key to self-knowledge. Candor is based in honesty of thought and action, a steadfast devotion to principle, and a fundamental soundness and wholeness. . . .

Even though I talk about basic ingredients, I'm not talking about traits that you're born with and can't change. As countless deposed kings and hapless heirs to great fortunes can attest, true leaders are not born, but made, and usually self-made. Leaders invent themselves. They are not, by the way, made in a single weekend seminar, as many of the leadership-theory spokesmen claim. I've come to think of that one as the microwave theory: pop in Mr. or Ms. Average and out pops McLeader in sixty seconds. . . .

PROBLEM 1-1

One key quality of leaders is self-knowledge. Understanding your core values, aspirations, and identity can help guide you to positions in which you can develop as a leader. To that end, complete two of the following self-assessment exercises.

A. What are four qualities that best define you on the dimensions relevant to leadership? Ask someone who knows you well the same question. Compare your lists.[102]

B. Name three leadership positions that you would like to have, or three organizations in which you would like a leadership position. What is distinctive about these work settings? What does creating the list tell you about your most important values?

C. Create a list of key personal values and priorities relevant to leadership. For example:
   - What are your professional goals?
   - What do you most want to accomplish in your career? What will make your work meaningful?
   - What is your tolerance for risk, conflict, stress, pressure, and extended work hours?
   - What balance do you want between professional, personal, and family commitments?

- What kind of work do you like most and least? In what professional contexts do you feel most challenged and effective?[103]

D. Complete either the Myers-Brigg Types Inventory of personal characteristics, which rates individuals on four dimensions (introversion-extraversion, sensing-intuition, thinking-feeling, and judging-perceiving), or the Five Factor Model of personality, which uses five factors (neuroticism, extraversion, openness, agreeableness, and conscientiousness).[104] What does this assessment suggest about the kinds of leadership positions in which you would be most effective?

NOTES AND QUESTIONS

1. How would you define leadership?
2. Think of three leaders from history or personal experience whom you most admire. Do you see common characteristics that are particularly critical?
3. What makes leaders effective in some contexts but not in others? Break into groups and identify a leader who both succeeded and failed. What accounts for the different outcomes?
4. Does effective leadership presuppose ethical leadership? Were Hitler, Mao, and Lenin effective leaders?[105] Is the ultimate test of leadership influence, or does it presuppose something more? Richard Nixon once claimed that in "evaluating a leader, the key question about his behavioral traits is not whether they are attractive or unattractive, but whether they are useful."[106] Do you agree? Does the research summarized below suggest that these criteria are related?
5. What is the relationship between power and leadership? In *The Power Paradox*, Dacher Keltner defined power as the capacity to influence others and make a difference in the world.[107] Harvard Professor Rosabeth Moss Kanter claimed that power was "America's last dirty word." And despite its importance for leaders, "it is easier to talk about money—and much easier to talk about sex—than it is to talk about power."[108] John Gardner famously observed that in most democracies "power has such a bad name that many good people persuade themselves they want nothing to do with it." Yet in Gardner's view, the negative connotations are undeserved. "To say a leader is preoccupied with power, is like saying that a tennis player is preoccupied with making shots his opponent cannot return. Of course leaders are preoccupied with power! The significant questions are: What means do they use to gain it[?] . . . To what ends do they exercise it?"[109] How comfortable would you be if someone accused you of being focused on power? Would you be satisfied giving Gardner's response? Does gender matter? Are women less comfortable than men in seeking power or being seen as doing so? See the discussion in Chapter 8.

   Harvard psychologist David McClelland famously distinguished between power exercised to control others and power exercised to enable them. Building on that distinction, a growing number of leadership experts emphasize the value of using power to empower.[110] Have you observed that distinction? Consider its importance in light of the discussion of leadership styles in Chapter 2, and relationships with followers in Chapter 4.

Are the qualities necessary to gain leadership the same as those necessary to gain power? Stanford Business School professor Jeffrey Pfeffer maintains that power is a function of "will and skill." Will includes ambition, energy, and focus; skill includes self-knowledge, confidence, empathy, and capacity to tolerate conflict.[111] To what extent do these overlap with the qualities of effective leadership described below?

6. One interesting finding of some research on leadership traits is that although intelligence correlates with perceived leadership effectiveness and emergence, typical leaders are only slightly more intelligent than the groups they lead, and the most intelligent person in a group is not the one most likely to become its leader.[112] In general, people do not like to be led by those who seem very much smarter than themselves.[113] Nor is intelligence a good predictor of power.[114] This disconnect between leadership and intelligence is captured in titles of books about the leaders responsible for the Vietnam War (*The Best and the Brightest*) and the Enron scandal (*The Smartest Guys in the Room*). What accounts for this disconnect? Arrogance? Overconfidence? Inability to understand or value others' concerns and perspectives?[115] What implications do these findings have for aspiring leaders?

C. WHAT QUALITIES ARE CRITICAL FOR LEADERSHIP?

Although, as noted earlier, researchers have identified no single personality trait that correlates with successful leadership across all circumstances, they have identified qualities that tend to make leaders effective. These qualities cluster in five categories:
- Values (integrity, honesty, trust, service);
- Personal skills (self-awareness, self-control, conscientiousness);
- Interpersonal skills (social intelligence, empathy, persuasion, collaboration);
- Vision (forward-thinking, , inspirational); and
- Technical competence (knowledge, preparation, judgment).[116]

A Pew survey of the American public found that the leadership traits rated most important were honesty, intelligence, decisiveness, and organization.[117]

Other experts have looked at leadership in law and related fields. Maureen Broderick's study of personal service firms, including law firms, identified the capacity to influence and build coalitions, to inspire and be visionary, and to listen and communicate effectively.[118] The federal Office of Personnel Management and experts on government leaders emphasize integrity, decisiveness, self-direction, resilience, flexibility, emotional maturity, and an ethic of service.[119]

At the abstract level, few would disagree about the desirability of these characteristics. At the practical level, however, not all of them always correlate with objective measures of effectiveness, such as financial outcomes.[120] Moreover, in many contexts, competing values and situational pressures tug in different directions. For example, is empathy always the best policy? Empathy for whom? To what extent do we want leaders to empathize with the inevitable civilian casualties of military operations—euphemistically identified as "collateral damage"? Many brutal leaders are selectively empathetic; Hitler, for example, was responsive to concerns of the great majority of the German people.

In the excerpt below, Ben Heineman, a lawyer who has also held general counsel and public-policy positions, describes what he sees as the primary leadership challenges for the legal profession. Are the capacities that he sees as desirable for lawyers the ones you would emphasize? How can they be effectively developed?

BEN W. HEINEMAN JR., LAW AND LEADERSHIP

56 Journal of Legal Education 596 (2006)

My thesis is that law school graduates should aspire not just to be wise counselors but wise leaders; not just to dispense "practical wisdom" but to be "practical visionaries"; not just to have positions where they advise but where they decide. I wish to redefine, or at least reemphasize, the concept of lawyer explicitly to include "lawyer as leader." I do this with the hope that the law schools and the profession will more candidly recognize the importance of leadership and will more directly prepare and inspire young lawyers to seek roles of ultimate responsibility and accountability than is the case today. These are roles which those with core legal training have in fact assumed throughout our history and which Alexis de Tocqueville recognized and celebrated more than 150 years ago.

Why do I advance this thesis? First, our society—national and global—suffers from a leadership deficit. We need our brightest, toughest, most ethical, most broad-gauged to combine strong substantive visions with an ability to get things done. Surely, our law school graduates can try—and I emphasize try—to address that deficit if they are so motivated. The core competencies of law are as good a foundation for broad leadership as other training. . . .

Second, the legal profession, by many accounts, is suffering from a crisis that is "the product of growing doubts about the capacity of a lawyer's life to offer fulfillment. . . ." An important dimension of this problem is the disconnect between personal values and professional life, especially the possible amorality of serving clients' interests in an adversary mode. Providing leadership can certainly be an affirmation—and a testing—of one's vision and one's values. So providing leadership may serve both social and individual needs. . . .

Whatever the setting and whatever the style, the lawyer as leader is focused on making decisions for institutions or causes or ideas that . . . have as a driving force the desire to make our national or global society a "better place," however difficult that goal is to define, much less achieve. . . .

[What kind of lawyers should we be educating for leadership roles?] Most generally, we are seeking lawyers who *have a creative and constructive, not just a critical, cast of mind*, who relish asking "ought," not just answering "is," questions. How do we—how can we—build, not just deconstruct, an argument in a brief, a regulation, a complex piece of legislation, a business plan, the agenda of an NGO, a foreign policy, a cross-border strategy for global issues like energy and the environment?

 We are seeking lawyers who, in asking the "what ought we to do" questions, *can articulate powerfully a set of systematic and constructive options that expose and explore the value tensions inherent in most decisions . . . [and] can find a fair balance . . . between legitimate competing values. . . .*

We are seeking lawyers who *think about the ethical, reputational, and enlightened self-interest of their client or the institution they are leading*, not just about what is strictly legal or advantageous in the short term. . . .

We are seeking lawyers who, in making recommendations or decisions, *are capable of assessing all dimensions of risk but who are not risk-averse*. Taking chances is not a quality of mind customarily associated with lawyers but is often vital to innovation and change in the public and private sectors.

We are seeking lawyers who *have the ability to understand how to make rules realities*: lawyers who understand, *inter alia*, institutions, history, culture, resources, and psychology and who can identify, and develop, strategies to mitigate the obstacles to meaningful implementation.

We are seeking lawyers who *understand and respect the hurly burly world of politics, media and power*, not just the more intellectual world of policy prescriptions and legal rules. . . .

We are seeking lawyers who are not just strong individual contributors but who *have the ability to work cooperatively and constructively on teams*. . . .

We are seeking lawyers who are not just strong team members but who *can lead and build organizations*: create the vision, the values, the priorities, the strategies, the people, the systems, the processes, the checks and balances, the resources, and the motivation. Working on teams and leading them are interconnected: much of leadership today is not command and control of the troops but persuasion, motivation, and empowerment of teams around a shared vision.

We are seeking lawyers who, in developing positions, whether in an article, brief, regulation, legislation, code of corporate conduct, or a myriad other rule-announcing activities, *have the ability to understand the value, and limits, of related disciplines*—including economics, anthropology, history, political science, psychology, statistics, sociology, [public policy management,] and organizational theory—to increase the accuracy and sophistication of those positions. Lawyers cannot all have joint degrees, but they need the aptitude and capacity to envision the relevance and then, through the expertise of others, mine these other fields of knowledge—to understand their strengths and the limitations inherent in their assumptions and methods.

Most importantly, we are seeking lawyers who understand the methods of thinking and analysis taught in the business and public policy schools. . . .

We are seeking lawyers who have global understanding, intuition, and perspective.

We are seeking lawyers who can perform early in their careers as outstanding specialists so that they truly understand what analytic rigor and excellence are, but can then have the vision, breadth and inclination to be outstanding generalistleaders later in life. The quintessential quality of the great generalist is envisioning and understanding the multiple dimensions of issues—to define the problem or issue properly—and the ability to comprehensively integrate those dimensions into the decision. . . .

———

James Kouzes and Barry Posner's *The Leadership Challenge*, excerpted below, identifies practices that are key to effective leadership: model the way, inspire a shared vision, challenge the process, enable others to act, foster trust and collaboration, and <u>encourage the heart.</u> Do these seem adequate descriptions? Can you identify examples of such practices in leaders whom you admire?

JAMES M. KOUZES AND BARRY Z. POSNER, THE LEADERSHIP CHALLENGE (4TH ED.)

(San Francisco: Jossey-Bass, 2007), pp. 14-23, 28-30, and 32-35

The Five Practices of Exemplary Leadership

We began our research on what constituents expect of leaders more than twenty-five years ago by surveying thousands of business and government executives. We asked the following *open-ended* question: "What values, personal traits, or characteristics do you look for and admire in a leader?". . .

From [the responses], we developed a survey questionnaire called "Characteristics of Admired Leaders." We've administered this questionnaire to over seventy-five thousand people around the globe, and we update the findings continuously. We distribute a one-page checklist and ask respondents to select the seven qualities that they "most look for and admire in a leader, someone whose direction they would <u>willingly</u> follow." We tell them that the key word in this question is *willingly*. What do they expect from a leader they would follow, not because they have to, but because they want to?

The results have been striking in their regularity over the years, and they do not significantly vary by demographic, organizational, or cultural differences. Wherever we've asked the question, it's clear, as the data in [the following t]able illustrate, that there are a few essential "character tests" someone must pass before others are willing to grant the designation *leader*.

Although every characteristic receives some votes, and therefore each is important to some people, what is most striking and most evident is that only four over time (with the exception of Inspiring in 1987) have always received over 60 percent of the votes. And these same four have consistently been ranked at the top *across different countries.* . . .

What people most look for in a leader (a person that they would be willing to follow) has been constant over time. And our research documents this consistent pattern across countries, cultures, ethnicities, organizational functions and hierarchies, gender, educational, and age groups. For people to follow someone willingly, the majority of constituents believe the leader must be

- Honest
- Forward-looking
- Inspiring
- Competent. . . .

Honest

In almost every survey we've conducted, honesty has been selected more often than any other leadership characteristic; overall, it emerges as the single most important factor in the leader-constituent relationship. The percentages vary, but the final ranking does not. Since the very first time we conducted our studies honesty has been at the top of the list.

It's clear that if people anywhere are to willingly follow someone—whether it's into battle or into the boardroom, the front office or the front lines—they first want to assure themselves that the person is worthy of their trust. They want to know that the person is truthful, ethical, and principled. When people talk to us about the qualities they admire in leaders, they often use the terms *integrity* and *character* as synonymous with honesty. . . .

We want our leaders to be honest because their honesty is also a reflection upon our own honesty. Of all the qualities that people look for and admire in a leader, honesty is by far the most personal. More than likely this is also why it consistently ranks number one. It's the quality that can most enhance or most damage our own personal reputations. . . .

Forward-Looking

A little more than 70 percent of our most recent respondents selected the ability to look ahead as one of their most sought-after leadership traits. People expect leaders to have a sense of direction and a concern for the future of the organization. This expectation directly corresponds to the ability to envision the future that leaders described in their personal-best cases. Whether we call that ability vision, a dream, a calling, a goal, or a personal agenda, the message is clear: leaders must know where they're going if they expect others to willingly join them on the journey. . . .

We want to know what the organization will look like, feel like, and be like when it arrives at its destination in six quarters or six years. We want to have it described to us in rich detail so that we can select the proper route for getting there and know when we've arrived.

Clarity of vision into the distant future may be difficult to attain, but it's essential that leaders seek the knowledge and master the skills necessary to envision what's across the horizon. Compared to all the other leadership qualities constituents expect, this is the one that most distinguishes leaders from other credible people. Expecting leaders to be forward-looking doesn't mean constituents want their leaders to set out on a solitary vision quest; people want to be engaged in the search for a meaningful future. . . . But this expectation does mean that leaders have a special responsibility to attend to the future of their organizations.

Characteristics of Admired Leaders

Characteristic	Percentage of Respondents Selecting Each Characteristic (2007 ed.)
HONEST	89
FORWARD-LOOKING	71
INSPIRING	69
COMPETENT	68
Intelligent	48
Fair-minded	39
Straightforward	36
Broad-minded	35
Supportive	35
Dependable	34
Cooperative	25
Courageous	25
Determined	25
Caring	22
Imaginative	17
Mature	15
Ambitious	16
Loyal	18
Self-Controlled	10
Independent	4

Note: These percentages represent respondents from six continents: Africa, North America, South America, Asia, Europe, and Australia. The majority of respondents are from the United States. Since we asked people to select seven characteristics, the total adds up to more than 100 percent.

how do we inspire people?

Inspiring

People expect their leaders to be enthusiastic, energetic, and positive about the future. It's not enough for a leader to have a dream. A leader must be able to communicate the vision in ways that encourage people to sign on for the duration and excite them about the cause. . . .

Inspiring leadership also speaks to constituents' need to have meaning and purpose in their lives. Being upbeat, positive, and optimistic about the future offers people hope. . . .

Competent

To enlist in a common cause, people must believe that the leader is competent to guide them where they're headed. They must see the leader as having relevant experience and sound judgment. If they doubt the person's abilities, they're unlikely to join in the crusade.

Leadership competence refers to the leader's track record and ability to get things done. . . .

Another key characteristic of effective leaders is what Daniel Goleman, Richard Boyatzis, and Annie McKee describe as "emotional intelligence": (1) personal competence, involving self-awareness and self-management; and (2) social competence, involving social awareness (i.e., empathy) and relationship management (i.e., persuasion, conflict management, and collaboration). Their research suggests that these skills enable individuals to find resonance with wide groups, identify common ground, build rapport, and move people toward a common vision.[121]

DANIEL GOLEMAN, RICHARD BOYATZIS, AND ANNIE MCKEE, PRIMAL LEADERSHIP: LEARNING TO LEAD WITH EMOTIONAL INTELLIGENCE

(Boston: Harvard Business School Press, 2002),
pp. 38-40 and 45-52

. . . Interestingly, no leader we've ever encountered, no matter how outstanding, has strengths across the board in every one of the many EI [(emotional intelligence)] competencies. Highly effective leaders typically exhibit a critical mass of strength in a half dozen or so EI competencies. Moreover, there's no fixed formula for great leadership: There are many paths to excellence, and superb leaders can possess very different personal styles. Still, we find that effective leaders typically demonstrate strengths in at least one competence from each of the four fundamental areas of emotional intelligence.

Self-Awareness

Simply put, self-awareness means having a deep understanding of one's emotions, as well as one's strengths and limitations and one's values and motives.

People with strong self-awareness are realistic—neither overly self-critical nor naively hopeful. Rather, they are honest with themselves about themselves. And they are honest about themselves with others, even to the point of being able to laugh at their own foibles.

Self-aware leaders also understand their values, goals, and dreams. They know where they're headed and why. They're attuned to what "feels right" to them. For example, they're able to be firm in turning down a job offer that's tempting financially but doesn't fit with their principles or long-term goals. Conversely, a person lacking self-awareness will likely make decisions that trigger inner turmoil by treading on buried values. "The money looked good so I signed on," someone might say two years into a job, "but the work means so little to me that I'm constantly bored." Because the decisions of self-aware people mesh with their values, they more often find their work energizing.

Perhaps the most telling (though least visible) sign of self-awareness is a propensity for self-reflection and thoughtfulness. Self-aware people typically find time to reflect quietly, often off by themselves, which allows them to think things over rather than react impulsively. Many outstanding leaders, in fact, bring to their work life the thoughtful mode of self-reflection that they cultivate in their spiritual lives. For some this means prayer or meditation; for others it's a more philosophical quest for self-understanding.

All of these traits of self-aware leaders enable them to act with the conviction and authenticity that resonance requires. . . .

In short, intuition offers EI leaders a direct pipeline to their accumulated life wisdom on a topic. And it takes the inner attunement of self-awareness to sense that message.

The Leader's Primal Challenge: Self-Management

From self-awareness—understanding one's emotions and being clear about one's purpose—flows self-management, the focused drive that all leaders need to achieve their goals. Without knowing what we're feeling, we're at a loss to manage those feelings. Instead, our emotions control us. That's usually fine, when it comes to positive emotions like enthusiasm and the pleasure of meeting a challenge. But no leader can afford to be controlled by negative emotions, such as frustration and rage or anxiety and panic.

self-awareness
⇓
self-managment

The problem is that such negative emotional surges can be overwhelming; they're the brain's way of making us pay attention to a perceived threat. The result is that those emotions swamp the thinking brain's capacity to focus on the task at hand, whether it's strategic planning or dealing with news of a drop in market share. . . .

Self-management, then—which resembles an ongoing inner conversation—is the component of emotional intelligence that frees us from being a prisoner of our feelings. It's what allows the mental clarity and concentrated energy that leadership demands, and what keeps disruptive emotions from throwing us off track. Leaders with such self-mastery embody an upbeat, optimistic enthusiasm that tunes resonance to the positive range. . . .

Similarly, leaders who can stay optimistic and upbeat, even under intense pressure, radiate the positive feelings that create resonance. By staying in control of their feelings and impulses, they craft an environment of trust, comfort, and fairness. And that self-management has a trickle-down effect from the leader. No one wants to be known as a hothead when the boss consistently exudes a calm demeanor. . . .

Social Awareness and the Limbic Tango

After self-awareness and emotional self-management, resonant leadership requires social awareness or, put another way, empathy. . . .

While empathy represents a necessary ingredient of EI leadership, another lies in leaders' ability to express their message in a way that moves others. Resonance flows from a leader who expresses feelings with conviction because those emotions are clearly authentic, rooted in deeply held values. . . .

Social awareness—particularly empathy—is crucial for the leader's primal task of driving resonance. By being attuned to how others feel in the moment, a leader can say and do what's appropriate—whether it be to calm fears, assuage anger, or join in good spirits. This attunement also lets a leader sense the shared values and priorities that can guide the group. By the same token, a leader who lacks empathy will unwittingly be off-key, and so speak and act in ways that set off negative reactions. Empathy—which includes listening and taking other people's perspectives—allows leaders to tune into the emotional channels between people that create resonance. And staying attuned lets them fine-tune their message to keep it in synch.

Empathy: The Business Case

Of all the dimensions of emotional intelligence, social awareness may be the most easily recognized. We have all felt the empathy of a sensitive teacher or friend; we have all been struck by its absence in an unfeeling coach or boss. But when it comes to business, we rarely hear people praised, let alone rewarded, for their empathy. The very word seems unbusinesslike, out of place amid the tough realities of the marketplace.

But empathy—the fundamental competence of social awareness—doesn't mean a kind of "I'm okay, you're okay" mushiness. It doesn't mean that leaders should adopt other people's emotions as their own and try to please everybody. That would be a nightmare—it would make action impossible. Rather, empathy means taking employees' feelings into thoughtful consideration and then making intelligent decisions that work those feelings into the response. . . .

Empathetic people are superb at recognizing and meeting the needs of clients, customers, or subordinates. They seem approachable, wanting to hear what people have to say. They listen carefully, picking up on what people are truly concerned about, and they respond on the mark. . . .

Finally, in the growing global economy, empathy is a critical skill for both getting along with diverse workmates and doing business with people from other cultures. Cross-cultural dialogue can easily lead to miscues and misunderstandings. Empathy is an antidote that attunes people to subtleties in body language, or allows them to hear the emotional message beneath the words.

Relationship Management

The triad of self-awareness, self-management, and empathy all come together in the final EI ability: relationship management. Here we find the most visible tools of leadership—persuasion, conflict management, and collaboration among them. Managing relationships skillfully boils down to handling other people's emotions. This, in turn, demands that leaders be aware of their own emotions and attuned with empathy to the people they lead.

If a leader acts disingenuously or manipulatively, for instance, the emotional radar of followers will sense a note of falseness and they will instinctively distrust that leader. The art of handling relationships well, then, begins with authenticity: acting from one's genuine feelings. Once leaders have attuned to their own vision and values, steadied in the positive emotional range, and tuned into the emotions of the group, then relationship management skills let them interact in ways that catalyze resonance.

Handling relationships, however, is not as simple as it sounds. It's not just a matter of friendliness, although people with strong social skills are rarely mean-spirited. Rather, relationship management is friendliness with a purpose: moving people in the right direction, whether that's agreement on a marketing strategy or enthusiasm about a new project.

That is why socially skilled leaders tend to have resonance with a wide circle of people—and have a knack for finding common ground and building rapport. That doesn't mean they socialize continually; it means they work under the assumption that nothing important gets done alone. Such leaders have a network in place when the time for action comes. And in an era when more and more work is done long distance—by e-mail or by phone—relationship building, paradoxically, becomes more crucial than ever.

Given the primal task of leadership, the ability to inspire and move people with a compelling vision looms large. Inspirational leaders get people excited about a common mission. They offer a sense of purpose beyond the day-to-day tasks or quarterly goals that so often take the place of a meaningful vision. Such leaders know that what people value most deeply will move them most powerfully in their work. Because they are aware of their own guiding values, they can articulate a vision that has the ring of truth for those they lead. That strong sense of the collective mission also leaves inspirational leaders free to direct and guide with firmness.

NOTES AND QUESTIONS

1. Some experts believe that for the nation's most significant leadership positions, temperament is critical to success.[122] Supreme Court Justice Oliver Wendell Holmes famously described Franklin Roosevelt as a "second class

intellect. But a first class temperament."[123] Yet not all leaders seem to have the temperament and emotional intelligence that Goleman, Boyatzis, and McKee describe. Many politicians including Margaret Thatcher and Donald Trump have been portrayed as abrasive, arrogant, narcissistic, or lacking in interpersonal skills.[124] Even such legendary leaders as Steve Jobs have frequently lost positions in part due to arrogance and inability to relate well to others.[125] Traits such as hubris (an exaggerated sense of pride or arrogance) and narcissism (grandiosity, an excessive need for admiration, and a strong sense of entitlement) help explain the emergence of leaders but often undermine their effectiveness.[126] What do you think accounts for the success of narcissistic individuals in gaining leadership positions? Why do followers not anticipate the problems that narcissism will create?[127]

2. Recent polls find that 95 percent of Americans believe that character is important for the nation's president and two thirds think that it is very important.[128] Yet two thirds of the public did not think that Donald Trump had "strong moral character," and less than a third considered him "honest and trustworthy."[129] What accounts for the disconnect between what voters say they value and the leaders they select? Research summarized in Chapter 5 indicates that Trump is not an exceptional case, and explores some of the reasons why integrity is devalued in political contexts.

3. Some leaders, such as George H. W. Bush, have dismissed the "vision thing," and many have improvised in the face of changing circumstances. Historians note that Franklin Roosevelt was "following no master program" in his initial handling of the Depression, "no fancy plans." Rather, he boasted of "playing by ear."[130] However, most research underscores the importance of an inspiring and credible mission, however general.[131] How would you describe the vision of a leader or an organization that you admire?

4. Recent research suggests that self-awareness is the primary characteristic that distinguishes successful leaders; it provides the foundation for professional development.[132] How would you rate yourself on that dimension? What might you do to increase your self-awareness?

5. Global research finds that some traits are valued for leaders throughout the world, such as foresight, trustworthiness, and positive attitudes. Other characteristics, such as risk-taking, sensitivity, compassion, and ambition are more culturally contingent.[133] Leaders in individualist cultures such as the United States tend to prioritize their own careers and emphasize assertiveness, innovation, and self-confidence.[134] East Asian leaders who are influenced by Confucian principles tend to place more value on group rather than individual interests, and Middle East and Latin American leaders generally place a premium on "saving face" and maintaining their dignity and reputation.[135] How might these cultural differences affect the way that leaders negotiate or give feedback? What other cultural differences might be important for global leaders to recognize?

PROBLEM 1-2

Create a list of seven qualities that you think would be most useful for a leadership position that you could envision yourself occupying. Rate yourself from one to five on each of those characteristics. Ask several individuals who know you reasonably well to do the same on an anonymous form and develop a mean for each of these traits. How do your self-ratings compare with their ratings?[136] What areas of improvement do the ratings suggest?

MEDIA RESOURCES

Many films and television series offer useful snapshots of leadership. The opening scenes of *Primary Colors*, a film based on Bill Clinton's initial presidential primary campaign, show the magnetism and empathetic responses that enabled him to connect so well with voters. Many episodes in the television series *The West Wing*, *Madame Secretary*, *House of Cards*, and *Veep* offer interesting portraits of political leadership. *The Good Wife* features law firm leaders coping with ethical and leadership dilemmas, and *Billions* profiles the U.S. Attorney for the Southern District of New York as he seeks to prosecute a leading hedge fund manager. *Michael Clayton*, starring George Clooney as a fixer for a prominent corporate law firm, shows lawyers exercising a range of soft and hard power. *The Children's Act*, starring Emma Thompson, portrays a British judge struggling to balance empathy and the rule of law in a case involving a minor's right to refuse a blood transfusion that would violate his religious beliefs.

The confirmation hearings of Justice Brett Kavanaugh offer a window on the meaning and importance of temperament for judicial leaders. As Chapter 7 indicates, his vitriolic tone, accusations of partisanship, and lack of respect toward certain female senators prompted widespread concern. Following his testimony, the American Bar Association rescinded its rating of his qualification for appointment.[137]

END NOTES

[1] Neil W. Hamilton, *Ethical Leadership in Professional Life*, 6 ST. THOMAS L. REV. 358, 361 (2009). In 2019, 40 percent of Congress attended law school. Thomas Lewis, INSIGHT: Law School Popular for Congress, with Harvard, Georgetown Topping List, BLOOMBERG LAW, Jan. 25, 2019, https://news.bloomberglaw.com/us-law-week/insight-law-school-popular-for-congress-with-harvard-georgetown-topping-list.

[2] For lawyers' representation in the population, see James Podgers, *State of the Union: The Nation's Lawyer Population Continues to Grow, But Barely*, ABA J. (July 1, 2011), http://www.abajournal.com/magazine/article/state_of_the_union_the_nations_lawyer_po pulation_continues_to_grow_but_bare.

Approximately 10 percent of the CEOs of Fortune 50 companies are lawyers. *See* Mark Curriden, *CEO, Esq.*, ABA J. (May 1, 2010), http://www.abajournal.com/magazine/article/ceo_esq/.

[3] S.A. Rosenthal, NATIONAL LEADERSHIP INDEX 2012: A NATIONAL STUDY OF CONFIDENCE IN LEADERSHIP (Center for Public Leadership, Harvard University, 2012).

[4] Gallup, *Honesty/Ethics in Professions* (Dec. 3-12, 2018), http://www.gallup.com /poll/1654/honesty-ethics-professions.aspx.

[5] Ann Swanson, *How the Most Disliked—and Elected—Profession Is Disappearing from Politics*, WASH. POST, Jan. 19, 2016; Lewis, INSIGHT.

[6] *The Harris Poll Annual Confidence Index Rises 10 Points*, BUSINESS WIRE (Mar. 5, 2009), https://www.businesswire.com/news/home/20090305005071/en/Harris-Poll%C2%AE-Annual-Confidence-Index-Rises-10.

[7] PEW RESEARCH CENTER, PUBLIC TRUST IN GOVERNMENT, 1958-2017 (Dec. 14, 2017).

[8] The Editorial Board, *Pick Your Favorite Ethics Offender in Trumpland,* N.Y. TIMES, Apr. 1, 2017; Mark Landler & Glenn Thrush, *Trump Denies any Collusion Between his Campaign and Russia*, N.Y. TIMES, May 18, 2017; Amy B. Wang, *Trump Lashes Out at "So-Called Judge" Who Temporarily Blocked Travel Ban*, WASH. POST, Feb. 4, 2017.

[9] In his classic 1954 book on management, Peter Drucker summed up conventional wisdom: "Leadership cannot be taught or learned." PETER E. DRUCKER, THE PRACTICE OF MANAGEMENT 194 (1954). For contemporary research, see, e.g., ROGER GILL, THE THEORY AND PRACTICE OF LEADERSHIP 271 (2006); for Drucker, see Peter Drucker, *Foreword,* in THE LEADER OF THE FUTURE xi (Frances Hesselbein & Marshall Goldsmith eds., 1996) (noting that "leadership must be learned and can be learned").

[10] Richard D. Arvey, Nan Wang, Zhaoli Song & Wendong Li, *The Biology of Leadership*, in THE OXFORD HANDBOOK OF LEADERSHIP AND ORGANIZATIONS 79 (David V. Day ed., 2014). For studies on twins suggesting that 70 percent of leadership skills are acquired, not genetically based, see Richard D. Avery, Maria Rotundo, Wendy Johnson, Zhen Zhang & Matt McGue*, The Determinants of Leadership Role Occupancy: Genetic and Personality Factors*, 17 LEADERSHIP Q. 1 (2006); Bruce Avolio, *Pursuing Authentic Leadership Development*, in HANDBOOK OF LEADERSHIP THEORY AND PRACTICE 739, 752 (Nitin Nohria & Rakesh Khurana eds., 2010). *See also* WARREN G. BENNIS & BERT NANUS, LEADERSHIP: STRATEGIES FOR TAKING CHARGE 207 (1997).

[11] KEITH GRINT, LEADERSHIP: CLASSICAL, CONTEMPORARY, AND CRITICAL APPROACHES 2 (1997).

[12] Jacob Heilbrunn, *Interim Report*, N.Y. TIMES BOOK REV., May 30, 2010, at 12.

[13] WILLIAM A. COHEN, DRUCKER ON LEADERSHIP 204 (2010).

[14] Ben Brooks & Natasha H. Chapman, *Leadership is Learned,* 12 J. LEADERSHIP STUD. 72, 73 (2018).

[15] For expenditures, see Gillian Pillans, *Leadership Development: Is It Fit For Purpose*, CORP. RES. FORUM, May, 2015; Sara Canaday, *Shedding Light on Our Leadership Development Crisis,* HUFFINGTON POST (Apr. 9, 2016), http://www.huffingtonpost.com/sara-canaday/shedding-light-on-our-leadersip_b_9649 906.html.

[16] For growing recognition of the need for leadership education, see Richard Greenwald, *Today's Students Need Leadership Training Like Never Before*, CHRON. OF HIGHER EDUC. (Dec. 6, 2010), http://chronicle.com/article/Todays-Students-Need/125604.

[17] BERNARD M. BASS, BASS AND STOGDILL'S HANDBOOK OF LEADERSHIP: THEORY, RESEARCH, & MANAGERIAL APPLICATIONS (3d ed. 1990); Gareth Edwards, *In Search of the Holy Grail: Leadership in Management* (Working Paper LT-GE-00-15 Ross-on-Wye, United Kingdom, Leadership Trust Foundation, 2000).

[18] ROGER GILL, THEORY AND PRACTICE OF LEADERSHIP (2006); JOSEPH C. ROST, LEADERSHIP FOR THE TWENTY-FIRST CENTURY 38 (1991).

[19] NICK PETRIE, FUTURE TRENDS IN LEADERSHIP DEVELOPMENT 21-22 (Center for Creative Leadership, 2014); RONALD H. HUMPHREY, EFFECTIVE LEADERSHIP: THEORY, CASES, AND APPLICATIONS 246-248 (2014); CRAIG PEARCE & JAY CONGER, SHARED LEADERSHIP REFRAMING THE HOW AND WHYS OF LEADERSHIP (2002).

[20] JOHN W. GARDNER, ON LEADERSHIP 3 (1990).

[21] David V. Day & John Antonakis, *Leadership: Past, Present, and Future,* in THE NATURE OF LEADERSHIP 5 (DAVID V. DAY & JOHN ANTONAKIS eds., 2d ed. 2012); PETER NORTHOUSE, LEADERSHIP: THEORY AND PRACTICE 3 (7th ed. 2015).

[22] Deborah L. Rhode, *Where Is the Leadership in Moral Leadership?*, in MORAL LEADERSHIP: THE THEORY AND PRACTICE OF POWER, JUDGMENT, AND POLICY 1, 4 (2006).

[23] Thom Shanker, *Retiring Army Chief of Staff Warns against Arrogance*, N.Y. TIMES, June 12, 2004, at 32.

[24] MONTGOMERY VAN WART, DYNAMICS OF LEADERSHIP IN PUBLIC SERVICE: THEORY AND PRACTICE 113 (2005).

[25] GARDNER, ON LEADERSHIP, 34.

[26] Max Weber, *The Sociology of Charismatic Authority*, in FROM MAX WEBER: ESSAYS IN SOCIOLOGY 245-246 (H. H. Gerth & C. Wright Mills trans. and eds., 2009).

[27] GILL, THEORY AND PRACTICE OF LEADERSHIP, 253; Robert C. Solomon, *The Myth of Charisma,* in THE ETHICS OF LEADERSHIP 202 (Joan B. Ciulla ed., 2003); RONALD E. RIGGIO, THE CHARISMA QUOTIENT (1987) (chapters 2 and 3 discuss emotional and social sensitivity, expressiveness, and control).

[28] *See* Ketan H. Mhatra & Ronald E. Riggio, *Charismatic and Transformational Leadership: Past, Present and Future*, in THE OXFORD HANDBOOK OF LEADERSHIP 221-25 (David v. Day ed., 2014); R.J. House, *Path-Goal Theory of Leadership: Lessons, Legacy and Reformulated Theory*, 7 LEADERSHIP Q. 323 (1996); Michael E. Brown & Linda K. Trevino, *Is Values-Based Leadership Ethical Leadership?*, in EMERGING PERSPECTIVES ON VALUES IN ORGANIZATIONS 151, 168 (Stephen Gilliland, Douglas Steiner & Daniel Skarlicki eds., 2003).

[29] JAY A. CONGER & RABINDRA N. KANUNGO, CHARISMATIC LEADERSHIP IN ORGANIZATIONS (1998).

[30] RABINDRA N. KANUNGO & MANUEL MENDONCA, ETHICAL DIMENSIONS OF LEADERSHIP 20 (1996); Solomon, *Myth of Charisma,* 202 (noting the role of crisis).

[31] Herbert Spencer, *The Great Man Theory Breaks Down*, in POLITICAL LEADERSHIP: A SOURCE BOOK, Chap. 13 (Barbara Kellerman ed., 1986).

[32] JOSEPH NYE, THE POWERS TO LEAD 5 (2008).

[33] NYE, THE POWERS TO LEAD, 15.

[34] DORIS KEARNS GOODWIN, LEADERSHIP IN TURBULENT TIMES, xiii-xiv (2018).

[35] GARDNER, ON LEADERSHIP, 5-6, 47.

[36] GOODWIN, LEADERSHIP IN TURBULENT TIMES, 41-42.

[37] *See* Cheryl Lavin, *Nader the Dragonslayer Still Breathing Fire*, CHI. TRIB., July 13, 1986, at C1; Tamara Straus, *From Hero to Pariah in One Documentary*, S.F. CHRON., Mar.

11, 2007, at PK-28 (reviewing the documentary, *An Unreasonable Man*); JUSTIN MARTIN, NADER: CRUSADER, SPOILER, ICON, 267-69 (2002).

[38] BROWN, MYTH OF THE STRONG LEADER, 54-55.

[39] Marcia Coyle, *A Supreme Court Memoir*, NAT'L L.J., Oct. 3, 2011, at 27 (quoting Stevens); BOB WOODWARD & SCOTT ARMSTRONG, THE BRETHREN: INSIDE THE SUPREME COURT 66, 174, 256 (1979); JEFFREY TOOBIN, THE NINE: INSIDE THE SECRET WORLD OF THE SUPREME COURT 29 (2008) (quoting Rehnquist).

[40] WALTER R. NEWELL, THE SOUL OF A LEADER 81-84 (2009).

[41] NYE, THE POWERS TO LEAD, 21-22 (quoting Bill George et al., *Discovering Your Authentic Leadership*, HARV. BUS. REV., Feb. 2007, at 129).

[42] GILL, THEORY AND PRACTICE OF LEADERSHIP, 39.

[43] JAMES MACGREGOR BURNS, LEADERSHIP 244 (1978). Robert Solomon argues that "charisma doesn't refer to any character trait or quality in particular, but is rather a general way of referring to a person who seems to be a dynamic and effective leader. And as a term of analysis in leadership studies, . . . it is more a distraction than a point of understanding." Robert C. Solomon, *Ethical Leadership, Emotion and Trust: Beyond "Charisma,"* in ETHICS: THE HEART OF LEADERSHIP 98 (Joanne B. Ciulla ed., 2d ed. 2004). *See also* GARDNER, ON LEADERSHIP, 35.

[44] Bradley Agle et al., *Does CEO Charisma Matter? An Empirical Analysis of the Relationships Among Organizational Performance, Environmental Uncertainty, and Top Management Team Perception of CEO Charisma*, 49 ACAD. MGMT. J. 161 (2006).

[45] Jasmine Vergauwe et al., *Too Much Charisma Can Make Leaders Look Less Effective*, HARV. BUS. REV. (2017).

[46] Gary Yuki, *Leading Organizational Learning: Reflections on Theory and Practice*, 20 LEADERSHIP Q. 49, 50 (2010).

[47] Jim Collins, *Level 5 Leadership: The Triumph of Humility and Fierce Resolve*, HARV. BUS. REV. 73 (Jan. 2001); GILL, THEORY AND PRACTICE OF LEADERSHIP, 253.

[48] Michael Hiltzik, *Peter Drucker's Revolutionary Teachings Decades Old but Still Fresh*, L.A. TIMES, Dec. 31, 2009.

[49] Michael Hiltzik, *Peter Drucker's Revolutionary Teachings Decades Old but Still Fresh*, L.A. TIMES (Dec. 31, 2009). Peter F. Drucker, *Forward*, in THE LEADER OF THE FUTURE 2: NEW VISIONS STRATEGIES AND PRACTICES FOR THE NEXT ERA xi-xii (Frances Hesselbein, Marshalll Goldsmith & Richard Beckhard eds., 2006).

[50] ARCHIE BROWN, THE MYTH OF THE STRONG LEADER 76 (2004) (quoting Churchill).

[51] STANLEY MCCHRYSTAL, JEFF EGGERS & JASON MANGONE, LEADERS: MYTH AND REALITY 193 (2018).

[52] DREW WESTEN, THE POLITICAL BRAIN: THE ROLE OF EMOTION IN DECIDING THE FATE OF THE NATION 125 (2007). *See also* BROWN, MYTH OF THE STRONG LEADER, 50.

[53] MCCHRYSTAL, EGGERS & MANGONE, LEADERS, 48.

[54] James O'Toole, *When Leadership Is an Organizational Trait*, in THE FUTURE OF LEADERSHIP 159 (Warren Bennis, Gretchen M. Spreitzer & Thomas G. Cummings eds., 2001).

[55] J. Richard Hackman, *What Is This Thing Called Leadership?*, in HANDBOOK OF LEADERSHIP THEORY AND PRACTICE 110 (Nitin Nohria & Rakesh Khurana eds., 2010); Joel L. Podolney, Rakesh Khurana & Max L. Besharov, *Revisiting the Meaning of Leadership*, in HANDBOOK OF LEADERSHIP THEORY AND PRACTICE 53, 66 (Nohria & Khurana eds., 2010).

[56] JOHN W. GARDNER, LIVING, LEADING, AND THE AMERICAN DREAM 122 (Francesca Gardner ed., 2003).

[57] McCHRYSTAL, EGGERS & MANGONE, LEADERS, 376-382.

[58] FRED GREENSTEIN, THE PRESIDENTIAL DIFFERENCE (2009); Mathew N. Beckmann, *A President's Decisions and the Presidential Difference,* in LEADERSHIP IN AMERICAN POLITICS 69-70 (Jeffery A. Jenkins & Craig Volden eds., 2017).

[59] GEORGE EDWARDS, AT THE MARGINS: PRESIDENTIAL LEADERSHIP OF CONGRESS 211 (1989).

[60] Philip B. K. Potter, *Presidential Leadership in American Foreign Policy*, in LEADERSHIP IN AMERICAN POLITICS, 91-97.

[61] MARK PETERSON, LEGISLATING TOGETHER: THE WHITE HOUSE AND CAPITOL HILL FROM EISENHOWER TO REAGAN 267 (1990).

[62] Noria & Khurana, *Advancing Leadership Theory and Practice*, in HANDBOOK OF LEADERSHIP THEORY AND PRACTICE 9 (Nohria & Khurana eds., 2010); Noah Wasserman, Bharat N. Anand & Nitin Nohria, *When Does Leadership Matter? The Contingent Opportunities View of CEO Leadership,* in HANDBOOK OF LEADERSHIP THEORY AND PRACTICE 27, 30-32, 49 (Nohria & Khurana eds., 2010); Hackman, *What Is This Thing Called Leadership?*, 110.

[63] Mats Alvesson & André Spicer, *Critical Perspectives on Leadership*, in THE OXFORD HANDBOOK ON LEADERSHIP AND ORGANIZATIONS 43-45 (David V. Day ed., 2014).

[64] David Denyer & Kim Turnbull James, *Doing Leadership-as-Practice Development*, in LEADERSHIP AS PRACTICE: THEORY AND APPLICATION 264 (Joseph A. Raelin ed., 2016); Lucia Crevani & Nada Endrissat, *Mapping the Leadership-as-Practice Terrain: Comparative Elements*, in *Id.*, at 31.

[65] For example, a recent statistical study by Laurie Bassi & Daniel McMurrer found that the most powerful predictor of large firm profitability is "the quality of the partners' leadership skills." Laurie Bassi & Daniel McMurrer, *Leadership and Large Firm Success: A Statistical Analysis*, McBASSI & Co. 5 (Feb. 2008), http://www.leadershipforattorneys.org/articles/WhitePaper-LeadershipAndLawFirmSuccess%20Feb%208.pdf. For other evidence on the importance of leadership, see Jennifer A. Chatman & Jessica A. Kennedy, *Psychological Perspectives on Leadership*, in HANDBOOK OF LEADERSHIP THEORY AND PRACTICE 159, 160 (Nohria & Khurana eds., 2010).

[66] JOE A. WALLIS & BRIAN E. DOLLERY, MARKET FAILURE, GOVERNMENT FAILURE, LEADERSHIP, AND PUBLIC POLICY 119, 125 (1999).

[67] For overviews, see GILL, THEORY AND PRACTICE OF LEADERSHIP; PETER GUY NORTHOUSE, LEADERSHIP: THEORY AND PRACTICE (3d ed. 2004).

[68] BROWN, THE MYTH OF THE STRONG LEADER, 25.

[69] For early development of the theory, see FRED E. FIEDLER, A THEORY OF LEADERSHIP EFFECTIVENESS (1967); Fred E. Fiedler, *Leadership: A New Model*, in LEADERSHIP 230-241 (C.A. Gibb ed., 1969).

[70] NORTHOUSE, LEADERSHIP, 111-123; EDWIN P. HOLLANDER, INCLUSIVE LEADERSHIP: THE ESSENTIAL LEADER-FOLLOWER RELATIONSHIP 28 (2009).

[71] NORTHOUSE, LEADERSHIP, 93-107; HOLLANDER, INCLUSIVE LEADERSHIP, 27.

[72] Deanne N. Den Hartog & Marcus W. Dickson, *Leadership and Culture*, in THE NATURE OF LEADERSHIP 404-419 (DAVID V. DAY & JOHN ANTONAKIS eds., 2d ed. 2012). For other differences, see Mansour Javidan et al., *In the Eye of the Beholder: Cross Cultural Lessons in Leadership from Project GLOBE*, 20 ACAD. MGMT. PERSP. 67, 72-73 (2006).

[73] Paul Hersey & Kenneth H. Blanchard, *The Life Cycle Theory of Leadership*, 23 Training and Development J. 26 (1969); PAUL HERSEY & KENNETH H. BLANCHARD, MANAGEMENT OF ORGANIZATIONAL BEHAVIOR: UTILIZING HUMAN RESOURCES (6th ed. 1993); NORTHOUSE, LEADERSHIP, 89-90.

[74] Joshua Rothman, *Shut Up and Sit Down: Why the Leadership Industry Rules*, NEW YORKER, Feb. 29, 2016.

[75] WALLIS & DOLLERY, MARKET FAILURE, GOVERNMENT FAILURE, LEADERSHIP AND PUBLIC POLICY, 145.

[76] See Robert Goffee & Gareth Jones, *Why Should Anyone Be Led by You?*, HARV. BUS. REV. 63, 64 (Sept.-Oct. 2000); Jay W. Lorsch, *A Contingency Theory of Leadership*, in HANDBOOK OF LEADERSHIP THEORY AND PRACTICE 411-424 (Nohria & Khurana eds., 2010). For the importance of cultural and organizational context generally, see Roya Ayman & Susan Adams, *Contingencies, Context, Situation, and Leadership*, in THE NATURE OF LEADERSHIP 234 (David V. Day & John Antonakis eds., 2012).

[77] NYE, THE POWERS TO LEAD, 22.

[78] GILL, THEORY AND PRACTICE OF LEADERSHIP, 49; NORTHOUSE, LEADERSHIP, 115-116.

[79] Nohria & Khurana, *Advancing Leadership Theory and Practice*, 17.

[80] NORTHOUSE, LEADERSHIP, 176, 185; BERNARD M. BASS & RONALD E. RIGGIO, TRANSFORMATIONAL LEADERSHIP 3-4 (2d ed. 2006).

[81] BURNS, LEADERSHIP, 20, 46. *See also* Bernard M. Bass & Paul Steidlmeier, *Ethics, Character, and Authentic Transformational Leadership Behavior*, 10 LEADERSHIP Q. 181, 181-83 (1999).

[82] BASS & RIGGIO, TRANSFORMATIONAL LEADERSHIP, 6-7.

[83] The leading texts are by ROBERT K. GREENLEAF, SERVANT LEADERSHIP (1977), and ROBERT K. GREENLEAF, THE SERVANT AS LEADER (1991). The term is used in many leadership contexts. The motto of Sandhurst, the United Kingdom's Royal Military College is "serve to lead," and its prayer states: "Help us to be masters of ourselves that we may be servants of others and teach us to serve to lead."

[84] For an overview, see GILL, THEORY AND PRACTICE OF LEADERSHIP, 54, 59-60; JOAN B. CIULLA, *Leadership Ethics: Mapping the Territory*, in ETHICS: THE HEART OF LEADERSHIP (Joan B. Ciulla ed., 1998). For visionary leadership, see Marshall Saskin, *The Visionary Leader*, in CHARISMATIC LEADERSHIP: THE ELUSIVE FACTOR IN ORGANIZATIONAL EFFECTIVENESS (Jay A. Conger & Rabindra N. Kanungo eds., 1988). For strategic leadership, see GERRY JOHNSON & KEVAN SCHOLES, EXPLORING CORPORATE STRATEGY (6th ed. 1998); MICHAEL A. HITT, R. DUANE IRELAND & ROBERT E. HOSKISSON, STRATEGIC MANAGEMENT: COMPETITIVENESS & GLOBALIZATION (1995); Katherine Beatty & Laura Quinn, *Strategic Command: Taking the Long View for Organizational Success*, 22 LEADERSHIP IN ACTION 3 (2002).

[85] BERNARD M. BASS & BRUCE J. AVOLIO, *Introduction*, in IMPROVING ORGANIZATIONAL EFFECTIVENESS THROUGH TRANSFORMATIONAL LEADERSHIP (Bernard Bass & Bruce J. Avolio, 1994).

[86] Michael Keeley, *The Trouble with Transformational Leadership: Toward a Federalist Ethic for Organizations*, in ETHICS: THE HEART OF LEADERSHIP 111, 124 (Joanne B. Ciulla ed., 1998).

[87] KEOHANE, THINKING ABOUT LEADERSHIP, 43.

[88] BENNIS & NANUS, LEADERS: THE STRATEGIES FOR TAKING CHARGE 21 (1985).

[89] GARDNER, LIVING, LEADING, AND THE AMERICAN DREAM, 117. See WARREN BENNIS & JOAN GOLDSMITH, LEARNING TO LEAD 8 (2003); GILL, THEORY AND PRACTICE OF LEADERSHIP, 26; Abraham Zaleznik, *Managers and Leaders: Are They Different?*, HARV. BUS. REV. 74 (1977); JOHN P. KOTTER, A FORCE FOR CHANGE: HOW LEADERSHIP DIFFERS FROM MANAGEMENT 3-8 (1990).

[90] John P. Kotter, *What Leaders Really Do*, 68 HARV. BUS. REV. 74 103 (May-June 1990).

[91] Kotter, *What Leaders Really Do*, 104.

[92] Kotter, *What Leaders Really Do*, 104-05.

[93] Kotter, *What Leaders Really Do*, 104.

[94] JOANNE B. CIULLA, *Leadership Ethics* 1, 13.

[95] NORTHOUSE, LEADERSHIP, 10.

[96] GARDNER, LIVING, LEADING, AND THE AMERICAN DREAM, 116.

[97] GILL, THEORY AND PRACTICE OF LEADERSHIP, 28-30; Bruce A. Pasternak, Thomas D. Williams & Paul F. Anderson, *Beyond the Cult of the CEO: Building Institutional Leadership*, STRATEGY + BUS. 22 (2001); James O'Toole, *When Leadership is an Organizational Trait*, in THE FUTURE OF LEADERSHIP 160 (Warren Bennis, G.M. Spreitzer & T.G. Cummings eds., 2001).

[98] Elihu Root, *Lincoln as a Leader of Men,* in MEN AND POLICIES: ADDRESSES BY ELIHU ROOT 75 (Robert Bacon & James B. Scott eds., 1924).

[99] J. Patrick Dobel, *Managerial Leadership and the Ethical Importance of Legacy*, in PUBLIC ETHICS AND GOVERNANCE: STANDARDS AND PRACTICES IN COMPARATIVE PERSPECTIVE 201 (Denis Saint-Martin & Fred Thompson eds., 2006).

[100] Doebel, *Managerial Leadership*, 202.

[101] RAY BLUNT, LEADERS GROWING LEADERS FOR PUBLIC SERVICE, reprinted in THE JOSSEY-BASS READER IN NON-PROFIT PUBLIC LEADERSHIP 41 (James L. Perry ed., 2010) (quoting Noel Tichy).

[102] For similar exercises, see ROBERT E. QUINN ET AL., BECOMING A MASTER MANAGER 37 (5th ed. 2010).

[103] For a more complete list, see MARY C. GENTILE, GIVING VOICE TO VALUES app. Table 1 (2010).

[104] *See* QUINN et al., BECOMING A MASTER MANAGER, 40-41; Oliver P. John, Laura P. Naumann & Christopher J. Soto, *Paradigm Shift to the Integrative Five Factor Trait Taxonomy*, in HANDBOOK OF PERSONALITY: THEORY AND RESEARCH (Oliver P. John, Richard W. Robins & Lawrence A. Pervin eds., 3d ed. 2008).

[105] Leadership experts are divided. Burns claims Hitler was not a leader but a tyrant; Bass & Heifetz disagree. *See* Joanne Ciulla, *Leadership Ethics: Mapping the Territory*, 12-13, 74; BURNS, LEADERSHIP, 27, 240. BERNARD M. BASS, LEADERSHIP AND PERFORMANCE BEYOND EXPECTATIONS 183-185 (1985).

[106] RICHARD NIXON, LEADERS 324 (1982).

[107] DACHER KELTNER, THE POWER PARADOX: HOW WE GAIN AND LOSE INFLUENCE 3, 7 (2016).

[108] Rosabeth Moss Kanter, *Power Failure in Management Circuits*, 57 HARV. BUS. REV. 65 (July-Aug. 1979).

[109] GARDNER, ON LEADERSHIP, 55, 57.

[110] LIZ WISEMAN WITH GREG MCKEOWN, MULTIPLIERS: HOW THE BEST LEADERS MAKE EVERYONE SMARTER 20-22, 100-121 (2010); Scott N. Spreier, Mary H. Fontaine & Ruth L. Malloy, *Leadership Run Amok: The Destructive Potential of Overachievers*, HARV. BUS. REV. 74-79 (June 2006).

[111] JEFFERY PFEFFER, POWER: WHY SOME HAVE IT—AND OTHERS DON'T 43-47 (2010).

[112] For the correlation, see studies cited in RONALD H. HUMPHREY, EFFECTIVE LEADERSHIP: THEORY, CASES, AND APPLICATIONS 63 (2014).

[113] EDWIN P. HOLLANDER, INCLUSIVE LEADERSHIP: THE ESSENTIAL LEADER-FOLLOWER RELATIONSHIP 25 (2009); MCCHRYSTAL, EGGERS, AND MANONE, LEADERS, 148; BERNARD BASS AND RUTH BASS, THE BASS HANDBOOK OF LEADERSHIP: THEORY, RESEARCH & MANAGERIAL APPLICATIONS 148 (4th ed. 2008).

[114] PFEFFER, POWER, 55.

[115] PFEFFER, POWER, 56.

[116] NORTHOUSE, LEADERSHIP, 19; Robert Hogan and Robert B. Kaiser, *What We Know About Leadership*, 9 REV. GEN. PSYCHOL. 169, 172 (2005). *See also* MICHAEL GENOVESE, BUILDING TOMORROW'S LEADERS TODAY: ON BECOMING A POLYMATH LEADER (2013); MARSHALL SASHKIN & MOLLY G. SASHKIN, LEADERSHIP THAT MATTERS 183 (2003); HUMPHREY, EFFECTIVE LEADERSHIP, 69, 97-98; MIHALY CSIKSZENTMIHALYI, GOOD BUSINESS: LEADERSHIP, FLOW, AND THE MAKING OF MEANING 157 (2003); HOWARD GARDNER, MIHALY CSIKSZENTMIHALYI, AND WILLIAM DAMIN, GOOD WORK: WHEN EXCELLENCE AND ETHICS MEET 293 (2001).

[117] *Women and Leadership*, PEW RESEARCH CENTER (Jan. 4 2015), http://www.pewsocialtrends.org/2015/01/14/women-and-leadership/.

[118] MAUREEN BRODERICK, THE ART OF MANAGING PROFESSIONAL SERVICES: INSIGHTS FROM LEADERS OF THE WORLD'S TOP FIRMS 267 (2011).

[119] MONTGOMERY VAN WART, DYNAMICS OF LEADERSHIP IN PUBLIC SERVICE: THEORY AND PRACTICE 16, 92-119 (2005).

[120] NORTHOUSE, LEADERSHIP, 27.

[121] DANIEL GOLEMAN, RICHARD BOYATZIS & ANNIE MCKEE, PRIMAL LEADERSHIP: REALIZING THE POWER OF EMOTIONAL INTELLIGENCE 253-256 (2002).

[122] RICHARD E. NEUSTADT, PRESIDENTIAL POWER AND THE MODERN PRESIDENTS 153 (1980).

[123] GEOFFREY C. WARD, A FIRST-CLASS TEMPERAMENT: THE EMERGENCE OF FRANKLIN ROOSEVELT, 1905-1928 xv (2014).

[124] For discussion of Thatcher's domineering, overconfident, and sometimes acerbic style, see HOWARD GARDNER, LEADING MINDS 238 (2005); Ben Fenton, Daniel Pimlott & Vanessa Houlder, *Iron Lady Was Advised How to Dominate Cabinet*, FINANCIAL TIMES, Dec. 30, 2010, at 1. For Trump, see Amy Elliss Nutt, *Is Donald Trump a Textbook Narcissist?*, WASH. POST, July 22, 2016.

[125] For descriptions of Jobs, see PFEFFER, MANAGING WITH POWER, 109; QUINN et al., BECOMING A MASTER MANAGER, 186.

[126] JEAN M. TWENGE & W. KEITH CAMPBELL, THE NARCISSISM EPIDEMIC: LIVING IN THE AGE OF ENTITLEMENT 44-45 (2009); Joyce E. Bono, Winny Shen & David J. Yoon, *Personality and Leadership: Looking Back, Looking Ahead*, in OXFORD HANDBOOK OF LEADERSHIP AND ORGANIZATIONS, 20-207 (David V. Day ed., 2014); Robert B. Kaiser & S. Bartholomew Craig, *Destructive Leadership in and of Organizations*, in THE OXFORD HANDBOOK OF LEADERSHIP AND ORGANIZATIONS, 269 (David V. Day ed., 2014); Seth A. Rosenthal & Todd L. Pittinsky, *Narcissistic Leadership*, 17 LEADERSHIP Q. 617, 618-624 (2006); Emily Grijalva, Peter D. Harms, Daniel A. Newman, Blaine H. Gaddis & R. Chris Graley, *Narcicissm and Leadership: A Meta-Analytic Review of Linear and Nonlinear Relationships*, 68 PERS. PSYCHOL. 1 (2014) (meta-analysis finding that narcissism predicts emergence of leaders due to extraversion and that moderate narcissism may aid effectiveness but that high levels of narcissism sabotages it).

[127] Rosenthal & Pittinsky, *Narcissistic Leadership*, 619-624; Jeffrey Pfeffer, *Donald Trump: The Unproductive Narcissist*, FORTUNE.COM (June 20, 2016), http://fortune.com/2016/06/20/donald-trump-the-unproductive-narcissist/; JEFFREY PFEFFER, LEADERSHIP BS: FIXING WORKPLACES AND CAREERS ONE TRUTH AT A TIME 73-76, 81-82 (2015).

[128] Theodore Bunker, *Poll: Voters Rate Candidate's Policies More Important Than Character*, NEWSMAX (Oct. 19, 2016), https://www.newsmax.com/t/newsmax/article/754289.

[129] Campaign 2016, PollingReport.com, https://www.pollingreport.com/wh16.htm; Mark Blumenthal, *The Underpinnings of Donald Trump's Approval Rating*, HUFFINGTON POST (Feb. 11, 2017), https://www.huffpost.com/entry/the-underpinnings-of-donald-trumps-approval-rating_b_589e4206e4b080bf74f03c20.

[130] JAMES MACGREGOR BURNS, ROOSEVELT: THE LION AND THE FOX 171 (1956). See also GOODWIN, LEADERS, 293.

[131] QUINN et al., BECOMING A MASTER MANAGER, 183.

[132] JEAN B. LESLIE, CENTER FOR CREATIVE LEADERSHIP, WHAT YOU NEED AND DON'T HAVE WHEN IT COMES TO LEADERSHIP TALENT 4 (2009); Kevin Cashman, *Return on Self-Awareness: Research Validates the Bottom Line of Leadership Development*, FORBES (Mar. 17, 2014), https://www.forbes.com/sites/kevincashman/2014/03/17/return-on-self-awareness-research-validates-the-bottom-line-of-leadership-development/#1e44f9b33750.

[133] *How Cultural Factors Affect Leadership*, Knowledge@Wharton, Wharton School of the University of Pennsylvania (July 23, 1999), https://knowledge.wharton.upenn.edu/article/how-cultural-factors-affet-leadersip. For a general discussion of cultural influences that leaders should take into account, see RICHARD D. LEWIS, WHEN CULTURES COLLIDE: LEADING ACROSS CULTURES (3d ed. 2005).

[134] Gus Lubin, *24 Charts of Leadership Styles Around the World*, BUSINESS INSIDER (Jan. 6, 2014), https://www.businessinsider.com/leadership-styles-around-the-world-2013-12.

[135] Lubin, *24 Charts*; Sue Bryant, *8 tips on how to impress senior leaders across cultures*, COUNTRY NAVIGATOR (June 26, 2018), https://countrynavigator.com/blog/global-talent/leaders-across-cultures-2/.

[136] For an example of such a rating form, see NORTHOUSE, LEADERSHIP, 34-35.

[137] Deborah L. Rhode, *The Public Deserves Better*, POLITICO (Oct. 6, 2018), https://www.politico.com/magazine/story/2018/10/06/kavanaugh-confirmation-reaction-221087.

CHAPTER 2

LEADERSHIP STYLES AND DEVELOPMENT

Leadership is not simply a matter of personal characteristics or formal position. It is, most importantly, a process of building relationships. Recall the metaphor by Harvard government professor Joseph Nye, quoted in Chapter 1: "[H]olding a formal title is like having a fishing license; it does not guarantee you will catch any fish."[1] This chapter begins by exploring the challenges confronting those who seek to exercise leadership and the styles that are most effective. Discussion then turns to an analysis of how the core competencies of leadership can be learned.

A. CONTEMPORARY CHALLENGES

Whatever their differences, experts on leadership generally agree that its exercise has grown more challenging in recent decades. Military leaders have coined the acronym VUCA to describe this environment, one characterized by volatility, uncertainty, complexity, and ambiguity.[2] For some lawyer leaders, these characteristics define most of their decisions. Law professor Anthony Thompson notes the challenges for Barack Obama, who, in the first weeks of his presidency, had to decide how to cope with a major economic recession and whether to assist General Motors and Chrysler as they verged on bankruptcy.[3]

Although the contexts of contemporary leadership vary, most share some common features, including an increase in competition, complexity, scale, pace, and diversity. Change is happening more rapidly and on a larger scale, and the future is increasingly uncertain.[4] In private practice, competitiveness has grown within and across organizations. Law firm partnership means less and is harder to attain, and attention has increasingly centered on bottom-line financial performance. In the public sector, competition for attention, support, and resources has intensified.[5] These pressures pose difficulties on both the organizational and financial level. As one commentator quips, "[C]ompetition brings out the best in products and the worst in people."[6] Leaders face growing "pressure to perform, to be constantly competitive, constantly innovative, constantly communicative, constantly at the top of their game, constantly at the service of followers whose level of patience with those in charge has dropped to new, arguably precipitous lows."[7]

Other challenges arise from the growth in scale and complexity of legal organizations, as well as the problems that they confront. Over the last half century, the size of the 50 largest firms has increased more than 10 times, and the staffs of the most prominent public interest legal organizations have more than doubled.[8] The in-house offices of large corporations have also grown, and they confront more issues involving multiple states, countries, and stakeholders. Summarizing these developments, the title of a prominent *Economist* article put it bluntly: It's "tough at the top."[9] In organizations with multiple offices and hundreds or even thousands of employees, the advantages that come from "leadership by walking around" and personal interactions are harder to realize. If, as John Gardner argued, "nothing can substitute for a live leader . . . listening attentively and responding informally," the challenges of achieving such responsiveness are daunting.[10]

This increase in size, together with other social, economic, legal, and technological changes, has significantly complicated the role of leaders. As the president of the Institute for the Future has noted, governments, markets, organizations, and professions are interacting in more complex ways, and the decisions of those in charge often play out on a larger social, international, and environmental stage.[11]

The technological advances that have encouraged such growth have also posed additional challenges. Over the last decades, both the pace of decision-making and the accessibility of decision makers have dramatically increased. Leaders often face an information overload, along with pressure to make complex decisions instantly.[12] As one former deputy attorney general noted, "if you don't like an issue before you, wait fifteen minutes. . . . Somebody will give you a new one."[13] Leaders remain tethered to their workplaces through electronic communication, and the personal costs can be substantial: stress, burnout, substance abuse, and related mental health difficulties.[14] The risks and consequences of bad decisions are also amplified by an ever more present media.

Additional challenges involve increased diversity. As Chapter 8 notes, this trend has had many payoffs for organizations and underrepresented groups, but it has also complicated the lives of leaders. In the United States, organizations are focusing increased efforts on reducing barriers based on sex, race, ethnicity, age, disability, sexual orientation, and gender identity. In virtually every industrialized nation, leaders of global corporations are attempting to accommodate cultural variations in leadership styles and practices. The GLOBE study of some 17,000 leaders in 62 societies identified some important cultural differences in perceptions of leaders' effectiveness. For example, more egalitarian societies valued participatory leadership approaches, while societies that attached high priority to empathy and altruism viewed these qualities as particularly important in leaders.[15] Creating institutions that can deal productively with cultural and identity-related differences is a crucial skill in an increasingly interconnected world.

The challenges that leaders face vary across contexts. The concerns that arise in managing a 1000-person law firm with multiple branches in multiple countries differ from those involved in running a state attorney general's office, or a small disability rights organization. The United States Secretary for Housing and Urban Development and the head of a nonprofit community association are both exercising policy influence, but their roles and responsibilities are quite different.

Consider the following contextual factors:

- Organizational characteristics: size, complexity, structure, resources, and competitive position;
- Stakeholder characteristics: expectations, needs, and values; and
- Positional characteristics: forms of hard and soft power, relationships with stakeholders (including clients), criteria for success, and structures of accountability.

How might these factors affect the qualities of leadership that will be most successful in a given context? Compare, for example, the variety of settings in which lawyers exercise leadership. Their role is often analogized to "servant leadership."[16] In effect, the lawyer serves both clients and colleagues by enabling them to realize their highest aspirations and their organizations' best interests. Much of lawyers' work, both as leaders and advisors to leaders, involves soft power. Unlike top executives in hierarchical corporate structures, these lawyer leaders often lack the structural power to make important decisions themselves. They need to rely on "persuasion, political currency, and shared interests to create conditions for the right decisions to happen."[17] Qualities essential to leadership in these contexts involve active listening, communication, and self-reflection.[18]

Relationships with followers pose another cluster of challenges. Although the extent and complexity of demands on contemporary leaders often argue for shared authority, many stakeholders retain a desire for a single heroic figure at the helm. As Joseph Nye describes it, this "Mt. Rushmore syndrome" rests on a fundamental "leader attribution error"—a tendency to ascribe undue credit or blame to the person at the top.[19] The problem is common in both the public and the private sectors. People often expect quick fixes to complex social problems and intractable market dynamics. Unrealistic expectations by followers encourage unrealistic promises by would-be leaders. The result is that those individuals often "fail upwards" because their grand visions inevitably fall short.[20]

A further difficulty is that although followers might want, or benefit from, the results of strong leadership, they may not like to be led, and may not welcome the changes and sacrifices that it demands. This problem is particularly common in legal- and public-sector workplaces. By training and temperament, lawyers tend to value independence and are well prepared to challenge authority when they disagree. As consultants note, lawyers are experts at locating loopholes and are attached to precedent; any new leadership proposal is likely to be met with skepticism and counterexamples—hardly a "recipe for a strategic advantage" or innovation.[21] In public-sector bureaucracies, rigid rules, job protection for civil servants, insulation from market pressures, and potential political landmines can often foster resistance to innovation.[22] Policy settings also tend toward what experts describe as "organized anarchy." No one is in charge: Power is dispersed across shifting coalitions and interest groups, which require considerable leadership skills to align in pursuit of societal goals.[23]

Other challenges arise from the disconnect between the qualities that enable individuals to achieve leadership roles and the qualities they need once they have those positions. The following excerpt describes such challenges.

DEBORAH L. RHODE, LEADERSHIP IN LAW

69 Stanford Law Review 1603, 1620-1623 (2017)

The Paradoxes of Leadership

The practice of leadership involves a number of paradoxes. One arises from the disconnect between some of the motivations that drive lawyers to achieve leadership positions and the motivations that are necessary for lawyers to succeed once they get there. What makes leaders willing to accept the pressure, hours, scrutiny, and risks that come with their role? For many lawyers, it is not only commitment to a cause, an organization, or a constituency. It is also ambition: attraction to money, power, status, and recognition. As one observer noted, there are some "colossal egos" among lawyer leaders: "everyone wants their own fiefdom." Yet successful leadership requires subordinating self-interests to a greater good. The result is what is often labeled the "leadership paradox." Individuals reach top positions because of their high needs for personal achievement. But to perform effectively in these positions, they need to focus on creating the conditions for achievement by others. As the philosopher Laotse famously put it, a leader is most effective when people barely know he exists; when his work is done, "[t]he people all remark, 'we have done it ourselves.'"

A second paradox arises from the way that positive qualities such as empathy, which can help leaders gain power, are eroded by the exercise of that power. Psychologist Dacher Keltner labels this "the power paradox." He notes that groups tend to give authority to individuals whom they believe have empathy and a willingness to advance the common good. But once individuals obtain that authority, they tend to lose focus on the needs of others. Leaders need to resist that tendency. For as Keltner points out, empathy and a commitment to the welfare of stakeholders is the best guarantee of continued influence. So too, those holding top positions must be willing to let go of their power when the organization would benefit from change.

A third paradox arises from the disconnect between qualities that people say they value in leaders and qualities that they actually use to select leaders. Law firms have a tendency "to put [people] in a leadership position . . . often not because of leadership skills but because of [rainmaking capabilities] . . . and hope they don't drive into a ditch." Similarly, people say they highly value honesty in leaders, but it is not a quality that receives much weight in elections. The 2016 presidential contest is a case in point. Only about a third of Americans thought Hillary Clinton and Donald Trump were honest and trustworthy. That election is not exceptional. As one commentator notes, "integrity has rarely been a trait that has been commonly associated with U.S. presidential candidates . . . ."

One other quality that people value in leaders but discount when selecting them is modesty. Humility is a key trait of what Jim Collins calls "Level 5 leaders," the highest performing executives who create extraordinary results over long periods. These leaders give others credit for collective accomplishments, and it should come as no surprise that this is a productive technique. People are more likely to work hard for a project that they identify as "their" project or "our" project. Humble leaders are more open to new ideas and critical feedback. And because they are less preoccupied with self-promotion, they also have more time to focus on organizational objectives. Yet Collins was studying people who had already attained the role of CEO; humility does not appear to be a trait that helps people make it to the top. Stanford Professor Jeffrey Pfeffer's book, *Leadership BS*, has a chapter titled "Modesty: Why Leaders Aren't," which makes the obvious point that self-promotion is often essential for actual promotion. Narcissistic individuals are frequently selected for leadership positions because people are attracted to the confidence, charisma, and grandiosity they project. . . . Those same characteristics, however, can translate into a sense of entitlement, overconfidence, and an inability to learn from mistakes. If left unchecked, the ambition, self-confidence, and self-centeredness that often enable lawyers to achieve leadership roles may sabotage their performance once in those roles.

B. STYLES OF LEADERSHIP

To meet these challenges, leaders need to develop diverse styles that can accommodate different leadership contexts.[24] The following excerpt describes common approaches. Consider their advantages and disadvantages for positions that you might occupy.

DEBORAH L. RHODE, LAWYERS AS LEADERS

(Oxford University Press, 2013), pp. 12-22

Harvard psychology professor Daniel Goleman is unusual among experts in that his conclusions about effective leadership have a broad empirical base. Drawing on a sample of almost 4,000 leaders worldwide, Goleman has identified six styles, each reflecting distinctive forms of "emotional intelligence." Effective leaders "do not rely on only one leadership style; they use most of them in a given week—seamlessly and in different measure—depending on the [situation]." Goleman summarizes the styles as follows:

Coercive leaders demand immediate compliance.

Authoritative leaders mobilize people toward a vision.

Affiliative leaders create emotional bonds and harmony.

Democratic leaders build consensus through participation.

Pacesetting leaders expect excellence and self-direction.

Coaching leaders develop people for the future.

All of these styles are readily recognizable among lawyer leaders, and other commentators have added variations that are relevant for professional development.

The Coercive or Intimidating Style.

Coercion, the style most often associated with positions of power, is typically the least effective. Goleman suggests a number of reasons why. A leader's "extreme top-down decision making" kills new ideas. People feel so "disrespected that they . . . won't even bring . . . ideas up" or so "resentful that they adopt the attitude, 'I'm not going to help this bastard.'" Because the leader has not conveyed a sense of shared mission, people can become "alienated from their own jobs, wondering, 'How does any of this matter?'" Research on lawyers similarly suggests that while this approach may accomplish short-term results, it often does so at the expense of longer-term problems of morale.

That is not to suggest that coercive styles are always ineffective. They are often useful in conditions of crisis or emergency, or with "'problem' employees with whom all else has failed." Stanford business school professor Roderick Kramer also suggests that a certain form of coercion, practiced by "great intimidators," can yield impressive bottom-line results. These leaders, while not above using a few "ceremonial hangings" are not your "typical bullies." Their motivation does not involve "ego or gratuitous humiliation"; rather, they are impatient with impediments, including human ones, and willing to use anger to achieve their ends. One of Kramer's examples is Clarence Thomas, whose capacity for intimidation was on display during Senate confirmation hearings on his appointment to the Supreme Court. In response to questions about whether he had sexually harassed Anita Hill, Thomas accused Senate committee members of engaging in a "high tech lynching for uppity blacks". . . .

The biographies of famous lawyers are laced with examples of coercion and intimidation. Wisconsin Senator Joseph McCarthy was one of the profession's most infamous bullies. His abusive tactics ruined countless careers of suspected communist sympathizers until his cruelty in televised congressional hearings appalled the nation and eroded his political support. Less extreme examples involve leaders whose desire for control sapped the morale and initiative of those around them. A profile of Paul Cravath, founder of Cravath Swaine and Moore, noted that "most of the young men who worked in his offices disliked him heartily" largely because of his insistence that "everything be done his way." Washington insider Edward Bennett Williams, founder of Williams Connolly, and Califano, could be similarly autocratic. He demanded "total control" over firm decision making, was notoriously "unforgiving of errors" by others, and could fly into a "rage on demand." Jeff Kindler, the lawyer who became CEO of Pfizer, reportedly lost his position because of a combative, abusive micromanagement style. Ralph Nader, another "micromanager," structured the public interest organizations that he founded so that "everything passed through [him]." Nader even opposed unionization in those organizations, a position hard to square with his progressive ideals. As one staffer put it, Nader just felt that the workplace was "his baby and he want[ed] to run things his way." That way included a ban on soft drinks in his flagship organization, the Center for the Study of Responsive Law. On discovering a contraband Coca-Cola can in the trash, Nader personally telephoned the staffer responsible. "This is a breach of trust," he explained to an incredulous reporter. "Soda is bad all the way around. It has no nutrition. It causes cavities. It is taste manipulation. Companies that make it should not be supported." Steven Kumble, the founder of Finley Kumble, similarly obsessed about lawyers and clients who carried coffee cups without lids, threatening the firm's $300,000 carpet. "I think I'm just going to have to take the coffee away from them," he announced.

Coercive and intimidating styles are less common in women leaders. Not only are they socialized differently, they also are punished for such "unfeminine" conduct. What seems merely assertive in a man can seem abrasive in a woman. "Attila the Hen" and "the Dragon Lady" have difficulty gaining respect, support, and cooperation from coworkers. Indeed, some leadership coaches have developed a market niche in rehabilitating "bully broads"—women who come across as insufficiently feminine. Still, the history of the legal profession offers many examples of unrepentant female leaders who were at least partly successful despite their intimidating styles. Congresswoman Bella Abzug, a leader on many women's rights issues, was known as "rude," "cantankerous," "abusive" to her staff, and "not kind to stupid people." That insensitivity to the needs of others exacted a heavy toll. She experienced constant turnover among employees, and was fired as chair of an influential Presidential Advisory Committee on Women, because of her inability to "cooperate" with the administration, including President Carter himself.

Kramer claims that the "great intimidators" are not "typical bullies" because their motive is not humiliation. But it is by no means clear how much motive matters to those who are on the receiving end of abusive conduct. Most research suggests that likeability is correlated with effective leadership and that continued bullying impairs the performance both of leaders and their subordinates. About half the targets of such abuse leave their job as a result. Those who stay are unlikely to volunteer constructive criticism to leaders with the attitude of Hollywood's Darryl Zanuck, known for suggesting that subordinates "don't say yes until I stop talking."

Another form of intimidating behavior involves the use of knowledge in ways that preempt competing views. "Informational intimidators," as Kramer terms them, "always have an abundance of facts, and intentionally or unintentionally invoke them in ways that suppress opposition." This, of course, can be a highly useful skill for lawyers, particularly in litigation. But in leadership contexts, where the goal is to understand and inspire others, this behavior can be counterproductive. It is especially damaging if done with insufficient concern for truth. In the short run, as Kramer notes, "[o]ften, it doesn't even matter all that much whether the "facts" are right. . . . Even the misleading or inaccurate factoid—when uttered with complete confidence and injected into a discussion with perfect timing and precision—can carry the day." But in the long run, that tactic can be costly, particularly if the errors are made in public and someone has sufficient incentive and ability to expose them. Given the importance that people attach to honesty among leaders, informational intimidators can suffer serious credibility costs if they are flexible with facts.

A final type of coercive tactics arises from what is sometimes labeled a "drive to overachievement." Leaders with this tendency focus too much on their own performance and need to surpass not only competitors but also subordinates. They don't truly listen to others; they soak up "all the oxygen in the room" by pushing their own ideas and even answering their own questions. This approach may yield some short-term advantages if the leader is gifted, but the ultimate result is likely to be disengagement and dependency among followers.

The Authoritative Style

Goleman's research suggests that the authoritative style is generally the most effective. This approach combines clarity about ends with flexibility about means. . . . Yet as Goleman also notes, the authoritative style is not effective in every situation. It fails, for example, "when a leader is working with a team of experts or peers who are more experienced than he is; they may see the leader as pompous or out-of-touch. Another limitation . . . [is that] if a manager trying to be authoritative becomes overbearing, he can undermine the egalitarian spirit of an effective team." These circumstances are particularly common in law firms; many partners are reluctant to cede too much power to a single individual.

So too, an authoritative manner in women bumps up against the gender stereotypes noted earlier. An overview of more than a hundred studies confirms that women are rated lower as leaders when they adopt authoritative, seemingly masculine styles, particularly when the evaluators are men, or when the role is one typically occupied by men. This leaves female leaders in a double bind. They risk seeming too feminine or not feminine enough. Those with a soft-spoken approach may appear unable or unwilling to make the tough calls that leadership positions require. Those who lean in the opposite direction are often viewed as strident, arrogant, or overly aggressive. During her presidential campaign[s], Hillary Clinton sought to strike an elusive balance, described as "something between a country-club, golf playing, hedge fund executive, with a whiff of bingo games, Sunday churchgoing, supermarket aisles, and coffee clatches." . . . [T]hese persistent, often unconscious gender biases help explain women lawyers' continued underrepresentation in leadership roles. One recommended response is to modify traditional styles by being "relentlessly pleasant" without backing down. Researchers propose frequently smiling, expressing appreciation and concern, invoking common interests, focusing on others' goals as well as their own, and taking a problem-solving rather than a critical stance. In assessing Sandra Day O'Connor's prospects for success in the Arizona state legislature, one political commentator noted, that "Sandy . . . is a sharp gal" with a "steel-trap mind, and a large measure of common sense. . . . She [also] has lovely smile and should use it often."

The Affiliative Style

The "affiliative" style of leadership puts people first. Its adherents focus on maintaining satisfaction and harmony among followers. They tend to be "natural relationship builders" who supply frequent positive feedback, value personal relationships, and celebrate group accomplishment. The result is a high level of trust, loyalty, communication, and innovation.

Many successful politicians and heads of law firms and in-house counsel offices have been known for such relational skills. Robert Kennedy was a prominent example. Shortly after his appointment as Attorney General, he astonished Justice Department lawyers by walking into their offices announcing, "I'm Bob Kennedy" and then asking where they had gone to law school and what they were working on. He got minor officials their first invitation to the White House, sent thank you notes to staff whom he saw working on holidays, and called or wrote lawyers with congratulations when they had accomplished some difficult task. As Victor Navasky summed it up, this leadership style "brought out the best in others and enlarged their sense of possibility." Hillary Clinton . . . earned similar praise in her position as Secretary of State. She [was] famously "big on feedback"; an Internet "Secretary's Sounding Board is bringing the suggestion box into the modern age." Clinton also gain[ed] respect for following through on the ideas that she hears. After receiving complaints that full benefits for domestic partners were not yet available, she cut through bureaucratic obstacles with a simple directive: "Fix it."

Similar examples are common in the private sector. Michael Kelly's *Lives of Lawyers Revisited* profiles a general counsel who made it a priority to sponsor social events and to meet individually with staff and find out what they would like changed. Larry Sonsini, one of the founders of the Silicon Valley legal establishment, including the law firm that bears his name, is legendary for "bridge build[ing]" and having "a firm grasp of what is important to others." Louis Brandeis, who distinguished himself in many leadership positions on and off the bench, recognized the value of knowing the affairs of others, including clients, "better than they do" and using that knowledge to forge personal relationships. As he advised a young lawyer, "the ability to impress [others] grows from . . . confidence [that] can never come from books; it is gained by human intercourse."

Used exclusively, however, the affiliative approach has its limitations. Too much praise and desire for harmony "can allow poor performance to go uncorrected" and internal conflicts to go unresolved. Whatever its short term advantages in minimizing stress and unpleasantness, conflict avoidance should be avoided. . . . [U]naddressed problems can fester, impair performance, and lead to more costly confrontations later on.

The Democratic Style

One way to handle conflicts, as well as other leadership challenges, is through democratic processes. By giving stakeholders a say in decisions that affect them, leaders can generate new ideas, encourage buy-in, and build morale, trust, respect, and commitment. Many heads of public interest legal organizations employ this approach and rely heavily on legal staff to shape organizational priorities.

However, as experts including Goleman note, the democratic style has drawbacks that make it ill-suited for many leadership contexts. Most lawyers have had experience with the problems, such as "endless meetings where ideas are mulled over, consensus remains elusive, and the only visible result is scheduling more meetings." Participatory processes can also defer decisions in ways that leave individuals "confused and leaderless." Many accomplished leaders have paid a price for this approach. Observers of Hillary Clinton's [2008] presidential campaign chronicled the downsides of her democratic style and refusal to resolve internal staff conflicts. A year into her campaign, her advisors were still "squabbling over [the] message," and, rather than establish clear lines of authority, Clinton allowed them to share power. The result was that "nobody knew who was in charge. Nobody wanted to be in charge."

The broader lesson from such examples is that democratic processes work best when leaders are themselves uncertain about the best direction to take and need ideas and commitment from stakeholders. Alternatively, even when leaders have a strong vision of what needs to change, democratic styles can generate constructive strategies for making that change happen, and buy-in from those most affected. But there are also times when leaders simply have to decide; the problem with democracy can be the same as with socialism, which in a classic phrase, "takes too many evenings."

The Pacesetting Style

A fifth leadership style emerging from large-scale research involves pacesetting. A leader employing this approach "sets high performance standards and exemplifies them himself. . . . He quickly pinpoints poor performers and demands more from them. If they don't rise to the occasion, he replaces them with people who can."

This is a readily recognizable strategy among prominent lawyers. A textbook example comes from the autobiography of the prominent criminal defense attorney William Kuntsler. In *My Life as a Radical Lawyer*, he describes his first meeting with a law student intern who had just started working for the firm. Kuntsler handed him a motion to file immediately and added, with little more by way of instruction, "If you screw this up, don't come back." In explaining his strategy, Kuntsler noted, "Clearly I had no time to babysit law students if they couldn't do the work. . . . My goal for anyone who works with me is, simply, to get the job done. . . . I expect a lot from people . . . and I don't want to hear . . . [their] complaints or problems. I often yell when someone makes a mistake, which, I admit, is not pleasant, but that's how I function."

If subordinates couldn't handle the pressure, Kuntsler had a simple solution: "I let them quit."

Ralph Nader [was another pacesetter]. He created an entire consumer movement by recruiting students and recent law graduates and giving them substantial responsibility. "I'm not interested in the Lone Ranger effect," he famously insisted. "The function of leaders is to produce more leaders." To that end, he looked for Nader Raiders who would be "highly self-directed as well as highly motivated." "Advice–giving [was] a luxury he [didn't] have much time for." "Don't ask me questions," he told his staff. "Just go get at them."

This style has some of the same downsides as the coercive approach. According to Goleman, "Many employees feel overwhelmed by the pacesetter's demands for excellence, and their morale drops. . . . Work becomes not a matter of doing one's best along a clear course so much as second-guessing what the leader wants."

Of course, as Goleman notes, "the pacesetting style isn't always a disaster. The approach works well when all employees are self-motivated, highly competent, and need little direction or coordination." . . . Ralph Nader was revered by many staff for being "the best teacher in the world . . . partly because he doesn't teach you." He gave junior lawyers major policy, press, and political organizing responsibilities and enabled them to rise to the occasion. Their efforts laid foundations for major consumer, environmental and occupational safety regulations, and many of those lawyers went on to lead other public interest initiatives. Yet not all "Nader's Raiders" were up for the pressure and the "hundred hour work week" that Nader thought was "perfect"; "flameout" was a significant problem. The lesson is that pacesetting, like other styles, requires discretion. Leaders need to exercise judgment about when those on the receiving end are up to the task.

The Coaching Style

A final style involves coaching. Leaders taking this approach "help employees identify their unique strengths and weaknesses and tie them to their personal and career aspirations. . . . Coaching leaders excel at delegating; they give employees challenging assignments, even if that means the tasks won't be accomplished quickly. . . .

Leaders who have made coaching a priority have been responsible for some of the profession's greatest achievements. Charles Houston, the Dean of Howard Law School and head of the NAACP legal office in the 1930s and 1940s, nurtured the careers of many civil rights leaders including Thurgood Marshall, who did the same for others. Former Secretary of State Warren Christopher was revered for supporting junior lawyers; one of his mentees recounted thirty years of assistance, ranging from recruitment to Stanford law school, to critical support and advice concerning his appointment as an associate attorney general and judge on the 9th circuit court of appeals. . . .

Yet despite its frequent effectiveness, the coaching style is the least common leadership approach that Goleman's research identified. The reason, according to interviewed leaders, is that they "don't have the time in this high-pressure economy for the slow and tedious work of teaching people and helping them grow." Other explanations involve interpersonal obstacles to candid feedback, such as leaders' desires to be liked or to avoid conflict, and concerns about damaging relationships and reducing chances of retention. Particularly in large organizations with high turnover rates, leaders often see little reason to invest in subordinates who are likely to leave. As a consequence, many legal workplaces lack adequate mentoring and leadership development. The problem is compounded by some leaders' lack of skills and comfort in coaching those who are different along lines of race, ethnicity, or gender. Although increasing numbers of legal workplaces have responded by creating formal mentoring programs, these initiatives often lack effective oversight and reward structures. Mentors take a "call me if you need me approach" that leaves subordinates uncomfortable in asking for assistance. Also lacking are well-designed leadership development strategies. Only a quarter of surveyed firms have leadership succession plans. . . .

[Yet] [f]ailure to develop subordinates has been identified as one of the "fatal flaws" of unsuccessful leaders. In today's increasingly competitive climate, organizations need those who occupy positions of power to support and model effective mentoring. Indeed, Goleman puts the point directly; "[a]lthough the coaching style may not scream "bottom-line results," it delivers them. . . .

As this overview makes clear, no single leadership style is effective in all contexts, although some are more likely to be effective than others. Leaders need multiple approaches and an understanding of when each is most appropriate. The best leaders are "exquisitely sensitive to the impact they are having on others," and able to adjust their styles accordingly.

The preceding excerpt section identified a repertoire of styles that can be effective for leaders. In the following excerpt, Jack Zenger and Joseph Folkman identify styles that can be fatal. As you read their description, think about other characteristics that you might add and whether your leadership has fallen short in any of the ways that they describe.

JACK ZENGER AND JOSEPH FOLKMAN, TEN FATAL FLAWS THAT DERAIL LEADERS

Harvard Business Review, June 2009, p. 18

Poor leadership in good times can be hidden, but poor leadership in bad times is a recipe for disaster. To find out why leaders fail, we scrutinized results from two studies:

In one, we collected 360-degree feedback data on more than 450 Fortune 500 executives and then teased out the common characteristics of the 31 who were fired over the next three years. In the second, we analyzed 360-degree feedback data from more than 11,000 leaders and identified the 10% who were considered least effective.

We then compared the ineffective leaders with the fired leaders to come up with the 10 most common leadership shortcomings. Every bad leader had at least one, and most had several.

The Worst Leaders:

Lack energy and enthusiasm. They see new initiatives as a burden, rarely volunteer, and fear being overwhelmed. One such leader was described as having the ability to "suck all the energy out of any room."

Accept their own mediocre performance. They overstate the difficulty of reaching targets so that they look good when they achieve them. They live by the mantra "Underpromise and overdeliver."

Lack clear vision and direction. They believe their only job is to execute. Like a hiker who sticks close to the trail, they're fine until they come to a fork.

Have poor judgment. They make decisions that colleagues and subordinates consider to be not in the organization's best interests.

Don't collaborate. They avoid peers, act independently, and view other leaders as competitors. As a result, they are set adrift by the very people whose insights and support they need.

Don't walk the talk. They set standards of behavior or expectations of performance and then violate them. They're perceived as lacking integrity.

Resist new ideas. They reject suggestions from subordinates and peers. Good ideas aren't implemented, and the organization gets stuck.

Don't learn from mistakes. They may make no more mistakes than their peers, but they fail to use setbacks as opportunities for improvement, hiding their errors and brooding about them instead.

Lack interpersonal skills. They make sins of both commission (they're abrasive and bullying) and omission (they're aloof, unavailable, and reluctant to praise).

Fail to develop others. They focus on themselves to the exclusion of developing subordinates, causing individuals and teams to disengage.

These sound like obvious flaws that any leader would try to fix. But the ineffective leaders we studied were often unaware that they exhibited these behaviors. In fact, those who were rated most negatively rated themselves substantially more positively. Leaders should take a very hard look at themselves and ask for candid feedback on performance in these specific areas. Their jobs may depend on it.

One much debated leadership style is intimidation. Although frequently condemned, it can also achieve desired results. In the following excerpt, Stanford Business School professor Roderick Kramer explores the capacities and constraints of leading by intimidating.

Roderick M. Kramer, The Great Intimidators

Harvard Business Review, February 2006

"Since when has being a difficult boss been a disqualifier for a job?" asked *Nightline*'s Ted Koppel after several abrasive, intimidating leaders of major corporations—Disney's Michael Eisner, Miramax's Harvey Weinstein, and Hewlett-Packard's Carly Fiorina—fell from their heights of power. Picking up on what seemed to be a new trend in the workplace, the business media quickly proclaimed that the reign of such leaders was over. From now on, the *Wall Street Journal* predicted, "tough guys will finish last."

But wait a minute, you might think. If they're just plain bad for their organizations, why have so many of these leaders made it to the top in the first place? Wouldn't the ones who've wreaked nothing but havoc have plateaued or been weeded out long before they could inflict too much damage? Yet many leaders who rule through intimidation have been doing just fine for a very long time. Before we proclaim their extinction, then, it's worth taking a close look at the pros as well as the cons of their tough-minded approach. Doing so might cast light on some subtle dimensions of effective leadership, especially in organizations or industries that were once rigid or unruly, stagnant or drifting—places where it took an abrasive leader to shake things up a little and provide redirection.

Consider Ed Zander, who's been hailed as "Motorola's modernizer." When Zander took over as CEO of Motorola in January 2004, the company was in steep decline. After being in the high-velocity world of Silicon Valley, Zander found himself at the helm of a company that seemed to be running, in his words, "on autopilot." In taking on the challenge of turning Motorola around, Zander described his guiding philosophy as, "Whack yourself before somebody whacks you." He observed, "A lot of companies have clogged arteries." In Motorola's case, Zander found that much of the problem was at the VP level. "I don't know how many dozens of VPs are no longer with us," he reported in one interview. "Some have left on their own accord, some have not." The transformation at Motorola is far from complete, but it is off to a good start. . . .

[Leaders such as Zander] are examples of what I call *great intimidators.* They are not averse to causing a ruckus, nor are they above using a few public whippings and ceremonial hangings to get attention. And they're in good company. A list of great intimidators would read a bit like a business leadership hall of fame: Sandy Weill, Rupert Murdoch, Andy Grove, Carly Fiorina, Larry Ellison, and Steve Jobs would be just a few of the names on it. These leaders seem to relish the chaos they create because, in their minds, it's constructive. Time is short, the stakes are high, and the measures required are draconian.

But make no mistake—the great intimidators are not your typical bullies. If you're just a bully, it's all about humiliating others in an effort to make yourself feel good. Something very different is going on with the great intimidators. To be sure, they aren't above engaging in a little bullying to get their way. With them, however, the motivating factor isn't ego or gratuitous humiliation; it's vision. The great intimidators see a possible path through the thicket, and they're impatient to clear it. They chafe at impediments, even those that are human. They don't suffer from doubt or timidity.

They've got a disdain for constraints imposed by others. . . . Beneath their tough exteriors and sharp edges, however, are some genuine, deep insights into human motivation and organizational behavior. Indeed, these leaders possess what

I call *political intelligence*, a distinctive and powerful form of leader intelligence that's been largely ignored by management theorists and practitioners. . . .

Political Intelligence at Work

. . . Over the past decade, management theorists and practitioners alike have come to appreciate the roles that different forms of human intelligence play in effective leadership. Psychologist Howard Gardner—who first articulated the theory of multiple intelligences—suggested, for example, that social intelligence is what makes some leaders so adept at getting others to follow them and at extracting maximum performance from subordinates. Gardner defined social intelligence in terms of leaders' interpersonal skills, such as empathy and the ability to influence others on the basis of that understanding.

There's no question that it's important for all leaders to have these skills. Indeed, social intelligence is the sort of competency leaders rely on every day to accomplish the routine work of an organization. However, it's not the *only* kind of intelligence they need. What's more, in some settings (a rigidly hierarchical organization, for example), other forms of intelligence may be more useful. That's when the application of political intelligence, the hallmark of great intimidators, can make the difference between paralysis and successful—if sometimes wrenching—organizational change.

In understanding the distinction between socially intelligent and politically intelligent leaders, it's important to realize that they share certain skills. Both types of leaders are adept at sizing up other people. Both possess keen, discriminating eyes—but they notice different things. For instance, socially intelligent leaders assess people's strengths and figure out how to leverage them, while politically intelligent leaders focus on people's weaknesses and insecurities. Speaking of President Lyndon B. Johnson, one of history's truly great intimidators, former press secretary Bill Moyers noted that he possessed "an animal sense of weakness in other men." As one political scientist elaborated, Johnson "studied, analyzed, catalogued, and remembered the strengths and weaknesses, the likes and dislikes, of fellow politicians as some men do stock prices, batting averages, and musical compositions. He knew who drank Scotch and who bourbon, whose wife was sick . . . who was in trouble . . . and who owed him."

Not only do socially intelligent and politically intelligent leaders notice different things; they also *act* differently on the basis of their divergent perceptions. While leaders with social intelligence use empathy and soft power to build bridges, politically intelligent leaders use intimidation and hard power to exploit the anxieties and vulnerabilities they detect. Both kinds of leaders are good judges of character. But instead of having empathy for others, the politically intelligent leader adopts a dispassionate, clinical, even instrumental view of people as resources for getting things done. This absence of empathy opens up branches of the decision tree, exposing options that other leaders might reject.

Perhaps the starkest point of contrast between these two kinds of leaders is how willing they are to use hard power. Politically intelligent leaders appreciate the power of fear and its close relation, anxiety. As Harvard University's [former]

[handwritten margin note: difference appears to lie in how these leaders view the people around them]

[handwritten margin note: "how willing they are to use hard power"]

president, Larry Summers, once observed: "Sometimes fear does the work of reason." He went to Harvard determined to shake up the institution—and whatever else may be said about him, he has succeeded in doing just that. Interviews with faculty, staff, and students at Harvard who've had close encounters with Summers reveal a common pattern in his interactions: initial confrontation, followed by skeptical and hard questioning. "Perhaps we don't really even need a department like this at Harvard," he is said to have told one group of faculty at a "let's get acquainted" session.

Such questions may not make a leader popular, but they certainly wake people up. And they sometimes compel people to think more deeply about their purpose in an organization and the value they add to it. In asking them to justify their existence, for instance, Summers has forced professors and administrators at Harvard to become more thoughtful about what they do. . . .

Summers' sentiments regarding the virtues of inculcating a little fear echo one of President Richard Nixon's convictions: "People react to fear, not love—they don't teach that in Sunday school, but it's true." For Nixon, leadership wasn't about inspiring others or being liked; it was about producing tangible results. And although too much fear or anxiety may induce trepidation and paralysis, too little may result in lackluster effort and complacency. . . .

The Intimidator's Tactics

 . . . *Get up close and personal.* . . . In addition to aggressive physical demeanors, intimidators routinely use the weapons of language—taunts and slurs—to provoke their victims. This behavior is designed to throw others off balance. It's hard to think clearly and follow your own game plan when your buttons are being pushed. Clarence Thomas, associate justice of the U.S. Supreme Court, used this tactic to browbeat his Democratic opponents on the Senate judiciary committee during his nomination hearings. When accused by Anita Hill of sexual harassment, he asked the members of the committee how they would like to be so accused. The discomfort of the committee (which included an understandably subdued Ted Kennedy) was palpable. To complete the trick, he threw the race card down on the table, calling the procedure "a high-tech lynching for uppity blacks who in any way deign to think for themselves . . . [and don't] kowtow to an old order." By putting the committee on the defensive, Thomas pulled the moral high ground right out from under their feet.

Be angry. Most intimidators use anger and rage to get their way. A calculated "loss of temper" does more than help intimidators prevail in the heat of the moment, though. It also serves as a chilling deterrent for potential challengers. While in some instances they are clearly putting on an act, intimidators aren't always in full control of their emotions when they go off on tirades. But even then a loss of control can be useful. As political pundit Chris Matthews once said, "Don't have a reputation for being a nice guy—that won't do you any good." He cited his experience working with former Maine senator Ed Muskie: "Muskie was the best of them all, the absolute best, because nobody wanted to tangle with the guy. You know, why tangle with the guy? Why ruin your day?". . .

Know it all. Mastery of the facts—or at least the appearance of it—can also be hugely intimidating. "Informational intimidators" always have facts and figures at their fingertips, while their opponents are still trying to formulate an argument or retrieve something from memory. British prime minister Margaret Thatcher was legendary for her ability to silence or paralyze her opponents with her superior command of whatever topic was being debated. As one observer noted, Thatcher was a "demon for information, for research, for numbers. She devoured them, [and] she remembered them. . . . No one could out-study or out-prepare her." In one famous confrontation in the House of Commons, Thatcher took on and "battered into submission" the able and respected Richard Crossman. "It was obvious," recalled John Boyd-Carpenter, the cabinet minister in charge at the time. "She had done her homework, and he had not done his."

Often, it doesn't even matter all that much whether the "facts" are right. When it comes to making a good impression or anchoring an argument, the truly great intimidator seizes the advantage. Even the misleading or inaccurate factoid—when uttered with complete confidence and injected into a discussion with perfect timing and precision—can carry the day. In a negotiation or board meeting, less confident individuals are likely to remain silent and avoid challenging someone presenting her case with assurance. It's only later, when there might be time to check out the accuracy of a statement, that people realize they've been hoodwinked. By then, however, it's too late: The moment is gone, and the informational intimidator has walked away with all the marbles. Robert McNamara raised this technique to the level of an art. When he and Lee Iacocca were at Ford, Iacocca once commented to another executive, "That son of a bitch [McNamara] always has an answer, and it always sounds good. But you know," he added, "I checked some of it out after a meeting, and some of it is really bullshit. Stuff he just made up." . . .

So before we throw out all the great intimidators—and turn the organizational helm over to those gentle, humble, self-effacing leaders who've apparently been waiting in the wings—we might stop to consider what we would lose. Great intimidators may create disharmony, but they also can create value.

Former Secretary of Defense and CIA Director Robert Gates has a different view than Kramer. Which do you find more compelling?

ROBERT M. GATES, A PASSION FOR LEADERSHIP: LESSONS ON CHANGE AND REFORM FROM FIFTY YEARS OF PUBLIC SERVICE

(New York: Alfred A. Knopf, 2016), pp. 160-161, 166-167, 169-172

The last thing the egotist wants is candor, particularly if that includes implied criticism or even a hint that the boss is somehow shy of perfection in all things. It stifles creativity. If someone comes up with a good idea, the egotist is quick to dismiss it because it was someone else's—or take credit for it with superiors. The sharpest, best people will do whatever they can to avoid serving with such people.

To determine your leadership philosophy, you must ask yourself, "How do I want my subordinates to feel?"

Subordinates will hesitate about making decisions for fear of the egotist's wrath at independent thinking or action, much less the consequences of something going wrong. In short, the environment created by an egotist is the antithesis of what is required to lead reform successfully. An egotist cannot help being an autocrat, the type of boss who unilaterally decides what changes are needed and implements them by fiat from above—the thunder-bolt approach to leading change. It is nearly always guaranteed to fail.

. . . You can't tell arrogant leaders anything they don't already know. They disdain advice, especially from underlings but even from peers and superiors. They often operate just barely inside the rules. They are supremely self-confident, amazingly lacking in self-awareness, incapable of introspection, and generally unpleasant to deal with. They are usually bullies. And they can be found throughout the ranks of management, not just at the top.

Arrogant egotists also are people who crave power. Like a black hole in space, they draw to themselves all decision-making authority and constantly seek to expand their bureaucratic empires, to continue growing their power. They weaken everyone around them. The power hungry have no sense of limits.

"Never miss a good chance to shut up!"

An arrogant egotist is exactly the wrong person to lead reform. . . . A favorite saying of mine is "Never miss a good chance to shut up." I won't tell you how many times in a congressional hearing I just wanted to scream. How often in the White House Situation Room I wanted to say, "That's the dumbest idea I ever heard." How often in a briefing at the CIA or the Pentagon I wanted to tell someone where to stick his PowerPoint slides. Senior leaders want to blow off steam—shout at people—all the time. But to be an effective leader, you have to suppress those urges.

Two common threads through this book have been the needs to listen and to empower subordinates. The corollary to both is to know when to keep quiet and when to keep your hands off the steering wheel. The temptation to weigh in with your own opinions or to take over a problem is constant. Being an effective leader, especially a reform leader, requires a lot of self-control. Silence and restraint are essential, if undervalued, tools of leadership. . . .

When you are talking, you are not learning!

It is a simple truth that when you are talking, you are not learning. . . . One of the reasons I believe the leader of an institution—any reformer—must exercise great self-discipline has to do with subordinates. If the boss can't control himself, that sends a signal to those at lower levels that such behavior is acceptable, and that hardly creates an environment in which inclusive, participatory reform can take place. It sounds old-fashioned, but the leader of an institution needs to be a role model. . . . Intellectual and professional intimidation, characteristic of those who believe they are the smartest people in the room, is a poor way to solicit good ideas and avoid big mistakes. . . .

Over the years, I have worked for and with a number of people who thought they were the smartest in the room. A couple were presidents of the United States. I can think of at least two White House chiefs of staff, a handful of cabinet secretaries, a few corporate executives, and assorted others in less august positions. A leader who feels that way has a tough time taking seriously what anyone else thinks, especially if he disagrees. Such a leader might solicit opinions from others on a particular subject, but it quickly becomes apparent to all others that his interest is phony: he believes he has already thought about everything everyone has said—and made up his mind before walking in the door. The folks who believe themselves to be the smartest in the room tend to condescend and subtly or not so subtly bully their interlocutors. Sometimes they can be downright insulting. They are not much fun to work for—or with. There is a remarkable overlap between arrogant egotists and those who believe they are the smartest people in the room. A telltale sign of both is, in the middle of a meeting, a long-suffering sigh intended to convey impatience at having to put up with inferior minds.

The Supreme Court justice Oliver Wendell Holmes Jr. once observed of Franklin D. Roosevelt that he had a second-rate intellect but a first-rate temperament. I believe most of our greatest presidents fit that description: George Washington, Abraham Lincoln, FDR, Truman, Eisenhower, Reagan. No one around any of them ever forgot who was in charge, but each surrounded himself with extremely capable people, listened to them, integrated their opinions with his own judgment and instincts, and made historic decisions. . . .

Leaders of institutions who approach their jobs with some humility are far more likely to get from subordinates the kinds of ideas and advice critical to success and to build a solid team than those who presume to know all the answers. No matter what room I was in, I always knew I was not the smartest person there. This was not false modesty. . . .

NOTES

In the years since Kramer wrote about the "great intimidators," workplace bullying has gained increasing attention. It has also emerged as a significant leadership issue because some leaders exhibit abusive behaviors and others fail to create cultures that adequately address them. My forthcoming book on ambition summarizes major research findings as follows:

Under conventional definitions, workplace bullying involves "vindictive, cruel, or malicious attempts to humiliate or undermine other employees." By that definition, over half of Americans report experiencing or witnessing persistent bullying behaviors, although less than 1 percent admit engaging in them. Such conduct imposes enormous costs on individuals and organizations. For individuals, the consequences include physical disorders (such as insomnia, substance abuse, and ulcers); mental health disorders (such as stress, depression, anxiety, panic, and suicide); and behavioral disorders (including emotional outbursts, loss of concentration, and violence). For organizations, the consequences include eroding employee motivation, engagement, morale, productivity, and cooperation, along with increasing absenteeism, attrition, legal liability, and retaliation by targets of abuse. Studies by the Workplace Bullying

Institute find that four-fifths of employees subject to bullying ultimately leave or lose their jobs compared with less than one- fifth of bullies. . . .

Causes of bullying behavior involve both individual and organizational characteristics. Most obviously, people bully because they can; they believe that their workplace will tolerate such behavior or that targets and witnesses will be unwilling to incur the costs of reporting it. There is ample basis for those beliefs. In a Workplace Bullying Institute Survey, less than 2 percent of employees thought that employers conducted a fair investigation that protected the victim from further bullying and resulted in negative consequences for the bully. In a majority of cases, the employer reportedly did nothing, and in almost three- quarters of cases, the victim experienced retaliation. Other contributors to bullying involve personality traits, abusive childhood experiences, poor social skills, workplace stress, and biases toward less privileged groups.

Some researchers distinguish between dispute-related bullying, which grows out of interpersonal conflicts between the parties, and predatory bullying, which occurs without any triggering conduct by the victim. Predatory bullying may be directed at individuals because of their race, ethnicity, gender, or sexual orientation, or because they are an easy target for frustration and stress caused by other factors.[25]

Whatever their motives, bullies generally share an "entrenched sense of entitlement" that insulates them from complaints. They believe that they are "special, that the normal rules of conduct don't apply" to them.[26]

Much of what we have learned about bullying behavior over the past decades casts some of Kramer's "great intimidators" in a different light. The sense of entitlement that enables bullying in general also enables serial sexual abuse by otherwise talented leaders such as Harvey Weinstein. Even Steve Jobs, who was highly successful in most aspects of his career, was in the view of most observers, ill served by his intimidating tactics. Apple co-founder Steve Wozniak believed that Jobs could have made his contributions without "terrorizing folks."[27] Biographer Walter Isaacson summarized prevailing views: "Nasty was not necessary. It hindered him more than helped him."[28] Contemporary research suggests that focusing on practices such as empathy, gratitude, and generosity are most likely to promote effectiveness in even cut-throat work environments.[29]

One reason that bullying by leaders is especially toxic is that their conduct is likely to be noticed and mimicked. If they respond to stress by blaming others and losing their tempers, it sends unintended messages about what constitutes acceptable workplace behaviors.[30] They also lose opportunities for candid feedback. Donald Trump's 2004 book, How to Become Rich, put it bluntly: "Do not intimidate people. If you do, you'll never get a straight answer from anyone, and you'll be defeating your own purpose."[31] Would he be a more effective leader if he followed that advice?

Prominent lawyer leaders in other countries have developed highly successful styles that are the opposite of the intimidating or directive models profiled above.

For example, Mahatma Gandhi famously advocated what he called Satyagraha, meaning firmness in truth.[32] This strategy sought to convert others, including adversaries, by "suffering in one's own person."[33] Its aim was to arouse the conscience of the oppressor and to build a sense of moral urgency and agency among the oppressed. This philosophy underpinned Gandhi's non-violent protests, life-threatening fasts, and renunciation of personal comforts unavailable to the poor. These techniques inspired millions of followers to not only challenge British colonial rule, but also resist violence against and repression of other Indians based on religion and caste.

Nelson Mandela, who received a Nobel peace prize for helping to dismantle apartheid in South Africa, also modeled a leadership style that promoted reconciliation and respect. After 27 years in prison, he displayed remarkably little rancor towards former adversaries, as well as collaborative, egalitarian attitudes towards followers. He invited former guards to his inauguration as president, included white opposition leaders in his government, spent ceremonial occasions talking with support staff, and introduced visiting dignitaries to the woman who served them tea.[34] When asked about his role in creating a democratic South Africa, he insisted that credit belonged to the African National Congress political party: "I don't think there is much history can say about me," he claimed. "I just want to be remembered as part of that collective."[35] He was wrong about history.

QUESTIONS

1. Have you observed the paradox of power described above, in which the qualities that propel people into leadership are not what they need to exercise it effectively? Researchers have documented examples in a wide range of settings. Sam Walker analyzed the captains of the most dominant athletic teams in history to look for qualities of leadership that made them successful. He found that the best captains were generally not the best athletes and weren't fond of the spotlight. They focused on team success, not their own. This led Walker to identify a related paradox: that "the people who pursue leadership positions the most ardently are often the wrong people for the job. They're motivated by the prestige the role conveys rather than the desire to promote the good . . . of the organization."[36] To what extent is that true of lawyer leaders? What follows from that paradox for the way we select leaders?

2. Some experts emphasize the importance of "executive presence," which typically includes the "ability to project mature self-confidence, a sense that you can take control of difficult, unpredictable situations, make tough decisions in a timely way, and hold your own with other talented and strong-willed [colleagues]."[37] These are leaders who can "stay composed and levelheaded . . . even when—in fact particularly when—everyone else is losing their composure."[38] Think about leaders that you have admired. Did they have this quality? How did they project it?

3. In the aftermath of the 2016 election, commentators observed that Hillary Clinton's famed skills as a "listener" fell short and that it was Donald Trump

who heard the deep disaffection and desire for change among voters in key battleground states.[39] Is that a fair criticism? Was she too much of a "policy wonk" in her responses?[40] Do you agree with commentators who have argued that the styles and skills (such as listening and managing) that make someone an effective leader do not necessarily match the skills that will help individuals obtain leadership positions? Is that particularly true in politics where campaigning is very different from governing? Is it also true for lawyers in firms, in-house counsel office, and nonprofit organizations? If so, what can help lawyers make the transition?

4. Another lawyer/politician famous for his listening abilities is Cory Booker, who as mayor of Newark made available to residents his e-mail address and cell phone number.[41] Are there downsides of this strategy? What would you do in his position to communicate responsiveness?

5. Consider two leaders whom you have especially admired. How did their styles match up to Goleman's categories and to Gates's ideal prototype? What made their approaches effective?

6. Hay/McBer's research finds that "coaching" is the least common style of leadership. In explaining why, experts identify not only lack of time and interest but also interpersonal obstacles to candid feedback, such as the desire to be liked or to avoid conflict, and concerns about damaging the relationship. Even leaders who attempt to provide coaching may sabotage their efforts by lack of sensitivity. Common problems include becoming antagonistic or defensive; losing sight of others' needs; failing to be specific about what needs to change and why; getting locked into one approach and not being responsive to the impact of criticism or to new information and behavior; and failing to follow up on plans for improvement. Think about contexts in which you have given or received feedback. What has been most and least effective? Assess your approach again in light of the discussion of followers and feedback in Chapter 4.

7. When Rudy Giuliani was Manhattan's U.S. attorney, a common joke was that the most dangerous place to be in the city was between Giuliani and a newscaster's microphone. This preoccupation with self-promotion reportedly "left a trail of resentment" among other New York prosecutors, "many of whom thought he made the office about one person—himself—and used publicity about his case as a way to further his political ambitions rather than doing justice."[42] Has Giuliani been well served by these priorities? To what extent have they helped him reach positions of power, such as mayor of New York and counsel to President Trump? To what extent have they sabotaged his performance by encouraging him to sound off without knowing the facts or thinking through the implications of disclosures about his client?

8. Are the "fatal flaws" of leadership that Zenger and Folkman identify ones that you have observed or studied? How might they be remedied, other than by removing the individual from office?

9. Shortly after Minnesota Senator Amy Klobuchar entered the 2020 presidential race, the *New York Times* ran a front-page story titled "Klobuchar's Taunts and

Temper Stand Out in a Sea of Tough Bosses." The story recounted the view of many former aides that "she was not just demanding but often dehumanizing." She reportedly threw small office objects, including binders and phones, in the direction of staff. She assigned them demeaning tasks like washing her dishes, or even her combs, "a possible violation of Senate ethics rules." She reportedly told a succession of media aides that they were the "worst press staff I ever had," and blamed their errors for "standing in her way." For years, she had one of the highest rates of staff turnover in the Senate, and imposed unrealistic hours and time demands. [43]

How do you assess this criticism? Would the same behavior by a male candidate have gotten the same degree of attention? Should it have? How relevant is it for assessing her fitness for office? Consider Bill Clinton, who was legendary for losing his temper, being abusive to staff, and expecting 24/7 availability. He left office with one of the highest performance ratings in history.[44]

10. Kramer claims that the "great intimidators" are "not your typical bullies." What is the difference? How much does motive matter to those who are on the receiving end of abusive conduct? Most research suggests that pervasive bullying impairs performance, and that likeability is correlated with effective leadership. Surveys also find that about a third of employees report being bullied, and of these, about half leave their jobs as a result.[45] Women are particularly likely to be disliked for intimidating and domineering styles.[46] Although some forceful female leaders manage to be viewed positively— Golda Meir was thought a "femme formidable"—Chapter 8 notes the difficulty that women have in negotiating the "too assertive/not assertive enough" double bind.[47] What strategies might best enable female leaders to cope with this challenge?

11. For every example that Kramer cites of successful bullying, other experts offer counterexamples or disagree with his characterization of success. Kramer's assessment of Lawrence Summers differs sharply from those of many observers, including that of Harvard professor Howard Gardner, discussed in Chapter 4. In your view, what separates the successful from the unsuccessful intimidators? Have you ever worked for an individual with that style? How would you assess its effectiveness?

12. A recent account of "destructive leadership," defines it as undermining the goals, well-being, or effectiveness of a group. Behaviors that meet that description fall across a spectrum, and include everything from ethical violations and abusive conduct to neglectful laissez-faire styles that fail to hold individuals accountable.[48] How can these leadership patterns be prevented and constrained? What role can boards of directors, news media, government regulators, and followers play?

PROBLEM 2-1

Barack Obama is a leader whose personal style has been much admired and much criticized. Supporters point to capabilities of listening and consensus building that he exhibited early in his career. Obama was the first African American to serve a president of the *Harvard Law Review*, and his election to that position occurred at a time when the organization was highly polarized. As one of his coeditors put it, "Barack was the one who was truly able to move between different groups and have credibility with all of them. . . . I don't think he was agenda driven. I think he genuinely thought, 'Some of these guys are nice, all of them are smart, some of them are funny, all of them have something to say.'"[49] Another editor similarly noted that he "earned the affection and trust of almost everyone."[50] A professor observed that Obama's talent was "his openness in engaging people with whom he disagrees."[51] One African-American editor who lambasted him at the time for his conciliatory attitudes later came to recognize its strength. "I had no patience for the idiots on the other side and Barack did, which annoyed me, even angered me sometimes, but it made him the better person, certainly a better one to be president of the Law Review."[52] Obama also had a helpful capacity to keep in-fighting in perspective. When arguments got out of hand, Obama would say, "Remember folks, nobody reads it."[53]

Obama's style as president gets more mixed reviews. Critics charge that he is "aloof, insular, diffident, arrogant, inert, unwilling to jolly his allies along the fairway and take a 9-iron to his enemies."[54] They believe that his unwillingness to socialize with members of Congress has impaired his ability to build coalitions. As one Democratic Senator put it, "When you don't build those personal relationships, it's pretty easy for a person to say, 'Well, let me think about it.'"[55]

Obama himself concedes that having two young daughters compromised his ability to "work the social scene in Washington."[56] However, Obama and his aides believe that the significance of this failure has been vastly overstated. When Obama has reached out, his invitations have sometimes been declined, and aides note that they could "invite every Republican in Congress to play golf until the end of time . . . and never cut the Gordian knot of contemporary Washington."[57] As Obama told one reporter, "There are some structural institutional realities to our political system that don't have much to do with schmoozing."[58]

What is your view? How would you evaluate Obama's style of leadership? What are its strengths and limitations?

MEDIA RESOURCES

Examples of different styles of leadership abound. Models of effective coaching appear in *Invictus* and *A Man for All Seasons*, described in Chapter 11, as well as in movies about teachers or athletes, such as *A League of Their Own*, *The Great Debates*, and *Chariots of Fire*. A particularly good example comes from season 4, episode 8 of the television series *Mad Men* ("The Summer Man"), in which Peggy, the female copywriter, asks her boss Don Draper to deal with sexual harassment and disrespect by a male freelance employee. Draper tells her to handle it herself and earn respect rather than a reputation as a tattletale. When she does so, she is told by the female office manager who was also a target of the harassment that the action succeeded only in establishing Peggy as a humorless bitch. The scene raises multiple issues of effective styles of coaching, as well as diversity and conflict management.

Profiles of intimidating leaders in television and film are in ample supply. Margaret Thatcher was known as "the Iron Lady" with good reason. Several portraits of Steve Jobs, including a *60 Minutes* documentary, suggest that he was a classic "great intimidator" who leveraged his charisma to compensate for callous behavior. The television series *Veep* portrays politicians and staff who display comically abusive and self-promoting behavior. *The Paper Chase* features a legendary scene in which a bullying law professor humiliates a first-year law student. *Legally Blonde* has a similar scene in which the bully is a woman. In *The Devil Wears Prada*, Meryl Streep plays the fictionalized version of a legendary head of a women's fashion magazine who terrorizes subordinates without ever raising her voice.[59] In a companion clip, Anna Wintour, who inspired Streep's character, denies being intimidating,[60] *The Proposal* features Sandra Bullock as the abusive head of a publishing company, whose morning entrance prompts an e-mail to the workforce that "the witch is on her broom." These portraits raise issues not only of effectiveness but also of gender stereotypes. As discussion in Chapter 8 indicates, behavior that appears assertive in male leaders often appears abrasive in their female counterparts. More positive portrayals of women leaders occur in *Madame Secretary*, in which a female secretary of state manages to be authoritative without being abrasive.

"Executive Wrath," the pilot episode of *The West Wing*, shows a more productive example of intimidation. President Bartlet, played by Martin Sheen, upbraids right-wing leaders who were trying to bully his staff into accepting legislative concessions; the conservatives were seeking payback for an insult that an administration official had delivered on morning television. Bartlet undercuts the conservatives' moral high ground by denouncing their failure to disavow tactics of a fundamentalist group that had sent graphic hate mail to his twelve-year-old granddaughter. A key issue is how much motive matters. Does Bartlet's wrath seem more justified because larger social values are implicated? Another core question is whether intimidation works in the absence of hard power to back it up.

Billions, a series featuring a conflict between a self-righteous U.S. Attorney and an arrogant hedge fund manager, shows repeated examples of unproductive intimidating behavior. In one key scene, a win-win plea bargain falls apart because of a clash of egos between these main characters.

C. LEARNING LEADERSHIP

1. THE STATE OF LEADERSHIP EDUCATION

Leadership education is a relatively recent phenomenon, and it has yet to secure widespread support and respect in many organizations and academic institutions. One survey of some 32,000 employees found that only a third of workers believed that their workplaces were effectively developing future leaders.[61] Law schools have been especially slow to embrace the need for formal training, which is particularly puzzling given the high proportion of their graduates who occupy leadership positions.[62] Lawyers' leadership responsibilities are a dominant theme in commencement speeches and mission statements, but the topic is often missing in action in day-to-day teaching and programming.[63] The most recent surveys reveal that only a small number of schools have some leadership program or course, or list leadership as one of their learning outcome objectives.[64]

The inadequate attention to leadership development is rooted in broader problems in legal education that are attracting increased concern. A LexisNexis survey on the state of the legal industry found that almost two-thirds of law students, and 90 percent of lawyers, felt that law school effectively teaches legal doctrine but not the practical skills necessary in the current economic climate.[65] Leaders of the bar have expressed growing discontent about the disconnect between academic preparation and the needs of practice.[66] So too, the consensus among experts, including authors of the widely respected Carnegie Foundation report *Educating Lawyers*, is that schools have not done enough to integrate issues of values into the core curriculum.[67]

The need for more effective training in social, interpersonal, and managerial capabilities is particularly pronounced at leadership levels.[68] Large law firms, in-house counsel offices, government agencies, and public-interest organizations are run by individuals who generally have had no leadership training, and whose abilities as lawyers do not necessarily meet the demands on leaders. This inattention to leadership development raises particular concern in light of a statistical study finding that the most powerful predictor of large-firm profitability is "the quality of partners' leadership skills."[69] Similar points apply to leaders in the nonprofit sector. In noting the current demands of his job, the executive director of the public-interest Immigrant Legal Resources Center wondered: "Why didn't I go to business school?"[70] What accounts for law schools' traditional lack of interest in leadership courses? Given the influence that the legal profession exercises, what can it do to train more members not just to think like lawyers but also to think like leaders?

2. THE LEARNING PROCESS

How then can lawyers learn to lead? Experience is, of course, critical. It is one thing to read about the Charge of the Light Brigade and quite another to lead soldiers into battle. Diverse leadership experiences supply the foundation for effective exercises of power and influence. But experience alone is not sufficient. As Mark Twain famously observed, a cat that sits on a hot stove will not sit on a hot stove again, but it will not sit on a cold one either. What is needed is reflection on experience: a capacity to learn from mistakes and to build on such knowledge in future action. Research on high performers who demonstrate leadership potential early in their careers finds that they are particularly gifted "catalytic" learners; that is, they are able to identify and absorb ideas and translate them into practical strategies.[71]

How then does one learn to be a learner? Individuals vary, and they need to seek out the structures that are most effective for them. Do they learn best by reading, discussion, observation, coaching, or group interaction?[72] For many people, courses and programs during and after their academic education can be valuable. They can enhance individuals' understanding of how to exercise influence and what cognitive biases, interpersonal behaviors, and organizational dynamics can sabotage effectiveness. Through exposure to leadership research, case studies, historical examples, role simulations, and guided analysis, individuals can prepare for dilemmas that they will face in practice.[73] Such settings can also provide a safe space to explore mistakes and their causes and correctives.

After law school, many leadership programs are available, but their lessons are not always transferable to particular workplace contexts, and long-term behavioral changes are unlikely unless they are reinforced and monitored.[74] Many individuals will profit most from experiential learning and "self-development" strategies, such as tailored on-the-job assignments, coaching, and mentoring.[75] To be effective, leadership development needs to be "professionalized." Yet current providers are not subject to a credentialing process or quality controls, and generally offer little evidence of long-term effectiveness.[76] Many programs also fail to provide what researchers believe is key to success: a continuing educational process supplying ongoing feedback.[77] Top-down, bottom-up "360" evaluations in a supportive organizational culture are critical for professional growth.[78] Mentoring programs should provide clear objectives and expectations, support for participation, and systematic evaluation.[79] Whatever the setting, the fundamental objective is to promote guided reflection that helps individuals become more effective life-long learners.

Part of that learning process involves leaders' reflection on their own strengths and weaknesses, and on the kinds of positions that will best match their talents and commitments. Many organizations and educational programs attempt to improve performance by focusing solely on deficiencies. Feedback becomes a predominately negative experience, which can discourage individuals from seeking it and erode self-confidence. Although constructive criticism is necessary for leadership development, it is not sufficient. Most individuals develop best by capitalizing on their strengths and pursuing their most fundamental goals and values.[80] That requires self-awareness and a plan for enhancing capabilities that are necessary to realize one's own aspirations. Beginning in law school and continuing throughout their careers, individuals need to become "self-directed learners." They must take the initiative in diagnosing their learning needs, formulating their learning goals, identifying necessary strategies and resources, and monitoring their progress.[81] Recent research in neuroscience underscores the importance of mindfulness: taking time to reflect on thoughts, emotions, and behaviors that may be undermining our ethical values and performance.[82]

3. OBSTACLES TO LEARNING

Chris Argyris argues in the excerpt below that most organizations not only have difficulty in addressing their "learning challenge, . . . they aren't even aware that it exists."[83] Part of the reason is misfocused attention. As Harvard psychology professor Howard Gardner notes, too often individuals engage in "Monday morning quarterbacking" of the substance of an erroneous decision, but fail to analyze the decision-making process, and the obstacles that prevent effective learning from mistakes.[84]

The first obstacle is the failure to acknowledge the need for continuous learning and to invite the criticism on which it depends. Leadership experts James Kouzes and Barry Posner put it bluntly: "[M]ost leaders don't want honest feedback, don't ask for honest feedback, and don't get much of it unless it's forced on them."[85] Of course, leaders are scarcely unique in this respect. But the understandable human tendency toward self-protection is particularly problematic for leaders, because of both the power they hold and the reluctance of subordinates to volunteer criticism. In Kouzes and Posner's survey of some 70,000 individuals, the statement that ranked the lowest in a list of 30 leadership behaviors was that the leader "asks for feedback on how his/her actions affect others' performance."[86] Only 40 percent of law firms offer associates the opportunity to evaluate their supervisor, and of those who engage in the process, only 5 percent report a change for the better.[87]

Yet, without such feedback, leaders may fail to identify problems in their own performance. Harvard economist John Kenneth Galbraith once noted that "[f]aced with the alternatives between changing one's mind and proving it unnecessary, just about everybody gets busy on the proof."[88] Defensiveness and denial are particularly apparent when individuals' own self-evaluations are at issue, and the cognitive biases discussed more extensively in Chapter 3 can reinforce this tendency. One common bias is the fundamental attribution error: people's tendency to attribute success to their own competence and character, and failure to external circumstances. A related problem stems from confirmation and assimilation biases. People tend to seek out evidence that confirms their preexisting, typically favorable, vision of themselves, and avoid evidence that contradicts it. They also assimilate evidence in ways that favor their preexisting beliefs and self-image.[89] In one random sample of adult men, 70 percent rated themselves in the top quarter of the population in leadership capabilities, and 98 percent rated themselves above average.[90]

As experts often note, the leaders' "most difficult and daunting task" is leading themselves.[91] Part of the reason is that those who achieve leadership positions are individuals with high needs for approval. For those individuals, as one consultant notes, "the intention to *look* good displaces the intention to *be* good" and to pay attention to needs that do not translate into immediate recognition.[92] Researchers including psychologist Carol Dweck find that people learn better when they are driven by learning goals rather than performance goals.[93] Those who focus on showing that they have a valued performance characteristic are less effective than those who seek to learn how to develop that characteristic. Truly effective leaders are those who have consistent curiosity and a desire to learn.[94]

Other obstacles to learning involve the time demands of lawyering and skepticism about leadership development programs. The pace and pressure of work often crowds out space for sustained reflection and efforts to do things differently.[95] In the nonprofit sector, with its fierce competition for scarce resources, leaders may be so focused simply on survival that they have little opportunity to attend to anything else.[96] "I don't have time" is a common response to opportunities for leadership training or coaching.[97] Avoiding these opportunities can also help individuals to evade their own responsibility for performance problems and to stay within their comfort zones.[98] These learning obstacles are compounded by the common assumption that leadership education is a "touchy-feely" process, unworthy of attention from intellectually sophisticated individuals. Yet as one prominent consultant puts it, "[T]he soft stuff is the hard stuff."[99] Effective leadership requires more than analytic skills, and high achievers in intellectual domains may not have developed corresponding interpersonal capabilities. In today's increasingly diverse work environments, development of cross-cultural competence should be a key priority, and it does not come naturally to many lawyer leaders.[100] They don't know what they don't know.

A final set of obstacles involves organizational failures. Overcommitted supervisors are often reluctant to invest the time in mentoring others, planning an appropriate sequence of developmental opportunities, or taking risks in giving inexperienced employees the new responsibilities that would best expand their competence.[101] Organizations have also been slow to address concerns that narcissistic individuals are particularly likely to seek positions of influence and to need programs and coaching that counteract unduly self-interested and self-aggrandizing tendencies.[102] Developing leadership requires leadership, and it is not always forthcoming.[103]

4. LEARNING STRATEGIES

The first step in overcoming these obstacles to effective learning requires self-knowledge. Lawyers must be reflective about what they want and what experiences and abilities will be necessary to achieve it.[104] Over five centuries ago, Michel de Montaigne famously wrote:

> A man who has not directed his life as a whole toward a definite goal cannot possibly set his particular actions in order. A man who does not have a picture of the whole in his head cannot possibly arrange the pieces

. . . . No one makes a definite plan of his life; we think about it only piecemeal . . . . Our plans go astray because they have no direction and no aim.[105]

Leaders and prospective leaders need a sense of their "ideal selves": what positions they aspire to hold, what qualities they are missing, and what is standing in their way.[106] One often unacknowledged obstacle is what psychologists call "self-handicapping."[107] Individuals avoid making efforts that might fail and thus put their own self-esteem at risk. Procrastinating, refusing to compete, or failing to prepare adequately for an interview, exam, or other competitive selection process gives people an explanation for their lack of success other than that they were not good enough.[108] By contrast, successful leaders have what Dweck terms "a growth mindset;" a belief that they can develop necessary capabilities through their own efforts.[109] For those unaccustomed to self-scrutiny, formal educational programs may help by forcing them to think deeply about their values, passions, and priorities, and what personal changes and sacrifices they are prepared to make to realize their professional aspirations. In gauging their leadership objectives, individuals need to be honest about their tolerance for risk, failure, conflict, competition, pressure, and sweatshop schedules. At various stages of their careers, lawyers should examine their current job and determine how much of their time goes to work that they really enjoy and find meaningful. If the ratio is too low, they should think about how to move to a position that is a better match for their interests and talents.[110]

Lawyers also need a plan for diagnosing their learning needs; formulating goals; identifying the resources, experiences, and capabilities that they will need to advance to their desired leadership roles; choosing learning strategies; and evaluating outcomes.[111] At the most general level, that plan should include a mix of methods: learning through doing, learning through analysis, and learning through social interaction.[112] Lawyers should consider how they learn best, and decide whether to read, take a course, watch on-line presentations, get a coach, or attend programs.[113]

They should also develop a "nose for opportunity," and be proactive in seeking positions and "stretch assignments" that develop new skills.[114] Exceptional performers are those who constantly seek to improve, and look for developmental opportunities outside their comfort zone.[115] The prominent Wall Street lawyer Arthur Liman recalled that early in his career the New York District Attorney Robert Morgenthau invited him to run a special unit prosecuting securities fraud. Liman raised concerns that he "knew almost nothing about stocks, let alone stock fraud. He had never studied securities at Yale nor even so much as read the federal securities statutes."[116] Morgenthau reassured him, "Arthur, neither have the crooks."[117] Sometimes lawyers have to seize an opportunity even if the timing or their qualifications are not ideal. Barack Obama did just that in 2008, when he ran for president despite concerns about his relative lack of experience and his two small children. As his strategist David Axelrod put it, "usually the politician chooses the moment, [but] sometimes the moment chooses the politician."[118]

So too, law students and junior lawyers can seek volunteer positions that give them leadership experience. They can also sometimes benefit from those positions and from job rotation that broadens and develops their skills.[119] High levels of responsibility and pressure, coupled with adequate organizational coaching and support, often provide .the best learning experiences.[120] Training in cultural competence is also critical.[121] Warren Bennis emphasizes the importance of "taking risks as a matter of course, with the knowledge that failure is as vital as it is inevitable . . . [and thinking through mistakes to] see where we went wrong, mentally revise what we're doing, and then act on the revisions . . . ."[122] What matters is not the number of mistakes aspiring leaders make, but rather the number of times that they make the same mistake, or fail to admit it.[123] The key is to "crash and learn . . . [not] crash and burn."[124] Successful learners also need "grit"—a combination of passion and perseverance that researchers find is more important than innate talent in accounting for outstanding performance.[125]

A key aspect of an effective learning process is feedback. As experts often emphasize, the "more elevated your position, the more important it is to solicit feedback," because candid criticism is unlikely to be volunteered by subordinates.[126] The feedback can come in varying forms in both educational and real-life settings: objective measures of behavior, observations by others, bottom-up 360-degree evaluations, and mentoring.[127] Enlisting trusted and respected mentors is critical and not always easy. Ideally, advisors should have honesty, knowledge of their advisee's work setting, and effective interpersonal and communication skills.[128] As Chapter 8 notes, demand for mentors frequently outpaces supply, particularly for women and minorities. For individuals at early stages of their leadership development, the best strategy may be not to seek "perfect mentors," but rather to become "perfect protégés," so superiors will want to provide coaching.[129] That means being respectful of mentors' own needs and constraints, responding positively to advice, and finding ways to reciprocate or to express gratitude.

For individuals already holding top positions, the most useful advice may come from predecessors, from those who hold comparable positions in other settings, or from experts in the field. Psychologists Ann Colby and William Damon studied exemplary leadership by individuals who had maintained ethical commitments and had made exceptional contributions in the face of significant hardship. One distinguishing characteristic of these individuals was their willingness to subject their views to challenge and criticism. They developed leadership skills by actively seeking advice from others who shared their fundamental moral goals but had a different perspective on how to realize them.[130]

Leaders also can benefit from formal networks and individualized coaching. Networks can connect individuals in similar positions who can be a source of advice, support, and innovative ideas. Herminia Ibarra recommends developing diverse networks.[131] If lawyers work just with people like themselves, they may remain caught in an echo chamber that fails to promote new skills and perspectives. Yet as other experts note, superficial outreach efforts can be overrated or even counterproductive if the self-promotion is too overt. The best way to attract useful attention is to accomplish something worthy of it; that way, "instead of having to push your way in, you'll get pulled in. The network comes to you."[132] Professional coaching can also supply the kind of expert assessment and candid evaluation that may be unavailable from other sources. An example comes from an executive coach profiled in the *New Yorker*, who told the leader who had hired him, "I can't help you make money. You're already making more than God. But do you want a funeral that no one attends? Because that's where this train is heading."[133]

Both public- and private-sector organizations need to help individuals develop leadership potential and to engage in their own succession planning. Many experts have been highly critical of programs that are removed from actual workplace challenges, and that fail to provide adequate evaluation and follow-up.[134] As a consequence, a growing trend is toward customized in-house programs and "action learning"—team-based experiential exercises involving issues of immediate relevance to the organization.[135] Successful initiatives generally require identification of clear goals and competencies, continuing reinforcement and feedback, and rewards for mentoring prospective leaders. The limited research available suggests that a combination of coaching, classroom instruction, multisource feedback, and experiential training is most likely to improve individual and organizational performance.[136] Such initiatives should be a priority for the legal profession. As one *Harvard Business Review* study notes, just as we need more people to provide leadership in complex organizations that dominate our world today, we also need more people to develop the cultures that will create that leadership. Institutionalizing a leadership-centered culture is the ultimate act of leadership.[137]

5. ORGANIZATIONAL LEARNING

Experts stress the need for both leader development (individual skills) and leadership development (structures and processes).[138] Efforts need to focus both on enhancing individual skills and on creating structures and processes that will foster learning, collaboration, adaptation, and innovation. A growing number of researchers stress "leadership as practice," which emphasizes practices not practitioners, and the importance of productive, collaborative relationships.[139]

In effect, leaders need to focus not only on their own learning process, but also on creating what Peter Senge termed "learning organizations." By his definition, these are institutions in which individuals are "continually learning how to learn together to expand their capacity to create the results they truly desire."[140] Other experts describe a learning organization as one "skilled in creating, acquiring and transferring knowledge, and at modifying its behavior to reflect new knowledge and insights."[141] Leaders can foster such learning environments by becoming "multipliers" of collective intelligence; they can take advantage of talent by extending opportunities and sharing credit, control, and ownership of organizational objectives.[142] Leaders can also set goals and hold individuals accountable for meeting them in performance reviews.[143] And they can support innovation along the lines described in Chapter 4. They can reward experimentation, demand better evaluation and monitoring of leadership development programs, and create networks for collaboration and information exchange.[144]

Learning organizations can also make it safe for individuals to acknowledge mistakes. An example involves Tom Watson, the legendary founder of IBM. During his leadership, a junior executive involved the company in a risky venture that proved financially disastrous. When Watson called the man into his office, he offered his resignation. Watson responded, "You can't be serious. We just spent $10 million educating you."[145]

These kinds of learning environments treat individual mistakes not simply as discrete events but as possible signals of broader organizational problems. Too many organizations experience difficulty in leadership development because they reward employees for being the smartest people in the room, not for nurturing the careers of others.[146] Workplaces that are serious about mentoring can adjust their incentive structure. They can also seek feedback on their own performance through benchmarking: finding out how other high-performing organizations handle similar functions.[147] Leaders can also look for ways to institutionalize organizational learning. As FBI director, James Comey oversaw a training curriculum that explored prior abuses by the Bureau, such as the surveillance of Martin Luther King's extramarital relationships. That curriculum required trainees to visit the Martin Luther King memorial and write an essay about FBI values.[148]

Leaders can also do their part, as John Gardner noted, to "create or strengthen systems that will survive them."[149] That includes legal, political, and regulatory structures that will serve public as well as organizational interests. Consider these approaches to individual and organizational learning in light of the readings that follow. What insights do they suggest about your own experience in learning to lead?

CHRIS ARGYRIS, TEACHING SMART PEOPLE HOW TO LEARN

Harvard Business Review 69(3) (1991): 99-109

Any [organization] that aspires to succeed in [today's] tougher business environment . . . must first resolve a basic dilemma: success in the marketplace increasingly depends on learning, yet most people don't know how to learn. What's more, those members of the organization that many assume to be the best at learning are, in fact, not very good at it. I am talking about the well-educated, high-powered, high-commitment professionals who occupy key leadership positions in the modern corporation.

Most companies not only have tremendous difficulty addressing this learning dilemma; they aren't even aware that it exists. The reason: they misunderstand what learning is and how to bring it about.

As a result, they tend to make two mistakes in their efforts to become a learning organization.

First, most people define learning too narrowly as mere "problem solving," so they focus on identifying and correcting errors in the external environment. Solving problems is important. But if learning is to persist, managers and employees must also look inward. They need to reflect critically on their own behavior, identify the ways they often inadvertently contribute to the organization's problems, and then change how they act. In particular, they must learn how the very way they go about defining and solving problems can be a source of problems in its own right.

I have coined the terms "single loop" and "double loop" learning to capture this crucial distinction. To give a simple analogy: a thermostat that automatically turns on the heat whenever the temperature in a room drops below 68 degrees is a good example of single-loop learning. A thermostat that could ask, "Why am I set at 68 degrees?" and then explore whether or not some other temperature might more economically achieve the goal of heating the room would be engaging in double-loop learning.

Highly skilled professionals are frequently very good at single-loop learning. After all, they have spent much of their lives acquiring academic credentials, mastering one or a number of intellectual disciplines, and applying those disciplines to solve real-world problems. But ironically, this very fact helps explain why professionals are often so bad at double-loop learning.

Put simply, because many professionals are almost always successful at what they do, they rarely experience failure. And because they have rarely failed, they have never learned how to learn from failure. So whenever their single-loop learning strategies go wrong, they become defensive, screen out criticism, and put the "blame" on anyone and everyone but themselves. In short, their ability to learn shuts down precisely at the moment they need it the most.

The propensity among professionals to behave defensively helps shed light on the second mistake that companies make about learning. The common assumption is that getting people to learn is largely a matter of motivation. When people have the right attitudes and commitment, learning automatically follows. So companies focus on creating new organizational structures—compensation programs, performance reviews, corporate cultures, and the like—that are designed to create motivated and committed employees.

But effective double-loop learning is not simply a function of how people feel. It is a reflection of how they think—that is, the cognitive rules or reasoning they use to design and implement their actions. Think of these rules as a kind of "master program" stored in the brain, governing all behavior. Defensive reasoning can block learning even when the individual commitment to it is high, just as a computer program with hidden bugs can produce results exactly the opposite of what its designers had planned.

Companies can learn how to resolve the learning dilemma. What it takes is to make the ways managers and employees reason about their behavior a focus of organizational learning and continuous improvement programs. Teaching people how to reason about their behavior in new and more effective ways breaks down the defenses that block learning. . . .

Defensive Reasoning and the Doom Loop

When you observe people's behavior and try to come up with rules that would make sense of it, you discover a very different theory of action—what I call the individual's "theory-in-use." Put simply, people consistently act inconsistently, unaware of the contradiction between their espoused theory and their theory-in-use, between the way they think they are acting and the way they really act. What's more, most theories-in-use rest on the same set of governing values. There seems to be a universal human tendency to design one's actions consistently according to four basic values:

- To remain in unilateral control;
- To maximize "winning" and minimize "losing";
- To suppress negative feelings; and
- To be as "rational" as possible—by which people mean defining clear objectives and evaluating their behavior in terms of whether or not they have achieved them.

The purpose of all these values is to avoid embarrassment or threat, feeling vulnerable or incompetent. In this respect, the master program that most people use is profoundly defensive. Defensive reasoning encourages individuals to keep private the premises, inferences, and conclusions that shape their behavior and to avoid testing them in a truly independent, objective fashion.

Because the attributions that go into defensive reasoning are never really tested, it is a closed loop, remarkably impervious to conflicting points of view. The inevitable response to the observation that somebody is reasoning defensively is yet more defensive reasoning. [In one representative team that we studied], whenever anyone pointed out the professionals' defensive behavior to them, their initial reaction was to look for the cause in somebody else—clients who were so sensitive that they would have been alienated if the consultants had criticized them or a manager so weak that he couldn't have taken it had the consultants raised their concerns with him. In other words, the case team members once again denied their own responsibility by externalizing the problem and putting it on someone else.

In such situations, the simple act of encouraging more open inquiry is often attacked by others as "intimidating." Those who do the attacking deal with their feelings about possibly being wrong by blaming the more open individual for arousing these feelings and upsetting them.

Needless to say, such a master program inevitably short-circuits learning. And for a number of reasons unique to their psychology, well-educated professionals are especially susceptible to this. . . . Behind this high aspiration for success is an equally high fear of failure and a propensity to feel shame and guilt when they do fail to meet their high standards. "You must avoid mistakes," said one. "I hate making them. Many of us fear failure, whether we admit it or not."

To the extent that these consultants have experienced success in their lives, they have not had to be concerned about failure and the attendant feelings of shame and guilt. But to exactly the same extent, they also have never developed the tolerance for feelings of failure or the skills to deal with these feelings. . . .

The consultants use two intriguing metaphors to describe this phenomenon. They talk about the "doom loop" and "doom zoom." Often, consultants will perform well on the case team, but because they don't do the jobs perfectly or receive accolades from their managers, they go into a doom loop of despair. And they don't ease into the doom loop, they zoom into it.

As a result, many professionals have extremely "brittle" personalities. When suddenly faced with a situation they cannot immediately handle, they tend to fall apart. They cover up their distress in front of the client. They talk about it constantly with their fellow case team members. Interestingly, these conversations commonly take the form of bad-mouthing clients. . . .

Learning How to Reason Productively

. . . The key to any educational experience designed to teach senior managers how to reason productively is to connect the program to real business problems. The best demonstration of the usefulness of productive reasoning is for business managers to see how it can make a direct difference in their own performance and in that of the organization. This will not happen overnight. Managers need plenty of opportunity to practice the new skills. But once they grasp the powerful impact that productive reasoning can have on actual performance, they will have a strong incentive to reason productively not just in a training session but in all their work relationships.

DAVID W. JOHNSON AND FRANK P. JOHNSON, JOINING
TOGETHER: GROUP THEORY AND GROUP SKILLS

(Allyn and Bacon, 2005), pp. 43-48

All humans need to become competent in taking action and simultaneously reflecting on their action to learn from it. Integrating thought with action requires that we plan our behavior, engage in it, and then reflect on how effective we were. . . . [Acquiring or altering leadership behaviors is more challenging than is often assumed.]

1. Information and knowledge can generate interest in changing, but will not bring about change. Knowing a rationale for change is not sufficient for motivating a person to change.
2. Firsthand experience alone will not generate valid knowledge. . . . Besides experience there must be a theoretical system that the expertise tests out and reflection on the meaning of the experience.
3. It takes more than engaging in a new behavior to result in permanent change. New skills may be practiced and mastered but will fade away unless action theories and attitudes also change.

To learn leadership skills, for example, the learner must develop a concept of what leadership is (knowledge), an action theory concerning what leadership behaviors will lead to effective group functioning, positive attitudes toward new leadership procedures, and perceptions that the new leadership actions are appropriate and that he or she is capable of performing them. Finally, the learner must develop the skills needed to perform the new leadership actions. . . . Experiential learning can be conceived of in a simplified way as a four-stage cycle: (1) take action on the basis of one's current action theory, (2) assess consequences and obtain feedback, (3) reflect on how effective actions were and reformulate and refine the action theory, and (4) implement the revised action theory by taking modified action. . . .

It takes more than firsthand experience to generate valid knowledge. Lewin used to state that thousands of years of human experience with falling bodies did not bring humans to a correct theory of gravity. Besides experience, there needs to be a theoretical system that the experience tests out and reflection on the meaning of the experience.

Behavior changes will be temporary unless the action theories and attitudes underlying them are changed. New behavioral skills may be practiced and mastered, but without changes in the person's action theories and attitudes, the new behavior patterns will fade away. . . . Learners must perceive themselves as capable of doing the needed behaviors and must see the behaviors as being appropriate to the situation before they will engage in them. . . . The more supportive, accepting, and caring the social environment, the freer a person is to experiment with new behaviors, attitudes, and action theories.

PROBLEM 2-2

1. Think about a leadership mistake that you have made or observed. What was responsible? What lessons did you draw from the experience at the time? What insights would you draw now?
2. Think about a leadership dilemma that you or someone you know resolved effectively. What did you or that person do well? Ask someone else knowledgeable about the situation if his or her perception is the same. What lessons did you both take away from the experience?
3. Construct a timeline in which you list your own greatest successes in leadership above the line, and your most significant failures below the line. Can you identify common patterns in the experiences in which you were most and least effective? What learning needs do they suggest?[150]

NOTES AND QUESTIONS

1. Chris Argyris distinguishes between single-loop and double-loop learning. The first involves finding a solution to a problem; the second involves understanding your own contribution to that problem. Can you identify leadership experiences where it would have been better for you or for your

leader to engage in double- rather than single-loop analysis? What got in the way?

2. David and Frank Johnson describe a process of experiential learning that involves taking action, assessing its consequences, reflecting on how effective it was, and modifying future action. Construct such a process for yourself on a quality you would like to improve and spend the next week attempting to follow your plan. How successful were you? What did you learn from the experience?

3. In his article "Financial Leaders Go AWOL in the Meltdown," Harvard lecturer and former general counsel for General Electric Ben Heineman writes:

> In all good business organizations, facing failures honestly, looking at root causes, disciplining individuals and implementing systemic change to prevent recurrences is as important as planning for new products, markets or technologies.
>
> Yet a voracious reader of economic and business reports would have a hard time finding a financial industry statesman talking candidly about the errors and flawed judgment among managers or directors [leading to the 2008 financial crisis]. Nor will you find a hint about how these private institutions should govern themselves in the future to avoid a recurrence of such widespread devastation.
>
> Instead, the chairman of a failed investment bank testifies on Capitol Hill that he is responsible—then blames everyone else. Financial CEOs at a session organized by the New York Stock Exchange call for more Wall Street tax breaks, repeal of the Sarbanes-Oxley Act, and limits on class-action lawsuits. . . . [Some suggest that acknowledgement of error appears too dangerous in a litigious society.] But retired leaders or sitting CEOs in institutions singed by the crisis can surely find a way to discuss these issues without putting their heads in a noose.[151]

If Heineman is right, what might encourage more self-critical reflection among those responsible for circumstances like those leading to the financial crisis? Think about a contemporary social problem in which leaders have seemed unwilling or unable to learn from experience. What accounts for their difficulty? What could be done to address it?

D. WELL-BEING AND TIME MANAGEMENT

1. WELL-BEING

Lawyer well-being is a critical leadership issue both because the pressures of their position make leaders particularly susceptible to stress and mental health difficulties, and because leaders bear part of the responsibility for workplace conditions that give rise to such difficulties in others and impair organizational performance.

DEBORAH L. RHODE, PREPARING LEADERS: THE EVOLUTION OF A FIELD AND THE CONDITIONS AND STRESS OF LEADERSHIP

58 SANTA CLARA LAW REVIEW 411, 418- 424 (2019).

In the summer of 2017, many in the legal and leadership community read with shock a front-page article in the Sunday *New York Times* business section. The author, Eilene Zimmerman, movingly described the death of her ex-husband, Peter, from an infection related to drug abuse. Peter Zimmerman was a leading partner at a leading Silicon Valley law firm who, for several years, had exhibited signs of serious ill health and substance abuse. It is, of course no secret that many highly successful lawyers suffer from such problems. But what the article brought home is just how serious and tragic their difficulties may be when others look away, or fail to look at all. Eilene Zimmerman writes:

> Of all the heartbreaking details of his story, the one that continues to haunt me is this: The history on his cellphone shows the last call he ever made was for work. Peter, vomiting, unable to sit up, slipping in and out of consciousness, had managed, somehow, to dial into a conference call.

. . . Peter Zimmerman's case is all too typical. The most comprehensive recent study of lawyers and substance abuse . . . was cosponsored by the American Bar Association and Hazelden Foundation. Based on responses from almost 13,000 attorneys, it found that about a fifth of lawyers (21 percent) qualify as problem drinkers and suffer from anxiety (19 percent), and over a quarter struggle with mild or more serious depression (28 percent). Figures on drug use are unreliable because three quarters of the survey participants declined to answer. . . .

The limited research available also suggests that lawyers report almost three times the rate of depression and almost twice the rate of substance abuse as other Americans. Law ranks among the top five careers for suicide. Primary reasons for legal professionals' particular vulnerability involve: first, the characteristics of individuals who become lawyers; second, the priorities and pressures that they receive in law school; and third, the conditions of practice that they encounter after graduating. As to the first reason, most research suggests that law attracts a disproportionate number of individuals with personality traits that make them susceptible to pressure, stress, and related mental health difficulties, such as competitiveness, combativeness, and pessimism.

The law school experience compounds the problem. Although entering students rank better than students in other fields with respect to mental health and substance abuse, they graduate with higher rates of problems. Reasons include the competition for jobs and grades, the pressure of overwork, the stress of crushing debt loads, and the lack of education and resources concerning psychological health. For students of color, both subtle and overt forms of racial bias, and feelings of isolation and exclusion, create further challenges. White students from socially and economically disadvantaged backgrounds experience related difficulties. Even students who recognize that they have problems are often unwilling to seek help. Major barriers include concerns about privacy, social stigma, financial implications, and potential threats to bar admission, employment, or academic status. In one recent survey of fifteen law schools, although over 40 percent of students thought that they had needed help for mental health problems in the prior year, only about half actually received counseling from a mental health professional. . . . Similarly disturbing is that only half of students say that their law school places substantial emphasis on preparing them to handles the stresses of law practice.

These stresses are increasing, and they set lawyers up for an array of health-related concerns. . . . For lawyers in firms, billable hours have sharply escalated, and what has not changed is the number of hours in the day. Law is the nation's second most sleep deprived occupation, which escalates the risk of anxiety and depression, and seriously impairs performance. All work and no play is increasingly the norm and, as a *New Yorker* cartoon notes, it "makes you a valued employee." . . . Unsurprisingly most surveyed lawyers report that they do not have sufficient time for themselves and their families, and overwork is a leading cause of lawyers' physical and psychological health difficulties.

In addressing these issues, technology has created as many problems as it has solved. Electronic communication has made it increasingly possible for lawyers to work at home or on vacation, but has also made it increasingly impossible for them not to do so. Lawyers remain tethered to their devices, as Eilene Zimmerman notes in describing Peter's memorial service. When a young associate from the firm "stood up to speak of their friendship . . . [q]uite a few of the lawyers attending the service were bent over their phones, reading and tapping out e-mails. Their friend and colleague was dead, and yet they couldn't stop working long enough to listen to what was being said about him."

Racial, ethnic, gender, and class bias also creates additional stress. Underrepresented groups often face isolation, denigration, harassment, and pressures to suppress aspects of their identity to fit the dominant culture. Chronic "micro-inequities"—subtle insults, denigrating messages, and patterns of being overlooked and undervalued—can impair performance and psychological wellbeing. . . .

Stress and overwork escalate for lawyers who lead given the pace and pressures of their position. . . . [These leaders also] have a responsibility to address the working conditions in their organizations that contribute to high rates of dysfunction. Although data are lacking on the prevalence and effectiveness of wellness programs in legal workplaces, the experience in other fields is not especially encouraging. All too often employers supply voluntary opportunities with or without modest incentives for participation, which do not attract most employees or address the root causes of stress (such as overwork, inflexible and unpredictable schedules, excessive competition, and unrealistic time pressure). Failure to modify these conditions is not only inhumane, it is economically unproductive; bleary, burned out, disaffected, and/or addicted lawyers are not delivering cost effective services. Leaders need to know more about how their policies and practices are exacerbating rather than combatting the problem.

PROBLEM 2-3

Break the class into teams of five. Each team should make recommendations about how leaders should address stress and well-being issues in different sectors of the profession including law schools, law firms, and bar associations. Discuss what strategies are most important and what obstacles stand in the way.

NOTES AND QUESTIONS

The American Bar Association has cosponsored a National Task Force on Lawyer Well-Being that has provided over 44 specific recommendations for legal employers, legal educators, bar regulators, and other stakeholders. The aim is to prevent problems, raise awareness, and encourage individuals to seek assistance. Leaders can play an important role in following these recommendations and implementing reforms that reduce billable hour requirements, improve flexible schedule options, encourage adequate vacations, and provide support to colleagues who are struggling.[152] Engaging in self-care is equally critical. Addressing their own health needs (diet, sleep, exercise, unplugged time) will enhance leaders' performance and make them better role models for others.

The proposals that have gotten the most traction from a subsequent ABA working group focus on providing education and confidential access to resources for attorneys facing these challenges.[153] There is, however, little evidence of a commitment to reducing the problems of overwork and inflexible schedules that compromise well-being. In a recent survey of law firm leaders, the majority saw stress and workload as the main drivers of mental health and substance abuse difficulties.[154] Addressing these issues is, of course, a tougher sell to firms concerned with productivity and profitability. But lawyer impairment also threatens these goals, as leaders readily acknowledge. Is it realistic to think that major progress is possible without addressing the profit structure that drives the problems? What can and should leaders do to respond to the causes, not simply the symptoms, of impairment?

That same survey of leaders found that although 94 percent believed that addiction to alcohol and drugs was stigmatized, 87 percent thought that getting treatment for addiction is not.[155] If those beliefs are accurate, what can leaders do to encourage more lawyers to obtain treatment?

2. TIME MANAGEMENT

Leaders can also be sabotaged by inadequate time-management skills, which may be a cause as well as a consequence of exceptional stress and pressure. To be sure, lawyers who reach positions of influence are generally skilled enough to avoid some of the problems that plague the profession generally, such as chronic procrastination.[156] Many leaders, however, can at times become overwhelmed by inexhaustible demands and information overload.[157] Some otherwise successful individuals suffer from "attention deficit." Its primary symptoms are distractibility, impatience, and lack of organization. The consequences include careless mistakes, inefficiency, impaired relationships, and underachievement.[158]

To address these issues, leaders need to take care of basic health needs (sleep, exercise, diet), monitor their time allocation to be sure it matches their priorities, and develop strategies to maximize efficiency.[159] Experts recommend handling paperwork only once; lawyers should try to act on it, file it, or discard it, and avoid pileups in their inbox or e-mails.[160] They should schedule crucial work for the time of day when they perform best, avoid distractions during these time blocks, and break daunting tasks into smaller manageable ones.[161] Effective performers generally minimize multi-tasking and try not to work too long or too short in a stretch; they also batch related work to avoid constantly switching gears.[162]

When leaders feel overwhelmed, they need to delegate, ask for assistance, avoid distractions, and focus on what is critical.[163] Setting boundaries, saying no, and avoiding perfectionism are critical skills for any lawyer, but are especially necessary for leaders, who often face an avalanche of demands and requests that they cannot adequately accommodate.[164] Leaders should be realistic about how much time given tasks require, and build in some margin for error and buffer zones between commitments. No one wants to work for a leader whose poor planning consistently subjects subordinates to excessive workloads and unrealistic deadlines. Constant directives to "just make it happen" breed a "trickle down toxicity [and] downward flowing distress."[165]

Although conventional wisdom is that people should not "sweat the small stuff," that advice can be misleading in professional contexts. Researchers find that conscientiousness is a key predictor of effective performance and that one of the best warning signs of ineffectiveness is the failure to handle small matters promptly and courteously. For example, responding promptly to e-mails is a signal that the leader is conscientious, organized, dependable, and hard-working.[166] That is not to suggest that leaders need to answer every inquiry or respond outside of normal working hours. But as Adam Grant notes, if "you're habitually 'too busy' to answer legitimate e-mails, there's a problem with your process. It sends a signal that you're disorganized—or that you just don't care."[167]

How would you evaluate your own time-management skills? What could you improve? Break up into groups and share strategies for effectiveness.

END NOTES

[1] JOSEPH S. NYE, JR., THE POWERS TO LEAD 19 (2008).

[2] Nathan Bennett & G. James Lemoine, *What VUCA Really Means for You*, HARV. BUS. REV. (Jan.-Feb. 2014).

[3] ANTHONY C. THOMPSON, DANGEROUS LEADERS: HOW AND WHY LAWYERS MUST BE TAUGHT TO LEAD 30-33 (2018).

[4] NICK PETRIE, FUTURE TRENDS IN LEADERSHIP DEVELOPMENT 7 (Center for Creative Leadership, 2014).

[5] For an overview for public interest organizations, see Deborah L. Rhode, *Public Interest Law: The Movement at Midlife*, 60 STAN. L. REV. 2027 (2008).

[6] MONTGOMERY VAN WART, DYNAMICS OF LEADERSHIP IN PUBLIC SERVICE: THEORY AND PRACTICE 186 (2005) (quoting David Sarnoff).

[7] BARBARA KELLERMAN, HARD TIMES: LEADERSHIP IN AMERICA 301 (2015).

[8] Scott L. Cummings, *The Politics of Pro Bono*, 52 UCLA L. REV. 1, 35 (2004-2005); Rhode, *Public Interest Law*, 2032.

[9] *Tough at the Top*, THE ECONOMIST, Oct. 25, 2003.

[10] JOHN GARDNER, ON LEADERSHIP 27 (1990).

[11] BOB JOHANSEN, LEADERS MAKE THE FUTURE: TEN NEW LEADERSHIP SKILLS FOR AN UNCERTAIN WORLD 11 (2009).

[12] MICHAEL FULLAN, LEADING IN A CULTURE OF CHANGE 2 (2001).

[13] ELIZABETH VRATO, THE COUNSELORS: CONVERSATIONS WITH 18 COURAGEOUS WOMEN WHO HAVE CHANGED THE WORLD 51 (2002) (quoting Jamie Gorelick).

[14] Deborah L. Rhode, *Preparing Leaders: The Evolution of a Field and the Stresses of Leadership*, 58 SANTA CLARA L. REV. 411, 417-425 (2018).

[15] Manseur Javidan, Peter W. Dorfman, Jon Paul Howell & Paul J. Hanges, *Leadership and Cultural Context*, in HANDBOOK OF LEADERSHIP THEORY AND PRACTICE 335, 366-368 (Nitin Nohria & Rakesh Khurana eds., 2010).

[16] Neil W. Hamilton, *Ethical Leadership in Professional Life*, 62 U. ST. THOMAS L.J. 383 (2009).

[17] Hamilton, *Ethical Leadership*, 363 (quoting Jim Collins).

[18] Hamilton, *Ethical Leadership*, 385-86.

[19] NYE, THE POWERS TO LEAD, 2.

[20] Warren Bennis & James O'Toole, *Don't Hire the Wrong CEO*, HARV. BUS. REV. 174 (May-June 2000); ROGER GILL, THEORY AND PRACTICE OF LEADERSHIP 20 (2d ed. 2011).

[21] David Maister, *The Trouble with Lawyers*, AM. LAW., Apr. 2006, at 100. For discussion of lawyers' need for autonomy and the difficulties that poses for leadership, see Larry Richard & Susan Raridon Lambreth, *What Does It Take to Develop Effective Law Firm Leaders?*, LAW PRAC. TODAY, Mar. 2006; *Leadership Partners or Managing Partners*, LAW OFF. MGMT. AND ADMIN. REP. 1, 5 (Oct. 2010).

[22] VAN WART, DYNAMICS OF LEADERSHIP IN PUBLIC SERVICE, 55-56.

[23] BARBARA C. CROSBY, LEADERSHIP FOR THE COMMON GOOD: TACKLING PROBLEMS IN A SHARED-POWER WORLD 161-62 (2005).

[24] There is no consistent evidence of a universally effective style. *See* David V. Day & John Anonakis, *Leadership: Past, Present and Future*, in THE NATURE OF LEADERSHIP 8 (David V. Day & John Antonakis eds., 2012).

[25] DEBORAH L. RHODE, AMBITION: FOR WHAT (forthcoming).

[26] AARON JAMES, ASSHOLES: A THEORY 5-6 (2012).

[27] Walter Isaacson, *The Real Leadership Lessons of Steve Jobs*, HARV. BUS. REV. 94, 99 (Apr. 2012) (quoting Wozniak).

[28] Tony Schwartz, *The Bad Behavior of Visionary Leaders*, N.Y. TIMES, June 26, 2018.

[29] Dacher Keltner, *Managing Yourself: Don't Let Power Corrupt You*, HARV. BUS. REV. 112, 114 (Oct. 2016).

[30] Robert S. Kaplan, *What to Ask the Person in the Mirror*, in ON MANAGING YOURSELF 151 (Harv. Bus. Rev. ed. 2010).

[31] DONALD J. TRUMP WITH MEREDITH MCIVER, TRUMP: HOW TO GET RICH 14 (2004).

[32] KATHRYN TIDRICK, GANDHI: A POLITICAL AND SPIRITUAL LIFE 81 (2006).

[33] MOHANDAS K. GANDHI, SATYAGRAHA IN SOUTH AFRICA 106 (2008).

[34] RHODE, CHARACTER.

[35] Alexander Abad-Santos, Abby Ohlheiser & Sara Morrison, *Nelson Mandela, "The Epicenter of Our Time," Has Died*, ATLANTIC, Dec. 5, 2013 (quoting Mandela).

[36] SAM WALKER, THE CAPTAIN CLASS: THE HIDDEN FORCE THAT CREATES THE WORLD'S GREATEST TEAMS 141 (2017).

[37] John Beeson, *Deconstructing Executive Presence*, in HARV. BUS. REV., LEADERSHIP PRESENCE 4-5 (2018).

[38] Rebecca Shambaugh, *To Sound Like a Leader, Think About What You Say, and How and When You Say It*, in HARV. BUS. REV., LEADERSHIP PRESENCE, 23, 33.

[39] For Clinton's listening skill and listening tours, see Klein, *Understanding Hillary.*

[40] Id. (quoting Robert Reich).

[41] David Giambusso, *Cory Booker's Legacy in Newark Under Spotlight as He Looks to Senate*, NJ.COM (Oct. 6, 2013), https://www.nj.com/politics/2013/10/cory_bookers_legacy_in_newark_under_spotlight_as_he_looks_to_senate.html.

[42] JAMES COMEY, A HIGHER LOYALTY: TRUTH, LIES, AND LEADERSHIP 21 (2018).

[43] Matt Flegenheimer & Sydney Ember, *Klobuchar's Taunts and Temper Stand Out in Sea of Tough Bosses*, N.Y TIMES, Feb. 23, 2019, A1.

[44] GEORGE STEPHANOPOULOS, ALL TOO HUMAN: A POLITICAL EDUCATION 286-288 (1999); DEBORAH L. RHODE, CHARACTER: WHAT IT MEANS AND WHY IT MATTERS (2019).

[45] NYE, THE POWERS TO LEAD, 82.

[46] For the research, see PFEFFER, POWER, 135, Alice H. Eagly & Linda L. Carli, Leadership and Gender, in THE NATURE OF LEADERSHIP, 453-455; DEBORAH L. RHODE, WOMEN AND LEADERSHIP 11, 80-81 (2016).

[47] RICHARD NIXON, LEADERS 287-88 (1982).

[48] Robert B. Kaiser & S. Bartholomew Craig, *Destructive Leadership*, in THE OXFORD HANDBOOK OF LEADERSHIP AND ORGANIZATIONS 262-67 (David V. Day ed., 2014).

[49] DAVID REMNICK, THE BRIDGE: THE LIFE AND RISE OF BARACK OBAMA 209 (2011) (quoting Christine Spurell).

[50] REMNICK, THE BRIDGE, 207 (quoting David Goldberg).

[51] REMNICK, THE BRIDGE, 206 (quoting Christopher Edley).

[52] REMNICK, THE BRIDGE, 209 (quoting Christine Spurell).

[53] REMNICK, THE BRIDGE, 210.

[54] David Remnick, *Going the Distance: On and Off the Road with Barack Obama*, NEW YORKER, Jan. 27, 2014.

[55] Remnick, *Going the Distance* (quoting Joe Manchin).

[56] Remnick, *Going the Distance* (quoting Obama).

[57] Remnick, *Going the Distance*.

[58] Remnick, *Going the Distance* (quoting Obama).

[59] http://www.youtube.com/watch?v=hA-xfaf8V_Y.

[60] http://www.youtube.com/watch?v=Eba6pf3HrtE.

[61] Andrea R. Steel & David V. Day, *The Role of Self-Attention in Leaders' Development*, 12 J. LEADERSHIP STUD. 17 (2018).

[62] *See* Deborah L. Rhode, *Lawyers and Leadership*, 20 THE PROF. LAW. 1 (2010). For the evolution of law school initiatives, see George T. "Buck" Lewis & Douglas A. Blaze, *Training Leaders the Very Best Way We Can*, 83 TENN. L. REV. 771, 773-776 (2016).

[63] Hamilton, *Ethical Leadership*, 362, 370. For an exception, see PAULA MONOPOLI & SUSAN MCCARTY, LAW AND LEADERSHIP: INTEGRATING LEADERSHIP STUDIES INTO THE LAW SCHOOL CURRICULUM (2013).

[64] Leah Witcher & Jackson Teague, *Training Lawyers for Leadership: Vitally Important Mission for the Future Success (and Maybe Survival) of the Legal Profession and Our Democracy,* 58 SANTA CLARA L. REV. 633, 655 (2018) (31 out of 204 schools have courses and/or programs); Neil W. Hamilton, *Leadership of Self: Each Student Taking Ownership Over Continuous Professional Development/Self-Directed Learning,* 58 SANTA CLARA L. REV. 567, 577 (2018) (8 out 138 schools list leadership).

[65] Lexis Nexis, *State of the Legal Industry Survey, Executive Summary.*

[66] For a sampling of the criticisms, see Harry T. Edwards, *The Growing Disjunction Between Legal Education and the Legal Profession*, 91 MICH. L. REV. 34 (1992); Thomas S. Ulen*, The Impending Train Wreck in Current Legal Education: How We Might Teach Law as the Scientific Study of Social Governance*, 6 U. ST. THOMAS L.J. 302 (2009); ABA SECTION ON LEGAL EDUCATION AND ADMISSION TO THE BAR, REPORT OF THE TASK FORCE ON LAW SCHOOLS AND THE PROFESSION: NARROWING THE GAP: AN EDUCATIONAL CONTINUUM (1997).

[67] WILLIAM SULLIVAN ET AL., EDUCATING LAWYERS: PREPARATION FOR THE PROFESSION OF LAW 87-89 (2007).

[68] David V. Day, *Leadership Development*, in SAGE HANDBOOK OF LEADERSHIP 38 (Alan Bryman, David Collinson, Keith Grint, Brad Jackson & Mary Uhl-Bien eds., 2011).

[69] Laurie Bassi & Daniel McMurrer, *Leadership and Large Firm Success: A Statistical Analysis*, http://www.leadershipforattorneys.org/articles/WhitePaper-LeadershipAndLawFirmSuccess%20Feb%208.pdf.

[70] Rhode, *Public Interest Law*, 2046 (quoting Eric Cohen).

[71] Douglas A. Ready, Jay A. Conger & Linda A. Hill, *Are You a High Potential?*, HARV. BUS. REV. 78, 82 (June 2010).

[72] GILL, THEORY AND PRACTICE OF LEADERSHIP, 275; Peter E. Drucker, *Managing Oneself*, HARV. BUS. REV.68-69 (Mar.-Apr. 1999); DOUG LENNICK & FRED KIEL, MORAL INTELLIGENCE: ENHANCING BUSINESS PERFORMANCE AND LEADERSHIP SUCCESS 239 (2008).

[73] NYE, THE POWERS TO LEAD, 24; Jay A. Conger, *Leadership Development Interventions*, in HANDBOOK OF LEADERSHIP THEORY AND PRACTICE 712, 714 (Nohria & Khurana eds., 2010).

[74] Michael Beer, Magnus, Finnstrom & Derek Schrader, *Why Leadership Training Fails—and What to Do About It,* HARV. BUS. REV. 52-53 (Oct. 2016); Pierre Gurdjian, Thomas Halbeisen & Kevin Lane, *Why Leadership-Development Programs Fail*, MCKINSEY Q., Jan. 2014; Harrison Monarth, *Evaluate Your Leadership Development Program*, HARV. BUS REV. (Jan. 22, 2015); David V. Day et al., *Advances in Leader and Leadership Development: A Review of 25 Years of Research and Theory*, 25 LEADERSHIP Q. 66-69 (2014).

[75] Deborah Rowland, *Why Leadership Development Isn't Developing Leaders*, HARV. BUS. REV. (Oct. 2016); Sydney Finkelstein, *Why We Loath Leadership Training,* BBC (July 20, 2016), http://www.bbc.com/capital/story/20160719-why-we-loath-leadership-training; Gurdjian, Halbeisen & Lane, *Why Leadership-Development Programs Fail*; Lisa A. Boyce, Stephen J. Zaccaro & Michelle Zaanis Wisecarver, *Propensity for Self-Development of Leadership Attributes: Understanding, Predicting, and Supporting Performance of Leader Self-Development*, 21 LEADERSHIP Q. 159 (2010); CYNTHIA D. MCCAULEY, LEADER DEVELOPMENT, 40.

[76] BARBARA KELLERMAN, PROFESSIONALIZING LEADERSHIP (2018); JEFFREY PFEFFER, LEADERSHIP BS: FIXING WORKPLACES AND CAREERS ONE TRUTH AT A TIME (2015).

[77] KELLERMAN, PROFESSIONALIZING LEADERSHIP; Day et al, *Advances in Leader and Leadership Development*, 80; George T. "Buck" Lewis & Douglas A. Blaze, *Training Leaders the Very Best We Can*, 83 TENN. L. REV, 771, 788-789 (2016).

[78] Day et al, *Advances in Leader and Leadership Development*, 71 CYNTHIA D. MCCAULEY, LEADER DEVELOPMENT: A REVIEW OF RESEARCH 31 (Sept. 2008) (noting that performance improvements are most likely where individuals perceive the need to change, view the feedback as accurate, work with a coach, and receive organizational support, and have high self-esteem).

[79] Lisa M. Finkelstein & Mark L. Poteet, *Best Practices in Workplace Formal Mentoring Programs*, in THE BLACKWELL HANDBOOK OF MENTORING: A MULTIPLE PERSPECTIVES APPROACH 345-368 (Tammy D. Allen & Lillian T. Eby eds., 2007).

[80] DOUG LENNICK & FRED KIEL, MORAL INTELLIGENCE: ENHANCING BUSINESS PERFORMANCE AND LEADERSHIP SUCCESS 245-48 (2008). For discussion of research showing performance improvement when people are told that they did a task well, see THOMAS J. PETERS & ROBERT H. WATERMAN, IN SEARCH OF EXCELLENCE: LESSONS FROM AMERICA'S BEST RUN CORPORATIONS 58-59 (2004).

[81] MALCOLM KNOWLES, SELF-DIRECTED LEARNING: A GUIDE FOR LEARNERS AND TEACHERS 18 (1975); Barry Zimmerman, *Theories of Self-Regulated Learning and Academic Achievement: An Overview and Analysis*, in SELF-REGULATED LEARNING AND ACADEMIC ACHIEVEMENT 1 (Barry J. Zimmerman & Dale H. Shunk eds., 2d ed. 2001).

[82] Keltner, *Managing Yourself*, 113.

[83] Chris Argyris, *Teaching Smart People How to Learn*, HARV. BUS. REV. 2 (1991).

[84] HOWARD GARDNER, CHANGING MINDS 110 (2004).

[85] KOUZES & POSNER, A LEADER'S LEGACY, 28. *See also* Richard, *Herding Cats*, 3 (noting that lawyers score low on resiliency, which means that they tend to be defensive and resistant to negative feedback).

[86] KOUZES & POSNER, A LEADER'S LEGACY, 28.

[87] National Association for Law Placement Foundation (NALPF), *How Associate Evaluations Measure Up: A National Study of Associate Performance Assessments* 74 (2006).

[88] ROBERT HARGROVE, MASTERFUL COACHING 302 (2008) (quoting Galbraith).

[89] For discussion of such biases, see Chapter 3 and PETERS & WATERMAN, IN SEARCH OF EXCELLENCE, 58.

[90] David G. Myers, *The Inflated Self: How Do I Love Me? Let Me Count the Way*s, PSYCHOL. TODAY, May 1980, at 16.

[91] MCKINSEY & CO., LEADERSHIP DEVELOPMENT AS A COMPETITIVE ADVANTAGE (2018) (quoting Alain Bejjani).

[92] HARGROVE, MASTERFUL COACHING, 124. *See also* Argyris, *Teaching Smart People How to Learn*, 2.

[93] CAROL DWECK, MINDSET: THE NEW PSYCHOLOGY OF SUCCESS (2008). *See also* RONALD H. HUMPHREY, EFFECTIVE LEADERSHIP: THEORY, CASES, AND APPLICATIONS 389 (2014).

[94] MIHALY CSIKSZENTMIHALYI, GOOD BUSINESS: LEADERSHIP, FLOW, AND THE MAKING OF MEANING 162 (2003); JOHN H. ZENGER & JOSEPH L. FOLKMAN, THE EXTRAORDINARY LEADER: TURNING GOOD MANAGERS INTO GREAT LEADERS 103-108 (2002).

[95] DIANE REINHOLD, TRACY PATTERSON & PETER HEGEL, MAKE LEARNING STICK: BEST PRACTICES TO GET THE MOST OF OUT OF LEADERSHIP DEVELOPMENT 1 (Center for Creative Leadership 2015).

[96] Sarah Smith Orr, *Soul-Based Leadership,* in IMPROVING LEADERSHIP IN NONPROFIT ORGANIZATIONS 269-270 (Ronald E. Riggio & Sarah Smith Orr eds., 2004).

[97] HARGROVE, MASTERFUL COACHING, 124.

[98] HARGROVE, MASTERFUL COACHING, 124; Argyris, *Teaching Smart People How to Learn.*

[99] Richard J. Leider, *The Ultimate Leadership Task: Self-Leadership*, in THE LEADER OF THE FUTURE: NEW VISIONS, STRATEGIES, AND PRACTICES FOR THE NEXT ERA 189 (Frances Hesselbein, Marshall Goldsmith & Richard Beckhard eds., 1996).

[100] For the importance of cross-cultural competence, see Scott A. Westfahl & David B. Wilkins, *The Leadership Imperative: A Collaborative Approach to Professional Development in the Global Age of More for Less*, 69 STAN. L. REV. 1667, 1709 (2017).

[101] Morgan W. McCall Jr., *The Experience Conundrum*, in HANDBOOK OF LEADERSHIP THEORY AND PRACTICE 679, 692-693 (Nohria & Khurana eds., 2010); Ben W. Heineman Jr. & David B. Wilkins, *The Lost Generation?*, AM. LAW, Mar. 1, 2008, at 85.

[102] Mathew M. Sowcik & Austin Council, *Developing the Next Generation of Narcissistic Leaders*, 12. J. LEADERSHIP STUD. 64, 66 (2018).

[103] McCall, *The Experience Conundrum*, 699; HUMPHREY, EFFECTIVE LEADERSHIP, 389.

[104] JOHN GARDNER, ON LEADERSHIP, 117; Steele & Day, *The Role of Self-Attention*, 18.

[105] MICHEL DE MONTAIGNE, *Of the Inconsistency of Our Actions*, in ESSAYS (1858), reprinted in LEADERSHIP: ESSENTIAL WRITINGS BY OUR GREATEST THINKERS 680 (Elizabeth D. Samet ed., 2015).

[106] LENNICK & KIEL, MORAL INTELLIGENCE, 239.

[107] PFEFFER, POWER, 13-14.

[108] Annalise Acorn & Jason Buttuls, *The Not Now Habit: Procrastination, Legal Ethics, and Legal Education*, 16 LEGAL ETHICS 73 (2013).

[109] DWECK, MINDSET.

[110] Leider, *The Ultimate Leadership Task*, 194-95.

[111] Boyce, Zaccaro & Wisecarver, *Propensity for Self-Development of Leaders*, 161.

[112] GILL, THEORY AND PRACTICE OF LEADERSHIP, 281.

[113] JAMES M. KOUZES & BARRY Z. POSNER, LEARNING LEADERSHIP: THE FIVE FUNDAMENTALS OF BECOMING AN EXEMPLARY LEADER 52-58 (2016).

[114] Ready, Conger & Hill, *Are You a High Potential?*, 82; Linda Hill, *Developing the Star Performer*, in LEADER TO LEADER 296 (Frances Hesselbein & Paul M. Cohen eds., 1999); David V. Day, *Leadership Development: A Review in Context*, 11 LEADERSHIP Q. 581 (2001); KOUZES & POSNER, LEARNING LEADERSHIP, 144.

[115] ZENGER & FOLKMAN, EXTRAORDINARY LEADER, 103-108.

[116] ARTHUR L. LIMAN with PETER ISRAEL, LAWYER: A LIFE OF COUNSEL AND CONTROVERSY 35 (1998).

[117] Id. (quoting Morgenthau).

[118] David Remnick, *The Joshua Generation: Race and the Campaign of Barack Obama,* NEW YORKER, Nov. 17, 2008, at 68 (quoting Axelrod).

[119] *See* William A. Cohen, DRUCKER ON LEADERSHIP: NEW LESSONS FROM THE FATHER OF MODERN MANAGEMENT 139-40, 193 (2009); John P. Kotter, *What Leaders Really Do*, 68 HARV. BUS. REV. 103 (May-June 1990); Sheri-Lynne Leskiw & Parbudyal Singh, *Leadership Development: Learning from Best Practices*, 28 LEADERSHIP AND ORGAN. DEV. J. 444, 450-54 (2007).

[120] Morgan W. McCall Jr., *The Experience Conundrum*, in HANDBOOK OF LEADERSHIP THEORY AND PRACTICE 679, 683-85 (Nohria & Khurana eds., 2010).

[121] Julie E. Owen, Sharrrell Hassell-Goodman & Aoi Yamanaka, *Culturally Relevant Leadership Learning: Identity, Capacity, and Efficacy*, 11 J. LEADERSHIP STUDIES 48 (2017).

[122] WARREN BENNIS, ON BECOMING A LEADER 108-09 (2002).

[123] JOHN MAXWELL, THE LEADERSHIP HANDBOOK 106-107 (2008).

[124] MICHELE COLEMAN MAYES & KARA SOPHIA BAYSINGER, COURAGEOUS COUNSEL: CONVERSATIONS WITH WOMEN GENERAL COUNSEL IN THE FORTUNE 500 122 (2011) (quoting Richard St. John).

[125] ANGELA DUCKWORTH, GRIT: THE POWER OF PASSION AND PERSEVERANCE (2016).

[126] LENNICK & KIEL, MORAL INTELLIGENCE, 97.

[127] GILL, THEORY AND PRACTICE, 273-77; Day, *Leadership Development*, 594.

[128] Day, *Leadership Development*; Doris Gomez, *The Leader as Learner*, 2.3 INT'L J. OF LEADERSHIP STUD. 283 (2007).

[129] Hill, *Developing the Star Performer*, 299.

[130] ANNE COLBY & WILLIAM DAMON, SOME DO CARE: CONTEMPORARY LIVES OF MORAL COMMITMENT 198-99 (1992).

[131] HERMINIA IBARRA, ACT LIKE A LEADER, THINK LIKE A LEADER 90 (2015).

[132] Adam Grant, *Good News for Young Strivers: Networking is Overrated,* N.Y. TIMES, Aug. 24, 2017.

[133] Larissa MacFarquhar, *The Better Boss*, NEW YORKER, Apr. 22, 2002, at 114. *See also* Gomez, *The Leader as Learner*, 280, 283.

[134] Pierre Gurdjian, Thomas Halbeisen & Kevin Lane, *Why Leadership-Development Programs Fail*, MCKINSEY Q. (Jan. 2014); Harrison Monarth, *Evaluate Your Leadership Development Program*, HARV. BUS. REV. (Jan. 22, 2015).

[135] Conger, *Leadership Development Interventions*, 714 (citing estimates that 75 percent of executive education dollars are spent on customized programs). For the trend to action learning, see Leskiw & Singh, *Leadership Development*, 154; REINHOLD, PATTERSON & HEGEL, MAKE LEARNING STICK, 5.

[136] Brett Seidle, Sergio Fernandez & James L. Perry, *Do Leadership Training and Development Make a Difference in the Public Sector? A Panel Study,* 76 PUB. ADMIN. REV. 603, 611 (2016).

[137] Kotter, *What Leaders Really Do.*

[138] David V. Day, *Leadership Development: A Review in Context,* 11 LEADERSHIP Q. 251 (2000).

[139] Lucia Crevani & Nada Endrissat, *Mapping the Leadership-As-Practice Terrain: Comparative Elements*, in LEADERSHIP-AS-PRACTICE: THEORY AND APPLICATION 31 (Joseph A. Raelin ed., 2016).

[140] PETER M. SENGE, THE FIFTH DISCIPLINE: THE ART & PRACTICE OF THE LEARNING ORGANIZATION 3 (1990).

[141] David A. Gavin, *Building a Learning Organization*, HARV. BUS. REV. 78, 79 (July-Aug. 1993).

[142] WISEMAN WITH MCKEOWN, MULTIPLIERS, 20-22.

[143] REINHOLD, PATTERSON & HEGEL, MAKE LEARNING STICK 7,10.

[144] Sean T. Hannah & Paul B. Lester, *A Multilevel Approach to Building and Leading Learning Organizations*, 20 LEADERSHIP Q. 34, 35 (2009); Gavin, *Building a Learning Organization.* For the inadequacy of leadership development evaluation, see Doris B. Collins & Elwood F. Holton III, *The Effectiveness of Managerial Leadership Development Programs: A Meta-Analysis of Studies from 1982 to 2001*, 15 HUM. RESOURCE DEV. Q. 217, 218 (2004). For strategies to monitor leadership development programs, identify barriers to their success, and design efforts to support individual growth, see KELLERMAN, PROFESSIONALIZING LEADERSHIP; Beer, Finnstrom & Schrader, *Why Leadership Training Fails*, 55-57.

[145] WARREN G. BENNIS & BURT NANUS, LEADERS: STRATEGIES FOR TAKING CHARGE (1985), as quoted in Elliot Aronson & Carol Tavris, MISTAKES WERE MADE (BUT NOT BY ME): WHY WE JUSTIFY FOOLISH BELIEFS, BAD DECISIONS, AND HURTFUL ACTS 225 n.9 (2007).

[146] Robert M. Fulmer & Byron Hanson, *Do Techies Make Good Leaders?*, WALL ST. J., Aug. 23, 2010, at 23.

[147] VAN WART, DYNAMICS OF LEADERSHIP IN PUBLIC SERVICE, 185-86.

[148] COMEY, A HIGHER LOYALTY, 136.

[149] JOHN W. GARDNER, LIVING, LEADING, AND THE AMERICAN DREAM 125 (2003).

[150] *See* BARBARA C. CROSBY & JOHN M. BRYSON, LEADERSHIP FOR THE COMMON GOOD: TACKLING PUBLIC PROBLEMS IN A SHARED-POWER WORLD 50 (2005).

[151] Ben W. Heineman Jr., *Financial Leaders Go AWOL in the Meltdown*, BLOOMBERG.COM, Nov. 4, 2008, at 1-2, http://www.law.harvard.edu/programs/corp_gov/articles/Heineman-Bloomberg-Financial-Sector-Leaders-Go-AWOL-Nov08.pdf.

[152] NATIONAL TASKFORCE ON LAWYER WELL-BEING: PRACTICAL RECOMMENDATIONS FOR POSITIVE CHANGE (2017).

[153] AMERICAN BAR ASSOCIATION, WORKING GROUP TO ADVANCE WELL-BEING IN THE LEGAL PROFESSION (2019).

[154] Patrick Krill, *ALM Survey on Mental Health and Substance Abuse: Big Law's Pervasive Problem,* LAW.COM, Sept. 14, 2018.

[155] Patrick Krill, *Big Law Leaders Say Stigma Comes with Addiction and Mental Health Problems*, RECORDER, Sept. 24, 2018.

[156] David Rasch & Meehan Rasch, *Overcoming Writer's Block and Procrastination for Attorneys, Law Students, and Law Professors,* 43 N.M. L. REV. 193 (2013); Hara Estroff Marano, *Procrastination: Ten Things to Know,* PSYCHOL. TODAY, Aug. 23, 2003.

[157] TRACEY WILEN-DAUGENTI, DIGITAL DISRUPTION: THE FUTURE OF WORK, SKILLS, LEADERSHIP, EDUCATION, AND CAREERS IN A DIGITAL WORLD 161 (2018).

[158] Edward M. Hallowell, *Overloaded Circuits*, in ON MANAGING YOURSELF 79, 82, 90-94 (HARV. BUS. REV. ed. 2010).

[159] Robert S. Kaplan, *What to Ask the Person in the Mirror*, in ON MANAGING YOURSELF 154, 150 (HARV. BUS. REV. ed. 2010).

[160] Hallowell, *Overloaded Circuits*, 82, 90-91.

[161] John Rampton, *Manipulate Time With These Powerful 20 Time Management Tips*, FORBES.COM (May 1, 2018), https://www.forbes.com/sites/johnrampton/2018/05/01/manipulate-time-with-these-powerful-20-time-management-tips?#5ec43fff57ab; Rasch & Rasch, *Overcoming Writer's Block*, 229.

[162] Rampton, *Manipulate Time*; Rasch & Rasch, *Overcoming Writer's Block*, 201.

[163] Hallowell, *Overloaded Circuits*, 82, 91-93.

[164] Rampton, *Manipulate Time*; Hallowell, *Overloaded Circuits*.

[165] Patrick Krill, *"Just-Make-It-Happen" Mentality Is Bad for Lawyer Well-being,* Law.com (Mar. 19, 2019), https://www.law.com/2019/03/19/just-make-it-happen-mentaility-is-bad-for-lawyer-well-being/?printer-friendly#.

[166] Adam Grant, *No, You Can't Ignore Email. It's Rude,* N.Y. TIMES, Feb. 17, 2019, SR 9.

[167] Grant, *No, You Can't Ignore Email.*

LEADERSHIP SKILLS

CHAPTER 3

LEADERS AS DECISION MAKERS

"I'm the decider" was President George W. Bush's much parodied response to criticism about his deference to his Defense Secretary's strategies concerning Iraq.[1] Whatever the adequacy of Bush's statement in that particular context, it does capture the centrality of decision-making in the leadership role. This chapter focuses on what enables leaders to make effective judgments, and the cognitive biases and organizational dynamics that can get in the way.

Decision-making generally has two core objectives: quality and acceptability. Both are subject to external constraints, such as time and cost, and trade-offs are often necessary. For example, broad participation will often enhance the soundness and legitimacy of decisions, but it will typically require more time, effort, and expense. In many contexts, the optimal decision is out of reach due to the complexity of issues, the limitations of information, and the costs of obtaining it. The "endless pursuit of perfect information" can both delay and impair decision-making.[2] The search can lead to policy paralysis. Even when it does not, the brain can process only so many facts at any one time, and an overload may misdirect our focus. As political scientist and Nobel Laureate Herbert Simon noted, "a wealth of information creates a poverty of attention."[3] Given these constraints, individuals often fall back on heuristics—simplifying processes based on intuition, habit, or rules of thumb. These mental shortcuts may not seem "rational" from a purely logical point of view, but they are reasonable responses to the social environment of decision-making.[4]

Decision makers are, however, subject to cognitive biases—inappropriate reliance on heuristics—that require conscious correctives. Psychological research popularized in Daniel Kahneman's *Thinking, Fast and Slow* suggests that people have two ways of evaluating information and making decisions. *System 1* thinking is automatic and instinctive; it operates with little or no effort and no sense of control. *System 2* is slower, logical and deliberate; it involves choice and concentration.[5] In making decisions, people are subject to "bounded rationality"—limitations of time and cost that constrain their judgments. And in light of these limitations, people "satisfice"; rather than examining all possible alternatives, they settle for a solution that meets an acceptable level of quality.[6]

One of leaders' important tasks is to create decision-making processes that are most cost effective and least subject to distortion. In designing such processes, leaders need to take into account concerns such as:

- How important is the quality of the decision?
- How much information is necessary to make a reasonably good decision?
- Who else has relevant information and can be involved in the process?
- Do those individuals share the organization's objectives or have other personal concerns that might skew their judgment?
- How important is followers' commitment to the outcome, and how much is it likely to depend on their involvement in the process?
- What values apart from efficiency and effectiveness are at stake?
- What are the time and cost constraints?[7]

Complex decisions need to take account of different time frames and different value metrics. What options are most appealing today, at the point of some future election or retention decision, or decades from now? What consequences are most critical: financial, political, personal, or moral?[8]

In addition to these concerns, leaders also need to consider the appropriate decision-making framework. Three approaches are common. The first, the "reasoned choice" framework, is the most typical. It takes a rational pragmatic approach to identifying objectives, analyzing options, and evaluating responses. However, in contexts where full information on these issues is impossible or too costly to obtain, an "incremental" strategy may be preferable. Under this framework, the decision maker takes small steps that can be assessed and adjusted in light of experience, thus avoiding major risks of failure.[9] A third possibility is a "mixed model" in which decision makers first survey the external environment for major economic, technical, political, competitive, or related trends that require a response. They then examine the internal organizational environment for significant problems, such as declines in profits, productivity, or employee retention. If any such warning signals are present, leaders should invest substantial effort in exploring solutions.[10] Otherwise, resorting to an incremental approach will be sufficient.

Decision-making is a continuing process. Even the most carefully considered judgment can be derailed by factors that leaders cannot control or anticipate. The key to success is constant assessment and midcourse corrective action.[11]

A common characteristic of effective leaders is their ability to analyze what issues are at stake in particular decisions and to design a process that will produce cost-effective responses. The readings that follow explore some of the challenges involved in that role.

A. THE DECISION-MAKING PROCESS AND COGNITIVE BIASES

Paul Brest and Linda Krieger begin their book on decision-making by noting that many problems facing lawyers, both as leaders and as advisors to clients who are leaders, "seldom conform to the boundaries that . . . divide different disciplines." So, for example, "most clients expect their lawyers to integrate legal considerations with other aspects of their problem. . . . Reflecting this reality, an American Bar Association report on the ten 'fundamental lawyering skills' that new lawyers should acquire places 'problem solving' at the very top of the list—even before legal analysis."[12] Those who wish to be leaders in law need the kind of decision-making skills described in the excerpts below.

PAUL BREST AND LINDA HAMILTON KRIEGER, PROBLEM SOLVING, DECISION MAKING, AND PROFESSIONAL JUDGMENT

(New York: Oxford University Press, 2010),
pp. 3, 11-23, 241-252, and 257-265

Problem Solving & Decision Making Processes:
Deliberation, Intuition, and Expertise

Deliberative Processes

An ideal deliberative model of decision making consists of the following steps or elements:

- State, or "frame," the problem to be solved;
- Identify and prioritize the relevant values, interests, and objectives;
- Identify and resolve major uncertainties concerning the cause of the problem;
- Generate a range of plausible solutions or alternative courses of action;
- Predict the consequences of the courses of action and assess their impact on the relevant interests or objectives;
- Select the course of action that optimizes the interests or objectives to be served (i.e., make a decision);
- Implement, observe, and learn from the outcome of the decision.

The process is recursive, beginning with the need to frame the problem in terms of the interests involved and to consider the interests in the context of the particular problem. After completing step 5 [predicting consequences], a decision maker would be wise to review the earlier steps, not just because he may have accidentally omitted something, but because the concreteness of positing solutions can reframe objectives and his conception of the overall problem.

Framing the problem. Problem solvers sometimes go about solving the wrong problem because they do not frame the issues adequately. They may mistake symptoms of a problem for the problem itself, or define the problem too narrowly, or define the problem in terms of a ready solution without taking account of the objectives they are actually trying to achieve. . . .

Identifying interests and objectives. The German philosopher Friedrich Nietzsche is reputed to have proposed, "To forget one's purpose is the commonest form of stupidity."

The best frame for a problem is the one that incorporates the broadest possible range of purposes, interests, objectives, and values implicated by the situation. . . .

Divergent and Convergent Thinking

The deliberative approach to problem solving combines elements of *divergent* and *convergent* thinking. Divergent thinking expands the range of perspectives, dimensions, and options relating to a problem. Convergent thinking eliminates possible alternatives through the application of critical analysis, thereby eventually reducing the number of available options. Divergent thinking conceives; convergent thinking critiques. Divergent thinking envisions; convergent thinking troubleshoots, fine tunes, selects, and implements. . . .

Intuitive Processes in Problem Solving and Decision Making

. . . Most of the time we solve problems without coming close to the conscious, step-by-step analysis of the deliberative approach. In fact, attempting to encounter even a small fraction of the problems we encounter in a full, deliberative manner would bring our activities to a screeching halt. Out of necessity, most of problem solving is intuitive. . . .

The Role of Schemas . . .

. . . In a classic article entitled *On Perceptual Readiness*, cognitive psychologist Jerome Bruner observed that when we perceive a stimulus from our environment, our first task is to fit that information into some existing knowledge structure represented in memory. Perception is given meaning only when filtered through and incorporated into preexisting cognitive elements, such as schemas. . . . A schema imposes meaning on the inherently ambiguous information supplied by raw perception. Once a schema is activated, we implicitly expect incoming information to be consistent with its elements. Schematic processing is both inevitable and a pervasive source of errors of judgment. Our need to impose order on the world leads us to see patterns even where they do not exist, and schemas lie at the core of inaccurate stereotypes based on race, sex, and other factors. . . .

The Role of Affect

The heart has its reasons that reason does not understand.
Blaise Pascal

Intuitive problem solving and decision making depends not only on the essentially mental processes of recognizing patterns, but on affect as well. . . . Without emotions, our decision making processes would be overwhelmed by the burdens of cognition. . . . Emotions and reasoning exist in a delicate balance, however, and . . . emotions can sometimes overwhelm reasoning to our detriment. . . . Among other things, the skilled professional must be able to differentiate between her own emotions and those of clients and others. This capacity is a component of so-called *emotional intelligence*. . . .

The Limits of Deliberation: Bounded Rationality

Problem solving and decision making in professional contexts and in everyday life call for a mixture of intuition and deliberation—of System 1 and System 2 processes. The predominance of intuitive decision making is an inevitable aspect of the human condition of limited cognitive ability and time—what Herbert Simon has called the condition of *bounded rationality*. . . . [T]o use Simon's evocative neologism, we *satisfice*, opting for a reasonably good outcome—often the first that meets some threshold of satisfaction—rather than devoting excessive cognitive energy to seeking the very best. . . .

Biases in Perception and Memory—Introduction: Stages of Information Processing

. . . Cognitive psychologists have likened a person making a judgment to an "information processor" that proceeds through a number of stages from the availability of information to the generation of a response to that information. . . . Every moment of our lives, we are bombarded with vast amounts of *information*, of which we *attend* to only a small fraction. We *encode* the information, structuring, evaluating, and interpreting it and transforming into some sort of mental representation. You might think of *perception* . . . as overlapping attention and encoding. We *store* information in memory and, on occasion, *retrieve* it from memory (i.e., become aware of it) and *process* it with respect to particular objectives. Our *response* to processing may be a factual judgment or inference, an evaluative judgment or opinion, a choice among alternatives or decision, or a solution to a problem. [A wide range of] . . . biases and distortions . . . can affect these stages of information processing. . . .

Biases in Acquisition, Retention, and Retrieval

. . . Our memory does not store complete representations of what was perceived, but only fragments of our *interpretations* of the relevant facts or events. Recollection requires reconstructing one's interpretation, often using (more or less) logical inferences to fill in missing details. [Bias can occur in acquiring, retaining, and retrieving information.] . . .

Dolly Chugh and Max Bazerman describe what they call *bounded awareness*—the phenomenon where "individuals fail to see, seek, use, or share highly relevant, easily accessible, and readily perceivable information during the decision-making process." Because our cognitive power is limited, we can focus only on a small part of everything that goes on around us—often only on one thing at a time.

Much of our daily experience involves multitasking, but we aren't as good at multitasking as we would like to believe. Most of the time, we just don't notice things that are not in our mental field of vision. . . . Chugh and Bazerman characterize the misalignment of available information of which one is unaware with the information needed for a decision as a *focusing failure*. . . .

[People also] interpret the same ambiguous information in different ways. . . . At the worst, from all the events going on in the environment, we sometimes notice those that are significant from our egocentric position, and fail to notice those that [aren't]. . . . [In one classic experiment,] participants who had previously identified themselves as pro-Arab, pro-Israeli, or neutral viewed extensive samples of media coverage of the massacre of Palestinians in Lebanese refugee camps by allies of Israel. . . . The pro-Arab participants saw the media as biased toward Israel; the pro-Israeli participants saw the news programs as biased against Israel. . . . [Researchers] concluded that "the pro-Arab and pro-Israeli participants 'saw' different news programs—that is, they disagreed about the very nature of the stimulus they had viewed." For example, the groups reported that a higher percentage of the references to Israel were, respectively, favorable or unfavorable. And each believed that the programs would lead an undecided or ambivalent viewer to favor the opposing position. . . .

[So too,] experiences after an event can distort one's recollection of the event. For example, people who read an inaccurate newspaper description of an event they personally witnessed are prone to incorporate the inaccuracies into their recollections. . . . Leading questions (which invite a particular answer) [and one's own intervening thoughts] can distort memory. . . .

Availability, Vividness and Inference

Richard Nisbett and Lee Ross note that "vivid information is more likely to be stored and remembered than pallid information," and thus more likely to be retrieved at some later date and to affect later inference. Factors that contribute to the vividness of information include:

- *Emotional interest.* Events in which we or people we know are involved have more emotional interest than those involving strangers.
- *Concreteness.* Even events involving strangers can be emotionally gripping if they are described in sufficient detail to prompt imagery. Compare "Jack was killed by a semi-trailer that rolled over his car and crushed his skull" to "Jack sustained fatal injuries in a car accident.". . . Statistics may be the least concrete form of information.
- *Direct experience.* First-hand information has more salience than the reports of others. By the same token, a face-to-face recommendation is likely to be more effective than the same recommendation in writing.

In addition to its availability, vivid information is more likely to recruit additional information from one's memory and people are more likely to rehearse, or mull over, vivid information, making it even more memorable.

The normative problem of using vividness, and availability more generally, as criteria for inference is that they are not always strongly correlated with their evidential value. This is illustrated by a number of experiments in which vividness caused participants to generalize from obviously biased samples. For example, Ruth Hamill, Timothy Wilson and Richard Nisbett showed participants a videotape interview of a prison guard, which depicted him as either humane or brutal. Some were told that the guard was typical, some that he was highly atypical. When later asked to generalize about prison guards, both groups of participants concluded that prison guards generally tended to be like the one they had seen in the interview [even participants who were told the portrayal was atypical]. . . .

Egocentrism: A Particular Memory Bias in Acquisition and/or Retrieval

. . . [P]eople's recollections and judgments tend to be clouded by an egocentric bias. When married couples estimate their proportionate contribution to household tasks, the sum exceeds 100 percent. So too of collaborators' estimates of their contributions to joint projects, such as this book. While the phenomenon may be partially explained by self-serving motives of having inflatedly positive views of oneself, it extends to negative behaviors as well. Spouses report *causing*, as well as resolving, most of the problems in their relationship, and people are prone to overestimate their own errors and unattractive behaviors.

One plausible explanation for the egocentric bias is that our own actions are more readily accessible to our memories than those of others. . . . Even when an individual holds himself accountable for an outcome vis-à-vis others, the question remains open whether the outcome was due to internal factors such as skill or its absence, or to external factors, such as bad luck. In an analysis of newspaper accounts of sporting events, Richard Lau and Dan Russell found that players attributed good outcomes to their skill 75 percent of the time, but took responsibility for bad outcomes only 55 percent of the time. . . . [E]ven sportswriters were more likely to provide internal attributions for their home teams' wins than for losses.

Egocentrism is often correlated with self-servingness. Among people working different amounts of time in a joint enterprise, those who work more believe they should be paid more, while those who work less believe that both parties should be paid equally. . . .

Conclusion: Naïve Realism

. . . The biases in the acquisition and recollection of information outlined above are exacerbated by three related convictions that people have about their perceptions and judgments and [those] of other people. These are the elements of what Lee Ross has termed *naïve realism*:

1. I see actions and events as they are in reality. My perceptions and reactions are not biased: rather, they are an unmediated reflection of the "real nature" of whatever it is I am responding to.
2. Other people, to the extent that they are willing and able to see things in a similarly objective fashion, will share my perceptions and reactions.
3. When others perceive some event or react to it differently from me, they (but not I) have been influenced by something other than the objective features of the events in question. Their divergent views probably result from an unwarranted ideological rigidity or a self-serving bias that I am not influenced by. The more extreme the view is in divergence from my own, the stronger their bias probably is.

Naïve realism can be especially pernicious in the context of disagreement or conflict. It has the practical implications that:

1. Partisans tend to overestimate the number of others who agree with their views—the *false consensus* effect—or at least overestimate the number who would agree with them if apprised of the "real" facts; partisans therefore assume that disinterested third parties would agree with them.
2. Partisans tend to see viewpoints that differ from their own as highly revealing both of personal dispositions (for example, gullibility, aggressiveness, pessimism, or charitableness), and of various cognitive and motivational biases. In fact, differences in judgment often reflect differences in the way a given issue or object of judgment is perceived and construed rather than a difference in the perceivers' values or personality traits. . . .
3. Partisans will be polarized and extreme in their view of others. Once they believe a person to be biased, they tend to discount his views entirely, and will underestimate areas of agreement and underestimate the prospects of finding "common ground" through discussion or negotiation.

We have seen that being asked to articulate the weaknesses of one's own position may counter perceptual biases in some situations. A broader hope . . . is that students and readers who understand[ ] those biases and the phenomena of naïve realism will be less likely to fall into their traps. But we should be among the first to admit that the hope does not rest on much of an empirical foundation.

NOTES ON COGNITIVE BIAS AND COGNITIVE CONSTRAINTS

Experts on decision-making have identified significant cognitive biases in addition to those identified by Brest and Krieger. The most important include:

Confirmation bias. We are most likely to seek out, recall, and value information that supports our preexisting beliefs and preferences.[13]

Overconfidence. We think we know more than we do about how the future will unfold. In Kahneman's phrase, we have an "almost unlimited ability to ignore our ignorance."[14]

Optimism. We overestimate the likelihood of positive events and our own capabilities.[15]

Anchoring. We root our decisions and estimates in an initial value and fail to make appropriate adjustments.[16]

Hindsight Bias. We revise the history of our beliefs in light of what actually happened; in hindsight, we exaggerate what could have been anticipated in foresight.[17]

Outcome Bias. We assess the quality of a decision not by whether the process was sound but by whether the outcome was favorable.[18]

Loss Aversion. We feel losses more acutely than gains of the same amount, which makes us more risk averse than a rational calculation would dictate.[19]

Self-Serving Attribution Bias. We accept too little responsibility for our failures and attribute them to external causes, while taking too much credit for successes and attributing them to internal explanations, such as our own merits.[20]

Status Quo Bias. We prefer the status quo to change.[21]

Sunk Cost Fallacy. We consider historical costs that are not recoverable when considering future courses of action.[22]

Escalation of Commitment. We continue to invest in losing propositions, partly to justify the time, effort and resources already invested.[23]

Not only are decision makers subject to these cognitive biases, they are also subject to cognitive constraints. One is the 'unknown unknowns," the things they don't know that they don't know.[24] In *Seeing What Others Don't*, Gary Klein explores what enables or blocks insights, and notes that decision makers often fail by dismissing anomalies or contradictions instead of looking for new information and theories that could explain them.[25] Decision-making is also impaired when individuals are fatigued, stressed, pressured, or multitasking.[26] "Incidental anger" triggered by an unrelated experience can also undermine rational thought processes and make individuals unresponsive to others' ideas and concerns.[27] Some of these biases are particularly pronounced for leaders. Power amplifies over-optimism and overconfidence; it heightens leaders' sense of control and infallibility, and decreases their willingness to take advice.[28] So too, leaders who signal "don't bring me problems, bring me solutions" often reinforce a culture of advocacy, not inquiry, and prevent the understanding necessary to evaluate options.[29]

Psychologists have been much more effective in identifying cognitive biases than in identifying correctives. Simply describing the direction of bias or warning individuals about its effects is generally not sufficient. More productive "debiasing" approaches involve receiving intensive feedback, taking a disinterested outsider's perspective, consulting an outsider, and considering the opposite of a preferred position.[30] Holding individuals accountable for their decisions and requiring them to give specific reasons behind their actions encourages more reflective "System 2" thinking.[31] Creating cultures that encourage leaders to consult experts and seek outside perspectives can be equally critical.[32] Leaders should also take their "emotional temperature" before making important decisions, and consider whether social influences are skewing their judgments.[33]

Other strategies involve changing the environment to reduce biases or to "nudge" individuals toward more rational decisions through "choice architecture." For example, Richard Thaler and Cass Sunstein's *Nudge* proposes ways of taking account of individuals' tendency to discount future risks by requiring them to opt out of policies that correct for that tendency.[34] Among lawyers, a common way to reduce problems arising from overconfidence and over-optimism is to build in "buffer time" on projects. Such automatic adjustments decrease the risk of missing crucial deadlines.[35]

Borrowing from design theory, some experts recommend dividing a large problem into sub-problems and assigning them to groups. The groups then deliberate and present their work to the whole team, receive feedback, regroup, and revise in a cycle that continues until a decision is made.

In *Decisive,* Chip and Dan Heath recommend four strategies reflected in the acronym WRAP:

- Widen your options;
- Reality test your assumptions;
- Attain distance before deciding; and
- Prepare to be wrong.[36]

For example, to widen options, Heath and Heath suggest benchmarking: finding others who have addressed your problem and identifying their best practices. Sam Walton, the founder of Walmart, made a habit of imitating competitors. As he acknowledged, "Most everything I've done I've copied from someone else."[37] To reality test assumptions, Heath and Heath recommend asking what would have to be true for this to be the right decision.[38] To prepare for the worst, experts advocate engaging in "premortems," in which decision makers ask what could go wrong at each step, how likely is the worst-case scenario, and what would the consequences be.[39] Could any of these approaches have helped in examples of bias you have observed, or in the problems and questions set forth below?

PROBLEM 3-1

You are general counsel for Sears. Yesterday, state and national media reported allegations by a former employee that Sears Auto Centers systematically defraud customers by selling them unnecessary car repairs. The employee told reporters that Sears uses a commission-based compensation system for its mechanics and requires them to meet mandatory quotas. He also described high-stakes contests that encourage mechanics to exceed the quotas.

Sears's CEO asks you to meet in his office first thing tomorrow. He is livid and says that he wants the publicity squashed immediately, whatever the cost. In quickly preparing for the meeting, you learn that the employee's description of the compensation practices is essentially correct—though Sears abandoned the contests several years ago. You also learn that the employee left Sears after being accused of sexually harassing a fellow worker. The employee disputed this allegation, and the matter was settled with a confidential termination agreement, in which both he and the company agreed to refrain from making negative public statements about the other.

Treat this as a problem of decision-making in which you:

- Frame the problem to be solved;
- Identify and prioritize the relevant values, interests, and objectives;
- Identify and resolve major uncertainties concerning the cause of the problem;
- Generate a range of plausible courses of action and predict their consequences;
- Select the course of action that best serves the relevant objectives and values; and
- Establish criteria for evaluating the outcome of the decision.

NOTES AND QUESTIONS

1. Consider an example of flawed decision-making that you have read about or observed. What accounted for the failures and what strategies might have improved the analytic process?
2. Some evidence suggests that cognitive biases were apparent in the run-up to the 2010 BP oil spill disaster. In a press conference following the explosion, a reporter asked President Barack Obama whether he regretted his earlier support for increased oil drilling. Obama responded:

> I continue to believe what I said at that time, which was that domestic oil production is an important part of overall energy mix. . . . Where I was wrong was in my belief that the oil companies had their act together when it came to worst-case scenarios. . . . Oil drilling has been going on in the Gulf, including deepwater, for quite some time. And the record of accidents like this we hadn't seen before. But it just takes one to have a wake-up call and recognize that claims that fail-safe procedures were in place . . . were faulty.[40]

What cognitive biases and group dynamics may have contributed to those faulty assumptions? Psychology professors David Messick and Max Bazerman note that leaders, like other decision makers, are prone to unrealistic optimism about the future, tend to discount low-probability events, and exaggerate their ability to avert errors and risks.[41] The result may be insufficient worst-case planning by both private-sector decision makers and their government regulators.

In the case of BP, ample evidence was available prior to the disaster concerning the company's abysmal safety record and federal regulators' inadequate responses. Obama acknowledged in his press conference that "[f]or years, there has been a scandalously close relationship between oil companies and the agency that regulates them."[42] In the years preceding the spill, BP reportedly accounted for 97 percent of flagrant violations of environmental standards in the refining industry. (760 offenses compared to 8 by the next highest offender).[43] Sanctions for these violations (including the largest fine ever administered by the Occupational Safety and Health Administration) were demonstrably ineffective. In its report on the disaster, the National Commission on the BP Deepwater Horizon Oil Spill and Offshore Drilling concluded that the blowout was not the result of "aberrational decisions . . . that could not have been anticipated or expected to recur again. Rather, the . . . missteps were rooted in systemic failures by industry management . . . and also by failures of government to provide effective regulatory oversight of offshore drilling." These failures included insufficient review of drilling procedures and inadequate safety testing requirements.[44]

A broader problem was that regulators lacked the resources and trained personnel necessary for oversight. They largely ignored scientists' warnings about the inevitable and potentially catastrophic risks accompanying deepwater drilling, and frequently rubber-stamped permits and proposed changes in well design.[45] Commenting on the problem, a Coast Guard officer noted: "The pace of technology has definitely outrun the regulators."[46]

Although risk management procedures for drilling can undoubtedly be improved, is that an adequate solution? Or does an accurate framing of the problem point to broader, costlier reforms aimed at reducing dependence on oil and preventing agency capture by the industry to be regulated?

3. As noted earlier, another factor that complicates decision-making is stress, which increases when both speed and precision are critical, and the stakes are substantial. Although moderate stress can be helpful in mobilizing energy, concentrating the mind, and eliminating distraction, intense stress generally impairs reasoning.[47] To reduce this risk, experts recommend building in opportunities for reflection that allow System 2 reasoning to take over.[48] Another antidote is a well-functioning team, which is why combat units and other dangerous occupations put such a high premium on group cohesion. To encourage effective team decision-making, sharing information is critical, as is knowing when to stop the search for perfect information.[49] In some contexts, timeliness is essential, and the worst decision is indecision, because it offers no basis for learning whether the most plausible alternative was right or wrong. The United States Marine Corps' widely emulated response to these circumstances is the "70 percent solution." Leaders are told to act if they have 70 percent of the necessary information, have performed 70 percent of the analysis, and feel 70 percent confident in their decision.[50] Can you identify situations where this approach makes sense? Situations where it does not?

Barack Obama has similarly noted that in top positions like the presidency, nothing comes to the leader's desk that is "perfectly solvable. Otherwise someone else would have solved it. So you wind up dealing with probabilities. Any given decision you make you'll wind up with a 30 to 40 percent chance that it isn't going to work. You have to own that and feel comfortable with the way you made the decision. You can't be paralyzed by the fact that it might not work out."[51] Nor can leaders always afford to acknowledge that fact. As Michael Lewis notes, "people being led do not want to think probabilistically."[52] During a crisis, leaders are generally advised to "keep messaging positive. Negativity feeds stress and fuels panic."[53] If that advice is correct, how should leaders balance the need for honesty and self-confidence in their communication strategies? What are examples of effective and ineffective approaches?

4. Group allegiance can also skew decision-making. A famous example comes from a study of Princeton and Dartmouth students who were asked to watch a film of a highly contentious football game between teams from their schools. Princeton students counted twice as many rule violations by Dartmouth players as by Princeton players. Dartmouth students reported seeing only half as many violations committed by their school's team as Princeton students reported.[54]

   Political affiliations produce similar biases. One study gave participants research overviews on gun control. Republicans who got a version suggesting that a gun-control measure was effective misread the results. Democrats who got research showing the measure was ineffective also got the calculations wrong.[55] Have you observed similar examples of biased decision-making? Were they effectively corrected? If not, how should they have been?

5. Self-serving attributions and interpretations of events often compromise leaders' decision-making and negotiating ability. A famous example involves the Iceland arms controls talks between President Reagan and General Secretary Gorbachev. On the same day that Reagan publicly denounced Gorbachev for rejecting a reasonable proposal, Gorbachev complained to the press that Regan had come to the meeting "empty-handed."[56] In legal settings, people tend to find that arguments supporting their position are more credible than those opposing it.[57] A wide array of evidence suggests that professionals are subject to this bias when looking for interpretations of information that will favor a client.[58] How can lawyers guard against these tendencies?

   The importance of framing came through clearly in a famous incident from the 1912 presidential campaign. Three million brochures with the photograph of candidate Theodore Roosevelt were printed and ready to be circulated when the campaign manager learned that copyright permission to use the photograph had not been secured. He immediately telegraphed the photographer and informed him, "We are pleased to distribute millions of pamphlets with Roosevelt's photo on the cover. It will be great publicity for the studio whose photograph we use. How much will you pay us to use yours? Respond immediately." The photographer offered $250.[59] Was that ethical? Can you think of other incidents in which framing a decision was equally critical?

6. In March 2004, the Sierra Club filed a motion in the U.S. Supreme Court asking Justice Antonin Scalia to recuse himself from *Cheney v. U.S. District Court*. The basis for the motion was that Scalia had hunted ducks in Louisiana with Vice President Dick Cheney earlier that year. At issue in the litigation was whether Cheney should be forced to provide information about the energy task force he led while the Bush administration was formulating its

environmental policy. The Sierra Club claimed that Scalia and Cheney's friendship could affect Scalia's objectivity in deciding that issue. Scalia rejected that claim and refused to recuse himself. He insisted that his friendship with the vice president would not distort his judgment. According to Scalia, "[i]f it is reasonable to think that a Supreme Court Justice can be bought so cheap, the nation is in deeper trouble than I had imagined."[60] Critics responded that Scalia's position ignored a vast array of psychological research on conflicts of interest, and the role of personal relationships in biasing judgments.[61] Despite efforts to be objective, people often succumb to "motivated reasoning." Such reasoning involves the "rationalization of preferred opinions," namely "our tendency to arrive, by seemingly purely rational reasoning, at the opinions that we prefer for other motives."[62] Given such cognitive tendencies, should a Supreme Court Justice have the final word on whether to recuse himself? Using choice architecture, could the Court construct a fairer decision process for recusal motions?

7. One other cognitive tendency common among leaders is "action bias," the tendency to seek ways of actively responding to risks and to discount the problems that these responses might entail. In policy-making settings, the bias is known as the "dangerous dog" effect, based on a clumsy legislative overreaction to several dog bite incidents.[63] When this tendency is combined with decision makers' overconfidence in their own competence, the result may be the reinforcement of naïve realism. To mitigate these biases, what correctives would you propose?

8. The result of confirmation bias is a "disagreement deficit." Most of us are "supremely unmotivated to educate ourselves about beliefs with which we disagree."[64] A European communist who was asked whether he had read any criticisms of communism responded, "A man does not sip a bottle of cyanide just to find out what it tastes like."[65] Similar tendencies are apparent in the current polarized political climate in the United States. In one study, when Republicans and Democrats were offered free research, members of both parties were eager to get intelligent arguments reinforcing their views, and were somewhat interested in arguments for the other side that were so weak that they could be readily mocked and caricatured. Neither Republicans nor Democrats were interested in intelligent arguments that challenged their views.[66] The same preferences are apparent among political leaders who get their news from media channels that skew conservative or liberal. A related problem is what psychologists call "motive attribution asymmetry": peoples' assumption that their own ideology is based in benevolence and societal interests and that the other side's is motivated by hatred and self interest—an assumption that blocks productive negotiations and compromise.[67]

Given the universal human tendency to prefer confirming information, experts consistently recommend that leaders proactively consult members of diverse networks. Such efforts reduce the possibilities of "echo chambers" in which decision makers become mired in consensus.[68] Why do you think so many leaders resist that advice? What might change their behavior?

PROBLEM 3-2

Henry Louis Gates Jr. is a professor at Harvard and one of the world's preeminent scholars of African-American studies. In July 2009, on returning home around noon from a "14-hour flight and nursing a bronchial infection," Gates found the front door to his Cambridge home jammed.[69] Gates, who is 58 and walks with a cane because of a lifelong disability, asked for help in forcing the door open from his cabdriver, a dark-skinned Moroccan.[70]

A concerned neighbor who saw two men of color struggle with the door called the Cambridge police to report a possible burglary. In the preceding six months, the neighborhood had 23 break-ins, many of which had occurred during the day.[71] The first on the scene was Sergeant James M. Crowley, an officer with 11 years of experience, an adviser to the Cambridge police commissioner, an instructor on methods to avoid racial profiling, and a role model for younger officers. He had the reputation of being a "by-the-book" sergeant.[72] Crowley saw Gates in the foyer and asked him to step outside. Gates refused.

What happened next is a matter of dispute. According to Charles J. Ogletree, a Harvard law professor who represented Gates in the matter, Gates explained that the house belonged to him and showed Crowley his Massachusetts and Harvard identification cards.[73] When Crowley questioned the explanation, Gates grew frustrated and asked for the sergeant's name and badge number.

According to the police report, Gates initially refused to show identification. Crowley explained to Gates that he was investigating a possible break-in, and Gates exclaimed, "Why, because I'm a black man in America?" and accused Crowley of racism.[74] Crowley further noted in the police report that he was led to believe Gates lived in the home but was "quite surprised and confused" by Gates's behavior.[75]

As the encounter escalated, the Cambridge police unsuccessfully tried to reach Crowley on his radio at least three times. When they received no response, they sent six cars to the scene, which surprised Gates as he exited his home.[76] A video showed Gates responding belligerently as he was charged with disorderly conduct and led in handcuffs from the house.[77] Charges were subsequently dismissed. A joint statement by Gates's lawyer, the Cambridge Police Department, the City of Cambridge, and the county district attorney's office called the incident "regrettable and unfortunate" and emphasized that it "should not be viewed as one that demeans the character and reputation of Professor Gates or the character of the Cambridge Police Department."[78]

Six days after Gates's arrest, President Obama was asked about the incident at the close of a press conference on health care. He responded:

Now, I don't know, not having been there and not seeing all the facts, what role race played in that, but I think it's fair to say, number one, any of us would be pretty angry; number two, that the Cambridge police acted stupidly in arresting somebody when there was already proof that they were in their own home; and, number three, what I think we know, separate and apart from this incident, is that there is a long history in this country of African-Americans and Latinos being stopped by law enforcement disproportionately. And that's just a fact.[79]

Obama's comments triggered widespread controversy. Critics claimed that he had prejudged the situation and had helped further "fuel the controversy" by charging the police with acting "stupidly."[80] According to Ben Heineman, a prominent commentator on lawyers and leadership, Obama missed a "teaching moment."[81] By relying on assumptions rather than facts about the incident in question, he undercut his own position on racial profiling. He also diverted attention from the theme of his press conference—the urgency of health care reform.[82]

In the wake of public criticism, Obama made another statement to the press acknowledging that he "could have calibrated" his words more carefully.[83] However he also stressed his conviction that the incident was "a sign of how race remains a factor in this society."[84] When the controversy persisted, Obama invited Gates and Crowley to the White House for a beer.

The gesture met with mixed reviews. Many of his African-American advisors thought that he should not have backpedaled, and that the meeting was, as one put it, "demeaning"; it "diminished his leadership and his voice."[85] Other observers were more forgiving. According to one black factory worker, Obama had "backtracked because he wanted to be everybody's president."[86]

Some commentators parodied the effort:

> President Obama today named this Thursday, Drink a Beer with Someone Who Arrested You Day. Explaining his decision, the President told reporters, "When tempers run a little high, there's one thing that always helps people think more rationally: beer." The President said he hoped that his proclamation would result in thousands of friendly get-togethers around the country between police officers and the innocent people they recently arrested.[87]

Considerable media attention focused on the types of beer chosen and whether Obama's beer selection (Bud Light) was "a safe political choice." After all, Jon Stewart noted, the parent company of that beer was Belgian. Wasn't this a moment to "buy American?"[88] David Letterman's Top Ten comments overheard at the meeting included, "Let's call Rush Limbaugh and take this party to the next level."[89]

The meeting generated relatively few substantive efforts to address the problems that the incident exposed. In a public statement following the "beer summit," Crowley indicated that he and Gates had "agreed to disagree" and "decided to look forward."[90] Gates reported that the meeting had helped them bridge their divide and "make a larger contribution to American society."[91]

1. What role might cognitive bias have played in the way that Gates, Crowley, and Obama each framed the incident? Was there evidence of:

- Recognition-primed decision-making (use of schemas to size up a situation);
- Bounded rationality (limitations of time and cognitive processes leading to reliance on intuitive rather than deliberative decision-making);
- Retention and retrieval biases (overreliance on vivid, personal, concrete information); or
- Naïve realism (assumptions that our view is neutral while others are biased)?

2. If they had been aware of these potential biases, might participants have responded differently? How should the Cambridge Police Department have handled the incident?

3. How should President Obama have responded to press questions? Do you agree that his statement inappropriately "fueled the controversy?" Ben Heineman proposed the following alternative statement:

> I don't know the facts of this local police matter. But there is a potential question of racial profiling. Without passing judgment on Professor Gates' arrest, let me address that larger problem which, in my judgment, clearly continues to exist in America today.[92]

Is that what you would have said? Why or why not?

4. Was the beer summit an example of effective leadership? If not, what would you have done?

5. According to one *New Yorker* account of the incident, the takeaway for Obama was that "talking about race, especially extemporaneously, was just not worth it."[93] Would that be your assessment? Given the climate at the time, could Obama have avoided talking about race? Valerie Jarrett, one of Obama's top advisors, said that what the incident taught them was that "you just have to be careful about the words that you choose. It doesn't mean you shy away from issues that arise that deal with race. . . . But you have to be sensitive to a long history of people reacting strongly to the topic."[94] In a later *New Yorker* interview at the close of his second term, Obama again reflected on the incident, and noted that in its aftermath, his poll numbers among white voters dropped around 10 percent. And he concluded, "If you don't stick your landing in talking about racial issues, particularly when it pertains to the criminal-justice system, then people just shut down. They don't listen."[95] What lessons can be drawn from that insight in framing future leadership choices on race and criminal justice issues?

6. In a 2016 memorial service in Dallas, following a series of police shootings of unarmed black men, and a black army veteran's shooting of five Dallas police officers, Obama spoke what the *New York Times* described as "hard truths to both sides."[96] He told police officers that Black Lives Matter activists were responding to legitimate grievances of systemic racial bias and that officers should not dismiss them as "troublemakers or paranoid." And he told blacks that "[w]e ask the police to do too much and we ask too little of ourselves." He

added that the Dallas killings had exposed the "deepest fault lines" of our democracy. But he said that people should not simply "retreat to their respective corners" and "give in to despair." He pointed out that both Dallas police and protestors had showed "incredible restraint" and helped each other when the bullets started flying. "That's the America I know," he concluded.[97] How would you evaluate that response? What else might you have said? Former President George W. Bush also spoke at the memorial, noting, "Too often we judge other groups by their worst examples while judging ourselves by our best intentions. And this has strained our bonds of understanding and common purpose."[98] Do you agree? How might leaders help bridge these racial tensions?

7. Another factor that can impair decision-making is what Zachery Shore labels "exposure anxiety": an unwillingness to appear weak or inadequate.[99] As Shore notes in *Blunder*, the dynamic plays out in many contexts where leaders worry that failure to take decisive action will weaken their authority.[100] In the following excerpt, George Orwell describes a famous example of what might qualify as exposure anxiety. Orwell intended his account as an indictment of imperialism. Does it also hold broader lessons for contemporary society?

GEORGE ORWELL, "SHOOTING AN ELEPHANT," IN NEW WRITING (1936)

[George Orwell was a British novelist, journalist, and political observer of the early 20th century. After attending school in England, he served with the Imperial Police in Burma during its time as a British colony. "Shooting an Elephant" describes an incident in which the police got a complaint that an elephant was ravaging a bazaar. It was a working elephant that had gotten loose and killed a coolie and a cow, raided fruit stalls, and turned over a van. When Orwell got to the scene, the elephant was peacefully eating, and he felt certain that he should not shoot the animal—that would be comparable to "destroying a large and costly piece of machinery." Alive the elephant was worth at least 100 pounds; dead, only about five. But he had been followed by a large crowd who expected him to kill the elephant. Orwell recalls his reaction.]

It was at this moment, as I stood there with the rifle in my hands, that I first grasped the hollowness, the futility of the white man's dominion in the East. Here was I, the white man with his gun, standing in front of the unarmed native crowd—seemingly the leading actor of the piece; but in reality I was only an absurd puppet pushed to and fro by the will of those yellow faces behind. I perceived in this moment that when the white man turns tyrant it is his own freedom that he destroys. . . . For it is the condition of his rule that he shall spend his life in trying to impress the "natives", and so in every crisis he has got to do what the "natives" expect of him. He wears a mask and his face grows to fit it. I had got to shoot the elephant. . . . A sahib has got to act like a sahib; he has got to appear resolute, to know his own mind and do definite things. To come all that way, rifle in hand, with two thousand people marching at my heels and then to trail feebly away, having done nothing—no, that was impossible. The crowd would laugh at me. And my whole life, every white man's life in the East, was one long struggle not to be laughed at. . . .

[Orwell shot the elephant multiple times, which felled him but didn't immediately kill him.]

It seemed dreadful to see the great beast lying there, powerless to move and powerless to die, and not even be able to finish him. I sent back for my small rifle and poured shot after shot into his heart and down his throat. They seemed to make no impression. The tortured gasps continued as steadily as the ticking of a clock.

In the end I could not stand it any longer and went away. I heard later that it took him half an hour to die. . . . Afterwards, of course, there were endless discussions about the shooting of the elephant. The owner was furious, but he was only an Indian and could do nothing. Besides, legally I had done the right thing, for a mad elephant has to be killed, like a mad dog if its owner fails to control it. Among the Europeans opinion was divided. The older men said I was right, the younger men said it was a damn shame to shoot an elephant for killing a coolie, because an elephant was worth more than any damn Coringhee coolie. And afterwards I was very glad that the coolie had been killed; it put me legally in the right and it gave me a sufficient pretext for shooting the elephant. I often wondered whether any of the others grasped that I had done it solely to avoid looking a fool.

NOTES ON ACKNOWLEDGING ERROR

In *Being Wrong*, Kathryn Schulz begins by quoting Moliere's famous quip: "It infuriates me to be wrong when I know I'm right."[101] She goes on to note:

As a culture, we haven't even mastered the basic skill of saying "I was wrong." This is a startling deficiency, given the simplicity of the phrase, the ubiquity of error, and the tremendous public service that acknowledging it can provide. Instead, what we have mastered are two alternatives to admitting our mistakes that serve to highlight exactly how bad we are at doing so. The first involves a small but strategic addendum: "I was wrong, *but . . . ,*" a blank we fill in with wonderfully imaginative explanations for why weren't so wrong after all. . . . The second (infamously deployed by, among others, Richard Nixon regarding Watergate and Ronald Reagan regarding the Iran-Contra affair) is even more telling: we say, "Mistakes were made.". . . [A]ll we really know how to do with our errors is not acknowledge them as our own.

By contrast, we positively excel at acknowledging other people's errors. . . . Witness, for instance, the difficulty with which even the well-mannered among us stifle to urge to say "I told you so." The brilliance of this phrase (or its odiousness, depending on whether you get to say it or must endure hearing it) derives from its admirably compact way of making the point that not only was I right, I was also right about being right.[102]

In Schulz's view, "our distaste for error and our appetite for being right . . . tends to be rough on relationships."[103] Yet the problem is difficult to avoid because "the whole reason it's possible to be wrong is that while it is happening, you are oblivious to it. . . . Whatever falsehoods each of us currently believes are necessarily invisible to us. . . . [E]rror-blindness helps explain why we accept fallibility as a universal phenomenon, yet are constantly startled by our own mistakes.[104] According to Schulz, people's first reaction if confronted with disagreement is generally "the ignorance assumption." "We assume that other people are ignorant because we assume that we are not. . . . When other people reject our beliefs, we think they lack good information. When we reject their beliefs, we think we possess good judgment."[105] Schulz further claims that if the ignorance assumption fails because people stubbornly persist in disagreeing even after we've tried to enlighten them, we move on to the "idiocy assumption" and the "evil assumption." We assume that people are either unable to comprehend the truth or "have willfully turned their backs on it."[106]

Because lawyer leaders occupy a pivotal role in our justice system, their refusal to acknowledge error carries special costs. An example involves prosecutors' response to evidence that exposes wrongful convictions. Peter Neufield, co-director and co-founder of the Innocence Project, reports that prosecutors frequently resist requests for DNA testing and, when confronted by exculpating evidence, demand that the tests be redone, or come up with a new theory of how the crime was committed that makes the DNA evidence irrelevant. Some prosecutors attempt to retry a defendant who is exonerated, and then dismiss the charges, not because they accept that the defendant is innocent, but because, they claim, that it is too difficult to get witnesses. Such prosecutors "give up the case, but not their convictions."[107]

An example that Schulz profiles is Michael McGrath, former Attorney General of Montana, who insisted on the guilt of a student, Jimmy Ray Bromgard. Bromgard was sentenced to 40 years for a child rape that DNA evidence demonstrated he did not commit. After 15 years in prison, Bromgard sued the state, and McGrath gave a deposition in which he suggested that the semen and hair found in the victim's underwear, which did not match Bromgard's, came from someone else with whom she was sexually active. The girl was eight years old. McGrath also insisted that she had given "quite significant identification testimony." He was then forced to acknowledge that she testified that she was "not very sure" that her rapist was Bromgard. The defendant settled his case for $3.5 million, and McGrath moved unsuccessfully to have the deposition sealed.[108] To Schulz, what was most disturbing about the story was that it wasn't "particularly unusual. . . . Being involved in a wrongful conviction challenges [prosecutors'] sense of themselves as basically good, honest, smart, reliable people, who are "on the side of the angels."[109]

Schulz wants decision makers to accept of the likelihood of errors, be more transparent in admitting them, place greater reliance on objective data, and actively encourage disagreement.[110] She also suggests that acknowledging uncertainty can be disarming, and can encourage those with opposing opinions to be more open to new arguments. She gives an example of a graduate student who prefaced a comment in a contentious discussion with "I might be going out on a limb here. . . ." That opening enabled classmates to contemplate the statement's merits instead of rushing to invalidate it.[111] According to Schulz, "embracing our fallibility simply acknowledges what philosopher Richard Rorty called 'the permanent possibility of someone having a better idea.'"[112]

Consider a situation in which you were in error. How well did you handle it? Do the preceding insights suggest anything that you might have done differently?

MEDIA RESOURCES

Ample media coverage is available on the Gates incident, including Obama's initial statement and participant interviews. Many news programs replayed Obama's statement about the BP disaster, and commentary on the underlying regulatory and risk prevention failures. A video of a classic psychology experiment can be used to explore perceptual errors. In the video, viewers are asked to count the passes made by teams in white shirts and black shirts passing a basketball, and then asked what they saw. What they did not see is equally instructive.[113] *Moneyball*, based on Michael Lewis' bestseller, explores what happened in professional baseball when the general manager of Oakland Athletics reduced cognitive biases in the market for baseball players.[114] The first season of *Billions* features a plea negotiation between a federal district attorney and Wall Street hedge fund manager that implodes at the last minute because the D.A. cannot resist the self-serving satisfaction of getting the final word.[115] In *The Children's Act*, Emma Thompson plays a British judge who must decide whether a minor should have the right to refuse a life-saving blood transfusion for religious reasons.

B. GROUP DECISION-MAKING

Although our image of a leader's decision-making tends to be a solitary individual "decider," that person's judgments are often the product of collective processes. The reasons are obvious. As Harvard Business School professor Harold Leavitt suggested in his classic article "Suppose We Took Groups Seriously," decision-making often benefits from the different information, values, skills, and perspectives that multiple individuals bring to the table.[116] Subsequent theorists have emphasized that group involvement in decision-making can also increase the legitimacy of the process and enhance the commitment of members who need to live with the outcomes. But as researchers have also noted, group decision-making takes more time and can result in poor decisions if the members lack sufficient expertise, if conflicts and power disparities are not well managed, and if tendencies to conformity are not well controlled. Social psychologist Irving Janis explored the latter problem. His widely discussed book and article in *Psychology Today* on "groupthink" described the ways that highly cohesive groups can suppress independent views and too quickly converge on ill-conceived decisions.[117]

1. THE PROBLEM OF GROUPTHINK

IRVING L. JANIS, GROUPTHINK

Psychology Today Magazine (1971), pp. 84-89

There is evidence from a number of social-psychological studies that as the members of a group feel more accepted by the others, which is a central feature of increased group cohesiveness, they display less overt conformity to group norms. Thus we would expect that the more cohesive a group becomes, the less the members will feel constrained to censor what they say out of fear of being socially punished for antagonizing the leader or any of their fellow members.

In contrast, the groupthink type of conformity tends to increase as group cohesiveness increases. Groupthink involves nondeliberate suppression of critical thoughts as a result of internalization of the group's norms, which is quite different from deliberate suppression on the basis of external threats of social punishment. The more cohesive the group, the greater the inner compulsion on the part of each member to avoid creating disunity, which inclines him to believe in the soundness of whatever proposals are promoted by the leader or by a majority of the group's members.

In a cohesive group, the danger is not so much that each individual will fail to reveal his objections to what the others propose but that he will think the proposal is a good one, without attempting to carry out a careful, critical scrutiny of the pros and cons of the alternatives. When groupthink becomes dominant, there also is considerable suppression of deviant thoughts, but it takes the form of each person's deciding that his misgivings are not relevant and should be set aside, that the benefit of the doubt regarding any lingering uncertainties should be given to the group consensus.

Stress. I do not mean to imply that all cohesive groups necessarily suffer from groupthink. All ingroups may have a mild tendency toward groupthink, displaying one or another of the symptoms from time to time, but it need not be so dominant as to influence the quality of the group's final decision. Neither do I mean to imply that there is anything necessarily inefficient or harmful about group decisions in general. On the contrary, a group whose members have properly defined roles, with traditions concerning the procedures to follow in pursuing a critical inquiry, probably is capable of making better decisions than any individual group member working alone.

The problem is that the advantages of having decisions made by groups are often lost because of powerful psychological pressures that arise when the members work closely together, share the same set of values and, above all, face a crisis situation that puts everyone under intense stress.

The main principle of groupthink, which I offer in the spirit of Parkinson's Law, is this: The more amiability and esprit de corps there is among the members of a policy-making ingroup, the greater the danger that independent critical thinking will be replaced by groupthink, which is likely to result in irrational and dehumanizing actions directed against outgroups.

Symptoms. In my studies of high-level governmental decision-makers, both civilian and military, I have found eight main symptoms of groupthink.

(1) *Invulnerability.* Most or all of the members of the ingroup share an *illusion* of invulnerability that provides for them some degree of reassurance about obvious dangers and leads them to become over-optimistic and willing to take extraordinary risks. It also causes them to fail to respond to clear warnings of danger. . . .

(2) *Rationale.* As we see, victims of groupthink ignore warnings; they also collectively construct rationalizations in order to discount warnings and other forms of negative feedback that, taken seriously, might lead the group members to reconsider their assumptions each time they recommit themselves to past decisions. . . .

(3) *Morality.* Victims of groupthink believe unquestioningly in the inherent morality of their ingroup; this belief inclines the members to ignore the ethical or moral consequences of their decisions.

Evidence that this symptom is at work usually is of a negative kind—the things that are left unsaid in group meetings. . . .

(4) *Stereotypes.* Victims of groupthink hold stereotyped views of the leaders of enemy groups: they are so evil that genuine attempts at negotiating differences with them are unwarranted, or they are too weak or too stupid to deal effectively with whatever attempts the ingroup makes to defeat their purposes, no matter how risky the attempts are. . . .

(5) *Pressure.* Victims of groupthink apply direct pressure to any individual who momentarily expresses doubts about any of the group's shared illusions or who questions the validity of the arguments supporting a policy alternative favored by the majority. . . .

(6) *Self-censorship.* Victims of groupthink avoid deviating from what appears to be group consensus; they keep silent about their misgivings and even minimize to themselves the importance of their doubts. . . .

(7) *Unanimity.* Victims of groupthink share an *illusion* of unanimity within the group concerning almost all judgments expressed by members who speak in favor of the majority view. This symptom results partly from the preceding one, whose effects are augmented by the false assumption that any individual who remains silent during any part of the discussion is in full accord with what the others are saying. . . .

(8) *Mindguards.* Victims of groupthink sometimes appoint themselves as mindguards to protect the leader and fellow members from adverse information that might break the complacency they shared about the effectiveness and morality of past decisions. . . .

Remedies. . . . 1. The leader of a policy-forming group should assign the role of critical evaluator to each member, encouraging the group to give high priority to open airing of objections and doubts. This practice needs to be reinforced by the leader's acceptance of criticism of his own judgments in order to discourage members from soft-pedaling their disagreements and from allowing their striving for concurrence to inhibit critical thinking.

2. When the key members of a hierarchy assign a policy-planning mission to any group within their organization, they should adopt an impartial stance instead of stating preferences and expectations at the beginning. This will encourage open inquiry and impartial probing of a wide range of policy alternatives.

3. The organization routinely should set up several outside policy-planning and evaluation groups to work on the same policy question, each deliberating under a different leader. This can prevent the insulation of an ingroup.

4. At intervals before the group reaches a final consensus, the leader should require each member to discuss the group's deliberations with associates in his own unit of the organization—assuming that those associates can be trusted to adhere to the same security regulations that govern the policy-makers—and then to report back their reactions to the group.

5. The group should invite one or more outside experts to each meeting on a staggered basis and encourage the experts to challenge the views of the core members. . . .

9. After reaching a preliminary consensus about what seems to be the best policy, the group should hold a "second-chance" meeting at which every member expresses as vividly as he can all his residual doubts, and rethinks the entire issue before making a definitive choice.

2. STRENGTHS, LIMITATIONS, AND STRATEGIES FOR IMPROVEMENT OF GROUP DECISION-MAKING

Groupthink is not the only way in which cognitive and interpersonal dynamics can compromise group decision-making. In the following excerpt, Paul Brest and Linda Krieger explore other biases as well as strategies to address them.

PAUL BREST AND LINDA HAMILTON KRIEGER, PROBLEM SOLVING, DECISION MAKING, AND PROFESSIONAL JUDGMENT

(New York: Oxford University Press, 2010), pp. 595-597, 604-608, 611, 614-618, and 623-629

Thinking about Group Decision Making

Three decades of research tell a more nuanced and complex story than many [accounts of collective decision making suggest]. . . . Groups can add value to a decision-making process, but they can also run it off the rails. Small groups often make better decisions than their average member would make alone, but they seldom outperform their best members. Small groups fall prey to virtually all of the cognitive biases that plague individual decision makers and sometimes actually amplify the effects of those biases. . . .

Aggregation without Group Process: The Wisdom of Crowds

In a phenomenon that James Surowiecki has termed the "wisdom of crowds," combining a sufficient number of diverse and independent judgments often yields a better outcome than the judgment of any isolated person, no matter how smart or well-informed he or she might be. The result requires that four conditions be met:

1. The "group" must reflect a *diversity* of skills, opinions, information, and perspectives.
2. Each member's judgments must be *independent* from the others. That is, an individual's knowledge and opinions cannot be influenced by the knowledge and opinions of other group members.
3. The members must make and report their "sincere" judgments rather than skewing them for strategic purposes.
4. The decision maker needs a mechanism for *aggregating* the individual judgments to turn large numbers of private judgments into a single one. . . .

The Common Knowledge Effect

[These conditions are not met in circumstances of groupthink, and where] . . . deliberations often focus on shared rather than unshared information. The so-called "common knowledge effect" biases group decision making in the direction supported by shared information. . . . [The strength of the common knowledge effect depends on several factors, including the verifiability of the unshared information, the number of members who have it, and contextual factors. For example,] time pressure increases reliance on common information, as does an increase in the decision's apparent importance and group members' sense of accountability for it. . . .

But, certain measures tend to reduce the common knowledge effect:

- *Framing* the task as a "problem to be solved," implying that it has a "correct" answer.
- *Publicly* assigning roles to different group members [and giving them] the responsibility to supply information on a particular decision-relevant topic.
- *Extending* the time for discussion, which results in the use of more unshared information.
- Increasing the number of options from which the group can choose, and explicitly listing those options.
- Providing an objective source of verification of unshared information. . . .

Group Polarization

. . . [P]eople generally want to be viewed well by others. In order to present themselves in a socially desirable light, they constantly monitor others' reactions to determine how to adjust their self-presentation. As group members see how others view the issue under discussion, they tend to present themselves to be congruent with the perceived emerging trend. Indeed, to be "distinct" from their peers in the socially valued direction they often go "one step further" in the direction of increasingly extreme positions. Seen in this way, group polarization can be understood as a type of bandwagon effect.

Second, people generally see themselves and like to be seen by others as moderate, and initially express positions that may be more moderate than their true beliefs. But after being exposed to others having their own viewpoints, people become disinhibited from expressing more extreme views and they become more confident of those views. Robert Baron and his colleagues demonstrated that discussion with like-minded people can move individuals to more extreme positions solely by virtue of this *social corroboration* effect.

A third account of polarization, *social identity*, concerns the relationship of the group to others outside the group. As group members begin interacting with each other, they collectively begin to identify the characteristics, behaviors, and norms that differentiate their group from other groups. To differentiate their group from others, members attribute more extremity to their own group than is objectively the case; they distinguish their group from others by accentuating the perceived distance between their group norm and the norms they attribute to out-groups. Group members then conform their own behaviors, norms, and self-conceptions to the group's. Polarization thus occurs through a process of contrast with other groups within a specific social context.

. . . Another cognitive account of group polarization understands group interaction as an exercise in *rationale construction* rather than information collection. This model posits that people bring to a discussion their ex ante preferences and that interaction calls upon them to explain these to other group members. As people explain their positions, they gain confidence in them, whether or not they are accurate. Indeed, as Chip Heath and Richard Gonzales have shown, interaction with others increases confidence in, but not accuracy of, judgments. A related causal theory draws on the *effects of repeated expression:* polarization occurs as people repeat their own arguments and are repeatedly exposed to particular arguments, evidence, or expressions of a conclusion by like-minded others.

Reducing the Tendency Toward Group Polarization

There has been very little research directly testing the effectiveness of particular interventions in reducing group polarization. However, some inferences can be drawn from research on the contextual factors that tend to reduce or exacerbate the effect:

- Polarization is moderated by heterogeneity of initial opinions within a deliberating group.
- As with groupthink, polarization is exacerbated where the group is an ideologically cohering, high-solidarity entity.
- Groups that work together over a sustained period of time, making numerous similar decisions, may get feedback on the quality of those decisions, which

may moderate overconfidence and lead to more effective use of information in subsequent decision making.

- Polarization is moderated where a group is subject to external shocks (e.g. losing an election, being sued, experiencing a severe policy failure) or where the group must temper its preferences to preserve its prestige with external constituencies.

- Polarization can be reduced by increasing decision-making independence through mechanisms like the Delphi technique ([below]), and through norms and facilitation that encourage open-mindedness, the inclusion of minority perspectives, and evidence-based decision making.

Strategic Participation in Group Decision Making

Group members' concerns about their relations with others in the group play a significant role in the pathologies of group decision making. Individual group members may have interests that differ from those of their colleagues. So, for example, in a meeting to help a company's managers decide whether to settle or litigate an employment discrimination case, the lawyer may be concerned to maintain the impression that she is "on their side" even as she attempts to impress upon them the nature of the exposure to risk that they face. She may also want to convey a gender counter-stereotypical "toughness" that she hopes will instill confidence in her competence as a vigorous advocate.

Other participants in the decision-making process may have their own sets of competing processing goals. The manager who made the now-challenged decision may seek to save face, preventing his colleagues from concluding that he made a mistake or otherwise acted imprudently. Yet another group member may simply want to create a good impression and be viewed as a "team player." And all (or almost all) of the group members will be attempting to maintain a certain level of social harmony, both during and after the decision-making process.

In other words, the goal of making of a "good" decision is only one of the items on members' individual and collective agendas. The susceptibility of a group to decision-making errors will depend in substantial measure on these often hidden competing motivations.

The Susceptibility of Groups to Biases and Heuristics

Overconfidence. . . . [I]ndividuals often are overconfident in the accuracy of their own judgment. It turns out that groups don't do better. . . . Group overconfidence may result from the group polarization effect. . . .

Confirmation bias. Small deliberating groups, no less than individuals, fall prey to the tendency to overweight information that confirms a prior position, theory, or attitude and to underweight information that would tend to disconfirm it. . . .

Improving Group Decision Making

Preventing Premature Convergence: Devil's Advocacy and Dialectical Inquiry

One of the most common structures for group-based strategic decision making is an "expert approach," where a group of individuals, selected for their presumed expertise, present and seek consensus for a single recommended course of action. This procedure invites premature convergence.

Devil's advocacy is one way to inhibit premature convergence. After a plan is proposed by an individual or subgroup, another individual or subgroup attempts to identify everything wrong with the plan. The larger group then uses this critique to improve or replace the original proposal. Problem-solving groups that use devil's advocacy have been shown to generate a wider range of alternative courses of action than do conventional deliberating groups. Janis cites President Kennedy's handling of the Cuban Missile Crisis as an example of successful use of devil's advocacy. During those critical days in October 1962, President Kennedy assigned his brother, Attorney General Robert F. Kennedy, the role of devil's advocate with the task of aggressively challenging the assumptions and analysis underlying any emerging consensus. Devil's advocacy is not without its limitations: for example, if group members view the devil's advocate as being insincere, they may ignore his critique.

In *dialectical inquiry*, the entire group plays the role of devil's advocate. After identifying and discussing an initial plan, the entire group develops a "counterplan." There follows a structured debate, in which those responsible for making an ultimate decision hear arguments for and against the plan and the counterplan, with the possibility that yet another plan may emerge. . . .

The Stepladder Technique

Many of the dysfunctions of small decision-making groups result from social processes that interfere with the group's ability to fully utilize the potential contribution of all of its members. The group may be dominated by particularly aggressive individuals who stifle input from others in the group. Some group members may engage in social loafing, depriving the group of their potential contribution. Social pressures and social conformity effects may cause group members to withhold valuable information, opinions, or perspectives.

In the 1990s, Steven Rogelberg and his colleagues developed a procedure known as the *stepladder technique* to minimize the impact of these negative dynamics on group deliberation. The stepladder technique structures the entry of individuals into a decision-making group so as to maximize their independence from other group members and highlight their uniquely held information, opinions, ideas, and perspectives.

Before entering the discussion, each member is presented with the group's task and sufficient time to think about it alone. After the first two members discuss the problem, new members join the group one at a time. When entering the group, each new member must present his or her preliminary solution to the problem before hearing what the other group members think. Then the group discusses the problem before another new member enters. No final decision is made until all group members have been incorporated into the group in this manner.

The stepladder technique tends to improve a group's decision performance. Stepladder groups outperformed both their average and best member more often than conventional deliberating groups.

Generating and Evaluating Alternatives with Nominal Groups: The Delphi Technique

As described [above], the members of a "nominal group" work alone to solve a problem and their individual solutions are then aggregated. In some situations, nominal groups are more effective than either individuals or interactive groups. For example, nominal groups tend to outperform face-to-face groups in brainstorming tasks, where the goal is to generate lots of ideas and eventually improve on them.

The *Delphi Technique* is a well-known form of nominal group brainstorming. A coordinator transmits questions to group members. Working alone, the members transmit their responses to the coordinator, who assembles the information and generates additional information requests. Suppose, for example, that a humanitarian relief NGO is deciding what precautions to take in a conflict-ridden country in which its workers are in physical danger, or whether to pull out altogether. The coordinator states the problem, and asks each participant to generate as many ideas as possible for dealing with the issue. The coordinator then asks for comments on their strengths and weaknesses, and asks for refinements and new ideas. The process continues, with eventual resolution either through the emergence of a consensus or through voting. . . .

The Effects of Accountability on Individual and Group Decision Making Performance

. . . Accountability has become a popular concept in business, politics, and elsewhere, but its effects are not always clearly understood. Received wisdom tells us that a decision maker's accountability to others improves the quality of the decision. Though this sometimes is true, accountability can also lead to poorer decision making. This section summarizes the literature on the effects of accountability.

All other things being equal, accountability is likely to reduce error and bias in contexts in which, for whatever reason, people tend to make mistakes that they could prevent with extra attention or effort. For example, the expectation that they will have to justify their decision leads people to think more carefully and logically, and not to be satisfied with using unarticulated criteria or unsubstantiated empirical judgments to arrive at answers. Moreover, accountability makes people more likely to identify their own sources of bias, because of the need to justify themselves to others who do not necessarily view the decision with the same biases.

But . . . the benefits of accountability depend on a number of factors, such as:

- *Whether the views of the audience are known or unknown.* Decision makers who know the views of the audience to whom they are accountable tend to conform decisions to gain the audience's favor. . . . When the audience's views are unknown, decision makers tend to engage in *preemptive self-criticism*, anticipating how the decision would be viewed from various perspectives.
- *Whether one is accountable for the quality of the decision process or the decision's substantive outcome.* For example, a foundation could hold its program officers accountable for the success of their grants each year, or it could focus instead on whether the program officers were making thoughtful, informed outcome-focused decisions. Ultimately, the proof of a good process is in its outcomes; but this may take many years. A program officer who is held accountable only for outcomes may be afraid to take appropriate risks in making grants since, even if the risks are well considered in terms of expected value, they could still fail and lead to a bad outcome. On the whole, accountability for the process tends to improve the decision's accuracy and calibration while accountability for outcome can reduce decision quality. . . . Accountability may actually lead to poorer decision making when a biased choice seems the easiest to justify. For example decision makers may anticipate less criticism of a decision if they choose the middle ground between two extreme values . . . or if they take into account all the information presented, including irrelevant information.

NOTES AND QUESTIONS

1. In *Wiser: Getting Beyond Group Think to Make Groups Smarter*, law professor Cass Sunstein and behavioral science professor Reid Hastie similarly argue that groups err for two reasons: incorrect informational signals, which lead members to misperceive information from others, and reputational pressures, which lead members to silence or change their views to avoid disapproval.[118] As a consequence, groups are even more likely than individuals to escalate their commitment to a failing course of action and to fall victim to the "cascade effect" in which they follow the statements or actions of those who spoke or acted first.[119] If most members of a group make certain errors, others will interpret that consensus as proof. And by focusing on what most people believe, they don't take into account critical information that only a few members have. The result is often that groups become polarized, and take positions more extreme than those that members had before deliberations.[120] Correctives include many of those suggested above: having leaders encourage critical thinking and silence their views until others have expressed theirs; assigning roles and appointing a devil's advocate; and using the Delphi method.

   Can you identify circumstances in which you observed failures in group decision-making? What effort was, or should have been, made to counteract them? How would you evaluate the strategies proposed by Sunstein, Hastie, Brest, and Krieger? Which strike you as most plausible for legal contexts?

2. Where there is complete consensus, experts agree that leaders should step back and ask what they are missing.[121] But it matters who they ask. A common tendency is to seek advice from friends and colleagues who share their perspective. But performance only improves when leaders gather advice from those outside the group who bring different insights and challenge the group to address possible mistakes and deficiencies.[122] Devil's advocates who are assigned positions are generally less persuasive than those who actually hold dissenting views. Those playing a role are less likely to argue forcefully enough for the opposing perspective, and group members are less likely to take them seriously.[123] Yet while team performance generally improves when members have different expertise and perspectives, it declines when they have different goals and values. Consider the implications of this finding for conflict management issues discussed in Chapter 4 and diversity initiatives discussed in Chapter 8.

3. In another essay on decision-making, Paul Brest highlights a number of biases that are particularly problematic in public-policy settings.[124] One involves confirmation bias, which makes it difficult to separate political preferences from fact-finding. So, for example, a legislator worried about the political and economic consequences of restricting greenhouse gas emissions may tend to discount the risks of global warming that the restrictions seek to address. A second problem is the "cognitive myopia" that leads to undervaluing future costs and benefits. When considering social investments, policy leaders tend to find the immediate costs more concrete, salient, and thus analytically "available" than long-term consequences. The problem is compounded by accountability to current constituents, who exhibit the same biases. A third difficulty arises from leaders' tendency to overvalue consistency and sunk costs. A representative case involves members of Congress who cited the dollars spent and lives lost in NASA's space shuttle program as a reason for its continued support.[125] Have you observed such tendencies in recent policy-making processes? Is the size of the federal budget deficit an example? What about failures to adopt sufficient climate change initiatives? How might such biases be overcome?

4. Some observers have argued that the Bush administration's decision to invade Iraq, and the faulty intelligence on which it was based, was an illustration of groupthink. In 2004, the Senate Intelligence Committee issued a report concluding that the intelligence community had seriously misjudged Iraq's military capabilities. One of the report's conclusions was that

> [t]he Intelligence Community (IC) suffered from a collective presumption that Iraq had an active and growing weapons of mass destruction (WMD) program [based on Iraq's prior deception and refusal to cooperate fully with UN inspectors]. This "group think" dynamic led Intelligence Community analysts, collectors, and

managers to both interpret ambiguous evidence as conclusively indicative of a WMD program as well as ignore or minimize evidence that Iraq did not have active and expanding weapons of mass destruction programs. This presumption was so strong that formalized IC mechanisms established to challenge assumptions and group think [such as devil's advocacy] were not utilized. . . . IC personnel involved in the Iraq WMD issue demonstrated several aspects of group think: examining few alternatives, selective gathering of information, pressure to conform within the group or withhold criticism, and collective rationalization.[126]

Other commentators noted that confirmation biases may also have inclined the intelligence community to interpret evidence in a way consistent with the political convictions of administration leaders.[127] According to one intelligence department chief, any skepticism about weapons of mass destruction was greeted with a suggestion to "think it over again."[128] Lawyers in the Bush administration have also received criticism for ignoring dissenting voices.[129]

If these accounts are correct, how could such misjudgments be prevented in the future? The report mentioned the need for the Intelligence Community to "make sure to question presumptions instead of rationalizing/explaining away lack of strong evidence with self-reinforcing premises."[130] How could this be achieved? What stands in the way?

A related problem is that the voters on whom we rely to check reckless political decisions are themselves subject to cognitive bias. Psychologists Carol Tavris and Elliot Aronson see a desire to reduce cognitive dissonance at work in the insistence of half of surveyed Republicans that weapons of mass destruction were found in Iraq, despite intensive news coverage to the contrary.[131] In some instances, individuals who are ideologically committed to a position will become even more entrenched in their views when presented with evidence exposing their error. Researchers found evidence of such "backfire" effects among conservatives who received the findings of the Duelfer Report, which documented the absence of stockpiles of such weapons or an active production program prior to the U.S. invasion.[132] What lessons should policy leaders draw from these examples?

5. Abraham Lincoln avoided some perils of groupthink by appointing a "team of rivals" in his cabinet, including his most formidable opponents.[133] President Obama also seemed sensitive to the potential pitfalls in group decision-making and the need to obtain diverse views. This tendency emerged early in his leadership experiences. As president of the *Harvard Law Review*, he avoided loading the masthead with liberals and students of color. Rather, he followed the traditional system of selection and ended up with three out of four executive editors who were conservatives.[134] According to one of his professors, Obama had a great "openness in engaging people with whom he disagrees."[135] In 2008, after appointing his national security team, which

included his primary election opponent, Hillary Clinton, he was asked about how he would ensure that the group would function as a team of rivals rather than a class of rivals. He responded:

> I assembled this team because I am a strong believer in strong personalities and strong opinions. I think this is how the best decisions are made. One of the dangers in a White House based on my reading of history is that you get wrapped up in group think and everybody agrees with everything and there is no dissenting view. So I am going to be welcoming a vigorous debate inside the White House.[136]

Subsequent news reports indicated that Obama had, in fact, developed a "culture of debate" on major foreign-policy decisions, such as expansion of the war in Afghanistan.[137] Although he was also criticized for failing to build a sufficiently diverse team of advisors on domestic policy issues, his approach was generally viewed as more open to contention than that of either his predecessor or his successor.[138] In an interview with Bob Woodward, George Bush described himself as a "gut player," someone who tends to "play by intuition" rather than extended debate.[139] Similarly, Donald Trump, despite his lack of international or domestic political experience, is famously confident in his own intuitions and unwilling to seek different perspectives. When asked during the 2016 presidential campaign whom he consulted on foreign policy, he said "my primary consultant is myself." When accepting the Republican nomination, he claimed, "Nobody knows the system better than me, which is why I alone can fix it."[140]

What accounts for the tendency toward insularity in political leadership? How can it be addressed?

6. Some experts have maintained that a major contributor to the 2008 financial recession was the investment community's misplaced faith in ever-rising real estate prices and in the market's self-policing capabilities. On this view, groupthink, overconfidence, and confirmation biases became a toxic combination resulting in "contagious wishful thinking."[141] According to an article by David Leonhardt in the *New York Times*, federal regulators, along with other analysts, "got trapped in an echo chamber of conventional wisdom" about rising real estate prices.[142] Robert Shiller, author of *Irrational Exuberance*, described the pressure he felt to avoid "deviating too far from consensus" in advising financial institutions. He didn't want to risk "ostracism," and feared criticism for "gratuitous alarmism" in his warnings about stock and housing market bubbles. In his view, another reason economists consistently underestimate the likelihood of bubbles is that they "aren't generally trained in psychology," and ignore cognitive bias; they prefer to focus on the "rational" behaviors that "they understand well."[143] Other commentators suggested that some policy leaders' prior commitment to deregulation may also have led them to overlook subprime lending abuses calling for greater oversight.[144] Malcolm Gladwell similarly faults

overconfidence in financial markets and concludes that leaders "saw the world that [they] wanted to see," not the one that existed.[145]

Neuroscientists have also joined the search for underlying causes of such market meltdowns. Some research on brain activity during simulated financial bubbles finds a physiological craving for rewards that come from early returns on investment. Dopamine neurons fire rapidly and stimulate the brain's nuclei, which increases individuals' excitement and encourages them to pour more money into the market. The rational centers of the brain then come up with all sorts of reasons why the market will not decline in order to sustain the heightened activity. This reasoning persists even after dopamine neurons cease firing shortly before the bubble bursts. High-risk activity is exacerbated by competition. The desire to outsmart others encourages ever more speculative behavior.[146] Such dynamics are at work in "deal fever," in which leaders are so anxious to beat out the competition and score a major merger or acquisition that they end up ignoring warning signals or overpaying to score a "big win."[147]

Consider the strategies for combating cognitive biases discussed above, and the problems in regulating unethical conduct explored in Chapter 5. What initiatives might have helped to avert unduly risky behavior? What might have prompted more executives to follow the example of Alfred Sloan, former chair of General Motors, who once adjourned a board meeting shortly after it began? "Gentlemen," he observed, "I take it we are all in complete agreement on the decision here. . . . Then I propose we postpone further discussion of this matter until our next meeting to give ourselves time to develop disagreement and perhaps gain some understanding of what the decision is all about."[148]

3. A CASE STUDY: THE HEWLETT PACKARD PRETEXTING SCANDAL

DEBORAH L. RHODE, DAVID LUBAN, SCOTT L. CUMMINGS, AND NORA FREEMAN ENGSTROM, LEGAL ETHICS

(New York: Foundation Press, 7th ed. 2016), pp. 664-667

In 2006, the Silicon Valley computer company, Hewlett-Packard, became embroiled in a highly publicized scandal. The problems arose from pretexting, the use of investigators to obtain confidential information through false pretenses. The case provides a highly illuminating portrayal of "how the good go bad"—how well intentioned lawyers and managers can become complicit in conduct widely viewed as unethical if not unlawful.

In 2005, leaks of confidential information accompanied the widely publicized firing of HP C.E.O. Carly Fiorina. Patricia Dunn, a member of the board of directors became its new chair and Mark Hurd became C.E.O. Neither had legal background; Dunn came from investment services and Hurd had headed a technology company. Among Dunn's first challenges was to address leaks that could only have come from board members or top executives. At the suggestion of an HP security manager, Dunn launched an investigation headed by a Boston-based private investigator, Ron DeLia, who had done work for HP in the past. In the late spring of 2005, DeLia sent a report to Dunn, which she forwarded to General Counsel Ann Baskins. In that report, and a subsequent June 15 telephone conference call, DeLia explained that investigators had obtained phone records through pretexting. Baskins expressed concerns about the legality of the process, and he responded that he was aware of no laws that made it illegal and no criminal prosecutions for such activities. Although the investigation failed to identify the leakers, HP leadership hoped that the process would deter future disclosures.

However, in January 2006, reporter Dawn Kawamoto ran a story on HP's long-term strategies. George Keyworth, a board member, later acknowledged having been the source. He did not believe he had disclosed any proprietary information and considered the story to be good press. Hewlett-Packard's leadership, by contrast, viewed the story with alarm, particularly because it addressed potential acquisitions. Baskins asked an HP employment lawyer, Ken Hunsaker, to head an investigation. Through pretexting, the investigation team obtained phone records of two HP employees, seven directors and nine reporters. It also created a fictional disgruntled HP employee who contacted Kawamoto by e-mail, and attached a file with tracking capability. Investigators hoped that she would forward the e-mail to her source for confirmation. Hurd, the C.E.O. authorized the process but later denied knowledge of the tracking aspect.

Around the same time, Baskins asked Hunsaker to explore the legality of pretexting. He put the question to Anthony Gentilucci, an HP security manager. Gentilucci responded that pretexting was common. In his view, although phone operators shouldn't give the information out and were in some sense "liable," the practice was "on the edge, but above board." Hunsaker's now infamous e-mail answer was "I should not have asked." Hunsaker also spent about an hour researching the issue on line. It is not clear what sources he consulted, but had he looked at the websites of the Federal Trade Commission or the Federal Communications Commission, he would have discovered that both considered the practice illegal.

In February, the issue arose again. Two HP security employees sent an e-mail to Hunsaker stating that pretexting "is very unethical at the least and probably illegal." So too, Baskins again asked Hunsaker about the legality of pretexting, and he again put the question to DeLia. This time DeLia consulted his outside counsel. That lawyer offered a quick judgment that pretexting was not illegal, based on research done by a summer associate the preceding year. DeLia then sent an e-mail to Hunsaker indicating that no state or federal laws prohibited pretexting but that there was "a risk of litigation."

In March, Hunsaker circulated a report connecting Keyworth to the leaks. In preparation for a meeting with Hurd, Baskins asked Hunsaker to talk to outside counsel about pretexting. . . . [In response, DeLia's] lawyer had a paralegal prepare a response. She told Gentilucci that she was unable to find any criminal charges to indicate that pretexting was illegal. In April, at Baskin's request, Hunsaker prepared a memo on the issues raised by pretexting. He noted his online research and his contacts with DeLia and his outside counsel. According to the memo, counsel's firm had conducted "extensive research" and found the practice "not unlawful." Mark Hurd then met with Keyworth privately and gave him an opportunity to acknowledge his leaks. Keyworth did not do so. As he later recalled the meeting, Hurd did not ask him about the reporter and Keyworth was not aware that her story was the focus of the investigation.

In May, a divided board asked Keyworth to resign. One of its most influential members, Tom Perkins, objected to the decision and resigned in protest. He also recalled objecting to the legality of pretexting. Dunn and other board members recalled no such objection and Dunn denied making any promise to keep the leaker's identity confidential. Larry Sonsini, HP's outside counsel then contacted Perkins about how to handle the resignation. Post-Enron reforms require that a company report board resignations to the SEC, and if the resignation stems from any disagreement with the company or the board, the reasons must also be disclosed. Perkins said his disagreement was with Dunn not the company, and the SEC report included no reasons.

Perkins subsequently consulted law professor Viet Dinh, who served with him on another board. Dinh raised concerns about pretexting that Perkins then conveyed to Sonsini. Sonsini responded that pretext calls were a "common investigatory method" and that "it appears, therefore, that the process was well done and within legal limits." Perkins relayed this to Dinh who then expressed doubts that the records could have been lawfully obtained. Perkins' dissatisfaction continued to escalate after receiving a notice from the phone company suggesting that his phone records were "hacked." He was also angry that the minutes of his final board meeting did not reflect the objections to pretexting that he recalled making. Perkins demanded that the minutes be amended, and that the company file a notice with the SEC since he now considered his dispute to be with the company. Baskins subsequently wrote to Perkins denying his requests, because the minutes had been approved and were accurate as drafted, and because he had earlier characterized the reasons for his resignation as personal. Perkins, represented by Dinh, then contacted the SEC, the California Attorney General, and the U.S. Attorney for the Northern District of California, which all launched investigations.

A national scandal erupted, fueled by Congressional hearings at which Dunn and Hurd testified and Baskins and Hunsaker invoked their 5th amendment privilege. Dunn, Baskins, Hunsaker, and Gentilucci were all forced to resign. The California Attorney General charged Dunn, Hunsaker, DeLia, and two private investigators with four felony counts: fraudulent wire communications, wrongful use of computer data, identity theft, and conspiracy. The counts were later reduced to misdemeanors. A state court dismissed the charges against Dunn, and then later against all other defendants based on evidence that they had performed community service. One investigator pleaded guilty to federal charges.

In his Congressional testimony, Hurd apologized for the "rogue" investigation and for authorizing the fake e-mail. While denying knowledge of certain other pretexting activity that others had permitted, he acknowledged that failing to read a report that described it was not "my finest hour." Patricia Dunn stated: "I do not accept personal responsibility for what happened." She added: "I relied on the expertise of others in whom I had full confidence. I deeply regret that so many people, including me, were let down." Larry Sonsini maintained that his response to Perkins about the legality of pretexting was not a "legal opinion. It was conveying the truth of what I was told." Ann Baskins made no public statement. Her lawyer told *New Yorker* reporter James Stewart: "A general counsel has to be able to rely on her senior counsel's research and advice, particularly when she has hundreds of lawyers working for her worldwide." Hunsaker's lawyer assured Stewart that "There cannot be a violation without intent to violate the law and Kevin absolutely believed that the investigation was being done in a legal and proper way."

The financial and personal effects of the scandal varied considerably. HP reimbursed Perkins for $1.5 million in legal expenses and agreed to pay Keyworth's as well. Ann Baskins, in exchange for cooperating with HP's investigation and releasing the company from liability, received the right to exercise stock options worth over $3.7 million, with another million in options to vest immediately. Mark Hurd, who according to Dunn, had received the same legal advice that she had received, got a bonus of $8.6 million in 2007, along with options on over 500,000 shares of stock. HP stock rose to its highest value in over six years.

———

Both Congress and the California legislature subsequently passed legislation making pretexting a criminal offense. Ann Baskins lost her job but not her license to practice law. Wilson Sonsini lost its long-standing role as HP's outside counsel.[149] HP settled litigation brought by the *New York Times* and three *Business Week Magazine* journalists for an undisclosed sum.[150]

ERIC DEZENHALL AND JOHN WEBER, DAMAGE CONTROL: WHY EVERYTHING YOU KNOW ABOUT CRISIS MANAGEMENT IS WRONG

(New York: Portfolio of Penguin Books, 2007), pp. 34-37

Hewlett-Packard: Overkill in Crisis Management

If ever there were a case of failing to differentiate between a nuisance, a problem, and a crisis, it was the bungled 2006 attempt by Hewlett-Packard's top brass to ferret out boardroom leaks by spying on their own board of directors, among others. In this notorious sin of excess, the cure became worse than the disease.

The scandal's climax came in the form of congressional hearings in which ten witnesses invoked their Fifth Amendment right against self-incrimination— sinister optics that helped turn a problem (a leaky board) into a crisis (Nixonian dirty tricks). . . .

[Board Chair] Dunn, who was indicted for fraud and conspiracy the following month, was not fundamentally wrong to be concerned about boardroom leaks. As CEO Mark Hurd said upon her resignation: "The intent of the investigation was proper and appropriate. The fact that we had leaks on the board needed to be resolved." The problem was that her team appeared to have been obsessed to the point of monomania.

Nor was Dunn wrong to entertain the use of private investigators, a practice that is indiscriminately branded as unethical in today's scandal climate. Some private investigations, dare we say, are good things. Without investigators, General Motors never would have learned that journalists at *Dateline NBC* had rigged a GM truck to explode in order to portray an alleged pattern of flammability. Indeed, our own experience has been that private investigations can identify and stop bad actors who have no God-given right to ignore the law in pursuit of their corporate quarry.

The problem with HP's actions was that they were undertaken without seasoned leadership, and whatever flimsy parameters were set apparently cascaded out of control and came to include tactics and targets that should have been off-limits. . . . There is such a thing as overresponding to a threat, which is what HP did when confronted by leaks. While as of this writing the facts of the case are still unfolding, one thing is certain: The operation that was put in place to plug the leaks did more damage to HP than the leaks ever did. . . .

"Tell it all," "Get it all out," went the extreme chants of the scandal's Greek chorus in the weeks before HP spoke publicly. One problem with these absolutes is that companies in crisis rarely know everything they need to know in order to make immediate and ideal decisions. That's why it's a crisis.

Another problem is that complete disclosures, while theoretically desirable, may be admissible in court and can place the company in legal jeopardy. If HP had begun speculating publicly about who did what, innocent people could have been smeared, forcing them to take legal action against the company. Moreover, HP didn't want to give fodder to prosecutors who were investigating the matter. Herein lies the tension between attorneys, who tend to counsel silence, and communicators, who tend to counsel openness. Who's right? Both are "right" within the context of their disciplines; however, each crisis has its own special set of considerations. It's up to the chief crisis officer (usually the CEO) to determine where on the silence-openness continuum public statements must fall.

On Friday, September 22, 2006, HP CEO Mark Hurd held a news conference (but took no questions) in which, for the first time since the affair broke in the press several weeks earlier, he commented at some length on the scandal and announced the resignation of chairman Dunn. Hurd also apologized to those who were spied upon and announced the appointment of former U.S. prosecutor Bart Schwartz to look into the investigative methods that were employed by the company in its attempt to plug leaks. . . .

Was Hurd's news conference held too late? In a perfect world, sure; but in the real world where a leader needs to know what he's talking about, it was the best of his bad options.

Hurd was criticized for not taking questions, but he was probably wise not to. When legal issues are at stake—especially when information is so limited—open-ended give-and-take with the news media is laden with mines. In the proverbial battle between lawyers and public relations people, the HP press conference was a thoughtful compromise between the two disciplines.

NOTES AND QUESTIONS

1. How would you evaluate the decisions of the leaders involved in the pretexting scandal? What accounts for their conduct? What role might cognitive biases have played? If the problem that HP officers identified was "find the leak," was this an adequate frame? Should they also have asked, "Why is this problem a problem?" and tried to get the entire board invested in the solution? Did their authorization of deceptive investigative techniques reflect a bias that psychologists label escalation of commitment, known colloquially as the "boiled frog" problem? Folk wisdom has it that a frog dropped into a pot of boiling water will hop out; a frog in water with gradually increasing temperatures will calmly boil to death.[151] This turns out to be untrue of frogs but metaphorically true of leaders. If this dynamic, along with other groupthink pathologies, was present among the HP leadership, what might have been done to counteract them?

2. Bart Schwartz, a former federal prosecutor later hired to evaluate HP's conduct, told a *New York Times* reporter that he was struck by the lack of consideration of ethical issues in the company's efforts to trace press leaks. In his view, "Doing it legally should not be the test; that is given. You have to ask what is appropriate and what is ethical."[152] What accounted for so many HP leaders' willingness to outsource ethics? What broader lessons does it suggest?

3. "Where were the lawyers?" asked one congressman in hearings on the HP scandal. "The red flags were waving all over the place," but "none of the lawyers stepped up to their responsibilities."[153] The same point has been raised about lawyers' complicity in other corporate scandals, and the search for explanations has led some commentators to build on identity theory and research. This framework demonstrates how individuals' role identification can encourage them to process information in ways that support their self-perception.[154] So, for example, in a survey of several hundred in-house counsel who evaluated a hypothetical ethical dilemma, those who identified themselves more as an employee than a lawyer were more likely to interpret an attorney's obligations in ways consistent with management's interests rather than with professional norms.[155] Could such dynamics have been at work in the HP scandal? What correctives might be effective?

4. HP delayed public statements regarding the scandal and when CEO Mark Hurd testified before Congress, he dismissed the incident as a "rogue investigation" that went against the company's "values."[156] Compare that strategy with Warren Buffett's response to rogue trading at Salomon Brothers, discussed in

Chapter 5. Buffett made immediate and full disclosure of corporate misconduct, and cooperated fully with government investigators, even when it meant waiving the corporation's attorney-client privilege. Would such a strategy have been preferable for HP, or do you agree with Dezenhall and Weber's endorsement of Hurd's approach?

5. What broader lessons does the HP case suggest about the role of attorneys charged with ensuring ethical compliance?

MEDIA RESOURCES

A Fox News report offered a groupthink explanation for the misdiagnosis of Iraq's military capabilities.[157] Hurd's congressional testimony on the pretexting scandal is also available, as is Patricia Dunn's.[158] *Twelve Angry Men* is a classic film portrayal of one man's efforts to overcome groupthink among his fellow jurors. *Philadelphia* portrays the stereotypes and group dynamics that lead a law firm to fire an attorney with AIDS. *Wall Street: Money Never Weeps*, a National Public Radio broadcast, includes illuminating interviews with financial services professionals who refused to believe that the Wall Street community was in any sense responsible for the 2008 economic crisis.[159]

C. COST-BENEFIT ANALYSIS

Some of leaders' most common decision-making challenges involve cost-benefit tradeoffs. Problems arise when values and risks cannot be definitively quantified and compared. The materials that follow explore these challenges in representative legal and policy settings.

PAUL BREST AND LINDA HAMILTON KRIEGER, PROBLEM SOLVING, DECISION MAKING, AND PROFESSIONAL JUDGMENT

(New York: Oxford University Press, 2010),
pp. 370-371, 373-374, 376-380, and 383-384

[T]he use of cost-benefit analysis to guide public or corporate policymaking has sometimes been criticized for requiring "immoral commodification" by placing a dollar value on life's unquantifiables—such as human life, health, or the existence of a wilderness area. [Jurors often impose punitive damages on corporate defendants who seem cold-blooded in engaging in cost-benefit analysis. . . .] To be sure, some decisions call for existential choices—for example, tradeoffs between peace and justice—that far transcend the capacity of cost-benefit analysis. But as Robert Frank notes:

Scarcity is a simple fact of the human condition. To have more of one good thing, we must settle for less of another. Claiming that different values are incommensurable simply hinders clear thinking about difficult tradeoffs. . . .

Policy makers (and others) use various strategies to avoid explicit tradeoffs between constitutively incommensurable values. When they cannot avoid a conscious or public tradeoff, they engage in buck-passing, procrastination, and obfuscation. And when responsibility for a decision cannot be avoided, they tend to "spread the alternatives," "playing down the strengths of the to-be-slighted value and playing up the strengths of the to-be selected value.". . .

Some of the most divisive debates surrounding CBA concern the valuation of human life—an issue that arises in government regulatory efforts to reduce workplace, toxic, and other risks. . . . Currently, there exist three main methods for the assessment of human life: VSL (Value of a Statistical Life), VSLY (Value of Statistical Life-Years), and QALYs (Quality Adjusted Life Years). . . .

Value of a Statistical Life (VSL). Perhaps the most widely used method, VSL assigns a fixed monetary value to every human life in a certain population. It does not seek to estimate the *intrinsic* value of an individual human life, but is based on people's willingness to pay (WTP) to avoid an aggregation of many small health and safety risks in their lives. . . . VSL can be determined through WTP by using:

(1) People's *stated preferences* for how much they would pay to eliminate risks, or
(2) People's *revealed preferences*, analyzing decisions that people have already made about risk tradeoffs for goods and/or workplace risk reductions.

Utilizing both these techniques, the Environmental Protection Agency reviewed 26 peer-reviewed value-of-life studies from academic literature to arrive at a single VSL of $6.3 million for the United States (in year 2000 dollars). Subsequently, however, an [EPA] work group asserted that, since VSL values vary widely by social and economic status, race, population, and country, there "does not appear to be a universal VSL value that is applicable to all specific subpopulations." Furthermore, the work group recommended that VSL studies using stated and revealed preferences be analyzed separately, since they sometimes lead to significantly different estimates.

Citizens of a developing country, such as India, have a lower WTP and thus a lower VSL than an economically developed country, such as the United States. In fact, VSL evaluations conducted around the world range from $70,000 to $16.3 million. Nonetheless, some scholars advocate, on moral grounds, the use of a universal VSL for all peoples, regardless of their economic status or willingness to pay. On the other hand, others, including Cass Sunstein, assert that policymakers should establish specific, local VSLs for communities and countries. Sunstein argues that VSLs should be assessed within the population where regulations force the beneficiaries to bear the costs. If an inflated VSL is used, poorer citizens may be forced to "spend" their money to reduce a workplace risk when they would prefer to put that money to other uses. . . .

Value of Statistical Life-Years (VSLY). VSL treats the lives of the very young and very old as equally valuable. Under the VSLY approach, benefits to individuals are assessed based on their estimated remaining years of life. . . . Michael J. Moore and W. Kip Viscusi, proponents of this approach, note that "in the case of fatalities, a young person loses a much greater amount of lifetime utility than does an older person," and thus assert that it doesn't make sense to use the same value for an elderly person with a remaining five-year life expectancy as for a 25-year-old. Critics of VSLY term it the "senior death discount.". . . [T]he U.S. Office of Management and Budget has encouraged federal agencies to conduct analysis using both approaches. . . .

Consider James Hammit's . . . letter to the editor of the *New York Times*:

> The Office of Management and Budget's interest in applying cost-benefit analysis to homeland security measures is laudable. Even if precise quantification of the benefits to security and harms to civil liberties is impossible, analytic consideration of the trade-offs is wise.
>
> As John Graham, director of regulatory affairs at O.M.B., says, "Simply identifying some of these costs will help understand them and get people to think about alternatives that might reduce those costs."
>
> Cost-benefit analysis should have also been used to evaluate the potential war in Iraq. The benefits of ousting Saddam Hussein should be measured against the costs of casualties, waging war, reconstruction, retaliatory terrorism and increased anti-Americanism. Such analysis would prompt us "to think about alternatives that might reduce those costs."]

PROBLEM 3-3

As the preceding materials note, jurors and the public have sometimes punished defendants for engaging in explicit cost-benefit analysis concerning the value of human life. A widely discussed example is the $176 million damage award (later reduced to $6.6 million) against Ford Motor Company for deaths resulting from a Pinto gas tank explosion. A company memo indicated that Ford had estimated the costs of improvements to the gas tank at $37 million ($11 per car), and determined that they exceeded the value of injuries averted and lives saved, estimated at $49.5 million ($67,000 per injury and $200,000 per life). The value of life figures came from federal studies on the costs to economy of lives lost in traffic accidents. Other federal agencies at the time used figures for the value of a life ranging from $70,000 to $132 million.[160] Jury verdicts around the time averaged $950,000 for the death of a man in his thirties, and $85,000 for a woman over 65.[161] The Ford Pinto model had a much worse safety record for rear-end collisions than other subcompact models, but a better overall safety performance, because a very small proportion of traffic fatalities are caused by rear-end fires.[162] Commentators on the case note that Ford's willingness to overlook its safety defect was a function of broader corporate priorities. As one engineer explained, "This company is run by salesmen, not engineers; so the priority is styling, not safety."[163] When a concerned engineer prepared a presentation on safer tank design and convinced his boss to invite all company engineers and product planning personnel, the only person who showed up was his boss.[164]

If you had been General Counsel at Ford, would you have engaged in similar cost-benefit calculations? If so, what figures would you have used for value of life? Would you have included other potential costs in the calculations, such as reputational injury? Is there an alternative approach to the decision that might have been preferable, such as analyzing whether the Pinto without the improvement would meet reasonable consumer expectations in light of industry standards? If so, how would you determine what is reasonable?

NOTES AND QUESTIONS

1. Another auto-safety issue that attracted widespread attention involved the first fatal crash in 2016 of a Tesla running on autopilot. The company responded that Tesla vehicles had driven 130 million miles before having a fatal crash, while the national rate is about 94 million miles per fatality.[165] Commentators responded that the comparison was flawed because the national rate is for driving on all roads and under all conditions, while the Tesla figures are only for conditions where autopilot can be activated, such as freeways and larger roads. Driving under those conditions results in disproportionately fewer accidents.[166] Commentators also objected that the Tesla sample size was too small for meaningful comparison; it involved only 130 million miles compared with the national statistics based on 3 trillion miles annually. As one critic noted, if another fatal accident had occurred the day after the first one, something certainly possible given the realm of standard probabilities, Tesla's rate would have been one death per 65 million miles, much worse than the national rate.[167]

   Commentators raised other concerns as well. One was that the vivid nature of the accident, with its identifiable victim, would cause consumers to overestimate risks, as the availability bias suggests. Another concern was that Tesla's marketing had oversold the autonomous feature of its autopilot. Although its manual cautioned that car drivers must remain alert, with their hands on the wheel in case they need to take over, "not all Tesla owners . . . read their manuals."[168] The driver in the fatality case was playing a Harry Potter DVD when his car ran into a tractor-trailer turning left in front of him.[169]

   In the aftermath of the accident, the National Highway Traffic Safety Administration launched an investigation. If you were in charge, how would you proceed? If you were Tesla's General Counsel, what recommendations would you make about how to handle the issue?

2. What follows from the wide disparity in measures of value of life for purposes of safety decisions? Brest and Krieger note the controversy over OMB's cost-benefit analysis concerning homeland security measures. What are the capabilities and limitations of such analysis in these circumstances?

Many cognitive biases affect the way people value life in cost-safety tradeoffs. One example is the underinvestment in prevention. The public is often willing to spend vast sums to save identifiable victims, such as a baby trapped in a well, or coal workers trapped in a mine, but unwilling to invest proportionate amounts in safety measures to prevent such tragedies.[170] A related dynamic is "psychosocial numbing: people value lives less as the number of lives at risk increases."[171] As Joseph Stalin famously put it, "[T]he death of a single Russian soldier is a tragedy. A million deaths is a statistic."[172] The problem is compounded in certain policy settings given the scale of potential consequences and the effort necessary to prevent them. Robert Weissman, president of Public Citizen, worries that under current frameworks "[t]he bigger picture is absent. How do you do cost benefit on global warming?"[173]

3. Do the preceding examples reflect irrational decision-making that policy leaders should strive to overcome? Or do they reflect inevitable, and to some extent commendable, tendencies to empathize with individuals whom we can visualize, and whose suffering is most cognitively "available?"[174] Some research suggests that the most significant reason for people's disproportionate concern for identifiable victims is that a high proportion of those apparently at risk can be saved. But as researchers point out, that factor bears no obvious normative relevance in policy making.[175] Yet telling people about their bias in favor of identifiable victims does not entirely solve the problem because it causes them to spend less on behalf of those victims rather than to spend more to save statistical lives.[176] In one telling experiment, subjects made lower financial contributions to famine relief when they received information about both an individual victim and statistics about hunger in Africa. Simply thinking about large numbers appeared to dampen the emotional responses that encouraged altruism.[177] In explaining these findings, social scientists note that what moves people to action is the emotion aroused by seeing a single suffering victim; focusing on facts and figures does not trigger the moral emotions that may be necessary to impel a compassionate response.[178]

4. What implications should policy leaders and heads of nonprofit organizations draw from such findings? What tradeoffs would you make between identifiable and statistical victims? Would you limit the resources you would invest in saving identifiable victims? On what basis?

END NOTES

[1] Peter Spiegel, *Rumsfeld Links Generals' Flak to Resentment over Shake-Ups*, L.A. TIMES, Apr. 19, 2006, at 14 (quoting Bush).

[2] MARTIN DEMPSEY & ORI BRAFMAN, RADICAL INCLUSION: WHAT THE POST-9/11 WORLD SHOULD HAVE TAUGHT US ABOUT LEADERSHIP 118 (2018).

[3] JONAH LEHRER, HOW WE DECIDE 159 (2009) (quoting Simon and citing research).

[4] Gerd Gigerenzer, *Heuristics*, in HEURISTICS AND THE LAW 17 (Gerd Gigerenzer & Christoph Engel eds., 2006).

[5] DANIEL KAHNEMAN, THINKING, FAST AND SLOW 21 (2011).

[6] MAX H. BAZERMAN, JUDGMENT IN MANAGERIAL DECISION MAKING 6 (2006).

[7] MONTGOMERY VAN WART, DYNAMICS OF LEADERSHIP IN THE PUBLIC SERVICE: THEORY AND PRACTICE 329-30 (2005).

[8] Joshua Rothman, *The Art of Decision-Making*, NEW YORKER, Jan. 21, 2019.

[9] VAN WART, DYNAMICS OF LEADERSHIP, 259-60. For a landmark formulation, see Charles E. Lindbloom, *The Science of Muddling Through*, 19 PUB. ADMIN. REV. 79 (1959).

[10] VAN WART, DYNAMICS OF LEADERSHIP, 260. For a classic description, see Amitai Etzioni, *Mixed-Scanning: A "Third" Approach to Decision-Making*, 27 PUB. ADMIN. REV. 385 (1967).

[11] RONALD A. HEIFETZ, ALEXANDER GRASHOW & MARTY LINSKY, THE PRACTICE OF ADAPTIVE LEADERSHIP: TOOLS AND TACTICS FOR CHANGING YOUR ORGANIZATION AND THE WORLD 257 (2009).

[12] PAUL BREST & LINDA HAMILTON KRIEGER, PROBLEM SOLVING, DECISION MAKING, AND PROFESSIONAL JUDGMENT: A GUIDE FOR LAWYERS AND POLICY MAKERS 289-293 (2010).

[13] CHIP HEATH & DAN HEATH, DECISIVE: HOW TO MAKE BETTER CHOICES IN LIFE AND WORK 11 (2013); John Beshears & Francesca Gino, *Leaders as Decision Architects*, HARV. BUS. REV. 57 (May 2015).

[14] KAHNEMAN, THINKING, FAST AND SLOW, 201. *See also* HEATH & HEATH, DECISIVE, 17.

[15] Beshears & Gino, *Leaders as Decision Architects*, 57; John R. Chapin & Grace Coleman, *Optimistic Bias: What You Think, What You Know, or Whom You Know*, 11 N. AM. J. PSYCHOL. 121 (2009): Neil D. Weinstein & William M. Klein, *Unrealistic Optimism: Present and Future*, 15 J. SOC. & CLINICAL PSYCHOL. 1 (1996).

[16] Beshears & Gino, *Leaders as Decision Architects*, 57; KAHNEMAN, THINKING, FAST AND SLOW, 119.

[17] KAHNEMAN, THINKING, FAST AND SLOW, 203; BREST & KRIEGER, PROBLEM SOLVING, DECISION MAKING, AND PROFESSIONAL JUDGMENT, 272-275.

[18] KAHNEMAN, THINKING, FAST AND SLOW, 203; Francesca Gino, Don A. Moore & Max H. Bazerman, *No Harm, No Foul: The Outcome Bias in Ethical Judgments*, (HARV. BUS. SCH. Working Paper, No. 08-080, 2009); Jonathan Baron, John C. Hershey, *Outcome Bias in Decision Evaluation*, 54 J. PERS. SOC. PSYCHOL. 569 (1988).

[19] Daniel Kahneman, Jack L. Knetsch & Richard H. Thaler, *Anomalies: The Endowment Effect, Loss Aversion, and Status Quo Bias*, in CHOICES, VALUES, AND FRAMES (Daniel Kahneman & Amos Tversky eds., 2000); Beshears & Gino, *Leaders as Decision Architects*, 57; MAX H. BAZERMAN & DON A. MOORE, JUDGMENT IN MANAGERIAL DECISION MAKING 55 (2013).

[20] BAZERMAN & MOORE, JUDGMENT IN MANAGERIAL DECISION MAKING, 71; Donelson Forsyth, *Self-Serving Bias*, INT'L ENCYCLOPEDIA OF SOC. SCI. (2007).

[21] BREST & KRIEGER, PROBLEM SOLVING, DECISION MAKING, AND PROFESSIONAL JUDGMENT, 421; Beshears & Gino, *Leaders as Decision Architects*, 57.

[22] Hal R. Arkes & Catherine Blumer, *The Psychology of Sunk Cost*, 35 ORG. BEHAV. & HUM. DECISION PROCESSES 124 (1985); Beshears & Gino, *Leaders as Decision Architects*, 57. For an argument that it is sometimes relevant to consider sunk costs, see R. Preston McAfee, Hugo Mialon & Sue H. Mialon, *Do Sunk Costs Matter?*, 48 ECON. INQ. 323 (2007).

[23] Dustin J. Sleesman, Donald E. Conlon, Gerry McNamara & Jonathan E. Miles, *Cleaning Up the Big Muddy: A Meta-Analytic Review of the Determinants of Escalation of Commitment*, 55 ACAD. MGMT. J. 541 (2012); Barry M. Staw, *The Escalation of Commitment: An Update and Appraisal*, in ORGANIZATIONAL DECISION MAKING 191 (Zur Shapira ed., 1997).

[24] David A Graham, *Rumsfeld's Known and Unknowns: The Intellectual History of a Quip*, ATLANTIC, Mar. 27, 2014.

[25] GARY KLEIN, SEEING WHAT OTHERS DON'T: THE REMARKABLE WAYS WE GAIN INSIGHTS (2013).

[26] Jack B. Soll, Katherine L. Milkman & John E. Payne, *Outsmart Your Own Biases*, HARV. BUS. REV. (May 2015).

[27] FRANCESCA GINO, SIDETRACKED: WHY OUR DECISIONS GET DERAILED, AND HOW WE CAN STICK TO THE PLAN 47 (2013).

[28] Leigh Plunkett Tost, Francesca Gino & Richard P. Larrick, *Power, Competitiveness, and Advice Taking: Why the Powerful Don't Listen*, 117 ORG. BEHAV. & HUM. DECISION PROCESSES 53, 54 (2012).

[29] ADAM GRANT, ORIGINALS: HOW NON-CONFORMISTS MOVE THE WORLD 197 (2016).

[30] Katherine L. Milkman, Dolly Chugh & Max H. Bazerman, *How Can Decision Making Be Improved?*, 4 PERSP. ON PSYCHOL. SCI. 379, 389-81(2009); BAZERMAN & MOORE, JUDGMENT IN MANAGERIAL DECISION MAKING, 194, 198-99.

[31] Jennifer S. Lerner & Philip E. Tetlock, *Accounting for the Effects of Accountability*, 125 PSYCH. BULL. 255 (199); BAZERMAN & MOORE, JUDGMENT IN MANAGERIAL DECISION MAKING, 79.

[32] Tost, Gino & Larrick, *Power, Competitiveness, and Advice Taking*, 63.

[33] GINO, SIDETRACKED, 61, 227.

[34] RICHARD H. THALER & CASS R. SUNSTEIN, NUDGE: IMPROVING DECISIONS ABOUT HEALTH, WEALTH, AND HAPPINESS (2008).

[35] Beshears & Gino, *Leaders as Decision Architects*, 60; HEATH & HEATH, DECISIVE, 209.

[36] HEATH & HEATH, DECISIVE, 25.

[37] HEATH & HEATH, DECISIVE, 69 (quoting Walton).

[38] HEATH & HEATH, DECISIVE, 99.

[39] HEATH & HEATH, DECISIVE, 190, 203.

[40] Remarks by President Obama on the Gulf Oil Spill, FEDERAL INFORMATION AND NEWS DISPATCH, May 27, 2010.

[41] David M. Messick & Max H. Bazerman, *Ethical Leadership and the Psychology of Decision Making*, 37 SLOAN MGMT. REV. 1, 4 (1996).

[42] Remarks by President Obama, 2.

[43] Frank Rich, *Don't Get Mad, Mr. President. Get Even*, N.Y. TIMES, June 6, 2010, at WK 10.

[44] National Commission on the BP Deepwater Horizon Oil Spill and Offshore Drilling (2011), https://www.govinfo.gov/content/pkg/GPO-OILCOMMISSION/pdf/GPO-OILCOMMISSION.pdf.

[45] *See* Michael T. Klare, *The Oil Catastrophe*, THE NATION, June 14, 2010, at 4, 6; Bryan Walsh, *The Spreading Stain*, TIME MAG., June 21, 2010, at 56; National Commission on the BP Deepwater Horizon Oil Spill.

[46] Ian Urbina, *At Issue in Gulf: Who Was in Charge*, N.Y. TIMES, June 6, 2010, at A1, 19 (quoting Odom).

[47] Michael Useem, *Decision Making as Leadership Foundation*, in HANDBOOK OF LEADERSHIP THEORY AND PRACTICE 507 (Nitin Nohria and Rakesh Khurana eds., 2010).

[48] Beshears & Gino, *Leaders as Decision Architects*, 58.

[49] MICHAEL USEEM, THE LEADERSHIP MOMENT: NINE TRUE STORIES OF TRIUMPH AND DISASTER AND THEIR LESSONS FOR US ALL 85-86 (1998), 85-86; Useem, *Decision Making*, 514.

[50] Useem, *Decision Making*, 514.

[51] Michael Lewis, *Obama's Way*, VANITY FAIR, Oct. 2012 (quoting Obama).

[52] Lewis, *Obama's Way*.

[53] Alicia Bassuk, *Leadership Crisis/Crisis Leadership*, HUFFINGTON POST (Oct. 12, 2017), https://www.huffpost.com/entry/leadership-crisiscrisis-leadership_b_59dfd639e4b09e31db97579e.

[54] Albert H. Hastorf & Hadley Cantril, *They Saw a Game: A Case Study*, 49 J. ABNORM. & SOC. PSYCHOL. 129 (1954).

[55] Nicholas Kristof, *You're Wrong! I'm Right!*, N.Y. TIMES, Feb. 18, 2018, SR9.

[56] Robert I. Sutton & Roderick M. Kramer, *Transforming Failure into Success: Impression Management, the Reagan Administration, and the Iceland Arms Control Talks*, in ORGANIZATIONS AND NATION-STATES: NEW PERSPECTIVES ON CONFLICT AND COOPERATION (Robert L. Kahn & Mayer N. Zald eds., 1990).

[57] *See, e.g.*, Linda Babcock, George Loewenstein, Samuel Issacharoff & Colin Camerer, *Biased Judgments of Fairness in Bargaining*, 85 AM. ECON. REV. 1337 (1995); Linda Babcock & George Loewenstein, *Explaining Bargaining Impasse: The Role of Self-Serving Biases*, 11 J. ECON. PERSPECTIVES 109 (1997).

[58] BAZERMAN & MOORE, JUDGMENT IN MANAGERIAL DECISION MAKING, 76.

[59] GINO, SIDETRACKED, 198.

[60] Michael Janofsky, *Scalia Refusing to Take Himself Off Cheney Case*, N.Y. TIMES, Mar. 19, 2004, at A1 (quoting Cheney).

[61] MAX H. BAZERMAN & ANN E. TENBRUNSEL, BLIND SPOTS: WHY WE FAIL TO DO WHAT'S RIGHT AND WHAT TO DO ABOUT IT 19 (2011).

[62] Slavisa Tasic, *Are Regulators Rational?* (Bruno Leoni Institute Working Paper); Matt Ridely, *Studying the Biases of Bureaucrats*, WALL ST. J., Oct. 23, 2010, at C4.

[63] Tasic, *Are Regulators Rational?*; Ridely, *Studying the Biases of Bureaucrats*, at C4.

[64] KATHRYN SCHULZ, BEING WRONG: ADVENTURES IN THE MARGIN OF ERROR 149 (2010).

[65] SCHULZ, BEING WRONG, 130.

[66] Kristof, *You're Wrong!*

[67] Arthur C. Brooks, *Our Culture of Contempt*, N.Y. TIMES, Mar. 3, 2019.

[68] HERMINIA IBARRA, ACT LIKE A LEADER, THINK LIKE A LEADER 90, 97 (2015).

[69] Don Van Natta Jr. & Abby Goodnough, *2 Cambridge Worlds Collide in Unlikely Meeting*, N.Y. TIMES, July 27, 2009, at A13.

[70] Van Natta Jr. & Goodnough, 2 *Cambridge Worlds Collide*, at A13.

[71] Van Natta Jr. & Goodnough, 2 *Cambridge Worlds Collide*, at A13.

[72] Van Natta Jr. & Goodnough, 2 *Cambridge Worlds Collide*, at A13.

[73] Abby Goodnough, *Harvard Professor Jailed; Officer Is Accused of Bias*, N.Y. TIMES, July 21, 2009, at A13.

[74] Gates Police Report (July 16, 2009), http://www.scribd.com/doc/17512830 /Gates-Police-Report.

[75] Goodnough, *Harvard Professor Jailed*, at A13.

[76] Van Natta Jr. & Goodnough, *2 Cambridge Worlds Collide*, at A13.

[77] *Henry Louis Gates Jr.: I'm Outraged* (Good Morning America, July 22, 2009), https://www.youtube.com/watch?v=AeRK_0lc3yQ.

[78] John Hechinger & Simmi Aujla, *Police Drop Charges Against Black Scholar*, WALL ST. J., July 22, 2009, at A6.

[79] Katharine Q. Seelye, *Obama Wades Into a Volatile Racial Issue*, N.Y. TIMES, July 23, 2009, https://www.nytimes.com/2009/07/23/us/23race.html.

[80] Anahad O'Connor, *Beer Summit Goes for a Second Round*, N.Y. TIMES, Oct. 30, 2009, http://thecaucus.blogs.nytimes.com/2009/10/30/beer-summit-goes-for-a-second-round/?scp=3&sq=obama%20%22acted%20stupidly%22%20blog&st=cse.

[81] Ben W. Heineman Jr., *A Due Process Teaching Moment—WASTED*, THE ATLANTIC, July 25, 2009, https://www.theatlantic.com/politics/archive/2009/07/a-due-process-teaching-moment-wasted/22124/.

[82] Heineman, *A Due Process Teaching Moment*.

[83] Jeff Zeleny, *Obama Expresses His Regrets on Gates Incident*, THE CAUCUS, N.Y. TIMES, July 24, 2009, http://thecaucus.blogs.nytimes.com/2009/07/24/obama-expresses-his-regrets-on-gates-incident/?apage = 4.

[84] Seelye, *Obama Wades into a Volatile Racial Issue*.

[85] Michael D. Shear & Yamiche Alcindor, *Finding His Voice on Race: Jolted by Deaths, Obama Abandoned His Early Reticence*, N.Y. TIMES, Jan. 15, 2017, 18.

[86] Id. (quoting Edward Robinson).

[87] The Borowitz Report, *Funny Times*, NEW YORKER, Sept. 2009, at 5.

[88] White House Beer Simulation (The Daily Show with Jon Stewart, July 30, 2009), http://www.cc.com/video-clips/oecqdo/the-daily-show-with-jon-stewart-white-house-beer-simulation.

[89] Top Ten Things Overheard at the White House Beer Summit (Late Show with David Letterman, July 30, 2009).

[90] Abby Goodnough, *Gates Reflects on Beers at the White House*, THE CAUCUS, N.Y. TIMES, July 31, 2009, http://thecaucus.blogs.nytimes.com/2009/07/31/gates-reflects-on-beers-at-the-white-house.

[91] Goodnough, *Gates Reflects on Beers at the White House*.

[92] Heineman, *A Due Process Teaching Moment*.

[93] Ken Auletta, *Non-Stop News*, NEW YORKER, June 25, 2010, at 38.

[94] Id. (quoting Jarrett).

[95] David Remnick, *It Happened Here*, NEW YORKER, Nov. 28, 2016, 63 (quoting Obama).

[96] Gardiner Harris & Mark Landler, *Obama Tells Mourning Dallas, "We Are Not as Divided as We Seem,"* N.Y. TIMES, July 11, 2016.

[97] Harris & Landler, *Obama Tells Mourning Dallas.*

[98] Harris & Landler, *Obama Tells Mourning Dallas.*

[99] ZACHARY SHORE, BLUNDER: WHY SMART PEOPLE MAKE BAD DECISIONS 14 (2008).

[100] SHORE, BLUNDER, 14.

[101] SCHULZ, BEING WRONG 3 (quoting Moliere).

[102] SCHULZ, BEING WRONG, 7-8.

[103] SCHULZ, BEING WRONG, 9.

[104] SCHULZ, BEING WRONG, 19

[105] SCHULZ, BEING WRONG, 107.

[106] SCHULZ, BEING WRONG, 107-08.

[107] SCHULZ, BEING WRONG, 233-34 (quoting Neufield).

[108] SCHULZ, BEING WRONG, 236-37 (quoting McGrath).

[109] SCHULZ, BEING WRONG, 238-39.

[110] SCHULZ, BEING WRONG, 304-05.

[111] SCHULZ, BEING WRONG, 308-09.

[112] RICHARD RORTY, PHILOSOPHY AND THE MIRROR OF NATURE 349 (1981); SCHULZ, BEING WRONG, 339.

[113] *See* Daniel J. Simons & Christopher Chabris's Gorilla Basketball Experiment clip, http://viscog.beckman.illinois.edu/grafs/demos/15.html, and http://www.youtube.com/watch?v=Ahg6qcgoay4.

[114] For an instructive review of Lewis' book and its lessons for decision-making in other contexts, see Richard H. Thaler & Cass R. Sunstein, *Who's on First*, NEW REPUBLIC, Aug. 31, 2003.

[115] Billions, Season One, https://www.youtube.com/watch?v=MfC54kLXNQg.

[116] Harold J. Leavitt, *Suppose We Took Groups Seriously*, in MAN AND WORK IN SOCIETY 67-77 (Eugene L. Cass & Frederick G. Zimmer eds., 1975).

[117] Janis revised his 1972 book in an expanded 1982 version. IRVING L JANIS, GROUPTHINK: PSYCHOLOGICAL STUDIES OF POLICY DECISIONS AND FIASCOES (1982).

[118] CASS R. SUNSTEIN & REID HASTIE, WISER: GETTING BEYOND GROUPTHINK TO MAKE GROUPS SMARTER (2015), adapted in Cass R. Sunstein & Reid Hastie, *Making Dumb Groups Smarter*, HARV. BUS. REV. 92 (Dec. 2014).

[119] Sunstein & Hastie, *Making Dumb Groups Smarter*, 92.

[120] Sunstein & Hastie, *Making Dumb Groups Smarter*, 92.

[121] ANTHONY C. THOMPSON, DANGEROUS LEADERS: HOW AND WHY LAWYERS MUST BE TAUGHT TO LEAD 53 (2018).

[122] ADAM GRANT, ORIGINALS: HOW NON-CONFORMISTS MOVE THE WORLD 184 (2016); Michael L. McDonald & James D. Westphal, *Getting By with the Advice of Their Friends: CEOS' Advice Networks and Firms' Strategic Responses to Poor Performance*, 48 ADMIN. SCI. Q. 1 (2003).

[123] GRANT, ORIGINALS, 192-193; Stefan Schulz-Hardt, Marc Jochims & Dieter Frey, *Productive Conflict in Group Decision Making: Genuine and Contrived Dissent as Strategies to Counteract Biased Information Seeking*, 88 ORG. BEHAV. & HUM. DECISION PROCESSES 563 (2002).

124 Paul Brest, *Quis Custodiet Ipsos Custodes?: Debiasing the Policy Makers Themselves*, in THE BEHAVIORAL FOUNDATIONS OF POLICY (Eldar Shafir ed., 2014).

125 *The Space Shuttle: Old, Unsafe, and Costly*, THE ECON., Aug. 28, 2003.

126 REPORT OF THE SELECT COMMITTEE ON INTELLIGENCE ON THE U.S. INTELLIGENCE COMMUNITY'S PREWAR INTELLIGENCE ASSESSMENTS ON IRAQ, 108TH CONG. 2D. SESS., S. REP. NO. 106-301, 18 (July 9, 2004).

127 Brest, *Quis Custodiet Ipsos Custodes?*

128 FRANK RICH, THE GREATEST STORY EVER SOLD: THE DECLINE AND FALL OF TRUTH FROM 9/11 TO KATRINA 97 (2016).

129 HAROLD H. BRUFF, BAD ADVICE: BUSH'S LAWYERS IN THE WAR ON TERROR (2009).

130 REPORT OF THE SELECT COMMITTEE, 22.

131 CAROL TAVRIS & ELLIOT ARONSON, MISTAKES WERE MADE (BUT NOT BY ME): WHY WE JUSTIFY FOOLISH BELIEFS, BAD DECISIONS, AND HURTFUL ACTS 19 (2007).

132 Brendan Nyhan & Jason Reifler, *When Corrections Fail: The Persistence of Political Misperceptions*, 32 POL. BEHAV. 303, 313-15, 323 (2010). For other research, see Joe Keohane, *How Facts Backfire*, BOSTON GLOBE, July 11, 2010.

133 DORIS KEARNS GOODWIN, TEAM OF RIVALS: THE POLITICAL GENIUS OF ABRAHAM LINCOLN (2005).

134 DAVID REMNICK, THE BRIDGE: THE LIFE AND RISE OF BARACK OBAMA 209 (2011).

135 REMNICK, THE BRIDGE, 206 (quoting Christopher Edley).

136 LIZ WISEMAN WITH GREG MCKEOWN, MULTIPLIERS: HOW THE BEST LEADERS MAKE EVERYONE SMARTER (2010).

137 WISEMAN WITH MCKEOWN, MULTIPLIERS (quoting David Brooks).

138 Peter Wallsten & Jonathan Weisman, *Pressure Builds on Obama to Shake Up Inner Circle*, WALL ST. J., Nov. 2, 2010, at A4.

139 BOB WOODWARD, STATE OF DENIAL: BUSH AT WAR, PART III 11 (2007) (quoting Frontline interview with Bush).

140 Doris Kearns Goodwin, *Teddy vs. Trump: The Art of the Square Deal,* VANITY FAIR, Nov. 2018, at 76 (quoting Trump).

141 *See* sources cited in Roland Bénabou, *Groupthink: Collective Delusions in Organizations and Markets*, (National Bureau of Economic Research Working Paper 14764, March 2009), and sources cited in notes 62, 63, 65, and 66.

142 David Leonhardt, *If Fed Missed This Bubble. Will It See a New One?*, N.Y. TIMES, Jan. 6, 2010, at A1.

143 Robert J. Shiller, *Challenging the Crowd in Whispers, Not Shouts*, N.Y. TIMES, Nov. 2, 2008, at BU5. Shiller was a member of an economic advisory panel for the Federal Reserve Bank of New York.

144 For wishful thinking, see Bénabou, *Groupthink*; for the commitment to deregulation, see Carol A. Needham, *Listening to Cassandra: The Difficulty of Recognizing Risks and Taking Action*, 78 FORDHAM L. REV. 2329 (2010).

145 Malcolm Gladwell, *Cocksure: Banks, Battles, and the Psychology of Overconfidence*, NEW YORKER, Jul. 20, 2009, at 28.

146 Jonah Lehrer, *Microscopic Microeconomics*, N.Y. TIMES MAG., Oct. 31, 2010.

147 SUSAN CAIN, QUIET 157 (2012).

148 LEHER, HOW WE DECIDE, 218 (quoting Sloan).

[149] Seth Hettena, *Ready for the Next Scandal*, AM. LAW., Oct. 2010, at 17.

[150] Matt Richtel, *Hewlett Packard Settles Spying Case*, N.Y. TIMES, Feb. 14, 2008.

[151] *See* the discussion in Deborah L. Rhode, *Where Is the Leadership in Moral Leadership?*, excerpted in Chapter 5.

[152] Damon Darlin, *Adviser Urges H.P. to Focus on Ethics over Legalities*, N.Y. TIMES, Oct. 4, 2006, at C3 (quoting Schwartz).

[153] HEARING BEFORE THE SUBCOMMITTEE ON OVERSIGHT AND INVESTIGATIONS OF THE HOUSE COMMITTEE ON ENERGY AND COMMERCE, HEWLETT-PACKARD'S PRETEXTING SCANDAL, 109TH CONG. 13 (2006).

[154] PETER J. BURKE ET AL., ADVANCES IN IDENTITY THEORY AND RESEARCH (2003); Sheldon Stryker & Peter J. Burke, *The Past, Present, and Future of an Identity Theory*, 63 SOC. PSYCHOL. Q. 28 (2000); Cassandra Burke Robertson, *Judgment, Identity and Independence*, 42 CONN. L. REV. 1, 14-20 (2009).

[155] Hugh Gunz & Sally Gunz, *Hired Professional to Hired Gun: An Identity Theory Approach to Understanding the Ethical Behavior of Professionals in Non-Professional Organizations*, 60 HUM. REL. 851, 882-86 (2007).

[156] Mark Hurd, *Prepared Statement Before the Subcommittee on Oversight and Investigations*, COMM. ON ENERGY AND COMMERCE, U.S. HOUSE OF REPRESENTATIVES, Sept. 28, 2006.

[157] Liza Porteus, *"Group Think" Led to Iraq WMD Assessment*, FOXNEWS.COM, July 11, 2004.

[158] TRANSCRIPT OF MARK HURD'S ORAL REMARKS BEFORE THE HOUSE OF REPRESENTATIVES ENERGY AND COMMERCE OVERSIGHT AND INVESTIGATIONS SUBCOMMITTEE (Sept. 28, 2006); Video: Hewlett-Packard Investigation (C-SPAN, Sept. 28, 2006), http://www.c-spanvideo.org /program/id/164745. For Dunn's testimony, see http://www.cbsnews.com/video/ watch/?id=2069751n.

[159] The segment aired on *This American Life*, "Crybabies," Episode 415 (WBEZ Chicago, Sept. 24, 2010), https://www.thisamericanlife.org/415/crybabies.

[160] For Ford's calculation and liability, see DEBORAH L. RHODE & DAVID LUBAN, LEGAL ETHICS 394-95 (2009). For federal figures, see Marianne Lavelle, *Placing a Price on Human Life*, NAT'L L.J., Oct. 10, 1988, at 1, 28-29. The low figure came from proposed regulations on space heaters; the high estimate came from an FDA decision to ban DES pesticide in cattle feed.

[161] Lavelle, *Placing a Price*, 28.

[162] Gary T. Schwartz, *The Myth of the Ford Pinto Case*, 43 RUTGERS L. REV. 1032 (1990-1991).

[163] BAZERMAN & TENBRUNSEL, BLIND SPOTS, 161.

[164] DOUGLAS BIRSCH & JOHN H. FIELDER, THE FORD PINTO CASE: A STUDY IN APPLIED ETHICS, BUSINESS, AND TECHNOLOGY 23 (1994).

[165] The Tesla Team, *A Tragic Loss* (June 30, 2016), https://www.tesla.com /blog/tragic-loss.

[166] Jan Dawson, *Tesla's Bigger Risk from the Autopilot Crash Is the Story Line Surrounding Self-Driving Cars*, MARKETWATCH.COM (July 17, 2016), http://www.marketwatch.com/story/teslas-bigger-risk-from-the-autopilot-crash-is-the-story-line-surrounding-self-driving-cars-2016-07-13.

[167] Dawson, *Tesla's Bigger Risk*.

[168] Greg Gardner, *What Tesla Autopilot Crash Means for Self-Driving Cars*, USA TODAY (July 17, 2016), http://www.usatoday.com/story/money/cars/2016/07/17/what-tesla-autopilot-crash-means-self-driving-cars/87219126/.

[169] Gardner, *What Tesla Autopilot Crash Means*.

[170] Karen E. Jenni & George Loewenstein, *Explaining the "Identifiable Victim Effect,"* 14 J. RISK & UNCERTAINTY 235 (1997). In 1987, people gave $700,000 in unsolicited funds to the family of Baby Jessica, who was trapped for 58 hours in a Texas well. *See "Baby Jessica" 20 Years Later*, TODAY (June 11, 2007), https://highered.nbclearn.com/portal/site/HigherEd/flatview?cuecard=58817.

[171] James Friedrich et al., *Psychophysical Numbing: When Lives Are Valued Less as the Lives at Risk Increase*, 8 J. CONSUMER PSYCHOL. 227, 285 (1999).

[172] RICHARD E. NISBETT & LEE ROSS, HUMAN INFERENCE: STRATEGIES AND SHORTCOMINGS OF SOCIAL JUDGMENT 43 (1980) (quoting Stalin).

[173] Id. (quoting Robert Weissman).

[174] For the social value of the identifiable victim response, see Douglas A. Kysar et al., *Group Report: Are Heuristics a Problem or a Solution?*, in HEURISTICS AND THE LAW 135 (Gigerenzer & Engel eds., 2006) (suggesting that the preference is socially "useful nonsense").

[175] Jenni & Loewenstein, *Explaining the Identifiable Victim Effect*, 254.

[176] Deborah A. Small, George Loewenstein & Paul Slovic, *Sympathy and Callousness: The Impact of Deliberative Thought on Donations to Identifiable and Statistical Victims*, 102 ORG. BEHAV. & HUM. DECISION PROCESSES 143 (2007).

[177] DAN ARIELY, THE UPSIDE OF IRRATIONALITY: THE UNEXPECTED BENEFITS OF DEFYING LOGIC 248 (2010); LEHRER, HOW WE DECIDE 188.

[178] BARRY SCHWARTZ & KENNETH SHARPE, PRACTICAL WISDOM: THE RIGHT WAY TO DO THE RIGHT THING 75-76 (2010).

CHAPTER 4

INFLUENCE

If, as Chapter 1 suggested, the core of leadership is influence, a key issue is how best to achieve it. What resources are available and what strategies are most effective? How do leaders influence followers? How do followers influence—or circumvent—leaders? How do those in positions of authority foster innovation and manage conflict? How do they communicate most persuasively?

A. FORMS OF INFLUENCE

As is clear from the readings below and the discussion of soft power in Chapter 1, the currency of influence can come in many forms. Strategies fall across a spectrum. Leaders compel, intimidate, pressure, bribe, negotiate, model, persuade, consult, co-opt, and inspire. They exercise such influence at personal, group, and organizational levels, with varying degrees of success. Influence comes from both the power of position (such as control over resources, rewards, sanctions, and information) and the power of the person (through experience, relationships, and loyalty).[1] Recent research identifies forms of influence that cluster under the following primary categories: authority, reciprocity, social influence, and association.

1. AUTHORITY

The most obvious source of influence stems from position: the power to reward and punish. This power does not need to be explicit to be effective. Colin Powell reportedly claimed that he never had to say, "This is an order." His authority was implicit in his position. Nor is leverage restricted to obvious forms of benefits and sanctions, such as promotions, bonuses, dismissals, or discipline. Authority can arise from the credibility that attaches to a particular status. Prominent examples include the doctors who received undeserved deference from nurses in the study that psychologist Robert Cialdini discusses below, and the researchers in the famous obedience experiments by Stanley Milgram, reviewed in Chapter 6. In Cialdini's example, 95 percent of nurses were willing to administer a dangerous dose of an unauthorized drug at a doctor's direction. In Milgram's experiments, two-thirds of subjects were prepared to deliver ostensibly dangerous levels of electric shocks when a person in authority gave them orders to do so. Such results speak volumes about people's willingness to obey leaders even in the absence of hard power.

2. RECIPROCITY

One of the most effective forms of soft power is reciprocity, an impulse that sociobiologists argue is hardwired through evolution. A widely shared and deeply held sense of obligation to return favors has been adaptive for human survival because it encourages individuals to share food, care, defense, and other forms of assistance.[2] Sociologists and anthropologists have documented the pervasiveness of this impulse in virtually every society, and psychologists have identified its influence in a wide variety of contemporary exchanges. For example, in one famous experiment by Cornell professor Dennis Regan, subjects bought twice as many raffle tickets when an experimenter did them a small unsolicited favor—bringing them a bottle of Coke during a break. Unlike other subjects, who had received no favor and whose purchase of raffle tickets was affected by how much they liked the experimenter, those who had received the drink felt a sense of obligation to repay the favor irrespective of how they felt about the experimenter.[3] Behavioral economists note a similar dynamic at work in circumstances modeled in the game "Ultimatum." There, one person (the proposer) receives ten dollars and a partner (the responder) receives nothing. The proposer suggests how the money should be divided and the responder can accept or reject the division. If he or she rejects it, both players walk away with nothing. Although, in theory, responders would benefit by receiving any amount, in practice they refuse what seems unjust. Anticipating that reaction, proposers typically offer around five dollars.[4] In *Influence: The Psychology of Persuasion*, Cialdini explores how reciprocity functions in real-world settings. For example, marketers have substantially increased response rates to surveys or charitable appeals by enclosing a nominal payment or gift, and sellers achieve similar results through free samples.[5] Another example is "reciprocity rings," in which participants present a request to a group and members respond with knowledge, resources, and connections to try and fulfill it. First developed for university classes, rings are now used by major companies such as IBM, Citigroup, UPS, Novartis, and Boeing. Many participants initially have reservations and are astonished to find how many people help in so many ways, both personal and professional. Givers make four contributions on average; takers give three times more than they get.[6]

Reciprocity is similarly effective in many leadership contexts. In politics, it underpins lobbying, campaign contributions, and legislative coalitions. Lyndon Johnson was legendary for his ability to trade favors when seeking support for policy initiatives.[7] The importance of "pay to play" in lobbying activities is well illustrated by a famous statement by banker and financier Charles Keating, who served prison time for assisting fraudulent conduct by savings and loans institutions. When asked whether a connection existed between the $1.3 million he had contributed to the campaigns of five U.S. senators and their subsequent interventions on his behalf with federal regulators, he responded, "I certainly hope so."[8] The same impulse is at work in current American foreign relations. Many nations receive substantial economic and military aid in exchange for their assistance in the war against terrorism and other U.S. policy objectives.

More subtle forms of reciprocity also underpin relationships between leaders and followers. When subordinates help superiors look good or perform well, superiors often respond in kind, not only through pay and promotions but also with verbal recognition, mentoring, and personal support. Leaders and aspiring leaders can similarly build loyalty by sharing information, credit, and other forms of recognition. Robert Kennedy was famous for motivating lower-level Justice Department employees to "pla[y] over their heads" by getting them invitations to the White House, sending notes to those who worked on holidays, and calling to congratulate those who achieved some small victory.[9] In *The Seven Habits of Highly Effective People*, Steven Covey advises cultivating a "mentality of abundance" in allocating rewards and recognition.[10] Flattery, even when transparent, is often effective partly because it evokes norms of reciprocity. When people give us compliments, our natural inclination is to respond in kind and to look for corresponding ways to think well of them.[11] Dacher Keltner, an influential expert on power, emphasizes three practices essential to effective leadership and organizational performance: empathy, gratitude, and generosity.[12]

3. SOCIAL INFLUENCE

As is clear from research summarized in Chapters 3 and 6, individuals are highly susceptible to social influence, which psychologists variously label "social proof" or "conformity." Some of the influence stems from self-doubt, and some from individuals' desire for social approval and inclusion. Particularly in contexts of imperfect information, individuals rely on the behaviors of others for cues or social proof about what is appropriate, and their desire for affiliation and a positive self-concept encourages them to conform.[13] The result in circumstances of collective decision-making is often the kind of groupthink described in the previous chapter. But the dynamic also affects individuals' behavior even when they have reason for confidence in their own judgments. In Solomon Asch's famous experiment asking subjects which of several lines was the same length as another "standard" line, about four-fifths of the subjects gave at least one wrong answer in order to conform to incorrect answers given by other members of a group.[14] When asked later about their reasons, some subjects acknowledged that they knowingly gave a wrong answer just to go along with the group; others reported that they thought that they must somehow have been misunderstanding the nature of the task. The same dynamic is apparent in famous *Candid Camera* scenes. In one, a man in an elevator, when surrounded by actors facing the wrong way, eventually turns around as well. In another, passengers in an airport are told that they need to lie down on a conveyor belt to go through a scanner. Eleven of twelve do so.[15] Someone responding to an advertisement for research, when surrounded by people who begin disrobing, does so as well without even asking for an explanation.[16] In *Thinking, Fast and Slow,* Daniel Kahneman summarizes research finding that "people can maintain an unshakable faith in any proposition, however absurd, when they are sustained by a community of like-minded believers."[17]

Leaders can harness social norms to encourage desirable behaviors. For example, a famous study demonstrated that the most effective way to encourage hotel guests to reuse their towels was providing a card asking them to "join your fellow guests in helping to save the environment" and telling them that a majority of guests reused their towels. This message was more effective than asking them to "help save the environment."[18] Similarly, a large-scale survey of residential energy users found that although users listed the actions of others as the least important influence on their own conservation behavior, compared with benefitting society or the environment or saving money, in fact, the belief that others were conserving was much more predictive of reported energy-saving efforts than other motivations.[19] People are most influenced by behaviors of those who are similar to them and are most open to such influence under conditions of uncertainty.[20]

4. ASSOCIATION

A final form of influence comes from association bias, which makes a message or messenger's impact depend on its relationship with events and individuals that evoke positive or negative reactions. The association principle can affect leaders' effectiveness in several ways. Positive spillover can come from endorsements by well-respected and well-connected individuals. So, for example, leaders who are seeking change within an organization or community can benefit from having such individuals become "early adopters" and speak in its favor. As experts note, "[I]nfluence is often best exerted horizontally rather than vertically."[21] Pleasant experiences at events can also have positive effects, which is why so many business dollars are spent on dining.

Negative spillover can be equally powerful. Leaders have to worry about both being damned by association and being shielded from information by others who do not want to be the bearer of unwelcome messages. In the excerpt below, Robert Cialdini describes a powerful example of association bias at work, as well as a chilling case study on the significance of authority.

ROBERT B. CIALDINI, INFLUENCE: THE PSYCHOLOGY OF PERSUASION

(New York: Harper Collins, 2007),
pp. 188-190 and 224-225

[Shakespeare captured the essence of the association bias] with one vivid line. "The nature of bad news," he said, "infects the teller." There is a natural human tendency to dislike a person who brings us unpleasant information, even when that person did not cause the bad news. The simple association with it is enough to stimulate our dislike. . . . [Consider the following example.]

Television weather forecasters make a good living talking about the weather, but when Mother Nature throws a curve ball, they duck for cover.

Conversations with several veteran prognosticators across the country this week turned up stories of them being whacked by old ladies with umbrellas, accosted by drunks in bars, pelted with snowballs and galoshes, threatened with death, and accused of trying to play God [or ruining a daughter's wedding].

"I had one guy call and tell me that if it snowed over Christmas, I wouldn't live to see New Year's," said [one weather reporter]. . . .

Most of the forecasters claimed they are accurate 80 percent to 90 percent of the time on one-day forecasts, but longer-range predictions get tricky. And most conceded they are simply reporting information supplied by computers and anonymous meteorologists from the National Weather Service or a private agency.

But it's the face on the television screen that people go after. . . .

As for the positive associations, . . . [consider how marketers are] incessantly trying to connect themselves or their products with the things we like. Did you ever wonder what all those good-looking models are doing standing around in the automobile ads? What the advertiser hopes they are doing is lending their positive traits—beauty and desirability—to the cars. The advertiser is betting that we will respond to the product in the same ways we respond to the attractive models merely associated with it.

And they are right. In one study, men who saw a new-car ad that included a seductive young woman model rated the car as faster, more appealing, more expensive looking, and better designed than did men who viewed the same ad without the model. Yet when asked later, the men refused to believe that the presence of the young woman had influenced their judgments. [The association bias is why celebrities are paid to peddle even products wholly irrelevant to their role] (soft drinks, popcorn poppers, panty hose). The important thing for the advertiser is to establish the connection; it doesn't have to be a logical one, just a positive one. . . .

[Authority can also exert profound influence. Consider the following example.] A group of researchers, composed of doctors and nurses with connections to three Midwestern hospitals, became increasingly concerned with the extent of mechanical obedience to doctors' orders on the part of nurses. . . . To twenty-two separate nurses' stations on various surgical, medical, pediatric, and psychiatric wards, one of the researchers made an identical phone call in which he identified himself as a hospital physician and directed the answering nurse to give twenty milligrams of a drug (Astrogen) to a specific ward patient. There were four excellent reasons for a nurse's caution in response to this order: (1) The prescription was transmitted by phone, in direct violation of hospital policy. (2) The medication itself was unauthorized; Astrogen had not been cleared for use nor placed on the ward stock list. (3) The prescribed dosage was obviously and dangerously excessive. The medication containers clearly stated that the "maximum daily dose" was only ten milligrams, half of what had been ordered. (4) The directive was given by a man the nurse had never met, seen, or even talked with before on the phone. Yet, in 95 percent of the instances, the nurses went straightaway to the ward medicine cabinet, where they secured the ordered dosage of Astrogen and started for the patient's room to administer it. It was at this point that they were stopped by a secret observer, who revealed the nature of the experiment. . . .

The following excerpt focuses on the role of social proof in skewing behavior, and on strategies that can counteract it.

PAUL BREST AND LINDA HAMILTON KRIEGER, PROBLEM SOLVING, DECISION MAKING, AND PROFESSIONAL JUDGMENT: A GUIDE FOR LAWYERS AND POLICYMAKERS

(New York: Oxford University Press, 2010), pp. 545-546, 554, and 556

Social Proof and Professional and Corporate Malfeasance

Many "ethical train wrecks" in law and business can be traced, at least in part, to social proof effects. Consider, for example, the ruin of in-house Enron lawyer Kristina Mordaunt, described by Kurt Eichenwald in his book, *Conspiracy of Fools*. In 2001, Ms. Mordaunt played a minor role in working out "LJM1," one of the shady partnerships (known in accountant-speak as a "special purpose entity") that had been used to manipulate Enron's apparent financial performance and enrich certain Enron executives. LJM1's status as a valid special purpose entity, which accorded it favorable accounting treatment, was highly questionable. But from Mordaunt's point of view, the relevant accounting rules were ambiguous, the deal had been approved by Enron financial officers and accountants, and the executives who had put it together were rising stars in one of the country's best-regarded corporations.

A short time after her work on LMJ1 was completed, Mordaunt was off-handedly asked by Enron Treasurer, Ben Glisan, Jr., whether she wanted to invest $10,000 in a similar special purpose entity, known by Enron insiders as "Southampton." She ended up investing only $5,800, but a few weeks later, when the Southampton deal wound down, she found in her bank account a return of over a million dollars. Weeks later, her career was ruined, and by the middle of 2002, prosecutors had filed a forfeiture action to seize her home and car.

It is easy—perhaps too easy—to conclude that Mordaunt was a knowing participant in a patently fraudulent scheme who got precisely what she deserved. But Eichenwald suggests an alternative explanation. Caught up in a web of mind-numbingly complex and ambiguous accounting rules, and watching apparently well-respected, successful high level executives participating in complex transactions like LJM1 and Southampton, Mordaunt could easily have concluded that the deals were legitimate, and that she was doing nothing wrong. The "proof" was all around her, in the actions of her superiors and colleagues.

The social proof phenomenon can explain lawyers' passive acquiescence in client misconduct in various legal contexts. For example, Donald C. Langevoort suggests that it can explain attorney inaction in the face of client fraud:

> [A]n attorney who is new to a situation, especially an inexperienced one, is particularly prone to rely on social learning as the basis for constructing a schema. The fact that those more senior and more familiar with the situation are behaving as if there is no problem provides a strong cue. This, indeed, is one explanation for the reduced tendency of people in groups to act heroically, since responsibility is effectively diffused. To this, naturally, must be added the situational pressures on junior members of groups to conform to apparent norms. . . .

Defusing the Impulses toward Obedience

. . . Psychologists Philip Zimbardo and Michael Lieppe suggest [the following approaches to inoculating oneself against automatic obedience]:

- remain engaged with alternate systems of authority, such as a those deriving from one's religious, spiritual, political, or philosophical commitments;
- trust your intuition when you find yourself thinking, "something is wrong here";
- when in doubt, seek out a knowledgeable—but independent—person to give you an "obedience check";
- mentally rehearse disobedience strategies and techniques for various situations;
- be particularly vigilant when you notice people using euphemisms to describe harmful behaviors or the people they harm;
- don't expect not to suffer adverse consequences when refusing to obey an authority figure—rather, consider the worst case scenario and act on that possibility;
- chose [sic] carefully the organizations and situations in which you place yourself, because it's all too easy to overestimate your powers to resist.

NOTES AND QUESTIONS

1. Might other dynamics besides social proof have been at work in explaining Mordaunt's conduct? Recall the material on self-serving cognitive biases in Chapter 3. In *The Smartest Guys in the Room,* a documentary on Enron, interviews with former employees suggest that part of what accounted for some extremely stupid decisions by some very intelligent leaders was the enormous amount of money they stood to gain from discounting risks and cutting ethical corners. Consider how psychological factors worked in tandem with skewed reward structures discussed in Chapter 5.

2. An increasing number of organizations are attempting to harness social proof in the service of progressive social change. For example, after a popular soap opera in Mexico City showed characters seeking adult literacy materials, a quarter million viewers did the same. A radio play in Tanzania had similar impact in changing AIDS prevention behavior among a quarter of the population in its broadcast area.[22] Can you identify similar efforts or opportunities in this country?

The currencies of influence come in many forms, and the following excerpt details the wide range of strategies available even to individuals who lack formal positions of authority. Consider how some of these currencies might have assisted you in a situation in which you failed to exercise as much influence as you hoped.

DAVID L. BRADFORD AND ALLAN COHEN, INFLUENCE WITHOUT AUTHORITY

Organizational Dynamics, American Management Association, Winter 1989, pp. 5-17

Currencies: The Source of Influence

If the basis of organizational influence depends on mutually satisfactory exchanges, then people are influential only insofar as they can offer something that others need. Thus power comes from the ability to meet others' needs.

A useful way to think of how the process of exchange actually works in organizations is to use the metaphor of "currencies." This metaphor provides a powerful way to conceptualize what is important to the influencer and the person to be influenced. Just as many types of currencies are traded in the world financial market, many types are "traded" in organizational life. Too often people think only of money or promotion and status. Those "currencies," however, usually are available only to a manager in dealing with his or her employees. Peers who want to influence colleagues or employees who want to influence their supervisors often feel helpless. They need to recognize that many types of payments exist, broadening the range of what can be exchanged.

Some major currencies that are commonly valued and traded in organizations are listed in Exhibit 1. Although not exhaustive, the list makes evident that a person does not have to be at the top of an organization or have hands on the formal levers of power to command multiple resources that others may value.

Part of the usefulness of currencies comes from their flexibility. For example, there are many ways to express gratitude and to give assistance. A manager who most values the currency of appreciation could be paid through verbal thanks, praise, a public statement at a meeting, informal comments to his peers, and/or a note to her boss. However, the same note of thanks seen by one person as a sign of appreciation may be seen by another person as an attempt to brownnose or by a third person as a cheap way to try to repay extensive favors and service. Thus currencies have value not in some abstract sense but as defined by the receiver.

Although we have stressed the interactive nature of exchange, "payments" do not always have to be made by the other person. They can be self-generated to fit beliefs about being virtuous, benevolent, or committed to the organization's welfare. Someone may respond to another person's request because it reinforces cherished values, a sense of identity, or feelings of self-worth. The exchange is interpersonally stimulated because the one who wants influence has set up conditions that allow this kind of self-payment to occur by asking for cooperation to accomplish organizational goals. . . .

Of course, the five categories of currencies listed in Exhibit 1 are not mutually exclusive. When the demand from the other person is high, people are likely to pay in several currencies across several categories. They may, for example, stress the organizational value of their request, promise to return the favor at a later time, imply that it will increase the other's prestige in the organization, and express their appreciation. . . .

Exhibit 1
Commonly Traded Organizational Currencies

Inspiration-Related Currencies

Vision	Being involved in a task that has larger significance for the unit, organization, customers, or society
Excellence	Having a chance to do important things really well
Moral/Ethical Correctness	Doing what is "right" by a higher standard than efficiency

Task-Related Currencies

Resources	Lending or giving money, budget increases, personnel, space, and so forth
Assistance	Helping with existing projects or undertaking unwanted tasks
Cooperation	Giving task support, providing quicker response time, approving a project, or aiding implementation

Position-Related Currencies

Advancement	Giving a task or assignment that can aid in promotion
Recognition	Acknowledging effort, accomplishment, or abilities
Visibility	Providing the chance to be known by higher-ups or significant others in the organization
Reputation	Enhancing the way a person is seen
Importance/Insiderness	Offering a sense of importance, of "belonging"
Network/Contacts	Providing opportunities for linking with others

Relationship-Based Currencies

Acceptance/Inclusion	Providing closeness and friendship
Personal Support	Giving personal and emotional backing
Understanding	Listening to others' concerns and issues

Personal-Related Currencies

Self-Concept	Affirming one's values, self-esteem, and identity
Challenge/Learning	Sharing tasks that increase skills and abilities
Ownership/Involvement	Letting others have ownership and influence
Gratitude	Expressing appreciation or indebtedness

The Process of Exchange

To make the exchange process effective, the influencer needs to (1) think about the person to be influenced as a potential ally, not an adversary; (2) know the world of the potential ally, including the pressures as well as the person's needs and goals; (3) be aware of key goals and available resources that may be valued by the potential ally; and (4) understand the exchange transaction itself so that win-win outcomes are achieved. . . . Unfortunately, people desiring influence are not always aware of precisely what they want. . . . They fail to think through which aspects are more important and which can be jettisoned if necessary. . . .

All of the preceding discussion needs to be conditioned by one important variable: the nature of the relationship between both parties. The greater the extent to which the influencer has worked with the potential ally and created trust, the easier the exchange process will be. Each party will know the other's desired currencies and situational pressures, and each will have developed a mutually productive interaction style. With trust, less energy will be spent on figuring out the intentions of the ally, and there will be less suspicion about when and how the payback will occur.

A poor relationship (based on previous interactions, on the reputation each party has in the organization, and/or on stereotypes and animosities between the functions or departments that each party represents) will impede an otherwise easy exchange. Distrust of the goodwill, veracity, or reliability of the influencer can lead to the demand for "no credit; cash up front," which constrains the flexibility of both parties. . . .

Few transactions within organizations are one-time deals. (Who knows when the other person may be needed again or even who may be working for him or her in the future?) Thus in most exchange situations two outcomes matter: success in achieving task goals and success in improving the relationship so that the next interaction will be even more productive. Too often, people who want to be influential focus only on the task and act as if there is no tomorrow. Although both task accomplishment and an improved relationship cannot always be realized at the same time, on some occasions the latter can be more important than the former. Winning the battle but losing the war is an expensive outcome. . . .

PROBLEM 4-1

Break into pairs. Construct a situation in which one of you attempts to persuade the other to alter some workplace behavior. Reverse roles. Which strategies were most and least effective? What might you do differently?

NOTES

Research suggests that the effectiveness of various forms of influence depends on three conditions. First, the individuals whom a leader seeks to influence must believe that their efforts can bring the desired results—that they have the necessary ability, training, resources, clarity about assignment, and so forth. Second, they have to believe that there will be an accurate linkage between performance and rewards or sanctions—for example, that shirking will be detected or that they, not just their supervisor, will reap the benefits of a job well done. Third, they have to fear or value the sanctions or rewards that are likely to follow. In some job settings, particularly those in the public and nonprofit sectors, additional compensation may be a less effective motivator than other factors such as job security or flexibility, recognition, challenge, and opportunities for professional development and making a meaningful contribution.[23] For example, what drives high satisfaction for mid-level law firm associates is interesting work, relations with colleagues, and support for pro bono involvement.[24] Some reward systems backfire because they are based on results that can be manipulated by dysfunctional behaviors or because workers perceive them as arbitrary. This dynamic, famously described as the "folly of rewarding A while hoping for B," explains why focusing only on productivity can lead to problems of quality and efficiency.[25] Among lawyers, high billable hour requirements can lead to padding, meter running, and other fee-related abuses.[26] Introducing fines for parents who were late to pick up their children at daycare were also counterproductive because they replaced a sense of moral obligation with a cost-benefit calculation.[27] Employee-of-the-month programs have led to widespread resentment from those who felt they should have won.[28] Such research underscores the importance of knowing, not simply assuming, what factors will be most effective in a given context.[29]

Although situational knowledge is crucial, social science research also suggests some general lessons on influence that can guide leaders' strategies. One is that sanctions are more difficult than rewards to use effectively. Discipline and disincentives can lead to poorer performance by undermining confidence and self-esteem, and by provoking resentment, sabotage, manipulation, and litigation.[30] Experts emphasize the need to investigate thoroughly before resorting to negative sanctions, and to use them sequentially, beginning with coaching and warnings, before escalation to more serious penalties or dismissals. A second finding is that public praise is a significant and surprisingly underutilized form of recognition.[31] A third is that extrinsic rewards are typically less effective than intrinsic motivation in promoting high performance, particularly in matters involving creativity and ethics.[32] For example, a survey of art institute students 20 years into their careers found that those who were most successful by external measures (such as recognition and income) were not those who had been most interested in such rewards, but rather were those with inner drives to achievement.[33] Other large-scale studies find that the factors most likely to produce high job satisfaction involve elements intrinsic to the work itself, including the sense of achievement, contribution, and opportunity for recognition that it creates. Factors most likely to contribute to dissatisfaction involved extrinsic considerations: workplace policies and conditions, salary, job security, and relationships.[34] In summarizing this research, an influential *Harvard Business Review* article noted that "kick in the pants" responses to job motivation problems were frequently ineffective. A better strategy typically involved job enrichment, which might provide greater opportunities for control and credit.[35]

QUESTIONS

1. What rewards and sanctions have been most effective in influencing your workplace performance? Did organizations where you have worked make use of the best strategies for affecting your behavior? If not, why not?
2. Albert Schweitzer, who won the Nobel Peace Prize for his work as a medical missionary, is credited with the observation, "Example is not the main thing in influencing others . . . it is the *only* thing."[36] Although not all leadership experts would go that far, they generally agree that leaders are crucial role models for followers. Can you identify situations where a leader's personal behavior made an important difference?
3. One expert on leadership in law identifies nine approaches for exerting influence: rational persuasion, inspirational appeal, consultation, ingratiation, exchange, personal appeal, coalition building, legitimating, and pressure.[37] Researchers find that non-coercive tactics that provide a rational and justifiable basis for compliance are more effective than pressure and express assertions of authority.[38] When a commitment feels involuntary, people are less likely to follow through and more likely to engage in resistance or retaliation.[39] Accordingly, leaders should begin with the most positive, least abrasive tactic.[40] They should establish credibility, frame goals in a way that identifies common ground with those they intend to persuade, and connect with their audience through compelling evidence and stories.[41] Empathic leadership has

been shown to positively affect job satisfaction and performance.[42] Personal meetings with key people can be critical to solicit their views, concerns, and buy-in. These individuals can also help predict how various proposals might affect others who need to be enlisted.[43] Consider those strategies in light of the excerpts below. What factors most influenced followers in those cases? Can you draw any general insights from these examples?

MEDIA RESOURCES

Descriptions of the Asch experiments and Cialdini's research are readily available, as are the elevator scenes from *Candid Camera*.[44] For an illustration of the association principle, season 36, episode 4 of *Saturday Night Live*, which aired on October 23, 2010, shortly before the midterm elections, opened with a parody of Harry Reid distancing himself from President Obama in a joint appearance, and Obama responding in kind. Materials on Enron and other more recent financial scandals in addition to *The Smartest Guys in the Room* are described in Chapters 5 and 7.

A masterful example of influence by a lawyer occurs in *Denial*, a film based on a true story of a British libel suit. The defendant is an American professor sued by a Holocaust denier. She wants to testify and to include testimony by former inmates of German concentration camps. The barrister representing her seeks to persuade her that this would risk losing the case.

B. FOLLOWERS

1. THE IMPORTANCE OF FOLLOWERS

Although leadership is widely recognized as involving a relationship, the study of leadership traditionally neglected followers. This has started to change, partly in recognition of their importance in influencing outcomes. As James Kouzes and Barry Posner note, "leadership is not a solo act, it's a team effort."[45] Warren Bennis similarly points out that "followers do the heavy lifting of any successful enterprise. No matter who is memorialized as founder, no nation or organization is built without the collective effort of a group of able, energetic, unsung followers."[46] Even achievements for which we credit leaders often involve collective efforts. Michelangelo worked with sixteen others to paint the ceiling of the Sistine Chapel.[47] "Not I but ten thousand clerks rule Russia," complained an eighteenth-century czar.[48] Leaders need followers and, as John Gardner noted, "[L]eadership is conferred by followers."[49] Some theorists have coined the term "leading in place" to refer to the behaviors of women and other underrepresented groups who exercise influence without formal leadership titles by virtue of their expertise and interpersonal skills.[50]

Moreover, followers' power is increasing in response to the decline of command-and-control managerial styles and the rise of technologies that facilitate ground-up communication and organization. The result is to blur the boundaries of leader and follower. Followers may lack authority, but they do not necessarily lack power. In some respects, all leaders are followers; to retain their influence, those in positions of authority have no choice but to "track, to follow their followers if only to be sure that they stay in line."[51] Leaders have long recognized as much. In the possibly apocryphal words of the French revolutionary leader Comte de Mirabeau, "There goes the mob, and I must follow them, for I am their leader."[52] Expressions such as "leading from behind" acknowledge the way that informal power structures may trump formal lines of authority.[53] Some leadership also involves shared authority or "distributed leadership" in which leaders defer to subordinates on particular issues.[54] Universities are a quintessential example of shared governance, as captured in the quip by Woodrow Wilson while president of Princeton: "How can I democratize this University if the faculty won't do what I ask?"[55]

So too, as international research by James Kouzes and Barry Posner makes clear, "the best leaders turn their followers into leaders, realizing that the journey ahead requires many guides."[56] Leaders' ability to enlist and engage followers is critical to their legacy. Andrew Carnegie recognized as much in asking that his tombstone read: "Here lies a man who attracted better people into his service than he was himself."[57] Given the relationship between leaders and followers, some commentators reject the dichotomy and even its terminology. For John Gardner, "the connotations of the 'follower' suggest too much passivity and dependence to make it a fit term for those who are at the other end of the dialogue with leaders."[58] Critical leadership theory similarly rejects the hierarchical assumptions built into terms that focus on position rather than practices.[59]

Yet while all leaders may in some sense be followers, the converse is not necessarily true. Rather, as Kellerman notes, although in some circumstances it may be possible for followers to "lead up," such initiatives from the bottom will not always be tolerated.[60] Hierarchies are real, and subordinates may be at the mercy of those in positions of authority. For that reason, the common trend in leadership studies is to maintain the distinction between leaders and followers, while recognizing the fluidity of boundaries and the complexity of power dynamics that do not run in only one direction. Most of the time, most lawyers "lead from the middle, attracting and persuading both upward and downward" to influence superiors and subordinates.[61] Our effectiveness depends on understanding the conditions of these leader-follower relationships.

In exploring such relationships, it is helpful to clarify what defines and also what differentiates followers. Most experts label someone a follower based on rank and responses. The category includes individuals who hold less formal authority than leaders and who generally defer to those holding leadership roles. Yet within that category are many different kinds and degrees of compliance. In *The Courageous Follower*, Ira Chaleff draws distinctions based on the amount of support and challenge that followers supply.[62] Some military leaders differentiate between those who will always "get it done" because they want the job above them, those who are "on the team" but lack the same degree of motivation, and those who are "least conformist" but sometimes the "most productive" because they argue about what *should* be done.[63] Other theorists explore differences in forms of resistance: strikes, whistle-blowing, sabotage, manipulation, and reduced effort.[64] Kellerman's typology of followers turns on their degree of engagement. She differentiates among isolates, bystanders, participants, activists, and diehards.

Why do followers follow? Common explanations include rewards and punishment; desires for stability, safety, security, and community; admiration, identification, and respect; and appeals to values and a vision of the future.[65] Barbara Kellerman explores those reasons, as well as some potential downsides of deference. As you read the excerpt below, think about the types of followers that you have seen in organizations and social movements. What accounts for the different levels of support, resistance, and engagement that you have observed? If, as a British government report on the public sector asserted, "responsible followers prevent irresponsible leaders," what can encourage subordinates to assume that role?[66]

BARBARA KELLERMAN, FOLLOWERSHIP: HOW FOLLOWERS ARE CREATING CHANGE AND CHANGING LEADERS

(Boston: Harvard Business Press, 2008), pp. 53-56, 57-59, 61, 65-68, 84-87, and 89-93

Why We Follow—Individual Benefits

Freud was first. He was the first to provide us with a psychological explanation of why followers follow their leaders. . . . Here, in part, was his answer:

Why the great man should rise to significance at all we have no doubt whatsoever. We know that the great majority of people have a strong need for authority which they can admire, to which they can submit, and which dominates and sometimes even ill-treats them. We have learned from the psychology of the individual whence comes this need of the masses. It is the longing for the father that lives in each of us from his childhood days.

The book *Moses and Monotheism* [also] . . . suggested that in all power relationships there are elements of admiration and envy on the one hand, and fear and loathing on the other. . . .

[T]hese "human desires" are strongest in times of uncertainty, especially in times of crisis. For example, if an election for mayor had been held in New York City on September 10, 2001, it is not at all clear that Rudolph Giuliani would have won. A poll taken earlier in the year showed that only 32 percent of New Yorkers approved of him as mayor, and his standing among African-American voters was "so low as to be virtually unmeasurable." But after the attacks on the World Trade Center, the situation changed dramatically: Giuliani became a hero. In good part this was because he performed admirably under impossibly difficult circumstances. In greater part this was because in that moment, a moment of crisis, his followers needed nothing so much as a leader to whom they could turn for comfort and guidance. . . .

Clearly, our needs and wants as individuals are met by our playing the part of follower, at least most of the time. We go along because we consciously or unconsciously determine it in our interest to do so. Here are only three of the reasons why: (1) leaders provide individuals with safety, security, and a sense of order; (2) leaders provide individuals with a group, a community, to which they can belong; and (3) leaders provide individuals with someone who does the collective work. Of course, some of the time, followers comply only involuntarily. Some of the time, their leader compels them to comply. . . .

[So too,] followers follow not only because it is in their interest to conform to their leaders, but also because it is in their interest to conform to their fellow followers. Followers provide each other with crucial reference points. . . . Followers also follow other followers for some of the same reasons they follow their leaders. That is, followers go along with other followers because they (1) lend stability and security, (2) provide order and meaning, and (3) constitute the group to which they want to belong. . . .

Why We Follow—Group Benefits

Freud was first here too. He was the first to provide us with a sophisticated psychological understanding of why *individuals* follow leaders. And he was the first to provide us with a sophisticated psychological understanding of why *groups* follow leaders. . . . Freud believed that we behave differently—worse—as members of groups than we do as individuals. In groups our "unconscious instinctual impulses" trump what turns out to be the fragile veneer of civilization. "By the mere fact that he forms part of an organized group," Freud wrote, "a man descends several rungs in the ladder of civilization. Isolated, he may be a cultivated individual; in a crowd he is a barbarian—that is, a creature acting by instinct," capable of committing acts in "utter contradiction with his character and habits." Therefore, like Thomas Hobbes, Freud concluded that groups need leaders, strong leaders, because without them they will revert to being "barbarian."

This, though, presented Freud with a dilemma. On the one hand, groups need leaders to, among other things, protect us from ourselves. But on the other hand, bad leaders can direct groups toward danger and destruction. Finally, Freud concluded, we have no choice: bad leaders are a risk we assume, if only because by nature we have what he called "an extreme passion for authority." Put another way, well before the worst of the twentieth-century dictators—Stalin, Hitler, Mao—Freud declared that we actually want "to be governed by unrestricted force."

As we have seen, Robert Michels also addressed the question of what benefits we derive from leaders. It turns out these benefits are bestowed not only on individuals but also on groups. Why the "iron law of oligarchy"? Because, as one observer put it, "Thirty people can sit around a campfire and arrive at a consensual decision; thirty million people cannot." Michels went even a step further. It is, he argued, "the incompetence of the masses" that makes leaders absolutely indispensable. Thus is the common good served by having the few (the leaders) assume responsibility for the many (the followers).

Since Freud and Michels, another leadership function has emerged, one also excluded from the standard leadership literature. It comes to us from the study of social movements and demonstrates that some people need leaders for the purpose of what in the late 1960s and early 1970s was called *consciousness-raising.* That is, some followers need leaders to show them the world has possibilities beyond anything they had previously conceived. [In addition,] . . . (1) leaders provide groups with a structure; (2) leaders provide groups with a goal; and (3) leaders provide groups with instruments of goal achievement. . . .

Follower-Leader Relations

. . . In his book *Domination and the Arts of Resistance,* James C. Scott makes this point: people who resist, who speak "truth to power," are rare, really rare. Scott does not claim that speaking truth to power is impossible, that subordinates can never speak freely and frankly to their superiors. But he does argue that when there is a high degree of control by the latter over the former, resistance is unlikely to be open. It's just too dangerous. What, then, is the alternative? Does this mean there is no resistance at all? Or do followers find other ways of opposing leaders who give them no way to say their piece?

Scott argues that what you see is *not* necessarily what you get. . . . Hidden transcripts tell us what is being said privately, behind closed doors. And they manifest themselves in secret acts of rebellion, such as sabotage, poaching, pilfering, and tax evasion. In short, hidden transcripts are "written" by the powerless in order to resist the powerful, without risking their lives in the process.

Scott's message is far-reaching in its consequences, for these private forms of resistance pave the way for public resistance later on. . . . [I]f it succeeds, its capacity to beat back oppression "is potentially awesome."

At the other end of the spectrum from totalitarian leadership is, of course, democratic leadership, leadership in keeping with a social contract, in which power between leaders and followers is shared. . . .

Present Types

Like the few who tilled this soil before me, I came to conclude that followers are different one from the other, and that they can and should be divided into at least a few different groups. . . . I settled finally on a typology based on a single, simple metric. It aligns followers along only one—the all-important one—axis. It is *level of engagement.* That is, I divide all followers into five different types, according to where they fall along a continuum that ranges from feeling and doing absolutely nothing on the one end to being passionately committed and deeply involved on the other. The five types are:

1. Isolate
2. Bystander
3. Participant
4. Activist
5. Diehard

Isolates

Isolates are completely detached. They do not care about their leaders, or know anything about them, or respond to them in any way. Their alienation is, nevertheless, of consequence. By default—by knowing nothing and doing nothing—Isolates strengthen still further leaders who already have the upper hand.

Consider the case of the American voter or, more precisely, the case of Americans who are eligible to vote but never do. . . . [Millions of Americans report that they have not voted because they are not interested in politics or the election. This disenchantment is] less with government as it is broadly conceived than it is with public officials, with leaders. "The vast majority of Americans find the playing field of politics to be tilted. Fifty-six percent agree that politics is a means for the already powerful to maintain advantage; just one third believe that politics is a way for the powerless to acquire equal footing." . . . Australia provides [an alternate] model: registered voters who do not go to the polls must either provide a reason for not voting or pay a modest fine that increases each time there is another offense. The result is a turnout rate of more than 95 percent. The fine is obviously a disincentive to stay home and not vote. But the system is about more than penalizing political truants. It instills the idea that voting is a social obligation and that it elevates the political dialogue. . . .

However, the problem of the Isolate is scarcely confined to the political realm. We know full well that the workplace similarly has a considerable contingent of subordinates who are totally detached, there to do what they must to get by and no more. Isolates in the workplace are uninformed, uninterested, and unmotivated. They have no relationship with their leaders or managers. They are alienated from the system, from the group or organization that constitutes the whole. Finally, they are silent because they are detached—and because they are silent, they are ignored. Isolates have a problem. Isolates *are* a problem.

Bystanders, Participants, Activists, and Diehards

The four other types of followers are all in some way engaged. They are engaged with their leaders, and with other followers, and with the group or organization in which they are embedded. Recall that they each presume subordinate rank, and they are ordered according to the level of their engagement.

1. *Bystanders observe but do not participate. They make a deliberate decision to stand aside, to disengage from their leaders and from whatever is the group dynamic. This withdrawal is, in effect, a declaration of neutrality that amounts to tacit support for whoever and whatever constitutes the status quo.*

2. *Participants are in some way engaged. They clearly favor their leaders and the groups and organizations of which they are members—or they are clearly opposed. In either case, they care enough to put their money where their mouths are—that is, to invest some of what they have (time, for example) to try to have an impact.*

3. *Activists feel strongly about their leaders and they act accordingly. They are eager, energetic, and engaged. Because they are heavily invested in people and process, they work hard either on behalf of their leaders or to undermine and even unseat them.*

4. *Diehards are as their name implies—prepared to die if necessary for their cause, whether an individual, or an idea, or both. Diehards are deeply devoted to their leaders; or, in contrast, they are ready to remove them from positions of power, authority, and influence by any means necessary. In either case, Diehards are defined by their dedication, including their willingness to risk life and limb. Being a Diehard is all-consuming. It is who you are. It determines what you do.*

. . . My primary point is this: we are followers. Followers are us. This does not, of course, mean that all of us follow all of the time—sometimes we lead. But all of us follow some of the time. It's the human condition.

NOTES AND QUESTIONS

1. Research finds that people are motivated by needs for achievement, power, affiliation, and security.[67] In workplace contexts, they are most likely to follow through on a leader's objective if they can perform the task adequately, they perceive it as worthwhile, they will be rewarded for effective performance, and they value the reward.[68] Creating a sense of belonging and shared purpose is crucial; as researchers note, in our increasingly competitive workplaces, "if people don't feel like they belong to your group . . . they easily can and probably will find something else to believe in and belong to."[69]

    Personal example and self-sacrifice can be crucial in creating such bonds, particularly in times of crisis or hardship.[70] Eleanor Roosevelt is credited with the observation, "It is not fair to ask of others what you are not willing to do yourself."[71] The truism holds in military contexts as well: "Good leaders eat after the troops are finished."[72]Consider a context in which a lawyer leader faces challenges in enlisting support. What strategies are most likely to be effective?

2. How might generational differences complicate relationships between and among leaders and followers? Do Millennials have different expectations than preceding generations that need to be accommodated?[73]

3. A growing number of organizations are encouraging shared leadership in contexts marked by common purpose, trust, and interdependence.[74] What do you see as the advantages and disadvantages of this approach in legal settings?

4. Even leaders who are in positions of enormous power are constrained by their inability to mobilize followers. The American presidency is one such position. When asked about the one thing he had learned being in government that he hadn't known before, George W. Bush responded that it featured a "lot of passive aggressive behavior."[75] *New York Times* columnist David Brooks has explained why that matters: "[T]he Civil Service has a thousand ways to ignore or sit on any presidential order."[76]

   For that reason, many commentators have faulted even highly charismatic leaders including Barack Obama for failures to persuade others, including civil servants, the public, and members of the opposing party. In commenting on this challenge, Obama noted that during his first term as president, people often wondered why he was pursuing certain policies that didn't poll well. He responded, "Well, I've got my own pollsters. I know it doesn't poll well. But it's the right thing to do for America."[77] In commenting on this approach, one observer noted, Obama is "so supremely confident in his intellect that he forgets, on his way to the correct decision, to slow down and pick up not so gifted stragglers."[78] Is that a fair criticism? If so, what could Obama have done differently?

5. What makes followers most effective? Researchers suggest that workers perform best when they feel that they have choice, they perceive the job to be meaningful, and they have opportunities to make an impact and participate in decision-making.[79] Ideal followers are informed, engaged, independent, and innovative.[80] In effect, they need a "courageous conscience."[81] Under some circumstances, this will require what Ira Chaleff terms "intelligent disobedience."[82] As Bennis notes, the "tools of great followership are not so different from those of leadership."[83] Yet such qualities are not always what supervisors or organizational structures foster. As is clear from the examples in Chapters 6 and 7, and Problem 4-3 below, peer pressure and institutional reward structures can produce dysfunctional patterns of conformity. Leaders unconsciously compound the problem when they discourage dissent and reward ingratiation. Followers' flattery can then become toxic; it reinforces leaders' narcissism and distances them from discomfiting realities.[84] Is there anything that leaders can do to inoculate themselves from ingratiation?

6. In a subsequent book, *The End of Leadership*, Kellerman writes:

   > Leading in America has never been easy. But now it is more difficult than ever—not only because we have too many bad leaders, but because we have too many bad followers. Many of us don't vote at all, or vote along strict or even extreme ideological lines, making it hard for political leaders to do what they must—to collaborate, to compromise. And many of us are too timid, too alienated, and/or, too disorganized to speak up and speak out, making it easy for corporate

leaders to do what they want—to do what's best for them and their bank accounts. Whatever it is that ails us, in other words, is not only about those at the top falling down on the job, but also about those in the middle and at the bottom falling down on theirs.[85]

Do you agree? If so, what can be done to address the problem?

7. Under what circumstances should followers assume the responsibility that Mary Gentile describes as "giving voice to values?"[86] The issue gained significant attention following the murder of Kitty Genovese in New York City's Kew Garden, in view of apartment residents who failed to call the police. Under what some philosophers subsequently labeled the "Kew Garden principles," individuals' responsibility to act depends on the significance of the need, their proximity, their capability, and the alternatives to their intervention. So, for example, ethical obligations are greatest when followers have the ability to prevent serious injury and are the parties of "last resort."[87] These principles of intervention underlie the bystander intervention training that is gaining prominence as a way to prevent sexual assault and other misconduct. Recent empirical research suggests that many followers do rise to the occasion. Conversely, seeing leaders remain silent in the face of injustice increases the likelihood that followers will not speak up themselves.[88]

8. What leadership behaviors can reinforce followers' sense of moral responsibility and encourage a culture of candor rather than conformity? The first step is recognition of the challenge. The art of leadership is not simply as Dwight Eisenhower once reportedly described it: "[G]etting someone else to do something you want done because he wants to do it."[89] Effective leadership also requires inviting constructive questions about *what* you want done and creating channels for internal dissent and whistle-blowing. Leaders often find that the more they listen to followers, the more followers listen to them, and that trust is the most important factor affecting follower satisfaction and performance.[90] Former Secretary of Defense, CIA director, and university president Robert Gates recommends that "before issuing a single directive or making a single decision, a leader should talk to people at every level of her organization, from the front office to the mail room."[91] He adds:

> Whatever a leader's place on the public or private bureaucratic ladder, she must provide the people working for her with the tools and opportunities for professional success and satisfaction. She must empower them and provide them with respect, motivation, job satisfaction, upward mobility, personal dignity, esteem, and, finally, the confidence that, as a leader, she genuinely cares about them collectively and as individuals. If a leader convinces them of that, employees will forgive a lot of the little mistakes that are inevitable.[92]

Common strategies for improving relationships with followers include: offering opportunities for 360-degree feedback and sharing information;

providing positive recognition and reinforcement for constructive criticism; creating a climate of transparency, responsiveness, accountability, and mutual respect; and involving individuals in key decisions that will affect their performance.[93] Pushing leadership opportunities down the ranks can help retain and engage subordinates.[94] Giving followers opportunities to evaluate leaders' fairness, accessibility, and skills in feedback and communication can enhance performance.[95] Personal and public expressions of gratitude can also be critical. In one study, they increased performance by 50 percent.[96] "Clap for every achievement," advise law firm consultants.[97] To earn professional respect and personal trust, leaders need to demonstrate a commitment to the well being of others. They either need to "actually care about [their] people or be remarkably good at faking it."[98]

What stands in the way of creating those conditions for effective followers? One difficulty is that leaders come to "believe their own press" and lose sight of the advice that cartoonist Hank Ketchum once offered: "Flattery is like chewing gum. Enjoy it but don't swallow it."[99] Leaders' tendency to micromanage or desire to retain control can also sap followers' initiative and commitment. When one leader in a Fortune 500 company put it, "[W]e can't afford loose cannons around here," a colleague responded, "When was the last time you saw a cannon of any kind around here?"[100] So too, although highly inclusive leadership styles that demonstrate openness and accessibility generally promote employee engagement, they also take time and can reduce efficiency.[101]

Recall the strategies for avoiding groupthink discussed in Chapter 3. What organizational structures and practices might prevent overly conformist cultures such as those involved in Problem 4-3 below?

9. If the problems that followers observe pose significant risk to the organization and/or third parties, what steps can they take to increase the effectiveness and lessen the risks of whistle-blowing? Research suggests that somewhere between half to two-thirds of whistle-blowers lose their jobs, and that retaliation is common for internal as well as external disclosures.[102] The consequences include ostracism, demotion, termination, vandalism, and assault. Even when dissenters do not go outside the organization, they remind colleagues "that there is an outside," which can have disruptive, discomfiting, and destabilizing effects.[103] Assertions of wrongdoing make "everyone wonder whose actions will next come under unwanted scrutiny with unforeseeable results. . . . Even those who welcome the consequences of betrayal mistrust the betrayer."[104] One lawyer who became unemployable after delivering an unwelcome message noted, "[P]eople think whistleblowers are great but they don't necessarily want one in their organizations."[105]

    Yet the benefits, both personal and societal, from whistle-blowing can be substantial. Such activism has been critical in exposing major governmental misconduct and preventing or remedying hazardous products and environmental disasters. For example, as subsequent chapters note, disclosures by whistleblowers were what revealed the "torture memos' under the Bush administration and the Watergate burglary coverup by the Nixon administration. Some individuals become heroes; others avoid guilt and experience the satisfaction of living up to their own best sense of themselves. As one whistle-blower in the Department of Energy explained her decision to expose risks at a nuclear reactor site: "I just couldn't stop imagining what would happen if children jumped over the fence and played in the radioactive dust." When asked why colleagues did not feel the same way, she responded: "They just didn't think about it. No one wanted to talk about it. Site protection wasn't our responsibility."[106]

Studies of whistle-blowers and other "change agents" within organizations suggest several strategies for success: identify whether concerns are widely shared, enlist allies, create a written record, appeal to shared values, explore possibilities for internal influence, and seek "small wins."[107] Incremental victories can be important in creating ripple effects and building confidence that change is possible.

10. Another way that followers exercise influence is by resigning in protest and publicizing the reasons for their resignation. Such resignations can be personally valuable in affirming moral commitment and establishing a reputation for integrity and self-sacrifice, but their effectiveness in influencing organizational behavior, raising public awareness, and mobilizing change depends heavily on context. For example, the Trump Administration has experienced a steady stream of resignations in protest, with no discernable effect on policy.[108] By contrast, the departure of the Attorney General and Assistant Attorney General who refused to fire the Special Counsel investigating Watergate (known as the "Saturday Night Massacre") triggered public outrage that helped force President Nixon from office. What do you think accounts for these different outcomes?

11. In "Tempered Radicals," Stanford professor Debra Meyerson explores strategies of organizational change through representative case studies. One involves Barb Waugh, a personnel director at Hewlett Packard and member of its Gay and Lesbian Employee Network. When the company's executive team initially decided not to offer domestic partner benefits, she considered resigning in protest. Instead, she began soliciting stories of how homophobia had harmed HP's productivity. She wrote up the most compelling accounts as a reader's theater piece, which was performed by thirteen employees. A Greek chorus in the background read out the names of HP competitors who offered domestic partner benefits. The script was emailed widely and the piece was performed some sixty times at HP sites across the globe, including one attended by the CEO and his executive staff. Within six months, the company reversed its decision and became the first Fortune 50 corporation to offer domestic partner benefits.[109]

Not every story has such a happy ending. Have you observed comparable examples of success or failure as a result of mobilization by followers? Consider situations such as those described in the problems below. What lessons do they suggest about how best to give "voice to values?"

PROBLEM 4-2

Think about a situation in which you were asked to do something contrary to your values. How did you respond? How satisfied are you with what you did and what happened as a result? What might have made it easier for you to gain a successful resolution of the issue?[110]

PROBLEM 4-3[111]

Suppose that you are an associate in the Wall Street law firm Donovan Leisure, under the circumstances that Steven Brill describes in the excerpt below. For the past two years you have worked principally for one senior partner on a large antitrust suit brought by Berkey Photo against your client, Eastman Kodak. One of the major issues in the suit concerns whether Kodak's acquisitions of early competitors or its superior product innovations were the primary cause of its dominant market position. In connection with that issue, Kodak has retained a highly regarded Yale economics professor to study the photography industry in the hope that he will develop an expert opinion that Kodak's innovations, rather than its acquisitions, enabled it to attain dominance. Ultimately, the professor does develop such a theory. However, in one early letter to the senior partner, the expert indicates that he is unable to explain how Kodak's early acquisitions could be irrelevant to its present market position.

Your firm has not provided this letter and certain documents reviewed by the economist in response to Berkey's demand in pretrial discovery proceedings for all such documents and for "interim reports" prepared by the economist. The partner in charge of the case has executed an affidavit under oath stating that he inadvertently destroyed the documents, believing them to be duplicates of material still available. The partner also privately maintains that he does not consider the economist's correspondence to be a "report" within the meaning of the discovery demand.

You find the interpretation contrived, and try unsuccessfully to convince the partner that the expert's preliminary expression of doubt is precisely the sort of interim statement that Berkey is seeking for cross-examination purposes. At the very least, you believe the trial court should be asked to rule on that question. You also know that the documents have not been destroyed, although they reveal nothing of substantive value to Berkey. You greatly respect the senior partner and are at a loss to explain his behavior. What is your response?

Suppose that Steven Brill's account of the Berkey-Kodak litigation excerpted below is essentially correct. Assume that you are a member of the firm's management committee. You have worked with the attorneys whose conduct is now open to question and, prior to this incident, you had respect for all those involved. What action do you believe the firm should take with regard to those individuals?

STEVEN BRILL, WHEN A LAWYER LIES

Esquire 23-24 (December 19, 1979)

Eighteen months ago, Joseph Fortenberry, Harvard College . . . and Yale Law [graduate], was on the perfect big-time lawyer's career path. At thirty-three, he had a federal court of appeals clerkship under his belt and was a senior associate at the New York law firm of Donovan Leisure Newton & Irvine working on the all-important antitrust case that Kodak was defending against Berkey Photo.

His prospects for being made partner at the prestige firm the following year were excellent: He was regarded not only as brilliant but also as engaging and enjoyable to work with; Kodak was the firm's biggest case (occupying twenty lawyers full time, with gross billings of some $4 million a year); and he was working hand in hand with Mahon Perkins Jr., one of the firm's most respected partners.

Then . . . [one] morning, in the middle of one of hundreds of depositions . . . that he had sat through for months, Joe Fortenberry's career unraveled.

Alvin Stein, the lawyer for Berkey Photo, was questioning a Kodak "expert witness," Yale economics professor Merton Peck, about files and other materials the professor had received from Kodak in order to prepare his testimony. In such suits, each side is allowed to obtain—or "discover"—almost any documents that the other side has used to prepare and bolster its case. Such materials can often be used to attack the credibility of witnesses.

Peck told Berkey lawyer Stein that he had shipped all the materials back to Perkins of Donovan Leisure earlier that year. What happened then, to the documents, Stein asked Perkins. I threw them out as soon as I got them, the Donovan Leisure partner replied.

Perkins was lying. He'd saved all the documents in a suitcase, frequently taking them back and forth between his office at the firm and a special office he'd leased near the federal courthouse for the trial. And Joe Fortenberry, sitting at Perkins's side during this deposition, knew his boss was lying. He'd worked with the suitcase full of documents, and at least once he'd carried it between Perkins's two offices. Two weeks later, Perkins submitted a sworn statement to the court confirming that he'd destroyed the documents. . . .

Perkins's perjury came to light when Stein, at the end of the Kodak-Berkey trial, asked Peck about any reports he had submitted prior to the trial to Kodak's lawyers. This led back to more probing questions about the materials Peck had used to prepare his testimony. Then—in what has since become a much-reported, pinstriped soap opera—on the Sunday night before the last week of trial, a frightened Perkins broke down and confessed to Kodak lead lawyer John Doar that he'd never destroyed the documents but had actually hid them in a cupboard in his office. Perkins told the judge the next day, then resigned from the firm; Stein used Donovan Leisure's withholding of documents to help convince the jury of Kodak's bad faith and guilt; Kodak lost the case in a spectacular $113 million verdict (since reduced to $87 million); Kodak dropped Donovan Leisure; and Perkins was convicted of contempt of court for his perjury and sentenced to a month in prison.

But what about Joe Fortenberry?

The rules by which the bar disciplines lawyers . . . require that "a lawyer who receives information clearly establishing that . . . a person other than his client has perpetrated a fraud upon the tribunal shall promptly reveal the fraud to the tribunal." Moreover, the [rules require] that a lawyer who knows that another lawyer has engaged in dishonesty, deceit, or misrepresentation must report the offending lawyer to proper prosecutorial authorities.

In short, Fortenberry was obligated to speak up when Perkins lied. Instead, he said nothing to anyone. To be sure, Perkins, perhaps thinking he was helping Fortenberry, told the federal prosecutors who later investigated the case that Fortenberry had whispered in his ear and reminded him of the existence of the documents when Perkins told Stein he'd destroyed them. Fortenberry denies this. What's undisputed, and more relevant, is that Fortenberry never said a word about Perkins's lie to the judge, as he was obligated to, or even to any other Donovan Leisure partner.

Throw the book at him, right? Wrong. Law firms teach young associates that they are apprentices to the partners, not whistle blowers. The partners, after all, are supposed to be the ones with the experience and standing to make decisions about right and wrong. Fortenberry had worked for Perkins for more than six months. . In an environment like Donovan Leisure, this means that he respected the fifty-nine-year-old "Perk," as his admiring partners called him, for the well-liked senior litigator that he was. It also means that he was intimidated by Perkins and, of course, that he knew Perkins was his ticket to partnership when the firm partners would decide in the following year which of the associates at Fortenberry's level would be offered that golden prize. "What happened to Joe" says a close associate "was that he saw Perk lie and really couldn't believe it. And he just had no idea what to do. I mean, he knew Perkins was lying, but he kept thinking that there must be a reason. Besides, what do you do? The guy was his boss and a great guy!" . . .

Donovan Leisure senior partner Murphy says that "the firm is trying to create an atmosphere in which associates in positions like Fortenberry's will feel free to take the story of one partner acting improperly to another partner." But Perkins's impropriety—a clear, deliberate lie—is an easy call. What about an associate who thinks his partner is filing a frivolous motion or is bilking his client? "You know, when you come to work at a big firm you do give up independence," Murphy concedes. "And a young lawyer's ideas about what is frivolous, for example, can't always be accepted, though we do encourage them to tell the partners they're working for what they think."

And what about firms other than Donovan Leisure that haven't been clubbed by a Perkins disaster into thinking about "open doors" and the like? I asked eight different associates, ages twenty-seven to thirty-two, at major firms around the country what they'd do in Fortenberry's situation. None said that they'd speak up to the judge in the case as their Code of Professional Responsibility requires; only four suggested that there was another partner at the firm they'd feel free to go to if their boss did something like that; and one told a story of watching a partner bill a client (a major utility) for three times the hours worked and, not knowing what to do, doing nothing.

Judge Marvin E. Frankel, the trial judge in the Kodak-Berkey case, was highly critical of Donovan Leisure's conduct during the trial and so outraged by Perkins's lie that he personally called it to the attention of the federal prosecutors. Frankel has since left the bench and become a partner at the midtown firm of Proskauer Rose Goetz & Mendelsohn. An associate there told me last week he'd "have no idea" what to do in a Perkins situation. "There isn't any way for an associate to handle that problem," Frankel concedes. Yet, unexplainably, the once-outraged judge shifts the direct responsibility from the individual law firm, where it belongs, to the organized bar generally: "All firms, including this one, should push the bar association to evolve procedures so that an associate doesn't have to be a hero to do what's ethical."

Every year more and more of the best brains in our society go from law school to firms like Donovan Leisure. And every year these firms get larger—and more competitive. Without some real effort from those at the top, this is an environment that is destined to make automatons out of those who get by and tragedies out of those, like Fortenberry, who have the bad luck to get tripped up.

NOTES

Following the trial, Judge Frankel made clear his own dissatisfaction with Donavan Leisure's performance. He criticized its lawyers' failure to let him determine whether Berkey Photo's counsel should see the expert's letter, and their failure to press Perkins about his explanation of the missing documents. To Frankel, this conduct reflected a "single-minded interest in winning, winning, winning" that he found inappropriate and "upsetting."[112]

The result was upsetting to others as well. Kodak eventually paid Berkey Photo $6.75 million to settle the case. Donovan Leisure paid Kodak $675,000 to prevent a malpractice claim for the firm's failure to turn over documents.[113] John Doar, who was widely criticized by Donovan Leisure colleagues for his arrogant and ineffective supervision of the Kodak litigation, resigned from the firm. Fortenberry's career reeled off track. According to an account in the *American Lawyer*:

The firm had actually passed him over two months before the Perkins matter ever came to light, partners there say. It later concealed its decision so as to enhance Fortenberry's chances of getting another job, keeping him working so that prospective employers would not see his immediate dismissal from the firm and conclude that Fortenberry was indeed implicated in Perkins's wrong-doing. Even so, Fortenberry was not hired by any private law firm to which he applied for a job.[114]

Ironically, of all the major players, Perkins ultimately came out the best. Although he served 27 days in jail for contempt of court, he was never disbarred. Subsequently, he traveled extensively, taught English in Japan, and served as president of his local orchestra. One of his former partners described him as "happier, I believe, than he had been as a practicing lawyer."[115]

In his midsixties, Perkins began working as a volunteer at the Center for Constitutional Rights, a prominent public-interest law firm. "Intellectually, the work here is every bit as satisfying as what I did before," he told a *New York Times* reporter. "And politically, I derive a lot more satisfaction than I did at Donovan Leisure. I'm helping in causes I believe in very deeply. This wasn't a very good way to have gotten out, but at this point, I'm very happy not to be there, and very happy to be here."[116]

QUESTIONS

1. Most large law firms have a designated attorney to provide advice on professional responsibility issues.[117] However, little research is available on the effectiveness of these individuals in circumstances such as those confronting Fortenberry. Not all procedures guarantee the confidentiality, credibility, and objectivity that experts believe is necessary.[118] What structural protections do you think might encourage junior lawyers to speak up?

2. The American Bar Association's current Model Rules of Professional Conduct, adopted after the Berkey-Kodak case, and enacted with some modifications in every state, now address this issue. Rule 5.1(a) makes partners in a law firm responsible for ensuring policies that give "reasonable assurance that all lawyers in the firm conform to the rules of professional conduct." Should firm leaders be subject to disciplinary liability based on this rule under circumstances such as Berkey-Kodak? Would it be preferable to hold the firm itself liable?[119] Another Rule, 5.2, provides that a lawyer is bound by professional rules "notwithstanding that the lawyer acted at the direction of another person." However, "a subordinate lawyer does not violate the rules of professional conduct if that lawyer acts in accordance with a supervisory lawyer's reasonable resolution of an arguable question of professional duty." Would that rule help an associate in Fortenberry's situation?

   Does the rule strike the right balance between competing values? Some law professors claim that it is neither necessary nor appropriate. In their view, lawyers do not need its protections because, even in states without the rule, discipline is virtually never imposed for "reasonable resolutions of an arguable question of professional duty."[120] From the standpoint of encouraging ethical debate, critics see the rule as inappropriate because it gives junior lawyers "little incentive to even consider tough ethical issues, let alone raise them.[121] By contrast, defenders claim that the rule encourages subordinate lawyers to "test supervisors' ethically questionable decisions or directives" because that is the only way they can be sure a resolution is "reasonable" and a shield against disciplinary liability.[122] What is your view? How would you draft a bar ethics rule to address the responsibilities of subordinate lawyers?

3. If you were the head of law firm, an in-house legal department, or a public agency, under what, if any circumstances, would you dismiss or sanction employees for not reporting unethical conduct? Would you promote, or terminate, someone who acted as Fortenberry or the GM junior attorney did?

MEDIA RESOURCES

For the general topic of followers, a documentary on Eichmann and footage showing rallies of the Third Reich or recent parades by the North Korean army offer chilling reminders of the costs of conformity. Clips from the television series *The Office* show different follower styles, including Stanley, the Isolate, and Dwight, the Diehard. *30 Rock* offers a parody of Tina Fey receiving a Followership award.[123] Other interesting portraits include a Chinese activist in the Tiananmen Square protest, and a Kamikaze pilot during World War II.[124] A chilling account of a high school teacher who created a cult is based on a real experience.[125] For discussion of whistle-blowing, *The Insider* chronicles the story of an executive willing to violate a confidential non-disclosure agreement in order to expose tobacco industry abuses on *60 Minutes*. A particularly compelling episode features a meeting between journalists and CBS corporate representatives (including a lawyer) who want to censor the story. *Billions* features a number of episodes in which a federal district attorney in Manhattan puts pressure on subordinate attorneys to engage in questionable conduct, including keeping him in the loop of an investigation from which he has recused himself. *The Good Wife* and *Suits* also feature many junior lawyers grappling with such issues. An episode from *The West Wing* features Sam Seaborn as a senior associate in a law firm, nearing partnership, when he jeopardizes his promotion by trying at the last minute to convince a client to buy safer boats that would reduce the risks of disastrous oil spills.[126]

Some more nuanced portraits of the follower's role appear in *The Remains of the Day*, discussed in Chapter 11, in which a butler played by Anthony Hopkins faces ethical conflicts with his employer, a Nazi sympathizer in the pre-World War II era. Other portraits emerge in the Netflix series, *The Crown*, which profiles the extent to which the power of Queen Elizabeth is constrained by the expectations of her followers. A particularly good illustration occurs in Season 1, in which a personal secretary tells her why she cannot have the person she chooses as the successor to his position.

2. ADAPTIVE LEADERSHIP

RONALD A. HEIFETZ, LEADERSHIP WITHOUT EASY ANSWERS

(Cambridge, MA: Belknap Press of Harvard
University Press, 1994), pp. 88-100

Tacoma

On July 12, 1983, the head of the U.S. Environmental Protection Agency (EPA), William Ruckelshaus, took unprecedented action in a case involving a copper plant owned by the American Smelting and Refining Company (Asarco) near Tacoma, Washington. The Asarco plant was the only one in the nation to use copper ore with a high content of arsenic, and arsenic had been found to cause cancer. As authorized by Amendments to the Clean Air Act of 1970, Ruckelshaus was expected to decide what to do about the plant; in particular, he had to determine what constituted an "ample margin of safety" in the plant's operation to protect public health.

This was both a technically and politically difficult question. In the years since the 1970 Clean Air Act Amendments had been written, scientists were discovering that many hazardous wastes lacked a clear threshold of safety. Even a minuscule amount of "nonthreshold chemicals" could produce adverse effects. As Ruckelshaus put it in his June 1983 address to the National Academy of Sciences, "We must assume that life now takes place in a minefield of risks from hundreds, perhaps thousands, of substances. No more can we tell the public: You are home free with an adequate margin of safety."

The Asarco plant had long been regarded as one of the major polluters in the Northwestern United States, but it had also provided employment to generations of people since its opening in 1890. By 1983, nearly one hundred years later, the plant employed about 575 workers in the town of Ruston with a payroll of $23 million. It contributed significantly to the local economy through its purchases of $12 million worth of supplies, and it provided $13 million of revenue to auxiliary businesses in addition to paying $3 million in state and local taxes. If Asarco were to close the plant, the state of Washington would have to pay as much as $5.5 million in unemployment benefits. Closing the plant would be a devastating blow to a region where several major industries had not yet recovered from recession.

. . . The Asarco company itself was well aware of the pollution problem. Under pressure from the regional air pollution authority, Asarco had spent about $40 million since 1970 in equipment and practices to reduce emissions. . . .Going further would require one of three options: develop a new technology to reduce emissions; ship in low arsenic ore at high cost; or convert the entire plant to electric smelting, a different process altogether, at a projected cost of $150 million.

According to the company, any of these three options would force the closing of the plant. World copper prices had crashed between 1980 and 1982 from $1.45

per pound to 60 cents per pound. To break even, the Asarco plant required 82 cents per pound, which meant that at current prices it was losing money already.

The battle, like many environmental battles, was pitched between jobs and health. According to the EPA, installing the converter hoods as planned would reduce the risk of arsenic related cancer from four persons a year to one. Would this be acceptable? Did an "ample margin of safety" to protect public health require more? Should regulations demand zero emissions? Or was the livelihood generated by the plant worth the added risk of one case of cancer per year?

Complicating these questions was the fact that the emissions, and thus the risks of cancer, were spread out over a twelve-mile area that involved people even at a distance from the plant and its jobs. For example, Vashon Island lay two miles offshore, but because of prevailing winds it became, as one resident put it, "the dumping grounds for these pollutants without any benefits such as jobs or Asarco tax payments." Many islanders were afraid of the high levels of arsenic found in the urine samples of their children and in the soil from their local gardens. Should they bear the side-effects of Asarco? People in the city of Tacoma were in the same predicament. Receiving tons of air pollution a year from the plant, and few tax benefits, one member of the Tacoma city council said it was as if "somebody [were] standing on the other side of the city line with a thirty-ought-six [rifle] and firing it into Tacoma."

Who should decide? By habit and statute, Ruckelshaus and the EPA were supposed to decide. The company and many of its workers looked to the EPA to confirm the acceptability of the actions they were about to take by spending $4 million on converter hoods. They were using the best available technology to reduce emissions from their plant. They looked to the EPA to resist taking action that would push them economically over the brink. Yet many area residents, along with environmental activists, looked to the EPA to provide "an ample margin of safety," and were quite willing to push the plant to the edge, if not over it, to reduce emissions significantly further.

Remarkably, Ruckelshaus, on July 12, 1983, refused publicly and dramatically to decide on his own. Going way beyond the perfunctory public hearings mandated by statute to accompany national rulemaking, Ruckelshaus proposed to engage the community at large in facing the problem. He announced the EPA's intention to solicit actively the views and wishes of the people that would be most affected by the EPA ruling. "For me to sit here in Washington and tell the people of Tacoma what is an acceptable risk would be at best arrogant and at worst inexcusable." As he later told the *Los Angeles Times*: "My view is that these are the kinds of tough, balancing questions that we're involved in here in this country in trying to regulate all kinds of hazardous substances. I don't like these questions either, but the societal issue is what risks are we willing to take and for what benefits?" Ruckelshaus even quoted Thomas Jefferson to back up his unprecedented stand: "If we think (the people) not enlightened enough to exercise their control with a wholesome discretion, the remedy is not to take it from them, but to inform their discretion." . . .

Few people reacted positively. The press framed the issue starkly: "What Cost a Life? EPA Asks Tacoma" (*Los Angeles Times*), "Smelter Workers Have Choice: Keep their Jobs or their Health" (*Chicago Tribune*). *The New York Times* ran an editorial that branded "Mr. Ruckelshaus as Caesar . . . who would ask the amphitheater crowd to signal with thumbs up or down whether a defeated gladiator should live or die." For Ruckelshaus to "impose such an impossible choice on Tacomans was . . . inexcusable." The head of the local chapter of the Sierra Club said, "It is up to the EPA to protect public health, not to ask the public what it is willing to sacrifice not to die from cancer." In the community's opinion as well, Ruckelshaus was neglecting his duties. Local citizens called it "copping out." "We elected people to run our government; we don't expect them to turn around and ask us to run it for them."

Ruckelshaus fought back in various encounters with the press. In a letter to *The New York Times*, he wrote, "Your Caesar analogy is seriously flawed. The Roman Caesars asked the crowd for thumbs up or down before sparing or condemning the gladiator. In Tacoma, the ones being asked for their reaction are at risk themselves. No one ever asked the gladiator his opinion, which may be the principal difference between Rome and the EPA." "Listen," he told the *Los Angeles Times*, "I know people don't like these kinds of decisions. Welcome to the world of regulation. People have demanded to be involved and now I have involved them and they say: 'Don't ask that question.' What's the alternative? Don't involve them?"

Resistance to Ruckelshaus also ran high within the EPA itself. Never before had the agency pushed problems back into the laps of a community. Like most government officials, managers within the EPA took seriously their charge to solve problems on behalf of the public. Indeed, public involvement seemed so messy a process compared with rational and expert decisionmaking that even the public hearings demanded by law were seen more as a formality to be suffered than an essential component of the problem-solving process. As a regional staff member described, "At headquarters [in Washington, D.C.] they thought we were a bunch of bozos out here in the region. They could not understand why we were scrambling and bending over backwards to organize the workshops and put out easily digestible information for the public."

As one might expect, the three public workshops held that August were controversial and packed with people, including a large number of smelter workers, union representatives, local citizen organizations, and environmental groups. The first workshop was held on Vashon Island, and the last two in Tacoma itself. The format was the same for all three, and all were covered by local and national television. After a formal presentation by the EPA staff, with graphs and charts to illustrate the technical facts regarding arsenic emission, dispersion, and the risk of illness, the audience was divided into smaller groups to facilitate individual responses. The EPA staff distributed several handouts with fact sheets, illustrations of how hooding helped control emissions, and excerpts from Ruckelshaus's National Academy of Sciences speech which outlined his philosophy (and Jefferson's) of public education. They then circulated among the groups to answer questions and record the comments of participants.

Many of the comments had little to do with verifiable facts. Hired by the EPA to observe, the dean of the School of Public Health at the University of Washington remarked on how "the personal nature of the complaints and questions made a striking counterpoint to the presentations of meteorological models and health effect extrapolations." People asked whether or not they could eat food from their Vashon Island gardens, how much soil should they remove to make it safe, how would their pets be affected. One woman asked, "Will my child die of cancer?"

The workshops had both immediate and subtle effects. Immediately, the EPA and the public learned some lessons. As one analyst for the EPA described, "We . . . got educated. The questions raised at the workshops sent some people back to the drawing board." Several public groups asked the EPA to postpone the formal hearings, scheduled for late August, to allow them more time to prepare testimony. In the meantime, the public held more workshops on its own under the sponsorship of the city of Tacoma and the Steel-worker's Union. Many more questions were raised, and not only questions about pollution and health, but about other options as well, like diversifying the local economy. Yet the EPA was still taking the heat. Some comments bordered on the openly hostile, "I have seen studies which show that stress is the main source of cancer; the EPA is one main cause of stress."

By the time of the hearings in November, the EPA had clarified several scientific questions raised by the public's involvement. Significantly, its computer model estimating the amount of arsenic emissions had been wrong. Yet the corrected model still predicted a risk of one additional cancer death per year from arsenic, even after placement of the new hooding devices.

The workshops and hearings surprised the staff at the EPA. As Ruckelshaus put it, local citizens had shown that they were "capable of understanding [the problem of the smelter] in its complexities and dealing with it and coming back to us with rather sensible suggestions." In fact, "the public—the non-technical, unschooled public—came back with some very good suggestions as to how they could reduce the emissions of arsenic in the plant [and still keep it open]."

Perhaps of greater import, local people began to see the situation in a new light. Rather than view it solely as a conflict between jobs and health, many people began to see a new possibility: the diversification of the local economy. Although no one knew whether or not the plant would have to close in the near future, many could see that remaining so dependent on this one struggling industry was a bad idea.

No one, including Ruckelshaus, saw the new possibility at the start. The idea of diversification, although obvious in retrospect, had not been part of anyone's mindset. The EPA, industry, labor, environmentalists, and local officials had been thinking in more narrow terms of emissions, health risks, and jobs. It took the noisy and conflictive process of public workshops, debates in the press, and the mobilization of neighborhoods to generate new ideas.

One year later, in June 1984, although Ruckelshaus had not yet come to a decision, Asarco announced that it would close the Tacoma plant the following year. Precipitated primarily by depressed copper prices and shortages of high-arsenic copper ore, Asarco nevertheless spread the blame for the shutdown to federal, state, and local environmental agencies for requiring it to install converter hoods costing $3 million by the end of that year. Furthermore, Asarco claimed that the EPA would require a great deal more investment in the future. Although this was not true, since Ruckelshaus had not yet made a final ruling, somebody would have to take the heat, and the EPA was the obvious lightning rod. As one worker told reporters, "I'll tell you something, it's the EPA's fault!"

Yet the community, however distressed, was also better prepared than it might have been. By the time the announcement came in 1984, the new goal had already been set: finding new jobs for the workers and attracting new industry to the region. When the plant closed in 1985, Tacoma and Ruston already had begun the task of diversifying its economy. People had come to the early workshops displaying buttons labeled either "Jobs" or "Health." By the final workshops, people were sporting buttons that said "BOTH."

In retrospect, nearly ten years later, Colin Conant, Executive Director of the Private Industry Council for Tacoma, looked back on the efforts of the Dislocated Workers Project for those laid off by Asarco:

> We created a model for re-training the workforce, and the community got behind it. We got many, many people involved on advisory committees: the labor union, United Way, the Private Industry Council, Asarco, the Economic Development Board, employees, and the State Employment Security Department. People might do it that way now, but back then nobody was. The support made a big difference in how well people adjusted. It could have been much more psychologically disruptive. There were far fewer casualties than there might have been without so many people and organizations backing us up. Since Asarco's closing, there have been several more closings in the area and we basically applied the same model. We learned a lot from how we did it then.

In addition to helping the workers adapt, the Asarco effort also served as a model in later years for resolving other environmental disputes in the Tacoma area. . . .

Implications

Ruckelshaus recognized that the Asarco situation represented an adaptive challenge rather than a technical problem. Consequently, he resisted pressures from within the EPA and from the public to provide an authoritative solution. Instead, he chose to engage people in facing the challenge. By doing so, he placed an unusual problem in the laps of his own agency. The EPA had no real experience in orchestrating public deliberation. Public hearings routinely had been pro forma, with presentations of technical arguments by interested parties and little more. Hearings tended to focus on narrowly defined issues, without much creativity in exploring new possibilities like diversifying a local economy. Parties did not talk to one another; they presented testimony to a panel of EPA administrators and experts.

The EPA had never seen itself in the role of orchestrating public thinking on problems. In the public workshops in Tacoma, it quickly found itself "over its head" in problems about which its technical expertise meant little. What could pollution experts say about the value of jobs versus the value of health, or ways to cope with a risk-filled life, or paths to economic diversification?

Bearing the brunt of managing the tasks of informing and involving the public, the regional EPA office exhausted itself in the undertaking. Roughly thirty people devoted full time for four months to this one case. Was it worth it? According to one official, the whole "process proved terrifically costly and time-consuming." And in the end, the decision was still the EPA's to make.

Yet there were at least three significant benefits. First, within the EPA itself, the staff at headquarters began to appreciate what it meant to be on the frontlines. Because the regional staff had frequent contact with area groups, they knew better how to engage with the public. On arriving in Tacoma, staff from Washington, D.C., had quickly found themselves out of touch with the real-world import of scientific findings at the local level. As one regional staff member put it, "When they arrived in Tacoma and found themselves face-to-face with a well-informed and often angry public, they began to appreciate our problem a little better." Now, information relevant to public policymaking would flow up from the frontlines rather than just down from headquarters. That made policymaking better. Routine procedures to involve the community began to change. In following years, the EPA began to act as a frequent sponsor and forum for negotiation among stakeholders to resolve environmental disputes. Furthermore, the agency began routinely to make use of the central distinction Ruckelshaus had made in Tacoma—between the science of assessing risk and the problem of managing the public implications of living with risk. The focus on risk management broadened the mission of the EPA, giving a larger context to its previously narrow scientific orientation.

Second, the Tacoma experiment in public deliberation restored the credibility of the EPA, which in 1983 had just come out of two years mired in public scandal. . . . As a member of the Washington Environmental Council put it, the EPA's cooperation and openness went "a long way toward restoring trust and confidence in the agency here in the region." Even previous skeptics of public deliberation later praised the effort. Ruth Weiner of the Sierra Club, who had criticized Ruckelshaus earlier for "copping out," stated at the conclusion of her public testimony that the Clean Air Act "requires public involvement." "Moreover," she said, "in becoming involved, the public begins to appreciate the difficulty attendant on making regulatory decision, the ease with which EPA can be made a scapegoat because the agency's blunders are so readily magnified, and the inadequacy of simply identifying 'heroes' and 'villains' in environmental protection. It may have been hard work and a headache for all of us, but the public involvement is most certainly worth it."

Third, and perhaps most significantly, the communities of Tacoma and Ruston began seeing the need to adapt. Certain facts were now being faced. Asarco's use of outdated technology in its Ruston plant made it only sporadically competitive in the world copper market. The town's reliance on a single industry placed it in a precarious position of dependence. In addition, some people were paying the price of the plant in terms of health, yet without benefit from jobs or tax revenues.

With the advantage of hindsight, we can see these benefits of public engagement. However, when Ruckelshaus broke precedent by involving the public in solving its problem, he met resistance from every quarter: industry, environmental interests, labor, the press, and within the EPA itself. With problems as tough as jobs, health, and economic diversification, it is no wonder that everyone expects authority to make the decision. That seems our inclination—to look to someone or some agency to take the heat in choosing what to do. Ordinarily, these expectations act as constraints on people in authority, inhibiting them from exercising leadership. Yet Ruckelshaus cut against the grain when he insisted that the public realize that the job of regulating pollutants was not simply a technical matter of setting safe thresholds of emission. Trade-offs would have to be made that involved value conflicts not amenable to scientific analysis. And if those trade-offs between jobs and health were to be faced, then perhaps new adaptations might be achieved in the face of loss.

Ruckelshaus insisted that these problems represented challenges to business-as-usual. At the very least, public attitudes toward living with risk had to change. Otherwise, agencies like the EPA would continue to be called upon to do the impossible, to provide fixes for what could not be fixed by fiat from above. Hard choices were necessary, requiring people to clarify and change their values. The EPA could stimulate those changes but it could not make them. . . .

NOTES AND QUESTIONS

1. According to Heifetz, "Ruckelshaus recognized that the Asarco situation represented an adaptive challenge rather than a technical solution." What made that characterization appropriate? Would the same kind of participatory process work for any situation requiring a trade-off between health and economic stability? If not, what distinguished the Asarco situation? Could you imagine some variation of Ruckelshaus's approach guiding the Obama administration's decision about whether to allow offshore drilling in the wake of the 2010 British Petroleum oil well disaster discussed in Chapter 3?

2. Heifetz describes three primary benefits from the way Ruckelshaus proceeded: it improved the decision-making process at EPA, it restored the public credibility of the agency, and it forced the community to diversify its economy. Do you think the leaders of Asarco would come to the same assessment? Are their perspectives important in evaluating the outcome?

3. What if Asarco had not decided to close the plant and Ruckelshaus had been forced to make a decision? Suppose that his view was different from that of the community. How would you weigh the risks and benefits of involving stakeholders if you are not prepared to defer to their decision?

4. Heifetz claims that the "most common leadership failure stems from trying to apply technical solutions to adaptive challenges," which he defines as requiring "changes in peoples' priorities, beliefs, habits, and loyalties."[127] In orchestrating change, a leader needs to ask the hard questions, name the elephant in the room, understand what parties care about and fear the most, and encourage them to take responsibility for key decisions.[128] Listening is a key skill. Heifetz claims that most of those who fail in leading adaptive change "go down with their mouths open. They get taken out of action because they keep talking beyond the point where key players are listening."[129]

Can you identify examples of such adaptive challenges? How well did leaders manage them? Consider a change initiative that you would like to lead. What challenges would you face and how would you address them?

3. FOSTERING INNOVATION AND MANAGING CHANGE

Former army chief of staff Eric Shinseki observed that "[i]f you don't like change, you're going to like irrelevance even less."[130] Any successful organization or movement needs to adapt to social, political, economic, and technological developments. Any effective leader needs to create the conditions for such adaptation. In the private sector, those that do not adapt do not survive. In the public sector, the insulation from competition may somewhat lessen the pressures for change, but organizations that lose touch with stakeholders' needs will eventually pay the price in diminished legitimacy and inadequate political and financial support.[131] As Chapter 2 noted, the pace of change has rapidly accelerated in recent decades and "digital disruptions" are constantly affecting every area of personal and professional life.[132]

Change comes in many forms, but much of the literature on leadership stresses innovation, defined as adaptation of an idea to a new setting.[133] Unlike invention or creativity, which refers to the development of something new, and may involve only individual effort, innovation requires collective practices that produce change.[134] Leadership behavior is a key driver of innovation.[135] Although leaders need not themselves be the source of innovative ideas, they do need to foster a culture that anticipates change and that positions their organizations accordingly. Many argue that Thomas Edison's greatest innovation was not the light bulb, but the concept of a research and development lab.[136] In times of heightened uncertainty, helping others "better understand and deal with the chaos will [make things] less chaotic."[137] Innovation is particularly critical in contexts of rapidly evolving technologies or shifting stakeholder expectations. As Peter Drucker famously observed, the "best way to predict the future is to create it," and "[w]hat brought you here won't get you there."[138]

Change occurs on a continuum, ranging in speed and scope. At one end of the spectrum lies incremental evolution of norms and practices; at the other end lies sudden and dramatic progress.[139] The impetus for such innovation varies. In *Seeing What Others Don't*, Gary Klein explores what enables or blocks insights by exploring 120 cases of breakthrough insights.[140] The most common method that leads to insights is using connections. People expose themselves to different ideas that can help them form new connections. Other strategies involve exploring coincidences, curiosities, or contradictions that rest on inconsistencies and anomalies. Finally, "creative desperation" occurs when people get stuck and use critical thinking to identify and correct flawed beliefs. The most successful innovators often use a "triple path," which combines using connections and exploring coincidences and curiosities—to anchor new understandings—along with analyzing contradictions and enlisting creative destruction to discard previous anchors.[141]

A crisis frequently dramatizes the need for change and creates the sense of urgency that makes it possible. A slow erosion of market power or public support can also propel organizations into action, as can regulatory reforms or recurrent problems that have yielded only temporary solutions.[142] Technological innovations can also make clear the need for organizational innovation. In *The Innovator's Dilemma: When New Technologies Cause Great Firms to Fail*, Harvard Professor Clayton Christensen argues that organizations often stumble because of "disruptive technologies" that are typically simpler, cheaper, and more convenient than they offer. Although the industry's most profitable customers don't initially want these innovations, they eventually become dominant. Established organizations lose out because they place too much emphasis on consumers' current preferences instead of adopting new technologies or strategies that anticipate future needs. This anticipation, which Christensen labels "disruptive innovation," is the key to high performance.[143] Christensen's examples have been subject to criticism claiming that what he labels as failures of innovation are often simply "bad management."[144] But almost no one disputes the central importance that innovation occupies in today's competitive cultures.

Experts identify three primary stages in which leaders can guide change.[145] The initial phase requires overcoming inertia and creating a compelling vision for the future.[146] According to Harvard Business School Professor John Kotter, most transformation efforts fail at this stage, in part because leaders underestimate how hard it can be to drive people out of their comfort zone, and overestimate how successful they have been in creating a sense of urgency. The tendency is to say "enough with the preliminaries; let's get on with it."[147] To avoid these pitfalls, leaders must understand the obstacles to change in their own organizations. In some contexts, the problem involves the "curse of homogeneity": too many insiders are drinking the same Kool-Aid, or have too much personal investment in outdated strategies.[148] To counteract these tendencies, leaders can identify looming problems or opportunities, and build coalitions to propose appropriate responses. An inclusive process is critical. Getting buy-in from key participants at an early stage can help minimize opposition later.[149] In-person, one-on-one meetings are generally the most effective strategy.[150] Reaching people on an emotional level through direct experience, compelling stories, and visual images can often create the urgency that inspires action. Demonstrating the costs of inaction is often key.

Taking a risk is more appealing when people are faced with a guaranteed loss if they don't change.[151]

Researchers on influence and innovation offer multiple examples. Asking senior medical care executives to investigate examples of fatal but preventable mistakes at their own hospitals gave them a sense of the human tragedies that are often masked by data spreadsheets; the result was a new commitment to specific remedial actions.[152] Requiring employees to listen to a recording of an angry business customer describing unresponsive sales personnel provided lessons in how to become better listeners.[153]

A second stage of organizational change involves developing a strategy for implementation and enlisting others in its support. That requires effectively communicating the mission, removing obstacles to its realization, encouraging innovation, and prioritizing popular improvements that can lay foundations for broader transformations.[154] Kotter claims that "if you can't communicate the vision to someone in five minutes or less and get a reaction that signifies both understanding and interest, you are not yet done with this phase of the transformational process."[155] Throughout that process, leaders also need to expect the unexpected, and be prepared to make midcourse corrections; patience, persistence, and flexibility are key.[156] Harvard professor Rosabeth Moss Kanter describes the need to support three levels of a pyramid. At the base should be a large number of incremental strategies that suggest promising directions. In the middle should be a portfolio of plausible early stage ventures or prototypes. At the top should be "a few big bets about the future."[157] In settings where innovation is especially critical, enabling employees to "fail early, fail often" without penalty may be necessary to encourage risk.[158] Franklin Roosevelt's success in crafting New Deal initiatives during the Depression was partly attributable to his willingness to innovate, improvise, and learn from mistakes. In his view, "the country needs . . . bold persistent experimentation. It is common sense to take a method and try it: if it fails, admit it frankly and try another. But above all, try something."[159]

Other common strategies for change include fostering friendly rivalry among divisions or branches; benchmarking through comparative analysis of other successful efforts; and establishing contests, team projects, and other support structures for creative problem solving.[160] Some professional service firms have sponsored brainstorming sessions and online resources to jump-start innovation programs in branch offices.[161] Many legal organizations are borrowing approaches from design thinking, a problem-solving process that helps generate and test options to identify innovative strategies.[162]

Where people are the problem, leaders can seek ways to address their concerns or to work around resisters. Transformative change generally requires dedication and creativity, which cannot be coerced; people need to be enlisted.[163] Finding areas of agreement, identifying what won't change, and stressing benefits from a new approach can all be critical.[164] The typical reasons why people oppose change are its threats to their status, power, autonomy, competence, comfort, and job security.[165] Leaders can allay such concerns by proactively helping employees adapt, retool, or find other assignments or positions.[166] Because people are more responsive to changing work methods than changing themselves, it is helpful to provide options that do not imply that the individual's personal characteristics are the problem.[167]

A third stage involves assessing and consolidating change. Here, the key is identifying the right time and metrics to evaluate progress. Premature assessment can stifle innovation. "Pulling up the radishes" to see how they are growing defeats the enterprise.[168] But at some point, the test of a good idea is whether it can be implemented effectively. Leaders ultimately will be judged less by their broad visions than by their actual accomplishments. In this final stage of change, leaders need to institutionalize what works, create systems and reward structures that reinforce progress, and look for ways to continue reinvigorating the process.[169] Declaring victory too soon kills momentum and empowers resisters; if leaders abdicate or delegate responsibility prematurely, it sends a signal that the project was just the flavor of the month and not a sustainable goal.[170] Poor succession planning can similarly undo years of hard work.[171]

Leaders sometimes underestimate the advantages of learning from the mistakes of others. Innovators have a "first-mover" advantage in capturing a market share, but research shows that the downsides of acting first are generally greater. Risk seekers who are drawn to being first are prone to making impulsive decisions without adequate analysis. Leaders waiting in the wings can also improve on first movers' initiatives and learn from their mistakes.[172] Some law firms have positioned themselves to encourage and build on innovations. Orrick, Herrington & Sutcliffe has created Orrick Labs to develop its capacity to use data analytics to study likely changes in legal practice and promote efficiency. Other firms have created incentives to invest in emerging technologies or used collaborative innovation methods to anticipate and address client problems.[173]

In *Switch*, psychologists Chip Heath and Dan Heath analogize the process of leading change to riding an elephant. The rider holds the reins, but if the elephant does not want to go, they are both stuck. To make progress, the rider needs to know the direction, motivate the elephant, and clear the path of obstacles.[174] If you wanted to change some aspect of your environment, what strategies might this metaphor suggest?

In *A Passion for Leadership*, excerpted below, Robert Gates generalizes from five decades of experience in reforming federal and academic bureaucracies. In his view, leaders of bureaucratic organizations must "always have an unfinished agenda," because the tendency of even reformed organizations is to drift back to their natural state of "torpor, complacency . . . inertia, and inefficiency." And to generate a successful agenda, leaders always have to keep "reinventing" themselves as well as their organizations.[175]

ROBERT M. GATES, A PASSION FOR LEADERSHIP: LESSONS ON CHANGE AND REFORM FROM FIFTY YEARS OF PUBLIC SERVICE

(New York: Alfred A. Knopf, 2016), pp. 90-94, 182, 208-209

Implementing reform, a leader must master the available information, make decisions, assign responsibility for action, have a regular reporting mechanism that allows her to monitor progress and performance, and hold people accountable. And then she must get out of the way. Micro-knowledge is necessary; micromanagement is not.

Leading change is hard work. The leader must do her homework to understand what change is needed, what change will work, who is a reliable source of information and who is not, whether recommendations will lead to the changes she wants, and whether her decisions are being effectively implemented. Broad perspective is always important, but a leader must get into the weeds as well. She must . . . know the innermost parts of the organization, get a sense of everyday life on the job from employees at every level. She must constantly be learning, listening, and asking questions. A leader must have sufficient detailed knowledge so she can recognize when someone is bullshitting her, when people are giving her inaccurate information (and whether it's because they don't know the facts themselves or are trying to mislead or steer her), whether options or recommendations are based on sound data.

When a leader is aware of the nitty-gritty, it doesn't take long for people to realize they had better double-check their work and that different organizations involved in the same briefing had better cross-check with each other before marching into a meeting. Such displays of micro-knowledge also send the message that it will be very hard to bamboozle the leader and the consequences of that or trying to bluff will be unpleasant. Moreover, micro-knowledge often allows a leader to better understand what she is being told, to place it in context, ask penetrating questions, and make smarter, better-informed decisions.

Too often, leaders think that knowing all these details is somehow unnecessary or "beneath" them, that their time is better spent on the "big picture." Such leaders will find themselves "kept" men and women of the organizations they purport to lead, dependent on others who may not have the same agenda or priorities to tell them what they need to know. For a leader to get the big things right depends a great deal on knowing the little things, especially when implementing difficult and controversial change. . . .

The point of a leader having micro-knowledge is neither to embarrass someone nor to nitpick. Both will make a leader look small and should be avoided. Everyone comes into a meeting with the boss with some measure of apprehension. Increasing people's anxiety or fear by faultfinding is counterproductive. If an error is meaningless to the larger discussion, ignore it; dwelling on typos, format, or some trivial issue in a chart suggests to people that the leader is not just in the weeds but lost in them. . . .

In trying to change any bureaucracy, especially in a large one, the leader must decide on the proper course of action and then assign responsibility for implementation to his subordinates and empower them to carry out the task. Give them space to show what they can do. Stay out of their hair. . . . [I]f a leader doesn't trust his lieutenants to carry out his strategy, he has chosen the wrong people.

Lasting change in a bureaucracy depends, above all, on those below you embracing the change and taking ownership, making it their own. The more frequently you intrude, implicitly reminding them it is your change, the less they will believe it is theirs. Successful implementation, in short, depends upon them. The leader cannot hold individuals accountable for driving change if he refuses to let go of the steering wheel. He must trust his subordinates, replace them if necessary. But he mustn't micromanage them. . . .

When you have accomplished your mission of reform, or taken it as far as you likely can, go home. Don't let power and position . . . go to your head. As the old saying goes, "The cemeteries are full of indispensable men."

One of the toughest decisions in life is knowing when to dance off the stage. We have all seen political and business leaders who stayed too long. Some get so enamored of the power, perks, and privileges they just can't bear to give them up. Or they don't want to give their critics inside and outside the organization the satisfaction. And so they remain in place, a growing liability to the very institution they might have ably led for a long time. I have always thought the sweet spot was to leave at a point when people would say "I wish he weren't leaving so soon" as opposed to "How the hell do we get rid of this guy?". . .

The Japanese some time ago developed a business practice called *kaizen*, which basically means continuing change for the better in all aspects of an organization. . . . Many companies around the world have adopted the practice, which includes a very open process encouraging suggestions for improvements large and small from employees at every level, including especially on the shop floor—the folks on the front lines. Developed for business, the concept of *kaizen* seems to me to have equal value for public sector bureaucracies as well.

The central idea behind *kaizen* is very important: understanding that everything in an organization can always be improved and that people at every level can make a contribution. It is in keeping with my view that the reformer's work is never done. How do you instill in a bureaucracy this notion of ongoing and dynamic change, which is so alien to bureaucratic culture?

As with the Japanese use of *kaizen*, a leader should provide incentives for his employees to come up with ideas on how to improve performance. She shouldn't just put up a suggestion box. She needs to get people at all levels thinking and working as a team. . . . Leaders need to break down silos and stovepipes and get people thinking beyond their own narrow piece of the action, get them thinking about how the organization as a whole can do better. People need to be incentivized to think "outside their lane." Managers at all levels should regularly sit down with their folks and talk about ways to do the work more efficiently. . . .

PROBLEM 4-4

1. Consider an example of organizational change with which you are familiar. What factors prompted the organization to act? What role did its leaders play? How successful were they? What resistance did they confront? What might you have done differently?
2. What are examples of "disruptive technologies" in law?[176] Is Legal Zoom, which markets on-line form preparation services, a case study? Bar associations in several states sued the company for unauthorized practice of law.[177] If you were the leader of an association whose members feared on-line competition, how would you respond?[178]
3. Meet with other members in your class in small groups to brainstorm about solutions to a problem at your institution or for lawyers in policy-making roles. Come up with a process for brainstorming and reaching consensus that avoids groupthink. After you decide on a solution, evaluate the process and the result.

4. FEEDBACK

One of the key ways that leaders can build effective relationships with followers is through constructive feedback. Candid dialogue is particularly critical when individuals are not performing in ways consistent with organizational needs and expectations. Yet as leaders themselves acknowledge, they often prefer to avoid having such difficult conversations.[179] And when they do, researchers find that most feedback is ineffective in producing the desired changes.[180] To address such performance difficulties, leaders should consider underlying causes.

- Awareness: Do individuals know how others perceive their work and how they are falling short?
- Competence: Do individuals have the right skills, experience, and knowledge?
- Barriers: Do individuals have adequate responsibility, authority, and support?
- Motivation: Do individuals want to do what is necessary, do they see a need to do it, and do they believe they will be rewarded for doing it?

In providing feedback around such issues, leaders need to structure candid dialogue that involves active empathic listening and mutual problem solving.[181] That means listening with an open mind, identifying needs, and brainstorming mutually acceptable solutions. Best practices for feedback include:

- making sure that the person in need of coaching is ready to hear it and has had time to prepare, and that there is sufficient time and privacy for honest conversation;
- providing support and encouragement as well as criticism; and emphasizing positive not just negative behaviors;
- helping individuals identify the causes of their problems and ways that they can improve to achieve their maximum potential;

- presenting specific and recent examples, and giving the other person full opportunity to respond, explain, and correct any misperceptions;
- developing a joint action plan, which includes specific performance goals and ways of helping the other person attain them; and
- expressing confidence in the individual's ability to improve.[182]

Some research suggests that the ratio of positive to negative comments in feedback should be at least 3 to 1, and preferably 5 to 1 in order to produce maximum improvement.[183] Experts also recommend that the feedback be honest, straightforward, and "problem-oriented" not "person-oriented." It should target behavior rather than personal characteristics.[184] The communication also needs to be two-way. Persons receiving feedback should have ample opportunity to express their views and leaders should treat them with respect. In *Practicing Positive Leadership,* Kim Cameron recommends that anyone giving feedback not speak for more than three or four sentences before giving the other person an opportunity to respond, and that parties should seek to identify areas of agreement.[185] Other ways to respond to problematic performance issues are reviewed in the section below on conflict management.

C. CONFLICT MANAGEMENT

A related way in which leaders exercise influence is through resolving, or at least managing, conflict. They play multiple roles: negotiating and mediating disputes, advising disputants, and structuring processes for dispute resolution. These roles are significant in terms of the time they require and the impact they have on performance. Estimates suggest that business leaders spend between 15 and 40 percent of their time dealing with conflicts.[186] For lawyers holding leadership positions, the percentage may be even higher. Not only do they face friction in their own workplaces, they also represent clients involved in disputes. Lawyers as policy leaders similarly confront conflict in multiple settings involving subordinates, peers, and other stakeholders.

Failure to handle conflict effectively carries substantial costs. Unresolved workplace disputes can lead to stress, mental health difficulties, turnover, absenteeism, non-cooperation, miscommunication, litigation, retaliation, and sabotage. Fear of conflict can inhibit constructive criticism. Mishandled legal disputes can cost millions, ruin reputations, and derail careers. In cases of international conflict or civil war, the human costs are staggering.

Yet, when managed effectively, conflict can be a source of productive communication and change. It can provide the catalyst for reform and a challenge to received wisdom. There is truth in the quip that when two people always agree, "one of them is unnecessary."[187] Conflict can also signal problems in relationships or organizational practices that need attention. In short, conflict can be a source of leaders' best ideas as well as worst failures.[188]

The following overview explores conflict resolution skills that are necessary for any leadership position. For those interested in the topic, it also provides references to more in-depth treatment of negotiation, mediation, international relations, interpersonal dynamics, alternative dispute resolution, and related topics. The point here is not to attempt an exhaustive summary, but rather to offer basic foundations for dealing with recurrent leadership challenges.

1. THE DYNAMICS OF CONFLICT

Definitions of conflict vary. Some experts include any situation involving "apparently incompatible interests, goals, principles, or feelings."[189] Others define it as a struggle over values, resources, needs, status, and power.[190] In some settings, it makes sense to distinguish between conflicts involving relationships and conflicts involving tasks or issues. In other settings, the distinction may be between disputes over process, and disputes over goals or values. Of the conflicts common in workplaces, employees express most frustration with those raising relational issues, such as clashing work styles or personalities.[191] Many circumstances hold potential for disputes, but whether they develop depends on factors including the importance of issues at stake, the costs of fighting for them, the resources available, and the likelihood of success.

The causes of conflict obviously vary, but certain patterns are common. Often a history of unresolved differences and repressed animosity will flare up in response to some precipitating event or change in conditions. Even relatively trivial incidents can become hot buttons for dispute when invested with deeper meaning.

The stakes in conflict can include values (such as priorities and ethical commitments), interests (such as money, status, or control) and underlying needs (such as security, recognition, or meaning).[192] Root causes frequently involve objective circumstances, such as insufficient resources; incompatible interests; power disparities; and differences in race, ethnicity, gender, religion, and culture. Subjective perceptions matter as well, particularly when fueled by incomplete information, miscommunication, and cognitive biases.[193] For example, a history of acrimony may result in attribution errors; parties may assign malicious motives to opponents' actions, rather than consider more benign explanations. Confirmation bias and selective perception can then kick in to reinforce prior assumptions and reduce cognitive dissonance.[194] People also tend to define fairness in terms of distributional principles that favor their own self interests: equality, need, merit, and precedent are invoked to justify preferred outcomes.[195] "Reactive devaluation" also fuels conflict; people react adversely to a proposal or concession if it comes from an opponent.[196] In one illustrative study, a researcher took peace proposals developed by Israeli negotiators and mislabeled them as Palestinian proposals, and mislabeled Palestinian proposals as Israeli proposals. When he asked Israeli citizens to evaluate the suggestions, they preferred those misattributed to Israelis. When he asked Palestinians to evaluate proposals, they preferred those misattributed to Palestinians.[197]

Once conflicts escalate, they are unlikely to be resolved as long as underlying causes remain unaddressed. Tensions may ebb and flow, but a cycle of resistance and retaliation will continue, sometimes resulting in intractable disputes that parties pursue as ends in themselves.

2. RESPONSES TO CONFLICT

Responses to conflict fall into certain common categories. Experts use somewhat different labels, but generally identify avoidance, contention, coercion, appeasement, compromise, and collaboration. No single approach is categorically preferable, and research on relative effectiveness is mixed.[198] On the whole, however, experts agree on certain general points.

Avoidance is many people's preferred response, and with reason.[199] Open confrontation risks unpleasantness, stress, and retaliation, and may seem pointless if the adversary has substantially greater power and a history of unresponsiveness. Leaders' desire for approval can also keep them from using their influence to broach difficult issues.[200] Yet, as a general matter, research suggests that avoidance should be avoided. Unresolved problems are likely to fester, impair productivity, and lead to more costly confrontations later. Franklin Roosevelt, an otherwise exemplary lawyer leader, hated firing people, and avoided such unpleasantness by simply moving them to the periphery of policy making. But as one expert notes, this is a "messy way of dealing with unsatisfactory performance and it often creates more problems than it solves. Sometimes, ruthless clarity is better for everyone concerned than too much empathy, avoidance, or denial."[201] Of course, under some circumstances, flight may be preferable to fight. A delayed response makes sense if it gives parties time to let their emotions cool and the adrenaline rush subside so they can carefully consider their reaction.[202] Temporary disengagement can be useful to prevent hostilities that will be difficult to remedy later, but it should not substitute for mutual problem solving under less volatile circumstances.

More direct responses to conflict involve contention or coercion. Openly vying for victory or imposing a solution authoritatively can seem satisfying to the winning party in the short run, but it is often counterproductive in the long term. In some instances, quick decisive action may be justifiable, and a prudent means of deterring further hostile acts. But outcomes that leave losers' fundamental needs or immediate interests unmet are likely to prove unstable, and to provoke resentment, resistance, or recurring confrontations. Competitive and coercive approaches also short-circuit opportunities for more creative, mutually acceptable solutions.

The same is true of appeasement. Parties who yield not because they believe the outcome is reasonable, but because they perceive no viable alternative, may nurse grievances that will erupt in more destructive fashion later. Moreover, capitulation may encourage even more oppressive behavior from a victorious bully. As experts note, "[T]he leader who always appeases is like someone who feeds crocodiles hoping that they'll eat him last."[203]

An often preferable option is compromise. Splitting differences may be productive particularly in contexts involving zero-sum trade-offs, in which no party can be made better-off without the other party suffering. But that approach risks leaving both sides dissatisfied, and it may fail to promote fair resolutions if the baseline for division is highly unequal.[204]

The alternative most experts promote is collaboration, or what some label integrative problem solving. Under this approach, parties work together to identify win-win outcomes that build on shared concerns and mutual respect.[205] Although this process has obvious advantages, it tends to be time consuming, and may not work if parties' differences are too great and their positions too entrenched.

Cultural as well as situational differences should inform the choice of responses. Groups vary in their tolerance for open disagreement and expression of emotion, and their preferences in negotiating styles and outcomes. Asian societies, for example, tend to be relatively restrained and accommodating, and to ascribe high value to harmonious relationships.[206] Yet individuals carry multiple identities—national, religious, racial, gender, occupational, and so forth. Stereotyping on the basis of any single attribute is bound to be misleading.[207] Leaders' responses to conflict thus need to be sensitive to diversity without making crude generalizations based on demographic characteristics.

3. STRATEGIES

Leaders play multiple roles in conflict management. They negotiate, mediate, facilitate, and advise concerning specific disputes, and they create organizational structures designed to prevent, resolve, or creatively use conflict. Each of these roles presents distinct challenges but also calls for certain common skills and strategies.

The first requirement is knowledge, both of self and others. In seeking to resolve conflicts in which they are personally involved, leaders need to be aware of their own "hot buttons," their underlying emotions, interests, and needs, and their "best alternative to a negotiated agreement" (BATNA).[208] So, for example, individuals who feel themselves losing control due to anger or anxiety can ask for a break, begin writing down constructive points that they wish to discuss later, or "freeze frames" by mentally imagining a pleasant situation or one in which they felt calm and self-confident.[209] An effective resolution often depends on learning as much as possible about the goals and concerns of everyone involved in the conflict. Seeking information from multiple sources is critical, as is active and empathic listening. Common techniques involve listening without interrupting; restating points to be sure that the other parties' meaning is understood; paying attention to body language and to what is unsaid as well as said; avoiding accusations, blame, moral judgment, or inflammatory rhetoric; probing for underlying reasons and concerns; and brainstorming about creative solutions.[210]

Experts also recommend "switching lenses:"

With the reverse lens, for example, people ask themselves, 'What would the other person in this conflict say and in what ways might that be true?' With the long lens they ask, 'How will I most likely view this situation in six months?' With the wide lens, they ask, 'Regardless of the outcome of this issue, how can I grow and learn from it?'[211]

In some contexts, it is helpful for leaders to identify the effects that the other person's behavior is having, and how those might be inconsistent with that person's goals.[212] Once parties have identified a solution, they need to agree on specific steps for implementation, which may include strategies for avoiding problems in the future.

In their landmark negotiation primer, *Getting to Yes,* Roger Fisher and William Ury similarly suggest focusing on interests, not on positions; insisting on objective criteria for assessing those interests; and inventing options for mutual gain.[213] Although the book also suggested the need to "separate the people from the problem," Fisher has subsequently acknowledged that "[i]n some cases the people are the problem; negotiating a good relationship with them may be more important than the substantive outcome of any one negotiation."[214] In commenting on resolving conflicts at the Supreme Court, Justice Elena Kagan emphasized a lesson she learned from Justice Scalia: "If you take it personally, you shouldn't be in this job." As she added, "there's always going to be the next case . . . and there's going to be the case after that and you better have continuing good relationships with your colleagues."[215]

To that end, other experts advise that leaders be willing to reach out to restore productive communication. An apology that is genuine and does not make unwarranted concessions of fault can often be a first step in building trust and empathy. In short, the overarching goal should be to reframe the conflict as an opportunity for collaborative problem solving and to create the conditions that will enable such a resolution to occur.

That same approach is useful for leaders who are mediating conflict among others or facilitating its resolution through advice and coaching. This role typically involves:

- establishing credibility and rapport by expressing concern for all parties and maintaining impartiality;
- insisting that parties remain civil, respectful, and committed to creating a productive working environment;
- helping parties identify the nature and causes of the problem, as well as shared values and objectives;
- encouraging parties to focus on underlying needs, priorities and concerns, and to identify plausible strategies for addressing them;
- providing a disinterested reliable source of information; and
- assisting the parties develop solutions and agree on a plan for action that is specific and that avoids "toothless" promises (such as a willingness to seek input in the future).[216]

Research on resolving contested issues in group settings emphasizes:

- creating common goals;
- maximizing information;
- multiplying proposed solutions;
- focusing the discussion on facts;
- ensuring that no significant issues are "undiscussable";
- maintaining a balanced power structure;
- injecting humor;
- asking people to look at multiple sides of the same question; and
- resolving issues without forcing consensus.[217]

When parties are unable to reach a sustainable agreement, the best strategy may be to let the dust settle and set a date for another meeting.

In *Say What You Mean*, Oren Sofer suggests language for certain "difficult conversations." For example, to avoid misunderstandings, lawyers can ask, "I'm not sure I was totally clear. What is your understanding?" or "I'd like to make sure we're on the same page. What are you taking away from this?"[218] To suggest solutions, lawyers could say, "Would you be willing to . . . ?" or "Could it work for you to . . . ?" or "How would it be for you to . . . ?"[219] When saying no, lawyers could say, "I hear how important this is to you, and I'm not seeing how I can make it work given that I also have a need for. . . . Could we explore some other options that might work for you?"[220]

Collaboration is one of the most effective strategies for managing conflict. Leaders can establish a collaborative process for gathering information about the problem and mutually acceptable solutions. Barbara Grey describes such an approach in the wake of the disaster at the Three Mile Island Nuclear Reactor. Community members were concerned about contamination and initially distrustful of the agencies charged with disseminating safety information. Officials at those agencies were, for their part, frustrated with what they considered irrational local responses. The solution was a Citizens Radiation Monitoring Program, which engaged concerned residents in assessing ongoing risk levels.[221] Such a process can enhance acceptance and commitment from affected parties.

Leaders can also play a crucial role in creating "conflict competent" organizations. That requires fostering cultures that value civility and constructive disagreement; provide multiple channels for dispute resolution; and offer support, training, and mediation for those involved in conflict.[222] Research makes clear that people's sense of the fairness of dispute resolution processes is even more important than substantive outcomes in promoting overall satisfaction and confidence. Given that fact, leaders should be sure that organizational structures are meeting participants' expectations of equity and legitimacy.[223]

In *Leading through Conflict*, Mark Gerzon describes an example of rethinking organizational structures for handling friction in a global company. Headquartered in the United States, the company had rapidly growing European and Asian divisions that came into conflict with American divisions over salary differentials, lack of follow-through for each others' multinational clients, and more subtle cultural tensions.[224] At prior meetings involving thirty senior executives of regional divisions, the practice had been to float ideas for new strategies and adopt those that received the most support. The result was that executives would spend countless hours giving examples about what someone else was doing wrong and needed to change. With the help of an international consulting group, the leader structured the meeting differently. Each executive was placed on a team charged with taking responsibility for the company's pressing problems and proposing solutions. The point was to force them out of their self-interested positions and make them wrestle with the big picture.

Consider circumstances in which you have faced significant conflicts. Would such a strategy have been effective? If not, what other approaches might have worked better?

PROBLEM 4-5

1. How would you evaluate your own strengths and weaknesses concerning conflict management?[225] Make a list of areas in which you could improve. If you have hot buttons, how could you better address them? Think of two recent situations in which you have experienced significant conflict. How well did you manage them? What could you have done differently? To aid your analysis, make a list of all the strategies that you pursued and all the barriers that you confronted. Make another list of all the thoughts and feelings that you did not express. Think about why you did not voice those concerns and whether a fuller discussion would have yielded a better resolution. Identify approaches that might be effective in similar future situations. Structure a conversation with someone with whom you have a significant disagreement. Actively listen to his or her views and try to understand the situation from your partner's point of view. Challenge yourself to gain new insights and information, and to avoid passing judgment. Ask your partner to listen to your responses and give you feedback on what was most and least persuasive.
2. Investigate a conflict that has generated significant public attention. What were its underlying causes and dynamics? What barriers to resolution did opposing sides face? How well did leaders handle the situation? What might you have done differently?

MEDIA RESOURCES

Masterful examples of conflict resolution, influence, and leader-follower behavior appear in *Invictus*, a film based on Nelson Mandela's early years as president of South Africa and his strategies to help the country overcome the bitter legacy of apartheid. Chapter 11 details examples. *Madame Secretary* offers countless examples of conflict resolution by the American secretary of state. In Season 3, for example, the secretary averts a world crisis by giving the Russian government a face-saving way of avoiding acknowledging that centrifuges were stolen from one of its nuclear facilities. In the last season of *Scandal*, the Attorney

General and the Independent Counsel also negotiate conflicts in which the stakes are global.

D. COMMUNICATION

One of the critical ways that leaders exercise influence is through communication. In one recent national survey of professionals, a majority rated communication as the most important capability for both political and business leaders.[226] In both public and private settings, leaders try to persuade followers, allies, adversaries, and the broader public. Although not everyone is equally skilled in all forums, any aspiring leader needs to master certain basic techniques of effective communication. The excerpts below set forth key principles, beginning with those applicable to public presentations.

1. STRATEGIES

DEBORAH L. RHODE, PUBLIC PRESENTATIONS

Excerpted in "Leadership in Law" 69 STANFORD LAW REVIEW 1603, 1629-1632 (2017)

Public speaking is an acquired skill, and many of its most effective practitioners did not start out that way. Abraham Lincoln's early efforts were, as one historian put it, "uniformly unhappy."[227] A widely acclaimed biography of Barack Obama similarly reported:

As a campaigner in Illinois in 1999 in an unsuccessful Congressional race against Bobby Rush, Obama was an awkward, if earnest novice. He was pedantic, distant, a little condescending at times, a better fit for the University of Chicago [Law School] seminar room than for the stump or the pulpit of a black church in Englewood. He had a tendency, as one of his staff noted, "to talk over, or down to people." A prominent Chicago lawyer and mentor Newton Minow, remembers that [Obama] "wasn't that good. Someone would ask a question and he would give a professorial answer. His answers were just too long and boring."[228]

Cory Booker, a Rhodes scholar and graduate of Stanford University and Yale Law School, also had to learn what campaign workers called a "more basic way . . . of communicating" with poor communities of color when he ran for mayor of Newark. Analogizing City Hall to a "Byzantine labyrinth" wasn't effective.[229]

Yet both of these leaders resisted the pressure to talk down to voters and speak in comforting soundbites. At the close of his presidency, Obama rejected suggestions that he use the term "radical Islam" because it was a "pithy phrase" that would arouse the public. As Obama put it, "I refuse to give in to the notion that the American people can't handle complicated information."[230] By contrast, California Congressman Adam Schiff, a former prosecutor, and then-chair of the House of Representatives Committee on Intelligence, drew a different lesson about the value of soundbites. By his own admission, he was initially an "awful candidate, pompous. . . [and] long winded."[231] As he told a *New Yorker* reporter, "I thought it was demeaning to have to answer questions on serious issues in thirty seconds. Now I know you have to do it in a tweet."[232]

Just as those politicians evolved, so do many leaders. That process requires several key strategies. The first is knowledge. Knowledge is power in leadership, and public presentations are no exception. The first step in preparation is to know your objectives, your audience, your occasion, and your substance.

Speakers often have multiple agendas and multiple constituencies that can pull in different directions. For example, politicians need to consider whether a particular speech is primarily intended to mobilize their base, persuade uncommitted voters, attract favorable media coverage, shore up their legacy, or send a message to other national and international leaders. Is a presentation to colleagues or potential clients designed mainly to convey information, build a relationship, sell an idea, or motivate change? What speakers most hope to accomplish needs to guide their style and substance. The importance of such choices is captured in a perhaps apocryphal observation attributed to various Roman historians: "When Cicero spoke, people marveled. When Caesar spoke, people marched." Much the same was said of Winston Churchill's World War II addresses to the British people: "He mobilized the English language and sent it into battle."[233]

Obvious though the need for clarity of purpose may seem, even seasoned speakers can lose sight of their main objective. Robert Reich, former Secretary of Labor in the Clinton administration wryly recalls his own foibles in preparing for his Senate confirmation hearing. When asked in practice sessions about any significant—and therefore potentially divisive—issue, his tendency as a professor of public policy was to elaborate his views. This was a mistake. As senior administration officials explained, "You have to respond to [Senators'] questions. You don't have to answer them. You *shouldn't* answer them. You're not expected to answer them." The main point of confirmation hearings, from Senators' point of view, was to give them, not the nominee, an opportunity to look learned and wise. The point from the nominee's point of view was to gain support, which called for dodging controversy while exuding deference. An ideal answer was something like, "Senator, you know far more about that issue than I do and I look forward to hearing your views in the months to come."[234] So too, lawyers seeking positions or pitching clients need to recall that their primary objective is to win support, not to score points by showing how much smarter they are than those asking questions.

In other contexts, however, leaders seek less to persuade a hostile audience than to escape after giving them as little ammunition as possible. In 2019, the Democrat-controlled House Judiciary Committee called the acting Attorney

General Mathew Whittaker to testify about any instructions that President Trump might have given to curtail the investigation by special counsel Robert Mueller. NPR coverage of the hearing revealed Whittaker masterfully running the clock, dodging, obfuscating, and "regularly declining to answer."[235] When asked for a simple "yes or no" answer, he fought the question and demanded to know "what is your basis for that question?" When the Chair, New York Representative and former lawyer Jerry Nadler finally asked him point blank if he had been asked to approve any action by the Special Counsel, Whittaker responded that the Chair's time for questions was up.[236]

That performance was an object lesson in staying on message. Leaders often need to exercise that skill and to avoid being thrown by minor distractions or technological malfunctions. Bill Gates famously experienced a computer shutdown during his public launch of Windows 98.[237] If it can happen to him, it can happen to anyone, so speakers should plan accordingly and have a backup strategy.

Knowledge of the audience is equally critical. Speakers too often suffer from one variation of the curse of knowledge: they don't know what others don't know.[238] They should strive to find out. How likely are audience members to be informed on the subject under discussion or sympathetic to the speakers' goals and objectives? How engaged or distracted will they be? Will they have read materials sent out in advance? Will they expect handouts, PowerPoints, or opportunities for interaction? What kind of arguments and evidence, and what combination of education and entertainment, will be most persuasive?

Humor tailored to the occasion can be highly effective. It can relieve tension, create a bond with the audience, draw media coverage, and promote greater recall of the message.[239] Chris Anderson, the curator of TED Talks, advises not jokes, but anecdotes relevant to the subject matter.[240] Bill Clinton was a master of this strategy. At a point in his presidency after his wife had taken enormous criticism for her role in health care reform and the Whitewater real estate scandal, Clinton opened his Gridiron speech before Washington journalists and politicians by expressing regret. "The First Lady is sorry she can't be with you tonight," he told them. "If you believe that, I've got some land in Arkansas I'd like to sell you."[241] Ronald Reagan scored a telling victory in his debates with presidential candidate Walter Mondale when he responded to a question about his age by stating, "I refuse to make age an issue in this election. I will not exploit, for political purposes, my opponent's youth and inexperience."[242] Humor can be especially useful for forceful female leaders by softening any perceived sharp edges.[243]

Rising above insults in a clever way can also be useful. A case in point involves Danica Roem, a transgender woman who defeated an opponent for the Virginia state legislature after an acrimonious and homophobic campaign. He refused to debate her and repeatedly referred to her using male pronouns. After her victory, Roem responded to a reporter's inquiry about his derogatory comments by explaining, "I don't attack my constituents. Bob is my constituent now." [244]

For all speakers, Self-deprecating humor tends to be particularly effective. In commenting on the conventional advice to speakers to "be yourself," Anderson adds, "the one exception to that is if you are arrogant and self-centered, then you should definitely pretend to be someone else."[245]

Finding ways to establish credibility and connect with audience members, collectively or individually, is always helpful. In some contexts, it makes sense to begin with the limitations of an idea or position, so as to build trust when talking about strengths.[246] The most effective communicators use emotionally charged language to engage a listener's self-concept. They rely on stories, metaphors, and repetition of simple concepts to amplify their messages.[247] Donald Trump's constant invocation of stock phrases—"build the wall," "lock her up"—were highly effective in galvanizing his base. Bill Clinton had exceptional empathetic and emotional appeal, which helps explain why he finished his presidency with some of the highest approval ratings in recent memory despite being dogged by scandal.[248]

In public speeches, if the introduction has not established the speaker's credibility, that is his or her first task, and the relevant credentials aren't always titles. Successful communicators have an art of finding or fabricating commonalities: a similar job, a family member who was from the area, a longstanding interest in a local product, athletic team, or landmark. It helps to make verbal or visual contact with as many members of the audience as possible, both before, during, and after the presentation. It is also important to gauge the audience's interest in the speaker's own experience. "Park your ego," advises Anderson.[249] Overly self-referential material can leave captive audience members feeling like the P.G. Wodehouse character, who complains: "The Agee woman told us for three quarters of an hour how she came to write her beastly book when a simple apology was all that was required."

Leaders also need to know their forum and to adapt their style accordingly. As Obama evolved as a speaker, one of his strengths was that he could change styles without relinquishing his genuineness. He subtly shifted accent and cadences depending on the audience:

> A more straight up delivery for a luncheon of businesspeople in the [Chicago] Loop; a folksier approach at downstate [rallies]; . . . echoes of the pastors of the black church when he was in one. Obama is multilingual, a shape shifter. . . . The greatest of all American speakers, Martin Luther King, Jr., did the same, shifting from one cadence and set of metaphors and frame of reference when speaking in Ebeneezer Baptist to quite another as he spoke to a national, multiracial audience on the steps of the Lincoln Memorial. There was, for King . . . a time to quote Tillich and a time to quote the blues. . . . Obama [also] crafted his speech to fit the moment.[250]

Obama himself has also noted the importance of tailoring a message to those who might find it threatening. As he told an audience at Howard University, effective communication "requires more than just speaking out":

It requires listening to those with whom you disagree, and being prepared to compromise. You know, when I was a state senator, I helped pass Illinois's first racial profiling law, and one of the first laws in the nation requiring the videotaping of confessions in capital cases. And we were successful because, early on, I engaged law enforcement. I didn't say to them, 'Oh you guys are so racist, you know you need to do something.' I understood, as many of you do, that the overwhelming majority of police officers are good and honest and courageous. . . . The point is, you need allies in a democracy. That's just the way it is.[251]

Obama's understanding about how to talk about such divisive issues also evolved during his presidency, as did other lawyers in his administration. James Comey, a former prosecutor and director of the FBI under Obama, recalls a conversation that they had about the use of the term "mass incarceration," which Comey had found problematic:

To my ears, the term "mass incarceration" conjures an image of World War II Japanese internment camps, where vast numbers of people were herded behind barbed wire. I thought the term was both inaccurate and insulting to a lot of good people in law enforcement who care deeply about helping people trapped in dangerous neighborhoods. It was inaccurate in the sense that there was nothing "mass" about the incarceration: every defendant was charged individually, represented individually by counsel, convicted by a court individually, sentenced individually, reviewed on appeal individually, and incarcerated. That added up to a lot of people in jail, but there was nothing "mass" about it, I said. And the insulting part, I explained, was the way it cast as illegitimate the efforts by cops, agents, and prosecutors—joined by the black community—to rescue hard-hit neighborhoods.

[Obama] responded by urging me to see how black people might experience law enforcement and the courts very differently, and that it was hard to blame them for seeing the jailing of so many black men, in numbers wildly greater than their proportion of the population, as anything other than "mass."[252]

One of leaders' most common mistakes is to assume that the essence of persuasion lies in presenting strong arguments. Yet researchers find that arguments are only part of what matters. Other factors are equally influential, such as the speaker's credibility, ability to connect on the right emotional level, and use of vivid language that makes arguments come alive.[253] Speakers always need to convey energy and enthusiasm, but strategies for doing so need to vary. For example, television is a notoriously cool medium, and calls for low-key conversational styles, not the flamboyant oratorical flourishes that are effective before large crowds. Body language and appearance are equally important. Some research finds that content is less important than voice and nonverbal expression as a factor in evaluations of performance.[254] Eye contact, a smile, and a manner that demonstrates self-confidence and engagement can be critical, as is eliminating "verbal graffiti" ("ah," "um," "so").[255] Speakers also need to avoid "uptalk," a tendency particularly associated with women, which involves concluding a sentence with rising inflection that sounds like a question, signaling weakness or self doubt. [256]

Clothes and grooming can also matter, particularly for women, who face more intense scrutiny and more severe consequences for falling short.[257] A "rumpled appearance" can convey a lack of "presence."[258] Elizabeth Warren was told she looked like a "school marm" and had to upgrade her glasses and overly "sensible" hairstyle.[259] Cory Booker's wardrobe got a makeover after an aide expressed the view that he dressed like a "goddamned white Republican."[260] First impressions are highly durable, and speakers benefit from meeting the audience's expectations.[261] Otherwise, if leaders don't know how to look the part, the public wonders what else they don't know.

Body language is also critical. If seated, speakers should lean inward in a non-aggressive way to indicate interest and engagement. If standing, they should aim for good posture and project warmth and strength. In either case, presenters should avoid "twitching, fidgeting, and other visual static signals" that suggest they are not in control. Poise telegraphs stability, which is important to a credible leadership presence."[262]

Conveying emotion is "a double-edged sword." It will make people who share your sentiments feel closer to you but will make others feel more distant and suspect you are being manipulative.[263] Hillary Clinton's tears during the 2008 New Hampshire primary reportedly humanized her and worked to her advantage with voters who found her cold and unfeeling. But in general, displays of emotion are riskier for women because they evoke gender stereotypes inconsistent with leadership.[264] Barack Obama has acknowledged working hard to avoid the stereotype of the "angry black man." In his campaigns and throughout his first term, any show of anger was off limits; in his second term he felt more able to express at least frustration.[265]

It is generally a mistake to "speak from the heart," even if that is what the occasion seems to demand. Effective speakers always prepare, even if they abandon or adapt their message in light of the circumstances. Anderson offers a cautionary tale from the first TED program. There one of the speakers began, "As I was driving down here wondering what to say to you. . . ." He then offered an unfocused list of random observations.[266] The opposite mistake is to remain tethered to a detailed script. If a talk is written out, speakers should know it well enough to avoid simply reading. If the presentation needs to look unrehearsed, that often requires rehearsal.

There are exceptions. Martin Luther King was able to "wing it" in his most famous "I have a dream" speech, before a crowd of 250,000 people and millions more on television, because he had used similar material in some 350 speeches the preceding year. When Mahalia Jackson, the famed Gospel singer, urged him from behind the podium, "Tell 'em about the dream, Martin," he improvised one of the nation's most soaring oratorical passages.[267] But less-experienced presenters need to practice until they can come across looking relaxed, confident, and unrehearsed. Speaking without notes is always impressive but doing it effectively generally requires substantial preparation. Even the ablest speakers recognize as much. Winston Churchill practiced in his bath, and when a startled valet once came rushing to the door, Churchill explained: "I was not speaking to you Norman, I was addressing the House of Commons."[268]

Finally, the speaker needs to know the subject. That means not just substantive knowledge, but what part of that knowledge is most important and accessible in the format available. Many otherwise impressive presentations suffer from one fact too many, or maybe more than one. Speakers need enough detail to make their arguments vivid, but not so much as to get bogged down in minor examples. For main points, communication experts suggest a rule of three. The goal is to provide enough to support the main theme but not so much as to dwarf the audience's normal attention span.

Prominent speakers also need to be mindful about how their remarks can be misinterpreted or taken out of context. In her autobiography *Becoming*, Michelle Obama describes how she learned that lesson after a statement she made in a campaign rally went viral. She said:

> [W]hat we've learned over this year is that hope is making a comeback! And let me tell you something, for the first time in my adult lifetime, I'm really proud of my country. Not just because Barack has done well, but because I think people are hungry for change.[269]

Opponents took the acknowledgement that this was the first time she was proud to be an American as evidence that "[s]he's not a patriot. This is who she really is."[270] And Obama felt responsible: "In trying to speak casually, I'd forgotten how weighted each little phrase could be. Unwittingly, I'd given the haters a fourteen-word feast."[271] Later, in watching recordings of her stump speeches, she realized that in trying to convey seriousness, she had come across as too severe. "I could see how the opposition had managed to dice up these images and feed me to the public as some sort of pissed-off harpy. . . . The easiest way to disregard a woman's voice is to package her as a scold. . . ." She adjusted her style accordingly.[272]

Communication research suggests a number of stylistic principles about what makes for an effective presentation. A compelling start and close are crucial, and they are particularly effective if tied together in a way that completes the circle and enhances coherence. A successful opening is often a story, an amusing quotation, or a surprising, counterintuitive claim that will attract audience interest. Humorist and screenwriter Nora Ephron makes the point with an account of her first day of a high school journalism course. The class was asked to write the lead for an article in the school newspaper about an upcoming conference. The entire faculty was to participate in an all-day program the following week in the state capitol, led by speakers including then California governor Pat Brown and the world-renowned anthropologist Margaret Mead. Ephron recalled that she and most of her classmates produced opening sentences explaining "who, what, where, and when." No one spotted the lead that their teacher suggested: "There will be no school next Thursday."[273]

The most memorable presentations are typically ones that express emotion, emphasize stories not statistics, propose solutions, and appeal to common concerns and values. Effective speakers often rely on metaphor, symbols, repetition, and terms of inclusion (we and our not them and they).[274] Franklin Roosevelt's fireside chats during the Depression were legendary because the President, though part of one of America's most elite families, was able to convey an understanding of the lives of ordinary Americans. His use of language that anyone could use and avoidance of empty promises conveyed respect, reassurance, and empathy. He "identified with those he never met or heard, and more important, they identified with him."[275]

Researchers find that speech imagery is positively correlated with outstanding communication and leadership.[276] Even highly educated audiences are more likely to remember facts and figures presented through stories than through statistics.[277] Hillary Clinton has been subject to criticism for being overly policy-oriented and "determinedly not dazzling."[278] As she herself recognized during the 2016 presidential campaign, "I've laid out all of these policies and people kind of made fun of it, because 'Oh there she goes with another policy.'"[279]

In *Made to Stick*, Chip and Dan Heath offer a framework for communicating messages that will be retained: they should be simple, unexpected, concrete, credible, emotional, and tell a story [SUCCESs].[280] An example that makes their messages stick comes from a campaign by the Center for Science in the Public Interest. Its challenge was to reduce consumption of popcorn popped in coconut oil. Movie theatres used the oil because it provided an appealing texture and aroma, but it also was extremely high in saturated fats; one typical popcorn carton had almost twice the U.S. Department of Agriculture's recommended average for the entire day. Center staff recognized that a campaign based on that fact would "have zero appeal. It's dry, it's academic, who cares?"[281] Instead they staged a press conference with the following message: "A medium-sized 'butter' popcorn at a typical neighborhood movie theatre contains more artery-clogging fat than a bacon and egg breakfast, a Big Mac and fries for lunch, and a steak dinner with all the trimmings—combined." The conference included a buffet table with all the fatty foods mentioned. The press had a field day. Typical headlines read: "Popcorn Gets an R Rating," "Lights, Action, Cholesterol," "Theatre Popcorn is a Double Feature of Fat."[282]

Effective communication often relies on such dramatic communication strategies. Mahatma Gandhi perfected methods of nonviolent protest including prayer, fasting, and marches against heavily armed opponents to highlight differences between colonial brutality and peaceful Indian resistance.[283] Nelson Mandela, at his inauguration as South Africa's first post-apartheid president, had one of his former white prison guards sit in the front row, thus underscoring his faith in racial reconciliation.[284] Margaret Thatcher won election as Britain's first female prime minister using clever visual campaign ads, such as a poster picturing a long queue outside a British unemployment office and a caption reading: "Labour isn't working."[285]

The growing influence of the mass media and Internet have amplified the importance of such graphic presentations. *An Inconvenient Truth*, Al Gore's documentary on global warming, brought public consciousness to new levels by showing footage of ice caps melting, polar bears stranded, and mockups of the potential environmental disasters of uncurbed temperature changes. Invisible Children's video *Kony 2012* on child soldiers attracted more than 50 million views and caused donations to spike from $14 million to $27 million in a single year.[286] Earth Island Institute's video of dolphins killed by tuna nets helped achieve customer boycotts, federal legislation, and corporate pledges to alter fishing methods.[287] Animal Rights activists convinced Pepsi Cola to withdraw support of bullfighting in Spain and Mexico by showing video footage of a bull bleeding to death in a fight; he was leaning for support against a billboard advertisement for Pepsi as he died. When the company refused to allow a stockholder activist to show the clip at a shareholders meeting, he positioned a van with television sets running the video in front of Pepsi headquarters. The film drew crowds of employees, shareholders, and the press, and Pepsi reversed its position on bullfights within the year.[288]

PowerPoint now makes such visual material available to any speaker, but too few take full advantage of the possibilities. Many make the mistake of simply presenting text, often in dense, list-like formats rather than relying on visually compelling images.[289] Such death-by-PowerPoint presentations leave many audiences if not half asleep then otherwise engaged—checking their cell phones or catching up on other work. The problem is compounded when speakers misjudge the length of their material, yet insist on getting through the entire slide collection either by speeding up or spilling over their allotted time. This leaves many audiences feeling about PowerPoint as Samuel Johnson did about Milton's *Paradise Lost*: "No one ever wished it longer."

Brevity is one of the best ways to maximize impact. Part of the reason is that it forces speakers to be self disciplined. When asked how long it took him to prepare a speech, Woodrow Wilson responded that it "depends on the length of the speech. If it is a ten-minute speech, it takes me two weeks to prepare it. If it is a half hour speech, it takes me a week. If I can take as long as I want to, it requires no preparation at all. I am ready now."[290] Brief eloquence is particularly likely to be memorable. Lincoln's Gettysburg Address was just over two minutes. The speaker before him droned on for two hours.[291] Bill Clinton was much mocked for his interminable Democratic Convention speech. And in some contexts, unwillingness to observe time limits or the audience's endurance can prove fatal. When I served as special counsel to the House of Representatives Committee on the Judiciary during the Clinton impeachment proceedings, I saw law professors from Harvard and Yale who were giving testimony ignore the red light signaling that their time was up. Committee members, who were unaccustomed to being treated like captive law students, were too annoyed by the speakers' arrogance to pay attention to the points being made in overtime. .

Crafting truly effective presentations requires time, skill, and effort, so leaders need one final form of knowledge: knowing how and when to delegate the drafting task. To take an obvious example, American presidents can ill afford to labor over what White House insiders label "Rose Garden rubbish." But they can issue clear instructions, along the lines of one of Dwight Eisenhower's directives: "tell them to go to hell but put it so they won't be offended."[292] There are, however, limits to what can be outsourced. Assistants can help in finding the right visuals and offering research and feedback, but at least for important occasions, speakers need to be sure that the material they are presenting reflects their own voice, vision, and values.

In the excerpt below, Heath and Heath summarize their strategies for effective communication, including ways to avoid another variation of the "curse of knowledge" that is common among lawyers.

CHIP HEATH AND DAN HEATH, MADE TO STICK: WHY SOME IDEAS SURVIVE AND OTHERS DIE

(New York: Random House, 2007), pp. 242-247

The Speakers and the Stickers

Each year in the second session of Chip's "Making Ideas Stick" class at Stanford, the students participate in an exercise, a kind of testable credential to show what kinds of messages stick and don't stick. The students are given some data from a government source on crime patterns in the United States. Half of them are asked to make a one-minute persuasive speech to convince their peers that nonviolent crime is a serious problem in this country. The other half are asked to take the position that it's not particularly serious.

Stanford students, as you'd expect, are smart. They also tend to be quick thinkers and good communicators. No one in the room ever gives a poor speech.

The students divide into small groups and each one gives a one-minute speech while the others listen. After each speech, the listeners rate the speaker: How impressive was the delivery? How persuasive?

What happens, invariably, is that the most polished speakers get the highest ratings. Students who are poised, smooth, and charismatic are rated at the top of the class. No surprise, right? Good speakers score well in speaking contexts.

The surprise comes next. The exercise appears to be over; in fact, Chip often plays a brief Monty Python clip to kill a few minutes and distract the students. Then, abruptly, he asks them to pull out a sheet of paper and write down, for each speaker they heard, every single idea that they remember.

The students are flabbergasted at how little they remember. Keep in mind that only ten minutes have elapsed since the speeches were given. Nor was there a huge volume of information to begin with—at most, they've heard eight one-minute speeches. And yet the students are lucky to recall one or two ideas from each speaker's presentation. Many draw a complete blank on some speeches—unable to remember a single concept.

In the average one-minute speech, the typical student uses 2.5 statistics. Only one student in ten tells a story. Those are the speaking statistics. The "remembering" statistics, on the other hand, are almost a mirror image: When students are asked to recall the speeches, 63 percent remember the stories. Only 5 percent remember any individual statistic.

Furthermore, almost no correlation emerges between "speaking talent" and the ability to make ideas stick. The people who were captivating speakers typically do no better than others in making their ideas stick. Foreign students—whose less-polished English often leaves them at the bottom of the speaking-skills rankings—are suddenly on a par with native speakers. The stars of stickiness are the students who made their case by telling stories, or by tapping into emotion, or by stressing a single point rather than ten. There is no question that a ringer—a student who came into the exercise having read this book—would squash the other students. A community college student for whom English is a second language could easily out-perform unwitting Stanford graduate students.

Why can't these smart, talented speakers make their ideas stick? A few of the villains discussed in this book are implicated. The first villain is the natural tendency to bury the lead—to get lost in a sea of information. One of the worst things about knowing a lot, or having access to a lot of information, is that we're tempted to share it all. High school teachers will tell you that when students write research papers they feel obligated to include every unearthed fact, as though the value were in the quantity of data amassed rather than its purpose or clarity. Stripping out information, in order to focus on the core, is not instinctual.

The second villain is the tendency to focus on the presentation rather than on the message. Public speakers naturally want to appear composed, charismatic, and motivational. And, certainly, charisma will help a properly designed message stick better. But all the charisma in the world won't save a dense, unfocused speech, as some Stanford students learn the hard way.

More Villains

. . . To beat decision paralysis, communicators have to do the hard work of finding the core. Lawyers must stress one or two points in their closing arguments, not ten. A teacher's lesson plans may contain fifty concepts to share with her students, but in order to be effective that teacher must devote most of her efforts to making the most critical two or three stick. Managers must share proverbs— "Names, names, and names," or "THE low-fare airline"—that help employees wring decisions out of ambiguous situations.

The archvillain of sticky ideas, as you know by now, is the Curse of Knowledge. The Stanford students didn't face the Curse of Knowledge because the data on crime were brand-new to them—they were more akin to reporters trying to avoid burying the lead on a news story than to experts who have forgotten what it's like not to know something.

The Curse of Knowledge is a worthy adversary, because in some sense it's inevitable. Getting a message across has two stages: the Answer stage and the Telling Others stage. In the Answer stage, you use your expertise to arrive at the idea you want to share. Doctors study for a decade to be capable of giving the Answer. Business managers may deliberate for months to arrive at the Answer.

Here's the rub: The same factors that worked to your advantage in the Answer stage will backfire on you during the Telling Others stage. To get the Answer, you need expertise, but you can't dissociate expertise from the Curse of Knowledge. You know things that others don't know, and you can't remember what it was like not to know those things. So when you get around to sharing the Answer, you'll tend to communicate *as if your audience were you.*

You'll stress the scads of statistics that were pivotal in arriving at the Answer—and, like the Stanford students, you'll find that no one remembers them afterward. You'll share the punch line—the over-arching truth that emerged from months of study and analysis—and, like the CEO who stresses "maximizing shareholder value" to his frontline employees, no one will have a clue how your punch line relates to the day-to-day work.

There is a curious disconnect between the amount of time we invest in training people how to arrive at the Answer and the amount of time we invest in training them how to Tell Others. It's easy to graduate from medical school or an MBA program without ever taking a class in communication. . . . Business managers seem to believe that, once they've clicked through a PowerPoint presentation showcasing their conclusions, they've successfully communicated their ideas. What they've done is share data. If they're good speakers, they may even have created an enhanced sense, among their employees and peers, that they are "decisive" or "managerial" or "motivational." But, like the Stanford students, the surprise will come when they realize that nothing they've said had impact. They've shared data, but they haven't created ideas that are useful and lasting. Nothing stuck.

Making an Idea Stick: The Communication Framework

For an idea to stick, for it to be useful and lasting, it's got to make the audience:

1. Pay attention
2. Understand and remember it
3. Agree/Believe
4. Care
5. Be able to act on it

PROBLEM 4-6

1. Select a policy issue about which you feel strongly. Prepare a three-minute speech attempting to convince someone not familiar with the topic of the merits of your position. Practice and time your presentation. Have another member of the class later recall your points and evaluate your effort.

2. Prepare a 45-second "elevator pitch" that summarizes the key points of your argument.

3. Prepare a PowerPoint or visual display that dramatizes your position.

4. Analyze a leader's speech that you have found particularly persuasive. What made it effective?

5. Write a one to two-page rebuttal to any of the speeches excerpted or listed in the media resources below, incorporating the insights summarized above. Ask someone else in the class to identify what he or she found most or least persuasive in your response.

2. EXAMPLES

Martin Luther King Jr. issued a Letter from a Birmingham Jail in 1963, following his arrest for peaceably marching to protest racial segregation. His march violated a city ordinance prohibiting parades without a permit and a court injunction against the demonstration. During his eight-day imprisonment, eight of Alabama's most prominent white religious leaders issued a public statement. It questioned why King and his followers did not pursue pressure by voters instead of protests and boycotts in seeking social justice. King's response, although addressed to these ministers, was in fact not sent to them but circulated to the national press, where it received widespread coverage.[293] His argument became the basis for *Why We Can't Wait*, a book chronicling the early civil rights campaign.

As you read this excerpt, consider what rhetorical techniques are most effective.

MARTIN LUTHER KING JR., LETTER FROM A BIRMINGHAM JAIL

April 16, 1963[294]

My Dear Fellow Clergymen:

While confined here in the Birmingham city jail, I came across your recent statement calling my present activities "unwise and untimely." Seldom do I pause to answer criticism of my work and ideas. If I sought to answer all the criticisms that cross my desk . . . I would have no time for constructive work. But since I feel that you are men of genuine good will and that your criticisms are sincerely set forth, I want to try to answer your statement in what I hope will be patient and reasonable terms.

I think I should indicate why I am here in Birmingham, since you have been influenced by the view which argues against "outsiders coming in." I have the honor of serving as president of the Southern Christian Leadership Conference, an organization operating in every southern state, with headquarters in Atlanta, Georgia. We have some eighty five affiliated organizations across the South, and one of them is the Alabama Christian Movement for Human Rights. . . . I, along with several members of my staff, am here because I was invited here [by this affiliate]. . . .

But more basically, I am in Birmingham because injustice is here. Just as the prophets of the eighth century B.C. left their villages and carried their "thus saith the Lord" far beyond the boundaries of their home towns, and just as the Apostle Paul left his village of Tarsus and carried the gospel of Jesus Christ to the far corners of the Greco Roman world, so am I compelled to carry the gospel of freedom beyond my own home town. Like Paul, I must constantly respond to the Macedonian call for aid.

Moreover, I am cognizant of the interrelatedness of all communities and states. I cannot sit idly by in Atlanta and not be concerned about what happens in Birmingham. Injustice anywhere is a threat to justice everywhere. We are caught in an inescapable network of mutuality, tied in a single garment of destiny. Whatever affects one directly, affects all indirectly. Never again can we afford to live with the narrow, provincial "outside agitator" idea. Anyone who lives inside the United States can never be considered an outsider anywhere within its bounds.

You deplore the demonstrations taking place in Birmingham. But your statement, I am sorry to say, fails to express a similar concern for the conditions that brought about the demonstrations. I am sure that none of you would want to rest content with the superficial kind of social analysis that deals merely with effects and does not grapple with underlying causes. It is unfortunate that demonstrations are taking place in Birmingham, but it is even more unfortunate that the city's white power structure left the Negro community with no alternative. . . .

Birmingham is probably the most thoroughly segregated city in the United States. Its ugly record of brutality is widely known. Negroes have experienced grossly unjust treatment in the courts. There have been more unsolved bombings of Negro homes and churches in Birmingham than in any other city in the nation. These are the hard, brutal facts of the case. On the basis of these conditions, Negro leaders sought to negotiate with the city fathers. But the latter consistently refused to engage in good faith negotiation.

Then, last September, came the opportunity to talk with leaders of Birmingham's economic community. In the course of the negotiations, certain promises were made by the merchants—for example, to remove the stores' humiliating racial signs. On the basis of these promises, the Reverend Fred Shuttlesworth and the leaders of the Alabama Christian Movement for Human Rights agreed to a moratorium on all demonstrations. As the weeks and months went by, we realized that we were the victims of a broken promise. A few signs, briefly removed, returned; the others remained. As in so many past experiences, our hopes had been blasted, and the shadow of deep disappointment settled upon us. We had no alternative except to prepare for direct action, whereby we would present our very bodies as a means of laying our case before the conscience of the local and the national community. Mindful of the difficulties involved, we decided to undertake a process of self purification. We began a series of workshops on nonviolence, and we repeatedly asked ourselves: "Are you able to accept blows without retaliating?" "Are you able to endure the ordeal of jail?" We decided to schedule our direct action program for the Easter season, realizing that except for

Christmas, this is the main shopping period of the year. Knowing that a strong economic-withdrawal program would be the by product of direct action, we felt that this would be the best time to bring pressure to bear on the merchants for the needed change.

[We then postponed the protest twice to avoid clouding issues in the mayoral election and runoff.] Having aided in this community need, we felt that our direct action program could be delayed no longer.

You may well ask: "Why direct action? Why sit ins, marches and so forth? Isn't negotiation a better path?" You are quite right in calling for negotiation. Indeed, this is the very purpose of direct action. Nonviolent direct action seeks to create such a crisis and foster such a tension that a community which has constantly refused to negotiate is forced to confront the issue. It seeks so to dramatize the issue that it can no longer be ignored. . . . My friends, I must say to you that we have not made a single gain in civil rights without determined legal and nonviolent pressure. Lamentably, it is an historical fact that privileged groups seldom give up their privileges voluntarily. Individuals may see the moral light and voluntarily give up their unjust posture; but, as Reinhold Niebuhr has reminded us, groups tend to be more immoral than individuals.

We know through painful experience that freedom is never voluntarily given by the oppressor; it must be demanded by the oppressed. Frankly, I have yet to engage in a direct action campaign that was "well timed" in the view of those who have not suffered unduly from the disease of segregation. For years now I have heard the word "Wait!" It rings in the ear of every Negro with piercing familiarity. This "Wait" has almost always meant "Never." We must come to see, with one of our distinguished jurists, that "justice too long delayed is justice denied."

We have waited for more than 340 years for our constitutional and God given rights. The nations of Asia and Africa are moving with jetlike speed toward gaining political independence, but we still creep at horse and buggy pace toward gaining a cup of coffee at a lunch counter. Perhaps it is easy for those who have never felt the stinging darts of segregation to say, "Wait." But when you have seen vicious mobs lynch your mothers and fathers at will and drown your sisters and brothers at whim; when you have seen hate filled policemen curse, kick and even kill your black brothers and sisters; when you see the vast majority of your twenty million Negro brothers smothering in an airtight cage of poverty in the midst of an affluent society; when you suddenly find your tongue twisted and your speech stammering as you seek to explain to your six year old daughter why she can't go to the public amusement park that has just been advertised on television, and see tears welling up in her eyes when she is told that Funtown is closed to colored children, and see ominous clouds of inferiority beginning to form in her little mental sky, and see her beginning to distort her personality by developing an unconscious bitterness toward white people; when you have to concoct an answer for a five year old son who is asking: "Daddy, why do white people treat colored people so mean?"; when you take a cross county drive and find it necessary to sleep night after night in the uncomfortable corners of your automobile because no motel will accept you; when you are humiliated day in and day out by nagging signs reading "white" and "colored"; when your first name becomes "nigger," your middle name becomes "boy" (however old you are) and your last name becomes "John," and your wife and mother are never given the respected title "Mrs."; when you are harried by day and haunted by night by the fact that you are a Negro, living constantly at tiptoe stance, never quite knowing what to expect next, and are plagued with inner fears and outer resentments; when you are forever fighting a degenerating sense of "nobodiness"—then you will understand why we find it difficult to wait. There comes a time when the cup of endurance runs over, and men are no longer willing to be plunged into the abyss of despair. I hope, sirs, you can understand our legitimate and unavoidable impatience. You express a great deal of anxiety over our willingness to break laws. This is certainly a legitimate concern. Since we so diligently urge people to obey the Supreme Court's decision of 1954 outlawing segregation in the public schools, at first glance it may seem rather paradoxical for us consciously to break laws. One may well ask: "How can you advocate breaking some laws and obeying others?" The answer lies in the fact that there are two types of laws: just and unjust. I would be the first to advocate obeying just laws. One has not only a legal but a moral responsibility to obey just laws. Conversely, one has a moral responsibility to disobey unjust laws. I would agree with St. Augustine that "an unjust law is no law at all."

Now, what is the difference between the two? How does one determine whether a law is just or unjust? A just law is a man made code that squares with the moral law or the law of God. An unjust law is a code that is out of harmony with the moral law. To put it in the terms of St. Thomas Aquinas: An unjust law is a human law that is not rooted in eternal law and natural law. . . .

Let me give another explanation. A law is unjust if it is inflicted on a minority that, as a result of being denied the right to vote, had no part in enacting or devising the law. Who can say that the legislature of Alabama which set up that state's segregation laws was democratically elected? Throughout Alabama all sorts of devious methods are used to prevent Negroes from becoming registered voters, and there are some counties in which, even though Negroes constitute a majority of the population, not a single Negro is registered. Can any law enacted under such circumstances be considered democratically structured?

Sometimes a law is just on its face and unjust in its application. For instance, I have been arrested on a charge of parading without a permit. Now, there is nothing wrong in having an ordinance which requires a permit for a parade. But such an ordinance becomes unjust when it is used to maintain segregation and to deny citizens the First-Amendment privilege of peaceful assembly and protest. . . .

Of course, there is nothing new about this kind of civil disobedience. . . . To a degree, academic freedom is a reality today because Socrates practiced civil disobedience. In our own nation, the Boston Tea Party represented a massive act of civil disobedience. We should never forget that everything Adolf Hitler did in Germany was "legal" and everything the Hungarian freedom fighters did in Hungary was "illegal." It was "illegal" to aid and comfort a Jew in Hitler's Germany. . . .

I must make two honest confessions to you, my Christian and Jewish brothers. First, I must confess that over the past few years I have been gravely disappointed with the white moderate. I have almost reached the regrettable conclusion that the Negro's great stumbling block in his stride toward freedom is not the White Citizen's Counciler or the Ku Klux Klanner, but the white moderate, who is more devoted to "order" than to justice; who prefers a negative peace which is the absence of tension to a positive peace which is the presence of justice; who constantly says: "I agree with you in the goal you seek, but I cannot agree with your methods of direct action"; who paternalistically believes he can set the timetable for another man's freedom; who lives by a mythical concept of time and who constantly advises the Negro to wait for a "more convenient season." Shallow understanding from people of good will is more frustrating than absolute misunderstanding from people of ill will. Lukewarm acceptance is much more bewildering than outright rejection. . . .

It is true that the police have exercised a degree of discipline in handling the demonstrators. In this sense they have conducted themselves rather "nonviolently" in public. But for what purpose? To preserve the evil system of segregation. Over the past few years I have consistently preached that nonviolence demands that the means we use must be as pure as the ends we seek. I have tried to make clear that it is wrong to use immoral means to attain moral ends. But now I must affirm that it is just as wrong, or perhaps even more so, to use moral means to preserve immoral ends. . . . [Southern police have too often] used the moral means of nonviolence to maintain the immoral end of racial injustice. As T. S. Eliot has said: "The last temptation is the greatest treason: To do the right deed for the wrong reason."

I wish you had commended the Negro sit inners and demonstrators of Birmingham for their sublime courage, their willingness to suffer and their amazing discipline in the midst of great provocation. One day the South will recognize its real heroes. They will be the James Merediths, with the noble sense of purpose that enables them to face jeering and hostile mobs, and with the agonizing loneliness that characterizes the life of the pioneer. They will be old, oppressed, battered Negro women, symbolized in a seventy two year old woman in Montgomery, Alabama, who rose up with a sense of dignity and with her people decided not to ride segregated buses, and who responded with ungrammatical profundity to one who inquired about her weariness: "My feets is tired, but my soul is at rest." They will be the young high school and college students, the young ministers of the gospel and a host of their elders, courageously and nonviolently sitting in at lunch counters and willingly going to jail for conscience' sake. One day the South will know that when these disinherited children of God sat down at lunch counters, they were in reality standing up for what is best in the American dream and for the most sacred values in our Judaeo Christian heritage, thereby bringing our nation back to those great wells of democracy which were dug deep by the founding fathers in their formulation of the Constitution and the Declaration of Independence.

Never before have I written so long a letter. I'm afraid it is much too long to take your precious time. I can assure you that it would have been much shorter if I had been writing from a comfortable desk, but what else can one do when he is alone in a narrow jail cell, other than write long letters, think long thoughts and pray long prayers?

If I have said anything in this letter that overstates the truth and indicates an unreasonable impatience, I beg you to forgive me. If I have said anything that understates the truth and indicates my having a patience that allows me to settle for anything less than brotherhood, I beg God to forgive me.

I hope this letter finds you strong in the faith. I also hope that circumstances will soon make it possible for me to meet each of you, not as an integrationist or a civil-rights leader but as a fellow clergyman and a Christian brother. Let us all hope that the dark clouds of racial prejudice will soon pass away and the deep fog of misunderstanding will be lifted from our fear drenched communities, and in some not too distant tomorrow the radiant stars of love and brotherhood will shine over our great nation with all their scintillating beauty.

Yours for the cause of Peace and Brotherhood,

Martin Luther King, Jr.

NOTES AND QUESTIONS

1. What did you find most and least effective about this letter? Was it, as he said, "much too long?" If so, what would you have advised him to cut?
2. King's Letter, excerpted in the *New York Post*, was highly influential and echoed strategies apparent in other influential speeches on racism and racial identity. In his famous 1964 address on the Washington mall, King again appealed to values in the nation's founding documents: "I still have a dream . . . deeply rooted in the American dream. I have a dream that one day this nation will rise up and live out the true meaning of its creed: that all men are created equal."[295]

    Barack Obama's references to race during his presidential campaign often employed rhetorical techniques advocated earlier—vivid narrative tied to expressions of hope and appeals to common values. When he announced his candidacy from Springfield, Illinois, his location and rhetoric evoked Abraham Lincoln's calls for a "more perfect union." Subsequent speeches invoked Martin Luther King Jr.'s references to the "moral arc" of the universe "bending toward justice."[296] Obama's address before the 2004 Democratic National Convention referred to his father's childhood herding goats in Kenya and maintained that "my story is part of the larger American story . . . and that in no other country on earth is my story even possible.[297] In his 2008 inaugural address, he made similar references to the "meaning of our liberty and our creed, why men and women and children of every race and every faith can join in celebration across this magnificent mall. And why a man whose father less than 60 years ago might not have been served at a local restaurant can now stand before you to take a most sacred oath."[298] His campaign slogan, often credited as one of the most memorable of American presidents, epitomized messages of hope and inclusion: "Yes, we can."[299]

As noted earlier, Obama is lauded as a "shape shifter" who can readily adjust his rhetorical style to church basements, huge stadiums, backyard barbeques, and elite policy forums.[300] Bill Clinton had similar skills:

> He seemed to sense what audiences needed and delivered it to them—trimming his pitch here, emphasizing different priorities, there, always aiming to please. This was one of his most effective, and maddening, qualities in private meetings as well. He always grabbed on to some points of agreement, while steering the conversation away from the larger points of disagreement, leaving his seducee with the distinct impression that they were in total harmony on just about everything.[301]

Yet Obama and other Democratic politicians have also been faulted for their communications on key policy issues. George Lakoff, one of the nation's leading experts on linguistics and political rhetoric, criticized Obama's early health care messages as a "policy-speak disaster." Is his criticism convincing? If you had been Obama's chief advisor, how would you have responded?

GEORGE LAKOFF, THE POLICY-SPEAK DISASTER FOR HEALTH CARE

Truthout, Aug. 20, 2009

Policy Speak is the principle that: *If you just tell people the policy facts, they will reason to the right conclusion and support the policy wholeheartedly.*

Policy speak is the policy behind the president's new Reality Check web site. To my knowledge, the Reality Check web site has not had a reality check. That is, the administration has not hired a first-class cognitive psychologist to take subjects who have been convinced by right-wing myths and lies, have them read the Reality Check web site, and see if the Reality Check web site has changed their minds a couple of days or a week later. I have my doubts, but do the test. . . . Truth matters. But it can only be comprehended when it is framed effectively and heard constantly. . . .

Policy Speak is supposed to be reasoned, objective discourse. [Yet] . . . [t]he scientific research in neuroscience and cognitive science has shown that most reason is unconscious. . . . Emotion is necessary for rational thought; if you cannot feel emotion, you will not know what to want or how anyone else would react to your actions. Rational decisions depend on emotion. Empathy with others has a physical basis, and as much as self-interest, empathy lies behind reason. . . .

Ideas are constituted by brain structures called "frames" and "metaphors," and reason uses them. Frames form systems called worldviews. All language is defined relative to such frames and metaphors. There are very different conservative and progressive worldviews, and different words can activate different worldviews [and different circuits in the brain]. . . .

Whenever brain circuitry is activated, the synapses get stronger and the circuits are easier to activate again. Conservative language will activate conservative frames, which will activate and strengthen the conservative worldview. Conservative tacticians may not know about brain research, but they know about marketing, and marketing theorists use that brain research. That is why conservatives place such importance on language choice, from the classic "socialized medicine," to [Frank] Luntz's "government takeover" [of health care] to [Sarah] Palin's "death panels." When repeated over and over, the words evoke a conservative worldview [and hold emotional appeal]. . . .

Conservative language will activate and strengthen conservative worldviews—even when negated! I titled a book "Don't Think of an Elephant!" to make this point. . . . I've heard President Obama say, "We don't want a government takeover," which activates the idea of a government takeover. Mediamatters.org's major story, as I write this, is: "The media have debunked the death panels—more than 40 times." It then gives a list of 40 cases of debunking, each one of which uses the term "death panels," [which assertedly would decide which individuals would be worthy of receiving subsidized medical treatments]. And you wonder, after so many debunkings, why it is still believed! Each "debunking" reinforced the idea. The first rule of effective communication is stating the positive in your own terms, not quoting the other side's language with a negation. . . . As I was writing this, I received the viral email written by David Axelrod, which he refers to as "probably one of the longest emails I've ever sent." It is indeed long. It is accurate. It lays out the president's list of needed reforms. It answers the myths. It appeals to people who would personally benefit from the president's plan. . . . And it is written in Policy Speak. It has 24 points—three sets of eight.

Ask yourself which is more memorable: "Government takeover," "socialized medicine" and "death panels"—or Axelrod's 24 points? Did the administration do a reality check on the 24 points? That is, did they have one of our superb cognitive psychologists test subjects who were convinced of the right-wing framing, have them read the 24 points and test them a couple days or a week later on whether Axelrod's 24 points had convinced them? Policy Speak folks don't tend to think of such things. . . . I respect Axelrod deeply. But the strategist who ran the best-framed campaign I've ever seen is giving in to Policy Speak. . . . In the Obama campaign, honest, effective framing was used with great success. But in the Obama administration, something has changed. It needs to change back.

NOTES AND QUESTIONS

1. Social critic Amitai Etzioni similarly claims that progressive leaders lack accessible and inspiring narratives. They too often produce "platformlike statements" without mobilizing power; they have no clear, concise explanation of why we are in difficulty and what will get us out. The need is not just for new rhetoric but for a more compelling narrative.[302] Political analyst George Packer summarized comparable criticisms by congressional representatives and staff. They viewed efforts by the Obama administration to have

sophisticated conversations on issues such as the mortgage crisis as "tone deaf." "You can't say to people whose homes are in foreclosure, who are losing their businesses, 'It's a complicated situation.' The President is having a very eloquent one-sided conversation. The country doesn't want to have the conversation he wants to have."[303] House Democratic Congressman Barney Frank agreed that Obama's "technocratic style" had been ineffective and that he would have been better-off with a more "adversarial approach" toward pharmaceutical firms, insurance companies, and banks.[304] How would you assess current political leaders' capacity to communicate? Can any progressives match Donald Trump's ability to energize voters with simple evocative messages ("build the wall," "lock her up")?

2. Some critics faulted Obama for his antagonistic approach toward Republicans in Congress, such as his claims that Mitch McConnell was "in bed with Wall Street movers and shakers" and was making "cynical and deceptive arguments for them."[305] Obama himself expressed concerns that he had sometimes failed to live up to his own aspiration that politicians "can disagree without being disagreeable."[306] In the current highly partisan political climate, how can leaders strike the right balance between mobilizing their base and reaching across the aisle?

3. Donald Trump's use of Twitter changed the conversation during and following his presidential campaign. What are the strengths and limitations of this communication strategy? What made Trump so effective?

4. George Packer notes that the public "wants many things these days, some of them contradictory. It wants the government to stop piling up debt and it also wants the government to spend aggressively on jobs, education, and health care."[307] Policy disputes over a replacement for Obamacare foundered on the public's competing desires for quality, affordability, and accessibility. Is there a way that the administration can better convey an unpopular message—that difficult trade-offs are inevitable? When should leaders force followers to have a conversation they do not want to have?

5. Lawyers often face similar challenges when clients are not interested in legal complexities or risk analysis and just want the lawyer to get the deal done or make the problem go away. What communication strategies might be helpful in packaging unwelcome messages?

6. Take a recent controversial policy issue and compare how leaders from different political perspectives frame their arguments. What techniques are most effective? How do they respond to opposition claims? How would you?

MEDIA RESOURCES

Many examples of inspiring leadership rhetoric are available in films and documentaries, as well as in political speeches and debates. Famous scenes of rallying the troops before battle provide classic illustrations: Henry IV on the eve of the Battle of Agincourt, Queen Elizabeth sending troops into France, and Julius Caesar asking for support in his march on Rome.[308] Exemplary fictional American presidential speeches appear in *The West Wing* and *The American President*. The trailer for *Up in the Air* features George Clooney's character giving a "backpack theory speech" that exemplifies many of the techniques advocated in the readings.[309] *Thank You for Smoking* portrays a lobbyist for tobacco companies doing a masterful job of making his clients appear sympathetic. Examples of successful and unsuccessful lawyers' speeches at meetings with clients in class actions appear in *Erin Brockovich* and *A Civil Action*. Interviews with professors Steven Pinker and Jonathan Haidt offer insights on political rhetoric and values.[310] Chip and Dan Heath explore their theory of how to make an idea stick as described in the readings.[311] Bill Gates shows how to get through a technology failure during a presentation.[312] Robin Williams' speech at a camp in Kuwait demonstrates the use of humor to cope with an interruption.[313] A *Saturday Night Live* parody of Donald Trump, played by Alec Baldwin, captive to his twitter habit during a security briefing, raises interesting questions about the role of social media as a leadership communication tool. The first season of the BBC series *Yes, Prime Minister* offers a humorous portrait of a United Kingdom prime minister being coached for a televised speech to the nation.

Examples of inspiring political speeches are in ample supply, many by lawyers. Those by civil rights leaders including King are described in Chapter 10's discussion of social movements. Barack Obama's Philadelphia 2008 speech on race, Michelle Obama's and Hillary Clinton's speeches at the 2016 Democratic Convention, and Donald Trump's speech at the 2016 Republican convention are worth exploring.[314] Widely acclaimed responses to tragedy include the address by New Zealand Prime Minister Jacinda Ardern following the mosque shootings in Christchurch, as well as presidential candidate Pete Buttigieg's statement of solidarity with the French people (delivered in French) following the 2019 Notre Dame Cathedral fire.[315]

END NOTES

[1] Gary Yukl, *Sources of Power and Influence*, in THE ETHICS OF LEADERSHIP 3-12 (Joanne B. Ciulla ed., 2003). See also Jay Conger, *The Necessary Art of Persuasion*, HARV. BUS. REV. 88 (May-June 1998); HOWARD GARDNER, CHANGING MINDS: THE ART AND SCIENCE OF CHANGING OUR OWN AND OTHER PEOPLE'S MINDS (2004) (stressing the role of reason, research, resonance, rewards, and resources).

[2] ROBERT B. CIALDINI, INFLUENCE: THE PSYCHOLOGY OF PERSUASION (2007); LIONEL TIGER & RICHARD FOX, THE IMPERIAL ANIMAL (1971); Alvin W. Gouldner, *The Norm of Reciprocity: A Preliminary Statement*, 25 AM. SOC. REV. 161 (1960).

[3] Dennis T. Regan, *Effects of a Favor and Liking on Compliance*, 7 J. EXP. SOC. PSYCHOL. 267 (1971).

[4] JONAH LEHRER, HOW WE DECIDE 181-82 (2009).

[5] CIALDINI, INFLUENCE, 30.

[6] ADAM GRANT, GIVE AND TAKE 239 -241, 244 (2013).

[7] CIALDINI, INFLUENCE, 27; *See also A Tutorial from Lyndon B. Johnson, Don't Let Dead Cats Stand on Your Porch*, N.Y. TIMES, Sept. 20, 2009, at WK 5.

[8] CIALDINI, INFLUENCE, 26 (quoting Keating).

[9] VICTOR S. NAVASKY, KENNEDY JUSTICE 347, 355, 359, 444 (1971).

[10] STEVEN R. COVEY, THE 7 HABITS OF HIGHLY EFFECTIVE PEOPLE 289-90 (1990).

[11] JEFFREY PFEFFER, POWER: WHY SOME PEOPLE HAVE IT AND OTHERS DON'T 33 (2010).

[12] Dacher Keltner, *Don't Let Power Corrupt You*, HARV. BUS. REV. 114 (Oct. 2016).

[13] Robert B. Cialdini & Noah J. Goldstein, *Social Influence: Compliance and Conformity*, 55 ANN. REV. PSYCHOL. 591, 613 (2004).

[14] Solomon E. Asch, *Effects of Group Pressure Upon the Modification and Distortion of Judgment*, in GROUPS, LEADERSHIP, AND MEN (Harold S. Guetzkow ed., 1951).

[15] Peter Funt, You're On Candid Scanner, WALL ST. J., Nov. 23, 2010.

[16] ROBERT H. FRANK, CHOOSING THE RIGHT POND: HUMAN BEHAVIOR AND THE QUEST FOR STATUS 15 (1985),

[17] DANIEL KAHNEMAN, THINKING, FAST AND SLOW 217 (2011).

[18] Vladas Griskevicius, Robert B. Cialdini & Noah J. Goldstein, *Social Norms: An Underestimated and Underemployed Lever for Managing Climate Change*, 3 INT'L J. SUSTAINABILITY COMM. 5, 10 (2008).

[19] Griskevicius, Cialdini & Goldstein, *Social Norms*, 7.

[20] Griskevicius, Cialdini & Goldstein, *Social Norms*, 11.

[21] Robert B. Cialdini, *Harnessing the Science of Persuasion*, HARV. BUS. REV. 76 (Oct. 2001). For early adopters, see KERRY PATTERSON ET AL., INFLUENCER: THE POWER TO CHANGE ANYTHING 148-150 (2008). *See also* Jay Conger, *The Necessary Art of Persuasion*, HARV. BUS. REV. 88 (May-June 1998).

[22] KERRY PATTERSON ET AL., INFLUENCER: THE POWER TO CHANGE ANYTHING (2008).

[23] For the motivations of government employees, see HAL G. RAINEY, UNDERSTANDING AND MANAGING PUBLIC ORGANIZATIONS 233 (2003).

[24] MP McQueen, *Happy To Be Here*, AM. LAW., Sept. 2016, at 76.

[25] PATTERSON ET AL., INFLUENCER, 209; Steve Kerr, *On the Folly of Rewarding A While Hoping for B*, 9 ACAD. OF MGMT. EXECUTIVE 7 (1995) (describing incentive structure that led some American troops in Vietnam to search and escape rather than search and destroy).

[26] DEBORAH L. RHODE, DAVID LUBAN, SCOTT CUMMINGS & NORA FREEMAN ENGSTROM, LEGAL ETHICS 811-813 (7th ed. 2016).

[27] SCHWARTZ & SHARPE, PRACTICAL WISDOM, 190-91; Uri Gneezy & Aldo Rustichini, *A Fine Is a Price*, 29 J. OF LEGAL STUD. 1 (2000).

[28] PATTERSON ET AL., INFLUENCER, 196 (quoting Demetri Martin).

[29] MONTGOMERY VAN WART, DYNAMICS OF LEADERSHIP IN PUBLIC SERVICE: THEORY AND PRACTICE 210 (2005).

[30] VAN WART, DYNAMICS OF LEADERSHIP, 209-213.

[31] James M. Kouzes & Barry Z. Posner, *Recognize Contributions Linking Rewards with Performance*, in LEADING ORGANIZATIONS 487 (GILL ROBINSON HICKMAN ed., 1998).

[32] DANIEL H. PINK, DRIVE: THE SURPRISING TRUTH ABOUT WHAT MOTIVATES US 45-46, 59 (2009).

[33] PINK, DRIVE, 46.

[34] Frederick Herzberg, *One More Time: How Do You Motivate Employees?*, HARV. BUS. REV. 6, 8-9 (Sept.-Oct. 1987).

[35] Herzberg, *One More Time*, 6-12.

[36] MARSHALL SASHKIN & MOLLY G. SASHKIN, LEADERSHIP THAT MATTERS: THE CRITICAL FACTORS FOR MAKING A DIFFERENCE IN PEOPLE'S LIVES AND ORGANIZATIONS' SUCCESS 118 (2003) (quoting Schweitzer).

[37] ROBERT W. CULLEN, THE LEADING LAWYER: A GUIDE TO PRACTICING LAW AND LEADERSHIP (2010).

[38] Gary Yukl & J. Bruce Tracey, *Consequences of Influence Tactics Used with Subordinates, Peers, and the Boss*, 77 J. APPLIED PSYCHOL. 525 (Aug. 1992); ANDREW J. DUBRIN, LEADERSHIP: RESEARCH FINDINGS, PRACTICE, AND SKILLS 249 (2004).

[39] Robert B. Cialdini, *Harnessing the Science of Persuasion*, HARV. BUS. REV. 77 (Oct. 2001).

[40] DUBRIN, LEADERSHIP, 250.

[41] Jay A. Conger, *The Necessary Art of Persuasion*, HARV. BUS. REV. 87, 90 (May-June 1988).

[42] Ned Kock et al., *Empathetic Leadership: How Leader Emotional Support and Understanding Influences Follower Performance*, J. LEADERSHIP & ORG. STUD. 1 (2018).

[43] Conger, *The Necessary Art of Persuasion*, 93.

[44] Robert Cialdini on the importance of reciprocity (July 8, 2009), http://www.youtube.com/watch?v=tkyGOAWoYxA. For Asch experiments, see https://www.youtube.com/watch?v=qA-gbpt7Ts8. For an experiment in which a person turns to the back of an elevator to conform to other passengers' behavior, see https://www.youtube.com/watch?v=BgRoiTWkBHU.

[45] JAMES M. KOUZES & BARRY Z. POSNER, THE LEADERSHIP CHALLENGE 223-224 (2003).

[46] Warren Bennis, *Introduction*, in THE ART OF FOLLOWERSHIP: HOW GREAT FOLLOWERS CREATE GREAT LEADERS AND ORGANIZATIONS xxiv, xxvi (Ronald E. Riggio, Ira Chaleff & Jean Lipman-Blumen eds., 2008).

[47] Warren Bennis, *The Secrets of Great Groups*, LEADER TO LEADER, 1997.

[48] Robert Dalling, THE STORY OF US HUMANS, FROM ATOMS TO TODAY'S CIVILIZATION 479 (2004).

[49] JOHN W. GARDNER, ON LEADERSHIP 24 (1990).

[50] RITA M. HILTON & ROSEMARY O'LEARY, LEADING IN PLACE: LEADERSHIP THROUGH DIFFERENT EYES 67, 83-84 (2018).

[51] BARBARA KELLERMAN, FOLLOWERSHIP: HOW FOLLOWERS ARE CREATING CHANGE AND CHANGING LEADERS 8 (2008).

[52] Joseph S. Nye Jr., *Power and Leadership*, in HANDBOOK OF LEADERSHIP THEORY AND PRACTICE 305, 312 (Nitin Nohria & Rakesh Khurana eds., 2010) (quoting de Mirabeau).

[53] NANNERL O. KEOHANE, THINKING ABOUT LEADERSHIP 30 (2010).

[54] RONALD H. HUMPHREY, EFFECTIVE LEADERSHIP: THEORY, CASES, AND APPLICATIONS 246-48 (2014); CRAIG PEARCE & JAY A. CONGER, SHARED LEADERSHIP: REFRAMING THE HOWS AND WHYS OF LEADERSHIP (2002); NICK PETRIE, FUTURE TRENDS IN LEADERSHIP DEVELOPMENT 21-22 (Center for Creative Leadership, 2014); Kathleen E.

Allen et al, *Leadership in the Twenty-First Century*, in LEADING ORGANIZATIONS 575 (GILL ROBINSON HICKMAN, ed, 1998).

[54] JAMES MACGREGOR BURNS, LEADERSHIP (1978).

[55] JOHN W. GARDNER, LIVING, LEADING, AND THE AMERICAN DREAM 145 (FRANCESCA GARDNER ed., 2003).

[56] JAMES M. KOUZES & BARRY Z. POSNER, A LEADER'S LEGACY 91 (2006).

[57] Peter F. Drucker, *Leaders Are Doers*, EXECUTIVE EXCELLENCE, Apr. 1996, at 8 (quoting Carnegie).

[58] JOHN GARDNER, THE NATURE OF LEADERSHIP: INTRODUCTORY CONSIDERATIONS 5-6 (1986).

[59] Jennifer L. S. Chandler & Robert E. Kirsch, *Addressing Race and Culture within a Critical Leadership Approach,* in GLOBAL AND CULTURALLY DIVERSE LEADERS AND LEADERSHIP 312 (JEAN LAU CHIN, JOSEPH E. TRIMBLE & JOSEPH E. GARCIA eds., 2018).

[60] KELLERMAN, FOLLOWERSHIP, 10.

[61] Nye, *Power and Leadership*, 312.

[62] IRA CHALEFF, THE COURAGEOUS FOLLOWER: STANDING UP TO AND FOR OUR LEADERS (2003).

[63] *A Military General's Leadership Lessons, Interview with Lieutenant General Russell Honoré,* GALLUP MGMT. J. (Jan. 8, 2009), https://news.gallup.com/businessjournal/113629/military-generals-leadership-lessons.aspx.

[64] David L. Collinson, *Conformist, Resistant and Disguised Selves: A Post-Structuralist Approach to Identity and Workplace Followership*, in THE ART OF FOLLOWERSHIP 309, 314 (Riggio, Chaleff, and Lipman-Blumen eds., 2008).

[65] KELLERMAN, FOLLOWERSHIP, 55-59.

[66] ROGER GILL, THE THEORY AND PRACTICE OF LEADERSHIP 12 (2006) (quoting Strengthening Leadership).

[67] KIM S. CAMERON, PRACTICING POSITIVE LEADERSHIP: TOOLS AND TECHNIQUES THAT CREATE EXTRAORDINARY RESULTS 52 (2013); ROBERT N. LUSSIER & CHRISOPHER F. ACHUA, LEADERSHIP: THEORY, APPLICATION, & SKILL DEVELOPMENT 75 (2nd ed. 2004).

[68] RICHARD I. HUGHES, ROBERT C. GINNETT & GORDON J. CURPHY, LEADERSHIP: ENHANCING THE LESSONS OF EXPERIENCE 262 (5th ed. 2006); CAMERON, PRACTICING POSITIVE LEADERSHIP, 52.

[69] MARTIN DEMPSEY & ORI BRAFMAN, RADICAL INCLUSION: WHAT THE POST 9/11 WORLD SHOULD HAVE TAUGHT US ABOUT LEADERSHIP 81 (2018).

[70] Alicia Bassuk, *Leadership Crisis/Crisis Leadership*, HUFFINGTON. POST (Oct. 12, 2019), https://www.huffpost.com/entry/leadership-crisiscrisis-leadership_b_59dfd639e4b09e31db97579e.

[71] Bassuk, Leadership Crisis (quoting Roosevelt).

[72] SIMON SINEK, LEADERS EAT LAST: WHY SOME TEAMS PULL TOGETHER AND OTHERS DON'T (2017).

[73] Heather J. Anderson et al., *What Works for You May Not work for (Gen)Me: Limitations of Present Leadership Theories for the New Generation,* 28 Leadership Q. 245 (2017).

[74] Qiong Wu, Kathryn Cormican & Guoquan Chen, *A Meta-Analysis of Shared Leadership: Antecedents, Consequences and Moderators,* J. LEADERSHIP & ORG. STUD. 1 (2018).

[75] David Brooks, *Politics and Culture in the Age of Obama*, COMMONWEALTH CLUB (Jan. 11, 2011), https://www.commonwealthclub.org/events/archive/transcript/david-brooks-politics-and-culture-age-obama (quoting Bush).

[76] David Brooks, *What a Failed Trump Administration Looks Like*, N.Y. TIMES, Feb. 17, 2017.

[77] Sheryl Gay Stolberg, *Obama Pushes Agenda Despite Political Risks,* N. Y. TIMES, July 15, 2010.

[78] Margaret Carlson, *Smart President Fails Test at Ground Zero*, BLOOMBERG, Aug. 18, 2010.

[79] HUMPHREY, EFFECTIVE LEADERSHIP, 242-43.

[80] GILL, THE THEORY AND PRACTICE OF LEADERSHIP, 12; Robert E. Kelley, *Rethinking Followership*, in THE ART OF FOLLOWERSHIP 13, 15 (Riggio, Chaleff & Lipman-Blumen, eds., 2008). *See generally* ROBERT E. KELLEY, THE POWER OF FOLLOWERSHIP (1992).

[81] Kelly, *Rethinking Followership*, 13, 15. *See also* Robert E. Kelley, *In Praise of Followers*, HARV. BUS. REV. 142, 146 (Nov.-Dec. 1988) (noting the importance of "initiative, self control, commitment, talent, honesty, credibility, and courage").

[82] IRA CHALEFF, INTELLIGENT DISOBEDIENCE: DOING RIGHT WHEN WHAT YOU'RE TOLD TO DO IS WRONG (2015).

[83] Bennis, *Introduction*, xxvi.

[84] Lynn R. Offerman, *When Followers Become Toxic*, HARV. BUS. REV. 55, 57, 59 (Jan. 2004); John P. Howell & María J. Méndez, *Three Perspectives on Followership*, in THE ART OF FOLLOWERSHIP 25, 35 (Riggio, Chaleff, and Lipman-Blumen eds., 2008).

[85] BARBARA KELLERMAN, THE END OF LEADERSHIP 123 (2012).

[86] MARY C. GENTILE, GIVING VOICE TO VALUES: HOW TO SPEAK YOUR MIND WHEN YOU KNOW WHAT'S RIGHT (2010).

[87] GENTILE, GIVING VOICE TO VALUES, 181.

[88] Alexander Zill, Michael Knoll, Alexandra (Sasha) Cook & Bertolt Meyer, *When Do followers Compensate for leader Silence? The Motivating Role of Leader Injustice*, J. LEADERSHIP & ORG. STUD. 1 (2018).

[89] JAMES W. ROBINSON, JACK WELCH ON LEADERSHIP: EXECUTIVE LESSONS FROM THE MASTER CEO 154 (2001).

[90] GILL, THEORY AND PRACTICE OF LEADERSHIP, 140.

[91] ROBERT M. GATES: A PASSION FOR LEADERSHIP: LESSONS ON CHANGE AND REFORM FROM FIFTY YEARS OF PUBLIC SERVICE 26 (2016).

[92] GATES, A PASSION FOR LEADERSHIP, 99.

[93] WILLIAM A. COHEN, DRUCKER ON LEADERSHIP: NEW LESSONS FROM THE FATHER OF MODERN MANAGEMENT 219 (2010); GILL, THEORY AND PRACTICE OF LEADERSHIP, 216; Bruce J. Avolio & Rebecca J. Richard, *The Rise of Authentic Followership*, in THE ART OF FOLLOWERSHIP 325, 329-35 (Riggio, Chaleff & Lipman-Blumen eds., 2008).

[94] ROBERT W. CULLEN, THE LEADING LAWYER: A GUIDE TO PRACTICING LAW AND LEADERSHIP 19 (2010).

[95] PATRICK J. MCKENNA & DAVID H. MAISTER, FIRST AMONG EQUALS: HOW TO MANAGE A GROUP OF PROFESSIONALS 246 (2002).

[96] FRANCESCA GINO, SIDETRACKED: WHY OUR DECISIONS GET DERAILED AND HOW WE CAN STICK TO THE PLAN 54 (2013). *See also* Adam M. Grant & Francesca Gino, *A Little Thanks Goes a Long Way: Explaining Why Gratitude Expressions Motivate Prosocial Behavior*, 98 J. PERS. & SOC. PSYCHOL. 946 (2010)

[97] MCKENNA & MAISTER, FIRST AMONG EQUALS, 45 (quoting General Electric CEO Jack Welch).

[98] MCKENNA & MAISTER, FIRST AMONG EQUALS, 33.

[99] Offerman, *When Followers Become Toxic*, 59 (quoting Ketchum).

[100] GILL, THEORY AND PRACTICE OF LEADERSHIP, 222.

[101] Ronald Busse & Sam Regenberg, *Revisiting the "Authoritarian Versus Participative" Leadership Style Legacy: A New Model of the Impact of Leadership Inclusiveness on Employee Engagement*, J. OF LEADERSHIP & ORG. STUD. 1, 11-13 (2018).

[102] C. Fred Alford, *Whistleblowing as Responsible Followership*, in THE ART OF FOLLOWERSHIP 309, 314 (Riggio, Chaleff & Lipman-Blumen eds., 2008); Jessica R. Mesmer-Magnus & Chokalingam Viswesvaran, *Whistleblowing in Organizations: An Examination of Correlates of Whistleblowing Intentions, Actions and Retaliation*, 62 J. BUS. ETHICS 277, 282, 288 (2005); David Culp, *Whistleblowers: Corporate Anarchists or Heroes? Towards a Judicial Perspective*, 13 HOFSTRA LAB. & EMP. L.J 109,112-113 (1995).

[103] Alford, *Whistleblowing as Responsible Followership*, 238.

[104] Robert Jackall, *Whistleblowing & Its Quandaries*, 20 GEO. J. LEGAL ETHICS 1133, 1134-1136 (2007).

[105] John Gibeaut, *Telling Secrets: When In-House Lawyers Sue Their Employers, They Find Themselves in the Middle of the Debate on Client Confidentiality*, ABA J. 73 (Nov. 2004) (quoting Susan W. Ausman).

[106] Alford, *Whistleblowing as Responsible Followership*, 240.

[107] ROBERTA ANN JOHNSON, WHISTLEBLOWING: WHEN IT WORKS AND WHY (2003); Alford, *Whistleblowing as Responsible Followership*, 241-242; DEBRA E. MEYERSON, TEMPERED RADICALS: HOW EVERYDAY LEADERS INSPIRE CHANGE AT WORK (2003).

[108] *See e.g.* Kevin Bogardus, *Members of Science Subcommittee Resign in Protest*, GREENWIRE, May 12, 2017; Matt Broomfield, *Environmental Justice Chief Resigns in Protest of Donald Trump's Plan to Slash EPA Funding and Support*, INDEPENDENT, Mar. 10, 2017; *CIA Analyst Edward Price Resigns in Protest of Trump*, DEMOCRACY NOW!, Feb. 22, 2017.

[109] Debra E. Meyerson, *The Tempered Radicals: How Employees Push Their Companies–Little by Little–to be More Socially Responsible*, STAN. SOC. INNOV. REV. 23 (Fall 2004).

[110] GENTILE, GIVING VOICE TO VALUES, 52.

[111] This problem is drawn from RHODE, LUBAN, CUMMINGS & ENGSTROM, LEGAL ETHICS, 676-77.

[112] Trial Transcript at 16,742, Jan. 21, 1978.

[113] Stephen Wermiel, *Lawyers' Public Image Is Dreadful, Spurring Concern by Attorneys*, WALL ST. J., Oct. 11, 1983, at 1.

[114] James B. Stewart Jr., *Kodak and Donovan Leisure: The Untold Story*, AM. LAW., Jan. 1983, at 24, 62.

[115] Stewart, *Kodak and Donovan Leisure*, 24, 62.

[116] David Margolick, Law; *The Long Road Back for a Disgraced Patrician*, N.Y. TIMES, Jan. 19, 1990, at B6.

[117] Ward Bower, *Report to Legal Management: Major Law Firms Embrace General Counsel Concept*, ALTMAN WEIL, INC. (2004) (finding that two-thirds of responding firms in a survey of the United States' 200 largest firms had designated counsel to provide ethics advice).

[118] Elizabeth Chambliss, *The Nirvana Fallacy in Law Firm Regulation Debates*, 33 FORDHAM URB. L.J. 119, 128-29 (2005).

[119] New York is one of the few states that permits firms to be subject to discipline, but such organizational sanctions are rare. For discussion, see RHODE & LUBAN, LEGAL ETHICS, 1001-1002.

[120] Andrew Perlman, *The Silliest Rule of Professional Conduct: Model Rule 5.2(b)*, 19 PROF. LAW. 14 (2009).

[121] Carol M. Rice, *The Superior Orders Defense in Legal Ethics: Sending the Wrong Message to Young Lawyers*, 32 WAKE FOREST L. REV. 887, 889 (1997).

[122] Douglas R. Richmond, *Academic Silliness about Model Rule 5.2(b)*, 19 PROF. LAW. 15, 20 (2009).

[123] Season 2, episode 4—Rosemary's Baby.

[124] Legacy of Tiananmen "tank man" lives on (June 4, 2009), http://www.youtube.com/watch?v=M5sNN9HvTgY&NR=1&feature= fvwp; Japanese war film tells kamikaze story; May open old wounds (June 6, 2007), http://www.youtube.com/watch?v=imtQEMU9BEg&.

[125] Cults: The Wave, Part 1 (Jan. 27, 2016), https://www.youtube.com /watch?v=ePiEyYlDWyw; Cults: The Wave, Part 2 (Jan. 27, 2016), https://www.youtube.com/watch?v=WOb1Iu-XhPw.

[126] West Wing, Second Season / Episode 2 / "In the Shadow of Two Gunmen Part II."

[127] RONALD A. HEIFETZ, ALEXANDER GRASHOW & MARTY LINSKY, THE PRACTICE OF ADAPTIVE LEADERSHIP: TOOLS AND TACTICS FOR CHANGING YOUR ORGANIZATION AND THE WORLD 71, 19 (2009).

[128] HEIFETZ, GRASHOW & LINKSKY, PRACTICE OF ADAPTIVE LEADERSHIP, 152, 169, 162.

[129] HEIFETZ, GRASHOW & LINKSKY, PRACTICE OF ADAPTIVE LEADERSHIP, 267.

[130] Interview by Peter Boyer with Deputy Secretary Paul Wolfowitz, NEW YORKER, June 18, 2002 (quoting Eric K. Shinseki).

[131] HAL G. RAINEY, UNDERSTANDING AND MANAGING PUBLIC ORGANIZATIONS 16-18 (2003) (discussing public opinion).

[132] TRACEY WILEN-DAUGENTI, DIGITAL DISRUPTION: THE FUTURE OF WORK, SKILLS, LEADERSHIP, EDUCATION, AND CAREERS IN A DIGITAL WORLD 5-7 (2018).

[133] MONTGOMERY VAN WART, DYNAMICS OF LEADERSHIP IN PUBLIC SERVICE: THEORY AND PRACTICE 40 (2005); Sanford Borins, *Loose Cannons and Rule Breakers, or Enterprising Leaders: Some Evidence about Innovative Public Managers*, 60 PUB. ADMIN. REV. 498, 499 (Nov.-Dec. 2000).

[134] MARK GERZON, LEADING THROUGH CONFLICT: HOW SUCCESSFUL LEADERS TRANSFORM INTO OPPORTUNITIES 208 (2006).

[135] DAVID MAGELLAN HORTH & JONATHAN VEHAR, INNOVATION: HOW LEADERSHIP MAKES THE DIFFERENCE 2 (Center for Creative leadership, 2015).

[136] Collins, *The Ultimate* Creation, 134.

[137] WILEN, DIGITAL DISRUPTION 65.

[138] COHEN, DRUCKER ON LEADERSHIP, 1; NEIL M. TICHY & WARREN G. BENNIS, JUDGMENT: HOW WINNING LEADERS MAKE GREAT CALLS 58 (2002) (quoting Drucker).

[139] Debra E. Meyerson, *Radical Change, The Quiet Way*, HARV. BUS. REV. 92, 94 (Oct. 2001).

[140] Gary Klein, Seeing What Others Don't: The Remarkable Ways We Gain Insights 31, 41 (2013).

[141] Klein, Seeing What Others Don't, 104-106, 190.

[142] VAN WART, DYNAMICS OF LEADERSHIP, 40; Borins, *Loose Cannons*, 503.

[143] CLAYTON M. CHRISTENSEN, THE INNOVATOR'S DILEMMA: WHEN NEW TECHNOLOGIES CAUSE GREAT FIRMS TO FAIL 221, 264-267 (2000).

[144] Jill Lepore, *The Disruption Machine: What the Gospel of Innovation Gets Wrong*, NEW YORKER, June 16, 2014.

[145] STEPHEN P. ROBBINS & TIMOTHY A. JUDGE, ORGANIZATIONAL BEHAVIOR 625-26 (13th ed. 2009); John P. Kotter, *Making Change Happen*, in LEADER TO LEADER 69-71 (Francis Hesselbein & Paul M. Cohen eds., 1999).

[146] Peter M. Senge, *The Practice of Innovation*, in LEADER TO LEADER 55, 60 (in Hesselbein & Cohen eds., 1999); John P. Kotter, *Leading Change: Why Transformation Efforts Fail*, HARV. BUS. REV. 61 (Mar.-Apr. 1995).

[147] JOHN P. KOTTER, LEADING CHANGE 61 (2012).

[148] PETER FIRESTEIN, CRISIS OF CHARACTER: BUILDING CORPORATE REPUTATION IN AN AGE OF SKEPTICISM 128, 133 (2009).

[149] ROBBINS AND JUDGE, ORGANIZATIONAL BEHAVIOR, 623-624; Kotter & Schlesinger, *Choosing Strategies for Change*, 109; GERZON, LEADING THROUGH CONFLICT, 209; GATES, A PASSION FOR LEADERSHIP, 63.

[150] Conger, *The Necessary Art of Persuasion*, 89.

[151] ADAM GRANT, ORIGINALS: HOW NON-CONFORMISTS MOVE THE WORLD 233 (2016); Alexander J. Rothman, Roger D. Bartels, Jhon Wlaschin & Peter Salovey, *The Strategic Use of Gain-and-loss Framed Messages to Promote Healthy Behavior: How Theory Can Inform Practice*, J. COMM. 56, 292 (2006).

[152] PATTERSON ET AL., INFLUENCER, 68-69, 102.

[153] JOHN P. KOTTER & DAN S. COHEN, THE HEART OF CHANGE 18, 30-31 (2002).

[154] KOTTER, MAKING CHANGE HAPPEN, 70; GATES, A PASSION FOR LEADERSHIP, 49-50.

[155] KOTTER, LEADING CHANGE, 63.

[156] MCKENNA & MAISTER, FIRST AMONG EQUALS, 128.

[157] ROSABETH MOSS KANTER, CREATING THE CULTURE FOR INNOVATION 6 (2000), reprinted in LEADING FOR INNOVATION: AND ORGANIZING FOR RESULTS 82 (Frances Hesselbein, Marshall Goldsmith & Iain Somerville eds., 2002).

[158] Jeffrey Pfeffer, *To Build a Culture of Innovation, Avoid Conventional Management Wisdom*, in LEADING FOR INNOVATION 101 (Hesselbein, Goldsmith & Summerfield eds., 2002) (quoting David Kelly); CHRISTENSEN, THE INNOVATOR'S DILEMMA, 260.

[159] Goodwin Leadership, 179, 181.

[160] VAN WART, DYNAMICS OF LEADERSHIP, 54; KANTER, CREATING THE CULTURE FOR INNOVATION, 4.

[161] MAUREEN BRODERICK, THE ART OF MANAGING PROFESSIONAL SERVICES: INSIGHTS FROM LEADERS OF THE WORLD'S TOP FIRMS 105-07 (2011).

[162] Paula Davis-Laack, *6 New Leadership Literacies Lawyers Must Build,* FORBES (Feb. 22, 2018), https://www.forbes.com/sites/pauladavislaack/2018/02/22/6-new-leadership-literacies-lawyers-must-build/#1824c6b82334.

[163] John P. Kotter, *Successful Change and the Forces that Drive It,* in LEADING ORGANIZATIONS, 464-465.

[164] CAMERON, PRACTICING POSITIVE LEADERSHIP, 34, 40.

[165] ROBBINS & JUDGE, ORGANIZATIONAL BEHAVIOR, 623; Kotter & Schlesinger, *Choosing Strategies for Change,* 107; LARINA KASE, THE CONFIDENT LEADER: HOW THE MOST SUCCESSFUL PEOPLE GO FROM EFFECTIVE TO EXCEPTIONAL 11 (2009).

[166] Barbara C. Crosby & John M. Bryson, *Implementing and Evaluating New Policies, Programs, and Plans,* in LEADERSHIP FOR THE COMMON GOOD: TACKLING PUBLIC PROBLEMS IN A SHARED-POWER WORLD 335 (Barbara C. Crosby & John M. Bryson eds., 2005).

[167] DUBRIN, LEADERSHIP, 375.

[168] Senge, *The Practice of Innovation,* 65 (quoting O'Brien).

[169] KOTTER, MAKING CHANGE HAPPEN, 71.

[170] KOTTER, LEADING CHANGE, 66; MCKENNA & MAISTER, FIRST AMONG EQUALS, 127.

[171] KOTTER, LEADING CHANGE, 66-67.

[172] GRANT, ORIGINALS, 106.

[173] Donald J. Polden, *Lawyers, Leadership, and Innovation,* 58 SANTA CLARA L. REV. 427, 449-450 (2019).

[174] CHIP HEATH & DAN HEATH, SWITCH: HOW TO CHANGE THINGS WHEN CHANGE IS HARD 16-20 (2010).

[175] GATES, A PASSION FOR LEADERSHIP, 202.

[176] *See* Raymond H. Brescia, *What We Know and Need to Know about Disruptive Innovation,* 67 S.C. L REV. 203 (2016).

[177] For bar efforts in Missouri, see *Janson v. LegalZoom,* 802 F. Supp. 1053 (D. Mo. 2011). For efforts in North Carolina, see *LegalZoom.com v. The North Carolina State Bar,* Complaint for Declaratory and Injunctive Relief (2011), http://online.wsj.com/public/resources/documents/LegalZoom.pdf.

[178] For discussion of bar strategies, see Deborah L. Rhode & Benjamin H. Barton, *Rethinking Self-Regulation: Antitrust Perspectives on Bar Governance Activity,* 20 CHAP. L. REV. 267 (2017).

[179] JAMES COMEY, A HIGHER LOYALTY: TRUTH, LIES, AND LEADERSHIP 134 (2018).

[180] David V. Day, *The Nature of Leadership Development,* in THE NATURE OF LEADERSHIP 124 (David V. Day & John Antonakis eds., 2012); James W. Smither, Manual London & Richard R. Reilly, *Does Performance Improve Following Multisource Feedback? A Theoretical Model, Meta-Analysis and Review of Empirical Findings,* 58 PERS. PSYCH. 33 (2005).

[181] *See* DOUGLAS STONE, BRUCE PATTON & SHEILA HEEN, DIFFICULT CONVERSATIONS: HOW TO DISCUSS WHAT MATTERS MOST (1998); Cynthia M. Phoel, *Feedback That Works,* 11 HARV. MGMT. UPDATE 3 (2006).

[182] For a similar list, see ROBERT E. QUINN ET AL., BECOMING A MASTER MANAGER: A COMPETING VALUES APPROACH 62 (2010); MCKENNA & MAISTER, FIRST AMONG EQUALS, 115. For evidence that specific goals are most effective, see Edwin A. Locke & Gary P. Latham, *New Directions in Goal-Setting Theory*, 15 CURRENT DIRECTIONS IN PSYCHOL. SCI. 265 (2006). For the importance of stressing positive contributions and specific goals, see CAMERON, PRACTICING POSITIVE LEADERSHIP, 82, 102.

[183] CAMERON, PRACTICING POSITIVE LEADERSHIP, 82; Marcial Losada & Emily Heaphy, *The Role of Positivity and Connectivity in the Performance of Business Teams: A Nonlinear Dynamics Model*, 47 AM. BEHAV. SCIENTIST 740, 747 (2004).

[184] CAMERON, PRACTICING POSITIVE LEADERSHIP, 85.

[185] CAMERON, PRACTICING POSITIVE LEADERSHIP, 92.

[186] Studies by the Leadership Development Institute and the Center for Creative Leadership estimate between 20 to 40 percent. CRAIG E. RUNDE & TIM A. FLANAGAN, BECOMING A CONFLICT COMPETENT LEADER: HOW YOU AND YOUR ORGANIZATION CAN MANAGE CONFLICT EFFECTIVELY 12 (2007). Other research estimates that the average executive spends the equivalent of seven weeks a year (roughly 15 percent of his or her time) dealing with workplace disputes. GERZON, LEADING THROUGH CONFLICT, 34.

[187] QUINN ET AL., BECOMING A MASTER MANAGER, 89 (quoting William Wrigley).

[188] BARBARA A. NAGLE-LECHMAN, CONFLICT AND RESOLUTION 4 (2008); RUNDE & FLANAGAN, BECOMING A CONFLICT COMPETENT LEADER, 115.

[189] RUNDE & FLANAGAN, BECOMING A CONFLICT COMPETENT LEADER, 21.

[190] HO-WON JEONG, UNDERSTANDING CONFLICT AND CONFLICT ANALYSIS 5 (2008); MCKENNA & MAISTER, FIRST AMONG EQUALS, 203.

[191] QUINN ET AL., BECOMING A MASTER MANAGER, 89.

[192] KENNETH R. MELCHIN & CHERYL A. PICARD, TRANSFORMING CONFLICT THROUGH INSIGHT 36-38 (2008).

[193] *See* JEONG, UNDERSTANDING CONFLICT AND CONFLICT ANALYSIS, 8-13; LECHMAN, CONFLICT AND RESOLUTION, 8; RUNDE & FLANAGAN, BECOMING A CONFLICT COMPETENT LEADER, 28-35.

[194] *See* JEONG, UNDERSTANDING CONFLICT AND CONFLICT ANALYSIS, 74; RUNDE & FLANAGAN, BECOMING A CONFLICT COMPETENT LEADER, 49 and Ch. 4.

[195] Richard Birke & Craig R. Fox, *Psychological Principles in Negotiating Civil Settlements*, 4 HARV. NEGOT. L. REV. 34-35 (1999).

[196] Robert H. Mnookin, *Why Negotiations Fail: An Exploration of Barriers to the Resolution of Conflict*, 8 OHIO ST. J. DISP. RESOL. 235, 246 (1993).

[197] CAROL TAVRIS & ELLIOT ARONSON, MISTAKES WERE MADE (BUT NOT BY ME): WHY WE JUSTIFY FOOLISH BELIEFS, BAD DECISIONS, AND HURTFUL ACTS 42 (2007).

[198] Connie Green, *Leader Member Exchange and the Use of Moderating Conflict Management Styles: Impact on Relationship Quality*, 19 INT'L J. CONFLICT MGMT. 92 (2008).

[199] JEONG, UNDERSTANDING CONFLICT AND CONFLICT ANALYSIS, 30; LECHMAN, CONFLICT AND RESOLUTION, 21-22.

[200] David L. Bradford & Allan R. Cohen, *Power Talk: A Hands-on Guide to Supportive Confrontation*, in POWER UP: TRANSFORMING ORGANIZATIONS THROUGH SHARED LEADERSHIP 321, 323, 345 (1998).

[201] NANNERL O. KEOHANE, THINKING ABOUT LEADERSHIP, 110-111 (2010). *See* FRANK FREIDEL, FRANKLIN D. ROOSEVELT: A RENDEZVOUS WITH DESTINY 124 (1990).

[202] RUNDE & FLANAGAN, BECOMING A CONFLICT COMPETENT LEADER, 117, 161.

[203] Manfred Kets de Vries & Elizabeth Engellau, *A Clinical Approach to the Dynamics of Leadership and Executive Transformation*, in HANDBOOK OF LEADERSHIP THEORY AND PRACTICE 183, 199 (Nohria & Khurana eds., 2010).

[204] Gary Goodpaster, *A Primer on Competitive Bargaining*, J. DISP. RESOL. 327 (1996).

[205] Green, *Leader Member Exchange*, 96; JEONG, UNDERSTANDING CONFLICT AND CONFLICT ANALYSIS, 40; RUNDE & FLANAGAN, BECOMING A CONFLICT COMPETENT LEADER, 44.

[206] RUNDE & FLANAGAN, BECOMING A CONFLICT COMPETENT LEADER, 45; Jeswald W. Salacuse, *Ten Ways That Culture Affects Negotiating Style: Some Survey Results*, 14 NEGOT. J. 221 (1998); DEBORAH A. PRENTICE & DALE T. MILLER, CULTURAL DIVIDES: UNDERSTANDING AND OVERCOMING GROUP CONFLICT (2001). *See also* discussion in Chapter 2.

[207] Kevin Avruch, *Culture as Context, Culture as Communication: Considerations for Humanitarian Negotiators*, 9 HARV. NEGOT. L. REV. 391, 392-398 (2004).

[208] For discussion of BATNAs and negotiation strategy generally, see Roger Fisher 7 WILLIAM URY, GETTING TO YES: NEGOTIATING AGREEMENT WITHOUT GIVING IN (2d ed. 1991).

[209] Robert S. Adler, Benson Rosen & Elliot M. Silverstein, *Emotions in Negotiation: How to Manage Fear and Anger*, 142 NEGOT. J. 161 (1998).

[210] MELCHIN & PICARD, TRANSFORMING CONFLICT THROUGH INSIGHT, 79; LECHMAN, CONFLICT AND RESOLUTION, 28 (noting that experts estimate that less than 10 percent of communication comes from substantive content; the rest comes from facial gesture, tone, and so forth).

[211] Tony Schwartz & Catherine McCarthy, *Manage Your Energy, Not Your Time*, in ON MANAGING YOURSELF 71-72 (Harv. Bus. Rev. eds., 2010).

[212] Bradford & Cohen, *Power Talk*, 331.

[213] FISHER & URY, GETTING TO YES, ix.

[214] James J. White, *The Pros and Cons of 'Getting to Yes'*, 34 J. LEGAL EDUC. 115, 123 (1984) (comments of Roger Fisher).

[215] Tony Mauro, *Kagan Dishes on Taking Changes, Anger at the Court and Going to Law School "For All the Wrong Reasons,"* NAT'L L.J., Nov. 1, 2016.

[216] MELCHIN & PICCARD, TRANSFORMING CONFLICT THROUGH INSIGHT, 79-80; MCKENNA & MAISTER, FIRST AMONG EQUALS, 205; VAN WART, DYNAMICS OF LEADERSHIP IN PUBLIC SERVICE, 222; OREN JAY SOFER, SAY WHAT YOU MEAN: A MINDFUL APPROACH TO NONVIOLENT COMMUNICATION 177 (2018); Bradford & Cohen, *Power Talk*, 340 (discussing toothless promises). *See also* GERZON, LEADING THROUGH CONFLICT, 50, 136 (suggesting open-ended questions, such as "What would it take to increase your trust?"); JEAN LEBEDUM, MANAGING WORKPLACE CONFLICT (1998).

[217] Kathleen M. Eisenhardt, Jean L. Kahwajy & L. J. Bourgeois III, *How Management Teams Can Have a Good Fight*, HARV. BUS. REV. 2 (July-Aug. 1997); ROBERT HARGROVE, MASTERFUL COACHING 235-45 (3d ed. 2008).

[218] SOFER, SAY WHAT YOU MEAN, 195.

[219] SOFER, SAY WHAT YOU MEAN, 198.

[220] SOFER, SAY WHAT YOU MEAN, 204.

[221] Barbara Gray, *Collaboration: The Constructive Management of Differences,* in LEADING ORGANIZATIONS, 476-78. *See also* BARBARA GRAY, COLLABORATING: FINDING COMMON GROUND FOR MULTIPARTY PROBLEMS 1-25 (1989).

[222] RUNDE & FLANAGAN, BECOMING A CONFLICT COMPETENT LEADER, 171; VAN WART, DYNAMICS OF LEADERSHIP, 221-224.

[223] TOM R. TYLER, WHY PEOPLE OBEY THE LAW (2006); TOM R. TYLER, READINGS IN PROCEDURAL JUSTICE (2005).

[224] GERZON, LEADING THROUGH CONFLICT, 69 (2006).

[225] For an example of a self-rating questionnaire, see Steven R. Wilson & Michael S. Waltman, *Assessing the Putnam-Wilson Organizational Communication Conflict Instrument (OCCI),* 1 MGMT. COMM. Q. 382-84 (Feb. 1988).

[226] *Fierce Leaders Survey* (2016), http://www.fierceinc.com/resources/surveys /leading-company-country.

[227] DAVID HERBERT DONALD, LINCOLN 164-65 (1995).

[228] DAVID REMNICK, THE BRIDGE: THE LIFE AND RISE OF BARACK OBAMA 324 (2011) (quoting Newton Minow).

[229] ANDRA GILLESPIE, THE NEW BLACK POLITICIAN: CORY BOOKER, NEWARK, AND POST-RACIAL AMERICA 60 (2012).

[230] Doris Kearns Goodwin, *Office Politics,* VANITY FAIR, Nov. 2016 (quoting Obama).

[231] Jeffrey Toobin, *Trump's Red Line,* NEW YORKER, Dec. 24 and 31, 2018, at 34 (quoting Brian Hennigen).

[232] Toobin, *Trump's Red Line,* at 34 (quoting Schiff).

[233] Edward R .Murrow offered this description in a broadcast celebrating Churchill's 80th birthday. IN SEARCH OF LIGHT: THE BROADCASTS OF EDWARD R. MURROW, 1938-1961, 237 (Edward Bliss Jr. ed., 1968).

[234] Robert Reich, *Locked in the Cabinet,* excerpted in NEW YORKER, Apr. 21, 1997, at 43.

[235] NPR, *Scrambling to Get Off the Ice,* THIS AMERICAN LIFE (2019), https://www.thisamericanlife.org/669/transcript.

[236] NPR, *Scrambling.*

[237] TIMOTHY J. KOEGEL, THE EXCEPTIONAL PRESENTER: A PROVEN FORMULA TO OPEN UP AND OWN THE ROOM 37 (2007).

[238] CHRIS ANDERSON, TED TALKS: THE OFFICIAL TED GUIDE TO PUBLIC SPEAKING 78 (2016) (quoting Robin Hogarth).

[239] John C. Meyer, *Humor as a Double-Edged Sword: Four Functions of Humor in Communication,* 10 COMM. THEORY 310, 319 (2000).

[240] ANDERSON, TED TALKS, 55.

[241] *"Hillary Gump" a Hit at Washington's Gridiron Club Dinner,* N.Y. TIMES, Mar. 27, 1995.

[242] KOEGEL, THE EXCEPTIONAL PRESENTER, 109.

[243] Wayne H. Decker & Denise M. Rotondo, *Relationships Among Gender, Type of Humor, and Perceived Leader Effectiveness,* 13 J. MANAGERIAL ISSUES 450, 452 (2001).

[244] CAITLIN MOSCATELLO, SEE JANE WIN; THE INSPIRING STORY OF THE WOMEN CHANGING AMERICAN POLITICS 63 (2019).

[245] ANDERSON, TED TALKS, 57 (quoting Salman Khan).

[246] ADAM GRANT, ORIGINALS: HOW NON-CONFORMISTS MOVE THE WORLD 73-74 (2016).

[247] John Antonakis, *Transformational and Charismatic Leadership*, in THE NATURE OF LEADERSHIP 276 (DAVID V. DAY & JOHN ANTONAKIS eds., 2012).

[248] ARCHIE BROWN, THE MYTH OF THE STRONG LEADER: POLITICAL LEADERSHIP IN THE MODERN AGE 81 (2004).

[249] ANDERSON, TED TALKS, 57.

[250] REMNICK, THE BRIDGE, 18.

[251] Adam Gopnik, *Liberal-In-Chief*, NEW YORKER, May 23, 2016, at 24 (quoting Obama).

[252] JAMES COMEY, A HIGHER LOYALTY: TRUTH, LIES, AND LEADERSHIP 150 (2018).

[253] Conger, *The Necessary Art of Persuasion*, 87.

[254] KOEGEL, THE EXCEPTIONAL PRESENTER, 14.

[255] KOEGEL, THE EXCEPTIONAL PRESENTER, 91-93.

[256] MOSCATELLO, SEE JANE WIN, 53.

[257] DEBORAH L. RHODE, THE BEAUTY BIAS: THE INJUSTICE OF APPEARANCE IN LIFE AND LAW 30-31 (2010).

[258] John Beeson, *Deconstructing Executive Presence*, in HARV. BUS. REV., LEADERSHIP PRESENCE 4-5 (2018).

[259] Deborah L. RHODE, WOMEN AND LEADERSHIP 45 (2017).

[260] GILLESPIE, THE NEW BLACK POLITICIAN, 91. Booker denied having heard the comment, but did acknowledge changing his wardrobe.

[261] For the importance of first impressions, see PFEFFER, POWER: WHY SOME PEOPLE HAVE IT AND OTHERS DON'T, 148-49.

[262] Amy J. Cuddy, Mathew Kohut & John Neffinger, *Connect, Then Lead*, in HARV. BUS. REV., LEADERSHIP PRESENCE 67 (2018). See also AMY CUDDY, PRESENCE: BRINGING YOUR BOLDEST SELF TO YOUR BIGGEST CHALLENGES (2015).

[263] *Are Leaders Getting Too Emotional*, in AUTHENTIC LEADERSHIP 128 (HARV. BUS. REV. eds., 2018) (quoting Gianpiero Petriglieri of INSEAD).

[264] *Are Leaders Getting Too Emotional*, 129-130 (quoting Gianpiero Petriglieri).

[265] *Are Leaders Getting Too Emotional*, 130 131 (quoting Guatam Mukunda of Harvard Business School).

[266] ANDERSON, TED TALKS, 24.

[267] GRANT, ORIGINALS, 100-102.

[268] WILLIAM MANCHESTER, THE LAST LION: WINSTON SPENCER CHURCHILL 1874-1932 (1983), quoted in GARDNER, ON LEADERSHIP, 51.

[269] MICHELLE OBAMA, BECOMING 260 (2018).

[270] OBAMA, BECOMING 260.

[271] OBAMA, BECOMING 260.

[272] OBAMA, BECOMING 260; Id. at 267.

[273] CHIP HEATH & DAN HEATH, MADE TO STICK: WHY SOME IDEAS SURVIVE AND OTHERS DIE 75 (2007).

[274] ROGER GILL, THEORY AND PRACTICE OF LEADERSHIP, 260-62 (2013); DAVID M. ARMSTRONG, MANAGING BY STORYING AROUND: A NEW METHOD OF LEADERSHIP (1992).

[275] JEREMI SURI, THE IMPOSSIBLE PRESIDENCY: THE RISE AND FALL OF AMERICA'S HIGHEST OFFICE 148 (2017). See also DORIS KEARNS GOODWIN, LEADERSHIP: IN TURBULENCE TIMES 291 (2018).

[276] For studies, see RONALD H. HUMPHREY, EFFECTIVE LEADERSHIP: THEORY, CASES, AND APPLICATIONS 354 (2014). *See also* Conger, *The Necessary Art of Persuasion,* at 92.

277 PATTERSON ET AL., INFLUENCER, 60 (describing experiment in which students were asked to recall information several weeks later).

278 Robert Draper, *How Hillary Became 'Hillary'*, N.Y. TIMES MAG., Oct. 11, 2016, at 65.

279 Mark Leibovich, *Her Way*, N.Y. TIMES MAG., Oct. 16, 2016, at 43 (quoting Clinton).

280 HEATH & HEATH, MADE TO STICK, 16-18.

281 HEATH & HEATH, MADE TO STICK, 6-7 (quoting Abe Silverman).

282 HEATH & HEATH, MADE TO STICK, 6-7.

283 GARDNER, CHANGING MINDS, 85, 101.

284 GARDNER, CHANGING MINDS, 86.

285 GARDNER, CHANGING MINDS, 76.

286 Ari-Decter-Frain, Ruth Vanstone & Jeremy A. Frimer, *Why and How Groups Create Moral Heroes*, in HANDBOOK OF HEROISM AND HEROIC LEADERSHIP 131 (SCOTT T. ALLISON, GEORGE R. GOETHALS, AND RODERICK M. KRAMER eds., 2017).

287 SARAH A. SOULE, CONTENTION AND CORPORATE SOCIAL RESPONSIBILITY (2009).

288 NORM PHELPS, THE LONGEST STRUGGLE: ANIMAL ADVOCACY FROM PYTHAGORAS TO PETA 293-297 (2007).

289 *See* CLIFF ATKINSON, BEYOND BULLET POINTS: USING MICROSOFT POWERPOINT TO CREATE PRESENTATIONS THAT INFORM, MOTIVATE, AND INSPIRE (2007); ANDERSON, TED TALKS, 117.

290 ANDERSON, TED TALKS, 35 (quoting Wilson).

291 ANDERSON, TED TALKS, 154.

292 William Safire, *Prolegemon*, in LEADERSHIP 19 (William Safire & Leonard Safire eds., 1990) (quoting Eisenhower).

293 S. JONATHAN BASS, BLESSED ARE THE PEACEMAKERS: MARTIN LUTHER KING, JR., EIGHT WHITE RELIGIOUS LEADERS, AND THE "LETTER FROM BIRMINGHAM JAIL" (2001); Foster Hailey, *Dr. King Arrested at Birmingham*, N.Y. TIMES, Apr. 13, 1963, at 1.

294 Available at https://www.africa.upenn.edu/Articles_Gen/Letter_Birmingham.html.

295 Martin Luther King Jr., *I Have a Dream*, Martin Luther King Papers, King Library, Stanford University (Aug. 28, 1963). For discussion of this speech and the Birmingham letter, see Mark Vail, *The "Integrative" Rhetoric of Martin Luther King Jr.'s, "I Have a Dream" Speech*, 9 RHETORIC AND PUB. AFF. 51 (2006).

296 Eric J. Sundquist, *"We Dreamed a Dream": Ralph Ellison, Martin Luther King, Jr., & Barack Obama*, DAEDALUS 114 (Winter 2011).

297 Barack Obama, Candidate for U.S. Senate in Illinois, *Keynote Address at the Democratic National Convention* (July 27, 2004).

298 Barack Obama, *Inaugural Address* (Jan. 20, 2009), http://www.presidency.ucsb.edu/ws/?pid=44.

299 Hillel Italie, *Capital Culture: Critics Assess Obama's Speeches*, PANTAGRAPH, Jan. 24, 2010.

300 Frank Rich, *It's a Bird, It's a Plane, It's Obama!*, N.Y. TIMES, Apr. 4, 2010, at WK 9.

301 JOE KLEIN, THE NATURAL: THE MISUNDERSTOOD PRESIDENCY OF BILL CLINTON 40, 79 (2002).

[302] Amitai Etzioni, *Needed: A Progressive Story Instead of an Endless Platform of Policy Ideas, Progressives Need to Tell a Shared Narrative*, THE NATION, May 24, 2010, at 22-23.

[303] George Packer, *Obama's Lost Year*, NEW YORKER, Mar. 15, 2010, at 46 (quoting aide).

[304] Packer, *Obama's Last Year*, 49 (quoting Frank).

[305] Jonathan Allen & Carol E. Lee, President *Obama's Strategy Gets Personal*, POLITICO, Apr. 27, 2010.

[306] CBS News, 60 MINUTES, Nov. 4, 2010.

[307] Packer, *Obama's Last Year*, 49.

[308] Caeser's Speech to 13th legion, *Rome* (Feb. 7, 2007), http://www.youtube.com/watch?v=5PeN1k9AAMg.

[309] http://www.youtube.com/watch?v=NSfXolCmnFo.

[310] Steven Pinker, *Political Rhetoric Explained* (Oct. 14, 2008), http://www.youtube.com/watch?v=DS4xVcko9qw; Jonathan Haidt, The moral roots of liberals and conservatives (Sept. 18, 2008), http://www.youtube.com /watch?v=vs41JrnGaxc.

[311] https://www.youtube.com/watch?v=2zlld9TA-Vg.

[312] https://www.youtube.com/watch?v=-NsXHPq71Bs.

[313] https://www.youtube.com/watch?v=QD9QAAEfQEA.

[314] Obama's keynote speech is available at https://www.youtube.com/watch?v=zrp-v2tHaDo. Another speech in which he speaks about loyalty and collective service is available at http://www.youtube.com/watch?v=Zgfi7wnGZlE.

[315] Anna Fifield, *New Zealand's Prime Minister Receives Wordwide Praise for Her Response to the Mosque Shootings*, WASH. POST, Mar. 18, 2019; *Pete Buttigieg Speaks on Notre Dame Cathedral Fire in French*, MSN.COM, Apr. 16, 2019.

PART III

ETHICS IN LEADERSHIP

CHAPTER 5

MORAL LEADERSHIP

In principle, the importance of moral leadership is never in dispute. But in practice, controversy arises over what exactly it requires and how it can be achieved. Conflicts are common between means and ends, and between personal principles and organizational interests. Leaders face challenges not only in resolving their own moral dilemmas but also in creating cultures that sustain moral values. Ethical leaders have a powerful influence on organizations by modeling appropriate behavior, setting appropriate standards, and holding employees responsible.[1] Studies find that the most important determinant of workplace climate is the day-to-day behavior of its leaders.[2] The materials that follow explore the importance and challenges of ethical leadership and begin by setting them in historical context.

A. HISTORICAL FRAMEWORKS

Niccolò Machiavelli is a much maligned and misunderstood thinker. His insights about political life are often reduced to simplistic sound bites, and his name carries pejorative connotations. Shakespeare referred to the "murderous Machiavel," and he was denounced as the "enemy of mankind" even by leaders such as Frederick the Great, who followed his advice.[3] Yet understood in context, Machiavelli offered a much more nuanced view of the role of leaders than is commonly acknowledged. Halfway through *The Prince*, he reminds readers of his goal: "Since my intention is to say something that will prove of practical use to the inquirer, I have thought it proper to represent things as they are in real truth, rather than as they are imagined."[4] Five centuries since its publication, the book remains one of the most realistic descriptions of the dilemmas of leadership.[5]

Machiavelli was very much a product of his time, but the problems he identified and the trade-offs he advocated have relevance for our own era. His insights can assist lawyers who are advisors as well as decision makers. Like Machiavelli, many lawyers are in the position of deciding, or counseling clients who are deciding, how to make the best of bad situations and how to balance their own moral principles with the practical realities of governance.

To understand *The Prince*, it is necessary also to understand its historical context. Niccolò Machiavelli was born in Florence, Italy in 1469. Although his family was not wealthy, his father had friends among the city's leading scholars, and Machiavelli received an extensive education in the classics, history, and moral philosophy.[6] The era was one of political instability. The Italian peninsula was fractured into several warring city-states and was vulnerable to outside invasion by aggressive European monarchies and the Ottoman Empire. Florence was plagued by competing factions among the richest families and social unrest among the poor. Machiavelli saw the Florentine government change hands three times during his lifetime as a result of bloody internal coups and invasions by French and papal troops.[7] In 1494, Savonarola, a Dominican friar, began a reign in which he plunged the city into four years of religious fanaticism, until he was charged with heresy, excommunicated, tortured, and burned at the stake.[8] Machiavelli received his first government appointment when Savonarola was excommunicated and the officials associated with him were expelled. At age 29, Machiavelli became head of the Second Chancery, which required him to help manage Florence's territories and to travel on diplomatic missions. After 14 years of service, he lost his position when Florence's republic fell in 1512. Papal troops invaded and reinstated the Medici family during a series of wars between Pope Julius II, Venice, Spain, and France. At first suspected of conspiracy against the new regime, Machiavelli was tortured, imprisoned, and fined.[9]

Machiavelli wrote *The Prince* in an effort to gain favor with the new Medici government. He dedicated the work to Lorenzo de Medici, and hoped to win a political appointment by displaying his considerable "knowledge of the actions of great men, learned by me from long experience with modern things and a continuous reading of ancient ones."[10] The book offers a straightforward presentation of different forms of governance, using classical and contemporary leaders as illustrative models of successes and failures. Ironically, although Machiavelli was highly critical of "unarmed prophets" such as Savonarola, he himself was "armed with only a pen when he became the prophet of a new understanding of politics."[11]

The Prince is famous for its recognition of the role of chance, and infamous for its conclusion that morality is situational and that rulers must do whatever is necessary to maintain the state, however incompatible with conventional moral principles. One of Machiavelli's core arguments is that a leader can be only as good as circumstances allow and that many individuals of great ability and integrity can be "ruined by fortune." Although often reviled for his elevation of prudence over principle, Machiavelli believed that the cruelties he advocated were morally justified to maintain social order and to prevent greater, more widespread brutality. Without a functioning state or a strong leader, "disorders . . . continue, from which come killings or robberies; for these customarily hurt a whole community."[12] In Machiavelli's view, individuals could not survive outside society, and society could not survive if led by those who put their own private morality first. From this perspective, a "virtuous" leader who failed to create "security and well-being" was unworthy of praise.[13] In effect, Machiavelli distinguished between public and private morality and argued that the "greatest good that one could do and the most gratifying to God is that which one does for one's country."[14] Contrary to popular views, Machiavelli did not lack a moral compass. It was rather, as he put it in a letter to a contemporary, he loved his country more than his soul.[15]

In the following excerpts from *The Prince*, Machiavelli elaborates on the qualities of successful leadership.

NICCOLÒ MACHIAVELLI, THE PRINCE (1532)

Harvey C. Mansfield, trans. (Chicago: University of Chicago Press, 2d ed. 1998)

Chapter VIII: Of Those Who Have Attained a Principality Through Crimes

[The test of leadership is whether] cruelties [are] badly used or well used. Those can be called well used (if it is permissible to speak well of evil) that are done at a stroke, out of the necessity to secure oneself, and then are not persisted in but are turned to as much utility for the subjects as one can. Those cruelties are badly used which, though few in the beginning, rather grow with time than are eliminated. Those who observe the first mode can have some remedy for their state with God and with men . . . ; as for the others it is impossible for them to maintain themselves.

Hence it should be noted that in taking hold of a state, he who seizes it should review all the offenses necessary for him to commit, and do them all at a stroke, so as not to have to renew them every day and, by not renewing them, to secure men and gain them to himself with benefits. Whoever does otherwise, either through timidity or through bad counsel, is always under necessity to hold a knife in his hand; nor can one ever found himself on his subjects if, because of fresh and continued injuries, they cannot be secure against him. For injuries must be done all together, so that, being tasted less, they offend less; and benefits should be done little by little so that they may be tasted better. And above all, a prince should live with his subjects so that no single accident whether bad or good has to make him change; for when necessities come in adverse times you will not be in time for evil, and the good that you do does not help you, because it is judged to be forced on you, and cannot bring you any gratitude. . . .

Chapter XV: Of Those Things for Which Men and Especially Princes Are Praised or Blamed

. . . For a man who wants to make a profession of good in all regards must come to ruin among so many who are not good. Hence it is necessary to a prince, if he wants to maintain himself, to learn to be able not to be good, and to use this and not use it according to necessity. . . .

Chapter XVII: Of Cruelty and Mercy, and Whether It Is Better to Be Loved Than Feared, or the Contrary

Descending next to the other qualities cited before, I say that each prince should desire to be held merciful and not cruel; nonetheless he should take care not to use this mercy badly. . . . A prince, therefore, so as to keep his subjects united and faithful, should not care about the infamy of cruelty, because with very few examples he will be more merciful than those who for the sake of too much mercy allow disorders to continue, from which come killings or robberies; for these customarily hurt a whole community, but the executions that come from the prince hurt one particular person. . . .

[D]ispute arises whether it is better to be loved than feared, or the reverse. The response is that one would want to be both the one and the other; but because it is difficult to put them together, it is much safer to be feared than loved, if one has to lack one of the two. For one can say this generally of men: that they are ungrateful, fickle, pretenders and dissemblers, evaders of danger, eager for gain. While you do them good, they are yours, offering you their blood, property, lives, and children, as I said above, when the need for them is far away; but, when it is close to you, they revolt. And that prince who has founded himself entirely on their words, stripped of other preparation, is ruined; for friendships that are acquired at a price and not with greatness and nobility of spirit are brought, but they are not owned and when the time comes they cannot be spent. And men have less hesitation to offend one who makes himself loved than one who makes himself feared; for love is held by a chain of obligation, which, because men are wicked, is broken at every opportunity for their own utility, but fear is held by a dread of punishment that never forsakes you.

The prince should nonetheless make himself feared in such a mode that if he does not acquire love, he escapes hatred, because being feared and not being hated can go together very well. This he will do if he abstains from the property of his citizens and his subjects, and from their women; and if he also needs to proceed against someone's life, he must do it when there is suitable justification and manifest cause for it. . . .

I conclude, then, returning to being feared and loved, that since men love at their convenience and fear at the convenience of the prince, a wise prince should found himself on what is his, not on what is someone else's; he should only contrive to avoid hatred, as was said.

Chapter XVIII: In What Mode Faith Should Be Kept by Princes

How praiseworthy it is for a prince to keep his faith, and to live with honesty and not by astuteness, everyone understands. Nonetheless one sees by experience in our times that the princes who have done great things are those who have taken little account of faith and have known how to get around men's brains with their astuteness; and in the end they have overcome those who have founded themselves on loyalty. . . .

A prudent lord, therefore, cannot observe faith, nor should he, when such observance turns against him, and the causes that made him promise have been eliminated. And if all men were good, this teaching would not be good; but because they are wicked and do not observe faith with you, you do not always have to observe it with them. Nor does a prince ever lack legitimate causes to color his failure to observe faith. One could give infinite modern examples of this, and show

how many peace treaties and promises have been rendered invalid and vain through the infidelity of princes. . . . But it is necessary to know well how to color this nature, and to be a great pretender and dissembler; and men are so simple and so obedient to present necessities that he who deceives will always find someone who will let himself be deceived. . . .

Thus, it is not necessary for a prince to have all the . . . [virtues] in fact, but it is indeed necessary to appear to have them. Nay, I dare say this, that by having them and always observing them, they are harmful; and by appearing to have them, they are useful as it is to appear merciful, faithful, humane, honest, and religious, and to be so; but to remain with a spirit built so that, if you need not to be those things, you are able and know how to change to the contrary. This has to be understood: that a prince, and especially a new prince, cannot observe all those things for which men are held to be good, since he is often under a necessity, to maintain his state, of acting against faith, against charity, against humanity, against religion. And so he needs to have a spirit disposed to change as the winds of fortune and variations of things command him, and as I said above, not depart from good, when possible, but know how to enter into evil, when forced by necessity.

A prince should thus take great care that nothing escape his mouth that is not full of the above-mentioned five qualities and that, to see him and hear him, he should appear all mercy, all faith, all honesty, all humanity, all religion. And nothing is more necessary to appear to have than this last quality. Men in general judge more by their eyes than by their hands, because seeing is given to everyone, touching to few. Everyone sees how you appear, few touch what you are; and these few dare not to oppose the opinion of many who have the majesty of the state to defend them; and in the actions of all men, and especially of princes, where there is not court to appeal to, one looks to the end. So let a prince win and maintain his state: the means will always be judged honorable, and will be praised by everyone.

NOTES AND QUESTIONS

1. Machiavelli is scarcely alone among politicians and theorists in viewing the stability and security of the state as the leader's preeminent responsibility. From their perspective, the rule of law and conventional moral values must sometimes be subordinated to national security because without such security, there can be no law or protection of values. In effect, desperate times require desperate remedies.[16] Yet what is distinctive about Machiavelli is that he saw such measures not as extraordinary interventions to preserve a system in which they would generally be unnecessary, but as ordinary demands of political life. Does his account adequately frame the issue and give due regard to the competing interests at issue? Many actions might somewhat enhance security compromise other core commitments (e.g., assassination, indefinite detention of suspected terrorists, or assistance to despotic allies). How should the trade-offs be made? Consider President Lincoln's decision to suspend habeas corpus protections, President Truman's decision to drop the atomic bomb on Japanese cities, or President Bush's decision to allow enhanced interrogation techniques

for suspected terrorists, discussed in Chapter 6.[17] What considerations should be most relevant in making such decisions?

2. Machiavelli argued that leaders should strive to be both feared and loved, but that if the combination proved elusive, it was "much safer to be feared." Is this generally true of leaders today? Contemporary researchers suggest that

> Machiavelli had it partly right. When we judge others—especially our leaders—we look first at two characteristics; how loveable they are (their warmth [or] . . . trustworthiness) and how fearsome they are (their strength, agency, or competence). . . . Why are these traits so important? Because they answer two critical questions: "What are this person's intentions toward me?" and "is he or she capable of acting on those intentions?"[18]

Leaders who stress strength without first establishing trust tend to evoke fear and undermine cooperation and creative problem solving. One large-scale study of some 51,000 leaders found that the chances that a leader who was feared and strongly disliked would also be considered successful were about one in 2,000.[19] So too, according to the renowned British philosopher Isaiah Berlin, Machiavelli's "psychology seems excessively primitive. He scarcely seems to allow for the bare possibility of sustained and genuine altruism."[20] Nor does his vision of followers seem plausible in light of what we now know about the importance of intrinsic motivation and the limits of hard power. How might a more complicated understanding of human psychology qualify his analysis?

3. Following Machiavelli, many theorists have debated the extent to which politics poses special demands on leaders to compromise personal moral principles in the service of the common good. Michael Walzer takes up that question in his celebrated essay on "dirty hands."

B. DIRTY HANDS

Michael Walzer, Political Action: The Problem of Dirty Hands

Philosophy & Public Affairs, 2(2) (Winter 1973): 160-180

[Are there moral dilemmas in which a man] must choose between two courses of action both of which it would be wrong for him to undertake[?] . . .

In modern times the dilemma appears most often as the problem of "dirty hands," and it is typically stated by the Communist leader Hoerderer in Sartre's play of that name: "I have dirty hands right up to the elbows. I've plunged them in filth and blood. Do you think you can govern innocently?" My own answer is no, I don't think I could govern innocently; nor do most of us believe that those who govern us are innocent—as I shall argue below—even the best of them. But this does not mean that it isn't possible to do the right thing while governing. It means that a particular act of government (in a political party or in the state) may be exactly the right thing to do in utilitarian terms and yet leave the man who does it guilty of a moral wrong. The innocent man, afterwards, is no longer innocent. If on the other hand he remains innocent, chooses, that is, the "absolutist" [position], . . . he not only fails to do the right thing (in utilitarian terms), he may also fail to measure up to the duties of his office (which imposes on him a considerable responsibility for consequences and outcomes). Most often, of course, political leaders accept the utilitarian calculation; they try to measure up. . . .

Let me begin, then, with a piece of conventional wisdom to the effect that politicians are a good deal worse, morally worse, than the rest of us (it is the wisdom of the rest of us). Without either endorsing it or pretending to disbelieve it, I am going to expound this convention. For it suggests that the dilemma of dirty hands is a central feature of political life, that it arises not merely as an occasional crisis in the career of this or that unlucky politician but systematically and frequently.

Why is the politician singled out? Isn't he like the other entrepreneurs in an open society, who hustle, lie, intrigue, wear masks, smile and are villains? He is not, no doubt for many reasons, three of which I need to consider. First of all, the politician claims to play a different part than other entrepreneurs. He doesn't merely cater to our interests; he acts on our behalf, even in our name. He has purposes in mind, causes and projects that require the support and redound to the benefit, not of each of us individually, but of all of us together. He hustles, lies, and intrigues *for us*—or so he claims. Perhaps he is right, or at least sincere, but we suspect that he acts for himself also. Indeed, he cannot serve us without serving himself, for success brings him power and glory, the greatest rewards that men can win from their fellows. The competition for these two is fierce; the risks are often great, but the temptations are greater. We imagine ourselves succumbing. Why should our representatives act differently? Even if they would like to act differently, they probably cannot: for other men are all too ready to hustle and lie for power and glory, and it is the others who set the terms of the competition. Hustling and lying are necessary because power and glory are so desirable—that is, so widely desired. And so the men who act for us and in our name are necessarily hustlers and liars.

Politicians are also thought to be worse than the rest of us because they rule over us, and the pleasures of ruling are much greater than the pleasures of being ruled. The successful politician becomes the visible architect of our restraint. He taxes us, licenses us, forbids and permits us, directs us to this or that distant goal—all for our greater good. Moreover, he takes chances for our greater good that put us, or some of us, in danger. . . . There are undoubtedly times when it is good or necessary to direct the affairs of other people and to put them in danger. But we are a little frightened of the man who seeks, ordinarily and every day, the power to do so. And the fear is reasonable enough. The politician has, or pretends to have, a kind of confidence in his own judgment that the rest of us know to be presumptuous in any man. . . .

No one succeeds in politics without getting his hands dirty. This is conventional wisdom again, and again I don't mean to insist that it is true without qualification. I repeat it only to disclose the moral dilemma inherent in the convention. For sometimes it is right to try to succeed, and then it must also be right to get one's hands dirty. . . .

It will be best to turn quickly to some examples. I have chosen two, one relating to the struggle for power and one to its exercise. . . . [L]et us imagine a politician . . . [who] wants to do good only by doing good, or at least he is certain that he can stop short of the most corrupting and brutal uses of political power. . . . In order to win the election the candidate must make a deal with a dishonest ward boss, involving the granting of contracts for school construction over the next four years. Should he make the deal? Well, at least he shouldn't be surprised by the offer, most of us would probably say (a conventional piece of sarcasm). And he should accept it or not, depending on exactly what is at stake in the election. But that is not the candidate's view. He is extremely reluctant even to consider the deal, puts off his aides when they remind him of it, refuses to calculate its possible effects upon the campaign. Now, if he is acting this way because the very thought of bargaining with that particular ward boss makes him feel unclean, his reluctance isn't very interesting. His feelings by themselves are not important. But he may also have reasons for his reluctance. He may know, for example, that some of his supporters support him precisely because they believe he is a good man, and this means to them a man who won't make such deals. Or he may doubt his own motives for considering the deal, wondering whether it is the political campaign or his own candidacy that makes the bargain at all tempting. Or he may believe that if he makes deals of this sort now he may not be able later on to achieve those ends that make the campaign worthwhile, and he may not feel entitled to take such risks with a future that is not only his own future. Or he may simply think that the deal is dishonest and therefore wrong, corrupting not only himself but all those human relations in which he is involved.

Because he has scruples of this sort, we know him to be a good man. But we view the campaign in a certain light, estimate its importance in a certain way, and hope that he will overcome his scruples and make the deal. It is important to stress that we don't want just *anyone* to make the deal; we want *him* to make it, precisely because he has scruples about it. We know he is doing right when he makes the deal because he knows he is doing wrong. I don't mean merely that he will feel badly or even very badly after he makes the deal. If he is the good man I am imagining him to be, he will feel guilty, that is, he will believe himself to be guilty. That is what it means to have dirty hands.

All this may become clearer if we look at a more dramatic example, for we are, perhaps, a little blasé about political deals and disinclined to worry much about the man who makes one. So consider a politician who has seized upon a national crisis—a prolonged colonial war—to reach for power. He and his friends win office pledged to decolonization and peace; they are honestly committed to both, though not without some sense of the advantages of the commitment. In any case, they have no responsibility for the war; they have steadfastly opposed it.

Immediately, the politician goes off to the colonial capital to open negotiations with the rebels. But the capital is in the grip of a terrorist campaign, and the first decision the new leader faces is this—he is asked to authorize the torture of a captured rebel leader who knows or probably knows the location of a number of bombs hidden in apartment buildings around the city, set to go off within the next twenty-four hours. He orders the man tortured, convinced that he must do so for the sake of the people who might otherwise die in the explosions—even though he believes that torture is wrong, indeed abominable, not just sometimes, but always. He had expressed this belief often and angrily during his own campaign; the rest of us took it as a sign of his goodness. How should we regard him now? (How should he regard himself?)

Once again, it does not seem enough to say that he should feel very badly. But why not? Why shouldn't he have feelings like those of St. Augustine's melancholy soldier, who understood both that his war was just and that killing, even in a just war, is a terrible thing to do? The difference is that Augustine did not believe that it was wrong to kill in a just war; it was just sad, or the sort of thing a good man would be saddened by. But he might have thought it wrong to torture in a just war, and later Catholic theorists have certainly thought it wrong. Moreover, the politician I am imagining thinks it wrong, as do many of us who supported him. Surely we have a right to expect more than melancholy from him now. When he ordered the prisoner tortured, he committed a moral crime and he accepted a moral burden. Now he is a guilty man. His willingness to acknowledge and bear (and perhaps to repent and do penance for) his guilt is evidence, and it is the only evidence he can offer us, both that he is not too good for politics and that he is good enough. Here is the moral politician: it is by his dirty hands that we know him. If he were a moral man and nothing else, his hands would not be dirty; if he were a politician and nothing else, he would pretend that they were clean. . . .

[The best way to escape this dilemma] recognizes the usefulness of guilt and seeks to explain it. There are, it appears, good reasons for "overvaluing" as well as for overriding the rules. For the consequences might be very bad indeed if the rules were overridden every time the moral calculation seemed to go against them. It is probably best if most men do not calculate too nicely, but simply follow the rules; they are less likely to make mistakes that way, all in all. And so a good man (or at least an ordinary good man) will respect the rules rather more than he would if he thought them merely guidelines, and he will feel guilty when he overrides them. Indeed, if he did not feel guilty, "he would not be such a good man." It is by his feelings that we know him. Because of those feelings he will never be in a hurry to override the rules, but will wait until there is no choice, acting only to avoid consequences that are both imminent and almost certainly disastrous.

The obvious difficulty with this argument is that the feeling whose usefulness is being explained is most unlikely to be felt by someone who is convinced only of its usefulness. He breaks a utilitarian rule (guideline), let us say, for good utilitarian reasons: but can he then feel guilty, also for good utilitarian reasons, when he has no reason for believing that he is guilty?. . . It is best to say only that the more fully they accept the utilitarian account, the less likely they are to feel that (useful) feeling. . . .

The first tradition [of thinking about dirty hands] is best represented by Machiavelli, the first man, so far as I know, to state the paradox that I am examining. The good man who aims to found or reform a republic must, Machiavelli tells us, do terrible things to reach his goal. . . . Sometimes, however, "when the act accuses, the result excuses." This sentence from *The Discourses* is often taken to mean that the politician's deceit and cruelty are justified by the good results he brings about. But if they were justified, it wouldn't be necessary to learn what Machiavelli claims to teach: how not to be good. It would only be necessary to learn how to be good in a new, more difficult, perhaps roundabout way. That is not Machiavelli's argument. His political judgments are indeed consequentialist in character, but not his moral judgments. . . . The deceitful and cruel politician is excused (if he succeeds) only in the sense that the rest of us come to agree that the results were "worth it" or, more likely, that we simply forget his crimes when we praise his success.

It is important to stress Machiavelli's own commitment to the existence of moral standards. His paradox depends upon that commitment as it depends upon the general stability of the standards—which he upholds in his consistent use of words like good and bad. If he wants the standards to be disregarded by good men more often than they are, he has nothing with which to replace them and no other way of recognizing the good men except by their allegiance to those same standards. It is exceedingly rare, he writes, that a good man is willing to employ bad means to become prince. Machiavelli's purpose is to persuade such a person to make the attempt, and he holds out the supreme political rewards, power and glory, to the man who does so and succeeds. The good man is not rewarded (or excused), however, merely for his willingness to get his hands dirty. He must do bad things well. There is no reward for doing bad things badly, though they are done with the best of intentions. And so political action necessarily involves taking a risk. But it should be clear that what is risked is not personal goodness—*that is thrown away*—but power and glory. If the politician succeeds, he is a hero; eternal praise is the supreme reward for not being good.

What the penalties are for not being good, Machiavelli doesn't say, and it is probably for this reason above all that his moral sensitivity has so often been questioned. He is suspect not because he tells political actors they must get their hands dirty, but because he does not specify the state of mind appropriate to a man with dirty hands. A Machiavellian hero has no inwardness. What he thinks of himself we don't know. I would guess, along with most other readers of Machiavelli, that he basks in his glory. But then it is difficult to account for the strength of his original reluctance to learn how not to be good. In any case, he is the sort of man who is unlikely to keep a diary and so we cannot find out what he thinks. Yet we do want to know; above all, we want a record of his anguish. That is, a sign of our own conscientiousness and of the impact on us of the second tradition of thought that I want to examine, in which personal anguish sometimes seems the only acceptable excuse for political crimes.

The second tradition is best represented, I think, by Max Weber, who outlines its essential features with great power at the very end of his essay "Politics as a Vocation." For Weber, the good man with dirty hands is a hero still, but he is a tragic hero. In part, his tragedy is that though politics is his vocation, he has not been called by God and so cannot be justified by Him. Weber's hero is alone in a world that seems to belong to Satan, and his vocation is entirely his own choice. He still wants what Christian magistrates have always wanted, both to do good in the world and to save his soul, but now these two ends have come into sharp contradiction. They are contradictory because of the necessity for violence in a world where God has not instituted the sword. The politician takes the sword himself, and only by doing so does he measure up to his vocation. With full consciousness of what he is doing, he does bad in order to do good, and surrenders his soul. . . .

Weber attempts to resolve the problem of dirty hands entirely within the confines of the individual conscience, but I am inclined to think that this is neither possible nor desirable. The self-awareness of the tragic hero is obviously of great value. We want the politician to have an inner life at least something like that which Weber describes. But sometimes the hero's suffering needs to be socially expressed (for like punishment, it confirms and reinforces our sense that certain acts are wrong). And equally important, it sometimes needs to be socially limited. We don't want to be ruled by men who have lost their souls. A politician with dirty hands needs a soul, and it is best for us all if he has some hope of personal salvation, however that is conceived. It is not the case that when he does bad in order to do good he surrenders himself forever to the demon of politics. He commits a determinate crime, and he must pay a determinate penalty. When he has done so, his hands will be clean again, or as clean as human hands can ever be. So the Catholic Church has always taught, and this teaching is central to the third tradition that I want to examine.

Once again I will take a . . . lapsed representative of the tradition and consider Albert Camus' *The Just Assassins.* The heroes of this play are terrorists at work in nineteenth-century Russia. The dirt on their hands is human blood. And yet Camus' admiration for them, he tells us, is complete. We consent to being criminals, one of them says, but there is nothing with which anyone can reproach us. Here is the dilemma of dirty hands in a new form. The heroes are innocent criminals, just assassins, because, having killed, they are prepared to *die—and will die.* Only their execution, by the same despotic authorities they are attacking, will complete the action in which they are engaged: dying, they need make no excuses. That is the end of their guilt and pain. The execution is not so much punishment as self-punishment and expiation. On the scaffold they wash their hands clean and, unlike the suffering servant, they die happy. . . .

[J]ust assassination, I want to suggest, is like civil disobedience. In both men violate a set of rules, go beyond a moral or legal limit, in order to do what they believe they should do. At the same time, they acknowledge their responsibility for the violation by accepting punishment or doing penance. But there is also a difference between the two, which has to do with the difference between law and morality. In most cases of civil disobedience the laws of the state are broken for moral reasons, and the state provides the punishment. In most cases of dirty hands moral rules are broken for reasons of state, and no one provides the punishment. There is rarely a Czarist executioner waiting in the wings for politicians with dirty hands, even the most deserving among them. Moral rules are not usually enforced against the sort of actor I am considering, largely because he acts in an official capacity. . . . I am nevertheless inclined to think Camus' view the most attractive of the three, if only because it requires us at least to imagine a punishment or a penance that fits the crime and so to examine closely the nature of the crime. . . . Without the executioner, however, there is no one to set the stakes or maintain the values except ourselves, and probably no way to do either except through philosophic reiteration and political activity.

"We shall not abolish lying by refusing to tell lies," says Hoerderer, "but by using every means at hand to abolish social classes." I suspect we shall not abolish lying at all, but we might see to it that fewer lies were told if we contrived to deny power and glory to the greatest liars—except, of course, in the case of those lucky few whose extraordinary achievements make us forget the lies they told. If Hoerderer succeeds in abolishing social classes, perhaps he will join the lucky few. Meanwhile, he lies, manipulates, and kills, and we must make sure he pays the price. We won't be able to do that, however, without getting our own hands dirty, and then we must find some way of paying the price ourselves.

NOTES AND QUESTIONS

1. Walzer takes his title from Sartre's play, *Dirty Hands*, and quotes the communist leader who acknowledges, "I have dirty hands right up to the elbows. Do you think you can govern innocently?" Walzer, like Machiavelli, answers no, but he also believes, unlike Machiavelli, that rulers should suffer anguish when they depart from moral principles. Machiavelli is known for the principle that when the act accuses, the result excuses. But according to Walzer, that cannot mean that wrongful acts are justified by good ends; if that were true, then the acts would not be wrongful, and Machiavelli would not need to provide instruction in how not to be good. In Walzer's view, the dilemma of political governance arises when leaders must choose between two wrongs. Do you agree? How should the politician deal with the dishonest ward boss? Is moral anguish sufficient absolution? Do all politicians who sacrifice moral conviction to win votes or campaign contributions dirty their hands? Or is Walzer talking about a different kind of dirt?

2. To what extent are Americans resigned to dirty hands among their political leaders? Recent polls find that 95 percent of Americans think that a president's character is important; two-thirds agree that it is very important.[21] When asked about relative importance, surveys find conflicting results. In one poll, Democrats and Independents ranked honesty as the most important trait, and Republicans ranked it second (after intelligence).[22] Integrity, however, came in fourth among Democrats and sixth for Independents and Republicans.[23] And

even Americans who claim honesty is crucial do not always vote that way. As Donald Trump began his presidency, less than a fifth of Americans considered him honest and trustworthy.[24]

Trump is an extreme case, but not an isolated one. As one researcher noted,

> Integrity has rarely been a trait that has been commonly associated with U.S. presidential candidates. . . . Since Eisenhower, it has been far more common for the losing candidate to be evaluated better on honesty than the winning candidate. In particular, incumbent presidents Lyndon Johnson, Richard Nixon, and Bill Clinton all survived their reelection bids with negative scores on integrity."[25]

Four-fifths of Americans believe that most politicians are more interested in winning elections than in doing what is right.[26] Three-quarters believe that most elected officials put their own interests ahead of the country's.[27] And only 7 percent have "a great deal of trust and confidence" in politicians.[28] What implications do these findings suggest for lawyers seeking careers in elective office?

3. How should political leaders deal with the need to buy influence through personal favors? As mayor of Newark, Cory Booker told a *New Yorker* author, "It's the Realpolitik that I'm living. Being someone who considers himself idealistic, you have a [member of the city council] . . . who comes to you and says, 'My cousin needs this . . .' and you know that it's going to control votes. . . . What do you do in that situation?"[29] How would you respond?

4. Are there parallels to dirty hands in legal contexts? Practices such as child labor abroad, corrupt payments to foreign governments, and environmental damage have often been justified as the lesser of two evils, and necessary to prevent dire economic consequences. Are these fair analogies? What other examples have you observed? Were they effectively addressed?

5. British playwright George Bernard Shaw captured the dirty hands dilemma in commenting on a Labor Party colleague who lost his seat in Parliament after refusing to compromise on an issue:

> When I think of my own unfortunate character, smirched with compromise, rotted with opportunism, mildewed by expediency . . . I do think Joe might have put up with just a speck or two on those white robes of his for the sake of the millions of poor devils who cannot afford any character at all because they have no friend in Parliament. Oh, these moral dandies, these spiritual toffs, these superior persons. Who is Joe anyhow, that he should not risk his soul occasionally like the rest of us?[30]

In this country, one of the most famous lawyer-politicians with dirty hands was Huey Long, a Louisiana governor and senator. He retained a commitment to democratic ideals but operated under no illusion that he could realize his populist reform agenda through democratic processes. "They say they don't like my methods," Long noted. "Well I don't like them either. . . . I'd do it some other way if there was one." But, he believed, "[y]ou've got to fight fire with fire."[31] Bribery, patronage, and smear tactics were, he thought, a necessary cost of consolidating control to achieve policy objectives that were "for the benefit of the people."[32] Are there circumstances under which you agree?

6. Some trade-offs between moral means and moral ends appear particularly necessary in government, because success is often "measured by a historian's yardstick" and undue insistence on principle can prevent compromises that are in society's long-term interests.[33]

As Richard Nixon put it:

> [A] leader has to deal with people and nations as they are, not as they should be. As a result, the qualities required for leadership are not necessarily those that we would want our children to emulate—unless we wanted them to be leaders. . . . Guile, vanity, dissembling—in other circumstances these might be unattractive habits, but to the leader they can be essential. . . . Roosevelt talked of keeping America out of war while maneuvering to bring it into war.[34]

Yet ironically enough, Nixon also claimed the moral high ground during the 1960 presidential campaign, when his opponent, John F. Kennedy, used questionable means in the service of civil rights and appeals to African American voters. The issue involved the arrest of Martin Luther King for a technical breach of his parole conditions, which he violated by participation in a sit-in. A Georgia state court judge sentenced King to hard labor for four months in a Georgia prison and many civil rights activists worried he would be lynched. Robert Kennedy called the Georgia judge to protest that King had a right to bail and appeal. King was freed on bond, and Kennedy's support in the African American community escalated. Nixon told his staff, "I think Dr. King is getting a bum rap. But despite my strong feelings in this respect, it would be completely improper for me or for any other lawyer to call the judge. And Robert Kennedy [as a lawyer] should have known better than to do so."[35] Do you agree? What would you have done in Kennedy's situation?

7. Although dilemmas of dirty hands do not yield categorical solutions, many theorists agree that they should be subject to moral reasoning of the sort that Walzer supplies. British philosopher Bernard Williams suggests that conflating Plato's question "how can the good rule?" and Machiavelli's question "how to rule the world as it is?" leads to cynicism unless one adjusts the definitions: "[T]he good need not be pure, so long as they retain some active sense of moral costs and moral limits and [the culture] has some genuinely settled expectations of civic respectability."[36] Williams adds:

It is a predictable and probable hazard of public life that there will be these situations in which something morally disagreeable is clearly required. To refuse on moral grounds ever to do anything of that sort is more likely to mean that one cannot seriously pursue even the moral ends of politics. . . . [But] only those who are reluctant and disinclined to do the morally disagreeable when it is really necessary have much chance of not doing it when it is not necessary. . . . A habit of reluctance is an essential obstacle against the happy acceptance of the intolerable.[37]

How do political leaders decide what is "really necessary?" What if the costs and benefits are uncertain, indeterminate, and/or incommensurable? Is the test of what is necessary look to what is essential for the public or for the politician? What if political leaders believe (as most do) that keeping themselves in office serves the people's interest? Consider Barack Obama's abandonment of his position on campaign finance in order to accept super PAC money in the 2012 presidential race? Although Obama had previously opposed super PACs, stating that American elections should not "be bankrolled by America's powerful interests," the Supreme Court decision permitting unlimited contributions by such PACs prompted change in his views. Obama's inability to match Republican donations without such support forced him to shift his position.[38] As his senior advisor David Axelrod explained, "[W]hether we liked or not, these [were] the rules of the game now. We just decided that we couldn't play touch while they were playing tackle."[39]

Compare Obama's change in position on campaign finance with John McCain's shift on issues—such as abortion, gun control, immigration, and tax cuts for the wealthy—when more conservative views proved necessary to gain the Republican presidential nomination in 2008. In a 2000 concession speech acknowledging his loss of the presidential nomination, McCain promised that "I will never . . . dishonor the nation I love or myself by letting ambition overcome principle. Never. Never. Never."[40] Many commentators viewed his "flip flop" in 2008 as evidence that he "ha[d] become the sort of politician he once despised."[41]

Would Obama's and McCain's decisions satisfy Williams' test? Would they satisfy yours?

8. In reflecting on these "dirty hands" dilemmas, Canadian politician and political science professor Michael Ignatieff argues that "good judgment in politics is messy. It means balancing policy and politics in imperfect compromises that always leave someone unhappy—often yourself. Knowing the difference between a good and a bad compromise is more important in politics than holding on to pure principle at any price."[42] An elected official's responsibility is to the voters and, he emphasizes, "you can't accomplish anything for them if you value your conscience more highly than you value their interests."[43] In Ignatieff's view,

Embracing a political life means shedding your innocence. It means being willing to pay the costs before you even know what they are going to be. It means knowing who you are and being adamant about what a political life is for. You can't succeed unless the people who elect you believe that you're in it for them. If you're not in it for them, you shouldn't be in politics. . . . [Thinking of politics as a calling] captures precisely what is so hard: to be worldly and sinful yet faithful and fearless at the same time. You put your own immodest ambitions in the service of others. You hope that your ambitions will be redeemed by the good you do. In the process you get your hands dirty for the sake of ends that are supposed to be clean. You use human vices—cunning and ruthlessness—in the service of the virtues—justice and decency. . . .

Cynics will dismiss this vision of politics as a piece of self-important delusion, but for those who have actually done it, like me, it has a ring of truth. It is a vision of what politics could be that enables you to understand what politics actually is. It is in the nature of a calling that it remains beyond our grasp. Those who are called know they are not worthy of it, but it inspires them all the same.[44]

Do you agree? How does this framework help in resolving the dilemma in Problem 5-1?

PROBLEM 5-1

Democracy, Henry Adams's celebrated nineteenth-century novel, involves an Illinois senator in the post-Civil War era. Senator Ratcliffe takes an unabashedly Machiavellian view of politics, particularly when rationalizing his own involvement in two election scandals. About the first scandal he says:

In the worst days of the war there was almost a certainty that my State would be carried by the peace party, by fraud. . . . Had Illinois been lost then, we should certainly have lost the Presidential election, and with it probably the Union. At any rate, I believed the fate of the war to depend on the result. I was then Governor, and upon me the responsibility rested.

To secure victory, Ratcliffe and his fellow party members stuffed the ballot boxes. He was "not proud of the transaction, but [he] would do it again, and worse than that, if [he] thought it would save this country from disunion."[45]

The second incident, according to Ratcliffe's account, occurred during a hotly contested postwar presidential election. Party leaders asked him to abandon his opposition to a steamship subsidy, whose backers were providing substantial financial support. Ratcliffe, who was eager to advance to higher office, did so, and he rationalized his decision as follows:

> I do not take to undertake to defend this affair. It is the act of my public life that I most regret—not the doing, but the necessity of doing. . . . [T]here are conflicting duties in all the transactions of life, except the simplest. However we may act, do what we may, we must violate some moral obligation. All that can be asked of us is that we should guide ourselves by what we think the highest. At the time this affair occurred . . . I owed duties to my constituents, to the government to the people. I might interpret these duties narrowly or broadly. I might say: Perish the government, perish the Union, perish this people, rather than that I should soil my hands! Or I might say, as I did, and as I would say again: Be my fate what it may, this glorious Union, the last hope of suffering humanity shall be preserved.[46]

At other points in the novel, Ratcliffe elaborates the view that underpinned his decisions:

> No representative government can long be much better or much worse than the society it represents. . . . If virtue won't answer our purpose, we must use vice, or our opponents will put us out of office, and this was as true in [George] Washington's day as it is now, and always will be. . . . In politics we cannot keep our hands clean. I have done many things in my political career that are not defensible. To act with entire honesty and self-respect, one should live in a pure atmosphere, and the atmosphere of politics is impure.[47]

1. Would Walzer or Ignatieff have agreed with Ratcliffe's reasoning and decisions? Do you? Does trading votes for money pose the same ethical issue as stuffing the ballot box if the ends are the same? Does it matter whether the opposition is also guilty? How different is Ratcliffe's argument from the one that Abraham Lincoln advanced for suspending certain constitutional rights (such as habeas corpus) during wartime? "My oath to preserve the constitution . . . imposed upon on me the duty of preserving by every indispensable means, that government—that nation—of which that constitution was the organic law. . . . I felt that measures otherwise unconstitutional, might become lawful, by becoming indispensable to the preservation . . . of the nation."[48]

2. Other characters in the novel come to view Ratcliffe's political agenda as motivated by his own ambition, rather than by some higher vision of the public interest. This is what some commentators have described as "Machiavellism without Machiavelli."[49] How much should motive matter in determining whether dirty hands are morally justified?

MEDIA RESOURCES

Dirty-hands dilemmas are common in many contemporary media portraits of war, national security, law enforcement, and politics.[50] *Madame Secretary*, a television series about an American secretary of state, features countless examples of dirty hands, including one in which a president facing reelection faces tradeoffs between doing what is right for his campaign and what is right for the country. Episode 11 of the third season portrays a president who has the opportunity to avert a challenge to his election by engaging in what he considers a dirty tactic: threatening to leak the fact that his challenger has a genetic predisposition for early Alzheimer's disease that he did not disclose during the election. The president instructs his chief of staff not to make the threat; the chief of staff does so anyway, on the ground that the end justifies the means. The second season of *Scandal* involves an incident of election rigging and voter fraud in a presidential campaign that poses problems similar to the ones in *Democracy*.[51] The final season presents multiple episodes in which government leaders, including the Attorney General, have to decide whether to violate rules of law and morality to prevent an existential national security threat. The television series *24* also features a number of episodes in which Jack Bauer is willing to dirty his hands for what he perceives as national security reasons.

In *The Good Wife*, the lead character, junior associate Alicia Florrick, faces an ethical dilemma when she is asked to be in charge of hiring new associates, and a powerful partner pressures her to hire his niece rather than a more qualified candidate. In later scenes from season six of that series, Alicia is running for political office and has to consider how to answer questions about whether a drug dealer has contributed to her campaign, and how to respond to one of her donor's demands that she put a person of his choosing in a powerful position. The *Godfather* has several scenes raising Machiavelli's question of whether it is better for a leader to be feared or loved. *Night Falls on Manhattan* profiles a newly elected district attorney's fight against corruption and offers some memorable examples of bad leadership. The Netflix series *House of Cards* depicts the climb to power of Frank Underwood, a politician who is more than willing to dirty his hands to accomplish his desired ends. The series *Billions* poses multiple dilemmas for Manhattan prosecutors who cannot prosecute a duplicitous hedge fund leader without crossing ethical lines. Season four of profiles the ethical trade-offs that one of these prosecutors needs to make to be elected state attorney general.[52]

Another particularly powerful example of dirty hands comes from season three, episode 21 of the series *West Wing*, in which President Bartlet debates whether to authorize an assassination of a foreign diplomat. The diplomat, a secretary of defense from a fictional Middle East nation, Qumar, had scheduled a visit to the United States before the Bartlet administration learned of the extent of his involvement in terrorist activities. He cannot be tried when he visits because of diplomatic immunity. However, a plane accident could be faked over the Caribbean on his return, which would presumably save many lives and avert a major security threat to the United States. The president's chief of staff, Leo

McGarry, has no doubt that the assassination is necessary. When Bartlet protests that it's "just wrong; it's absolutely wrong," McGarry responds, "But you have to do it anyway." "Why?" asks Bartlet. "Because you won," McGarry answers. What further complicates the analysis, both for Bartlet and for viewers assessing his conduct, is how the decision might affect his own reputation and political career. At one point in his discussion with McGarry, Bartlet expresses concern that Qumar would realize the accident was staged. In that case, it could trigger a war and put Bartlet's own reelection in further jeopardy. That too would have national security consequences, particularly given Bartlet's assessment of his opponent's inadequate foreign policy capabilities. The episode can spark discussion of what factors should most influence such decisions and what members of the class would have done in those circumstances. Related issues arise in the discussion of torture in Chapter 6.

Several of the films described in Chapter 11 involve such dilemmas—for example, *A Man for All Seasons*, *All the King's Men*, and *Primary Colors*. *Frost/Nixon*, a dramatization of David Frost's interview of Richard Nixon, includes a gripping exchange on Watergate. *The American President*, starring Michael Douglas, centers on a leader trying to rise above politics as usual. His televised press conference raises key questions about the difference between what he calls "keeping my job" and "doing my job." The movie *Spotlight*, which won an Oscar for best picture for its portrayal of the *Boston Globe* exposé of pedophilia among Catholic priests, includes issues of legal ethics for the Church's lawyer. *Michael Clayton* features George Clooney as a law firm's "fixer" of ethical problems, including fraud by a major client involving toxic chemicals.

C. ETHICAL CHALLENGES FOR LAWYER LEADERS

From the public's perspective, ethical leadership in law seems to be in short supply. Less than a fifth of Americans rate attorneys' honesty and ethical standards as high or very high.[53] Even fewer have confidence in lawyers who lead law firms or who occupy positions of political leadership.[54] For over a century, bar leaders themselves have lamented the loss of professionalism and lawyer-statesmen. In 1914, future Supreme Court Justice Louis Brandeis chastised prominent attorneys for becoming "adjuncts" of the wealthy and neglecting "to use their powers for the protection of the people."[55] Two decades later, Supreme Court Justice Harlan Fisk Stone similarly warned that the "learned profession of an earlier day [had become] the obsequious servant of business . . . tainted with the morals and manners of the marketplace in its most antisocial manifestations."[56] Contemporary commentators have painted the profession as "'lost," "betrayed," in "crisis," and in "decline," and an erosion in leadership is held partly responsible.[57]

Ethical leaders are critical in three respects: modeling integrity in their own behavior, setting appropriate standards, and holding employees responsible.[58]

Research suggests that the conduct of leaders is the most important factor in determining an organization's ethical climate, which includes awareness of ethical issues and desires to maintain ethical standards.[59] Employees who see leaders act with integrity are much less likely to engage in misconduct and much more likely to report misconduct by others.[60]

Ethical leadership is critical for lawyers who head firms, government agencies, and non-profit organizations, and for those who serve as in-house or outside counsel to clients who lead. In describing ethical leaders, individuals emphasize a willingness to communicate clear ethical boundaries and to look beyond the "bottom line."[61] Discussion here begins with an exploration of what constitutes moral leadership, what gets in the way, and what strategies could promote it.

DEBORAH L. RHODE, INTRODUCTION: WHERE IS THE LEADERSHIP IN MORAL LEADERSHIP?

Deborah L. Rhode, ed., Moral Leadership: The Theory and Practice of Power, Judgment, and Policy (San Francisco: Jossey-Bass, 2007), pp. 1-45 and 53

Moral Leadership Defined

Ethics and Effectiveness

. . . [A crucial threshold issue is] whether all leadership has a moral dimension. To borrow Machiavelli's classic formulation, can one be a "good" leader in terms of effectiveness without being a "good" leader in terms of morality? The limited leadership commentary that focuses on this question stakes out a range of views. . . .

An increasingly common position, encountered in both scholarly and popular literature, is that the essence of effective leadership is ethical leadership. The first prominent theorist to take this view was historian James MacGregor Burns. . . . [In *Leadership*, Burns advocated] transformational leadership, [in which] leaders and followers "raise one another to higher levels of motivation and morality," beyond "everyday wants and needs." They aspire to reach more "principled levels of judgment" in pursuit of end values such as liberty, justice, and self-fulfillment. Similarly, John Gardner, in *The Moral Aspect of Leadership,* argued that leaders should "serve the basic needs of their constituents," defend "fundamental moral principles," seek the "fulfillment of human possibilities," and improve the communities of which they are a part. To Gardner, like other contemporary commentators, men such as Hitler and Stalin can be considered rulers but not leaders.

Many scholars see this definition as too limiting. Some argue that effective leadership requires morality in means, although not necessarily in ends. Underlying this distinction is the assumption that widely shared principles are available for judging process but no comparable consensus exists for judging objectives. According to this view, leadership cannot be coercive or authoritarian, but it can seek ends that most people would regard as morally unjustified.

Yet this distinction is inconsistent with conventional understandings and not particularly helpful for most purposes. As Bennis notes, "People in top positions [can often be] doing the wrong thing well." "Like it or not," others point out, Hitler, Stalin, and Saddam Hussein were animated by a moral vision and were extremely effective in inspiring others in its pursuit. In her recent account, *Bad Leadership,* Barbara Kellerman similarly suggests that it is unproductive to exclude from definitions of leadership those whose means or ends are abhorrent but nonetheless effective, and therefore instructive. As she puts it, "How can we stop what we don't study?"

Values-Based Leadership

 . . . [A related problem is that] even commentators who see an ethical dimension to values leadership often discuss it in only the most perfunctory and platitudinous terms. Publications aimed at managerial audiences frequently just list a few key qualities that have "stood the test of time," such as integrity, honesty, fairness, compassion, and respect, without acknowledging any complexity or potential conflict in their exercise. Other commentators simply add "moral" as an all-purpose adjective in the mix of desirable characteristics: leaders should have "moral imagination," "moral courage," "moral excellence," and, of course, a "moral compass.". . .

Part of the problem is that few of the publications marketed to leaders make any concessions to complexity. Only rarely does a note of realism creep in, typically by way of acknowledgment that reconciling priorities may be difficult or that most people, including leaders, act from mixed motives, not all of them disinterested. But rarer still are any real insights about how to strike the appropriate balance among competing concerns. When examples are given, they generally appear as stylized, often self-serving morality plays in which virtue is its own reward and dishonesty does not pay. The party line is that violating "timeless values" is always wrong, "pure and simple." In this uncomplicated leadership landscape, the "right thing for business and the right thing ethically have become one and the same."

Would that it were true. But . . . [recent research] . . . paints a much more complicated portrait than the mainstream commentary conveys. . . .

Doing Good and Doing Well: When Does Ethics Pay?

"Ethics pays" is the mantra of most moral leadership literature, particularly the publications written by and for managers. *If Aristotle Ran General Motors* offers a representative sample of reassuring homilies: a "climate of goodness will always pay," "you can't put a simple price on trust," and "unethical conduct is self-defeating or even self-destructive over the long run." A dispassionate review of global business practices might suggest that Aristotle would need to be running more than GM for this all to be true. But no matter; in most of this commentary, a few spectacularly expensive examples of moral myopia will do: companies that make "billion-dollar errors in judgment" by marketing unsafe products, fiddling with the numbers in securities filings, or failing to report or discipline rogue employees. The moral of the story is always that if "values are lost, everything is lost."

Even more hard-headed leadership advice is often tempered with lip-service to the cost-effectiveness of integrity and reminders that profits are not an end in themselves. "The top companies make meaning, not just money," Peters and Waterman assure us. . . . [To test these homilies, a closer look at research on ethics and financial performance is necessary.]

Corporate Social Responsibility, Ethical Conduct, and Financial Performance

A wide range of studies have attempted to address the "value" of values. [They confront significant methodological challenges, including the absence of consistent definitions or metrics of social responsibility and the impossibility of drawing causal inferences from correlations between social and financial performance. However, most research findings suggest some positive relationship between ethics and financial results. For example, . . .] employees who view their organization as supporting fair and ethical conduct and its leadership as caring about ethical issues observe less unethical behavior and perform better along a range of dimensions; they are more willing to share information and knowledge and "go the extra mile" in meeting job requirements. Employees also show more concern for the customer when employers show more concern for them, and workers who feel justly treated respond in kind; they are less likely to engage in petty dishonesty such as pilfering, fudging on hours and expenses, or misusing business opportunities. The financial payoffs are obvious: employee satisfaction improves customer satisfaction and retention; enhances workplace trust, cooperation, and innovation; and saves substantial costs resulting from misconduct and surveillance designed to prevent it.

Such findings are consistent with well-documented principles of individual behavior and group dynamics. People care deeply about "organizational justice" and perform better when they believe that their workplace is treating them with dignity and respect and ensuring basic rights and equitable reward structures. Workers also respond to cues from peers and leaders. Virtue begets virtue, and observing moral behavior by others promotes similar conduct. Employers reap the rewards in higher morale, recruitment, and retention. . . .

Ethical Reputation and Financial Value

A reputation for ethical conduct by leaders and organizations also has financial value. Most obvious, it can attract customers, employees, and investors and can build good relationships with government regulators. . . . The reputational penalty from engaging in criminal or unethical conduct can be substantial and can dramatically affect market share and stock value. . . . A substantial body of research also suggests that the goodwill accumulated by doing good can buffer a company during periods of difficulty resulting from scandals, product or environmental hazards, or downsizing.

A celebrated case in point is Johnson & Johnson's decision to recall Tylenol after an incident of product tampering. It was a socially responsible decision that was highly risky in financial terms; pulling the capsules cost more than $100 million, and many experts at the time believed that it would doom one of the company's most profitable products. But Johnson & Johnson's reputation for integrity, reinforced by the recall decision, maintained public confidence, and the product bounced back with new safety features and no long-term damage. . . .

When Ethics Doesn't Pay: The Case for Values

Such examples are not uncommon. Business ethics textbooks offer countless variations on the same theme. But the reasons that the examples are so abundant also point out the problems with "ethics pays" as an all-purpose prescription for leadership dilemmas. As Harvard professor Lynn Sharp Paine puts it, a more accurate guide would be "ethics counts." Whether doing good results in doing well depends on the institutional and social context. The "financial case for values," Paine notes, is strongest when certain conditions are met:

1. Legal and regulatory systems are effective in enforcing ethical norms.
2. Individuals have choices in employment, investment, and consumption and are well informed concerning those choices.
3. The public expects organizations to operate within an ethical framework.

Berkeley professor David Vogel [makes a similar point, and notes that it is] . . . naive and misleading to suggest that [a "market for virtue" is] always in place. It is also self-defeating. To make the case for "values" turn solely on instrumental considerations is to reinforce patterns of reasoning that undermine ethical commitments. We respect moral conduct most when it occurs despite, not because of, self-interest. . . .

Ultimately what defines moral behavior is a commitment to do right whether or not it is personally beneficial. What defines moral leadership is adherence to fundamental principles even when they carry a cost. Our challenge as a society is to find ways of minimizing these costs and reinforcing such leadership. That, in turn, will require a clearer understanding of the dynamics of moral conduct. . . .

Individual and Contextual Dimensions of Moral Conduct

Moral Character and Moral Decision-Making

Moral and religious philosophers since Aristotle have generally assumed the existence of fixed character traits that are largely responsible for ethical and unethical behavior. Much of the widely read work on moral leadership shares that assumption. A recurrent theme is that "character is the defining feature of authentic leadership" and that most recent problems are a "function of flawed integrity and flawed character." The perception that personality traits are consistent, deeply rooted, and responsible for ethical conduct reinforces our sense of predictability and control. It is also consistent with a widely documented cognitive bias that psychologists label the "fundamental attribution error": our tendency to overvalue the importance of individual character and undervalue the role of situational factors in shaping behavior. Yet social science research makes clear that many such assumptions about personality traits are a "figment of our aspirations." As discussion below indicates, moral conduct is highly situational and heavily influenced by peer pressures and reward structures.

Although the importance of personal qualities should not be overstated, neither should their role be overlooked. Individuals vary in their approach toward ethical issues in ways that matter for understanding leadership. In his influential analysis of moral development, psychologist James Rest identified four "components of ethical decision-making":

1. Moral awareness: recognition that a situation raises ethical issues
2. Moral reasoning: determining what course of action is ethically sound
3. Moral intent: identifying which values should take priority in the decision
4. Moral behaviors: acting on ethical decisions

Moral Awareness and Ethical Culture

Moral awareness, the first element, reflects both personal and situational factors. One involves the moral intensity of the issue at stake. Intensity is, in turn, affected by both social consensus about the ethical status of the acts in question and the social proximity of their consequences. When issues arise in workplace contexts, it is the degree of consensus in these settings that has the greatest influence on moral awareness. Organizations that place overwhelming priority on bottom-line concerns encourage individuals to "put their moral values on hold." Such workplace cultures may help account for the large numbers of surveyed managers and [lawyers] . . . who claim never to have faced a [workplace] moral conflict.

A second influence on moral awareness involves the "feeling of nearness (social, cultural, psychological, or physical)" that the decision maker has for victims or beneficiaries of the act in question. Individuals' capacity for empathy and their sense of human or group solidarity positively affect ethical sensitivity, which encourages altruistic action and receptiveness to principles of justice, equality, and fairness. Conversely, people's capacity to distance, devalue, or dehumanize victims leads to moral disengagement and denial of moral responsibility. These capabilities are themselves influenced by childhood socialization, religious and political commitments, direct exposure to injustice, and educational approaches that build awareness of others' needs.

A wide array of quantitative and qualitative research also demonstrates the effect of workplace cultures on ethical sensitivity. . . . [One widely reported case study involves Enron. Its] plummet from the nation's seventh largest corporation to a bankrupt shell has been partly attributed to its relentless focus on "profits at all costs." The message conveyed by corporate leaders was that accounting and ethics rules were niceties made to be stretched, circumvented, and suspended when necessary. Those who advanced were those able to "stay focused" on corporate objectives "unburdened by moral anxiety."

Moral Reasoning, Situational Incentives, and Cognitive Biases

Rest's second key element in moral leadership is moral reasoning. Individuals vary in their analysis of moral issues, although here again, context plays an important role. . . .

One powerful influence involves compensation. In a culture where money buys not just goods and services but also power and status, economic rewards can skew decision-making processes in predictable ways. . . .

Other forms of self-interest can similarly skew ethical decision-making. Psychologists have documented a variety of cognitive biases that contribute to moral myopia. Those who obtain leadership positions often have a high confidence in their own capacities and judgment. That can readily lead to arrogance, over-optimism, and an escalation of commitment to choices that turn out to be wrong either factually or morally. As a result, individuals may ignore or suppress dissent, overestimate their ability to rectify adverse consequences, and cover up mistakes by denying, withholding, or sometimes destroying information. A related bias involves cognitive dissonance; individuals tend to suppress or reconstrue information that casts doubt on a prior belief or action. Such biases may lead individuals to discount or devalue evidence of the harms of their conduct or the extent of their own responsibility.

In-group biases similarly can result in unconscious discrimination or in ostracism of inconvenient and unwelcome views. Those dynamics in turn generate perceptions of unfairness and encourage team loyalty at the expense of moral candor and socially responsible decision-making.

Moral Intent, Moral Conduct, and Situational Pressures

Yet individuals' moral reasoning processes, however affected by these cognitive biases, are only part of what explains moral conduct. Indeed, most research finds only a modest correlation between ethical reasoning and behavior. It is not enough for people to make a sound moral judgment. They must also have "moral intent"—the motivation to give priority to moral values—as well as the ability to follow through and act on that intent. Moral motivations are in part a reflection of the centrality of moral concerns to individuals' identity and self-esteem. Much depends on how they weigh these concerns in relation to other needs for power, status, money, peer approval, and so forth. So too, what psychologists label "ego strength" will help determine whether individuals are able to put their moral values into action. Factors include the person's ability to work around impediments, cope with frustration, and remain focused on moral objectives. . . .

Moral Behavior: Diffusion of Responsibility, Socialization, and Peer Pressure

Studies on behavior in group settings similarly underscore the malleability of moral conduct. This research typically finds that individuals are more likely to engage in unethical conduct when acting with others. Three dynamics often work to "protect people from their own conscience": diffusion of responsibility, socialization to expedient norms, and peer pressure.

. . . [D]isplacement of responsibility may help account for the passivity of many corporate boards during periods of massive misconduct. . . . [Enron] directors approved grossly excessive compensation and failed to heed warning signals of financial and ethical difficulties. Indeed, Enron's board even twice suspended conflict-of-interest rules to allow [chief financial officer Andrew] Fastow to profit at the corporation's expense. Part of the problem, as a former Enron prosecutor notes, is that directors generally lack individual accountability for collective decision-making; their reputations rarely suffer and insurance typically insulates them from personal liability. . . .

Other group dynamics apart from diffusion of responsibility also help explain the gaps between personal principles and practices. Socialization and peer pressure play important roles in signaling what ethical norms are appropriate and in penalizing those who fail to comply. Under circumstances where bending the rules has payoffs for the group, at least in the short term, members may feel substantial pressure to put their moral convictions on hold. That is especially likely when organizations place heavy emphasis on loyalty and offer substantial rewards to "team players." Strategies of disengagement such as euphemistic labeling, reattribution of blame, and denigration of victims then enable individuals to deny problematic aspects of their collective conduct.

The cognitive biases described previously also conspire in this process. For example, once individuals yield to group pressure when the moral cost seems small, the commitment bias and the desire to reduce cognitive dissonance may kick in and entrap them in more serious misconduct. The result is what is known as "the boiled frog" problem: [folk wisdom has it that] a frog thrown into boiling water will jump out of the pot; a frog placed in tepid water that gradually becomes hotter and hotter will calmly boil to death.

In "The Inner Ring," C. S. Lewis describes the process by which people's need to belong to a favored circle undermines moral commitments:

Just at the moment when you are most anxious not to appear crude, or naif, or a prig—the hint will come. It will be the hint of something which is not quite in accordance with the rules of fair play: something which the public, the ignorant, romantic public would never understand . . . but something, says your new friend, which "we"—and at the word "we" you try not to blush for mere pleasure—something "we always do." And you will be drawn in, if you are drawn in, not by desire for gain or ease, but simply because at that moment you cannot bear to be thrust back again into the cold outer world. . . . And then, if you are drawn in, next week it will be something a little further from the rules, and next year something further still. . . . It may end in a crash, a scandal, and penal servitude; it may end in millions [and] a peerage. . . . But you will be a scoundrel.

Organizational Structure, Climate, and Reward Systems

Other characteristics of organizations can be similarly corrosive and add a further dimension to the personal frameworks that theorists like Rest propose. One such characteristic involves the fragmentation of information. The size and structure of bureaucratic institutions and the complexity of the issues involved may work against informed ethical judgments. In many of the recent scandals, as well as earlier financial, health, safety, and environmental disasters, a large number of the upper-level participants were not well informed. Lawyers, accountants, financial analysts, board members, and even officers often lacked knowledge about matters raising both moral and legal concerns. In some instances, the reason may have been willful blindness: keeping one's eyes demurely averted is a handy skill, particularly when the alternative might be civil or criminal liability. In other cases, the problem has had more to do with organizational structures and practices. Work has been allocated in ways that prevented key players from seeing the full picture, and channels for expressing concerns have been inadequate. Shooting the messenger was the standard response to unwelcome tidings in cases like Enron, and ultimately, it was not just the messenger who paid the price.

Additional aspects of the organizational culture play a critical role. As earlier discussion indicated, a key factor is ethical climate: the moral meanings that employees place on workplace policies and practices. Organizations signal their priorities in multiple ways: the content and enforcement of ethical standards; the criteria for hiring, promotion, and compensation; the fairness and respect with which they treat employees; and the social responsibility they demonstrate toward other stakeholders. . . .

In the moral meltdowns recently on display, a range of factors contributed to the unethical climates. However, the scandals generally shared one fundamental characteristic: the elevation of decision makers' short-term interests over moral values. In this respect, Enron was a "perfect storm." The corporation's hypercompetitive, profits-at-any-cost culture and reward structure had a predictably pathological impact on ethical commitments. Under the company's "rank and yank" evaluation system, employees who rated the lowest in financial performance were publicly demoted, passed over, or let go. Board directors who signed off on huge compensation packages for top managers were rewarded in kind. They all received highly generous option-based payments for service. Some who headed allied businesses got lucrative contracts with Enron; others who worked for nonprofit institutions got six-figure charitable donations. Many of the "independent" professionals—lawyers, auditors, and financial analysts—who blessed ethically problematic transactions were part of organizations with similarly skewed incentives. The leadership of Enron's outside law and accounting firms generally placed such a high priority on maintaining lucrative client business that they could not avoid complicity in client misconduct. Precisely how much complicity is unclear and likely to remain so, given the massive destruction of potential evidence and the protections of confidentiality for many key decisions. But what is abundantly clear about Enron and other major scandals is that many participants in leadership roles failed to exercise appropriate moral oversight and create a climate that would encourage it.

Yet these were not, for the most part, individuals who appeared demonstrably immoral. Rather, they were caught in corrosive cultures and seemed indifferent or insensitive to the ethical consequences of their activities. . . . Designing correctives for such ethical indifference is one of the central leadership challenges of our era. Addressing that challenge will require strategies on two levels. We need to enable those in positions of power to exercise moral leadership more effectively. And we need to increase the willingness of leaders to make moral leadership a priority.

Strategies of Moral Leadership

. . . [Significant progress will require] solidly grounded strategic analyses, packaged in forms accessible to those in leadership positions. At a minimum, such analyses should address the role of ethical codes and compliance programs, the importance of integrating ethical concerns and stakeholder responsibilities into all organizational functions, and the necessity for visible moral commitment at the top. That commitment must include adherence not only to legal requirements, but also to widely accepted principles of social responsibility. In contexts where there is no consensus about ethically appropriate conduct, leaders should strive for a decision-making process that is transparent and responsive to competing stakeholder interests.

Ethical Codes and Compliance Programs

The vast majority of large organizations have ethical codes and compliance programs. In principle, their rationale is clear. Codes of conduct can clarify rules and expectations, establish consistent standards, and project a responsible public image. If widely accepted and enforced, codified rules can also reinforce ethical commitments, deter ethical misconduct, promote trust, reduce the organization's risks of liability, and prevent free riders (those who benefit from others' adherence to moral norms without observing them personally).

In practice, however, the value of codes is subject to debate. [Vagueness and lack of enforcement are common problems.] . . . In many organizations, ethical codes and compliance structures are viewed primarily as window dressing—public relations gestures or formalities needed to satisfy the federal sentencing guidelines. . . . "Good optics" was how one manager discussed Enron's ethical code, and shortly after the company's collapse, copies of the document were selling on eBay, advertised as "never been read."

. . . An increasing array of research is also available that can guide program design and suggest best practice standards. One key finding is that employees should have opportunities for involvement in the development of codes, training, and evaluation structures. . . .

Most organizations also need to do a far better job of providing adequate power, status, and resources for compliance officers and of evaluating the performance of their ethics programs. How often are ethical issues raised? How well does the organization follow up on reports of misconduct? How effectively does it protect whistle-blowers from retaliation? How do employees perceive the program? Do they feel able to deliver bad news or make confidential reports without reprisals? These are all key factors in predicting ethical conduct, and too few organizations have made serious attempts to assess them. More systematic strategies of program evaluation are necessary, such as surveys of employees and stakeholders, exit interviews, focus groups, and independent audits.

Establishing an effective ethics and compliance structure is a demanding task. The common practice of offloading responsibility to an outside consultant or underfunded midlevel manager is a setup for failure. Efforts to institutionalize ethics can succeed only if they are integral to the workplace culture and taken seriously by those at leadership levels.

Integrating Ethics

A true commitment to moral leadership requires the integration of ethical concerns into all organizational activities. In business and professional contexts, that means factoring moral considerations into day-to-day functions, including planning, resource allocation, hiring, promotion, compensation, performance evaluations, auditing, communications, public relations, and philanthropy. Responsibilities to stakeholders need to figure in strategic decision-making at more than a rhetorical level. To that end, assessments of organizational performance need to reflect values in addition to profits.

. . . Yet obvious though this seems, many leaders appear oblivious to how it plays out in practice; neither the formal nor informal reward structures of many organizations pay serious attention to the ethics of upper-level personnel or of the units that they supervise. Performance evaluations that focus only on short-term, bottom-line outcomes are particularly likely to skew moral decision-making. Most of the scandals discussed earlier were partly attributable to reward structures that encouraged pushing the ethical edge and failed to sanction conduct on the fringes of fraud. . . .

The Ethical Commitment of Leaders

One consistent finding of research on organizational culture is the significance of leaders' own ethical commitments. That commitment is critical in several respects. First, leaders set a moral tone and a moral example by their own behavior. Employees take cues about appropriate behavior from those in supervisory positions. Whether workers believe that leaders care about principles as much as profits significantly affects the frequency of ethical conduct. . . . Hypocrisy may be the bow that vice pays to virtue, but it is a singularly unsuccessful leadership strategy.

. . . At a less obvious level, leaders face a host of issues where the moral course of action is by no means self-evident. Values may be in conflict, facts may be contested or incomplete, and realistic options may be limited. Yet while there may be no unarguably right answers, some will be more right than others: that is, more informed by available evidence, more consistent with widely accepted principles, and more responsive to all the interests at issue. A defining feature of moral leadership is a willingness to ask uncomfortable questions: Not just, "Is it legal?" but, "Is it fair?" "Is it honest?" "Does it advance societal interests or pose unreasonable risks?" "How would it feel to defend the decision on the evening news?"

Not only do leaders need to ask those questions of themselves, they also need to invite unwelcome answers from others. To counter the self-serving biases and organizational pressures noted earlier, individuals in positions of power should actively solicit diverse perspectives and dissenting views. That will require more protection for whistle-blowers and more channels for disagreement over ethical issues. Studies of whistle-blowing consistently find that those who seek to expose legal or ethical violations typically encounter harassment, ostracism, and retaliation; some become permanent pariahs in their fields. The costs do not appear significantly lower for those who report the misconduct to supervisors rather than to external agencies or the media. And all too often, disclosures go largely unheeded or produce no lasting change. In commenting on the odds of vindication, one whistle-blower wryly predicted, "If you have God, the law, the press, and the facts on your side, you have a 50-50 chance of [victory]." Fear of reprisals, along with lack of confidence that reports would be productive, are the major reasons that employees give for not disclosing abuses or airing ethical concerns. Many doubt that anonymous or confidential disclosures would remain so or that paper protections against job retaliation would prove effective.

Those who are seriously committed to moral leadership need to create more safe spaces for both reports of misconduct and moral disagreements generally. The problem in too many organizations, as one expert puts it, is "not only does no one want to listen but no one wants to talk about not listening." It is of course true that some dissenters are unbalanced or vindictive employees who air unmerited claims or self-serving grievances. But creating adequate internal channels even for these reports is the best way to prevent the far greater costs of external whistle-blowing. And even those whose motives are tainted may have valid concerns. A widely publicized case in point is the disgruntled Texaco employee who leaked tapes of racist slurs and plans for document destruction in order to protect his own job during restructuring. Whatever the costs of coping with unjustified internal dissent, the price of suppression is likely to be greater. Candid dialogue on ethical issues is essential for informed decision-making. Every leader's internal moral compass needs to be checked against external reference points. Recognizing ways in which they might be wrong is crucial in determining what is likely to be right.

NOTES ON ETHICAL DECISION-MAKING[62]

Recent research, informed by neuroscience, suggests that most of what constitutes "everyday morality" for leaders as well as other individuals is tacit, automatic, and intuitive, rather than the product of deliberative reasoning.[63] As Chapter 3 noted, this school of thought, popularized by psychologist Daniel Kahneman, explains moral behavior in terms of a dual process: "automatic intuitive responses with respect to familiar situations and conscious reasoning in response to situations for which no repetitive intuitive response has developed."[64] System 1 thinking is intuitive, "fast, automatic, effortless, and emotional." System 2 thinking is "slower, conscious, explicit, and logical."[65] As a general matter, our intuitive System 1 responses are more likely to be immoral than our reflective System 2 responses.[66] Decisions with ethical importance generally call for System 2 thinking, but individuals do not always put in the effort that it requires.[67]

However, even when individuals attempt to step back and engage in ethical reflection, they are subject to cognitive limitations that undermine moral analysis and encourage rationalization of behavior that their initial instincts suggest is wrong.[68] In effect, people are subject to "bounded ethicality."[69] They find it particularly hard to acquire and process information necessary for sound ethical decisions in the face of complexity, uncertainty, time constraints, and conflicts of interest. Physical or mental fatigue can also deplete individuals' resources for self-control, and impair their ethical awareness, all of which makes misconduct more likely.[70] Self-interest further skews the reasoning process. The more tempted we are to behave unethically, the more common—and thus acceptable—we perceive the unethical action to be.[71]

Psychologists Ann Tenbrunsel and David Messick similarly document the role of what they call "ethical fading," in which ethical consequences recede from consciousness.[72] This process preempts not only moral awareness but also "moral attentiveness": the extent to which individuals proactively consider moral issues.[73] Euphemisms often aid this ethical fading process. For example, lawyers use terms like "hard ball" to describe evasive or abusive litigation conduct.

Repeated exposure to misconduct can also produce a form of "ethical numbing."[74] Through habituation and desensitization, individuals become accustomed to minor forms of misconduct, and engage in it without significant reflection.[75] These small acts pave the way for greater misconduct, and over time, can become almost mindless.[76] One commentator describes lawyers' fraudulent billing practices this way:

> One day, not too long after you start practicing law, you will sit down at the end of a long, tiring day and you just won't have much to show for your efforts in terms of billable hours. It will be near the end of the month. You will know that all of the partners will be looking at your monthly time report in a few days, so what you'll do is pad your time sheet just a bit. Maybe you will bill a client for ninety minutes for a task that really took you only sixty minutes to perform. However, you will promise yourself that you will repay the client at the first opportunity by doing thirty

minutes of work for the client for "free." In this way, you will be "borrowing," not "stealing."

And then what will happen is that will become easier and easer to take these little loans against future work. And then, after a while, you will stop paying back these little loans. You will convince yourself that, although you billed for ninety minutes and spent only sixty minutes on the project, you did such good work that your client should pay a bit more for it. After all, our billing rate is awfully low, and your client is awfully rich.

And then you will pad more and more—every two minute telephone conversation will go down on the sheet as ten minutes, every three hour research project will go down with an extra quarter hour or so. You will continue to rationalize your dishonesty to yourself in various ways until one day you stop doing even that. And, before long—it won't take much more than three or four years—you will be stealing from your clients almost every day, and you won't even notice it.[77]

The normalization of misconduct is often so gradual that it is imperceptible.[78] People cross the line through a series of decisions without the benefit of thorough deliberation, and these decisions then shape future options in a way that they fail to anticipate. And because each decision may lead to only small deviations from prior behavior, the escalating misconduct does not raise moral alarms.[79] This is what the preceding excerpt termed the "boiled frog problem."[80] As noted in chapter 3, the folk wisdom is wrong about frogs but right about humans. That is one way that people fall victim to bounded ethicality and end up engaging in behavior contrary to their own values without awareness that they are doing so.[81]

Ethical awareness is affected by both social norms and social consequences concerning the acts in question.[82] People respond to cues from peers and leaders, and observing moral or immoral behavior by others promotes similar conduct.[83] A key factor is social consensus concerning the morality of the behavior.[84] When people think "everybody does it," the risks of moral myopia escalate. Ninety-two percent of surveyed lawyers believe that other lawyers at least occasionally pad their bills, and this perception becomes a rationalization for their own fudging.[85] Web Hubbell, onetime chief justice of the Arkansas Supreme Court, acknowledged some 400 instances of fraudulently padding bills and charging personal expenses as business expenses while in private practice, but characterized the matter as a "private financial dispute" within the firm.[86] In a tape-recorded conversation with his wife, he conceded the overbilling. When she responded, "You didn't actually do that, did you, mark up time for the client, did you?" he acknowledged, "Yes I did. So does every lawyer in the country."[87]

Firm leaders who are aware of billing abuses often engage in their own rationalizations; most fail to report such misconduct to bar disciplinary authorities and many refuse to acknowledge inadequacies in organizational oversight.[88] According to the managing partner of Hubbell's firm, "We thought and believe still we had good systems in place at the firm . . . but there is no system tight enough to prevent abuse by someone in a position of trust."[89] Experts, however, view that attitude as part of the problem, and fault bar leaders for "institutional ineptitude" and willful blindness.[90] Abuses by powerful partners often go unchecked because "[n]obody wants to kill a rainmaker."[91]

"Ethical dissonance" also skews the reasoning process. Borrowing from Leon Festinger's theory of cognitive dissonance, psychologists note that when a person's behavior is inconsistent with his or her values, an uncomfortable state of tension results.[92] Individuals generally care about being and appearing ethical.[93] When that desire clashes with incentives to engage in misconduct, people often attempt to reduce the "cognitive dissonance" by understating the harms of their behavior or deflecting responsibility for causing them. Lawyers' rationalizations for "creative" billing practices are again a case in point. Such practices include inflating hours, overstaffing cases, performing unnecessary work, padding expenses, and double-billing two clients for the same task or time.[94] Auditors find demonstrable fraud in 5 to 10 percent of lawyers' bills and questionable practices in another 25 to 35 percent. Yet lawyers often deny that these practices cause injury, on the theory that the work was "worth more" than the time it required, or that the client had refused to reimburse reasonable expenses.[95] Lawyers also resist responsibility on the ground that the fault lies with their firm's unreasonable billable hour quotas.[96]

QUESTIONS

1. Have you observed this kind of billing abuse or similar misconduct? If so, what do you think leaders could have done to curb it?
2. What do we mean by moral leadership? Does it imply morality in means, ends, or both? How do we judge the morality of ends? The preceding excerpt seems to assume that we want more values-driven leadership. Is that always true? Hitler believed that he was purifying German society. Terrorists who train suicide bombers are inspired by a moral vision. If such examples suggest that we want leaders who share *our* values, what follows from that fact? Consider Walter Lippman's definition of the public interest: "[W]hat men would choose if they saw clearly, thought rationally, and acted disinterestedly and benevolently."[97] Is that a helpful starting point, or a standard too vague to apply?
3. A leader's willingness to sanction unethical behavior by followers depends in part on his or her own accountability.[98] What can be done to increase that accountability? Can you identify some examples?
4. Consider the discussion in Chapter 7 of the role of social media and the 24-7 news cycle in increasing transparency and accountability. How can these forces be used to reinforce moral leadership?
5. Have you observed or experienced the pull of "the inner ring" that C. S. Lewis described? What enables individuals to resist such pressures? Consider the advice of innovation expert Clayton Christensen, who claims that one of the most important decisions of his life was to resist ever accepting the logic of "in this extenuating circumstance, just this once, it's okay." He explains:

My life has been one unending stream of extenuating circumstances. Had I crossed the line that one time, I would have done it over and over in the years that followed. The lesson I learned from this is that it's easier to hold to your principles 100 percent of the time than it is to hold to them 98 percent of the time. If you give in just this once, based on a marginal cost analysis . . . you'll regret where you end up.[99]

D. HOW THE GOOD GO BAD: ETHICAL MISCONDUCT AND INSTITUTIONAL RESPONSES

1. LEADERSHIP FAILURES IN THE FINANCIAL MARKETS

PROBLEM 5-2[100]

"Rogue traders" are experts in financial markets who make unauthorized purchases or sales of securities or commodities. The practice is long-standing; one of the most celebrated American scandals dates to the 1880s. But the issue has gained increasing attention, both because of the scale and persistence of misconduct despite efforts at internal control. In recent decades, rogue traders have sometimes made over a billion dollars in illicit trades before discovery.[101]

What drives the misconduct is readily apparent. In the financial world, money is the measure of success. As anthropologist Clifford Geertz notes, particularly in contexts "where the amounts of money are great, much more is at stake than material gain: namely esteem, honor, dignity, respect—in a word . . . status."[102] What prevents organizations from dealing adequately with the misconduct is less obvious, and provides a window into more general leadership issues: What can cause so many extremely smart people to make such disastrous decisions?

One of the most celebrated financial scandals involving lawyers arose from proceedings that the Securities and Exchange Commission (SEC) initiated against the CEO, top officers, and general counsel of Salomon Inc., one of Wall Street's leading investment companies. The action arose from the firm's failure to discipline and disclose securities law violations by Paul Mozer, the head of the Government Trading Desk of Salomon Brothers, the firm's main subsidiary. To settle the case, the firm ended up paying some $290 million in fines, one of the largest ever penalties for a financial institution. It also lost major clients and over $4 billion in trades during a brief suspension. Its stock price plummeted, and a year after the scandal, its share of the underwriting market had dropped from 8 to 2 percent. According to Deryck C. Maughan, the CEO who assumed the position after the SEC charges, the events constituted a "billion-dollar error of judgment."[103] How that error occurred provides an illuminating case history of failed leadership.

The culture at Salomon was highly competitive. Conventional wisdom was that although the CEO John Gutfreund may have sometimes "talked about values . . . his conduct often sent a contrary message. He ordered his staff to arrive each morning ready to 'bite the ass of a bear.'"[104] He was known for getting rid of individuals and divisions without warning if they failed to meet his bottom-line expectations.

Paul Mozer was a 34-year-old trader whose aggressive style fit the Salomon culture. He was very rich but from his vantage point, not rich enough. Although he had made over $4 million annually, he compared his compensation to an arbitrage trader whose bonuses yielded six times that amount.[105] His own income would turn on his ability to dominate the government securities market. That challenge was complicated by Treasury rules limiting traders at auctions of government securities to bids not exceeding 35 percent of the value of bonds being sold. Mozer slightly exceeded the limit by placing a false bid on behalf of S. G. Warburg, one of his customers, in addition to Salomon's own bid. The violation came to light when Warburg, without Mozer's knowledge, also placed its own bid at the auction. This caused Treasury staff to ask for an explanation. Mozer initially tried to dissemble his way out of it, but when that failed, he informed his supervisor, Salomon vice president John Meriwether. Although Mozer claimed that this had been his only transgression, other incidents during his decade at Salomon Brothers suggested cause for concern. He had been a highly aggressive trader, and had exploded in anger when Salomon Brothers' chief auditor requested a routine review.

Over Mozer's objections, Meriwether notified Salomon president Thomas Strauss, and they then discussed the matter with general counsel Donald Feurstein and CEO John Gutfreund. Without further investigation, the group accepted Mozer's characterization of the bid as an isolated incident. However, Feurstein believed that the conduct was "probably criminal" and the group agreed it should be reported to the New York Federal Reserve Bank.[106] A subsequent SEC report described the decision-making as follows:

> [E]ach of the four executives who attended meetings . . . placed the responsibility for investigating Mozer's conduct and placing limits on his activities on someone else. Meriwether stated that he believed that once he had taken the matter of Mozer's conduct to Strauss and Strauss had brought Feuerstein and Gutfruend into the process, he had no further responsibility to take action with respect to the false bid unless instructed to do so by one of those individuals. Meriwether stated that he also believed that, though he had the authority to recommend that action be taken to discipline Mozer or limit his activities, he had no authority to take such action unilaterally. Strauss stated that he believed that Meriwether, who was Mozer's direct supervisor, and Feuerstein, who was responsible for the legal and compliance activities of the firm, would take whatever steps were necessary or required as a result of Mozer's disclosure.

Feuerstein stated that he believed that, once a report to the government was made, the government would instruct Salomon about how to investigate the matter. Gutfreund stated that he believed that the other executives would take whatever steps were necessary to properly handle the matter. According to the executives, there was no discussion among them about any action that would be taken to investigate Mozer's conduct or to place limitations on his activities.

After that discussion, Meriwether admonished Mozer and told him that the firm would report his conduct to the government. Gutfreund and Strauss agreed to raise the issue with Gerald Corrigan, head of the Federal Reserve Bank in New York. However, their busy travel schedules made the meeting hard to arrange. Although Gutfreund expected to run into Corrigan at another event where he could arrange a discussion, that opportunity never arose and the issue fell through the cracks. Some speculated that Gutfreund was concerned that a public disclosure might have triggered fines, lawsuits, and adverse publicity, which could have jeopardized his already precarious leadership position.[107] According to one insider, Gutfreund "went to sleep hoping it would just go away."[108]

It did not. Three months later, Mozer again submitted an illegal bid, and effectively cornered the market at that auction. Traders who had been shut out complained to the SEC, which launched a confidential investigation. The public attention caused Salomon to launch its own internal investigation, which revealed that Mozer had exceeded the limit on three other occasions and that several other unauthorized bids had occurred since the Treasury imposed a 35 percent ceiling.[109] However, almost three months passed before Gutfreund notified the SEC and issued a press release acknowledging the misconduct. That release did not disclose management's prior awareness of the incident. A week later, Salomon Brothers issued another release acknowledging that the company had known about at least one illegal trade for about four months, but, due to a "lack of sufficient attention," its determination to report the matter "was not implemented promptly." An earlier draft of the release, which had incensed Salomon's board, had attributed the inaction to the "press of other business."[110]

This revelation set off a flood of efforts to unload Salomon stock, and trading was temporarily suspended. When Corrigan threatened "drastic action" by the Federal Reserve Bank unless the firm took immediate dramatic steps, Gutfreund, Strauss, and Meriwether resigned.[111] The board fired Mozer and three others implicated in the scandal. Gutfreund convinced Warren Buffet to take over as interim chair and CEO. Gutfreund had previously recruited Buffet to be a major investor, board member, and advisor. Ironically enough, part of what had originally attracted Buffet to the company had been Gutfreund's "principled" work for another client in which Buffet's company was heavily invested.[112] Although Gutfreund's mishandling of the false bid nearly torpedoed Salomon, his enlistment of Buffet may have saved it.

Buffet faced both external and internal challenges. His external efforts involved convincing the Treasury Department not to suspend the firm's privileges to bid at Treasury auctions, the Federal Reserve not to terminate the firm's status as a primary dealer, and the SEC not to bring criminal actions against the firm. The Treasury and Federal Reserve actions would likely have triggered Salomon's collapse, and might also have caused a major panic on Wall Street. Key factors in government officials' decisions included Buffet's own reputation and his willingness to cooperate fully with regulators. Over objection of counsel, he waived the attorney-client privilege concerning Salomon's internal reports of wrongdoing. He also assured the SEC that if anyone failed to provide information requested, the Commission staff could call him personally and they would "have a new person to deal with in twenty minutes."[113]

Buffet also took internal steps to change Salomon's culture and to restore public confidence. To that end, he issued a series of memos and letters underscoring the firm's commitment to integrity. In one he stated,

> I don't think we can do any better than go back to J. P. Morgan, 'First class business in a first class way.' . . . If you lose money for the firm by bad decisions, as I've done plenty of times for Berkshire, I will be very understanding. If you lose reputation for the firm, I will be ruthless. . . . We want people basically to get rich around here but we want them to get rich *through* the firm not *off* the firm.[114]

He designated himself "chief compliance officer," and informed all officers that they were "expected to report, instantaneously and directly to [him], any legal violation or moral failure on behalf of any employee of Salomon." He exempted parking tickets and listed his personal telephone number.[115] Under Buffet's leadership, the firm also instituted other compliance mechanisms designed to prevent concealment of illegal acts and to increase legal oversight. In addition, Salomon altered its compensation structure to reduce incentives for risky behavior and to give employees a greater stake in the firm's performance; for example, income was tied to departmental performance, and an increasing percentage of salary came in the form of restricted stock that could not be sold for five years.[116]

In an open letter to shareholders, published as an advertisement in the *New York Times, Wall Street Journal, Financial Times,* and *Washington Post,* Buffet emphasized the new compliance and compensation structures. He also quoted his directive to employees indicating that they should be guided

> by a test that goes beyond rules; contemplating any business act, an employee should ask himself whether he would be willing to see it immediately described by an informed and critical reporter on the front page of his local paper, there to be read by his spouse, children and friends. At Salomon, we simply want no part of any activities that pass legal tests but that we as citizens would find offensive. . . . Good profits simply are not inconsistent with good behavior.

Although acknowledging that some employees might leave as a result of the changes, Buffet maintained, "In the end we must have people to match our principles not the reverse."[117]

Buffett was right about departures. Salomon initially witnessed a mass exodus of talent. Many Wall Street insiders, including lawyers, condemned Buffet for "pandering to the regulators" and showing so little compassion to former officers, who were cut off without medical benefits and reimbursement of legal fees.[118] But his actions had the intended effect within the financial market. Major investors soon returned and earnings rebounded. Summing up the situation for a *Fortune* profile, Buffet concluded: "All's well that ends."[119]

For those responsible for the scandal, however, there was no such happy ending. Their experience reflected an insight that Gutfreund had once expressed but seemingly failed to internalize in the Mozer affair: The government bond market is a "world where mistakes are not charitably dealt with."[120] The SEC brought civil charges against Salomon officers under Section 15(b) of the 1934 Securities Exchange Act. That section authorizes the Commission to impose sanctions against a broker dealer who "failed reasonably to supervise, with a view to preventing violations [of federal securities laws], another person who commits such a violation, if such person is subject to his supervision." A settlement of those charges banned Gutfreund for life from serving as a chair or CEO of a securities firm and imposed a $100,000 fine. He also lost his Salomon stock options and retirement benefits. Strauss and Meriwether received lesser fines and suspensions from securities work. Paul Mozer pleaded guilty to criminal charges of lying to the Federal Reserve Bank through his false February auction bid. He served four months in prison and was banned from the securities industry for life.

General Counsel Donald Feurstein was not a direct supervisor of the trader and had made no false representations, so he escaped liability. However, the Commission also viewed the proceeding as an

> appropriate opportunity to amplify our views on the supervisory responsibilities of legal and compliance officers in Feuerstein's position. . . . Once a person in Feuerstein's position becomes involved in formulating management's response to the problem, he or she is obligated to take affirmative steps to insure that appropriate action is taken to address the misconduct. For example, such a person could direct or monitor an investigation of the conduct at issue, make appropriate recommendations for limiting the activities of the employee, or for the institution of appropriate procedures, reasonably designed to prevent and detect future misconduct, and verify that his or her recommendations, or acceptable alternatives, are implemented. If such a person takes appropriate steps but management fails to act and that person knows or has reason to know of that failure, he or she should consider what additional steps are appropriate to address the matter. These steps may include disclosure of the matter to the entity's board of directors, resignation from the firm, or disclosure to regulatory authorities.

In a footnote, the Commission added, "[o]f course, in the case of an attorney, the applicable [ethical rules] . . . may bear upon what course of conduct that individual may properly pursue."

QUESTIONS

1. Did the conduct of any of the major players in the Salomon saga seem to reflect the cognitive biases discussed in Chapter 3? Was Paul Mozer's recklessness attributable to overconfidence in his capacity to outsmart the regulators? Was his continuation of the unauthorized trading an example of escalation of commitment? When Salomon leaders accepted Mozer's characterization of his March trade as an "isolated incident," were they reducing cognitive dissonance?[121] What other factors might have been at work, and what correctives might have been useful?

   What accounts for the failure of Salomon Brothers officers to respond more forcefully to reports of Mozer's illegal bids? Does it reflect the pathology that Hannah Arendt described as "rule by Nobody"?[122]

2. Law professor Kimberly Krawiec argues that rogue trading persists because leaders and sometimes shareholders benefit from the extremely competitive, high-risk institutional cultures that produce it. In order to sustain short-term profits, management often supports internal compliance structures that are sufficient to satisfy regulators and investors, but insufficient to detect and deter unauthorized conduct.[123] How might Warren Buffett respond? How would you? If Krawiec is correct, what other strategies are necessary? How important are changes in compensation structures, government oversight, and the "tone at the top"?

3. Lawyers' conduct in circumstances such as that presented in the Salomon Brothers case is now governed by Rule 1.13 of the Model Rules of Professional Conduct and the Sarbanes-Oxley Act. Rule 1.13 provides that if a lawyer knows of illegal conduct likely to result in substantial injury to an organization, the lawyer must report the matter to a higher authority, and if necessary to its highest authority, typically the board of directors, unless the lawyer reasonably believes that it is not necessary in the best interest of the organization. If no adequate response is forthcoming, the lawyer may resign or reveal the information in order to prevent substantial injury to the organization. If the matter involves a material violation of the law by a client who issues securities, the lawyer also has internal reporting obligations under the Sarbanes-Oxley Act.[124] If Rule 1.13 had been in effect, and Feurstein had followed it, would the outcome for Salomon necessarily have been different? Note that Feurstein apparently did not believe that the firm was obligated to disclose the unlawful bid. Could he also reasonably have taken the view that Meriwether's admonishment of Mozer was a sufficient response to an "incidental mistake"? How would you have handled the situation? Should lawyers in leadership positions such as Feurstein's be enlisted as "gatekeepers" of regulatory policy?[125] If that would make management less willing to trust them with

potentially implicating information, would it be worth the price? How would you know? Who should decide?

4. Misconduct in the financial services industry has been a chronic problem. In one five-year period, the top 16 financial services institutions paid about $300 billion in penalties, settlements, and legal costs in cases involving fraud and other illegal actions.[126] One widely publicized example involved Wells Fargo. It agreed in September 2016 to pay a $185 million fine to federal regulators in a settlement acknowledging that thousands of the banks' employees, in response to aggressive sales goals, had opened up to two million sham accounts in customers' names without their knowledge.[127] News of the settlement caused a public outcry, and Wells Fargo CEO John Stumpf faced harsh questioning in a Congressional hearing. The bank fired more than 5000 employees who had participated in setting up unauthorized accounts. It also announced that it would get rid of its sales incentive program, and seek $19 million from the recently retired executive who ran the division where the fraud occurred, as well as $41 million in compensation from the CEO, who eventually resigned.[128]

According to investigators, Wells Fargo had known for several years that some employees were opening sham accounts to meet sales goals, and had repeatedly warned employees not to create fake bank accounts for customers without their knowledge. But the sales goals remained unchanged, and the behavior persisted. As one former banker explained, "They warned us about this type of behavior and said, 'You must report it,' but the reality was that people had to meet their goals. They needed a paycheck."[129]

If you were the general counsel of Wells Fargo, how would you advise the company going forward concerning the establishment and training around sales goals? Do you think eliminating the goals would be enough to eliminate the problem? Some commentators argued that the sales incentives were not the root of the problem, but rather "the symptom of a corrupt system that put profit and growth ahead of financial and customer responsibility"?[130] What other changes would you recommend?

5. Former U.S. Attorney for the Southern District of New York Preet Bharara recalls occasions when students have asked him about leaders' roles in ethical compliance. For example, one student asked:

> "Mr. Bharara, you've talked about making sure you don't cross the line and that it's dangerous to wander too close to the line. So, exactly how far from the line do you recommend people stay?" It is asked as if it were a geometry problem. I say, "Oh, about three and a half feet should do the trick."
>
> I am always a bit taken aback at these attempts to quantify ethics. I answer such questions by explaining that I disagree with the premise of the question; its orientation is unfortunate and off base: that if you are single-mindedly focused on walking the line, you are bound to end up afoul of regulators and, God forbid, criminal prosecutors. Even

more dangerous perhaps, you are sending a message to every other
person at the firm that line walking is a good idea. That can work for
a while, but not forever. A culture of minimalism is lethal.[131]

Does that describe part of what went wrong at Salomon Brothers, and in the
product safety scandals described below?

2. LEADERSHIP FAILURES INVOLVING PRODUCT SAFETY

PROBLEM 5-3[132]

In 2014, it came to light that millions of General Motors' automobiles had
faulty ignition switches, which made it easy for keys to slip out of the ignition.
Such slips would, in turn, disable power-assisted steering and brakes, as well as air
bags. This defect led to many collisions, over 185 serious injuries, and at least 124
deaths.

GM started manufacturing cars with defective ignition switches around 2001
and stopped using them in 2007. Yet at the time the company ceased production
of the defective switches, it did not conduct a recall to remove them from millions
of already-manufactured cars. It ultimately was forced to recall about thirty million
vehicles.

The delay cost the company dearly. The National Highway Traffic Safety
Administration imposed a $35 million fine, and the Justice Department imposed a
$900 million penalty. To avoid protracted litigation, GM set up a no-fault
compensation system expected to distribute $600 million to GM's victims. The
company was the target of numerous state and federal investigations and dozens
of lawsuits leading to billions of dollars in damages. The company fired fifteen
employees, including at least five lawyers, and its General Counsel resigned.[133]

GM CEO Mary Barra testified before Congress that she only learned about the
ignition switch issue on January 13, 2014 (two days before she was appointed
CEO), and that she made appropriate disclosures very soon after. She suggested
that if she, or GM's previous CEO, had learned of this defect sooner, appropriate
action would have been taken, and many lives would have been spared.[134]

In 2014, Barra hired law firm Jenner & Block to conduct an independent
investigation and released the report in redacted form.[135] Based on more than 350
interviews with 230 witnesses, the report blames the episode on ignorance,
dithering, and displacement of responsibility, rather than a deliberate cover-up.
According to the author, Anton Valukas:

The interviews here showed a troubling disavowal of responsibility made
possible by a proliferation of committees. It is an example of what
witnesses called the "GM salute," a crossing of arms and pointing outward
towards others, indicating that the responsibility belongs to someone else.

Here, because a committee was "responsible," no single person bore responsibility or was individually accountable.[136]

This phenomenon of "information silos" extended to GM's lawyers.[137] The Report concludes: "[F]aced with a pattern of crashes that had resulted in fatalities and an unexplained 'anomaly' that affected the deployment of airbags, [GM's lawyers] did not . . . elevate the issues to the General Counsel and do not appear to have insisted on a quick and concrete timetable for the safety investigation."[138] The General Counsel claimed that he never knew about the issue, but many commentators suggested that this was precisely the problem: he should have known.[139] Outside counsel in products liability litigation recommended settling cases quietly, which had the unintended effect of keeping the safety problem bottled up in a litigation committee that did not know the big picture.[140] At one meeting in 2012,

> A junior lawyer recalled asking whether there should be a recall. He was told that the issue had already been raised with engineering, that the engineers were working on it, and that they had not come up with a solution. This lawyer got the "vibe" that the lawyers had "done everything we can do."[141]

Commenting on such incidents, a *New York Times* op ed put the takeaway in its title: "How G.M.'s Lawyers Failed in Their Duties."[142]

1. Suppose you had been the junior in-house lawyer at that 2012 meeting. Assume that you knew at the time of the meeting that the defect in thousands of GM's cars had already caused many deaths. Assume as well that you were not certain whether GM's General Counsel or its CEO knew about the problem. What would you do? What risks would you face? What protections might, or should be, available to you?
2. If you were the new General Counsel at General Motors, how would you address the problems identified in the Valukas report?

NOTES AND QUESTIONS

General Motors is by no means unique among car manufacturers in its handling of ethical difficulties. Over the last 15 years, the industry has experienced a steady series of scandals, attributed partly to fierce competition coupled with stringent new safety and environmental regulations.[143] However, part of the problem has also been ethical tone-deafness at leadership levels. At a 2008 corruption trial that convicted one Volkswagen executive, the CEO referred to the widespread use of company funds to pay for prostitutes as mere "irregularities."[144] In 2015, falsified emissions test results emerged from a Volkswagen culture where top managers told engineers who couldn't come up with expedient results something like, "Please think again on that, and if you don't find a solution, we may need to find another engineer."[145] Volkswagen's installation of a "defeat device" designed to make engines appear to comply with regulatory standards is estimated to cost the company $18 billion in fines, legal claims, and recalls; its $14.7 billion settlement with U.S. owners is the largest auto scandal agreement in U.S. history.[146] At least one lawyer was implicated in advising document destruction.[147] So too, in 2016, Mitsubishi admitted cheating on fuel economy tests, despite a decade-long effort to recover from another scandal involving suppression of vehicle defects that almost bankrupted the company.[148] Since 2012, Hyundai, Kia, Ford, and BMW have all been found to have sold cars with inflated test ratings.[149]

Toyota's desire to become the leader in global automotive sales also led to an increasing focus on quantity over quality, and to leaders who became overconfident and insensitive to safety concerns.[150] When complaints about acceleration began surfacing in 2010, the company was slow to respond, and slower still in disclosing information to the National Highway Safety Administration and launching a recall.[151] The delays led to a record fine, congressional hearings, class action lawsuits, and plummeting sales figures.

1. What broader lessons do these scandals suggest? Some research on "moral credentialing" finds that Fortune 500 companies that tout their corporate social responsibility in areas such as product safety are more likely to behave irresponsibly and ignore safety warnings; leaders assume that their moral reputations lessen the risk of immoral conduct.[152] How can decision makers protect themselves from these tendencies? *Economist* commentator quotes the advice of Anne Mulcahy, former CEO of Xerox: "First, get the cow out of the ditch. Second, find out how the cow got into the ditch. Third, make sure you do whatever it takes so that cow doesn't go into the ditch again."[153] By virtually all accounts, car manufacturers have bungled all three efforts. If you were general counsel in one of those companies, what steps would you advise leaders to take?

2. To prevent tunnel vision at the top, commentators have proposed a range of strategies. These include ethical climate surveys, hotlines, ethics officers, and ombudspersons. Anonymous surveys can ask employees whether their workplace has a culture of integrity and whether they can raise concerns without fear of retaliation.[154] By preserving confidentiality, such interventions can encourage reporting by individuals wary of retribution.[155] Leaders can also solicit views from outside critics and experts.[156] In reflecting on Monsanto's disastrous handling of European concerns over genetically modified crops, then CEO Robert Shapiro observed: "Because we thought it was our job to persuade, too often we failed to listen."[157] To promote responsiveness, some companies have set up external advisory groups or monitoring structures. One model is the respected panel that British Petroleum established to make recommendations on safety and security issues in connection with a pipeline along the Caspian Sea.[158] Should

car manufacturers pursue such strategies? How would you assess their costs and benefits?

MEDIA RESOURCES

Corporate misconduct has generated a wide variety of media portraits. Particularly instructive documentaries include *Inside Job*, which chronicles the 2008 financial crisis; *The Smartest Guys in the Room*, which documents the rise and fall of Enron; and *The Inventor: Out for Blood in Silicon Valley*, which profiles Elizabeth Holmes' founding of Theranos, a fraudulent blood testing start up.[159] A case study of whistle-blowing traces Wendell Porter's experience with CIGNA.[160] GM's ignition switch failures have been the subject of a documentary and Congressional hearings.[161] Both Stephen Colbert and John Oliver have profiled the Wells Fargo scandal, and Colbert's coverage includes clips of Elizabeth Warren interviewing CEO John Stumpf.[162]

Among popular films, *The Informant, Michael Clayton, Duplicity, Margin Call, The Wolf of Wall Street*, and *The Firm* all have scenes that dramatize the personal ambitions and organizational pathologies that produce corporate misconduct. Many Congressional hearings on misconduct by automotive industries, banks, and financial services firms are available. For example, in Senate hearings, Mary Barra, General Motors CEO, defends her company's general counsel despite findings that the legal department failed to share details of crash settlements linked to the ignition problem.[163] Commentary by prominent business leaders also speak to these issues. Examples include Warren Buffet's congressional testimony concerning the Salomon scandal, as well as his appearance with Bill Gates at a Columbia Business School panel on leadership.[164]

The BBC series *Yes, Minister* also offers satirical treatment of the corrosive relationship between corporate interests and government officials. One episode, "The Moral Dimension," portrays a cabinet minister and his staff negotiating a trade deal in an Arab country. Several ethical issues arise: the Minister arranges to have liquor secretly available at an embassy function in violation of religious and cultural norms; one of his undersecretaries allows a gift from the country to be undervalued so the Minister's wife can keep it; and the Minister learns of bribes paid to secure the deal. When he self-righteously announces his intent to launch a full inquiry into the bribes, which would implicate his staff, his permanent undersecretary threatens to make a clean breast of the liquor on similar moral principles. Subsequent press inquiries into the gift force the Minister to lie about his intent to give it away, and the recognition of his own moral compromises ends any thoughts of launching a full inquiry. What makes the portrayal especially effective for leadership purposes is its exposure of how small indiscretions can create a climate that perpetuates serious corruption.

END NOTES

[1] David M. Mayer et al., *Encouraging Employees to Report Unethical Conduct Internally: It Takes a Village*, 121 ORGAN. BEHAV. & HUM. DECISION PROCESSES 89, 90 (2013).

[2] David. M. Mayer, Maribeth Kuenzi & Rebecca Lee Greenbaum, *Examining the Link Between Ethical Leadership and Employee Misconduct: The Mediating Role of Ethical Climate*, 95 J. BUS. ETHICS 7, 8 (2010).

[3] Isaiah Berlin, *A Special Supplement: The Question of Machiavelli*, N.Y. REV. OF BOOKS, Nov. 4, 1971 (quoting Frederick the Great), https://www.nybooks.com/articles/1971/11/04/a-special-supplement-the-question-of-machiavelli/.

[4] NICCOLÒ MACHIAVELLI, THE PRINCE 49 (Penguin Books, 1999) (1532).

[5] For the scope of his influence, see SILVIA R. FIORE, NICCOLO MACHIAVELLI: AN ANNOTATED BIBLIOGRAPHY OF MODERN CRITICISM AND SCHOLARSHIP (1990); JOSEPH V. FEMIA, MACHIAVELLI REVISITED (2004).

[6] QUENTIN SKINNER, MACHIAVELLI 3-4 (1981).

[7] CHRISTOPHER DUGGAN, A CONCISE HISTORY OF ITALY 46, 50-51, 57-59 (1994).

[8] Carol Bresnahan Menning, *Florence in the Renaissance*, in ENCYCLOPEDIA OF THE RENAISSANCE 377-79 (Paul F. Grendler ed., 1999).

[9] SKINNER, MACHIAVELLI, 3, 6, 19-20.

[10] NICCOLÒ MACHIAVELLI, THE PRINCE 3 (Harvey C. Mansfield trans., 2d ed. 1998) (1532).

[11] ANTHONY GRAFTON, INTRODUCTION, in MACHIAVELLI, THE PRINCE xxvii (1999).

[12] GRAFTON, INTRODUCTION, MACHIAVELLI, 65-66.

[13] GRAFTON, INTRODUCTION, MACHIAVELLI, 62.

[14] MICHAEL A. LEDEEN, MACHIAVELLI ON MODERN LEADERSHIP 117 (1999) (quoting Machiavelli).

[15] Berlin, *The Question of Machiavelli* (citing a letter to Guicciardini).

[16] For a review, see Berlin, *The Question of Machiavelli*.

[17] For overviews of the decision to use nuclear weapons, their devastating consequences for the populations affected, and their legitimacy in terms of theories of just wars, see RONALD TAKAKI, HIROSHIMA: WHY AMERICA DROPPED THE ATOMIC BOMB (1995); JOHN HERSEY, HIROSHIMA (1998); MICHAEL WALZER, JUST AND UNJUST WARS: A MORAL ARGUMENT WITH HISTORICAL ILLUSTRATIONS (1977).

[18] Amy J. Cuddy, Mathew Kohut & John Neffinger, *Connect, Then Lead*, in HARV. BUS. REV. LEADERSHIP PRESENCE 37-37 (2018).

[19] Cuddy, Kohut & Neffinger, CONNECT, THEN LEAD, at 39-40 (citing research by Zenger and Folkman).

[20] Berlin, *The Question of Machiavelli*.

[21] Rasmussen Report (Oct. 19, 2016), http://www.rasmussenreports.com/public_content/politics/elections/election_2016/voters_rate_a_candidate_s_policies_more_important_than_character. For discussion, see Theodore Bunker, *Poll: Voters Rate Candidate's Policies More Important than Character,* NEWSMAX (Oct. 19, 2016), https://www.newsmax.com/t/newsmax/article/754289.

[22] Stefan Hankin & Rasto Ivanic, *What Voters Most Want: Honesty or Intelligence?*, WASH. MONTHLY (Oct. 19, 2015), http://washingtonmonthly.com/2015/10/19/what-voters-most-want-honesty-or-intelligence/.

[23] Hankin & Ivanic, *What Voters Most.*

[24] Mark Blumenthal, *The Underpinnings of Donald Trump's Approval Rating,* HUFFINGTON. POST (Feb. 11, 2017), https://www.huffingtonpost.com/entry/the-underpinnings-of-donald-trumps-approval-rating_us_589e4206e4b080bf74f03c20.

[25] Martin P. Wattenberg, *The Declining Relevance of Candidate Personal Attributes in Presidential Elections,* 46 PRES. STUD. Q. 125, 137 (2016).

[26] JAMES DAVIDSON HUNTER, THE POLITICS OF CHARACTER 10 (2000).

[27] Pew Research Center, *Beyond Distrust: How Americans View Their Government* (Nov. 23, 2015), http://www.people-press.org/2015/11/23/beyond-distrust-how-americans-view-their-government/.

[28] Gallup, *Trust in Government* (Jan. 10, 2017), http://news.gallup.com/poll/5392/trust-government.aspx.

[29] Peter J. Boyer, *The Color of Politics: A Mayor of the Post-Racial Generation*, NEW YORKER, Feb. 4, 2008 (quoting Booker).

[30] JOHN ROHR, ETHICS FOR BUREAUCRATS: AN ESSAY ON LAW AND VALUES 8-9 (1978) (quoting Bernard Shaw); STEPHEN K. BAILEY, ETHICS IN POLITICS: ETHICS AND THE POLITICIAN 6 (1960).

[31] T. HARRY WILLIAMS, HUEY LONG 748 (1969) (quoting Long).

[32] WILLIAMS, HUEY LONG, 748 (quoting Long).

[33] Stuart Hampshire, *Public and Private Morality*, in PUBLIC AND PRIVATE MORALITY 50 (Stuart Hampshire et al. eds., 1978).

[34] RICHARD M. NIXON, LEADERS: PROFILES AND REMINISCENCES OF MEN WHO HAVE SHAPED THE MODERN WORLD 324 (1982).

[35] FAWN M. BRODIE, RICHARD NIXON: THE SHAPING OF HIS CHARACTER 430-31 (1981) (quoting Nixon).

[36] Bernard Williams, *Politics and Moral Character*, in PUBLIC AND PRIVATE MORALITY 69 (Hampshire et al. eds., 1978).

[37] Id., at 62.

[38] Glenn Thrush, *Obama Embraces the Super PAC,* POLITICO (Feb. 6, 2012), https://www.politico.com/story/2012/02/obama-prods-donors-for-super-pac-072531 (quoting Obama).

[39] Thrush, *Obama Embraces the Super PAC* (quoting Axelrod)

[40] David Grann, *The Fall: John McCain's Choices,* NEW YORKER, Nov. 8, 2008.

[41] Grann, *The Fall* (quoting Richard Cohen). See also Michael Dobbs, *Dancing With GOP Stars: McCain Romney Do Flip Flop*, WASH. POST, Feb. 5, 2008.

[42] Michael Ignatieff, *Gettting Iraq Wrong,* N.Y. TIMES MAG., Aug 5, 2007

[43] MICHAEL IGNATIEFF, FIRE AND ASHES: SUCCESS AND FAILURE IN POLITICS 148 (2013).

[44] IGNATIEFF, FIRE AND ASHES, 178, 182-183.

[45] HENRY ADAMS, DEMOCRACY: AN AMERICAN NOVEL 72-73 (1981).

[46] ADAMS, DEMOCRACY, 233-234.

[47] ADAMS, DEMOCRACY, 49, 94, 204.

[48] Abraham Lincoln, *Letter to Albert G. Hodges* (Apr. 4, 1864), in SELECTED SPEECHES AND WRITINGS: ABRAHAM LINCOLN 419, 419-20 (Don Fehrenbacher ed., 1992). *See* Dennis J. Hutchinson, *Lincoln the Dictator*, 55 S.D. L. REV. 284, 298, n.65 (2010). Richard Nixon quotes the passage in his book, RICHARD NIXON, LEADERS: PROFILES AND REMINISCES OF MEN WHO HAVE SHAPED THE MODERN WORLD 326 (1982).

[49] MICHAELA A. LEEDEN, MACHIAVELLI ON MODERN LEADERSHIP 139 (2000).

[50] The television series *24* includes many examples. A famous film depiction of political corruption is *All the Kings' Men*, based on Robert Penn Warren's fictionalized portrait of Huey Long's rise to power in Louisiana. For a discussion of *All the Kings' Men*, see Chapter 12. *Buddy* is a contemporary documentary about trade-offs for the mayor of Providence, Rhode Island.

[51] Netflix, Season 2, Episode 11 ("A Criminal, a Whore, an Idiot, and a Liar").

[52] Billions, Season 4, Episode 3, ("Chickentown").

[53] *Honesty/Ethics in Professions*, GALLUP (Nov. 28-Dec. 1, 2011), http://www.gallup.com/poll/1654/honesty-ethics-professions.aspx.

[54] Seven percent of Americans have high or very high confidence in Congressional representatives. *Honesty/Ethics in Professions*, GALLUP. For law firm leaders, confidence runs at 11 percent. *See* Chapter 1.

[55] LOUIS D. BRANDEIS, *The Opportunity in the Law*, in BUSINESS: A PROFESSION 313, 321 (1914).

[56] Harlan F. Stone, *The Public Influence of the Bar*, 48 HARV. L. REV. 1 (1934).

[57] ANTHONY T. KRONMAN, THE LOST LAWYER: FAILING IDEALS OF THE LEGAL PROFESSION (1993); SOL M. LINOWITZ WITH MARTIN MAYER, THE BETRAYED PROFESSION: LAWYERING AT THE END OF THE TWENTIETH CENTURY (1994), cited in Deborah L. Rhode, *The Professionalism Problem*, 39 WM. & MARY L. REV. 283, 284 (1998).

[58] David M. Mayer et al., *Encouraging Employees to Report Unethical Conduct Internally: It Takes a Village*, 121 ORGAN. BEHAV. & HUM. DECISION PROCESSES 89, 90 (2013).

[59] David M. Mayer, Maribeth Kuenzi & Rebecca L. Greenbaum, *Examining the Link Between Ethical Leadership and Employee Misconduct: The Mediating Role of Ethical Climate*, 95 J. BUS. ETHICS 7, 8 (2010).

[60] Mayer, Kuenzi & Greenbaum, *Examining the Link Between Ethical Leadership and Employee Misconduct*, 13; Linda Klebe Treviño, Gary R. Weaver & Scott J. Reynolds, *Behavioral Ethics in Organizations: A Review*, 32 J. MGMT. 951, 971 (2006); DEBORAH L. RHODE, CHEATING: ETHICS IN EVERYDAY LIFE (2018).

[61] Gary R. Weaver, Linda Klebe Treviño & Bradley Agle, *"Somebody I Look Up To": Ethical Role Models in Organizations*, 34 in ORGANIZATIONAL DYNAMICS 313, 318, 322 (2005).

[62] This note draws on RHODE, CHEATING: ETHICS IN EVERYDAY LIFE 5-18 2018.

[63] Ruodan Shao, Karl Aquino, and Dan Freeman, *Beyond Moral Reasoning: A Review of Moral Identity Research and its Implications for Business Ethics*, 18 BUS. ETHICS Q. 513, 516 (2008): Darcia Narvaez & Daniel K. Lapsley, *The Psychological Foundations of Everyday Morality and Moral Expertise*, in CHARACTER PSYCHOLOGY AND CHARACTER EDUCATION 140, 142 (Daniel K. Lapsley and F. Clark Power eds., 2005); DAVID EAGELMAN, INCOGNITO: THE SECRET LIVES OF THE BRAIN 4 (2011); Jonathan Haidt, *The*

Emotional Dog and its Rational Tail: A Social Intuitionist Approach to Moral Judgment, 108 PSYCHOL. REV. 814, 822-88 (2001*). See also* DANIEL K. LAPSLEY & DARCIA NARVAEZ, *A Social Cognitive Approach to the Moral Personality*, in MORAL DEVELOPMENT, SELF AND IDENTITY 189 (2004).

[64] Gary R. Weaver & Michael E. Brown, *Moral Foundations at Work: New Factors to Consider in Understanding the Nature and Role of Ethics in Organizations*, in BEHAVIORAL BUSINESS ETHICS: SHAPING AN EMERGING FIELD 144 (David De Cremer and Ann E. Tenbrunsel eds., 2011); Haidt, *The Emotional Dog*; Scott J. Reynolds, *A Neurocognitive Model of the Ethical Decision-Making Process: Implications for Study and Practice*, 91 J. APPLIED PSYCHOL. 736 (2006).

[65] DANIEL KAHNEMAN, THINKING, FAST AND SLOW (2011); Max H. Bazerman & Francesca Gino, *Behavioral Ethics: Toward a Deeper Understanding of Moral Judgment and Dishonesty*, 8 ANN. REV. L. & SOC. SCI. 85, 99 (2012); Daniel Kahneman and Shane Frederick, *Representativeness Revisited: Attribute Substitution in Intuitive Judgment*, in HEURISTICS AND BIASES: THE PSYCHOLOGY OF INTUITIVE JUDGMENT 49 (Thomas Gilovich, Dale Griffin, and Daniel Kahneman eds., 2002).

[66] MAX H. BAZERMAN & ANN E. TENBRUNSEL, BLIND SPOTS: WHY WE FAIL TO DO WHAT'S RIGHT AND WHAT TO DO ABOUT IT 93, 154 (2011); Don A. Moore & George F. Loewenstein, *Self-Interest, Automaticity, and the Psychology of Conflict of Interest*, 17 SOC. JUST. RES. 189 (2004).

[67] KAHNEMAN, THINKING, FAST AND SLOW; Bazerman & Gino, *Behavioral Ethics*, 99.

[68] DAVID DESTENO & PIERCARLO VALDESOLO, OUT OF CHARACTER: SURPRISING TRUTHS ABOUT THE LIAR, CHEAT, SINNER (AND SAINT) LURKING IN ALL OF US 33-35 (2011). *See also* BAZERMAN & TENBRUNSEL, BLIND SPOTS, 36. For examples, see Chen-Bo Zhong, *The Ethical Dangers of Deliberative Decision Making*, 56 ADMIN. SCI. Q. 1 (2011).

[69] Dolly Chugh, Max H. Bazerman & Mahzarin R. Banaji, *Bounded Ethicality as a Psychological Barrier to Recognizing Conflicts of Interest*, in CONFLICTS OF INTEREST: PROBLEMS AND SOLUTIONS FROM LAW, MEDICINE AND ORGANIZATIONAL SETTINGS 74 (Don A. Moore, Daylian M. Caine, George Lowenstein and Max Bazerman eds., 2005).

[70] Francesca Gino, Maurice E. Schweitzer, Nicole L. Mead & Dan Ariely, *Unable to Resist Temptation: How Self-Control Depletion Promotes Unethical Behavior*, 115 ORGAN. BEHAV. & HUM. DECISION PROCESSES 191, 199 (2011); Mark Muraven & Roy F. Baumeister, *Self-Regulation and Depletion of Limited Resources: Does Self-Control Resemble a Muscle?*, 126 PSYCHOL. BULL. (2000); Martin S. Hagger, Chantelle Wood, Chris Stiff & Nikos L. D. Chatzisarantis, *Ego Depletion and the Strength Model of Self-Control: A Meta-Analysis*, 136 PSYCHOL. BULL. 495 (2010); Nicole L. Mead et al., *Too Tired to Tell the Truth: Self-Control Resource Depletion and Dishonesty*, 45 J. EXP. SOC. PSYCHOL. 594 (2009); William D. Killgore et al., *The Effects of 53 Hours of Sleep Deprivation on Moral Judgement*, 30 SLEEP 345 (2007).

[71] BAZERMAN & TENBRUNSEL, BLIND SPOTS; Ann E. Tenbrunsel, *Misrepresentation and Expectations of Misrepresentation in an Ethical Dilemma: The Role of Incentives and Temptation*, 41 ACAD. MGMT. J. 330 (198).

[72] Ann E. Tenbrunsel & David M. Messick, *Ethical Fading: The Role of Self-Deception in Unethical Behavior*, 17 SOC. JUST. RES. 223 (2004). *See also* Ann E. Tenbrunsel, Kristina A. Diekmann, Kimberly A. Wade-Benzoni & Max H. Bazerman, *The*

Ethical Mirage: A Temporal Explanation as to Why We Aren't as Ethical as We Think We Are 159-62 (Harv. Bus. Rev., Working Paper 08-012, 2009).

[73] Scott J. Reynolds, *Moral Attentiveness: Who Pays Attention to the Moral Aspects of Life*, 93 J. APP. PSYCHOL. 1027-28 (2008).

[74] Tenbrunsel & Messick, *Ethical Fading*, 228.

[75] Blake E. Ashforth & Vikas Anand, *The Normalization of Corruption in Organizations*, 25 RES. ORGAN. BEHAV. 1, 14 (2003).

[76] David T. Welsh, Lisa D. Ordonez, Deirdre G. Snyder & Michael S. Christian, *The Slippery Slope: How Small Ethical Transgressions Pave the Way for Larger Future Transgressions*, 100 J. APP. PSYCHOL. 114 (2015): Celia Moore & Francesca Gino, *Ethically Adrift: How Others Pull Our Moral Compass from True North, and How We Can Fix It*, RES. ORGAN. BEHAV. 64 (2013).

[77] Patrick J. Schiltz, *On Being a Happy, Healthy, and Ethical Member of an Unhappy, Unhealthy, and Unethical Profession*, 52 VANDERBILT L. REV. 871, 917-18 (1999).

[78] For other examples, see Blake E. Ashforth & Vikas Anand, *The Normalization of Corruption in Organizations*, 25 RES. ORGAN. BEHAV. 1, 30 (2003).

[79] DONALD PALMER, NORMAL ORGANIZATIONAL WRONGDOING 122-123 (2012).

[80] Francesca Gino & Max Bazerman, *When Misconduct Goes Unnoticed; The Acceptability of Gradual Erosion in Others' Unethical Behavior*, 45 J. EXPERIMENTAL SOC. PSYCHOL. 708 (2009).

[81] Dolly Chugh, Mahzarin R. Banaji & Max H. Bazerman, *Bounded Ethicality as a Psychological Barrier to Recognizing Conflicts of Interest*, in CONFLICTS OF INTEREST: PROBLEMS AND SOLUTIONS FROM LAW, MEDICINE, AND ORGANIZATIONAL SETTINGS (Don A. Moore, Daylian M. Cain, George Loewenstein, and Max H. Bazerman eds., 2005).

[82] Kenneth D. Butterfield, Linda Klebe Treviño & Gary R. Weaver, *Moral Awareness in Business Organizations: Influences of Issue-Related and Social Context Factors*, 53 HUM. REL. 981-82 (2000); Thomas M. Jones, *Ethical Decision Making by Individuals in Organizations: An Issue-Contingent Model*, 16 ACAD. MGMT. REV. 366, 368, 379 (1991); LINDA KLEBE TREVIÑO & GARY R. WEAVER, MANAGING ETHICS IN BUSINESS ORGANIZATIONS: SOCIAL SCIENTIFIC PERSPECTIVES 171 (2003).

[83] LYNN SHARP PAINE, VALUE SHIFT: WHY COMPANIES MUST MERGE SOCIAL AND FINANCIAL IMPERATIVES TO ACHIEVE SUPERIOR PERFORMANCE 45-46 (2002); Kim S. Cameron, David Bright & Arran Caza, *Organizational Virtuousness and Performance*, 47 AM. BEHAV. SCIENTIST 766, 773 (2004); Brian Mullin, Carolyn Copper & James E. Driskell, *Jaywalking as Function of Model Behavior*, 16 PERS. & SOC. PSYCHOL. BULL. 320 (1990).

[84] Scott J. Reynolds & Tara L. Ceranic, *The Effects of Moral Judgment and Moral Identity on Moral Behavior: An Empirical Examination of the Moral Individual*, 92 J. APP. PSYCHOL. 1610, 1611 (2007); Kenneth D. Butterfield et. al., *Moral Awareness in Business Organizations: Influences of Issue-Related and Social Contextual Factors*, 53 HUM. REL. 981, 1001 (2000).

[85] William G. Ross, *The Ethics of Hourly Billing by Attorneys*, 44 RUTGERS L. REV. 1, 92 (1991).

[86] Claudia MacLachlan & Harvey Berkman, *Little Rock's Bar Shaken to its Core: Local Lawyers are Reeling as Washington Woes Come Home to Roost*, NAT'L L. J., Apr. 11, 1994, at 18.

[87] DONALD L. BARTLETT & JAMES B. STEELE, THE GREAT AMERICAN TAX DODGE: HOW SPIRALING FRAUD AND AVOIDANCE ARE KILLING FAIRNESS, DESTROYING THE INCOME TAX, AND COSTING YOU 219 (2002).

[88] Lisa G. Lerman, *Blue-Chip Bilking: Regulation of Billing and Expense Fraud by Lawyers*, 12 GEO. J. LEGAL ETHICS 276 (1999); Benjamin Wittes, *It Could Happen to You: Hubbell's Plea Spotlights Firm Billing Problems*, LEGAL TIMES, Dec. 12, 1994, at 7.

[89] Wittes, *It Could Happen to You*, 7.

[90] Lerman, *Blue Chip Bilking*, at 275; Wittes, *It Could Happen to You* (quoting the president of a fraud auditing company).

[91] Lerman, *Blue Chip Bilking*, at 281 (quoting Roy Simon). *See also* Lisa G. Lerman, *A Double Standard for Lawyer Dishonesty: Billing Fraud Versus Misappropriation*, 34 HOFSTRA L. REV., 847, 864-65, 872 (2006).

[92] The classic account of cognitive dissonance appears in LEON FESTINGER, A THEORY OF COGNITIVE DISSONANCE 128-34 (1957). For more recent accounts, see EDDIE HARMON-JONES & JUDSON MILLS, COGNITIVE DISSONANCE: PROGRESS ON A PIVOTAL THEORY IN SOCIAL PSYCHOLOGY (1999). For an application in contexts of ethical behavior such as cheating, see Shahar Ayal & Francesca Gino, *Honest Rationales for Dishonest Behavior*, in THE SOCIAL PSYCHOLOGY OF MORALITY: EXPLORING THE CAUSES OF GOOD AND EVIL 149-50 (Mario Mikulincer & Phillip R. Shaver eds., 2012); Elizabeth E. Umphress & John B. Bingham, *When Employees Do Bad Things for Good Reasons: Examining Unethical Pro-Organizational Behaviors*, 22 ORG. SCI. 621, 632 (2011).

[93] Lisa L. Shu, Francesca Gino & Max H. Bazerman, *Dishonest Deed, Clear Conscience: When Cheating Leads to Moral Disengagement and Motivated Forgetting*, 37 PERS. & SOC. PSYCHOL. BULL. 330 (2011); Karl Aquino & Americus Reed II, *The Self-Importance of Moral Identity*, 83 J. PERS. & SOC. PSYCHOL. 1443 (2002); Nina Mazar, On Amir & Dan Ariely, *The Dishonesty of Honest People: A Theory of Self-Concept Maintenance*, 45 J. MARKETING RES. 633-34 (2008).

[94] DEBORAH L. RHODE, DAVID LUBAN, SCOTT L. CUMMINGS & NORA FREEMAN ENGSTROM, LEGAL ETHICS 811 (7th ed. 2016).

[95] RHODE, LUBAN, CUMMINGS & ENGSTROM, LEGAL ETHICS, 812; Helen Coster, *The Inflation Temptation*, AM. LAW., Oct. 1, 2004, at 129.

[96] DEBORAH L. RHODE, IN THE INTERESTS OF JUSTICE: PERFORMING THE LEGAL PROFESSION 171-72 (2000). *See* Lerman, *Blue-Chip Bilking*, at 205; Lerman, *The Slippery Slope*, at 897.

[97] VIRGINIA HELD, THE PUBLIC INTEREST AND INDIVIDUAL INTERESTS 205 (1970) (quoting Lippman).

[98] Niek Hoogervorst, David De Cremer & Marius van Dijke, *Why Leaders Not Always Disapprove of Unethical Follower Behavior: It Depends on the Leader's Self-Interest and Accountability*, 95 J. BUS. ETHICS 29 (2010).

[99] Clayton Chrstensen, *How Will You Measure Your Life*, in Harv. Bus. Rev. ed., On Managing Yourself (Boston, MA: Harvard Business Review Press, 2010).

[100] This problem is based on facts set forth in *In re Gutfreund*, Sec. Exch. Release No. 34-31554 (Dec. 3, 1992); DEBORAH L. RHODE, PROFESSIONAL REGULATION: ETHICS BY THE PERVASIVE METHOD 579-82 (2d ed. 1998); DWIGHT B. CRANE & PATRICK MORETON, SALOMON AND THE TREASURY SECURITIES AUCTION TN (1992) (including 1992 update); Paine, *Salomon Brothers (B)*; Warren Buffet, *Statement of Salomon Inc.*, in testimony

before SECURITIES SUBCOMMITTEE ON BANKING, HOUSING AND URBAN AFFAIRS, U.S. SENATE, Sept. 10, 1991; MICHAEL USEEM, THE LEADERSHIP MOMENT: NINE TRUE STORIES OF TRIUMPH AND DISASTER AND THEIR LESSONS FOR US ALL 178-207 (1998); Loomis, *Warren Buffett's Wild Ride at Salomon*; Grant, *Taming the Bond Buccaneers at Salomon Brothers*.

[101] Kimberly D. Krawiec, *Accounting for Greed: Unraveling the "Rogue Trader" Mystery*, 79 OR. L. REV. 301 (2000).

[102] CLIFFORD GEERTZ, THE INTERPRETATION OF CULTURES 433 (1973), quoted in Krawiec, *Accounting for Greed*, at 310, n. 36.

[103] USEEM, THE LEADERSHIP MOMENT (quoting Maughan).

[104] Grant, *Taming the Bond Buccaneers*. For the Salomon culture generally, see MICHAEL LEWIS, LIAR'S POKER 63-67, 69-70, 73, 75-76, 81-83 (1989).

[105] USEEM, THE LEADERSHIP MOMENT, 186.

[106] Loomis, *Warren Buffet's Wild Ride*.

[107] Grant, *Taming the Bond Bucaneers*. According to insiders, some of the firm's top executives favored a change in leadership and Gutfreund had temporarily appeased them with inflated pay that might not be sustainable if a scandal broke.

[108] USEEM, LEADERSHIP MOMENT, 197.

[109] Paine, *Salomon Brothers (B)*, at 1.

[110] Loomis, *Warren Buffet's Wild Ride* (quoting release).

[111] Grant, *Taming the Bond Buccaneers* (quoting Corrigan).

[112] Loomis, *Warren Buffet's Wild Ride*.

[113] USEEM, THE LEADERSHIP MOMENT, 205-206 (quoting Buffett).

[114] USEEM, THE LEADERSHIP MOMENT, 192 (quoting Buffet Memo, Aug. 26, 1991).

[115] USEEM, THE LEADERSHIP MOMENT, 191.

[116] Paine, *Salomon Brothers (B)*, at 3.

[117] Paine, *Salomon Brothers (B)*, at 2 (quoting ad from Oct. 31, 2001).

[118] Grant, *Taming the Bond Buccaneers*.

[119] Loomis, *Warren Buffet's Wild Ride* (quoting Buffet). For the financial turnaround, see Paine, *Salomon Brothers (B)*.

[120] Sarah Bartlett, *A Career Skids to a Halt for "King of Wall Street"*, N.Y. TIMES, Aug. 17, 1991, at 33 (quoting Buffet).

[121] For discussion of these problems of cognitive bias in the context of rogue trading, see Krawiec, *Accounting for Greed*, 316-318.

[122] HANNAH ARENDT, ON VIOLENCE 38-39 (1970).

[123] Krawiec, *Accounting for Greed*; Kimberly D. Krawiec, *Organizational Misconduct: Beyond the Principal-Agent Model*, 32 FLA. ST. L. REV. 571, 602-610 (2005); Kimberly D. Krawiec, *Cosmetic Compliance and the Failure of Negotiated Governance*, 81 WASH. U. L. REV. 487, 492-493 (2003).

[124] *See* 17 C.F.R. Part 205 (2003). For discussion of lawyers' obligations under Sarbanes-Oxley, see RHODE, LUBAN, CUMMINGS, AND ENGSTROM, LEGAL ETHICS, 651-58.

[125] Reinier H. Kraakman, *Gatekeepers: The Anatomy of a Third-Party Enforcement Strategy*, 1. J. L. ECON. & ORG. 53 (1986).

[126] BEN W. HEINEMAN JR., THE INSIDE COUNSEL REVOLUTION: RESOLVING THE PARTNER-GUARDIAN TENSION 137 (2016)

[127] James B. Stewart, *For John Stumpf, the Buck Stopped Where It Should Have*, N.Y. TIMES) Oct. 12, 2016), http://www.nytimes.com/2016/10/13/business/for-john-stumpf-the-buck-stopped-where-it-should-have.html?_r=0.

[128] Stewart, *For John Stumpf, the Buck Stopped Where It Should Have*; Michael Corkery & Stacy Cowley, *Wells Fargo Chief Abruptly Steps Down*, N.Y. TIMES (Oct. 12, 2016), http://www.nytimes.com/2016/10/13/business/dealbook/wells-fargo-ceo.html.

[129] Michael Corkery & Stacy Cowley, *Wells Fargo Warned Workers Against Sham Account, but "They Needed a Paycheck"*, N.Y. TIMES (Sept. 16, 2016), http://www.nytimes.com/2016/09/17/business/dealbook/wells-fargo-warned-workers-against-fake-accounts-but-they-needed-a-paycheck.html.

[130] Jim Keenan, *Listen to Your Sales Team: What Business Leaders Could Learn from the Wells Fargo Debacle*, FORBES (Sept. 30, 2016), http://www.forbes.com/sites/jimkeenan/2016/09/30/under-fire-wells-fargo-goes-too-far/. *See also* Andris A. Zoltners, PK Sinha & Sally E. Lorimer, *Wells Fargo and the Slippery Slope of Sales Incentives*, HARV. BUS. REV. (Sept. 20, 2016).

[131] PREET BHARARA, DOING JUSTICE: A PROSECUTOR'S THOUGHTS ON CRIME, PUNISHMENT AND THE RULE OF LAW 195 (2019).

[132] This problem draws on RHODE, LUBAN, CUMMINGS & ENGSTROM, LEGAL ETHICS, AT 689-91.

[133] Aaron M. Kellser, *G.M. Names New Counsel After Wave of Recalls*, N.Y. TIMES, Feb. 19, 2015.

[134] For more on the GM ignition switch scandal, see NORA FREEMAN ENGSTROM, PLAINTIFFS' LAWYER: INSTITUTIONAL CONSTRAINTS AND ETHICAL CHALLENGES 478-515 (unpublished manuscript 2015); Matthew Goldstein & Barry Meier, *As Scandal Unfolds, G.M. Calls In the Lawyers*, N.Y. TIMES, Mar. 16, 2014, at BU1; Rebecca R. Ruiz, *Woman Cleared in Death Tied to GM's Faulty Ignition Switch*, N.Y. TIMES, Nov. 24, 2014, at A1.

[135] ANTON R. VALUKAS, REPORT TO THE BOARD OF DIRECTORS OF GENERAL MOTORS COMPANY REGARDING IGNITION SWITCH RECALLS (May 29, 2014), http://www.nytimes.com/interactive/2014/06/05/business/06gm-report-doc.html?_r=0.

[136] VALUKIS, REPORT, 68-69.

[137] VALUKIS, REPORT, 213.

[138] VALUKIS, REPORT, 154.

[139] HEINEMAN, THE INSIDE COUNSEL REVOLUTION, 97.

[140] VALUKIS, REPORT, 203-05, 213.

[141] VALUKIS, REPORT, 108.

[142] Peter J. Henning, *How G.M.'s Lawyers Failed in Their Duties*, N.Y. TIMES, June 9, 2014.

[143] For examples dating back to the late 1990s, see Benjamin Hulac, *U.S. Sues Volkswagen for Alleged Pollution Cheating*, SCIENTIFIC AM., Jan. 5, 2016; Jonathan Soble, *Behind Mitsubishi's Faked Data, Fierce Competition*, N.Y. TIMES, Apr. 21, 2016; Leah McGrath Goodman, *Why Volkswagen Cheated*, NEWSWEEK, Dec. 15, 2015 (describing difficulties company faced in finding technical solutions within the its "time frame and budget" to meet U.S. emission standards); *Mitsubishi Motors Admits Falsifying Fuel Economy Tests*, BBC (Apr. 20, 2016), https://www.bbc.com/news/business-36089558 (describing automotive scandals).

[144] Jerry Useem, *What Was Volkswagen Thinking?*, ATLANTIC, Jan./Feb., 2016.

[145] Goodman, *Why Volkswagen Cheated* (quoting Ferdinand Dudenhoffer).

[146] Peter J. Henning, *Volkswagen's Legal Endgame in Emissions Scandal*, N.Y. TIMES, Apr. 25, 2016; James F. Peltz & Samantha Masunaga, *The Biggest Auto-Scandal Settlement in U.S. History Was Just Approved. VW Buybacks Start Soon*, L.A. TIMES, Oct. 25, 2106. For an overview see JACK EWING, FASTER, HIGHER, FARTHER: THE VOLKSWAGEN SCANDAL (2017).

[147] Sue Reisinger, *Behaving Badly: VW's Lawyers*, NAT'L L.J. Jan. 16, 2016, 1

[148] Jonathan Soble, *Mitsubishi Admits Cheating on Fuel-Economy Tests*, N.Y. TIMES, Apr. 20, 2016; Soble, *Behind Mitsubishi's Faked Data.*

[149] Soble, *Mitsubishi Admits Cheating.*

[150] Bill Saporito & Joseph R. Szczesny, *Behind the Troubles at Toyota*, TIME.COM (Feb. 11, 2010), http://www.time.com/time/business/article/0,8599,1963595,00.html; Bill Saporito, *Toyota's Flawed Focus on Quantity over Quality*, TIME.COM (Feb. 4, 2010), http://www.time.com/time/business/article/0,8599,1958991,00.html; Alan Ohnsman, Jeff Green & Kae Inoue, *The Humbling of Toyota*, BLOOMBERG BUSINESSWEEK (Mar. 11, 2010), http://www.businessweek.com/magazine/content/10_12/b4171032583967.html; Saporito, *Behind the Troubles at Toyota*; Jeff Kingston, *A Crisis Made in Japan*, WALL ST. J. (Feb. 6-7, 2010), https://www.wsj.com/articles/SB10001424052748704533204575047370633234414 at W1, The quality control problems predated the 2010 scandal. *See A Wobble on the Road to the Top*, THE ECONOMIST (Nov. 8, 2007), https://www.economist.com/briefing/2007/11/08/a-wobble-on-the-road-to-the-top.

[151] James Kanter, Micheline Maynard & Hiroko Tabuchi, *Toyota Has Pattern of Slow Response on Safety Issues*, N.Y. TIMES, Feb. 7, 2010, at A1; Kate Linebaugh, Dionne Searcey & Norihiko Shirouzu, *Secretive Culture Led Toyota Astray*, WALL ST. J., Feb. 10, 2010, at A1.

[152] Margaret E. Ormiston & Elaine M. Wong, *License to Ill: The Effects of Corporate Social Responsibility and CEO Moral Identity on Corporate Social Irresponsibility*, 66 PERSONNEL PSYCH. 861 (2013).

[153] Schumpeter: *Getting the Cow out of the Ditch*, ECONOMIST (Feb. 11, 2010), http://www.economist.com/node/15496136 (quoting Mulcahy).

[154] HEINEMAN JR., THE INSIDE COUNSEL REVOLUTION, 119.

[155] Ashforth & Anand, *The Normalization of Corruption in Organizations*, 39; Vikas Anand, Blake E. Ashforth & Mahendra Joshi, *Business as Usual: The Acceptance and Perpetuation of Corruption in Organizations*, 18 ACAD. MGMT. EXEC. 49 (2004).

[156] Linda Klebe Treviño, *Out of Touch: The CEO's Role in Corporate Misbehavior*, 70 BROOKLYN L. REV. 1195, 1209 (2005); PETER FIRESTEIN, CRISIS OF CHARACTER: BUILDING CORPORATE REPUTATION IN THE AGE OF SKEPTICISM 24-29 (2009).

[157] FIRESTEIN, CRISIS OF CHARACTER.

[158] FIRESTEIN, CRISIS OF CHARACTER, 194.

[159] An Enron documentary is available at https://www.youtube.com/watch?v=BIwFO4_SWQQ. For a review of *Inside Job* see A. O. Scott, *Movie Review: Inside Job: Who Maimed the Economy, and How*, N.Y. TIMES, Oct. 8, 2010, at C1.

[160] *Health Insurance Exec. Turns Whistleblower*, ABC NEWS (Aug. 16, 2009), http://www.youtube.com/watch?v=ST5rimNAZN0.

[161] The documentary is available at https://www.youtube.com/watch?v=Pwt1Dc2XD6Q. Mary Bara's congressional testimony is available at https://www.youtube.com/watch?v=wjiHEYuOXSk.

[162] For Colbert, see *Elizabeth Warren Rips Wells Fargo's CEO A New One,* https://www.youtube.com/watch?v=SQ4EDwcfjt8.

[163] https://www.youtube.com/watch?v=eTK8N-uHKNk.

[164] For Buffett, see *Buffett on Salomon Brothers*, C-SPAN (Feb. 19, 2009), http://www.youtube.com/watch?v=O0R_9L_D2Yk. For Buffet and Gates, see Bill Gates & *Warren Buffett on Leadership*, CNBC (Nov. 14, 2009), https://www.youtube.com/watch?v=tgbZzgyHZgI.

CHAPTER 6

AUTHORITY AND ACCOUNTABILITY

How individuals exercise and respond to authority is central to leadership relationships. Those holding upper-level positions are on the giving and receiving end of various forms of hard and soft power. This chapter explores the structure of authority, the dynamics of obedience, and the strategies for resistance. It provides case histories and psychological accounts of leaders who both gave and followed orders in ways that compromised legal or ethical standards. Attention centers on the situational pressures, cultural norms, personal ambitions, and regulatory frameworks that permit abuse, and on appropriate policy responses.

A. FOLLOWING ORDERS

After World War II, increased attention focused on how obedience to authority led to the erosion of moral judgment. One of the most probing accounts was philosopher Hannah Arendt's review of the trial of Adolf Eichmann, a high-level Nazi official charged with crimes against humanity for facilitating the genocide of millions of European Jews. Her profile of his life and his rationalizations provides a chilling description of what she termed "the banality of evil."

HANNAH ARENDT, EICHMANN IN JERUSALEM: A REPORT ON THE BANALITY OF EVIL

(New York: Penguin Books, 1994), 22, 25-26, 135, and 276-279

[To Eichmann], the indictment for murder was wrong: "With the killing of Jews I had nothing to do. I never killed a Jew, or a non-Jew, for that matter—I never killed any human being. I never gave an order to kill either a Jew or a non-Jew; I just did not do it," or, as he was later to qualify this statement, "It so happened . . . that I had not once to do it"—for he left no doubt that he would have killed his own father if he had received an order to that effect. . . .

Throughout the trial, Eichmann tried to clarify, mostly without success, this second point in his plea of "not guilty in the sense of the indictment." The indictment implied not only that he had acted on purpose, which he did not deny, but out of base motives and in full knowledge of the criminal nature of his deeds . . . [But from his perspective, his was not a] case of insane hatred of Jews, of fanatical anti-Semitism or indoctrination of any kind. He "personally" never had anything whatever against Jews; on the contrary, he had plenty of "private reasons" for not being a Jew hater. . . .

So Eichmann's opportunities for feeling like Pontius Pilate were many, and as the months and the years went by, he lost the need to feel anything at all. This was the way things were, this was the new law of the land, based on the Führer's order; whatever he did he did, as far as he could see, as a law-abiding citizen. He did his *duty,* as he told the police and the court over and over again; he not only obeyed *orders,* he also obeyed the *law.* . . .

The trouble with Eichmann was precisely that so many were like him, and that the many were neither perverted nor sadistic, that they were, and still are, terribly and terrifyingly normal. From the viewpoint of our legal institutions and of our moral standards of judgment, this normality was much more terrifying than all the atrocities put together, for it implied—as had been said at Nuremberg over and over again by the defendants and their counsels—that this new type of criminal . . . commits his crimes under circumstances that make it well-nigh impossible for him to know or to feel that he is doing wrong. . . .

Because he had been implicated and had played a central role in an enterprise whose open purpose was to eliminate forever certain "races" from the surface of the earth, he had to be eliminated. And if it is true that "justice must not only be done but must be seen to be done," then the justice of what was done in Jerusalem would have emerged to be seen by all if the judges had dared to address their defendant in something like the following terms:

> "You admitted that the crime committed against the Jewish people during the war was the greatest crime in recorded history, and you admitted your role in it. But you said you had never acted from base motives, that you had never had any inclination to kill anybody, that you had never hated Jews, and still that you could not have acted otherwise and that you did not feel guilty. We find this difficult, though not altogether impossible, to believe....
>
> You also said that your role in the Final Solution was an accident and that almost anybody could have taken your place, so that potentially almost all Germans are equally guilty. What you meant to say was that where all, or almost all, are guilty, nobody is. This is an indeed quite common conclusion, but one we are not willing to grant you...
>
> In other words, guilt and innocence before the law are of an objective nature, and even if eighty million Germans had done as you did, this would not have been an excuse for you.

Luckily, we don't have to go that far. You yourself claimed not the actuality but only the potentiality of equal guilt on the part of all who lived in a state whose main political purpose had become the commission of unheard-of crimes. And no matter through what accidents of exterior or interior circumstances you were pushed onto the road of becoming a criminal, there is an abyss between the actuality of what you did and the potentiality of what others might have done. We are concerned here only with what you did, and not with the possible noncriminal nature of your inner life and of your motives or with the criminal potentialities of those around you. You told your story in terms of a hard-luck story, and, knowing the circumstances, we are, up to a point, willing to grant you that under more favorable circumstances it is highly unlikely that you would ever have come before us or before any other criminal court. Let us assume, for the sake of argument, that it was nothing more than misfortune that made you a willing instrument in the organization of mass murder; there still remains the fact that you have carried out, and therefore actively supported, a policy of mass murder. For politics is not like the nursery; in politics obedience and support are the same. And just as you supported and carried out a policy of not wanting to share the earth with the Jewish people and the people of a number of other nations—as though you and your superiors had any right to determine who should and who should not inhabit the world—we find that no one, that is, no member of the human race, can be expected to want to share the earth with you. This is the reason, and the only reason, you must hang."

QUESTION

If you had been Eichmann or his lawyer, how would you have responded to the judicial statement that Arendt proposes? One question that her account raises is why leaders in Eichmann's position felt that they had no choice but to "follow orders." Stanford psychologist Philip Zimbardo, author of the excerpt below, is one of the world's leading experts on the potentially corrosive influences of authority and the responses they require.

PHILIP G. ZIMBARDO, THE PSYCHOLOGY OF POWER: TO THE PERSON? TO THE SITUATION? TO THE SYSTEM?

Deborah L. Rhode, ed., Moral Leadership: The Theory and Practice of Power, Judgment, and Policy (San Francisco: Jossey-Bass, 2006), pp. 129-157

. . . The same human mind that creates the most beautiful works of art and extraordinary marvels of technology is equally responsible for the perversion of its own perfection. This most dynamic organ in the universe has been a seemingly endless source for creating ever more vile torture chambers and instruments of horror: the concentration camps of the Third Reich, the "bestial machinery" of Japanese soldiers in their rape of Nanking, and the recent demonstration of "creative evil" of 9/11 by turning commercial airlines into weapons of mass destruction. How can the unimaginable become so readily imagined?

My concern centers around how normal individuals can be recruited, induced, and seduced into behaving in ways that could be classified as evil and the role of leaders in that process. In contrast to the traditional approach of trying to identify "evil people" to account for the evil in our midst, I will focus on the central conditions that underpin the transformation of good, or average, people into perpetrators of evil.

Locating Evil within Particular People: The Rush to Judgment

"Who is responsible for evil in the world, given that there is an all-powerful, omniscient God who is also all-Good?" That conundrum began the intellectual scaffolding of the Inquisition in the sixteenth and seventeenth centuries in Europe. As revealed in *Malleus Maleficarum,* the handbook of the German Inquisitors from the Roman Catholic church, the inquiry concluded that the devil was the source of all evil. However, these theologians argued that the devil works his evil through intermediaries, lesser demons, and, of course, human witches. Therefore, the hunt for evil focused on those marginalized people who looked or acted differently from ordinary people, who might, under rigorous examination or torture, be exposed as witches and then put to death. . . .

Paradoxically, this early effort of the Inquisition to understand the origins of evil and develop responses to evil instead created new forms of evil. It exemplifies the risk of simplifying complex problems by blaming individual perpetrators.

The same risk emerged following World War II, when a team of psychologists sought to make sense of the Holocaust and the broad appeal of national fascism and Hitler. Their focus was on the authoritarian personality: a set of traits underlying the fascist mentality. However, what they overlooked was the host of processes operating at political, economic, societal, and historical levels of analysis that influenced so many millions of individuals to revere their dictator and hate Jews.

This tendency to explain observed behavior by reference to dispositions, while ignoring or minimizing the impact of situational variables, is what Stanford psychologist Lee Ross has called the fundamental attribution error. We are all subject to this dual bias of overemphasizing dispositional analyses and underemphasizing situational explanations. We succumb to this effect because so much of our education, training, and law enforcement are geared toward a focus on individual orientations. . . . Thus, it is individuals who receive praise, fame, and wealth for achievement and are honored for their uniqueness, but it is also individuals who are blamed for the ills of society. Our legal, medical, educational, and religious systems are all founded on principles of individualism.

Dispositional analyses always include strategies for behavior modification to assist deviant individuals, by education or therapy, or to exclude them from society by imprisonment, exile, or execution. Locating evil within selected individuals or groups has the virtue of rendering society blameless. The focus on people as causes for evil then exonerates social structures and political decision-making for contributing to underlying conditions that foster evil: poverty, racism, sexism, and elitism.

Most of us take comfort in the illusion that there is an impermeable boundary separating the evil (them) from the good (us). That view leaves us with less interest in understanding the motivations and circumstances that contributed to evil behavior. But in fact, as is clear from the Russian novelist Alexander Solzhenitsyn, a victim of persecution by the Soviet KGB, that the line between good and evil lies in the center of every human heart.

It has been my mission as a psychologist to understand better how virtually anyone could be recruited to engage in evil deeds that deprive other human beings of their lives, dignity, and humanity. . . .

Blind Obedience to Authority: The Milgram Investigations

Stanley Milgram developed an ingenious research procedure to demonstrate the extent to which situational forces could overwhelm individual will to resist. He shocked the world with his unexpected finding of extremely high rates of compliance to the demands of an authority figure to deliver apparently dangerous electric shocks to an innocent victim. He found that about 67 percent of research participants went all the way up to the top shock level of 450 volts in attempting to "help" another person learn appropriate behaviors. Milgram's study revealed that ordinary American citizens could so easily be led to engage in "electrocuting a nice stranger" as the Nazis had been led to murder Jews.

After this initial demonstration with Yale College students, Milgram went on to conduct eighteen experimental variations on more than a thousand subjects from a variety of backgrounds, ages, and educational levels. In each of these studies, he varied one social psychological variable and observed its impact on the extent of obedience by a subject to shock the "learner-victim," who pretended to be suffering. The data told the story of the extreme pliability of human nature. Almost everyone could be totally obedient, or almost everyone could resist authority pressures; it depended on situational differences. Milgram was able to demonstrate that compliance rates could soar to 90 percent of people who delivered the maximum 450 volts to the learner-victim, or could be reduced to less than 10 percent of total obedience by introducing one variable into the compliance recipe[—another participant who resisted].

Want maximum obedience? Provide social models of compliance by having participants observe peers behaving obediently. Want people to resist authority pressures? Provide social models of peers who rebelled. Interestingly, almost no one shocked the learner-victim when he actually asked to be shocked. They refused authority pressure when the target seemed to be a masochist. In each of the other variations on this diverse range of ordinary Connecticut citizens, low, medium, or high levels of compliant obedience could be readily elicited as if one were simply turning a human nature dial.

What is the expected rate of such obedience in the Milgram setting according to experts on human nature? When forty psychiatrists were given the basic description of this experiment, their average estimate of the number of United States citizens who would give the full 450 volts was only 1 percent. Only sadists would engage in such behavior, they believed. These experts on human behavior were totally wrong because they ignored situational determinants. Their training in psychiatry had led them to overly rely on dispositional explanations. This is a strong instance of the operation of the fundamental attribution error in action.

Ten Steps to Creating Evil Traps for Good People

What were the procedures in this research paradigm that seduces many ordinary citizens to engage in such apparently abusive behavior? These procedures parallel compliance strategies used in many real-world settings by "influence professionals" such as salespeople, cult recruiters, and national leaders.

These are the influences that will lead ordinary people to do things they originally believe they would not:

- Offering an ideology that justifies any means to achieve a seemingly desirable goal. In clinical experiments like Milgram's, the rationale is helping people improve their memories. For nations, it is often a "threat to national security" that justifies going to war or suppressing dissident political opposition. . . . As research by Susan Fiske and her colleagues indicates, that reasoning contributes to ordinary people's willingness to torture enemy prisoners in contexts like Abu Ghraib prison.
- Arranging some form of contractual obligation, verbal or written.
- Giving participants meaningful roles to play (teacher, student) that carry with them previously learned positive values and response scripts.
- Presenting basic rules to be followed that seem to make sense prior to their actual use, but then can be arbitrarily used to justify mindless compliance. Make the rules vague, and change them as necessary.
- Altering the semantics of the act, the actor, and the action (from hurting victims to helping learners); replace reality with desirable rhetoric.
- Creating opportunities for diffusion of responsibility or suggesting that others will be responsible or that the actor will not be held liable.
- Starting the path toward the ultimate evil act with a small, insignificant first step (only 15 volts in the Milgram experiment).
- Gradually increasing steps on the pathway to abuse, so that they appear no different from prior actions. Increases of only 30 volts presented no noticeable difference in harm to the Milgram participants.
- Changing the nature of the influence authority from initially "just" and reasonable to "unjust" and demanding, which elicits confusion but continued obedience.
- Making the exit costs high by allowing the usual forms of verbal dissent (that make people feel good about themselves), while insisting on behavioral

compliance ("I know you are not that kind of person; just keep doing as I tell you").

Such procedures can prepare people psychologically to do the unthinkable.

On Being Anonymous: Deindividuation and Destructiveness

. . . [One of my most important experiments] involved having young women deliver a series of painful electric shocks to each of two other young women whom they could see and hear in a one-way mirror before them. Half the subjects were randomly assigned to a condition of anonymity, or deindividuation, and half to one of uniqueness, or individuation. The four college student subjects in each deindividuation cluster were treated as members of a group, not as individuals; their appearances were concealed by hoods, and their names were replaced by numbers. The comparison group consisted of individuals who wore name tags and were made to feel unique. . . . The results were clear: women in the deindividuation condition delivered twice as much shock to both victims as did the women in the individuated comparison condition. Moreover, they shocked both victims, the one previously rated as pleasant and the other unpleasant victim, more over the course of the twenty trials, while the individuated subjects shocked the pleasant woman less over time than they did the unpleasant one. One important conclusion flows from this research and its various replications and extensions, some using military personnel from the Belgian army: anything that makes people feel anonymous reduces a sense of accountability and increases their propensity to evil under situations inviting violence. . . .

Moral Disengagement and Dehumanization

Psychologist Al Bandura has developed a model of moral disengagement that specifies the conditions under which anyone can be led to act immorally, even those who usually ascribe to high levels of morality. The model outlines a set of cognitive mechanisms that alter a person's (1) perception of the reprehensible conduct (engaging in moral justifications, making palliative comparisons, using euphemistic labeling); (2) sense of the detrimental effects of that conduct (minimizing, ignoring, or misconstruing the consequences); (3) sense of responsibility for the link between reprehensible conduct and its detrimental effects (displacing or diffusing responsibility); and (4) view of victims (dehumanizing or blaming them).

Bandura and his colleagues designed a powerful experiment that is an elegantly simple demonstration of the power of dehumanizing labels. It reveals how easy it is to induce normal, intelligent individuals to accept a dehumanizing label of other people and then to act aggressively based on that classification. A group of four participants were led to believe they were overhearing a research assistant tell the experimenter that the students from another college were present to start the study in which they were to deliver electric shocks of varying intensity (allegedly as part of a group problem-solving study). In one of the three randomly assigned conditions, the subjects overheard the assistant say to the experimenter that the other students seemed "nice." In second condition, they heard that the other students seemed like "animals." In a third variation, the assistant did not label the students.

This situational manipulation clearly affected behavior. Experimental subjects gave the most shock to those labeled "animals," and their shock level increased over the ten trials. Those labeled "nice" were given the least shock, and the unlabeled group fell between these extremes. Thus, a single word, *animals*, was sufficient to induce intelligent college students to treat others as if they deserved to be harmed.

What is also of interest is the progressive nature of abuse. On the first trial, there is no difference across the three experimental situations in the level of shock administered, but with each successive opportunity, the shock levels diverge. Those shocking so-called animals shocked them more and more over time, a result comparable to the escalating shock level of the deindividuated female students in my earlier study. That increase in aggression over time, with practice or with experience, illustrates a self-reinforcing effect of abuse. Perhaps its appeal is not so much in inflicting pain to others as in the sense of power and control in such a situation of dominance.

A more positive finding was that individuals receive more respectful treatment if someone in authority labels them positively. Those perceived as "nice" were least harmed. There is an important message here about the power of words, to be used for good or evil.

Suspension of the Usual Cognitive Controls Guiding Moral Action

Part of what is necessary to get good people to engage in evil is to minimize or reorient normal cognitive control processes. That process suspends conscience, self-awareness, sense of personal responsibility, obligation, commitment, liability, morality, and analyses in terms of costs and benefits of given actions. The two general strategies for accomplishing this objective are reducing cues of social accountability of the actor (no one knows who I am or cares to) and reducing concerns for self-evaluation. The first strategy minimizes concerns for social evaluation and social approval by making the actor feel anonymous. It works in an environment that masks identity and diffuses personal responsibility across others in the situation. The second strategy stops self-monitoring by relying on tactics that alter one's state of consciousness (such as by drugs, strong emotions, or hyperintense activity) and projecting responsibility outward onto others.

The Hostile Imagination Created by Faces of the Enemy

The importance of situational influences is also apparent in the ways that nations prepare soldiers to engage in wars and prepare citizens to support the risks of going to war, especially a war of aggression. This difficult transformation is accomplished by a special form of cognitive conditioning. Images of the "enemy" are created to prepare the minds of soldiers and citizens to hate those who fit the category. This mental conditioning is the military's most potent weapon. . . . The enemy is aggressor; faceless; rapist; godless; barbarian; greedy; criminal; torturer; death; a dehumanized animal, or just an abstraction. Alternatively, there is a vision of the enemy as worthy, combatant, a powerful opponent to be crushed in "mortal combat"—as in the video game of the same name.

Can Ordinary Old Men Become Murderers Overnight?

One of the clearest illustrations of the transformation of ordinary people into agents of mass atrocities comes from the chronicle of Nazi genocides [over 11 months] by British historian Christopher Browning. . . . In just four months they had shot to death at point-blank range at least thirty-eight thousand Jews and deported another forty-five thousand to the concentration camp at Treblinka. Initially their commander acknowledged that this was a difficult mission and any individual could refuse to execute these men, women, and children. Records indicate that at first, about half the German police reservists refused and let others engage in the mass murder. But over time, social modeling processes took their toll, as did guilt-induced persuasion by those who had been doing the shooting. By the end of their journey, up to 90 percent of the men in Battalion 101 were involved in the shootings, even proudly taking close-up photographs of their killings. Like the guards at Abu Ghraib Prison, these policemen put themselves in their "trophy photos" as proud exterminators of the Jewish menace.

Browning makes clear that there was no special selection of these men. They were as ordinary as can be imagined—until they were put into a situation in which they had official permission and encouragement to act sadistically against those labeled as the "enemy." He also compares the underlying mechanism operating in that far-off land at that distant time to both the psychological processes at work in the Milgram research and the Stanford Prison Experiment discussed below. . . .

The Stanford Prison Experiment:
Institutional and Systemic Power to Corrupt

My own 1971 prison experiment synthesized many of the processes and variables outlined earlier: anonymity of place and person, dehumanization of victims, and a setting with differentials in control and power. This experiment was designed to extend over a two-week period . . . [but] had to be terminated after only six days because of the pathology we were witnessing. Normal students were behaving sadistically in their role of guards, inflicting humiliation, pain, and suffering. Some guards even reported they were enjoying doing so. Others had "emotional breakdowns" and stress disorders so extreme that five of them had to be excused within that first week. Those who adapted better to the situation were prisoners who mindlessly followed orders, became blindly obedient to authority, and allowed the guards to dehumanize and degrade them. . . .

The Evil of Inaction

British statesman Edmund Burke aptly observed, "The only thing necessary for evil to triumph is for good men to do nothing." Our usual take on evil focuses on violent, destructive actions, but non-action can also become a form of evil, when assistance, dissent, or disobedience are called for. . . . A counter to this dispositional analysis came in the form of a series of classic studies by Bibb Latane and John Darley on bystander intervention. One key finding was that people are less likely to help when they are in a group, when they perceive others are available who could help, than when those people are alone. The presence of others diffuses the sense of personal responsibility of any individual.

A powerful demonstration of the failure to help strangers in distress was staged by John Darley and Dan Batson. Imagine you are a theology student on your way to deliver the sermon of the Good Samaritan in order to have it videotaped for a psychology study on effective communication. Further imagine that as you are heading from the Psychology Department to the videotaping center, you pass a stranger huddled in an alley in dire distress. . . .

The researchers randomly assigned students of the Princeton Theological Seminary to three conditions that varied how much time they had to get to the Communication Department to tape their Good Samaritan speeches. The conclusion: don't be a victim in distress when people are late and in a hurry, because 90 percent of them are likely to pass you by. The more time the seminarians believed they had, the more likely they were to stop and help. So the situational variable of time press accounted for the major variance in helping, without any need to resort to dispositional explanations about theology students being callous, cynical, or indifferent. . . .

In situations of evil, there are almost always those who know what is going on and do not intervene to help. There were "good" guards in the Stanford Prison Experiment who did no harm to the prisoners, but they never once opposed the demeaning deeds of the bad guards. In the recent Abu Ghraib Prison abuse case, it is clear that many people knew of the abuse, even doctors and nurses, but never intervened to prevent it. . . .

Understanding What Went Wrong in Abu Ghraib Prison

The situational influences of evil came to the fore in recent trials of American prison guards at Abu Ghraib. In October 2004, I testified via closed circuit television to the military trial judge in Baghdad in defense of one of the guards, Sergeant Ivan Frederick. . . .

With regard to disposition, this soldier was totally and unequivocally normal on all measures assessed by an army clinical psychologist (and independently validated by a civilian expert in assessment). There was no evidence of any psychopathology or sadistic tendencies. Rather, Frederick matches our stereotypes of the All-American man. He is a patriotic son of a West Virginia coal miner. He hunts, fishes, plays Softball, attends Baptist church services regularly, and has a strong marriage to an African American woman. As a reserve soldier, he had a blameless record as a guard in a low-security, small-town civilian prison with one hundred inmates. He was proud to serve in Iraq and initially worked with children in a small village where he was starting to learn Arabic.

The situational conditions, the behavioral context, involved working conditions that bordered on the inhumane for both guards and prisoners. The processes operating in that prison were directly comparable to those in the Stanford Prison Experiment: deindividuation, dehumanization, moral disengagement, social modeling, pressures for conformity, passive bystanders, power differentials, use of enforced nakedness, and sexually humiliating tactics. The worst abuses in both settings took place on the night shift. The working conditions for Frederick included twelve-hour night shifts (4:00 P.M. to 4:00 A.M.), seven days a week, for forty days with not a day off, then fourteen days after one day off. Exhaustion and stress were exacerbated by chaotic conditions: unsanitary and filthy surroundings that smelled like a putrid sewer, with limited water for showering. Frequent electrical blackouts created dangerous opportunities for prisoner attacks. This young man with no mission-specific training was put in charge of more than three hundred prisoners initially; that number soon swelled to more than a thousand. He was also in charge of twelve army reserve guards and sixty Iraqi police, who often smuggled contraband to the inmates. He rarely left the prison. When off duty, he slept in a cell in a different part of prison. He missed breakfasts and stopped exercising or socializing. Tier 1-A became his total reference setting.

This of itself would qualify anyone for total job burnout. But guards were also under the stress of frequent insurgency attacks. Five U.S. soldiers and twenty prisoners were killed, and many others were wounded by almost daily shelling during Frederick's service. Finally, there were abusive acts by the prisoners themselves. Seven had rioted in another part of the prison and were sent to Tier 1-A for "safe keeping." Four others had raped a fellow boy prisoner. Five separate military investigations concerning Abu Ghraib acknowledge its horrendous conditions. They also acknowledge "failures of leadership, lack of leadership, indifferent leadership, and conflicting leadership demands." What is clear from these independent investigations is a total absence of accountability and oversight and an encouragement of stress interrogation.

The military judge took none of these conditions into account when he issued his sentence. Frederick received the maximum penalty: imprisonment for eight years, a dishonorable discharge, and loss of twenty-two years of army reserve retirement funds. This verdict represents yet another failure of leadership. It ignores the systemic conditions encouraging abuse and absolves the military and political officials responsible.

Promoting Civic Virtue, Moral Engagement, and Human Goodness

There are no simple solutions for the evils addressed here; if there were, they would already have been enacted by those far wiser than I. But the past half-century of psychological research provides some insight about what might be done at the individual and situational levels. . . .

Some of the same social-psychological forces that fostered the abuses described could also be harnessed for positive ends. We could, for example, construct an eleven-step plan for promoting civic virtue that parallels the ten steps toward evil outlined earlier:

- Openly acknowledge errors in judgments. This reduces the need to justify mistakes and continue immoral action. It undercuts the motivation to reduce dissonance by reaffirming a bad decision.
- Encourage mindfulness. People need reminders not to live their lives on automatic pilot, but to reflect on the situation and consider its ethical implications before acting.
- Promote a sense of personal responsibility and accountability for all of one's actions. People need a better understanding of how conditions of diffused responsibility disguise their own individual role in the outcomes of their actions.
- Discourage minor transgressions. Small acts—cheating, gossiping, lying, teasing, and bullying—provide the first steps toward escalating abuses.
- Distinguish between just and unjust authority. The fact that individuals occupy a position of authority, as in the Milgram experiment, does not entitle them to obedience in unethical actions.
- Support critical thinking. People need to be encouraged to demand evidence and moral justifications and to evaluate their credibility.
- Reward moral behavior. More recognition needs to be available for those who do the right thing under difficult situations, such as whistle-blowers in public and private sector positions.
- Respect human diversity. Appreciating difference is key to reducing in-group biases and prejudices.
- Change social conditions that promote anonymity. Making people feel special and accountable can promote socially desirable actions and reinforce individuals' sense of self-worth.
- Challenge pressures for conformity. Individuals need strategies for resisting group influences and maintaining their own moral compass.
- Refuse to sacrifice crucial freedoms for elusive promises of security. These sacrifices are often the first step toward fascism, and the price is often prohibitive.

NOTES AND QUESTIONS

1. Psychologists Max Bazerman and Ann Tenbrunsel provide a recent overview of the Milgram experiments. As they note, the study has been replicated multiple times with more than 1000 participants.[1] While the exact methodology would not be approved in contemporary American research settings subject to informed consent requirements, a similar replication found that 70 percent of subjects were willing to deliver dangerous shocks.[2] So too, a 2010 French television show, *Game of Death*, pictured 64 of 80 participants

delivering shocks that appeared severe enough to cause death. One participant who had followed orders revealed later that her Jewish grandparents had been victims of the Holocaust. What lessons should be drawn from the persistence of these findings?

2. One irony of the Stanford and Milgram experiments is that they have not only made enormous contributions to our understanding of moral behavior, they have also been subject to widespread criticism on moral grounds. Since the experiments were conducted, ethical oversight of research has become more rigorous. In the United States, any institution that receives federal funds must establish an institutional review board (IRB) to approve research involving human subjects. Criteria for approval, set forth in federal regulations, include whether the risks to subjects have been reduced to those necessary to achieve valid research objectives; whether those risks are outweighed by benefits to the participants or society generally; and whether the subjects have given informed consent that includes their right to withdraw at any time.[3]

If you were the chair of an IRB, would you approve research modeled on the Stanford prison or Milgram shock experiments? What changes, if any, would you require? Would it affect your view if, as Zimbardo claims, all of his participants returned to "normal" after extensive debriefing and most claimed that participation in the experiment was a valuable experience.[4]

3. If you had been the judge in the case involving Ivan Frederick, what sentence would you have imposed? What reasoning would you provide for that sentence?

PROBLEM 6-1

Abuse of detainees held at the Abu Ghraib prison in Iraq received worldwide attention in 2004 through pictures and articles chronicling the degradation. Prisoners were subject to beatings, death threats, sleep deprivation, stress positions, forced nudity, forced masturbation, and sex with dogs or other prisoners. Some observers such as Senator James Inhofe discounted the abuse by demonizing the prisoners as "murderers" and "terrorists." Military experts, however, including Brigadier General Janis Karpinski, the commanding officer at the prison, estimated that about 90 percent of the detainees were innocent.[5]

The United States Department of Defense removed 17 members of the military from duty in response to the abuses. Eleven soldiers were convicted in courts martial. Most received relatively light sentences: several months in prison, financial penalties, demotions, and dishonorable discharges. Sergeant Ivan Frederick, however, for whom Philip Zimbardo gave supportive psychological testimony, received an eight-year prison sentence for abuses that included forcing three prisoners to masturbate and punching one so hard that he needed resuscitation. No officers were convicted. Brigadier General Karpinski was demoted to the rank of colonel, despite her claims that she had no knowledge of the abuse and that enhanced interrogation had been authorized by superiors and performed by subcontractors. Thomas Pappas, commander of the military brigade in charge of the prison, was reprimanded, relieved of his command, demoted, and fined $8000.

In testimony before the Senate Armed Services Committee, then Secretary of Defense Donald Rumsfeld stated:

> These events occurred on my watch. As secretary of defense, I am accountable for them. I take full responsibility. It is my obligation to evaluate what happened to make sure those who have committed wrongdoing are brought to justice and to make changes as needed to see that it doesn't happen again. . . . To those Iraqis who were mistreated by members of the U.S. armed forces, I offer my deepest apology. It was un-American. It was inconsistent with the values of our nation.[6]

Rumsfeld also denounced those who had illegally distributed photos to the media, and he declined to call the abuse "torture."[7] Although he offered to resign, he added, "What was going on in the midnight shift in Abu Ghraib prison halfway across the world is something that clearly someone in Washington, DC, can't manage or deal with. And so I have no regrets. . . . We've made a lot of corrections to make sure that those kinds of things [that] happened either don't happen again or are immediately found out and limited and contained."[8] His offers to resign were rejected by President Bush, who also denounced the incidents as un-American.[9]

The Final Report of the Independent Panel to Review DOD Detention Operations specifically found that no senior U.S. military or political leaders "were directly involved in the incidents at Abu Ghraib."[10] Discussion of the leaders involved in decisions to allow "enhanced interrogation" of terrorist suspects appears in Part C below.

1. If you had been the president or the secretary of defense in 2004, how would you have responded to the abuses at Abu Ghraib?
2. Was the allocation of responsibility for the Abu Ghraib abuses appropriate: lengthy prison sentences for a few of those who perpetrated the abuses, and no criminal or civil liability for those who allowed the conditions that encouraged it? A New York Times editorial claimed that "each new revelation [concerning the prison] makes it more clear that the inhumanity of Abu Ghraib grew out of a morally dubious culture" fostered by the administration.[11] If that is true, what follows in terms of appropriate sanctions and preventive conduct?
3. Philip Zimbardo would clearly take issue with Rumsfeld's claim that the Abu Ghraib abuse was "un-American." Would you? If the thrust of Zimbardo's argument is that many "normal" Americans would behave like the Abu Ghraib guards under similar stressful circumstances, does that lessen the gravity of the offenses committed? Should it mitigate the sentences? Consider that issue in light of Hannah Arendt's discussion of Third Reich officers in the reading above.
4. Not all the guards at Abu Ghraib participated in the abuse. One who was ordered to waterboard a prisoner responded that it would violate the Geneva

Convention against torture. When his supervisor persisted, the guard responded, "I will need that order in writing before executing it."[12] That ended the matter. How can such strategies of resistance be encouraged?

MEDIA RESOURCES

A narrated video on the original version of the Milgram experiment is available, as are replications with comparable results.[13] One of the most interesting variations sought to ensure that participants believed that the shocks were real. The experiment used a puppy rather than a person as the subject of the "learning" exercise. Each participant watched the puppy first barking, then jumping up and down, and finally howling in pain from the shocks. Participants were horrified. They paced back and forth, hyperventilated, and gestured with their hands to show the puppy where to stand. Many openly wept. Yet the majority of them, 20 out of 26, continued the shocks up to the maximum voltage. Contrary to gender stereotypes that women are more caring and empathetic than men, none of the 6 who refused to continue were female. All 13 women who participated in the experiment obeyed until the end.[14]

Another variation divided participants' role into two parts: a person who transmitted the order to shock and the person who administered it. Obedience among the transmitters was substantially greater than among the administrators, which underscores the role of distance from victims in moral meltdowns.[15] One of the most recent versions of the Milgram experiment occurred at Santa Clara University, with modifications to secure IRB approval. The revised experiment involved lower voltage and clear instructions that the participants could drop out at any time.[16]

In 2015, the movie *The Stanford Prison Experiment*, based on Zimbardo's book, was released. The prison experiment has also has generated an extensive video record, as has the scandal at Abu Ghraib.[17] Images of the Abu Ghraib abuses and interviews with guards are available.[18]

For another treatment of ethical issues raised by terrorism, see *Yes Minister,* Season 3, episode 6, the Whisky Priest.

B. MORAL MELTDOWNS

In the following essays, David Luban, John Dean, and Peter Irons describe forces that have led to certain widely publicized "moral meltdowns." Recall the cognitive biases described in Chapter 3. To what extent are they at work in the examples described? What other factors may have been at work?

DAVID LUBAN, MAKING SENSE OF MORAL MELTDOWNS

Deborah L. Rhode, ed., Moral Leadership: The Theory and
Practice of Power, Judgment, and Policy (San Francisco:
Jossey-Bass, 2007), pp. 57-75

My aim in this chapter is to explore why executive and professional leadership goes sour. The examination proceeds along four principal dimensions: ethical, cultural, economic, and psychological.

The Ethical Dimension: Adversarial Ethics

At its simplest, what we seem to have witnessed in . . . [high-profile scandals] of the past few years is an epidemic of dishonesty, self-dealing, cheating, and even outright theft—an incredible failure to honor the most basic rules of Sunday school morality by executives and professionals who people trusted to know better than that and to do better than that. . . .

What conclusions we should draw from pandemic business scandals is likely to depend on one's overall outlook on business regulation. Those who think that our economy works best when executives have lots of power and discretion to make innovative, high-risk decisions are likely to favor tough enforcement over new regulation. According to their view, the fraudulent executives are bad apples in a basically sweet barrel. Whatever we do, let us make sure we do not kill the apple tree with a regulatory chainsaw. Others argue that the problem is not a few bad apples but a system that allows gross conflicts of interest and cries out for regulation. Their view is that the rottenness goes a lot deeper into the barrel than the notorious bad apples on top. With a system that makes self-dealing so easy and so profitable, it is no wonder that basic honesty goes out the window.

I take a different outlook from both of these. My proposition is that most of the people who brought us these scandals have ethical belief systems that are not much different from yours and mine. I suspect that if you asked them whether they think lying and cheating are okay, they would answer with an indignant no, and if you gave them a lie detector test when they said it, the needle would not budge. I do not pretend to see into people's brains, but I would be willing to bet that virtually none of the architects of these scandals—not the executives, not the accountants, not the lawyers—really thinks he or she did anything wrong. In that case, you might be asking what planet these people come from, but the answer, of course, is that we are standing on it. In their basic moral outlook, most will not turn out to be that much different from anyone else.

The fact is that everyday morality does not have settled principles for hypercompetitive, highly adversarial settings. For example, when the other side fights dirty, can you fight dirty too? On this issue, most people's moral intuitions are conflicted. Even Sunday school sends a double message. On the one hand, we say that two wrongs do not make a right and tell ourselves to turn the other cheek. On the other hand, we say that turnabout is fair play, we say an eye for an eye, we say you have to fight fire with fire. . . . I am not suggesting that "everyone does it" is a legitimate moral excuse. Rather, I am suggesting that there are very few consensus moral rules for highly adversarial, competitive settings. That implies a lot of moral uncertainty and ambiguity in a culture as addicted to competition as ours is.

The Cultural Dimension: America's Love Affair with Winners

This takes me to the second point: the cultural obstacles to dealing with Enron-type ethical meltdowns. The fact is that our culture loves the Fastows and Skillings of the world as long as they succeed. . . . The employees, managers, accountants, and attorneys who work for the winners are no exception.

More than that, I think it is undeniable that American culture has always had a soft spot in its heart for bad boys who break rules to get results, as long as they do it in style. . . .

Having a soft spot for bad boy winners seems harmless enough, but the flip side is a little uglier. As a culture, we have little patience with losers. If they did something wrong, we do not cut them the same slack we do for winners. Even if they were blameless, we are unlikely to find them all that appealing. In a fascinating series of experiments, the social psychologist Melvin Lerner discovered that the worse someone is treated, the more likely observers are to rate the victim as an unattractive, flawed person. Lerner explains this phenomenon as an unconscious attempt to ward off the scary thought that if unfair stuff can happen to her, it can happen to me. We unconsciously disparage the victim in order to find a distinction, some distinction, between her and us in order to reassure ourselves that *we* will not get victimized next. I find this explanation entirely plausible. Whatever the explanation, though, the experiment provides powerful evidence that we do not tend to find losers beautiful.

I think everyone instinctively understands this, and the implications for business ethics are disturbing. Given the choice between breaking rules and winning or being a law-abiding loser, you are far more likely to win friends and influence people if you break the rules—especially if you can portray the rules as red tape crying out to be cut. No wonder that Enron executives took the most aggressive accounting positions they possibly could. Pushing rules as hard as you can in order to be a winner is exactly what our culture prizes. . . .

The accountants' and lawyers' job is to keep the flamboyant bad boys out of trouble. The problem is that when a successful client is flying high, as high as Enron flew, no one wants to be the doomsayer who puts on the brakes. A hundred years ago, Elihu Root, one of the founders of Cravath, Swaine & Moore, said, "The client never wants to be told he can't do what he wants to do; he wants to be told how to do it, and it is the lawyer's business to tell him how." The same ethos permeates large accounting firms. The culture's love affair with bad boy businessmen creates a behavioral echo among the employees whose job is to hold them in check but who may see their real job as guarding the CEO's back.

The Economic Dimension:
The Feudal and Socialist Character of American Capitalism

. . . [The third major challenge to reform] is the economic fact that a capitalist economy always produces losers. . . . It does not matter how smart executives are or how fast on their feet. The world around them is faster. Inevitably they set their quarterly targets based on inadequate or obsolete information. And sometimes reality catches up with them. The economy goes south just when they have placed their bets on a few more golden quarters of going north. . . . In an odd way, executives fighting desperately to hide their losses and stay in business act in part out of a warped sense of fiduciary obligation to other people in the company. The moral pressure to meet your numbers, combined with self-interest, is overwhelming. . . .

What do you do when you cannot keep your promises and meet your targets? You have four choices. One is to pin the blame on someone else. Claiming you did not know what others were doing is the simplest way, but more subtle methods exist as well. For example, [sociologist Robert] Jackall discovered a system of "milking" factories in the chemical giant he studied. A manager struggling to meet his numbers shortchanges essential maintenance on the equipment. Eventually the equipment breaks down in a very expensive way, but by that time the manager has been promoted, and the meltdown happens on someone else's watch. Top management had little interest in tracking accountability, because in Jackall's company, everyone knew that the boss got to the top the same way.

If you cannot pin the blame on someone else, a second option is to arrange things so the losses fall on your customers, your shareholders, your employees—anywhere but yourself. . . . Option three, Enron's main strategy, is to smear on the cosmetics, cover up the losses as long as possible, and hope for a miracle turnaround to pull you from the fire. Rational managers should know better than to rely on miracles. But look at the character traits that make for successful entrepreneurs: boundless optimism, big egos, a taste for risk, unwillingness to take no for an answer. Exactly these traits predispose high-flying CEOs to bet the farm on one last roll of the dice and assume that Lady Luck will smile on them. Surely the economy will rebound and get you out of your troubles. Only sometimes it does not.

These are the three dishonest strategies: blame someone else, shaft someone else, or cover up and hope against hope. The fourth strategy is to accept that you have lost, take your lumps, and move on. . . . What we now see is that the failures that drive executives to cheat and cover up are built into the very nature of a corporation, which is a planned economy that cannot avoid placing high-risk bets. Put these three factors together, and you have a recipe for scandals. The conclusion seems unavoidable: the crooks, like the poor, will always be with us.

The Psychological Dimension: Cognitive Dissonance and Moral Compass

But none of this explains our original puzzle of why the crooks continue to think they are not crooks. Here social psychology offers an answer. The basic reason is cognitive dissonance. Whenever our conduct and principles clash with each other in a way that threatens our self-image as an upstanding person, the result is a kind of inner tension—dissonance. And dissonance theory tells us that wired into us is a fundamental drive to reduce dissonance. How do you accomplish that? Obviously, you cannot change your past conduct. Instead, you change your beliefs. That is what fifty years of research have taught. In situation after situation, literally hundreds of experiments reveal that when our conduct clashes with our prior beliefs, our beliefs swing into conformity with our conduct, without our noticing that this is going on. . . .

How can this happen? The answer, as any psychiatrist will tell you, is that we do not automatically know our own beliefs. Instead, we figure them out by examining our own behavior. . . . If I covered up losses with smoke-and-mirrors accounting, I must think that smoke-and-mirrors does not really count as a cover-up. And what if this contradicts what I have always been taught and always thought I believed in the past? I tell myself that only a fanatic refuses to learn from experience—and I am no fanatic.

One surprising result follows. Most of us are inclined to think that the big problem in the ethics scandals is lack of integrity on the part of the principals. But if integrity means doing what you think is right, these men and women had integrity to burn. They got it the cheap way: once they did things, they believed those things were right. Integrity does not help very much when you are in the grips of self-deception.

The problem is not simply that we unconsciously adjust our moral beliefs so they inevitably make us look good. Psychologists have also shown that our judgment is deeply affected by the people around us. Show a group of people two lines, and if eleven of them say that the shorter line is longer, the twelfth is likely to see it that way as well.

The same thing is true with moral judgment, and that is the special problem that organizational settings create: you are always in the room with eleven other people. In the 1960s, a young woman named Kitty Genovese was assaulted and murdered in Queens, New York, as dozens of people in their apartments witnessed the assault. Not a single person called the police. The media were filled with dismay at this sign of social indifference. But two social psychologists had a different explanation: they conjectured that groups of people are usually less likely to help out in emergencies than single individuals are. To test their hypothesis, they had subjects fill out questionnaires in a room. While a subject worked on the questionnaire, a staged emergency happened—either the sound of crashing equipment and screams from the next room or smoke billowing into the room where the subject was sitting. The results were remarkable: when subjects were by themselves, most responded quickly to the emergency. But when another person sat next to them and failed to respond, they mimicked the other person and did nothing themselves. Evidently we respond to unusual situations by first checking to see how other people respond. And just as we take cues from the other person, he or she takes cues from us. . . .

The Kitty Genovese effect goes a long way toward explaining why no one blew the whistle on the corporate scandals: insiders simply took their cues from each other. They saw everyone else acting as though everything was perfectly all right, and they acted that way themselves, each reinforcing the others' passivity.... The desire to fit in with those around us helps explain how [managers,] . . . lawyers and accountants become fatally implicated in corporate wrongdoing. In large organizations, decisions get parceled out among many people, and every piece of work is the product of many hands. Information filters in piecemeal, a little at a time. As a result, decisive moral moments are not obvious. They are not really moments at all. They do not scream out, "You've reached the crossroads!" Changes come gradually, like walking in a very large circle. Not only that, the consequences of decisions are often nearly unfathomable. And working in teams, it is seldom obvious whose responsibility any choice ultimately is. It may be everyone's or nobody's at all. The ground is fertile for the Kitty Genovese effect. . . .

Suppose, for example, that a chief financial officer calls in an in-house lawyer, and a consultant, and an accountant, and says that he would like to structure some deals that will help push accounting losses off the books. (Think Andrew Fastow [at Enron].) The lawyer may not know off the top of her head whether there is a legal way to do it, but that is what she gets paid to figure out. The last thing the lawyer thinks about is that an ethical rule forbids her from counseling or assisting in a client fraud. The conversation is about business goals, not about fraud (such an ugly word!). The lawyer, accountant, and consultant accept the business goal of making business losses vanish from the balance sheets, and reason backward to whatever complicated structure it will take to achieve it. So what if the law requires a proper business purpose other than sanitizing an annual statement? The whole lawyering problem is figuring out some way to package the client's goal as a proper business purpose, although that might require drifting into the gray zone at the margin of the law. Transparency avoidance feels to the lawyer, accountant, and consultant like little more than a formalistic game, not much different from tax avoidance.

The trouble is that transparency is what the law requires, and transparency avoidance bears an uncanny resemblance to fraud. . . . In a corporate culture, the incredible plasticity of conscience that social psychology reveals creates perhaps the biggest challenge to reformers. If you cannot trust your own conscience to tell you the difference between right and wrong, how are you supposed to do what is right? Remember what we have learned so far: the stakes in business are high, the corporate culture puts out powerful cues, the wider culture reinforces them, and no settled guidelines about morality in competitive settings push hard in the opposite direction. It should hardly astonish us that the result is ethical self-deception on a grand scale.

It may sound as though I am saying dishonesty is a social disease that is nobody's fault. That is not my intention at all. The goal is to understand, not to make excuses. In fact, I am not a great believer in the idea that to understand all is to forgive all. People make their choices under constraints, including psychological ones, but in the end, all sane adults are still accountable for the choices they make. We should never forget that not everyone gives in to social pressures. If my conscience lets me down, the fact remains that it is *my* conscience, not the company's conscience and not society's conscience.

Lessons for Leaders?

. . . What advice can I offer to managers, accountants, and lawyers in corporate settings? Is it really true that forces you are barely aware of can disconnect your conscience as thoroughly as the Stanford prison guards or the administrators of electric shocks? If the answer is yes, then how can anyone deal with forces they are barely aware of?

I have three suggestions. First, all the experimental studies suggest that cognitive dissonance disconnects the wires of conscience slowly and one step at a time. . . . For that reason, it becomes critically important to give ourselves some kind of warning. Set yourself some telltale sign—something that you know is wrong. Write down on a piece of paper, "I will never backdate a document." Or "I will never let a coworker get blamed for something that was my fault." Or "I will never paper a deal that I don't understand." Or "I will never do anything that I couldn't describe to my dad while looking him in the eye." Pick your telltale sign carefully, and the moment the alarm rings, evacuate the building.

Second, we may take a cue from Stanley Milgram's electric shock experiments. When Milgram debriefed his compliantly murderous subjects afterward, he asked them whose fault the shocks were: the scientist who ordered the shocks, the victim who provoked them by getting wrong answers on a test, or the subject who administered them. Not too surprisingly, the compliant subjects usually blamed the other two (while the defiant subjects, who refused to follow murderous orders, took on themselves primary responsibility for their conduct). My advice, then, is to notice when you are blaming someone else. Right or wrong, the very fact that you are blaming it on the CFO or the accountant is a telltale sign that your own conscience is on the road to perdition.

Finally, I suggest that a certain amount of self-doubt and self-skepticism is not such a bad thing. Moral meltdowns happen when the reactor overheats. There is a kind of euphoria that comes from working on big cases, big deals, for high-energy businesses and high-powered clients. Intoxicating though it may be, it is a bad idea to trust euphoria. My version of Socrates' "know yourself!" is "doubt yourself!" This is hard advice in a nation that admires self-confident, don't-look-back leaders. "Doubt yourself!" sounds like a recipe for neurosis. But without some healthy skepticism, the temptation to take your cues from the client-executive with the most hubris may be unavoidable. Icarus makes a terrible role model.

The Watergate scandal offers a particularly illuminating case history of how the good go bad, in part because of the sheer number of lawyers involved. The scandal owes its name to a Washington D.C. hotel and office complex, the site of a bungled burglary of the Democratic National Committee headquarters orchestrated by Nixon administration officials. Almost every major participant in the cover up was an attorney, and 20 ended up on the wrong side of the law.[19] Lawyers who occupied leadership positions in the Nixon administration and his re-election campaign, including two former attorney generals, were convicted of crimes including perjury, fraud, obstruction of justice, burglary, and conspiracy.[20] Nixon, also a lawyer, resigned to avoid impeachment for obstruction of justice and abuse of power. In testimony before a Senate Select Committee, John Dean, then Counsel to the President, recalled that he had "prepared a list of who was likely to be indicted as the investigation proceeded. . . . [M]y first reaction was . . . how in God's name could so many lawyers get involved in something like this."[21] In his own memoir, Dean provides a partial explanation.

JOHN W. DEAN III, BLIND AMBITION

(New York: Simon and Schuster, 1976), pp. 32-35,
38-39, 47-48, 52-55, 58-59, and 62-63

THE TESTS STARTED that first day at the White House. After a brief examination of my meager quarters, I had sat down at my desk. I didn't have anything to do, but then my secretary brought me a sealed envelope with a small red tag. I asked her what it was. She had not opened it; it was stamped "CONFIDENTIAL," and the red tag meant "priority." Someone had been planning work for the new counsel. The cover memorandum was a printed form, with striking blue and red instructions filled in . . . :

SUBJECT: Request that you rebut the recent attack on the Vice-President.

An attached "confidential memorandum" said that a new muckraking magazine called *Scanlan's Monthly* had published a bogus memo linking Vice-President Agnew with a top-secret plan to cancel the 1972 election and to repeal the entire Bill of Rights. Agnew had publicly denounced the memo as "completely false" and "ridiculous," and the editors of *Scanlan's* had replied: "The Vice President's denial is as clumsy as it is fraudulent. The document came directly from Mr. Agnew's office and he knows it." My instructions were clear: "It was noted that this is a vicious attack and possibly a suit should be filed or a federal investigation ordered to follow up on it."

"Noted" by whom? Since the memorandum was signed by John Brown, a member of Haldeman's staff, I called him to find out. The "noter" was the President, I was told; he had scrawled my orders in the margin of his daily news summary. No one had to explain why the President's name was not used. He was always to be kept one step removed, insulated, to preserve his "deniability."

So this is my baptism, I thought. I was astounded that the president would be so angrily concerned about a funny article in a fledgling magazine. It did not square with my picture of his being absorbed in diplomacy, wars and high matters of state. Was it possible that we *had* a secret plan to cancel the election and the Bill of Rights? I was embarrassed by the thought. Now I cannot look back on this episode without laughing, but then I was not at all loose about it. It was the President of the United States talking. Maybe he was right.

On the due date, I wrote my first memorandum to the President, explaining the hazards of a lawsuit and the wisdom of waiting to see what an FBI investigation produced. I thought the affair had been put to rest. Not so. Back came another action memorandum from the staff secretary. The President agreed with my conclusions, but he wasn't yet content. "It was requested," said the memorandum, "that as part of this inquiry you should have the Internal Revenue Service conduct a field investigation on the tax front."

This was the "old Nixon" at work, heavy-handed, after somebody. I began to fret. How could anything be at once so troubling and so absurd? The President was asking me to do something I thought was dangerous, unnecessary and wrong. I did nothing for several days, but the deadline was hard upon me. I couldn't simply respond, "Dean opposes this request because it is wrong and possibly illegal." I had to find some practical reason for doing the right thing or I would be gone. I called [White House lawyer] Bud Krogh several times, but he was out. Then I thought of my recent acquaintance, Murray Chotiner, [a Washington lawyer who advised the administration] and arranged to meet him.

"I need some counsel, Murray."

"You're the lawyer. You're the one who is supposed to give counsel around here," he said with a chuckle.

"I'm still trying to find the water fountains in this place," I said. "Murray, seriously, I need some advice. The President wants me to turn the IRS loose on a shit-ass magazine called *Scanlan's Monthly* because it printed a bogus memo from the Vice-President's office about canceling the 'seventy-two election and repealing the Bill of Rights."

Murray laughed. "Hell, Agnew's got a great idea. I hope he has a good plan worked out. It would save us a lot of trouble if we dispensed with the 'seventy-two campaign." Murray wasn't taking my visit as seriously as I was. We joked about Agnew for a few minutes before I could get him to focus on my problem, and he had the answer. "If the President wants you to turn the IRS loose, then you turn the IRS loose. It's that simple, John."

"I really don't think it's necessary, Murray. The President's already got Mitchell investigating it. The FBI, I guess."

"I'll tell you this, if Richard Nixon thinks it's necessary you'd better think it's necessary. If you don't, he'll find someone who does."

I was not convinced and said so, but nicely. "Okay, but let me ask you this, Murray. You're a lawyer. Isn't it illegal and therefore crazy to use IRS to attack someone the President doesn't like?"

"Not so," he snorted. He stopped and retrieved the calm he rarely lost. "John, the President is the head of the executive branch of this damn government. If he wants his tax collectors to check into the affairs of anyone, it's his prerogative. I don't see anything illegal about it. It's the way the game is played. Do you think for a second that Lyndon Johnson was above using the IRS to harass those guys who were giving him a hard time on the war? No sir. Nor was Lyndon above using

IRS against some good Republicans like Richard Nixon. I'll tell you he damn near ruined a few."

Murray was testy, or maybe defensive—I couldn't decide. It was clear that he didn't want to discuss the matter further. I thanked him and left. If I was going to play ball in Richard Nixon's league, I would have to get over my squeamishness. I am not sure what I would have done if John J. Caulfield had not walked into my office.

Jack Caulfield . . . had moved up the ranks of the New York police force, from a street beat to detective, arriving at the White House after an assignment as candidate Nixon's personal bodyguard in 1968. Bob Haldeman had assigned him to me without telling me why. Caulfield explained that he was White House liaison with the Secret Service and the local police, but his principal assignment was to investigate Senator Edward M. Kennedy's conduct in the Chappaquiddick accident for John Ehrlichman.

Jack was a bountiful source of information. He knew what everybody was doing. He could tell you how to get a refrigerator or parking privileges and who was sleeping with whose secretary. And he wanted to help me find my bearings. He seemed a natural person to turn to with my IRS orders, and I decided to show him the memos. "How would you handle this assignment?" I asked.

"This isn't any problem. I'll take care of it for you with a phone call," he answered confidently. He returned the next day to report that a tax inquiry would be fruitless because the magazine was only six months old and its owners had yet to file their first return. Being resourceful, however, he had asked the IRS to look into the owners themselves. "You can tell the President everything is taken care of," he assured me. . . .

I summarized the tax situation in my report. "The fact that *Scanlan's* is a new entity does not make the tax inquiry very promising," I concluded. "Accordingly, I have also requested that the inquiry be extended to the principal organizers and promoters of the publication." Thus, within a month of coming to the White House, I had crossed an ethical line. I had no choice, as I saw it. The fact that I had not carried out the assignment myself eased my conscience slightly. I had no idea how Jack had done it so easily, nor did I ask, and I never found out what became of the IRS inquiry. . . .

I [now] had learned to expect anything in special assignments. But I also focused on my regular duties and was adjusting my instincts to what I saw daily in the White House. . . . Although our work was technical and legal, we discovered that we could use it to get a foothold in substantive areas. If we were alert in conflict-of-interest reviews and investigations, we would have a small say in Presidential appointments. As with any law firm, our influence depended largely on our reputation, and our reputation was good. We cultivated it with care.

Haldeman's assignments always received priority, of course, and he fired questions at us regularly. A Presidential fact-finding committee had returned from Vietnam with two captured Chinese rifles for the President, and the Treasury Department wanted to disallow the gifts because they had been illegally imported. What could we do? After a crash study of the relevant law, we had no trouble persuading Treasury to classify the rifles as legal "war trophies" for the Commander in Chief. A corporation, said Haldeman, had upset the President by marketing a replica of the Presidential seal. Could anything be done? A few statutes cited on White House stationery made the company desist. Congress wanted the General Accounting Office to audit the White House budgets in which the redecorating expenses had been buried. Haldeman wanted to know if the audit could be blocked legally. We let the auditors in but assured Haldeman we could stall them for four years. . . .

Back in Washington, I was visited by Bud Krogh. . . . As part of his mandate to stop leaks, he wanted to harass the Brookings Institution in any way he could, and he was checking in with me. . . . He seemed almost apologetic, and I sensed he was slightly embarrassed at being chosen to head an intelligence operation that should logically have been mine. It was an uneasy conversation, with much nonverbal communication, and Bud was finally moved to offer an explanation: "John, I guess there are some people around here who think you have some little old lady in you.". . .

I was upset that they thought of me as a little old lady, but I tried not to let on. Later, as if to prove myself again, I had Caulfield obtain the tax records of Brookings from IRS as Bud had requested and sent them to him with a covering memo, noting that Brookings received many government contracts we might cut off. I also told him there were Nixon loyalists on the Brookings board whom we might use clandestinely. A week later I sent Bud another terse and self-serving memo, offering to help "turn off the spigot" of funds to Brookings, but he never called on me. . . .

[In 1972 an antitrust settlement with ITT] exploded in the Administration's face when Jack Anderson published a memo purportedly written by ITT lobbyist Dita Beard, in which she baldly told her boss that the antitrust suit against ITT would be dropped in return for a $400,000 contribution of ITT cash and services to the GOP convention in San Diego. The next day Anderson lobbed another bombshell: he charged that Kleindienst, who had just been appointed Attorney General (Mitchell having left to head the Committee to Reelect the President), had lied "outright" about the settlement of the ITT case. Impulsively, Kleindienst demanded that his confirmation hearings be reopened so that he could clear his name.

As usual, John Ehrlichman took charge at the White House. On March 8, 1972, I was invited to his office for my first of many meetings on the Kleindienst-ITT matter, along with Chuck Colson, public relations pros and Congressional-liaison men. . . . "Kleindienst is a damn fool," Colson said instantly. "Jim Eastland tried to talk him out of going back to the Hill, but Kleindienst charged off after his honor like Sir Galahad. We wouldn't be in this mess if he wasn't so stupid." . . . From the beginning, Colson's extraordinary efforts centered upon his conviction that the Dita Beard memo was a forgery. If he could prove it, he would expose the Democrats as hucksters. . . . Since J. Edgar Hoover did not like Colson, I was sent to enlist the director's cooperation; a delicate mission. . . .

"Mr. Hoover, we, the White House that is, Mr. Ehrlichman and others"—I wanted to get my authority established—"have good reason to believe the so-called Dita Beard memorandum is a phony, and we'd like to have your lab test it because we are sure that your test will confirm that it is forgery." . . .

"I understand exactly, Mr. Dean, what you need," the director said with emphasis, "and I'm delighted to be of service. Jack Anderson is the lowest form of human being to walk the earth. He's a muckraker who lies, steals, and let me tell you this, Mr. Dean, he'll go lower than dog shit for a story.". . . [However the FBI lab found that] the Dita Beard memo was legitimate. . . . Colson carried the FBI's draft letter to the President's office, and when he returned he said he had never before seen the President so furious. The President penned a note to his friend Edgar, asking him to "cooperate," then gave it to Ehrlichman with instructions to turn Hoover around. Ehrlichman could not budge the director an inch. When the President was told, he mused, "I don't understand Edgar sometimes. He hates Anderson." . . .

A fresh wave of anti-Hoover sentiment lapped through the Administration. Had he deliberately doctored the lab reports after discovering the work of ITT's experts? . . . Colson wanted to fire Hoover. The idea was, as always, discarded. There was a question on Hoover in each secret poll of public opinion conducted by the White House, and he always ranked extremely high. This piece of political realism, more than fear of blackmail, probably guaranteed Hoover his job until he died, unexpectedly, a few months later. . . .

Looking back, I wonder that I failed to see the signs of worse to come. At the time, I was relieved to have passed. The ITT scandal at last melted to the back pages of the papers, and Kleindienst was confirmed. . . .

"Well, Johnny," [a colleague] said as we walked slowly back from lunch one day in mid-May, "I read back in January where Jeane Dixon predicted Nixon would have a serious scandal this year but would survive it. It's amazing, she was right. We've had it, and the President was untouched." I agreed.

We were all wrong, of course. The machinery had long been cranking through the White House toward a scandal that would grind down the President himself. And I was part of the machinery. . . .

NOTES AND QUESTIONS

1. *Blind Ambition* is a case study of the moral meltdowns that Zimbardo's and Luban's essays describe. To what extent was John Dean's misconduct a function of character weaknesses, that is, blind ambition? To what extent was it attributable to situational pressures that might have resulted in similar conduct by many governmental officials? Under psychologist James Rest's framework described in the Rhode excerpt in Chapter 5, which of Dean's ethical lapses reflected inadequate moral awareness or moral reasoning, and which involved inadequate moral intent and disposition? Does it matter for purposes of preventing future scandals like Watergate?

2. Dean describes a number of dynamics that are common contributors to individual and organizational misconduct:
   - *Diffusion and displacement of responsibility*
     - Murray Chotiner tells Dean that if "Richard Nixon thinks it's necessary, you better think it's necessary. If you don't, he'll find someone who does."
     - After requesting Jack Caufield to have the IRS investigate political opponents, Dean notes: "The fact that I had not carried out the assignment myself eased my conscience slightly. I had no idea how Jack had done it so easily, nor did I ask. . . ."
   - *Willful ignorance*
     - Dean notes: "I never found out what became of the IRS inquiry."
   - *Peer pressure*
     - Bud Krogh warns Dean: "[T]here are some people around here who think you have some little old lady in you."
     - Dean notes: "If I was going to play ball in Richard Nixon's league, I would have to get over my squeamishness."
   - *Euphemistic descriptions*
     - "Squeamishness" is how Dean describes his sense of ethics.
   - *Social Proof*
     - "It's how the game is played" is how Murray Chotiner describes the use of IRS tax investigations to harass political opponents.
   - *Demonization of opponents and rationalization of retaliation*
     - J. Edgar Hoover's description of columnist Jack Anderson as the "lowest form of human being to walk the earth."
     - Murray Chotiner's assertion that Lyndon Johnson "damn near ruined a few" good Republicans through his use of IRS investigations.

   These cognitive biases were widely shared among Watergate lawyers. Demonization of the opposition and self-serving characterizations of their own motives were especially common and highly corrosive. After Daniel Ellsberg leaked the Pentagon Papers to the *New York Times*, Nixon told Colson, "We've got a counter-government here and we've got to fight it. I don't care how."[22] In a discussion with his chief of staff, H.R. Haldeman, the President stated, "We're up against an enemy. A conspiracy. They're using any means. We are going to use any means. Is that clear?"[23] Nixon never expressed any qualms about authorizing IRS investigations of political opponents. As he explained in his memoirs, "When Democrats controlled the White House, I was routinely subjected to politically instigated IRS audits. . . . I was simply trying to level the playing field. . . . In any case, I see nothing wrong with getting wealthy people to pay their taxes."[24] Nixon's views were contagious and helped to create a bunker mentality within his administration. "It was us against them," Colson recalled.[25] In a television interview when David Frost asked whether the president could "decide that it's in the best interests of the nation, and do something illegal," Nixon famously responded, "Well, when the president does it, that means it's not illegal."[26]

In this morally toxic setting, how would you have responded if you had been in Dean's position? Would you have been willing to stall the IRS audit or pull the Brookings contracts? Do these cross the moral trip wires that Luban advises setting? Is there anything Dean could have done differently, short of resignation?

3. Jeb Stuart Magruder, Nixon's special assistant who was involved in authorizing the Watergate burglary, describes another cognitive bias that affected decision-making. The break-in was proposed by G. Gordon Liddy, Magruder's general counsel, after the Committee to Reelect the President rejected more extreme ideas—such as mugging squads that would rough up anti-Nixon demonstrators, or "high class" prostitutes, who would seduce and blackmail leading Democratic politicians. Committee members, who included Attorney General John Mitchell, felt that they "needed" Liddy and were "reluctant to send him away with nothing." Yet, according to Magruder, if Liddy had come to them at the outset with the idea to break into the Democratic National Headquarters at the Watergate and install wiretaps, committee members would have "reject[ed] the idea out of hand."[27] In commenting on the legacy of Watergate, my earlier book *Lawyers as Leaders* notes,

> [N]ot every lawyer involved in Watergate succumbed to group pressures. Archibald Cox, the first Watergate special prosecutor, sought to compel Nixon to produce tapes of White House conversations, despite the President's claim of executive privilege. When Nixon asked Attorney General Elliot Richardson to fire Cox, Richardson instead resigned, as did his deputy William Ruckelshaus. The official next in line then followed the President's orders and abolished the office. The public was outraged over what became known as the Saturday Night Massacre. Nixon's approval ratings dropped to 17 percent, and he yielded to pressure to reinstate the special prosecutor. The steadfast adherence to principle by Cox, Richardson, and Ruckelshaus was critical in keeping the Watergate investigation alive. As their examples suggest, distinguished leaders often are remembered not only for what they do, but also for what they refuse to do.
>
> With four decades hindsight, Watergate offers some lasting leadership lessons. One is that the combination of insecurity, ambition, and arrogance can be toxic. The Nixon administration's insatiable desire for political intelligence and retaliation also reflected a particularly irrational form of group think. The president had no real need to risk so much for so little. As he later acknowledged, "in view of the 30 percent lead I had in the polls it made no sense to take such a risk [in burglarizing opposition headquarters] because the likely Democratic nominee, Senator George McGovern, stood virtually no chance of winning. . . . To paraphrase Tallyrand, Watergate was worse than a crime—it was a blunder. "But as Colson put it, "we wanted a

coronation," not just a victory.[28] Ironically, that same ambition and concern for his historical legacy contributed in other ways to Nixon's downfall. He created the White House taping system to assist him in writing memoirs that would secure his place in the pantheon of great presidents. Yet it was the material on those tapes, including his instructions to halt the FBI's Watergate investigation, that forced his resignation and marred his legacy.

For other members of his staff, the ambition to move up also ensured a move down. As Dean realized, "advancement would come from doing those things which built a common bond of trust—or guilt—from my superiors. . . . Slowly, steadily, I would climb toward . . . the President's inner circle until I finally fell into it, thinking I had made it to the top just as I began to realize I had actually touched bottom."[29]

What lessons do you draw from the Watergate scandal?

4. Are there other contemporary examples that suggest similar truths? Consider the congressional testimony of President Trump's personal lawyer Michael Cohen, who was sentenced to three years in prison for his tax fraud and perjury. He states:

> I knew early on in my work for Mr. Trump that he would direct me to lie to further his business interests. I am ashamed to say that when it was for a real estate mogul in the private sector, I considered it trivial. As the President, I consider it significant and dangerous. But in the mix, lying for Mr. Trump was normalized, and no one around him questioned it. In fairness, no one around him today questions it, either. . . . Over the past year or so, I have done real soul searching. I see now that my ambition and the intoxication of Trump's power had much to do with the bad decisions I made."[30]

————————————

Darryl Zanuck, the legendary Hollywood studio head, was famous for saying, "Don't say yes until I've finished talking."[31] Corporate and political leaders accustomed to getting their way may have little patience for legal technicalities or for the messengers who invoke them. What strategies are available to advisors who want to do right without losing their jobs? What were the options for the government lawyers in the problem below?

PROBLEM 6-2

Peter Irons's *Justice at War* (1983) provides another case history of the ethical dilemmas that can confront government lawyers. His account chronicles dilemmas for individuals defending the detention and relocation of Japanese Americans during World War II.

One such dilemma involved Edward Ennis, the director of the Alien Enemy Control Unit in the Justice Department. He had primary responsibility for presenting the Department's position supporting internment in *Hirabayashi v. United States*, 320 U.S. 81 (1943), and *Korematsu v. United States*, 323 U.S. 214 (1944). Although Ennis had opposed the policy, he was initially prepared to defend it. However, during the course of his work on *Hirabayashi,* he discovered a crucial internal memorandum by staffers in the Office of Naval Intelligence. That memo, by the military unit most knowledgeable on the issue, reached conclusions that directly undercut the rationale for the wholesale evacuation. In particular, the memo concluded that the "Japanese Problem" had been magnified out of proportion, that the small number of Japanese Americans who posed potential threats were in custody or were already known and subject to apprehension, and that case-by-case determinations of dangerousness were preferable to a categorical internment.

Ennis believed that this report should be called to the Supreme Court's attention, and he so advised the Solicitor General, Charles Fahy:

> Appealing to Fahy's sense of rectitude and his responsibility as Solicitor-General, Ennis argued that "in view of the fact that the Department of Justice is now representing the Army in the Supreme Court of the United States and is arguing that a partial, selective evacuation was impracticable, we must consider most carefully what our obligation to the Court is in view of the fact that the responsible Intelligence agency regarded a selective evacuation as not only sufficient but preferable." Ennis further noted that "one of the most difficult questions" in the Hirabayashi case is raised by the fact that the Army did not evacuate people after any hearing or any individual determination of dangerousness, but evacuated the entire racial group.". . . "[T]he Government is forced to argue that individual selective evacuation would have been impractical and insufficient when we have positive knowledge that the only Intelligence agency responsible for advising General DeWitt gave him advice directly to the contrary." Ennis phrased his final plea to Fahy in terms that waved a warning flag before the Solicitor General: "I think we should consider very carefully whether we do not have a duty to advise the Court of the existence of the [internal] memorandum and of the fact that this represents the view of the Office of Naval Intelligence. It occurs to me that any other course of conduct might approximate the suppression of evidence."[32]

Ennis's position did not prevail. Rather, Arnold Raum, the author of the brief for the government in *Hirabayashi,* maintained that

> [t]he rationale behind [military] orders was "not the loyalty or disloyalty of individuals but the danger from the residence of the class as such within a vital military area." Such a judgment about the "danger" posed by Japanese Americans as a group, however, necessarily required as the

"rational basis" demanded by the due process clause some reasonable estimation of loyalty within the group. In searching for such rationality, Raum retreated to speculation and supposition. Japanese Americans had been "treated as a group," he wrote, because some of them were "thought" to be dangerous. Raum did not identify those who harbored these thoughts, nor did he explain why it would be a "virtually impossible task" to determine loyalty on the basis of hearings. . . . Rebuffed in his attempt to alert the Supreme Court . . . , Ennis gave up for the time his objection to Fahy's "suppression of evidence." As a loyal government lawyer, Ennis swallowed his doubts and added his name to the Hirabayashi brief along with those of Fahy [and] Raum.[33]

A similar problem arose a year later in preparing the government's brief in *Korematsu*. Ennis had cause to be skeptical of certain assertions in the military's final report justifying the evacuation. At his request, the Attorney General authorized an FBI and FCC investigation of allegations regarding Japanese espionage efforts (including radio signaling) on the West Coast. Both agencies concluded that some assertions in a report justifying evacuation were false. It also appeared that the errors were known to General DeWitt, who had authorized the report and supported the evacuation.

Ennis and one of his staff members, John Burling, who was working on the *Korematsu* brief, were determined to avoid reliance on the final report in presenting the government's case. They added a footnote acknowledging that certain evidence, particularly about espionage, was "in conflict with information in possession of the Department of Justice." Accordingly, the government was not asking the Court to "take judicial notice" of those facts set out in the DeWitt report. This attempt to "wave the red flag" met opposition from the Solicitor General and the Assistant Attorney General. They substituted a footnote that eliminated any reference to the espionage allegations in the report. Instead, the footnote ambiguously stated:

We have specifically recited in this brief the facts relating to the justification for the evacuation, of which we ask the Court to take judicial notice; and we rely upon the Final Report only to the extent that it relates to such facts.[34]

Ennis and Burling signed the brief urging that the Supreme Court affirm Korematsu's conviction. In Irons' view, "institutional loyalty had prevailed over personal conscience."[35] He believed that if Ennis and Burling had been willing to resign in protest and disclose their reasons, it could have changed the Court's decision and repudiated the Government's policy.

In subsequent interviews reflecting on these incidents,

Ennis offered an explanation of why he and John Burling (who died in 1959) had swallowed their doubts and continued to work on the internment cases. . . . "I really believe we didn't [quit] . . . because we didn't want to put it in the hands of Justice Department lawyers who were gung-ho for the Army's position. I think we felt that we'd just stay with it and do the best that we could, which wasn't a hell of a lot." Ennis also confessed . . . that "when I look back on it now I don't know why I didn't resign."

Ennis had in fact talked of resigning [in protest of the evacuation order]. . . . There seems little doubt that his resignation at that point would not have affected Roosevelt's decision. . . . It seems more likely, however, that had Ennis and Burling resigned in October 1944, in protest at Solicitor General Fahy's capitulation to McCloy over the disputed footnote in the Korematsu brief, such a dramatic step might well have changed the outcome of that crucial case.[36]

1. How would you have handled the problems confronting Ennis and Burling in the wartime evacuation cases? Does preparing a brief from the solicitor general's office carry special responsibilities to present a full and fair record? Consider the view of former Solicitor General Archibald Cox, who maintained that the office would maximize its credibility if it was willing to take a "somewhat disinterested and wholly candid position even when it means surrendering a victory."[37]

On the one hand, it is clear that the record was inadequate to support the military's justification for the evacuation. A fuller factual record might have led to a better Supreme Court decision. Concealment ultimately damaged the credibility of all concerned: the Court, the army, and the government's lawyers. Given the enormous harm to Japanese Americans, should attorneys in the Solicitor General's office have taken special care to ensure the integrity of military and judicial decision-making?

On the other hand, how would you assess the costs of provoking a confrontation with high-level army officials during wartime and eroding their trust in government attorneys? Are you persuaded by Ennis's argument that he wanted to prevent the case from falling into the hands of more "gung-ho" pro-military lawyers? Consider Bernard Williams's observation that the rationale of "working from within" has kept many "queasy people tied to many appalling ventures for remarkably long periods."[38] Is this an example?

2. For lawyers, the difficulties of making such moral judgments are further complicated by questions of role. Where trade-offs between ethical principles and political expediency appear necessary, who should decide what balance to strike? In legal practice generally, bar ethical rules provide that lawyers "shall abide by a client's decisions concerning the objectives of representation . . . and shall consult with clients as to the means by which they are to be pursued."[39] Who is the client of the government lawyer? If, as many commentators insist, it is the public generally, and not any particular government agency or decision maker, how is the public's interest to be determined?

University of Chicago law professor Geoffrey Miller notes:

Despite its surface plausibility, the notion that government attorneys represent some transcendental "public interest" is, I believe, incoherent. It is commonplace that there are as many ideas of the "public interest" as there are people who think about the subject. . . . If attorneys could freely sabotage the actions of their agencies out of a subjective sense of the public interest, the result would be a disorganized, inefficient bureaucracy, and a public distrustful of its own government. More fundamentally, the idea that government attorneys serve some higher purpose fails to place the attorney within a structure of democratic government.[40]

Miller concludes that although government attorneys should not assist clearly illegal conduct, neither should they substitute their judgment for that of a political process that is generally accepted as legitimate.

Many practitioners take a similar view. As one study concluded, "most Justice Department lawyers continue to believe that most agencies, most of the time, are entitled to their day in court and to have the best said in their behalf that the legal imagination can devise—the more so because the agencies are captive clients who cannot seek representation elsewhere." On this analysis, a government lawyer who attempts to further the public interest is "not a lawyer representing a client but a lawyer representing herself."[41]

By contrast, other lawyers argue that government counsel have obligations as public servants to "pursue justice" and to avoid assisting an action that they believe is unconstitutional. From this perspective, "where the client is the Government itself, he who represents this vague entity often becomes its conscience, bearing a heavier responsibility than usually encountered by . . . lawyers."[42]

What is your view? If you had been Ennis, how would you have defined your responsibilities? What situational pressures might have influenced your view?

3. Consider the decision of Deputy Attorney General Sally Yates, who refused to allow the Department of Justice to defend President Trump's January 27, 2017, Executive Order banning immigration from seven Muslim-majority countries.[43] In defending her refusal as not just a policy difference, Yates explained: "President Trump asserted [the ban] had nothing to do with religious discrimination, yet he'd stated [the contrary] . . . many times on the campaign trail. How could I dispatch Department of Justice lawyers to argue something that wasn't grounded in truth?"[44] She released a statement saying, "I am responsible for ensuring that the positions we take in court remain consistent with this institution's solemn obligation to always seek justice and stand for what is right. At present, I am not convinced that the defense of the Executive Order is consistent with these responsibilities nor am I convinced that the Executive Order is lawful."[45] In a later speech at Harvard, when asked why she didn't just resign, Yates stated, "[M]y resignation would have

protected my own personal integrity . . . but I believed, and I still think, that I had an obligation to also protect the integrity of the Department of Justice."[46]

Shortly after Yates released her statement refusing to defend the Executive Order, President Trump fired her. He explained that "the Acting Attorney General, Sally Yates, has betrayed the Department of Justice by refusing to enforce a legal order designed to protect the citizens of the United States."[47] Commentators were divided on Yates's conduct. Some thought that she should have resigned if she thought the president's policy was an unconstitutional infringement on religious liberty.[48] Others thought that she was right to assert the independence of the Attorney General's position and to force Trump to fire her.[49] What is your view? What would you have done in her place?

4. Another Trump lawyer took a different view of how to respond to what he considered unlawful decisions by the President. Trump waived executive privilege and allowed White House Counsel Donald McGahn to testify before Special Counsel Robert Mueller during his investigation into Russian hacking of the 2016 presidential election. According to Mueller's Report, Trump ordered McGahn to fire Mueller based on pretextual claims of conflicts of interest.[50] McGahn had to threaten to resign to stop the President's repeated demands that he remove Mueller. When the story became public, President Trump demanded that McGahn deny the allegations, insisted on creation of a false record to substantiate the lie, and had a staff secretary warn McGahn that Trump would fire him if he refused to comply. McGahn refused. Trump denounced him as a "lying bastard," but did not fire him.[51] The Special Counsel Report found McGahn to be a credible witness with no motive to lie, and accepted his account, but stopped short of determining whether the President's actions constituted attempted obstruction of justice. McGahn subsequently left the White House Counsel office to join a private law firm, and acquiesced in President Trump's refusal to let him testify before a House congressional committee investigating these and related issues. How would you assess McGahn's actions?

PROBLEM 6-3

One of the most contested issues in the 2016 presidential election was the decision by Democratic candidate Hillary Clinton to use a private e-mail server for government business while she was Secretary of State. She claimed that it had been more convenient to have a single account and that she had not used the private account for classified material. The FBI, headed by former federal prosecutor James Comey, opened an investigation.

Comey's handling of the investigation was controversial from the outset. According to his account in *A Higher Loyalty*, Attorney General Loretta Lynch early on requested him to refer to the inquiry as a "matter" rather than an "investigation." He refused, interpreting the request as politically motivated, noting the "FBI doesn't do matters." He did not head the "Federal Bureau of Matters."[52] After Loretta Lynch had an informal meeting on an airport tarmac with

Bill Clinton while the investigation was ongoing, public outcry forced her to recuse herself from oversight. That left Comey in the uncomfortable position of having to decide whether, when, and how to discuss the scope and findings of the investigation.

His first controversial decision was to depart from longstanding FBI practice and comment publicly on the Bureau's finding that Clinton had used her personal e-mail account to review at least 36 classified e-mails. Comey characterized the conduct as "extremely careless" rather than criminal.[53]

His second decision, two weeks before the 2016 election, was to disclose that the FBI had reopened the investigation after discovering hundreds of thousands more emails from Hillary Clinton on the personal computer of one of Clinton's staff members. The discovery occurred during an unrelated inquiry into sexting by former New York congressman Anthony Weiner, who was married to one of Clinton's top advisors. Comey was concerned that he could not complete an investigation of the newly discovered e-mails before the election in November and felt that he faced two "terrible options" regarding whether to disclose the inquiry. As he saw it, "[T]o speak might affect the election. To fail to speak would be an affirmative act of concealment."[54] He decided that concealment would be worse. If he remained silent and the investigation revealed criminal activity by Clinton, the fallout would be "catastrophic to the integrity of the FBI and the Department of Justice."[55] When a member of his staff asked, "Should you consider that what you are about to do might elect Donald Trump?" he responded, "It is a good question but not for a moment can I consider it. Because down that path lies the death of the FBI as an independent force in American life. If we start making decisions based on whose political fortunes will be affected, we are lost."[56]

Two days before the election, he released a statement indicating that the investigation had not revealed any new incriminating information. Many viewed that statement as too little too late. In his memoir, Comey concludes, "[T]he idea that my decision had any impact on the outcome leaves me feeling mildly nauseous."[57]

Should it?

NOTES AND QUESTIONS

1. In a review of Comey's memoir describing his dilemma, Ronald Goldfarb states:

> How ironic it is that former FBI Director James Comey, the man whose behavior critics claim—and polls show—cost candidate Clinton the 2016 election, was fired by the man who was elected in her place, a man who Comey now says is morally unfit to hold that office. . . . Comey is a preachy, moralizing, self-promoting man who made a historic blunder, one he still doesn't understand.[58]

What is your view? What would you have done in his place?

2. After his election, Trump fired Comey for his refusal to curtail the investigation by Robert Mueller into Russian election interference. Comey subsequently wrote an op-ed in the *New York Times* commenting on the failure of other Trump administration lawyer leaders to stand up to the president's subversion of the rule of law. According to Comey, accomplished attorneys such as Attorney General William Barr and Assistant Attorney General Rob Rosenstein, had compromised their reputations by inaction. Comey wrote,

> Trump eats your soul in small bites. It starts with your sitting silent while he lies, both in public and private, making you complicit by your silence. In meetings with him, his assertions about what "everyone thinks" and what is "obviously true" wash over you, unchallenged . . . because he's the president and he rarely stops talking. As a result, Mr. Trump pulls all of those present in a silent circle of assent. Speaking rapid fire with no spot for others to jump into the conversation, Mr. Trump makes everyone a co-conspirator to his preferred set of facts or delusions. . . . From the private circle of assent, it moves to public displays of personal fealty. . . . To stay you must be seen as on his team, so you make further compromises. . . . And then you are lost. He has eaten your soul.[59]

   If Comey is right about that process, what could help lawyer leaders avoid it?

3. At the end of his essay on moral meltdowns, Luban suggests several lessons for leaders: draw lines in the sand, accept personal responsibility for your actions, and retain the capacity for self-doubt. Another possibility is the mental exercise colloquially known as the "60 Minutes" or "New York Times" test: how would this decision look on prime-time television or the front page of an international newspaper as presented by a skeptical reporter? Would any of those strategies have been useful for Dean, Ennis, or McGahn? What might have helped you or a leader you respect in situations posing analogous moral dilemmas?

4. Another issue raised by the Japanese internment cases involves the distribution of ethical responsibility between leaders and their subordinates. For example, Rule 5.2 of the American Bar Association's Model Rules of Professional Conduct provides that lawyers are bound by ethical rules when they act at another's direction, but that they do not violate those rules if they act in accordance with a supervisory lawyer's "reasonable resolution of an arguable question of professional duty." How helpful is this rule on the facts of the *Korematsu* case, or on the problem on torture set forth below? Does it resolve lawyers' moral responsibility as well as their disciplinary liability?

C. ACCOUNTABILITY

Torture is a longstanding leadership dilemma that has resurfaced with new force during America's "war on terror." The materials that follow explore the issues it poses for government officials, including lawyers, who have been instrumental in shaping American policy.

PHILIP BOBBITT, TERROR AND CONSENT: THE WARS FOR THE TWENTY-FIRST CENTURY

(New York: Alfred A. Knopf, 2008), pp. 361-366, 369-370, 373, 376, 387-388, 390-392

[On] the awful subject of torture . . . I am anxious to make one overriding point: the moral rules that govern the official of a state of consent impose a "duty of consequentialism"—that is, any contemplated course of action must be measured in terms of the foreseeable costs and benefits that are its result and not against any absolute or categorical rule. . . .

Let me deal at once with the notorious hypothetical of the "ticking bomb." The . . . hypothetical is usually posed like this: Imagine that interrogators learn that a terrorist in custody knows where a bomb has been planted [and refuses to disclose the information]. . . . Threats, harsh words, unpleasant behavior escalating to beatings and other violence, are suggested, and the question is asked: At which of these methods would one cavil?

The right answer—the only answer available to the official of the state of consent who has taken up the responsibility of protecting the safety of the public whose endorsement has put him in this position of authority—is that whatever methods are most effective must be employed. Indeed, Judge Richard Posner has argued, "If the stakes are high enough [even] torture is permissible. No one who doubts that should be in a position of responsibility." It is an easy question.

But look closely at the assumptions the hypothetical enfolds. We are to assume (1) that we have a person in custody, (2) that the person is a terrorist who (3) actually knows the location of a bomb that (4) is about to go off, and that (5) under torture he will accurately disclose the location of the bomb, that (6) cannot be determined by any other means. In such a situation, only a self-absorbed monster would say, sweetly, "Oh no, I mustn't (even if I wish I could), sorry," thus deliberately sentencing unnumbered innocents to death and dismemberment in order to protect the manifestly guilty.

The real difficulty does not lie in such a situation, as we shall see, but rather with cases whose contours are not so carefully shaped so as to provide such perfect information. Suppose the person we have in custody is a roommate—someone otherwise unimplicated who can lead us to the terrorist but who refuses to give this information. Suppose that person is suspected of terrorist activity, but there is substantial doubt about his involvement. Suppose his pleas that he really doesn't know the location of the bomb are plausible. Suppose there is no bomb—yet—but the person knows of plans to acquire such weapons. Suppose he is so averse to pain that he will say anything that he believes will appease his captors and in his fear provides the most plausible, but not the most accurate, information. Suppose an inhibition-reducing drug, coupled with a friendly and trusted interrogator, is a more effective means than violence, or that data cross-correlation, sensors that detect explosives, or other methods are more effective. Suppose that all these suppositions are in fact true or, more likely, suppose that we don't really know which ones are true.

This is not to assume that coercive interrogations and even torture are necessarily ineffective, a claim that will be discussed below. It is rather that their potential effectiveness depends upon a great many factors and that the "ticking bomb" hypothetical tends to focus our attention away from those contextual factors.

The preliminary claim I wish to make is simply that anyone with the responsibility for protecting others must discharge that responsibility with an eye firmly on the consequences—that is, the relationship between means and ends must govern the decision. If, for the public official whose role has been authorized by the consent of the governed, anything else trumps this relationship, he or she should resign. A pacifist should not be asked (or allowed) to be a general. . . .

The origin of the "duty of consequentialism" lies in the constitutional makeup of the state of consent. That is because the officials of a state of consent are bound to behave, in their official capacity, in a way that maximizes the "ends" or goals of the persons in whose name they govern. It is this delegation that imposes the duty of evaluating means in terms of the ends they serve, and that displaces the deontological or a priori moral rules that are so much a part of personal life. . . .

If the customary institutions of a state of consent have forbidden the torture and the cruel and degrading treatment of prisoners, then the conscientious official has little choice but to obey. He cannot substitute his personal moral imperatives as if he were acting as a nongovernmental agent. So what does he do when the "ticking bomb" case actually does arise? He disobeys the treaty, the statute, the regulation, and saves the city, of course. It is the right thing to do, not because of his private morality (which might in any case vary from official to official), but rather because the consequentialist calculus of obeying the law is so clear and so absolutely negative. This was, it will be recalled, Lincoln's position when he suspended habeas corpus during the American Civil War—in direct contradiction of a specific provision of the U.S. Constitution—in order to arrest some 13,000 persons under martial law. Defending his decision in a message to Congress on July 4, 1861, he wrote:

> To state the question more directly, are all the laws, but one, to go unexecuted and the government itself go to pieces, lest that one be violated? Even in such a case, would not the official oath be broken, if the government should be overthrown, when it was believed that disregarding the single law, would tend to preserve it?

This is plainly a consequentialist argument, but look carefully at how it sorts out ends and means. The objective sought (the end) that justifies the violation of law (the means) is in fact the preservation of the rule of law, which is shall we say "dented" by the very means that avoid a catastrophic collision. . . .

The Prevailing Law

Following the exposure of German and Japanese practices in World War II, the U.N. General Assembly adopted in 1948 the Universal Declaration of Human Rights, which contains an absolute ban on torture in order to eliminate, according to the drafters, "methods of torture and cruel punishment which were practiced in the recent past by the Nazis and fascists." Article 5 of the declaration provides: "No one shall be subjected to torture or to cruel, inhuman or degrading treatment or punishment."

This ban has been incorporated into the International Covenant on Civil and Political Rights (ICCPR) and into the Convention Against Torture or Other Cruel, Inhuman or Degrading Treatment or Punishment (the Torture Convention), which provides in Article 2 that "No exceptional circumstances whatsoever, whether a state of war or a threat of war, internal political instability or any other public emergency, may be invoked as a justification of torture." . . .

It may be, as Sanford Levinson has argued, that the very categorical nature of these prohibitions against torture has tempted states—including the U.K. and the U.S.—to write definitions of torture that are rather narrow. Indeed, because the U.S. administration at one time appeared to have interpreted away the restraints created by conventions to which it is a signatory, partly on the basis of Senate reservations made at the time of U.S. consent to these conventions, the U.S. Congress in 2005 adopted the McCain amendment, which provides: "No individual in the custody or under the physical control of the United States Government, regardless of nationality or physical location, shall be subject to cruel, inhuman, or degrading treatment or punishment."

[The distinction between torture and cruel and degrading treatment] . . . has been recognized by the European Court of Human Rights, the Israeli Supreme Court, and the U.S. Department of State. The importance of this distinction, since both are unlawful, is that the U.S. Supreme Court has recognized a "necessity" exception with respect to cruel and degrading treatment. This takes us a long way toward the recognition of certain otherwise unlawful methods that was at the core of the Bush administration's efforts to legitimate coercive interrogation techniques.

Ends and Means

There are three basic objectives (ends) sought by states when they employ torture. They can be categorized as evidentiary, political, and informational.

Evidentiary

. . . At present, there is no move in either the American or British jurisdictions to use information gained by torture conducted by their officials as evidence in court. And this in turn has led to rather absurd efforts to prosecute persons believed to be lethal terrorists on other, trivial grounds so as to continue their detention. . . .

Political

Torture is undertaken for political purposes when the object is less to coerce than to intimidate. This may be aimed at the victim himself, if he is subsequently released, or his family and associates, or even an entire society. Rather than hiding its hideous acts, if torture is employed for political ends, then it must be advertised. Although there is an ancient history of such practices, in the current day nothing is quite so exemplary as the practice of human beheadings by al Qaeda and its franchisees. . . . [An example was the video posted in 2004 of a Philadelphia businessman, Nicholas Berg, who was kidnapped while working on an Iraq construction project. He was pictured screaming in agony as his captors] appeared to saw through his neck, shouting, "God is great!" . . .

Informational

The infliction of pain and the fear of pain can also be used simply to extract information. It is in this context that the subject of torture was raised after 2001, when the urgency of preventing another 9/11 attack suggested to many that harsher methods of interrogation were necessary in order to thwart terrorist plots.

"Terrorists" was the term used by the Nazis in France for the Free French partisans known as the Resistance. Jean Moulin was called "the martyr of the Resistance" because following his capture by the Gestapo he was tortured so violently that he died on the way to a German prison. . . . [O]thers claim that [the torturers of Nicholas Berg], too, are resisters to an unlawful occupation. These complexities demand that we be able to tell the difference, and explain the difference, between those who wish to impose terror through an occupation and those occupiers who come to dispel terror and are risking their lives to do so.

It is of course tempting to shun this difficult task and simply to say that the use of violence in interrogation, for any purpose, is always impermissible; that it is the means, and not the ends, that must guide our judgment. This move is made immeasurably easier by making the assumption that torture simply never works. Persons in pain and afraid are unlikely to give correct information in their eagerness to appease their tormenters. Consider then this account, however, told to Bruce Hoffman by a Sri Lankan army officer charged with fighting the Tamil Tigers:

> [His] unit had apprehended three terrorists who, it suspected, had recently planted somewhere in the city a bomb that was then ticking away, the minutes counting down to catastrophe. The three men were brought before [him]. He asked them where the bomb was. The terrorists—highly

dedicated and steeled to resist interrogation—remained silent. [He] asked the question again, advising them that if they did not tell him what he wanted to know, he would kill them. They were unmoved. So [he] took his pistol from his gun belt, pointed it at the forehead of one of them, and shot him dead. The other two, he said, talked immediately; the bomb, which had been placed in a crowded railway station and set to explode during the evening rush hour, was found and defused, and countless lives were saved.

If we put this in the context that the Tamil insurgency had already claimed the lives of more than 60,000 people and that it was arrayed against a democratically elected government whose president, candidate for president, and the Indian prime minister Rajiv Gandhi it had murdered, one is hard-pressed not to conclude that the putative victims of an atrocity deserve more care than the would-be perpetrators.

Ends do matter. As we shall see, however, only when they are related to means can we derive usable rules.

Means

The problem is made more realistic by assuming that, in some circumstances, torture and assassination are effective—an assumption as to which there is some debate. Nevertheless, it must be obvious that at least in some situations this will prove to be the case and that these are the situations for which we require an answer, not a blithe assuming away of the problem. Because these activities are conducted in the dark, there is little adequate data to confirm an assumption either way. Occasionally, there are reports in open sources such as the case of an Al Qaeda terrorist, Jamal Beghal. He was arrested in the Dubai airport in October 2001. His lawyer subsequently charged that he had been "tossed into a darkened cell, handcuffed to a chair, blindfolded and beaten and that his family was threatened." It is not unreasonable to conclude that these measures had some effect: after some weeks in captivity, he suddenly decided to cooperate and "out poured a wealth of information" that thwarted a planned bombing of the U.S. embassy in Paris and could have prevented the 2001 bombing of the World Trade Center in New York had it come earlier.

I will discuss four alternatives prescribing what means of coercive interrogation are permissible. These are (1) an absolute ban; (2) a qualified ban, perhaps permitting some forms of cruel and degrading treatment but banning torture; (3) a ban with exceptions, perhaps permitting torture and any lesser means in certain certifiable circumstances; (4) rendition to a lawful authority, permitting some forms of coercive interrogation, including even torture, depending on the willingness of the State transparently to acknowledge its role.

Absolute Ban

The first thing to recognize about an absolute ban is that it will not prevent all torture any more than an absolute ban on smoking in elevators means that every cigar is extinguished by every solitary passenger. Even draconian penalties like stoning to death have not stopped adultery in Saudi Arabia; nor has capital punishment in America stopped capital crimes. . . . Indeed, the most important moral lesson of the "ticking bomb" problem is that no rule can entirely govern our conscience. That is the lesson of free will, which makes the conscience and thus morality itself possible. Free will makes alternative worlds possible, and one of these must always be a future in which a crime is committed rather than a law obeyed.

This means that an "absolute ban" is actually more like a lottery: it leaves to chance when torture occurs by refusing to specify the precise exculpatory circumstances. On the other hand, an absolute ban can be enforced with greater consistency and, if the penalties are significant, can bring about the highest level of deterrence. Indeed, an absolute ban has to be tightly enforced, or it loses its point. . . .

"No torture" rules sound fine, but the world in which they are to be applied can present situations in which such rules should not be followed. Is the "absolute ban" the right rule for the real world? In such a world, an order by the president to torture a captive would be an unlawful order, regardless of even the most extreme circumstances, and therefore it is highly unpredictable whether it would be obeyed.

Qualified Ban

This reflects an effort to capture in law and regulations those truly exceptional situations in which there is a political consensus that highly coercive methods, even torture, should be tried. Perhaps the most imaginative of these proposals is the suggestion by Alan Dershowitz, that courts—perhaps special courts—be authorized to issue "torture warrants." Studying practices in Israel—which is "the only country at the end of the twentieth century officially to sanction the intentional infliction of pain and suffering during interrogation"—Dershowitz concluded that the "ticking bomb" scenario had led officials to an increasing use of torture and highly coercive means of interrogation in cases quite remote from the assumptions of the scenario.

In 1987, the Landau Commission in Israel authorized the use of "moderate physical pressure" in ticking-bomb situations. A practice initially justified as rare and exceptional, taken only when necessary to save lives, gradually became standard procedure. Soon, some 80 to 90 percent of Palestinian security detainees were being tortured. . . .

Dershowitz argued that judicial oversight would curtail or eliminate these practices in a way that "don't ask, don't tell" rules and paper prohibitions had failed to do; he believed that requiring a warrant of some kind as "a precondition to the infliction of any type of torture under any circumstances" would accomplish this. When torture was taken out of the clandestine area of government activity and exposed to visibility and accountability, Dershowitz held, torture would drastically decline. In such circumstances, the "ticking bomb" hypothetical might actually serve as a limiting, rather than expanding, engine because a judicial warrant could be granted in this, but in no other, situation.

Notable objections have been made to this proposal: . . . that even with respect to warrants, the affidavits supporting them, the requests for them, and the judges' decisions granting them are all likely to be secret, which does little for transparency; that, because warrants are issued in ex parte proceedings before judges or magistrates chosen by the applicant, they are an ineffective check on executive discretion. What makes them effective in the ordinary criminal context is the use of materials gained by warrant in subsequent trials. That presumably is unlikely to be a significant motivation in a war against terror, particularly if enemy agents can be indefinitely detained without the usual trial proceedings. Finally, if torture is written into law—even if only for extreme situations—its use is bound to become routine, as interrogators test the limits of the law.

Ban with Exceptions

This proposal probably comes closest to the customary way in which such matters are usually dealt with in the democracies. In *Leon v. Wainwright* the Eleventh Circuit considered the following facts. Two kidnappers seized a taxi driver and held him for ransom. One of them was apprehended while collecting the ransom. The court found that

> [w]hen he refused to tell them the location, he was set upon by several of the officers . . . they threatened and physically abused him by twisting his arm and choking him until he revealed where [the cab driver] was being held. . . . This was . . . a group of concerned officers acting in a reasonable manner to obtain information they needed in order to protect another individual from bodily harm or death. [The acts of torture] were motivated by the immediate necessity to find the victim and save his life.

Sanford Levinson, who more than anyone courageously broke the silence of the academy on this subject, has concluded that such extraordinary methods must always be forbidden by law. This view need not make terrorists of those who protect us in the most perilous cases, however, because the last word rests with the juries and publics that are unlikely to condemn those persons who have acted wisely out of pity and not irresponsibly out of cruelty. Levinson holds that it is better wholly to outlaw such activities by the military and the police knowing that, on occasion, they may breach the law out of necessity. This is an appealing approach because it attempts to preserve our values in the face of anguishing choices. . . .

This approach relies upon a necessity defense to the purportedly "absolute" ban. Of course, the officers couldn't know for certain that the courts would exonerate them, any more than the intelligence officers who torture a terrorist to locate a ticking bomb are certain they will not be prosecuted. But it can be assumed that no jury is likely to convict the men who saved their city, especially if the alleged offense is committed against a person attempting mass murder.

The principal virtues of such uncertainty are three-fold. First, it allows us to state that we have an absolute ban on torture (in principle), not unlike the absolute prohibition against congressional action that abridges the freedom of speech, which in its application makes room for laws against disclosing classified documents, colluding to fix prices, and libel. Second, it depends upon the "bracketing" of the calculus of necessity, forcing the agent who must decide whether to disobey the law, to determine if torture would really save sufficient lives to justify its terrible imposition. As Henry Shue put one variation on this:

> An act of torture ought to remain illegal so that anyone who sincerely believes such an act to be the least available evil is placed in the position of needing to justify his or her act morally in order to defend himself or herself legally. . . . Anyone who thinks an act of torture is justified should have no alternative but to convince a group of peers in a public trial that all necessary conditions for a morally permissible act were indeed satisfied. . . . If the situation approximates those in the imaginary examples in which torture seems possible to justify [such as the "ticking bomb" scenario], a judge can surely be expected to suspend the sentence.

Third, it avoids the real cost of giving potential adversaries and terrorists extensive knowledge about what to expect when they are captured. As with nuclear deterrence, governments have been unwilling to spell out exact limits to the action they would regard as tolerable in extremis.

This proposal has widespread support among civil libertarians, philosophers, and jurists who "want nonlethal torture to be used if it could prevent thousands of deaths, but [do] not want torture to be officially recognized by our legal system." "It is better," wrote Judge Richard Posner, "to stick with our perhaps overly strict rules, trusting executive officials to break them when the stakes are high enough to enable the officials to obtain political absolution for their illegal conduct."

Nevertheless, this approach is not without its flaws. Far from prompting the rigorous analysis that its proponents imagine, because it is essentially a customary approach it relies upon our intuitive sense of our values, which is specific to every particular culture. The reason to debate an issue openly and write our conclusions into law is to overcome the many different attitudes that prevail in the military, among lawyers, in religious circles, and so on. . . .

At what point does custom become law, whatever the actual provisions of the law? . . . [I]f the answer is "sometimes," then how can we expect conscientious men and women to obey the law—whatever it may be—the law being so uncertain?

None of these approaches seems fully satisfactory. Absolute bans on torture, absolutely enforced, are essentially lotteries, and while they are admirably conscientious about the rights of prisoners, they are studiedly indifferent to the fate of the terrorist's victims. Qualified bans are legalistic, political attempts to manage torture. They are, nevertheless, inconsistent with international law, import a judicial process into warfare, and as currently proposed, are probably unconstitutional on the grounds that they authorize punishment without a jury's determination of guilt. Bans on torture that depend upon exceptional behavior can call on the legitimating ethos of society because they are "customary" approaches.... Yet for that very reason, such an approach can be highly unreliable, especially in a complex society that holds many cultures within it. An approach that depends upon guessing how a court would calculate the necessity of breaking the law is a pretty uncertain one. To save a million lives, anyone ought to be willing to brutalize a terrorist in the midst of his fevered attempt to become a mass murderer. But what about five lives, when the person to be tortured may or may not have the crucial information—or may or may not be a terrorist?

Implications of an Ends and Means Analysis

... The use of violence in the Wars against Terror is justified by our claims of self-defense. Having been attacked, we have the right to defend our societies.... In the Wars against Terror, violence can be used when a state of consent is threatened with violence by the agents of states or inchoate would-be states of terror.... The argument from *self-defense*, however, permits [only measures against the suspected terrorist, not a terrorist's child or an]... innocent bystander who may have crucial information but declines to give it up.... There must be some independent authority whose incentives are not so wholly driven by the desire to maximize the amount of information gathered, who is trustworthy enough not to disclose the secrets of operations and intelligence sources, and who is sophisticated enough to be able to accurately assess the claims of the interrogator. Moreover, such authority must be accorded legal status under international law.

What is needed is not a judge so much as a jury—that is, not an official who represents the government seeking information but a group of persons chosen from a pool of responsible people who represent, not the government, but the society in whose name the government is acting. Their identities can be secret in order to avoid reprisal, but they should be chosen randomly from the largest number that is practicable. Unless they can be persuaded that the detainee is in fact a terrorist with valuable information, he cannot be coercively interrogated. Unless they can be persuaded that he has lied—unless, that is, his claims cannot be persuasively disconfirmed—any coercive methods beyond the mildest cannot be used. Such procedures, it apparently needs to be added, must be created pursuant to statutory action by legislative bodies, and whatever they authorize must be clearly distinguished from the infliction of pain that is tantamount to torture under existing law. I have in mind coercive methods such as sleep deprivation, isolation, and the administration of drugs. Where there is no pain, there is no torture. The terrifying prospect of pain is a kind of terror itself, and thus once a state of consent is believed to practice torture as a matter of course, then—even if some progress is made in a War against Terror by such practices—that state will have suffered a considerable blow in the Wars against Terror. To reiterate: it is terror that we are fighting, not simply terrorists....

Summary

There must be an absolute ban on torture and coercive interrogations of any kind for political or evidentiary purposes. There ought to be an absolute ban on torture or coercive interrogations for the purpose of collecting tactical information, with the acceptance that this ban will be violated in the "ticking bomb" circumstances: the prosecutions that must follow will allow juries to consider the mitigating question of whether a reasonable person, motivated by a sincere desire to protect others, would have violated the law. . . .

Bruce Hoffman and others have argued that it was the use of terror against captives in Algiers in 1957 that outraged public opinion in France while alienating the Muslim community in North Africa, swelling the ranks of the FLN and increasing its popularity even while French forces relying on information gained from torture were breaking the back of the revolt. The French army's tactical success in the Battle of Algiers led, in other words, to the strategic defeat of the overall endeavor. So it will be with the wars against global, networked terror if we do not openly and transparently confront these issues, writing laws that reflect a democratic debate, and applying those laws sensitively in those rare contexts when an heroic official risks prosecution to save the rest of us. Otherwise, when the dreadful truth emerges, domestic opinion will abandon its government's war efforts in disgust. . . . [We must not] forget precisely what we are fighting for in the effort to ensure that we win.

NOTES AND QUESTIONS

1. In *Unspeakable Acts, Ordinary People*, John Conroy notes that "throughout the world torturers are rarely punished, and when they are, the punishment rarely corresponds to the severity of the crime."[60] One reason for this, according to Conroy, is that torturers are generally not sadists who are easy to condemn. Rather, they typically view themselves as servants of the state, engaged in a just war. To reduce cognitive dissonance, they often engage in the kind of euphemistic recharacterizations of the issue described in Chapters 3 and 5. So, as psychologists Carol Tavris and Elliot Aronson note, one strategy "is to say that if we do it, it isn't torture. 'We do not torture,' said George Bush, when he was confronted with evidence that we do. 'We use an alternative set of procedures'"—that is, "enhanced interrogation."[61] Another reason for the inadequacy of sanctions is that government leaders are often reluctant to expose their own administration's complicity in abuse. Is the United States an exception? Consider that issue in light of the materials below on Justice Department officials who gave advice on interrogation policy in the war on terror.

2. In the preceding excerpt, Bobbitt quotes federal judge and law professor Richard Posner, who has argued that even if torture is "always wrong, there is such a thing as a lesser wrong committed to avoid a greater one."[62] "If the stakes are high enough," Posner claims, "torture is permissible. No one who

doubts that this is the case should be in a position of responsibility."[63] Do you agree?

3. Law professor David Luban acknowledges that the "ticking time bomb" scenario is not "completely unreal." One example he cites is a 1995 airline bomb and assassination attempt that was thwarted by Philippine police, who tortured a Pakistani conspirator. Other commentators including Bobbitt have identified further examples.[64] However, as Luban notes, the difficulty in formulating policy based on the ticking-bomb hypothetical is that it "cheats its way around [real-world] difficulties by stipulating that the bomb is there and that officials know it and know they have the man who planted it."[65] But in all but the rarest circumstances, interrogators are dealing in probabilities. There may be a plot, the prisoner may know enough to prevent it, and may break under torture. Then the questions are, how likely do those circumstances need to be? How many lives need to be at stake? What techniques should be permissible? Should we torture the prisoner's wife or children? "Do you really want to make the torture decision by running the numbers?" Luban asks. And if only the numbers matter, he notes, "then torturing loved ones is almost a no brainer if you think it will work." A further problem with the ticking-bomb hypothetical is that it assumes a "single, ad hoc decision . . . in a desperate emergency. But . . . the real world is a world of policies, guidelines, and directives. It is a world of practices. . . ." That world requires addressing issues such as whether we want a "professional cadre of trained torturers" or federal grants for research on torture techniques. For Luban, the question then becomes: "Do we really want to create a torture culture and the kind of people who inhabit it?"[66]

Is that question rhetorical? Even Posner warns against creating rules that legitimize torture in specified circumstances: "Having been regularized, the practice will become regular. Better to leave in place the formal and customary prohibitions, but with the understanding that they will not be enforced in extreme circumstances."[67] But is that solution open to the problems of uncertainty and inconsistency that Bobbitt raises? Is there a better alternative?

4. In 2009, the CIA released three documents on the intelligence that had been gained from detainees. A 2004 report by its inspector general and memos from 2004 and 2005 failed to show that "enhanced interrogation techniques" such as waterboarding, which many consider torture, prevented a single imminent terrorist act.[68] Does that affect your assessment of the conduct of any of the lawyers involved in government decisions on the issue? Suppose there had been a successful example of prevention. Would that change your view? Consider Justice Holmes's classic dissent in a case involving illegal wiretaps. It should not, in his view, matter whether the wiretaps yielded important evidence:

> In a government of laws, existence of the government will be imperiled if it fails to observe the law scrupulously. Our Government is the potent, the omnipresent teacher. For good or for ill, it teaches

the whole people by its example. Crime is contagious. If the Government becomes a lawbreaker, it breeds contempt for law; it invites every man to become a law unto himself; it invites anarchy.[69]

Do the same arguments apply to torture, and to governments that determine when violation of international conventions on torture are justified? How would Bobbitt respond? How would you?

5. To what extent should public opinion matter? A 2016 Reuters poll asked participants if torture could be justified "against suspected terrorists to obtain information about terrorism." About 25 percent said it is "often" justified and 38 percent said it is "sometimes" justified. Only 15 percent said it is never justified.[70] A 2015 Roper poll found Americans more closely divided, with 51 percent saying torture is often or sometimes justified to gain information from suspected terrorists, and 47 percent saying it is rarely or never justified.[71] According to a Pew International survey of 38 nations, Americans are more likely to say torture is justified (58 percent) than the global mean (40 percent).[72] However, most Americans (58 percent) think rules against torture should be maintained because it is morally wrong and weakening these rules may lead to torture of U.S. soldiers abroad.[73] As a policy leader, how would these views affect your position?

6. What role should global opinion play in shaping policy? For example, the American public strongly opposes prosecuting terrorism suspects in civilian courts. The international community, however, is deeply suspicious of any verdicts reached in military proceedings that have fewer procedural protections and less transparency than criminal trials.[74] Attorney General Eric Holder was caught in the middle. As Elisa Massimino, the president of Human Rights First, noted, "Politically, these issues are poisonous. . . . You can't finesse it."[75] Holder himself believed that trying 9/11 terrorism suspects in civilian courts conveys an important moral message: "Values matter in this fight. We need to give those who might follow these mad men a good sense of what America is and what America can be. We are militarily strong, but we are morally stronger."[76] Critics, however, charged that Holder was trying to "protect his own image," and public opposition forced him to back down from his initial decision to try 9/11 defendants in Manhattan.[77]

If you had been in Holder's position, what factors would have been most important in your decision?

PROBLEM 6-4[78]

Consider the leadership roles of government officials who either authorized enhanced interrogation tactics or advised those who did. As noted earlier, public servants are often thought to have a special responsibility to the public as well as to the administration or agency that they serve.[79] The materials that follow explore this responsibility in several contexts related to the war on terror.

The first involves a 2002 meeting at Guantanamo Naval Base to discuss the use of enhanced interrogation techniques on detainees. Two of the ten participants listed in the meeting minutes were lawyers: one, a Lieutenant Colonel, was Staff Judge Advocate to the task force commander at Guantanamo; the other was assistant general counsel to the CIA [CIA AGC] and chief counsel to the CIA's counterterrorism center. The other participants were military and intelligence officers.[80] Nine days after this meeting, the Lieutenant Colonel provided a legal memorandum that approved more than a dozen aggressive interrogation techniques, including stress positions, sleep deprivation, intimidation through the use of military dogs, forced nudity, and the "wet towel" form of waterboarding, a technique of simulated drowning.[81] Many of these techniques were used on detainees in Guantanamo and Abu Ghraib Prison in Iraq.

According to minutes taken at the meeting, the Lieutenant Colonel first acknowledged that "we may need to curb the harsher operations while ICRC [the International Committee of the Red Cross] is around. It is better not to expose them to any controversial techniques." When informed that sleep deprivation was being reported at Bagram, a U.S. base in Afghanistan, the Lieutenant Colonel responded: "True, but officially it is not happening. It is not being reported officially. The ICRC is a serious concern. They will be in and out, scrutinizing our operations, unless they are displeased and decide to protest and leave. This would draw a lot of negative attention. . . ."

The following exchange occurred.

CIA AGC: The DOJ has provided much guidance on this issue. The CIA is not held to the same rules as the military. In the past when the ICRC has made a big deal about certain detainees, the DOD has "moved" them away from the attention of ICRC. Upon questioning from the ICRC about their whereabouts, the DOD's response has repeatedly been that the detainee merited no status under the Geneva Convention. The CIA has employed aggressive techniques against less than a handful of suspects since 9/11. Under the Torture Convention, torture has been prohibited under international law, but the language of the statutes is written vaguely. Severe mental and physical pain is prohibited. The mental part is explained as poorly as the physical. Severe physical pain described as anything causing permanent physical damage to major organs or body parts. Mental torture described as anything leading to permanent, profound damage to the senses or personality. It is basically subject to perception. If the detainee dies you're doing it wrong. . . . Any of the techniques that lie on the harshest end of the spectrum must be performed by a highly trained individual. Medical personnel should be present to treat any possible accidents. The CIA operates without military intervention. When the CIA has wanted to use more aggressive techniques in the past, the FBI has pulled their personnel from theatre. In those rare instances, aggressive techniques have proven very helpful.

Lieutenant Colonel: We will need documentation to protect us.

CIA AGC: Yes, if someone dies while aggressive techniques are being used, regardless of cause of death, the backlash of attention would be severely detrimental. Everything must be approved and documented.

When told that law enforcement agency [LEA] personnel would not participate in harsh techniques, the Lieutenant Colonel responded: "There is no legal reason why LEA personnel cannot participate in these operations. . . . [The] LEA choice not to participate in these types of interrogations is more ethical and moral as opposed to legal." The CIA AGC then added: "The videotaping of even totally legal techniques will look 'ugly.'"

This memo drew internal criticism at the Department of Defense, including this e-mail from Mark Fallon, the deputy commander of DOD's Criminal Investigation Task Force:

This looks like the kinds of stuff Congressional hearings are made of. Quotes from [the Lieutenant Colonel] regarding things that are not being reported give the appearance of impropriety. Other comments like "It is basically subject to perception. If the detainee dies you're doing it wrong" and "Any of the techniques that lie on the harshest end of the spectrum must be performed by a highly trained individual. Medical personnel should be present to treat any possible accidents" seem to stretch beyond the bounds of legal propriety. Talk of "wet towel treatment" which results in the lymphatic gland reacting as if you are suffocating, would in my opinion shock the conscience of any legal body looking at using the results of the interrogations or possibly even the interrogators. Someone needs to be considering how history will look back at this.[82]

A second context posing similar issues involved lawyers in the Department of Justice's Office of Legal Counsel (OLC) who participated in drafting what have become known as the "torture memos." They became public shortly after the revelation in 2004 of prisoner torture and humiliation at Abu Ghraib. OLC, which provides legal advice to the executive branch, has a distinguished staff, some of whom go on to become Supreme Court justices and high-ranking officials. OLC opinions are generally taken as authoritative statements of the law governing the executive branch of the federal government.[83] The OLC publishes some of its opinions, but others, including the torture memos, are intended to remain secret. The best known memo was signed by then OLC head Jay S. Bybee (now a federal court of appeals judge), but was written by another OLC lawyer, Berkeley law professor John Yoo.[84] It analyzes federal statutes making torture a crime, which implement the United States' commitment under the international Convention Against Torture (CAT). CAT requires signatories to criminalize torture, defined as government agents' intentional infliction of severe mental or physical pain or suffering. CAT also requires signatories to "undertake to prevent" cruel, inhuman, and degrading treatment that does not rise to the level of torture. The United States banned such treatment in 2005. Two other OLC memos concluded that the Geneva Conventions do not protect either Al Qaeda members or members of the Taliban. These conclusions were relevant in the war against terror because the Geneva Conventions prohibit not only torture but also "outrages against personal dignity, including humiliating and degrading treatment" of captives. Although the State Department's legal advisor and many legal experts strongly criticized the OLC analysis, in 2002 President Bush adopted its conclusions.[85]

Federal law prohibiting torture defines it as "severe physical or mental pain or suffering." In interpreting that prohibition, the Bybee-Yoo memo looked to a definition of "severe pain" in legislation entitling patients to Medicare benefits for emergency medical conditions. Based on that legislation, the memo concluded that the pain

> amounting to torture must be equivalent in intensity to the pain accompanying serious physical injury, such as organ failure, impairment of bodily function, or even death. For purely mental pain or suffering to amount to torture . . . , it must result in significant psychological harm of significant duration, e.g., lasting for months or even years. . . . A defendant must specifically intend to cause prolonged mental harm for the defendant to have committed torture.

The memo also concluded that

> even if an interrogation method arguably were to violate [federal law on torture, it] would be unconstitutional if it impermissibly encroached on the President's constitutional power to conduct a military campaign. As Commander-in-Chief, the President has the constitutional authority to order interrogations of enemy combatants to gain intelligence information concerning the military plans of the enemy. . . . [Those who engaged in such interrogation could also raise] a defense of necessity . . . [or self-defense]. Clearly, any harm that might occur during an interrogation would pale in significance compared to the harm avoided by preventing such an attack, which could take hundreds or thousands of lives.

A third context involving leadership issues involved how to respond in the wake of public criticism that the Bybee-Yoo memo attracted. Although a few law professors pronounced it "standard lawyerly fare," almost all other experts were highly critical.[86] In their view, the lack of public scrutiny or adversarial safeguards for OLC decisions imposed a special responsibility on the office's lawyers to act as "honest brokers," not "hired guns."[87]

Eventually, OLC itself took the highly unusual step of withdrawing the Bybee-Yoo memo, and replacing it with an alternative memo that had a less restrictive view of torture, but still justified enhanced interrogation techniques. On his first day in office, President Obama withdrew all the torture memos and issued an executive order prohibiting enhanced interrogation techniques.

Controversy also centered on whether the lawyers who wrote or approved the torture memos should be subject to any disciplinary action. The Department of Justice's Office of Professional Responsibility (OPR) launched an investigation, the District of Columbia and Pennsylvania Bar associations received disciplinary complaints, and a detainee subject to enhanced interrogation sued Yoo in federal court for violation of his civil rights.[88] A Spanish court also opened a criminal investigation against Bybee and Yoo under the universal jurisdiction provision of the Convention on Torture. None of these actions resulted in sanctions.

In 2010, the Department of Justice released both the report by the OPR and a decision by David Margolis, Associate Deputy Attorney General, rejecting its conclusion. The OPR found that Bybee and Yoo had committed misconduct by failing "to exercise independent legal judgment and render thorough, objective, and candid legal advice" as required by bar ethical rules.[89] Under OPR rules, attorneys engage in professional misconduct when they "intentionally violate or act in reckless disregard of a known unambiguous obligation imposed by law, rule of professional conduct, or Department regulation or policy." According to an OLC memo defining best practices, the office's role is to provide "candid, independent and principled advice—even when that advice may be inconsistent with the desires of policy makers." In general, opinions should strive for a "balanced presentation of arguments on each side of an issue. . . . OLC's interest is simply to provide the correct answer on the law, taking into account all reasonable counterarguments . . . ."[90] The report also noted that OLC lawyers must abide by professional rules of conduct. Under the District of Columbia's Rule 1.1, a lawyer must provide "competent representation, [which] requires the legal knowledge, skill, thoroughness, and preparation reasonably necessary for the representation." Under Rule 2.1, a lawyer must provide "independent professional judgment" and "candid advice."

In the view of OPR, the Bybee-Yoo memo fell short in several respects. It took its definition of torture from the use of "severe pain" in a medical benefits statute rather than from directly applicable precedents, failed to consider adverse authority, and misstated supporting authority.[91] Bybee was faulted for inadequate supervision and failure to consider relevant material, such as the military's determination that waterboarding constituted torture. Yoo's conduct was considered intentional, based both on the extent of his errors and on evidence that the CIA officials who had asked for the opinion were not interested in objective analysis, but rather in language that would protect interrogators from subsequent prosecution.[92] Accordingly, the OPR concluded that Yoo and Bybee should be referred to appropriate bar disciplinary agencies.

By contrast, Margolis determined that although both lawyers had exercised "poor judgment," they had not violated rules of professional conduct. The "memos contained some significant flaws," and constituted "an unfortunate chapter" in the history of the office, but in Margolis's view, they did not rise to the level of reckless or intentional misconduct.[93] The Department's inability to produce e-mails from around this period made it difficult to know the state of mind of the participants, but the record failed to show that Yoo's conclusion was the result of pressure from administration officials. To Margolis, it appeared that Yoo's "loyalty to his own ideology and convictions clouded his view of his obligation to his client and led him to author opinions that reflected his own extreme, albeit sincerely held, views of executive power."[94]

This conclusion met with mixed reviews. Supporters applauded the decision not to use disciplinary sanctions to resolve policy disagreements. Critics, including the *New York Times'* editorial board, viewed "poor judgment" as an "absurdly dismissive" way to characterize facilitation of torture.[95] Some saw the result less as a vindication of Yoo and Bybee than as an indictment of bar disciplinary standards and structures. According to many commentators, the case underscored the need for a "credible" oversight mechanism, "independent of the very department implicated" in the matter."[96]

QUESTIONS

1. What would you have done if you had been a participant in the 2002 meeting discussing enhanced interrogation? What would you have done in Mark Fallon's position after learning of the substance of that meeting? Might you have leaked the minutes?

2. Under what, if any, circumstances should lawyers working in government ever make anonymous disclosures to expose ethically problematic conduct?[97] Note that the public learned of the torture memos through such a leak. Is such disclosure ever an example of the kind of courageous follower behavior discussed in Chapter 4?

3. Those who formulated U.S. interrogation policy emphasize that at the time the torture memos were written, government leaders had great concern about a possible Al Qaeda attack on or around the anniversary of 9/11. According to General Richard Myers, who then chaired the Joint Chiefs of Staff, "There was a sense of urgency that in my forty years of military experience hadn't existed in other contingencies. [We had a] real fear that one of the detainees might know when the next attack would happen, and that [we] would miss vital information."[98] Margolis's report also made reference to the security context in which the memos were drafted. Should such considerations influence legal conclusions about what constitutes torture? Or is it precisely in times of stress that government leaders should be most careful not to stretch the law to reach expedient results?

4. If you had been in Margolis's position, would you have reached the same conclusions? What are the best arguments for and against sanctions?

5. Some commentators believed that Yoo's interpretation of the law on torture may have been skewed by the self-serving bias discussed in Chapter 3. Because he was heavily involved in policy decisions governing the war on terror, his political allegiances may have colored his legal judgments. If that is true, what is the appropriate response? If you were a bar leader, how would you assess the standards for assessing OLC lawyers? Note that its rules require "intentional" or "reckless" violations of clear duties, while bar disciplinary

rules make any violation a basis for sanctions. What accounts for the restricted liability of government lawyers? Is it justifiable?

6. If you were the attorney general, how would you respond to criticism of the OLC oversight process? Are there strategies, apart from criminal, civil, or disciplinary liability that might make government officials more accountable for their decisions? For example, should Congress require that all or certain specified OLC opinions be public, as some commentators and legislators have recommended? An unsuccessful proposed "OLC Reporting Act" would have obligated the attorney general to report to Congress in a timely fashion any OLC opinions that expanded executive power at the expense of Congress or the courts.[99] If you were in Congress, would you support such legislation? Would Yoo and Bybee have been likely to draft their opinion the same way if that act had been in force?

7. In his 2010 memoir *Decision Points*, former President Bush justified his actions as follows:

> CIA experts drew up a list of enhanced interrogation techniques. . . . At my direction, Department of Justice and CIA lawyers conducted a careful legal review. The enhanced interrogation program complied with the Constitution and all applicable laws, including those that ban torture. There were two I felt went too far, even if they were legal. I directed the CIA not to use them. Another technique was waterboarding, a process of simulated drowning. No doubt the procedure was tough, but medical experts assured the CIA that it did no lasting harm. . . . Had I not authorized waterboarding on senior al Qaeda leaders, I would have to accept a greater risk that the country would be attacked. In the wake of 9/11, that was a risk I was unwilling to take. . . . The new techniques proved highly effective. Zubaydah revealed large amounts of information on al Qaeda structure and operations. . . . Khalid Sheikh Mohammed [provided information that revealed terrorist plots and the location of key operatives].[100]

In an interview following the book's publication, Matt Lauer asked Bush: "Why is waterboarding legal in your opinion?" Bush responded: "Because the lawyer said it was legal. He said it did not fall within the Anti-Torture Act. I'm not a lawyer, but you gotta trust the judgment of people around you and I do." When Lauer then asked whether it would be "okay for a foreign country to waterboard an American citizen," Bush replied, "all I ask is that people read the book."[101]

Many commentators raised concerns with these defenses. One criticism was that Bush's legal team had offered an opinion that was inconsistent with the consensus of the expert international community. Another was that he had vastly overstated the value of intelligence obtained through enhanced interrogation and understated the pervasiveness of its use. Investigative journalists, and one of the interrogators involved, agreed that no actionable intelligence was gained from Zubaydah's treatment and that his false confessions sent CIA and FBI investigators "scurrying in pursuit of phantoms."[102] Although Khalid Sheikh Mohammed had provided some useful information, none of it was shown to have thwarted well-developed plots or to have saved lives. Nor did the record in either case indicate that the information could not have been obtained through accepted interrogation methods.[103] Critics also noted that the techniques Bush authorized were not reserved to a few senior terrorist leaders, but were employed on countless detainees in Afghanistan, Iraq, and Guantanamo Bay.

What is your view? How would you have advised President Bush? Does his reliance on lawyers affect your views of the gravity of conduct by Yoo and Bybee?

8. The issue of torture resurfaced in the 2016 presidential campaign. Although Donald Trump was not entirely consistent in his statements, he repeatedly maintained that the country "should go tougher than waterboarding." When pressed about whether military officers would carry out orders such as directives to kill terrorists' family members, a violation of the Geneva Conventions, Trump replied, "If I say do it, they're going to do it."[104] On other occasions, he promised to bring back waterboarding and a "hell of a lot worse" because "torture works" and even if it doesn't work, "they deserve it anyway."[105] After his inauguration, Trump called for a review of government policy on torture and overseas prisons where it occurred.[106] If you had been a lawyer advising Trump during this period, how would you have responded?

MEDIA RESOURCES

Many interviews with John Yoo are available, including one on *The Daily Show* with Jon Stewart from January 11, 2010, as are documentaries on the War against Terror.[107] Among the best are Frontline's *Cheney's War* and *Reckoning with Torture*, a documentary by the ACLU and PEN American Center, which features actors reading from official memos, e-mails, and speeches, as well as interviews with victims of torture. A *60 Minutes* interview with George Tenet explains the administration's interrogation policy.[108] An interesting comparison of views on interrogation comes from former President Clinton's 2008 interview with Tim Russert on *Meet the Press*, former President Bush's 2010 NBC interview with Matt Lauer, President Obama's public statement repudiating torture, and Donald Trump's support for it.[109] An illuminating portrayal of waterboarding shows a conservative talk show host, Erich "Mancow" Muller, recanting his views about the severity of the tactic after experiencing it personally.[110] Torture, rendition, and related practices also figure in many television plots, including segments of *24* and *The Wire*, and films such as *The Kingdom*, *Rendition*, and *Syriana*. The documentary, *Taxi to the Dark Side*, explores enhanced interrogation techniques used at Bagram Air Base. The film *A Few Good Men* also includes a relevant scene in which a hardened military officer upbraids an idealistic army lawyer for his inability to understand military necessities.

END NOTES

[1] MAX H. BAZERMAN & ANN E. TENBRUNSEL, BLIND SPOTS: WHY WE FAIL TO DO WHAT'S RIGHT AND WHAT TO DO ABOUT IT 12-13 (2012); Jerry M. Burger, *Replicating Milgram: Would People Still Obey Today?*, 64 AM. PSYCHOL. 1 (2009).

[2] BAZERMAN & TENBRUNSEL, BLIND SPOTS; IRA CHALEFF, INTELLIGENT DISOBEDIENCE 74 (2015).

[3] 45 C.F.R. § 46 (2009).

[4] PHILIP ZIMBARDO, THE LUCIFER EFFECT: UNDERSTANDING HOW GOOD PEOPLE TURN EVIL 238-39 (2007).

[5] Senator Inhofe made his comments on May 11, 2004, during the Senate Armed Services Committee hearings regarding prison abuses. For estimates of innocence rates, see Jen Banbury, *"Rummy's Scapegoat,"* SALON.COM (Nov. 10, 2005), http://www.salon.com/2005/11/10/karpinski/; and REPORT OF THE INTERNATIONAL COMMITTEE OF THE RED CROSS (ICRC) ON THE TREATMENT BY THE COALITION FORCES OF PRISONERS OF WAR AND OTHER PROTECTED PERSONS BY THE GENEVA CONVENTIONS IN IRAQ DURING ARREST, INTERNMENT AND INTERROGATION (Feb. 2004).

[6] Testimony as Prepared by Secretary of Defense Donald H. Rumsfeld, THE SENATE AND HOUSE ARMED SERVICES COMMITTEES, Friday, May 07, 2004, available at http://www.defense.gov/speeches/speech.aspx?speechid=118.

[7] Adam Hochschild, *What's in a Word? Torture,* N.Y. TIMES, May 23, 2004, at 11.

[8] *Rumsfeld Twice Offered to Resign,* BBC NEWS (Feb. 4, 2005), http://news.bbc.co.uk/2/hi/americas/4235045.stm.

[9] *Rumsfeld Twice Offered to Resign*, BBC NEWS.

[10] FINAL REPORT OF THE INDEPENDENT PANEL TO REVIEW DOD DETENTION OPERATIONS, Aug. 2004, at 43, available at http://www.defense.gov/news/Aug2004 /d20040824finalreport.pdf.

[11] *The Roots of Abu Ghraib,* N.Y. TIMES, June 9, 2004, at A24.

[12] CHALEFF, INTELLIGENT DISOBEDIENCE, at 77.

[13] https://www.youtube.com/watch?v=fCVlI-_4GZQ.

[14] *See* Charles Sheridan & Richard King, *Obedience to Authority with an Authentic Victim,* 7 PROCEEDINGS OF THE 80TH ANNUAL CONVENTION OF THE AMERICAN PSYCHOLOGICAL ASSOCIATION 165 (1972).

[15] This variation is described in Wesley Kilham & Leon Mann, *Level of Destructive Obedience as a Function of Transmitter and Executant Roles in the Milgram Obedience Paradigm,* 29(5) J. PERS. SOC. PSYCHOL. 696, 696-702.

[16] Available at https://www.psychologicalscience.org/observer/replicating-milgram#. WPfooRLytE4.

[17] Zimbardo's presentation on the Lucifer effect is available at https://www.youtube.com/watch?v=BYre8SlOO_k; http://www.prisonexp.org/book. For video links aside from Zimbardo's presentation, see *The Daily Show: Philip Zimbardo* (Mar. 29, 2007).

[18] For images, available at, http://www.antiwar.com/news/?articleid=2444; http://www.afterdowningstreet.org/sites/afterdowningstreet.org/files/images/abu2.jpg; http://traceyricksfoster.files.wordpress.com/2009/05/abu-ghraib.jpg.

[19] Robert Pack, *The Lawyers of Watergate,* WASH. LAWYER, July/Aug., 1999, at 25; John Dean, *Watergate: Lessons for Today, Nearly 40 Years Later,* OHIO LAWYER, July/Aug., 2011, at 11. Half of those indicted or named as coconspirators were lawyers. Richard Harris, *The Watergate Prosecutions,* NEW YORKER, June 10, 1974, at 46, 51. Of the key participants in the cover up, only H. R. Haldeman was not a lawyer.

[20] For a list of lawyers and offenses see Kathleen Clark, *The Legacy of Watergate for Legal Ethics Instruction,* 51 HASTINGS L.J. 673, 678-82 (1999).

[21] Watergate and Related Activities, PHASE I: WATERGATE INVESTIGATION, SENATE SELECT COMMITTEE ON PRESIDENTIAL CAMPAIGN ACTIVITIES, Presidential Campaign Activities of 1972, Book 3, 1013, 1054 (June 25-26, 1973).

[22] MICHAEL A GENOVESE & IWAN W. MORGAN, INTRODUCTION: REMEMBERING WATERGATE, in WATERGATE REMEMBERED: THE LEGACY FOR AMERICAN POLITICS 7 (Michael A. Genovese & Iwan W. Morgan eds., 2012).

[23] GENOVESE & MORGAN, INTRODUCTION, at 7.

[24] RICHARD NIXON, IN THE ARENA: A MEMOIR OF VICTORY, DEFEAT, AND RENEWAL 34 (1990).

[25] GENOVESE & MORGAN, INTRODUCTION, at 7.

[26] David Frost's interview with Richard Nixon in *Great Interviews of the 20th Century,* THE GUARDIAN (May, 1977), at https://www.theguardian.com/theguardian /2007/sep/07/greatinterviews1.

[27] JEB STUART MAGRUDER, AN AMERICAN LIFE: ONE MAN'S ROAD TO WATERGATE 214 (1974).

[28] GENOVESE & MORGAN, INTRODUCTION, at 13 (quoting Colson).

[29] DEBORAH L. RHODE, LAWYERS AS LEADERS 6-97 (2013).

[30] *Hearing on Michael Cohen, Former Attorney to President Donald Trump Before the H. Comm. on Oversight and Reform,* 116th Cong. Feb. 27, 2019 (statement of Michael Cohen), https://docs.house.gov/meetings/GO/GO00/20190227/108969/HHRG-116-GO00-Wstate-CohenM-20190227.pdf.

[31] MEL GUSSOW, DON'T SAY YES UNTIL I FINISH TALKING: A BIOGRAPHY OF DARRYL F. ZANUCK (NEW YORK: POCKET BOOKS, 1983).

[32] PETER H. IRONS, JUSTICE AT WAR: THE STORY OF THE JAPANESE AMERICAN INTERNMENT CASES 204 (1993).

[33] IRONS, JUSTICE AT WAR, 205-06.

[34] IRONS, JUSTICE AT WAR, 290-91.

[35] IRONS, JUSTICE AT WAR, 290-91.

[36] IRONS, JUSTICE AT WAR, 350-51.

[37] LINCOLN CAPLAN, THE TENTH JUSTICE: THE SOLICITOR GENERAL AND THE RULE OF LAW 10 (1987).

[38] Bernard Williams, *Politics and Moral Character,* in STUART HAMPSHIRE, ED., PUBLIC AND PRIVATE MORALITY 58 (1978).

[39] AMERICAN BAR ASSOCIATION, MODEL RULES OF PROFESSIONAL CONDUCT RULE 1.2 (2008).

[40] Geoffrey P. Miller, *Government Lawyers' Ethics in a System of Checks and Balances,* 54 U. CHI. L. REV. 1293, 1294-95 (1987).

[41] William Josephson & Russell G. Pearce, *To Whom Does the Government Lawyer Owe the Duty of Loyalty When Clients Are in Conflict?*, 29 HOW. L.J. 539, 565 (1986).

[42] Judge Charles Fahy, *Special Ethical Problems of Counsel for the Government,* 33 FED. B.J. 331, 333-34 (1974); Jack B. Weinstein & Gay A. Crosthwait, *Some Reflections on Conflicts Between Government Attorneys and Clients,* 1 TOURO L. REV. 1 (1985). *See also* Catherine J. Lanctot, *The Duty of Zealous Advocacy and the Ethics of the Federal Government Lawyer: The Three Hardest Questions,* 64 S. CAL. L. REV. 951 (1991).

[43] Sally Yates, letter from Acting United States Attorney General, Jan. 30, 2017, https://www.nytimes.com/interactive/2017/01/30/us/document-Letter-From-Sally-Yates.html.

[44] Sally Yates, *Not on My Watch,* N.Y. MAG., Oct. 18, 2018.

[45] Id.

[46] Anemona Hartocollis, *Sally Yates Tells Harvard Students Why She Defied Trump,* N.Y. TIMES, May 24, 2017.

[47] Id. (quoting statement)

[48] Jack Goldsmith, *Quick Thoughts on Sally Yates' Unpersuasive Statement,* LAWFARE, (Jan. 30, 2017), https:www.lawfareblog.com/quick-thoughts-sally-yates-unpersuasive-statement; Alan M. Dershowitz, *Sally Yates Was Wrong and Should Have Resigned,* THE HILL (Jan. 31, 2017), http://thehill.com/blogs/pundits-blog/the-administration/317081-shes-no-hero-sally-yates-should-have-resigned.

[49] Amy Davidson, *What Sally Yates Proved About Donald Trump,* NEW YORKER, Jan. 31, 2017.

[50] Robert S. Mueller III, *Report on the Investigation Into Russian Interference in the 2016 Presidential Election* (2019).

[51] Bob Bauer, *How Don McGahn Handled a Dishonest President*, N.Y. TIMES, Apr. 19, 2019.

[52] JAMES COMEY, A HIGHER LOYALTY: TRUTH, LIES, AND LEADERSHIP 170 (2018).

[53] COMEY, A HIGHER LOYALTY, at 187.

[54] COMEY, A HIGHER LOYALTY, at 194-195.

[55] COMEY, A HIGHER LOYALTY, at 195.

[56] COMEY, A HIGHER LOYALTY, at 196.

[57] COMEY, A HIGHER LOYALTY, at 206.

[58] Ronald Goldfarb, *James Comey's Conflicted Loyalty*, WASH. LAWYER, Aug./Sept., 2018

[59] James Comey, *How Trump Co-opts Leaders Like Bill Barr,* N.Y. TIMES, May 1, 2019.

[60] JOHN CONROY, UNSPEAKABLE ACTS, ORDINARY PEOPLE: THE DYNAMICS OF TORTURE 25-26 (2000). *See also* Sanford Levinson, *Contemplating Torture: An Introduction,* in SANFORD LEVINSON ED., TORTURE: A COLLECTION 36 (2004).

[61] CAROL TAVRIS & ELLIOT ARONSON, MISTAKES WERE MADE (BUT NOT BY ME): WHY WE JUSTIFY FOOLISH BELIEFS, BAD DECISIONS, AND HURTFUL ACTS 202-03 (2008).

[62] Richard Posner, *Torture, Terrorism, and Interrogation,* in LEVINSON ED., TORTURE, at 294.

[63] Richard A. Posner, *The Best Offense,* THE NEW REPUBLIC, Sept. 2, 2002, at 28, 30.

[64] STEPHEN L. CARTER, THE VIOLENCE OF PEACE: AMERICA'S WARS IN THE AGE OF OBAMA 43-44 (2011) (discussing French resistance fighters tortured by Nazis, and United States CIA officer tortured by Ethiopians).

[65] David Luban, *Liberalism, Torture and the Ticking Bomb,* 91 VA. L. REV. 1425, 1442-44 (2005).

[66] Luban, *Liberalism*, at 1445-46.

[67] Posner, *The Best Offense*, at 30.

[68] Ali H. Soufan, *What Torture Never Taught Us,* N.Y. TIMES, Sept. 5, 2009, at WK 9.

[69] *Olmstead v. United States,* 277 U.S. 438, 485 (1927) (Holmes, J., dissenting).

[70] Chris Kahn, *Most Americans Support Torture Against Terror Suspects,* REUTERS (Mar. 30, 2016), http://www.reuters.com/article/us-usa-election-torture-exclusive-idUSKCN0WW0Y3.

[71] *A Public Divided: Americans' Attitudes About Torture,* ROPER (Apr. 22, 2015), http://ropercenter.cornell.edu/a-public_divided_americans_attitudes_about_torture/.

[72] Richard Wike, *Global Opinion Varies Widely on Use of Torture Against Suspected Terrorists,* PEW RESEARCH CENTER (Feb. 9, 2016), http://www.pewresearch.org/fact-tank/2016/02/09/global-opinion-use-of-torture/.

[73] *A Public Divided* (citing 2010 poll). For an overview of Americans' opposition, see Paul Gronke, Darius Rejali & Peter Miller, *No, Americans Aren't "Fine with Torture." They Strongly Reject It,* WASH. POST, Dec. 11, 2014.

[74] Jane Mayer, *The Trial,* NEW YORKER, Feb. 15 and 22, 2010, at 57, 60.

[75] Luban, *Liberalism*, at 60 (quoting Massimino).

[76] Luban, *Liberalism*, at 62 (quoting Holder).

[77] Luban, *Liberalism*, at 57 (quoting anonymous source).

[78] Some of the following material is adapted from DEBORAH L. RHODE, DAVID LUBAN, SCOTT L. CUMMINGS & NORA FREEMAN ENGSTROM, LEGAL ETHICS 613-23 (7th ed. 2016).

[79] For discussion of the heightened public-interest obligations of government lawyers, see, e.g., Steven K. Berenson, *Public Lawyers, Private Values: Can, Should, and Will Government Lawyers Serve the Public Interest?*, 41 B.C. L. REV. 789 (2000).

[80] This document was released during Senate hearings on detainee abuse in June 2008.

[81] Legal Brief on *Proposed Counter-Resistance Strategies* from Diane Beaver to Gen. James T. Hill, Oct. 11, 2002, in KAREN J. GREENBERG & JOSHUA L. DRATEL, THE TORTURE PAPERS: THE ROAD TO ABU GHRAIB 229 (2005). The techniques are listed in Beaver, Legal Brief, at 227-28.

[82] Memorandum from Mark Fallon to Sam McCahon (Oct. 28, 2002).

[83] Some dispute centers on whether they are binding as a matter of law or custom. Randolph D. Moss, *Executive Branch Legal Interpretation: A Perspective from the Office of Legal Counsel,* 52 ADMIN. L. REV. 1303, 1318-20 (2000).

[84] Memorandum from Jay S. Bybee to Alberto Gonzalez (Aug. 1, 2002).

[85] The OLC memos and President Bush's order are reproduced in GREENBERG & DRATEL, THE TORTURE PAPERS, at 38-79, 81-117, 134-135. The State Department's critique is Memorandum from William Howard Taft IV to John Yoo (Jan. 11, 2002), available at http://nsarchive.gwu.edu/torturingdemocracy/documents/20020111.pdf. For critiques of government policy, see DAVID COLE, THE TORTURE MEMOS: RATIONALIZING THE UNTHINKABLE (2009).

[86] Eric Posner & Adrian Vermeuele, *A "Torture" Memo and Its Tortuous Critics,* WALL ST. J., July 6, 2004, A22; David Luban, *The Torture Lawyers of Washington,* in DAVID LUBAN, LEGAL ETHICS AND HUMAN DIGNITY (2007); Robert K. Vischer, *Legal Advice as Moral Perspective,* 19 GEO. J. OF LEGAL ETHICS 225 (2006); Jeremy Waldron,

Torture and Positive Law: Jurisprudence for the White House, 105 COLUM. L. REV. 1681 (2005); W. Bradley Wendel, *Legal Ethics and the Separation of Law and Morals,* 91 CORNELL L. REV. 67 (2005); Ruth Wedgwood & R. James Woolsey, *Law and Torture,* WALL ST. J., June 28, 2004, at A10.

[87] David Cole, *Introductory Commentary,* in COLE ED., THE TORTURE MEMOS, at 13.

[88] Press Release, *Disbar Torture Lawyers, Disciplinary Complaint Against Torture Memo Lawyers,* LEGAL ETHICS FORUM (Nov. 30, 2009), http://www.legalethicsforum.com/blog/2009/11/disciplinary-complaint-against-torture-memo-lawyers.html; *Padilla v. Yoo,* 633 F. Supp. 1005 (U.S.D. 2009) (partly denying motion to dismiss).

[89] Office of Professional Responsibility, Department of Justice, Investigation into the Office of Legal Counsel's Memoranda concerning Issues Relating to the Central Intelligence Agency's Use of Enhanced Interrogation Techniques on Suspected Terrorists (July 29, 2009) [OPR REPORT].

[90] Steven G. Bradbury, Principle Deputy Assistant Attorney General, Memorandum for Attorneys of the Office Re: Best Practices for OLC Opinions (May 16, 2005), quoted in OPR REPORT, at 15.

[91] OPR REPORT, at 228.

[92] OPR REPORT, at 226-37.

[93] David Margolis, Memorandum for the Attorney General of Decision regarding the Objections to the Findings of Professional Misconduct in the Office of Professional Responsibility's Report of Investigation (Jan. 5, 2010).

[94] Margolis, Memo, at 67.

[95] *The Torture Lawyers,* N.Y. TIMES, Feb. 25, 2010, at A26.

[96] Stephen Gillers, *Letter to the Editor,* N.Y. TIMES, Mar. 4, 2010, at A26; David Cole, *Torture Lawyers on Trial,* THE NATION, Mar. 1, 2010, at 7.

[97] Peter Van Buren, *When It's Time to Blow the Whistle,* N.Y TIMES, Feb. 19, 2017.

[98] PHILIPPE SANDS, TORTURE TEAM: RUMSFELD'S MEMO AND THE BETRAYAL OF AMERICAN VALUES 88 (2008).

[99] S. 3501, 110TH CONG. 2D. SESSION (2008). Text of bill available at http://www.fas.org/irp/congress/2008_rpt/srpt110-528.html. Other commentators have proposed that all OLC opinions public. See Norman W. Spaulding, *Professional Independence in the Office of the Attorney General,* 60 STAN. L. REV. 1931, 1978 (2008).

[100] GEORGE W. BUSH, DECISION POINTS 169-70 (2011).

[101] NBC NEWS SPECIAL, *Decision Points,* interview of George W. Bush by Matt Lauer, Nov. 8, 2010, available at http://www.msnbc.msn.com/id/40076644/ns/politicsw-decision_ points.

[102] Dan Froomkin, *The Two Most Essential, Abhorrent, Intolerable Lies of George W. Bush's Memoir,* HUFFINGTON POST, Nov. 22, 2010, https://www.huffpost.com/entry/the-two-most-esssential-a_n_786219 (quoting Washington Post and citing other sources); Ali Soufan, *My Tortured Decision,* N.Y. TIMES, Apr. 22, 2009.

[103] Froomkin, *The Two Lies,* quoting sources; Soufan, *My Tortured Decision.*

[104] *A Trump Sampler: His Changing Views,* N.Y. TIMES, May 7, 2016 (quoting Trump).

[105] Charlie Savage, *Trump Poised to Lit Ban on C.I.A. "Black Site" Prisons,* N.Y. TIMES Jan. 25, 2017 (quoting Trump).

[106] Savage, *Trump Poised.*

[107] For John Yoo interviews, see *The Daily Show: John Yoo* (Jan. 1 2010); http://www.pbs.org/wgbh/pages/frontline/torture/interviews/yoo.html. For documentaries on the War on Terror, see https://www.pbs.org/wgbh/pages/frontline/terror/]. For George Tenet on 60 MINUTES, see http://www.cbsnews.com/videos/former-cia-director-we-dont-torture-people/.

[108] https://www.cbsnews.com/video/former-cia-director-george-tenet-denies-torture-claims/.

[109] For Bush's interview with Matt Lauer, see http://www.nbcnews.com/id/40076644/ns/politicsw-decision_points#.UwEp_EJdXQw; Part I. For an earlier claim by Bush that the United States does not engage in torture, see http://www.youtube.com/watch?v=g6LtL9lCTRA. For Obama's statement, see http://www.youtube.com/watch?v=XM5FKawx1No.

[110] http://www.youtube.com/watch?v=qUkj9pjx3H0.

CHAPTER 7

SCANDAL: PRIVATE LIVES, PUBLIC RESPONSIBILITIES, AND CRISIS MANAGEMENT

Scandals, notes Professor Laura Kipnis, will always be with us, "sniffing at the back door, nosing around for cracks in the façade." Because the "human personality is helpless against itself, we will always see leaders "orchestrating their own downfalls, crashing headlong into their own inner furies."[1] And we, the public, the "collective superego" cannot resist the spectacle. Nor can we sometimes help but "relish the pleasure of knocking the excessively privileged . . . down a notch or two" when they violate norms that inconveniently constrain our own behavior.[2]

However, what is distinctive about the modern era are the social, economic, and technological forces that have increased the visibility of scandals. Growing competition among media is one factor. As sociology professor Ari Adut notes in *On Scandal*, "[T]he proliferation of the media sources and the establishment of the round-the-clock cable news cycle have stoked the demand for scandal and facilitated its publicization process. The effects of the citizen-journalism of YouTube, which allows almost anyone to put any kind of compromising images about elites into the public domain, are obvious. . . ."[3] The rise in watchdog groups that trade in publicity, and communications strategists who specialize in spin, has brought heightened transparency to leadership missteps. Technology has also provided more ways to obtain information and more ways of making it instantly accessible. Those in positions of power are increasingly vulnerable to exposure for their own frailties, as well as increasingly responsible for messes not of their own making. Some experts suggest that close to two-thirds of a company's worth is tied to reputation, and lawyers have become increasingly central advisors in how to manage reputational issues that arise in scandals.[4] As the following discussion indicates, lawyers in leadership positions have also been the architects of their own free-falls.

This chapter explores the dynamics of scandal. What enmeshes leaders in political, financial, and sexual misconduct? Under what circumstances does their private conduct become a subject of legitimate public concern? How relevant is hypocrisy, and how relevant should it be? What are the most effective ways of managing reputational crises? How can leaders prevent their own or their organization's mistakes from mushrooming into public relations disasters?

A. HYPOCRISY

Hypocrisy is at the foundation of many leadership scandals. This should come as no surprise. If, as conventional usage suggests, hypocrisy means assuming a false appearance of virtue, or failing to practice what one preaches, it is endemic to public life. As Somerset Maugham once quipped, hypocrisy is unlike other vices like gluttony or adultery, which can be "practiced at spare moments. It is a whole time job."[5] Leaders are not only subject to normal human frailties, but also exposed to the temptations of power, and expected to rise above both. Psychologists have identified two cognitive biases that contribute to hypocrisy at leadership levels. One is people's tendency to see themselves as unique and superior to others, particularly concerning moral conduct.[6] This uniqueness bias is exacerbated by conditions of power. Leaders live in what consultant Eric Dezenhall labeled a "mental aquarium," an environment of admiration that fosters an inflated sense of self-confidence and self-importance.[7] A second cognitive bias encourages individuals to view their own transgressions as less objectionable than identical actions by others.[8] Placing individuals in positions of power increases the likelihood of such hypocrisy.[9] Although social disapproval normally helps check self-interest, power tends to reduce exposure and sensitivity to that constraint.[10]

Yet, while no one doubts the pervasiveness of hypocrisy, commentators are divided on its significance and on the value of pointing it out. In sorting through these arguments, it is often useful to distinguish between individual and institutional hypocrisy. Leaders can be criticized either for failing to live up to their own principles, or for failing to ensure that an institution does so. For example, Thomas Jefferson can be faulted for violating his professed commitment to liberty and equality because he owned slaves, or for designing a constitutional system that proclaimed adherence to those principles but ignored their meaning for African Americans.[11] Recent research finds that people feel deceived by hypocrites because they misrepresent their own moral behavior in the hope of enhancing their reputations.[12] That deceit appears profoundly offensive. Researchers find that hypocrites are viewed as more dishonest than people who openly lie.[13]

Some commentators view hypocrisy in politics as a special case, and one in which criticism on that ground is often unrealistic and unproductive. Political theorists Judith Shklar and Ruth Grant both argue that conventional definitions presuppose hypermoralistic, "overinclusive" standards: "[T]o define hypocrisy as [failing to] practice what one preaches . . . allows no distinction between hypocrisy and moral weakness. To profess principles that one has no intention of following is hypocrisy: to be unable to live up to our best expectations of ourselves is human nature."[14] Grant argues further that political hypocrisy is sometimes appropriate in democratic regimes in which compromise and coalitions are necessary, and "the frank exposure of self-interested motivations is often a threat to that [collaborative] process."[15] Hypocrisy, she notes, "only occurs where people try to appear better than they are. . . . Where there is political hypocrisy, there is a . . . significant moral impulse."[16] That can be a positive influence in politics: "Every act of hypocrisy involves a pretense of virtue, which necessarily includes public acknowledgement of moral standards for political action, and sometimes, that public statement is the best that can be done."[17]

Shklar also worries that a focus on hypocrisy diverts attention from the substance of the conduct at issue.[18] Other commentators express concern that this focus will "drive our best hypocrites out of public life." Many talented leaders, who are basically "decent and well meaning" have also made some "significant missteps they would rather not read about in the morning paper."[19] By the same token, journalists end up in an "appallingly wasteful" diversion of scarce resources by duplicating each others' efforts to "sniff out the latest scandal."[20]

Yet exposure of hypocrisy can also serve legitimate functions. Political scientist Peter Furia argues that "when the very leaders who advocate morally demanding principles are unable to live up to them," it sparks a useful debate about the "practicability" of those principles.[21] Concerns about hypocrisy can also discourage overreaching, unprincipled, or self-righteous conduct that undermines the legitimacy of those in power.

Taken together, these arguments may suggest the need for a contextual approach to hypocrisy. Such an approach would evaluate the reasons why leaders have violated professed principles, and the consequences of their actions. Consider these arguments in light of the readings that follow. When do debates about leaders' hypocrisy serve a useful function and when are they counterproductive? Why?

JUDITH N. SHKLAR, ORDINARY VICES

(Cambridge, MA: The Belknap Press of Harvard University Press, 1984), pp. 47-48 and 77-78

Hypocrisy has always been odious. What is less obvious is just what hypocrisy is and why it should be so intensely resented. The *Oxford English Dictionary* is always helpful. Originally hypocrisy meant acting a part on the stage. For practical purposes the definition that counts is: "assuming a false appearance of virtue or goodness, with dissimulation of real character or inclination, especially in respect of religious life or belief." . . . The moral hypocrite . . . pretends that his motives and intentions and character are irreproachable when he knows that they are blameworthy. Then there are complacency and self-satisfaction, the hypocrisies of the wealthy and powerful. . . . Whatever is in their interest somehow is always also for the public good, in this best of all possible social worlds. There is, finally, a cluster of attitudes that taken together we call insincerity and inauthenticity. These need not express themselves in conduct that injures others directly, but they are said to deform one's personality. . . .

[Charges of hypocrisy are pervasive in political life because it] is not difficult to show that politicians are often more interested in power than in any of the causes they so ardently proclaim. It is, therefore, easier to dispose of an opponent's character by exposing his hypocrisy than to show that his political convictions are wrong. . . . The paradox of liberal democracy is that it encourages hypocrisy because the politics of persuasion require, as any reader of Aristotle's *Rhetoric* knows, a certain amount of dissimulation on the part of all speakers. On the other hand, the structure of open political competition exaggerates the importance and the prevalence of hypocrisy because it is the vice of which all parties can and do accuse each other. It is not at all clear that zealous candor would serve liberal politics particularly well. Nevertheless, the distance between the demand for sincerity and the actualities of politics can become a great distraction, especially in time of social stress. . . .

[W]e assume that our public roles carry greater moral responsibilities than our private ones. We expect to behave better as citizens and public officials than as actors in the private sphere. The whole concern about corruption in government turns on that, and it does yield immense hypocrisy; but pretended virtue may curtail graft and similar vices as well. It is, far more significantly, no longer acceptable in the United States to make racist and anti-Semitic remarks in public [even though they appear in private.] . . . Would any egalitarian prefer more public frankness? Should our public conduct really mirror our private, inner selves? Often our public manners are better than our personal laxities. That "sugary grin" is, in any case, not a serious issue. On the contrary, it is a very necessary pretense, a witness to our moral efforts no less than to our failures.

Indeed, one might well argue that liberal democracy cannot afford public sincerity. Honesties that humiliate and a stiff-necked refusal to compromise would ruin democratic civility in a political society in which people have many serious differences of belief and interest. . . .

DAVID RUNCIMAN, POLITICAL HYPOCRISY: THE MASK OF POWER, FROM HOBBES TO ORWELL AND BEYOND

(Princeton, NJ: Princeton University Press, 2008), pp. 222-226

Hypocrisy and the Environment

. . . Early in 2007 newspapers on both sides of the Atlantic were full of either deeply critical or sympathetically agonised articles about whether [Al] Gore's personal hypocrisy mattered, once it was discovered that the energy needs of his private home produced a carbon footprint many times the size of others in his neighborhood. Clearly, for any possible Gore candidature this was bad politics— blatant hypocrisy of this sort always gives your enemies a stick to beat you with. On the other hand, it is not clear that this kind of hypocrisy is the obstacle it sometimes appears, because there seems to be quite wide acceptance that some personal hypocrisy of this kind (not always practicing in the private sphere what you preach in public) is unavoidable in those who seek political power: they are like us, but they are not like us, and in some aspect of their lives the gap will show.

This kind of mismatch between public pronouncements and private practice is the [first-order] hypocrisy we tend to hear most about, because it is the easiest to find, and the easiest to exploit to provoke a reaction. In many settings, and above all in the more censorious branches of the media (particularly online), not practicing what you preach is what hypocrisy has come to mean. . . . But the reaction to this sort of hypocrisy is often short-lived, and frequently surprisingly tolerant. . . . [V]oters seem far more censorious about public inconsistencies—"flip-flopping" in the jargon—than they do about private lapses from the highest public standards. So perhaps the more serious charge of hypocrisy to which a politician like Gore is vulnerable is that he didn't do much about global warming when he was in office. . . .

There is[, moreover,] a big difference between those who do not live up to the standards they ask of others, and those who make a parade of their own ability to set an example. [An example of the latter type of politician is] British Conservative leader David Cameron, who has gone to great lengths to "green" his own personal lifestyle, and to make political capital out of that fact. When it emerged that Cameron's much publicised bicycle rides to the House of Commons involved the use of a car to ferry his personal belongings behind him, he revealed himself to be a second-order hypocrite. Second-order hypocrisy, because it makes a mockery of the whole business of public enactment, is corrosive in ways that first-order hypocrisy is not.

But even this is in a sense trivial. Far more significant than the question of whether individual politicians are hypocrites on environmental issues is the question of whether the most advanced democracies can cope with the charge of hypocrisy that is likely to be leveled against them by the rest of the world. . . . [I]it will be easy to portray the demand by developed nations like the United States or Britain for equivalent sacrifices by developing nations that have yet to enjoy the full benefits of economic growth as a kind of hypocrisy. How then will democratic politicians in the most advanced countries be able to persuade their own electorates of the sacrifices needed if the burdens of those sacrifices are not more widely shared? It will be relatively easy for democratic politicians in the West to portray politicians elsewhere in the world (particularly in China) as hypocrites if they expect the West to take a lead in adopting growth-restricting measures while the Chinese economy continues to grow apace. But it will be relatively easy for Chinese politicians to portray democratic politicians as hypocrites if they expect the rest of the world to follow their lead without taking account of the unequal states of development of the various economies. Equal sacrifices are hard to justify in an unequal world. But unequal sacrifices will be hard to justify in the democratic world. And there lies the problem.

. . . [A]t the heart of this issue lies a dilemma that the prevalence of hypocrisy poses for all forms of modern politics. Some hypocrisy seems unavoidable when it comes to environmental politics—in relation both to personal conduct, and to the behavior of different regimes that will seek to hold each other to standards that they cannot readily meet themselves—and it would be a mistake to imagine that hypocrisy must cease before any real progress can be made. Equally, however, it would be a mistake to be too sanguine about hypocrisy in this context, given its capacity to generate political conflict, and to spill over into the most destructive forms of self-deception. So we must try to distinguish between different kinds of hypocrisy, and to decide which ones are worth worrying about.

NOTES AND QUESTIONS

1. Runciman draws a distinction between "first order hypocrisy," the practice of "concealing vice as virtue," and "second order hypocrisy," the practice of "concealing the truth about this practice." It is the latter conduct that he finds troubling: "[W]e may need to hide the truth about ourselves in order to get by in this world, but we oughtn't to hide the truth from ourselves that this is what we are doing."[22] Is that a useful distinction? Think of examples of political hypocrisy that you find most offensive. Were they first order or second order? How much do you think it matters to the public?

2. Consider John Edwards's much-mocked $400 haircuts during the 2008 presidential campaign. Following a YouTube video of him fussing with hair and makeup, to the tune of "I Feel Pretty," Edwards reimbursed his campaign $800 for two Beverly Hills salon visits while insisting that he did not know how much they cost.[23] His gesture did little to quiet critics. As Maureen Dowd noted in the *New York Times*, "[S]omeone who aspires to talk credibly about [poverty and] the two Americas can't lavish on his locks what working families may spend on electricity in a year. You can't sell earnestness while indulging in decadence."[24] As Dowd also noted, Edwards at the time was living in a 28,000-square-foot North Carolina mansion with a basketball court, squash court, and swimming pool. Did that also undermine his ability to speak credibly about poverty? High-profile politicians and their families are routinely coached to give up preferences that seem too upscale. John Kerry's windsurfing did not poll well during his presidential campaign. Does that suggest a public ambivalence about authenticity? Voters sometimes demand that candidates look like "one of us" and then are disappointed when the pretense is revealed. Is that public response productive? Do charges of hypocrisy sometimes serve to discourage wealthy leaders from running for office or from taking politically progressive positions? What do you make of Donald Trump's boasts about his personal wealth and his support among blue-collar voters?

3. How would you evaluate the claims of hypocrisy leveled against leaders whose personal conduct is inconsistent with their public positions on immigration? For example, Meg Whitman, in her race for California governor, ran on a platform advocating tough sanctions for those who hire illegal immigrants. In the wake of public disclosures that she had employed an undocumented woman as her housekeeper for nearly a decade, she summarily fired the woman. Although Whitman claimed she was unaware of the woman's status,

she and her husband had received correspondence from the Social Security Administration advising them of a problem.[25] Political commentator Lou Dobbs, who has been highly critical of employers who hire undocumented workers, has similarly faced charges that he has long retained such workers as gardeners and as stable hands for his daughter's show horses.[26]

B. THE PARADOX OF POWER: THE CORROSION OF JUDGMENT

Leadership scandals invite public attention not only because they offer the perverse pleasure of seeing the mighty fallen but also because they often present such a curious paradox. How can leaders who seem so smart in other aspects of their lives be so clueless in the matters that can cost them their positions? Why do such ambitious individuals risk so much for relatively inconsequential rewards? Social scientists label this the paradox of power and suggest that much of the explanation lies in the cognitive biases and structural conditions noted earlier: leaders' tendencies to see themselves as unique and invulnerable, and to have those perceptions reinforced by the perks and deference that accompany powerful positions.[27] In the following excerpt, Stanford Business School professor Roderick Kramer explores these dynamics and identifies some strategies for leaders who otherwise might find themselves tottering toward an abyss.

RODERICK KRAMER, THE HARDER THEY FALL

Harvard Business Review 81(10) (Oct. 2003): 58-66

[When scandal sets in, once feted and envied leaders find themselves falling hard and fast. Admired leaders] not just in business but also in politics, religion, and the media—are finding themselves in a similar free fall. One moment they are masters of their domain. The next they are on the pavement looking up, wondering where it all went wrong.

At first glance, these [leaders] are unlikely candidates for such swift and ignoble falls. In their brilliant and rapid ascents, "star" leaders repeatedly demonstrate the intelligence, resourcefulness, and drive to go the distance. They prove adept at overcoming whatever obstacles they encounter along the way. And they display a dazzling ability to woo investors, enchant employees, and charm the media with their charisma, grandiose visions, and seemingly unlimited strategic acumen. Yet just when they appear to have it all, these A-list performers demonstrate uncharacteristic lapses in professional judgment or personal conduct. . . .

[This article explores] what I like to call the *genius-to-folly syndrome*—a swift and steady rise by a brilliant, hard-driving, politically adept individual followed by surprising stints of miscalculation or recklessness. Why do so many individuals seem to fall prey to stunning bouts of folly once they seize power? Attributing it to personal failings or lack of moral fiber seems too glib—after all, wouldn't the flaws have emerged earlier in the leaders' careers? As a psychologist and consultant to many businesses, I've spent most of my career researching the process of getting to the top. . . . I've found that there is something about the pursuit of power that often changes people in profound ways. Indeed, to get to the apex of their profession, individuals are often forced to jettison certain attitudes and behaviors—the same attitudes and behaviors they need for survival once they get to the top. During the high-tech boom, we saw risk-taking and rule-breaking as markers of good leadership. As a result, we often ended up with leaders who lacked the prudence, sense of proportion, and self-restraint needed to cope with the trappings of power.

Winner Wants All

In any attractive professional domain—be it Silicon Valley, Washington, or Hollywood—there are lots of extremely smart and ambitious individuals vying for just a few top slots. Moving up the ranks can be like competing in a high-stakes tournament: As you make it through successive rounds, the pool of worthy candidates narrows, the margin for error is much smaller, and the competition intensifies. This winnowing process means just a handful of people will attain prominence or success. In some contests—such as those for CEO of a major corporation, head of a mainstream motion picture studio, dean of an elite law school, or president of the United States—there can be only one winner.

Researchers Robert Frank and Philip Cook have characterized such tournaments as "winner-take-all markets"—a very few star performers generate most of the value and *end* up enjoying the lion's share of the spoils. I interviewed leaders from the worlds of business, politics, and entertainment and found that the intense competition in these winner-take-all markets creates players who suffer from a "winner-wants-all" mind-set. These elite performers expect everything—but often end up with nothing.

There are many explanations for this. For a start, because there are so many talented, determined people competing for just one top slot, the players in winner-take-all markets must be extraordinarily aggressive about taking risks . . . [and] willing to act quickly on those impulses—often before there is time for dequate reflection. "It's a very steep climb . . . and a fast one. You have to seize every handhold that appears and learn to take advantage of it instantly," one former film studio executive told me. "If you lean back on your ropes to look up and ponder the risks, the moment may be gone." Indeed, the most ambitious and competitive players in winner-take-all markets often perceive that introspection is antithetical to success. As a result, these individuals develop a dangerous aversion to moderation.

Rules Are for Fools

Another conspicuous feature of the winner-wants-all mind-set has to do with individuals' attitudes about the rules of the game. Many players in winner-take-all markets believe that getting ahead means doing things differently from ordinary people—for instance, finding a back door to success that others have not been smart enough to spot.

Consider the case of legendary African-American entrepreneur Reginald Lewis. At the time of his death at age 50 from a brain tumor, Lewis had earned a spot on *Forbes*'s list of the 400 wealthiest Americans, with a net worth estimated at around $400 million. More than 2,000 people attended his funeral, including former presidents Ronald Reagan and Bill Clinton as well as U.S. Secretary of State Colin Powell and entertainer Bill Cosby. Lewis not only orchestrated one of the biggest leveraged buyouts of his era, he also gave away millions, including $3 million to Harvard Law School. In his eulogy for Lewis, Cosby said, "We are all dealt a hand to play in this game of life, and believe me, Reg Lewis played the hell out of his hand."

But Lewis started life with a weak hand. The cards didn't get better until he came up with some new rules to play by. As an undergraduate at Virginia State, Lewis decided that a degree from Harvard Law School was just what he needed to get started on the path to prominence. But given his relatively undistinguished background, it was far from clear that he would be admitted to Harvard. Then he learned about a new Rockefeller Foundation-funded program at the law school that was aimed at minority students. Lewis devised a strategy to get into the program. In his own words, "First, have a tremendous final year in college. Second, know the objectives of the program. Third, break your ass over the summer, eliminate all distractions. Prove that you can compete. Do the job." These were the standards Lewis had set for himself, and he excelled, impressing everyone he met with his enthusiasm, intelligence, self-confidence, ambition, and hard work.

Unfortunately, there was a fly in the ointment. In setting up the summer program, Harvard had established a strict prohibition against using it as an entree into the law school. Undaunted by what seemed like yet another closed door, Lewis tirelessly started knocking on other doors, pitching himself as the ideal candidate for Harvard Law to anyone who would listen. Ultimately, it paid off. Lewis received a personal invitation to meet with the school's dean of admissions. And whatever was said during that meeting, it worked. Lewis became a member of the first-year class without even having filled out an application. He was reputedly the first person in the 148-year-history of Harvard Law ever admitted *before* he had applied.

People like Lewis are not the exception in high-stakes games; they are often the ones who win. Consider the case of David Geffen, cofounder of DreamWorks and currently worth an estimated $3.8 billion. When Geffen managed to wangle an entry-level job in the mail room at the William Morris Agency early in his career, he learned to his dismay that all employees had to provide proof of a college degree before they could advance. Geffen hadn't graduated from college. But unwilling to be held back by the facts, he dissembled on his application form that he had graduated from UCLA. When he learned that his employer would do a routine check on his credentials, Geffen got to work early every morning to intercept the incoming mail. When the letter from UCLA finally arrived, Geffen trashed it and replaced it with a forged letter indicating that he had indeed graduated from the university.

Lewis and Geffen broke the rules—and were deemed resourceful and enterprising by their bosses and peers, rather than immoral or criminal. Indeed, many players in winner-take-all markets believe that breaking the rules is not only necessary for getting ahead, it is virtually an act of creativity. "The rules are meant to be broken," one major automotive executive told me. "If you aren't willing to test the limits of what's acceptable and what works . . . you'll never make it to that next level of performance or attainment." An executive from the petroleum industry echoed that sentiment: "If you're too afraid of stepping over the foul line, you'll never figure out how close to it you can get."

Unfortunately, this disdain for the rules puts risk-taking leaders on a very slippery slope. They may consider themselves exempt from the rules that govern other people's behavior. Even more dangerous, leaders who want it all and who break the rules to get it often develop contempt for those who *do* play by the rules. Those who follow the letter of the law are seen as timid and unimaginative conformists who "just don't get it." As one advertising executive put it, "Frankly, it's hard to respect individuals who plod along by just following the rules." A highly successful Hollywood agent told me several years ago—and the quote seems ironic today—"If you want to follow all the rules, become an accountant. You'll be happier and live longer." It doesn't take too much imagination to see how, taken to the extreme, such attitudes foster the sort of can-do—yet ultimately dysfunctional—corporate cultures we observed in troubled companies such as Enron, Tyco, and WorldCom.

A Hefty Price Tag

[Leaders who get to the top under highly competitive conditions can become] extremely vulnerable to the heady effects of power's rewards. Leaders who've "made it" suddenly have to start coping with lavish expense accounts, travel in corporate jets, and a plethora of other compensations. Beyond these are innumerable social perks. Leaders find that their presence is desired at glamorous social gatherings. . . . Other people, including the rich and famous, treat these newly arrived leaders as equally important members of the in crowd. And as Henry Kissinger once pointed out, "Power is the ultimate aphrodisiac." . . .

But as enjoyable as they can be, the trappings of power only serve to feed the dangerous illusions people already have about themselves. Decades of psychological research on self-enhancing illusions suggest that most people have highly (and overly) positive views of their abilities. Most people, for example, believe they are better-than-average drivers, lovers, and leaders. Without the steadying influence of a robust personal life and a network of friends who can help you maintain a healthy perspective, easy access to corporate jets and unlimited expense accounts turns those unrealistic beliefs into certain knowledge, resulting in a potentially fatal overconfidence. "Looking back on it, my judgment was often terribly wrong," said one young entrepreneur who had burned through more than

$20 million trying to launch a Web-based business. "Unfortunately, I was never in doubt."

The sacrifices an individual makes on the way to the top not only make it harder to cope with the rewards when they do come, they also make the person greedier for more of the same. Indeed, getting more becomes "just deserts" for having paid such a high price for success. According to one report, former Tyco CEO Dennis Kozlowski spent millions on art and elaborate home furnishings. He allegedly charged to his company purchases of a $15,000 umbrella stand, a $17,000 traveling toilette box, a $5,900 set of bed sheets, and a $2,200 wastebasket. However easy it may be for leaders to rationalize such an exaggerated sense of entitlement, they create trouble for themselves when their indulgences become too out of sync with what other people believe is right or fair. While followers will experience obvious pleasure in seeing their beloved leaders work their way up the ranks, they will also get equal satisfaction out of seeing them brought down a notch. . . .

The Sins of Omission

It's not only what new leaders *do* when they get to the top that gets them into trouble; it's also what they *don't* do. They get distracted by all the temptations— and often abandon the practices that helped them capture the crown. They may spend less time, for example, conscientiously monitoring their environments. They may pay less attention to what others around them are thinking or doing— especially their critics and potential enemies.

Of course, like everyone else, leaders like to have the positive images they have of themselves reflected back. But then, leaders are in a unique position: Their followers are keen to praise and defend the person on whom their livelihood depends. Most executives don't question this ingratiating behavior as much as they should. After all, even if they recognize their subordinates' ingratiation as slightly exaggerated, leaders like to think there is at least a kernel of truth to the nice things other people are saying about them. Thus, despite their best intentions, leaders may find that every mirror held up to them says, in effect, you *are* the fairest of them all.

One might think that reality would splash a little cold water now and then on leaders' splendid illusions. At the very least, one would expect some high-ranked lieutenant or trusted adviser to sound the alarm. In fact, this rarely happens because close subordinates are often more deferential to leaders than lower-ranked employees are. The people who most closely surround a leader often occupy a precarious perch, and they often don't want to risk their place by being labeled a disloyal doubter or naysayer. Thus, paradoxically, at the same time that people serving the leader are paying such close attention to every wrinkle on the leader's brow, they also tend to look the other way whenever he or she does something unseemly. "I can remember being in meetings where people's faces were absolutely impassive when the CEO said something truly stupid," one financial services executive told me. "But I have to confess, my face was just as impassive as everyone else's."

How to Have It All

A lauded leader can indeed succumb to recklessness once power has been achieved. But not all executives lose their footing. The behaviors and values of the leaders I interviewed who got to the top and managed to stay there are quite similar. They had different personalities and management styles, but they all seemed to retain a remarkable sense of proportion and displayed a high degree of self-awareness. When I asked them how they had been able to remain effective for so long, I learned that each had developed a certain combination of psychological and behavioral habits that helped them stay grounded.

Keep your life simple. "It helps to remain *awfully* ordinary," one CEO told me. . . . Such normal behavior may seem lackluster, but it helps leaders stay in touch with themselves and with other ordinary people, including their customers and employees. Indeed, if high-flying leaders hope to stay on top, they would do well to nurture their humility. It helps people view their accomplishments, and their foibles, with detachment. It also helps people to see adversity through a healthy lens. The best way of developing humility is to remind ourselves of what really matters in life. Take it from Warren Buffett. When asked how he learned to handle his enormous power and wealth, he said, "I live now the way I lived 30 years ago."

Hang a lantern on your foibles. Few leaders manage to reach the top and remain there very long without suffering from some occasional blunders. We all have shortcomings, and they always interfere to some extent. The natural tendency with flaws and imperfections is to deny them or cover them up. But what we really need to do is to shine a light on our weaknesses to understand them better. What's more, acknowledging our shortcomings or mistakes helps to prevent others from punishing us too much for those failures. After the Bay of Pigs, for example, President Kennedy accepted full responsibility for the disastrous operation, and his popularity soared higher than ever. . . .

Sweat the small stuff. Some self-help books exhort people not to sweat the small stuff, and in many arenas of life, that's sound advice. But when it comes to running a film studio, a country, or a company, leaders *do* need to sweat the small stuff. They need to worry about what might be ahead so they can anticipate what might go wrong. . . . Perhaps the most famous practitioner of "sweating the small stuff" is former Intel CEO Andrew Grove, who explained it this way: "I believe in the value of paranoia. . . . I worry about factories not performing well, and I worry about having too many factories. I worry about hiring the right people, and I worry about morale slacking off. And, of course, I worry about competitors. I worry about other people figuring out how to do what we do better or cheaper and displacing us with our customers."

Reflect more, not less. Successful leaders strive to become more reflective. That's paradoxical given that today's business culture celebrates action over hesitancy. Americans in particular admire leaders who break new ground, transform industries, and smash glass ceilings. Given this overemphasis on *doing*, perhaps it's not surprising that many of the fallen leaders I studied appeared to have a strikingly impoverished sense of self. Though they often know how to read others brilliantly, they remain curiously oblivious to many of their own tendencies that expose them to risk. When Bill Clinton was interrogated about his relationship with Monica Lewinsky, for example, he made the startling disclosure that he assumed all along that Monica would tell some of her friends about what was going on. Perhaps he should have spent a little more time reflecting about which friends—and with what consequences. . . .

Each year, to encourage my students to become more mindful of the effects that success and power might have on their behavior as future business leaders, I ask them to write their obituaries. I encourage them to be as realistic as possible. Given the high caliber of these students, it is hardly surprising that most imagine their lives copiously filled with significant achievements. They expect to become CEOs, philanthropists, best-selling authors, and the like. The personal lives they accord themselves are no less spectacular. They describe large, happy families, wonderful vacations at summer and winter retreats, and a full complement of personal accomplishments. But when I ask the students to estimate how the process of attaining those achievements will change them, they rather uniformly report "very little" or "not at all." They don't expect, for example, their core values to change. Strikingly, they anticipate having to make few, if any, trade-offs in the pursuit of professional and personal success. Miraculously, they argue, they will manage to have it all.

When I ask respondents to explain why they think the process of experiencing great success will not change them in any fundamental way, they typically say something along the lines of, "Because I know what kind of person I am." These nascent leaders believe their personal characters and core values will buffer them from any temptation or travail that might be thrown at them on their paths to power. It is as if in finding success they will become merely bigger and better versions of what they are now. They can't even imagine that they could ever fall from grace. And that, of course, guarantees that some of them will. . . .

Recognizing the Symptoms of Reckless Leadership

When I talk to business executives and government leaders about the genius-to-folly syndrome, one of the questions I am asked most frequently is: "How will I know I'm in danger of falling?" There is no universal set of early warning signs, but there are some useful questions leaders can routinely ask themselves to find out how close to the precipice they really are. Just as shrewd leaders use accounting audits to see how financially healthy their organizations are, so too can they use *personal leader audits* to find out how robust their leadership is and to assess whether they are drifting toward disaster. These audits can help leaders reflect on the consequences of their actions. The questions might include the following:

Are you spending most of your time plugging holes and papering over cracks? In organizations headed for disaster, the leader has lost sight of the big picture. Instead, her attention is often myopically focused on staving off imminent disaster. Substantive problems are swept under the rug or pushed out of mind as she spends every waking moment obsessively focused on putting the best spin on the latest bad news. . . . This frenetic sleight of hand is usually accompanied by the leader's rationalization that she is simply buying time and will get to the big fixes later. If you relentlessly find yourself hoping tomorrow will be a better day, maybe you should change what you are doing right now. How do you respond to those annoying, dissenting voices in your organization? In almost every instance of leadership folly I've studied, one or more individuals in the organization recognized trouble was brewing and earnestly tried to alert the CEO to the dangers. Instead of applause, however, they got tomatoes. As a result, these good corporate citizens swallowed their whistles instead of blowing them. Even worse, many fled from what they viewed as a sinking ship. Leaders should think long and hard about how they—and those closest to them—really respond to the bearers of bad news.

Who can you really trust to tell you the emperor has no clothes? It's great to have a chorus of loyal aides and advisers who march to your orders. But you also need someone to let you know when the team is marching toward an abyss. Bill Gates—a man who clearly knows his own mind and who has all the brainpower one could ask for—has Steve Ballmer to bounce ideas off of and to provide those much-needed reality checks. "We trusted each other from the beginning in a very deep way," Gates says. Having a doubting Thomas (or Ballmer) is especially important because those leaders most prone to recklessness and folly are often too adept at creating an organizational world that reflects their own optimistic values and forward-charging inclinations. It's critical for such leaders to have someone who can speak up and give them an honest assessment of the situation. Not having such a person on your staff—or in your life—is one of the first signs that you may be getting dangerously isolated and insulated.

Do you have illusions of grandeur? In the humorous film *Defending Your Life*, Albert Brooks's character finds himself forced to witness and defend the many misdeeds of his life, including his acts of hubris, selfishness, and cowardice. Ideally, none of us will ever have to answer for our actions in such a demanding court. However, in the personal audit it definitely helps to ask yourself, "Has my behavior changed since I became chief?" Have you grown so important that virtually everyone you know cowers before you or defers to your every whim and demand? Are you sometimes wrong but never in doubt? Be honest. If you can answer yes to any of these queries, you are in danger of becoming grandiose.

Are you too greedy for your own good? It's difficult for most of us to think of ourselves as greedy. We all know how hard we've worked to get to the top. Yet if there is one hallmark of the winner-wants-all mind-set, it's the acquisitive instinct gone wild. The relentless, competitive quest for more power and status becomes an end in itself. The real problem begins when the appetite to acquire more comes to dominate every decision. Suddenly, we not only want it all. We actually feel entitled to it all. This can happen all too easily given the human propensity to take for granted things that were previously benchmarks of progress or success. The alert leader tries to combat his greediness by giving something back to society.

Is this a good time to pause, consider doing something different, or even do nothing at all? This is a simple question to ask, but one of the hardest to answer—especially in moments when we seem in full control of our destiny, and there isn't a cloud in the sky. Many of the fallen leaders I've studied stumbled just when the waters seemed calmest. So sometimes slowing the pace or even calling a time-out to reassess your path may be the best strategy of all. . . .

NOTES AND QUESTIONS

1. Psychologist Dacher Keltner, in *The Power Paradox*, summarizes research indicating that power increases the prevalence and acceptance of unethical behavior.[28] Like Kramer, he identifies the "practice of humility" and a focus on others as important correctives.[29] How can these be encouraged?
2. Have you ever observed symptoms of reckless leadership in yourself or others? What were the causes? What responses were, or would have been, most effective?
3. Consider one of the leadership scandals described in the materials in this chapter or in recent news coverage. What factors contributed to the misconduct? Could they have been averted through interventions of the sort that Kramer describes?
4. Social scientists often suggest that the best response to abuses of power is transparency: an active board of directors, government regulators, or consumer watchdogs who remind leaders that they are being monitored. In effect, the corner office needs windows.[30] If that is true, what might promote such oversight? Are scandals sometimes necessary to prevent further scandals?

C. CRISIS MANAGEMENT: APOLOGIES AND CORRECTIVE ACTION

Leaders confront crises of reputation based on their own conduct, their organization's conduct, or some combination. Whatever the context, the most fundamental challenges are similar. A case in point involves Mike Brown, the director of FEMA, the federal agency responsible for disaster relief efforts following hurricane Katrina. Expressing widely shared views, one commentator noted that Brown had handled the situation "perfectly, except for understanding what was happening and actually doing something about it."[31] The quip captures the essential tasks of crisis management: gaining a full appreciation of the causes and consequences of the situation and formulating a response that will both address the immediate problem and prevent a recurrence. Because leaders' responses are often widely disseminated through mainstream and social media, the stakes in getting the message right have escalated. [32]

An obvious point, but one sometimes overlooked when the behavior that results in scandal first surfaces internally, is that leaders should evaluate the situation in terms of reputational as well as legal consequences. Ethicists have often recommended what is colloquially known as the *New York Times* or *Sixty Minutes* test: how would this look if the details were fully aired on the front page of a national newspaper or major television program. As the examples later in this chapter make clear, leaders could have saved themselves a multitude of troubles if they had seriously considered the reputational consequences of full exposure at a time when they were positioned to take preventive actions.

Once a crisis has leaders, leaders' first question is often, "What do we do?" Experts on crisis management view this as the wrong question. The right one is, "What do we know?" Although the need for full information is obvious, it is often difficult or impossible to assemble before the pressures for action become overwhelming. During the BP oil spill, when *Today* show host Matt Lauer suggested to President Obama that he needed to "kick some butt," Obama responded that he was doing his best to find "whose ass to kick."[33] How to respond in situations of uncertainty is one of the challenges of leadership that Dezenhall and Weber discuss in the excerpt below. On some points, however, experts are in agreement. Leaders should be responsive to media and stakeholder questions, be honest about what they know and don't know, refuse to speculate, and anticipate difficult questions.[34] They should also get all the bad news out at once, rather than let it dribble out over successive news cycles.[35]

Once a crisis develops, leaders have four main options in terms of public statements: (1) a denial of wrongdoing, (2) a refusal to comment, (3) an expression of sympathy or regret (often termed a partial apology or non-apology apology), or (4) a full apology accepting responsibility. Each strategy has its advantages and limitations.

Denials take multiple forms. Leaders may claim that:

- No wrongful act occurred ("I did not have sex with that woman");
- "Mistakes were made" but not by me or my organization (I didn't know, a subsidiary or supplier was accountable for defects, customers were negligent);
- The acts were attributable to a rogue employee or a few bad apples, and were not typical of the organization.[36]

In some instances, those accused of wrongdoing may also attempt to reclaim the moral high ground by accusing their accusers of improper tactics or motivations. Richard Nixon, in his famous "Checkers speech," saved his spot on the vice presidential ticket by painting himself as the innocent victim of a political vendetta. After denying that he had misused a special campaign fund, he detailed his modest financial status and acknowledged having accepted only one gift from a Republican contributor—a cocker spaniel named Checkers that he refused to return because his daughters loved the dog so much.[37] A more recent example occurred in the Senate confirmation hearing of Supreme Court Justice Brett Kavanaugh, when he denied committing sexual assault as a teenager and characterized accusations of inappropriate sexual conduct as an "orchestrated political hit."[38]

If they are credible, denials are typically the most effective response in a scandal, particularly if the conduct involves integrity.[39] Part of the reason is that when evaluating ethical behavior, people tend to weigh negative acts more heavily than positive acts, so any statement that suggests moral culpability will be hard to remedy.[40] So too, if the conduct could create legal liability, stakeholders are likely to respond negatively to anything other than a denial.[41] However, if the facts are not strong enough to support a denial, or at least to create reasonable doubts, a refusal to acknowledge responsibility is counterproductive. When wrongdoing seems clearly to have occurred, the public expects conciliatory statements and corrective action.

Under these circumstances, excuses, denials, or minimization of harms fuel anger because they compound the misconduct and suggest the likelihood of future abuses.[42] Research suggests that the duration, rather than the initial impact of a crisis, is what determines its long-term repercussions, and an ineffective apology is what allows a scandal to fester.[43] One study that examined 150 press releases over a 15-year period found that companies that blamed others for a major scandal experienced continued decline in financial performance while companies that accepted responsibility experienced an uptick.[44]

In the face of conflicting or unfavorable information, a *New Yorker* cartoon captures the relevant trade-off. It pictures a corporate meeting in which the chair says, "Let's never forget that the public's desire for transparency has to be balanced by our need for concealment."[45] Refusals to comment are a common strategy for striking that balance when leaders believe that: evidence of culpability is unlikely to surface; the risks of creating potential liability for themselves or others are too great; more time is necessary to gain information; or the issues are so personal that full disclosure seems unwarranted.

However, in terms of public relations, silence is often the least effective option. It is less reassuring than a denial, because it fails to disclaim guilt, and less satisfying than an apology, because it fails to signal remorse and promise corrective action.[46] If the goal is to convince others to withhold judgment, silence seldom succeeds, particularly when evidence of culpability has surfaced. A representative example involved Merrill Lynch's recommendations of stocks that analysts had characterized in e-mails as "dogs," "trash," and "piece[s] of s—." The purpose of the recommendations was to retain banking business from issuers of these stocks. To settle charges, the firm paid a $100 million fine without admitting misconduct. But as then New York Attorney General Eliot Spitzer pointedly noted, "You don't pay a $100 million fine if you didn't do anything wrong."[47]

Partial apologies that express sympathy without acknowledging responsibility also present trade-offs. As common sense suggests and psychological research confirms, they are never as effective as full apologies in suggesting that the speaker is "aware of the social norms that have been violated" and therefore likely to "avoid the offense in future interactions."[48] Ritualistic apologies can also backfire. Those who utter frequent statements of regret may end up appearing weaker, less confident, and less sincere than those who do not apologize at all.[49] Yet, in some settings, expressions of sympathy are better than other options. If litigation is likely, acknowledging any responsibility is risky: "[E]very word used to persuade the public is a word that may be used to persuade a judge."[50] But some conciliatory statement may be necessary to avoid making the leaders or their organizations appear callous and unresponsive. Carefully crafted partial apologies can help reduce hostility, restore respect, and resolve conflict.[51]

Full apologies are, however, generally more effective in defusing anger, rebuilding relationships, and encouraging confidence that the misconduct will not recur.[52] In politics, apologies by leaders have often served a largely symbolic role; they have expressed collective remorse for wrongdoing ranging from the internment of Japanese Americans to abusive practices by the Internal Revenue Service.[53] In contexts involving legal liability, apologies have reduced financial demands and the chance of lawsuits.[54] To encourage expeditious settlements, about two-thirds of states have statutes that limit or prevent the use of apologies as evidence of wrongdoing in subsequent litigation.[55] Even in cases that go to trial, apologies that accept responsibility can help mitigate guilt, and are much more likely to have a positive influence than those that simply express sympathy and remorse.[56]

The most effective apologies are ones in which leaders

- promptly acknowledge wrongdoing;
- are specific about the wrongs inflicted;
- convey sincere emotions;
- ask for forgiveness;
- promise not to repeat the conduct; and
- indicate a desire to do what is necessary to put things right.[57]

Genuine apologies are always a work in progress. Their effectiveness will depend on whether the promised changes and reparations are forthcoming.[58]

Apologies that fall short of this ideal can still serve their intended objective. For example, in describing his own strategy for handling questions about youthful indiscretions while later campaigning for president, George W. Bush relied on advice from his pastor: "[Don't] talk about the details of [your] transgressions, but talk about what [you] have learned."[59]

Leaders can often amplify the persuasiveness of apologies through symbolic gestures. Holy Roman Emperor Henry IV set the gold standard in 1077 when apologizing to Pope Gregory VII for church-state conflicts by standing barefoot in the snow for three days.[60] Japanese leaders have perfected the contemporary equivalent. A rich literature is available to advise them on the art of the apology, complete with photographs comparing the angles of leaders' bows and tips on wardrobe. Suits in "sedate, calming colors" like black or navy are recommended.[61] As that advice suggests, leaders need to be aware of cultural differences in what constitutes an adequate apology. When Toyota CEO Akio Toyoda failed to come to America to manage the 2010 accelerator pedal recall problem, he earned a new nickname, "no show Akio."[62]

Even more important is what leaders promise, and deliver, in long-term correctives. Auto manufacturers have, for example, reformed policies on reporting possible defects, and run advertisements like Ford's, which pledged that in the future, "When we know it, so will the world."[63] In the aftermath of a highly publicized plagiarism scandal, the *New York Times* fired its editor, formed a task force to recommend preventative strategies, and followed up one and two years later to determine the effectiveness of those correctives.[64] Some organizations enhance their credibility by engaging critics or outside experts in the reform process. Tyco retained a Wharton School professor of corporate governance to help redesign its oversight policies.[65] In the wake of the #MeToo movement, some organizations hired outside law firms to assess their organizational culture and handling of accusations of sexual misconduct.[66]

Because the best response to scandal is always prevention, an increasing number of organizations conduct risk or reputation audits.[67] Stakeholder surveys and anonymous hotlines can serve as early warnings systems. Despite, or sometimes because of, their position, leaders are often insulated from negative information.[68] Subordinates may see too little to gain and too much to lose from being the bearer of unwelcome tidings. As earlier chapters suggested, leaders need to be proactive about soliciting candid information and protective of anyone who supplies it.

They should also use the occasion that scandal supplies to address fundamental problems. Experts recommend having participants compile a list of lessons learned. Questions worth addressing include:

- Were there early warning signs that could have been recognized sooner?
- How effective was the response?
- What was done right and what could have been done better?
- What will prevent such situations from happening again?
- If we could replay this entire event, what would we do differently?[69]

"Never waste a good crisis," was the advice that Harvard professor William George offered to Toyota following its accelerator pedal recall. This was a "unique opportunity to make fundamental changes required to restore Toyota quality."[70] Similarly, Barack Obama characterized the BP oil spill as the "most painful and powerful reminder yet that the time to embrace a clean energy future is now."[71] Boeing Aircraft's CEO James McNerney also used a scandal involving government contracting to convey the need for broader cultural change. One of his first efforts after assuming the leadership was to address top management with a PowerPoint presentation displaying two numerical sequences on large video screens. "These are not ZIP codes," he noted. They were the prison numbers of the Boeing executive and Air Force procurement officer convicted in the scandal.[72] That was a message "made to stick."[73]

PROBLEM 7-1

Consider the following apologies. Which seem most and least effective? Why? If you were the leader, or a lawyer advising the leader, what changes would you recommend?

Public Safety and Product Defects

- We are "deeply sorry that we have broken the trust of customers and the public. We do not and will not tolerate violations of any kind of our internal rules or of the law." We will "cooperate fully" with the EPA investigation and conduct "an external investigation of this matter." Martin Winterkorn, Volkswagen CEO, statement concerning fraudulent emissions standard compliance data.[74] The company also ran full-page ads in 30 newspapers pledging, "We're working to make this right," and offered a goodwill package to customers of affected vehicles of a $500 Visa gift card and a $500 subsidy toward a purchase of a new Volkswagen vehicle.[75]

- "I am very, very sorry that this accident occurred, very sorry. . . . And I do believe that it's right to investigate it fully and draw the right conclusion. . . . This is a complex accident, caused by an unprecedented combination of failures." Tony Hayward, CEO British Petroleum, apologizing for an explosion killing 11 people and causing a massive oil spill.[76]

- "We're sorry for the massive disruption it's caused to their lives. There's no one who wants this thing over more than I do. I'd like my life back." Tony Hayward, CEO British Petroleum, following the massive 2010 oil spill in the Gulf of Mexico.[77]

- "Our lawyers tell us it's not our fault, but it sure feels like our fault and we'll do anything we can to fix it." British Petroleum executive, following oil spill off San Diego.[78]

- "I myself, as well as Toyota, am not perfect. At times, we do find defects. But in such situations we always stop, strive to understand the problem, and make changes to improve further. . . . It has taken us too long to come to grips with a rare but serious set of safety issues, despite all of our good faith efforts." Jim Lentz, president and COO of Toyota Motor Sales, U.S. Congressional Testimony concerning accelerator pedals.[79]

- "I come before you to apologize to you, the American people—especially to the families who have lost loved ones in these terrible rollover accidents. I also come to accept full and personal responsibility on behalf of Bridgestone/Firestone." Masatoshi Ono, CEO Bridgestone/Firestone, U.S. Congressional Testimony in 2000 concerning tire malfunctions in Ford Explorers.[80]

- "Nobody took responsibility. . . . We are going to fix our mistakes and we are going to be a better, stronger company." Mary Barra, CEO General Motors, U.S. Congressional Testimony about ignition switch defect. Barra also indicated that the company would not expand its victim compensation program, share documents from its internal investigation, or dismiss its general counsel.[81]

Politics

- "Last night I was 'grossly generalistic' and that's never a good idea. I regret saying 'half'—that was wrong." Hillary Clinton apologizing for the following statement made during her 2016 presidential campaign: "To just be grossly generalistic, you can put half of Trump supporters into what I call the basket of deplorables. Right? Racist, sexist, homophobic, xenophobic, Islamophobic, you name it."[82]

- "I regret deeply any injuries that may have been done in the course of events that have led to this decision [to resign]. I would say only that if some of my judgments were wrong, and some were wrong, they were made in what I believed at the time to be in the best interest of the nation." Richard Nixon, resigning from the presidency.[83]

- "Mistakes were quite possibly made by the administrations in which I served." Henry Kissinger, responding to charges that he committed war crimes in his role as Secretary of State overseeing actions in Vietnam, Cambodia, and South America in the 1970s.[84]

- "This administration intends to be candid about its errors; for as a wise man once said: 'An error does not become a mistake until you refuse to correct it. . . . [The final responsibility for the failure of the Bay of Pigs invasion was] mine and mine alone." President John F. Kennedy.[85]

- "Bear in mind that this is a freewheeling anything-goes Internet radio show that is broadcast from a pub. It's like a political version of Saturday Night Live. Since my intended humorous context was lost in translation, I apologize. I still believe Ms. Haley is pretending to be someone she is not, much as Obama did, but I apologize to both for an unintended slur." Jake Knotts, South Carolina state senator, running for governor, after a statement concerning his primary opponent, Nikki Haley, who was raised as a Sikh: "We already got one raghead in the White House. We don't need another in the governor's mansion."[86]

- "To this day, I regret I couldn't give her the kind of hearing she deserved." Presidential candidate Joe Biden apologizing for his decisions as Chair of the Senate Judiciary Committee during the Clarence Thomas confirmation hearings, which refused to allow other witnesses to corroborate testimony by Anita Hill.[87]

Financial Management

- "This is a painful decision for me to make after five years at H.P., but I believe it would difficult for me to continue as an effective leader. . . . As the investigation progressed, I realized that there have been instances in which I did not live up to the standards and principles of trust, respect and integrity that I have espoused at H.P." Mark Hurd, resigning as CEO of Hewlett-Packard, after revelations of favoritism toward an attractive female HP contractor that raised concerns about conflicts of interest and fraudulent expense accounts totaling up to $20,000.[88]

- "Let me start by saying I'm sorry. I'm sorry that the financial crisis has had such a devastating impact for our country. I'm sorry about the millions of people, average Americans, who lost their homes. And I'm sorry that our management teams, starting with me, like so many others could not see the unprecedented market collapse that lay before us." Charles O. Prince III, former chair and CEO of Citigroup.[89]

Sex

- "Anyone who knows me knows these words don't reflect who I am, I said, I was wrong, and I apologize." Donald Trump, commenting on a taped interview that revealed him bragging about grabbing women's "pussy," a claim that he had earlier dismissed as "locker room banter."[90]

- "In many years on the campaign trail and in public life, I have offered countless handshakes, hugs, expressions of affection, support and comfort. And not once—never—did I believe I acted inappropriately. If it is suggested I did so, I will listen respectfully. But it was never my intention."[91] "I'm sorry I didn't understand more. . . . I'm not sorry for anything that I have ever done. I have never been disrespectful intentionally to a man or woman." Joe Biden, responding to claims of inappropriate touching of women.[92]

- "I've always had a broad sense of humor and a candid way of speaking to both male and female law clerks alike. In doing so I many not have been mindful enough of the special challenges and pressures that women face in the workplace. It grieves me to learn that I caused any of my clerks to feel uncomfortable; this was never my intent. For this I sincerely apologize." Ninth Circuit Judge Alex Kozinski, responding to allegations of inappropriate sexual conduct by female clerks.[93]

- "My hearing testimony was forceful and passionate. . . . At times, my testimony—both in my opening statement and in response to questions—reflected my overwhelming frustration at being wrongly accused, with corroboration, of horrible conduct completely contrary to my record and character. My statement and answers also reflected my deep distress at the unfairness of how this allegation has been handled. I was very emotional last Thursday, more so than I have ever been. I might have been too emotional at times. I know that my tone was sharp and I said a few things I should not have said. I hope everyone can understand that I was there as a son, husband, and dad. I testified with people foremost in my mind: my mom, my dad, my wife, and most of all, my daughters. Going forward, you can count on me to be the same kind of judge and person I have been for my entire 28-year legal career: hardworking, even-keeled, open-minded, independent, and dedicated to the Constitution and the public good."[94] Supreme Court Justice Brett Kavanaugh.

- "Earlier today, I tendered my resignation from the position of Dean of UC Berkeley Law School, effective immediately. I took this step because the pending [sex harassment] lawsuit, against the university and me, appears to have become a distraction for the law school, the university and our community, an outcome I had hoped could be avoided. I have received many requests to respond to, or comment on, the allegations that are the subject of the pending lawsuit. On my counsel's advice—and in order to have this case tried in a court of law, and not in the press—I am refraining from doing so at this juncture. I will defend, in the litigation, against the claims and allegations made against me. I respectfully ask that fair-minded persons understand that there are two sides to every narrative, and that the university and I should have an opportunity to mount a full defense in court, the only forum in which the claims and allegations against us can be fairly adjudicated." Sujit Choudhry, announcing his resignation as Dean of UC Berkeley School of Law a few days after his former assistant filed a sexual harassment lawsuit.[95]

NOTES AND QUESTIONS

1. Which of these apologies might constitute evidence of civil or criminal liability? In his deposition in a class action lawsuit against Firestone, CEO Ono claimed that his congressional testimony was not an admission of guilt. Rather, it was "sympathy expressed for those individuals who operated vehicles using our products and got into accidents. . . . So it's not . . . an issue of a defect."[96] How do you think Ono's statements played among the American public? What about potential jurors? Ono resigned the day after his deposition, citing health reasons. In the wake of a congressional investigation, product recall, and multiple lawsuits, the company forecast that its 2000 profits would fall over 80 percent.

    Subsequent independent investigations suggested that vehicle rollovers were attributable to a combination of faulty tire and vehicle design, as well as poor consumer care.[97] If you had been in Ono's position, and that was the information you had available at the time of the congressional hearings and depositions, what would you have said?

2. The U.C. Berkeley Provost conducted a four-month investigation that concluded that Dean Sujit Choudhry had violated the university's sexual harassment policy by kissing, hugging, and caressing his executive assistant after she made clear that the conduct was unwelcome. The university's sanction for the misconduct was a one-year 10 percent reduction in his $472,917 salary, and requirements that he undergo counseling and write a letter of apology. In a public statement, the Provost said, "We can and must do better as a campus administration. We must move in the direction of stronger sanctions, and in doing this we want and need the broad input of the campus community. We are sharply focused on this issue and committed to ensuring a supportive and safe environment for every single person on this campus. We will act quickly to generate action that will produce lasting change in our culture and practices."[98] How would you evaluate this sanction and statement?

    The controversy resurfaced six months after Choudhry stepped down when he filed a race discrimination suit against the university. It claimed that "when the University's inconsistent response to sexual harassment became the subject of national media attention, University President Janet Napolitano chose to use the case of Sujit Choudhry . . . as a means to try to improve the University's image as well as her own."[99] If you had been Choudhry's lawyer, would you have advised him to file suit? If you were Janet Napolitano, how would you respond?

3. Many women found Joe Biden's apologies inadequate. Anita Hill told reporters that she did not find his statement to be an apology, noting, "I cannot be satisfied by simply saying, I'm sorry for what happened to you. I will be

satisfied when I know there is real change and real accountability, and real purpose."[100] Hill, along with other commentators, claimed that Biden, as Chair of the Senate Judiciary Committee, failed in multiple ways to ensure a minimally fair process; he failed to allow corroborating witnesses to testify; he failed to allow objections to abusive cross-examination of Hill; and he allowed Clarence Thomas to have the opening and closing statements.[101] Biden gave further fuel to critics when he stated on ABC that "I did everything in my power to do what I thought was with the rules. I don't think I treated her badly."[102] If you had been Biden's chief of staff, what you would have advised him to say?

Critics were equally put off by his partial apologies for groping, for which he had long been subject to jokes and annoyed comments. House Speaker Nancy Pelosi stated that although she did not find his conduct "disqualifying," it was "important for the Vice President and others to understand it isn't how it was intended it's how it was received. . . . To say, 'I'm sorry that you were offended' is not an apology."[103] What would have been a more effective response?

Cass Sunstein, after conducting a small online poll based on responses to hypothetical apologies, concluded that apologies for minor misconduct by public figures can backfire.[104] They can make the leader seem weak and more in need of punishment. In Sunstein's view, "[a]s a matter of simple strategy, apologies may not be a great idea. It is sometimes smarter for public figures to remain silent—or to change the subject."[105]

By contrast, other commentators were critical of some of the "putative apologies" prompted by the #MeToo movement. One *New York Times* columnist noted that many of those accused

> claim that the behavior is in the past and seem irritated to have to answer for it. . . . Almost all the accused lean on abstract language and passive voice. They are sorry women "felt disrespected," "were hurt," felt pain." [106] That construction distances them from responsibility, and they seem to expect that after a decent interval passes, they are entitled to "resume [their] place in line exactly where [they] were kicked out."[107]

What is your view? Which of the apologies involving sexual conduct in Problem 7-1 seem problematic? What would you have advised instead?

4. Mark Hurd's resignation came after Jodie Fisher, a former reality TV actress and HP contractor, claimed that he had sexually harassed her in connection with marketing events that she had planned for the company. HP's investigation revealed no basis for the claims and no evidence of a sexual relationship. It did, however, find that Hurd had violated the company's Standards of Business Conduct in submitting false expense reports, including instances where Fisher had received compensation for no business purpose. Hurd settled the claims for an undisclosed amount and received a severance package estimated at $35 million including stock options).[108]

Hurd's conduct met with widespread astonishment. Ben Heineman, former GE General Counsel, captured common reactions: "I am staring at the headlines and asking, like so many others and on so many recent occasions, '[W]hat was he thinking?'"[109] Why didn't Hurd just pay the "business expenses" himself? Why didn't he take the chance that the contractor had initially offered to settle the claim privately without it reaching the company?

The board's decision initially met with mixed reactions. *New York Times* business columnist Joe Nocera doubted that expense misstatements were, or should have been, the real reason for Hurd's resignation. "If everyone who ever fudged an expense report or flirted with an outside contractor were fired, there wouldn't be many people left in the American workforce."[110] Oracle CEO Larry Ellison weighed in on the side of leniency. He lambasted the HP board for "cowardly corporate political correctness."[111] Within a month, Ellison hired Hurd as Oracle's co-president.[112] Columbia Law School professor John Coffee noted, "If all you're concerned about is an expense account, there are other sanctions. You could have taken away his bonus for the year. Most companies would not have treated a peccadillo with this severity, particularly when it inflicts such a penalty on shareholders."[113]

By contrast, others wondered how meaningful denial of a bonus would have been to someone whose take-home pay the previous year totaled about $24 million. Could Hurd have credibly enforced HP's standards after his own violations? According to Ben Heineman, "[F]or a CEO seeking to lead a company through word and deed—including a commitment to honest accounts . . . —the corporate death penalty that follows from violating such a standard cannot be stayed because Hurd is of great value to the company. As one of the HP investigators said, 'It had to do with integrity. . . .'"[114]

Months after the scandal broke, *Wall Street Journal* and *Fortune* profiles revealed further details about Hurd's conduct. Fisher's letter seeking compensation claimed that Hurd had told her about a plan to acquire Electronic Data Systems Corp. before the acquisition became public. HP investigators also revealed inconsistencies between what Hurd told the board and what the record showed. For example, Hurd initially claimed that he did not know Fisher well and was unaware of her prior career in adult movies. However, investigation revealed that he had visited Web pages showing her in pornographic scenes and that he had dined with her privately on many occasions, including several that involved no HP event.[115]

Why do you suppose that HP did not reveal these details of its investigative report at the time it terminated Hurd? Rather, the General Counsel simply cited his "profound lack of judgment," and the company gave him a generous severance package.

Suppose that Hurd had been forthcoming with the board about his relationship with Fisher, and had offered to repay the expenses and settle her claims privately. If you had been General Counsel, would you have recommended that he be allowed to retain his position? Consider the research summarized in Chapter 5, suggesting a link between leaders' ethics and employee conduct? If you had been on the board, how would you have balanced Hurd's ability to generate short-term profit increases averaging 18 percent a year, which doubled stock prices, against his ethical lapses in this case and in the pretexting scandal discussed in Chapter 3? How would you have recommended handling publicity surrounding the event? What considerations would affect your decision? What advice might damage control experts Dezenhall and Weber have provided in light of the views expressed below?

ERIC DEZENHALL AND JOHN WEBER, DAMAGE CONTROL: WHY EVERYTHING YOU KNOW ABOUT CRISIS MANAGEMENT IS WRONG

(New York: Portfolio of Penguin Group, 2008), pp. 79-92

Damage Control Means More than Having to Say You're Sorry

When they invented "I'm sorry," honor was lost.

—Greek proverb

The most common question a crisis manager gets at a barbecue: "Why don't your clients just fess up and apologize?" The question is often smugly followed by, "If Nixon had just admitted 'I screwed up' and said he was sorry, the whole thing would have blown over. . . ."

Wrong. Instead of resigning and rising off into the heavens on Marine One in anticipation of a pardon, Nixon would probably have been tried in a court of law, convicted, and dragged down Pennsylvania Avenue chained to a pickup truck.

The scandal-plagued refuse to apologize because they don't think they're guilty. Sometimes they're not. Guilty or innocent, a protective enzyme kicks in that creates a barrier between one's actions and one's self-perception. No matter how wicked an individual or institution is, what's universal is the desire to be loved and respected independent of one's actions.

But a more strategic reason clients in crisis don't "fess up" is because it's often a very bad idea.

Crises have legal implications. Despite pretrial cries for Martha Stewart to apologize for her involvement in her alleged insider trading scandal, she couldn't, because in a court of law, an apology may be interpreted by a judge and jury as an admission of guilt. One cannot, after all, apologize for what one did not do. This logic applies to civil litigation as much as it does to criminal trials, which is why we see so few corporate apologies.

The tension between legal and public relations considerations should be adjudicated by the answer to one question: Would you rather be loved or acquitted? If the latter is the answer, silence is golden—especially for corporations, which are almost always seen as being guilty, not to mention irredeemable.

The apology has its practical origins in ancient Greek culture. When Plato issued his "Apologia" on behalf of Socrates, he was offering a defense, not suggesting Socrates was sorry for anything.

The mission of the apology shifted with the rise of Christianity, where winning God's love and forgiveness became the goal. In order for one to restore one's self to God's grace, one needed to convey remorse and sustain a punishment of some kind in order to demonstrate that a valuable lesson had been learned. Reparations then needed to be made to the injured parties, to God. In Catholicism particularly, confessions occur privately with a cleric, so it's possible that one can return to God's good graces without a media advisor.

Not so in the court of public opinion. Public apologies can come, at a very high price, such as when former New Jersey governor James McGreevey announced in 2004 that he was gay and then resigned when allegations surfaced that he had appointed a purported love interest to a government job. The good news was that the story quickly evaporated. The bad news was that McGreevey was out of a job.

The Transactional Apology

In crisis management, an apology is a transaction whereby the accused humbles himself in exchange for mercy. It is offered as a gesture marking the end of the play, the final encore permitting the audience to go home, the turning of the proverbial page so that a new chapter can begin. It most certainly does not necessarily equate with repentance or sorrow.

The contemporary apology is cheap. Everybody's doing it, from presidents to deranged ear-chomping prizefighters. The apology is the tactic du jour of the public relations industry because it is seen as a way for the mighty to show human qualities. The apology often stops short of confession, employing weasel words that give the apologizer immunity from the consequences of the original sin.

The key question is "Do apologies *work* as a crisis management technique?" An apology "works" when a transaction occurs whereby something small is surrendered (pride) but something of value—such as one's freedom—is preserved. Transactional apologies can be effective, but there's a catch: The *carrot* of apology works best when accompanied by the *stick* of personal exposure for the adversary. . . .

Why Three Apologies Don't Add Up to Forgiveness

On January 14, 2005, Harvard University president Lawrence Summers spoke at a conference on women in science. He was under the impression that his remarks would be off the record. This was his first mistake. His second was choosing as his subject speculation on how biological differences between men and women might account for why women aren't more successful in math and science. Outrage broke out on campus.

In a letter posted on Harvard's Web site several days later, Summers wrote, "I deeply regret the impact of my comments and apologize for having not weighed them more carefully. . . . I was wrong to have spoken in a way that was an unintended signal of discouragement to talented girls and women." Summers apologized three different times.

He wasn't forgiven.

Pointing out biological differences has a certain Third Reich whiff about it. Saying, for example, that blacks predominate in athletics is perceived as a backhanded way of saying (wink, wink), "they" aren't as smart scholastically. Saying that women are weaker in math and science validates the stereotype that women are emotional (read: not rational).

Despite his contrition, Summers didn't fare as well with women in his ordeal as his former boss, President Clinton, did during his.

Professor Harvey Mansfield believed that Summers received bad advice from Kennedy School of Government professor and political advisor David Gergen: "He said if you apologize, you'll make yourself look weak and vulnerable, and women will feel sympathetic. . . . He took that advice and, of course, the women despised him for looking weak, just as men would have done. So his backpedaling was a big mistake and hasn't been successful. . . ."

Indeed, one of the great mirages of crisis management is the notion that an apology will lead to catharsis, the sense of relief associated with absolution. The problem is that human affairs are not static, they are dynamic, with an ever-shifting cast of characters and agendas vying for dominance.

In Summers's case, his apology served to validate, not neutralize, the hard nugget that lay at the core of an acute cultural conflict. In an age where agendas have multiple media in which to play out at lightning speed, Summers's original sin became a political football, forever in play.

Simple mistakes often are forgiven with an apology. Ideological shibboleths related to gender and race are not. Women in academia didn't find enough else to like about Summers and his policies to stand by him in his hour of need. Digging himself more deeply into his position wasn't a great option either, since he had already offended progressives in 2002 in a dispute with black studies professor Cornel West that drove the charismatic scholar out of Harvard to Princeton. Summers had no great options, but one thing became clear: There isn't always a correlation between apology and forgiveness. Summers announced his resignation in February 2006. . . .

In Western culture, it's understandable that we tie apology to forgiveness. This is especially tempting since the public relations industry, in a desperate attempt to win the respect of the broader culture, preaches this line so zealously. Hard evidence from the PR war zones, however, suggests that apologies work best when the violation is either aberrant or isolated. As for defusing more chronic offenses, one is more likely to be forgiven if instead of using kid gloves, one takes out the brass knuckles. . . .

NOTES AND QUESTIONS

1. Do you agree with Dezenhall and Weber's analysis? Why or why not? Do statutes barring the use of apologies in subsequent legal proceedings adequately reduce the concerns about apologies that they raise?

2. In a follow-up article, Dezenhall elaborates on ways that leaders often get crisis management wrong. One common myth is that they need to "get out in front of the story" by telling their side. In fact, Dezenhall argues, when you do not have a good side, sometimes the "less bad" solution is to just take the hit. Following allegations of chronic philandering, Tiger Woods would not have been better-off calling a press conference to "rattle through a list of lady friends declaring, 'Tiffany, yes; Trixy, no; Amber, don't remember. . . .'"[116]

3. Equally implausible, says Dezenhall, are assumptions that a crisis is primarily a communications problem and that public displays of corporate social responsibility can help. As he notes, the people whose lives were obliterated by the BP oil spill "don't want a more artfully crafted apology; they want their lives and their ecosystem back. . . . Perhaps if BP had diverted some of its PR resources to safety in recent years, they wouldn't be in this mess."[117] Consider the parody running under the title "Experts Propose Plugging Oil Leak with BP Executives":

   > "We've tried containment domes, rubber tires, and even golf balls," said William Cathermeyer of the National Oil Leakage Institute, a leading consultancy in the field of oil leaks. "Now it's time to shove some BP executives down there and hope for the best."
   >
   > "Submerging the oil company executives thousands of feet below the ocean's surface could be a 'win-win' situation," Mr. Cathermeyer said.
   >
   > "Best case scenario, they plug the leak," he said. "And at the very least, they'll shut the f—up."[118]

   What should Woods and BP have done once their respective crises unfolded?

4. One byproduct of our online culture is the practice of "digital shaming," which enables instant humiliation on an unprecedented scale for an indefinite period. In some instances, this practice can bring much needed accountability for conduct that would otherwise go unsanctioned. A case history is that of Uber engineer Susan Fowler. Her supervisor propositioned her on her first day on the job, and when she presented a screen shot of the offending e-mail to the company's Human Relations officers, they told her to let it pass because this was the perpetrator's "first offense," and he was a "high performer."[119] She subsequently learned that other female engineers had been told the same thing about this harasser, and her other efforts to report up the management chain proved equally fruitless. After learning that she was "on thin ice" at the company because of her repeated complaints, she left Uber.[120] But rather than let the incident pass, she blogged about it, and included other data on women's underrepresentation and marginalization at the company. Her post went viral

and eventually resulted in an investigation by former Attorney General Eric Holder that toppled the careers of 20 executives.[121]

But other cases have less happy outcomes. Sometimes the response is disproportionate to the offense, and an "Internet pitchfork mob" unleashes fury, threats, and social ostracism that have devastating consequences.[122] When a viral post gets the facts wrong or targets the wrong person, the damage is hard to remedy. And even if the initial outrage is deserved, the enduring and instant accessibility of damning evidence makes it hard for people to learn, grow, and move on from their mistakes. As one commentator noted, "[P]eople change, pictures don't."[123]

What implications does the growth of online shaming have for leaders? That their reputations are more at risk? That they should create structures of accountability that would lessen the need for posts such as Fowler's? What other lessons would you draw?

D. POLITICS

ARI ADUT, ON SCANDAL, MORAL DISTURBANCES IN SOCIETY, POLITICS, AND ART

(New York: Cambridge University Press, 2008), pp. 73-77, 80-81, 107-114, and 123-128

Political Scandal

A scandal is political to the extent that it affects the exercise of political power. Such events are almost always about high-status politicians, whose real or alleged transgressions pollute themselves and those they represent: their offices, parties, associates as well as the values they are supposed to stand for. The trust vested in these entities is thereby vitiated and the political process disrupted. The most common offenses that might give rise to political scandals are various uses of public office for private financial gain, abuse of power, and treason. Yet other transgressions, like sexual misconduct by politicians, can occasion political scandals as well by blotting the public persona of the offender as well as the office they represent. . . .

There is thus no sharp break between scandal and politics as usual. Rather we are presented with a continuum, at the one end of which we will find picayune, unexceptional bickering about morals and policy and on the other events such as Watergate with seismic effects. . . .

Nevertheless, political scandals seem to be on the rise in many Western democracies. . . . What would affect the frequency of scandals in a political system? The objectivist paradigm perceives political scandal as the manifestation of corruption and puts the blame on the growing dependence of politicians on money and on the languishing internal controls on their comportment. Draconian measures along with more transparency are proposed. The constructivist perspective, in contrast, points the finger to media and elite activism. . . . Scholars have pointed to collusions among publicity-hungry prosecutors, belligerent investigative bodies of Congress, and the scoop-oriented press. Regardless of their differences, both objectivist and constructivists bemoan that political scandals erode public trust in government.

The Presidency after Watergate

. . . [T]he 1980s and 1990s [continued] to yield high levels of executive branch scandal activity, which affected the presidency in varying degrees. More than 100 administration officials were accused of criminal or ethical misconduct during the two terms of the Reagan's presidency. Attorney General Edwin Meese [resigned and] . . . many staffers, including two national security advisors, were convicted with a host of charges including conspiracy and lying to Congress [in connection with the Iran Contra affair.] . . .

The Clinton years were remarkably rocky. . . . [In addition to his impeachment for lies regarding a sexual affair with Monica Lewinsky,] the president found himself ensnared in (1) Whitewater, which revolved around allegations of real estate fraud; (2) Cattlegate, which involved the first lady's cattle futures that earned questionably high returns; (3) Travelgate, in which the administration was battered for firing the members of the White House travel office; (4) Filegate, which broke with the charges that the White House had improperly obtained FBI files on more than 900 individuals, some of them prominent Republicans; (5) the Paula Jones sexual harassment case, in which the president was the defendant; and (6) the campaign finance scandal, during which the White House was accused of receiving illegal donations from foreign operatives and Asian-American donors. . . . Despite the general assumption of guilt in most of these affairs and despite the fact that the presidency itself did not inspire much confidence, the public ratings of Clinton's job performance, mainly thanks to the healthy economy, stayed high. Scandals could easily break against him and disrupt governance, but Clinton had the gumption, luck, and popular accommodation to fight them.

Imperial Tendencies in the 2000s

. . . An important question that arises out of [this] analysis is whether the low trust in the presidency and the multiplication of presidential scandals reveal a legitimacy crisis in the American political system. I don't think so. Degradation of their institutional authority makes life more difficult for presidents and renders governing harder. And a certain level of trust in public institutions is a public good . . . . [A]s allegations about presidents become more and more a routine element of political life, their impact tends to decline. There is in fact a trade-off, a negative relationship between the intensity and the frequency of political scandals. One reason why there are more scandals is because they are less intense [and] . . . the anticipated collective costs [are lower].

PROBLEM 7-2

While she was Secretary of State, Hillary Clinton chose to use a private e-mail address and server, which she and her lawyers attributed to a desire for "convenience." That decision came under increasing fire and several investigations during her 2016 presidential campaign. In response to these probes, Clinton turned over what she claimed were all official e-mails from that period and argued that her actions had been legally "allowed."[124] When aides advised her to apologize, she initially responded that opponents were manufacturing a controversy that she did not want to legitimize by acknowledging error.[125] But with polls showing that large percentages of voters did not consider her trustworthy, she began softening her stance. At a campaign rally in the summer of 2015, she acknowledged that her use of a personal e-mail server "clearly wasn't the best choice," and that "I take responsibility for that decision."[126] Finally, after supporters and focus group results argued for a more forthright apology, Clinton delivered it on ABC News in the fall of 2015. She stated that using a private e-mail account had been "a mistake," and "I'm sorry about that. I take responsibility"[127] However, she also maintained in other statements that her personal account was "aboveboard," and that "nothing I ever sent or received was marked classified at the time."[128]

Clinton's apology did little to appease critics, and even supporters such as former political strategist David Axelrod, called her handling of the issue "abysmal."[129] A trusted legal advisor warned her to "lawyer up," and suggested that her previous tendency to deny the seriousness of the issue and treat it as purely political could hurt her with the Justice Department and FBI investigators looking at the issue. "Insulting [those career] investigators is a very bad and ill-advised strategy."[130] The problem was compounded when the FBI determined that although Clinton had turned over roughly 55,000 pages of work-related e-mails, she had failed to supply several thousand more, and the lawyers whom she employed to sift through the e-mails and delete personal ones did not have security clearances.[131] Contrary to Clinton's representations, the FBI found that she had sent and received classified information on her personal account, and that it was possible that hostile forces had gained access to that account.[132]

Despite such findings, the FBI Director James Comey recommended that the Justice Department not pursue criminal charges against Clinton. Although the report found that she had been "extremely careless," it did not find that she had "intentionally transmitted or willfully mishandled classified materials," or that she had intentionally deleted or withheld work-related e-mails from investigators.[133] Attorney General Loretta Lynch accepted that recommendation, but her decision did not put the matter to rest, in part because of a further misstep by the Clinton campaign. While the FBI was completing its investigation, Bill Clinton boarded Lynch's plane when they were both waiting on the tarmac at the Phoenix airport. Lynch insisted that the meeting was purely social, and that the e-mail probe never came up. Nonetheless, she acknowledged that it was "casting a shadow over how people are going to view [the investigation]," and she "certainly wouldn't do it again."[134] She also said that she would "be accepting" whatever recommendation

FBI Director Comey would bring her about possible prosecution.[135] Neither Bill nor Hillary Clinton commented on the propriety of the meeting.[136]

1. If you had been Hillary Clinton, how would you have handled initial disclosures concerning the e-mails?
2. What do you think Bill Clinton and Loretta Lynch were thinking when they had their social conversation about what Lynch claimed was "grandchildren and golf and such?"[137] In commenting on the meeting and on the legal advice Hillary Clinton received concerning e-mails, *New York Times* columnist Maureen Dowd noted, "So many lawyers . . . so little law."[138] If you had been leading the Clinton campaign, how would you have advised handling the fallout from the scandal?

PROBLEM 7-3

Van Jones is a prominent CNN commentator and a globally recognized lawyer leader of the environmental and social justice communities. From his base in San Francisco, he has launched several not-for-profit organizations, including the Ella Baker Center for Human Rights and Green for All. In 2008, President Obama appointed him as a Special Advisor for Green Jobs, Enterprise and Innovation and a member of the White House Council for Environmental Quality (CEQ).[139] As special advisor for Green Jobs, Jones's responsibilities were to "advance the administration's climate and energy initiatives, with a special focus on improving vulnerable communities."[140]

Before joining the Obama Administration, Jones had been affiliated with a number of left-wing organizations, and had made statements that subsequently attracted widespread criticism.[141] In 2004, he signed a petition suggesting that President George W. Bush had knowingly allowed the terrorist attacks of 9/11 to occur in order to advance the administration's military objectives in the Middle East.[142] In a 2009 appearance before the Berkeley Energy & Resources Collaborative (BERC) event, a member of the audience asked why Republicans were more successful than Democrats in achieving legislative objectives; Jones replied, "They're assholes."[143]

After that last statement, leaders of the conservative news media began publicizing his prior comments and affiliations with "radical protest movements" and calling for his resignation.[144] Some also vowed "to dig deeper into the past of other policy 'czars' to raise questions about the President's judgment and policies."[145] Fox News host Glenn Beck led the campaign to oust Jones, which many believed was payback for Jones's work with an organization that had pressured advertisers to stop sponsoring Beck's television program.[146]

In response to the public outcry, Jones and the Obama administration issued a series of statements expressing regret and attempting to put his conduct in context. An administration source said that Jones had not carefully reviewed the language of the 9/11 petition, and Jones added that "the petition does not reflect [his] views now or ever."[147] When these statements did little to halt the criticism, Jones resigned. In a statement accompanying his resignation, Jones maintained: "On the eve of historic fights for health care and clean energy, opponents of reform have mounted a vicious smear campaign against me. . . . They are using lies and distortions to distract and divide. . . . I cannot in good conscience ask my colleagues to expend precious time and energy defending or explaining my past. We need all hands on deck, fighting for our future."[148] The White House Council on Environmental Quality accepted his resignation without comment.[149]

The fairness of Jones's treatment has been subject to debate. Howard Dean, the former chairman of the Democratic National Committee, claimed that Jones was being unjustly penalized for unwittingly signing a petition, an incident that was not reflective of his capabilities. Dean stated, "This guy's a Yale-educated lawyer . . . and best-selling author about his specialty."[150] By contrast, Jerry Taylor, a senior fellow with the Libertarian Cato Institute, saw scrutiny of Jones as "standard operating procedure," not as some "right wing conspiracy."[151] Ron Bonjean, former press secretary to Senate Majority Leader Trent Lott, argued that Obama had created a "boomerang effect" by appointing so many advisers who were not subject to the Senate confirmation process. As a result, "there could be plenty of past controversial positions taken by these czars that are just waiting to be found and explode like ticking time bombs."[152]

1. If you had been in Jones's position, how would you have responded to the criticism? What information about your political past would you have volunteered to administration officials prior to your appointment?
2. If you had been one of President Obama's chief advisors, how would you have suggested that the administration respond to the criticisms? Is there anything that the White House could or should have done to prevent the scandal? Should Jones's past statements and political affiliations have been fully vetted before his appointment? Should any of them have been disqualifying? Was his resignation necessary? Should the administration have made any statement concerning his resignation?
3. A year after his resignation, Jones wrote a *New York Times* op-ed suggesting that he had been a victim of the media's "rush to judgment." According to Jones,

> Life inside the Beltway has become a combination of speed chess and Mortal Kombat; one wrong move can mean political death. In the era of YouTube, Twitter, and 24-hour cable news, nobody is safe. . . . The result is that people at all levels of government are becoming overly cautious, unwilling to venture new opinions or even live regular lives for fear of seeing even the most innocuous comment or photograph used against them. . . .
>
> [T]he breakthrough will come not when we are better able to spot the lies. It will come when we are better able to handle the truth about people. We are complex beings; no one is all good or all bad. And people do evolve . . . —just look at Senator Robert Byrd, who died

this month and who entered politics as a segregationist and left as a statesman. . . . When it comes to politics in the age of Facebook, the killer app to stop the "gotcha" bullies won't be a technological one—it will be a wiser, more forgiving culture.[153]

Do you agree? If so, what could political and media leaders do to bring us closer to the world Jones envisions?

PROBLEM 7-4

For decades, Massachusetts Senator Elizabeth Warren claimed that she was of Native American ancestry and that her family stories indicated that her great-great-great-grandmother was Cherokee. After she launched her campaigns for Senate and then for president, reporters discovered that she had listed herself as Native American in faculty directories while she was a law professor, and that she had identified herself as "American Indian" on her 1986 Texas bar registration card.[154] After Donald Trump mocked her claims and called her Pocahontas, Warren took a DNA test that she said confirmed that she may have had Native American ancestors six to ten generations ago, making her possibly 1/1024th Native American.[155] The claim infuriated members of the Cherokee Nation. Its Secretary of State issued a statement saying that using a "DNA test to lay claim to any connection to the Cherokee Nation or any tribal nation, even vaguely, is inappropriate and wrong."[156]

"I can't go back," Warren told the *Washington Post*. "But I am sorry for furthering confusion on tribal sovereignty and tribal citizenship, and for the harm that resulted." As she explained, "Tribes and only tribes determine tribal citizenship," and "I am not a tribal citizen. . . . Family stories are not the same as tribal citizenship and this is why I have apologized." She also emphasized that "nothing about my background ever had anything to do with any job I got in any place," a claim that news reports have verified.[157]

Conservatives, however, argued that Warren was obviously invoking Native American identity for "career advancement," as a way to capitalize on affirmative action.[158] Liberals responded that there was no evidence that she had claimed minority status to gain preferential treatment, and that the media should be focusing on her policy proposals, not stoking anti-affirmative rhetoric and Native American slurs.[159] How would you respond? How would you assess Warren's handling of the issue once it surfaced during her political campaigns?

PROBLEM 7-5

In 2010, the U.S. House of Representatives censured Charles Rangel, a lawyer and former Assistant U.S. Attorney, based on findings of its ethics committee that the congressman had committed eleven violations of House Ethics Rules. The violations included failing to pay income tax and sending letters on congressional stationary seeking donations to New York City College's Charles B. Rangel Public

Service Center. The letters targeted individuals and entities with interests that could be affected by legislation before the House Ways and Means Committee, which Rangel chaired. The committee also found that Rangel used House resources, including staff and supplies, to support these fund-raising efforts.[160] While these charges were pending, a *New York Times* investigation revealed about a dozen current or former lawmakers who had been similarly honored by academic institutions through donations from companies that had business before Congress.[161] In some instances, the legislators personally solicited contributions or appeared at events to thank donors. Some of the amounts were quite substantial, and in excess of amounts that would be permissible as direct campaign contributions. For example, defense contractor Northrop Grumman donated $1 million to help establish the Trent Lott National Center at the University of Mississippi, and pharmaceutical company Amgen donated $5 million to the Edward Kennedy Institute while Kennedy was pushing legislation that would better protect companies, including Amgen, from competition from generic brands.

The House Ethics Committee concluded that Rangel's conduct was more egregious than that of others because he had used government stationery and staff to solicit contributions from entities with major concerns before his committee. According to a *New York Times* account, in one case the committee helped preserve tax loopholes worth millions of dollars for an oil-drilling company that had pledged $1 million.[162] Senator Mitch McConnell, who had sought funds for the McConnell Center for Political Leadership at the University of Louisville, went further in defending his own conduct. He told Fox News commentators that his situation was "totally different" from Rangel's. "This is a scholarship program for young people in Kentucky. They benefited from it, not me. It's a pure charitable activity."[163] Could Rangel make the same argument? Is it convincing? Is his conduct qualitatively different from that of other congressional leaders?

NOTES AND QUESTIONS

1. Norman Ornstein, an expert in campaign finance at the American Enterprise Institute, argues that "[t]he simple fact is these things should not be named after people when they are in office. We all know what is going on here; the donors are trying to influence the lawmakers."[164] But isn't that also true of many donations to political campaigns? What makes this practice seem more offensive? Is it the lack of transparency, the absence of limits on amounts, or something else?

2. Harvard government professor Dennis Thompson argues that congressional ethics rules serve three functions that are relevant to leaders' credibility: independence (making sure decisions are on the merits); fairness (playing by the rules); and accountability (maintaining public confidence).[165] What approach to donations honoring lawmakers would best serve these objectives? If you had been general counsel of City College of New York or the University of Louisville, would you have supported creation of centers honoring current

congressional leaders? Once the centers were in place, how would you respond to public criticism?

MEDIA RESOURCES

All the scandals noted above received widespread media coverage. Clips are available of Rangel's, Clinton's, and Warren's press statements, and of Fox News's coverage of Van Jones.[166] Jon Stewart offered critical accounts of many of these incidents, with especially biting coverage of Rangel and Hayward.[167] Radio interviews are available with David Runciman on political hypocrisy.[168] Nixon's Checkers speech, Gloria Allred's press conference with Whitman's housekeeper Nicky Diaz Santillan, and Tony Hayward's and Mark Hurd's public statements all vividly illustrate the challenges of crisis management. *The Contender* features Joan Allen playing a politician whose chance to become the first female vice president is at risk because of her unwillingness to respond to accusations of misconduct. The television series *Scandal, Veep,* and *House of Cards* include well-drawn fictional portraits of the kind of political misconduct and crisis management described above.

E. MONEY

Money plays a prominent, or at least walk-on, role in many leadership scandals. Although it might seem that affluence should insulate most leaders from temptation, in fact, research indicates that the rich are more susceptible to financial misconduct. Social psychologists hypothesize that increased wealth and independence from others is associated with increased willingness to prioritize self-interest and more favorable attitudes toward greed.[169] Whatever the causes, many leaders' careers have been derailed or tarnished by corruption in amounts that seem trivial given their economic status. Ethical problems take a variety of forms, some more serious than others. The following materials explore two common contexts in which it figures in a leader's downfall. In the first case, the problem comes from paying too much attention to money—from letting it become the preeminent measure of personal status and well-being. In the second case, the difficulties arise from not paying enough attention to money—from skating too close to the line in accounting matters and not considering how certain personal and institutional expenditures would look to those footing the bill.

BRYAN BURROUGH, MARC DREIER'S CRIME OF DESTINY

Vanity Fair, November 2009

. . . Marc Dreier [is] 59 years old, and his life is over. . . . Dreier was once a hotshot New York litigator with multi-millionaire clients. Then he stole $380 million from a bunch of hedge funds, got caught, and was arrested in Toronto under bizarre circumstances, having attempted to impersonate a Canadian pension-fund lawyer as part of a scheme to sell bogus securities to the big American hedge fund Fortress Investment Group. . . .

Maybe you remember the Dreier case. . . . If he's remembered today, it's probably for the details of his arrest, the sheer audacity of impersonating that Toronto attorney inside the man's own offices.

The Canadian incident turned out to be the tip of one very dirty iceberg. Re-arrested upon his return to La Guardia Airport, Dreier was revealed to have defrauded more than a dozen hedge funds, not counting the $45 million or so he stole from his own clients' escrow accounts. His 270-lawyer Park Avenue firm, Dreier L.L.P., imploded practically overnight. . . . In June[2009,] . . . he pleaded guilty to all charges. A judge sentenced him to 20 years in prison. . . .

Dreier's downfall left half the New York bar scratching their heads. Here was a lawyer who seemingly had every toy a middle-aged American man could want: not one but two waterfront homes in the Hamptons, condominiums in the Caribbean, a 120-foot yacht moored in St. Martin, a $200,000 Aston Martin, an oceanside condominium in Santa Monica, plus his own Los Angeles sushi restaurant, not to mention a collection of modern art that included works by Warhol, Hockney, Picasso, Matisse, and Lichtenstein.

There were all kinds of theories, though, most assuming that Dreier had resorted to theft to cover losses at his firm, or perhaps to support his outsize lifestyle. . . . They were all wrong. What no one understood is . . . that [t]his wasn't the case of a man who had everything going bad. . . . What no one understood is that everything Dreier owned—the cars, the mansions, the yacht, the sushi restaurant, even the law firm itself—was made possible by his crimes. This was a man who went bad to have everything.

I Confess

. . . "Obviously, people who knew me are puzzled by what I did," Dreier says, "and I hope talking to you helps begin to explain it. I obviously am sincerely, deeply remorseful and sorry about what I did, and hopefully an interview can convey to people I hurt how remorseful I am. That's the truth. I am deeply sorry. And the frustrating thing is not to be able to say that." He wants the world to see he is not some comic-book villain, he says, that he was once a decent man who found himself swept up in a culture that rewards material gains. All he ever wanted, Dreier says, was to be viewed as a success, and when he wasn't, he began to steal to get the things he craved.

"Even a good person can lose their way," he goes on. "This is not just a story about someone who engaged in a significant crime, but the less dramatic point, you know, is people who are following a certain path, who go to the right schools, who do the right things. . . . You can still lose your way. In a terrible way. As I did."

. . . "I [grew] up experiencing a lot of success, even in elementary school," Dreier says. "I had always been a leader. Things just came easy to me. People expected I would achieve real success in my life."

He got into Yale, earned a degree in 1972, and went on to Harvard Law School, where he graduated in the middle of his class in 1975. He was hired as a litigation associate at the white-shoe Manhattan firm of Rosenman & Colin. . . . As they had since he was a child, people predicted great things.

In 1985, to no one's surprise, [Dreier] made partner. . . . But if Dreier's career was thriving, Rosenman wasn't. . . . Older lawyers jealously guarded their clients, frustrating their younger colleagues, many of whom, especially the litigators, began to grow restless. Some attorneys began to leave. . . .

Dreier, for one, found making partner didn't bring him the money or the responsibility he felt he deserved. "Life didn't change as much as I would've wanted it to change," he says. "I was disappointed the position didn't mean everything I had hoped for. I guess you would say I didn't get either the financial success or the recognition I would've liked."

Just as Dreier's eye began to roam, he received a job offer from Fulbright & Jaworski, the massive Houston firm, which was opening a New York office. Dreier leapt at the chance to head Fulbright's New York litigation section. The move meant more money and more recognition, and Dreier hoped he would be representing Fulbright's big Texas clients in their courtroom battles. Instead, as at Rosenman, he found older lawyers not willing to let go of their clients. For the most part, Dreier and his group were obliged to find their own clients, which was difficult. . . .

[After an ugly dispute with Fullbright's management committee and an unsuccessful stint at a small firm, Dreier decided to strike out on his own.] Dreier rented a small office suite in Rockefeller Center and hired a few associates. Shortly after, in 1996, he agreed to partner with a friend of his brother-in-law's, Neil Baritz, who practiced in Boca Raton, Florida. Their new firm, Dreier & Baritz, muddled along for several years with little distinction; Dreier argued a string of cases for various small businesses, and for a time he felt content. "I was much happier," Dreier says. "I loved being my own boss. For the first time I felt like I was doing something meaningful."

Running his own firm, however, presented a host of new challenges, chiefly the pressure of luring clients. That meant entertaining, and Dreier quickly realized that prospective clients judged him in large part not on his legal talent but on the trappings of his success. He moved his family into a duplex on 76th Street, then into a far larger apartment on 58th Street, which he rented because he couldn't afford to buy it. He spent nearly $1 million on renovations, then thousands more buying art and furnishings. In 1998 he moved his offices to 499 Park Avenue, designed by I. M. Pei.

"I needed to give people the idea I was doing very well," he says. "That was the first step in a pattern toward living above my means." His new surroundings, in fact, soon drove Dreier into debt. The only way to get out, he realized, was to expand his firm and its revenues. . . .

By 2000, after two full years, the expanded firm was having "modest success," Dreier says. "We were paying the bills." Dreier turned 50 that year, a point when many men assess their lives. As he took stock, Dreier began to realize he hadn't fulfilled the potential so many had seen in him. Friends from Harvard were heading giant firms and bringing in multi-million-dollar judgments. It was depressing that, after all those years as a golden boy, Dreier was still mired in a small firm, still hustling to pay his bills. It was then that 9/11 hit, bringing on the dark days when Dreier's world began to collapse. . . .

"I had a very emotional response to [9/11]," he says. "I remember feeling an emptiness I couldn't shake in the last quarter of '01, feeling emotionally drained and looking to find myself.". . . "I was very distraught," he says. "I was very disappointed in my life. I felt my career and my marriage were over. I was 52 and [I felt] maybe life was passing me by. . . . I felt like I was a failure." His feelings of despair were deepened by his keen, lifelong sense of entitlement, a hard-core belief that he was destined to achieve great things.

And now, suddenly, he realized he hadn't. . . . "I thought I was too smart, I was too confident," he says finally. "You can lose your way a little bit. It was all my fault. I didn't have a therapist, a wife, or a friend. I didn't have anyone I could talk to. I don't do that. I kept everything inside.". . .

For months he brooded over the wreckage of his life [and eventually] . . . came to two conclusions. He would buy himself a big house on the beach. And he would get the money by dramatically expanding his firm, now renamed Dreier L.L.P. Dreier knows how ridiculous this sounds, that his criminal behavior can be traced to his yearning for a better beach house. . . .

He returned to his Park Avenue office that fall determined to lure teams of all-star lawyers to Dreier L.L.P. Each would get a guaranteed salary, plus a bonus based on performance. But unlike other major U.S. firms, Dreier L.L.P. would not be a partnership. Dreier himself would own it all.

The plan looked promising on paper, but in practice there was one major problem. "It required a lot of cash," Dreier admits. Each lawyer had to be paid up front, and as more came on board Dreier was obliged to lease an entire new floor of offices, complete with furniture and computers. Every penny had to come from his own pocket—money, needless to say, that he simply didn't have. . . .

Easy Money

. . . Dreier says he can't remember the moment he actually began considering fraud. But he acknowledges the decision was made easier by a long track record of what he calls "cutting corners." As he acknowledges, "Yeah, I took advantage of expense accounts, statements on tax returns, that kind of thing. You know, I discovered once you cross a gray line it's much easier to cross a black line." And once he did begin thinking about fraud, he rationalized it as a onetime event that was necessary to fuel his expansion plans. "I thought I could do what I had to do, and get out of it relatively quickly," he explains. "How much did I struggle with the ethical issue? I'd like to say I have a clear recollection of going through some great ethical analysis and agonizing over it. But I don't believe I did. I should have. I just don't remember that kind of angst. I don't." . . .

[Dreier created a fictitious real estate development company and borrowed $20 million. Further fraudulent loans eventually totaled $200 million, and the firm grew to 175 lawyers. But during the 2008 audit crunch, hedge funds wanted out. One of the hedge fund's auditors discovered a forged financial statement, and one of Dreier's partners discovered funds missing from a firm escrow account. In a desperate effort to replace the necessary cash, Dreier staged an elaborate hoax requiring him to impersonate an executive of a former client, the Ontario Teachers' Pension Plan. The investor was suspicious and his efforts led to Dreier's arrest.]

There's a Moral to Draw

. . . [Dreier] didn't bother with denials for long. He would admit everything: four long years of fraud, 80 or more bogus notes, . . . everything. His glorious new life, the firm, the "Dreier Model"—it had all been built on lies. Within days, attorneys began resigning [and] . . . Dreier L.L.P. simply imploded. . . .

"I expect to spend most of the rest of my life in prison," he tells me. "I hope I don't die there. . . ." [S]ome of his final words were instructive. "Many people," he observed, "are caught up in the notion that success in life is measured in professional and financial achievements and material acquisitions, and it's hard to step back from that and see the fallacy. You have to try and measure your life by the moments in your day. I see people my children's age first coming into finance, the working world, as having to make basic choices about how to define happiness and success. Obviously, I made the wrong choices."

"But they don't have to."

NOTES AND QUESTIONS

1. The dynamics that Dreier describes are common in many Ponzi schemes, including Bernie Madoff's well-documented scam. Such practices have been less common in law firms because leaders with substantial assets typically include equity partners, who exercise some collective oversight of financial practices. However, in Dreier's firm, with only one equity partner, non-equity practice leaders never saw the firm's books until after his arrest.[170] Does that suggest that the Model Rules of Professional Conduct should ban single-person equity partnerships or require them to meet special financial accountability standards?

2. Such reforms would not, of course, prevent all such scandals. South Florida lawyer Scott Rothstein managed to perpetrate a scheme similar to Dreier's by consolidating control and paying his two other name partners sufficiently well to avert unwelcome inquiries. Before Rothstein's arrest in 2009, his firm had defrauded investors of nearly $1.6 billion based on shares that they had purchased in non-existent case settlements.[171] Like Dreier, Rothstein had cultivated an image of accomplishment through lavish expenditures and political and philanthropic contributions. Also like Dreier, Rothstein exhibited a toxic combination of over-optimism and narcissism. As he put it in a suicide text message to his partners, "I am a fool. I thought I could fix it but got trapped by my ego and refusal to fail."[172] His partners, for their part, engaged in willful ignorance. The signs of problems were clearly visible. Rothstein was

obsessively secretive and isolated himself in an office protected by a bullet-proof door, special entry key card, and security guard.[173] In the year before the fraud was discovered, Rothstein paid himself $10 million, and one of his partners, $6 million. In a firm that was generating only about $8 million in genuine business, that should have triggered internal inquiries.[174]

In such cases, money plays a corrosive role not just for leaders but also for followers, who are reluctant to voice concerns about practices that seem exceptionally profitable. Often subordinates, and sometimes investors, suspect that ethical corners are being cut; they just assume that they will not be the victims. What, if anything, can be done to counteract such dynamics and ensure greater transparency in financial governance?

3. A more recent example involves Michael Avenatti, the celebrated Los Angeles plaintiff's lawyer who represented porn star Stormy Daniels in her dispute with President Donald Trump. Despite some impressive multimillion-dollar class action judgments, Avenatti's earnings couldn't keep up with his lifestyle, which included a $19 million Newport Beach mansion, several race cars, and shares in two private jets, along with debt resulting from years of unpaid taxes and bad investment decisions.[175] In an effort to address his increasingly desperate cash flow, he took a hardline stance in bargaining with Nike in a case involving a high school basketball coach who claimed that the company had paid off high school players. Avenatti offered that if Nike paid his client $1.5 million and hired him to conduct an internal investigation, which was estimated to cost $15 to $25 million, he would not disclose the allegations. Alternatively, for $22.5 million, he offered "full confidentiality, we ride off into the sunset."[176] Avenatti was indicted for extortion, and then, in unrelated matters, for bank and wire fraud based on false loan documents and for misappropriation of client funds. He had allegedly withheld millions of dollars allegedly owed to multiple clients, including a paraplegic personal injury victim and the porn star Stormy Daniels.[177]

In speculating on the causes of Avenatti's meteoric rise and fall, commentators pointed to a number of factors: his outsized ego, unbounded narcissism, "false sense of invincibility," and "insatiable, unsupportable lifestyle."[178] Avenatti was also known for his grandiose and ungrounded optimism about his prospects, which extended to predictions that he could be the next president.[179] Although denying any criminal conduct, Avenatti acknowledged that he often skated close to the edge. As he told a reporter, "[T]he good news is that I'm incredibly fearless. The bad news it that I'm incredibly fearless."[180] How would you characterize him? Could anything have helped keep his high-risk behavior in check?

4. The celebrated litigator and law firm chair David Boies came under considerable criticism for his role in representing and sitting on the board of Theranos, the Silicon Valley start-up that peddled a fraudulent blood testing device. Founder Elizabeth Holmes, who modeled herself on Steve Jobs, orchestrated a marketing scheme that blocked peer reviews and evidence of failures, and sold imperfect versions of the device to Walgreens, which led to

erroneous diagnoses for patients.[181] Through lucrative stock options and charismatic presentations, Holmes attracted a distinguished board of directors. It included several former cabinet secretaries, CEOs, and senators, who had insufficient voting power to perform meaningful oversight.[182]

Part of what enabled Holmes's con was her willingness to fire and silence any potential whistle-blower. She enlisted Boies Schiller in that effort, put David Boies on the Board of Directors, and arranged to pay half of his and the firm's fees in Theranos stock.[183] Many questioned whether this fee arrangement and dual role for Boies raised concerns about conflicts of interest, and his ability to exercise unbiased judgment both as a director representing the interests of investors and a lawyer representing the interests of management.[184] Concerns also surfaced about the firm's "thuggish" tactics in preempting dissent.[185] Litigators exposed one young employee to hundreds of thousands of dollars in legal fees and threatened another possible whistleblower with bankrupting him and his entire family.[186] The firm also threatened to sue the *Wall Street Journal* for defamation and disclosure of trade secrets if it published an article raising questions about the effectiveness of the blood testing technology.[187] After the article ran and most of the ex-statesmen members of the board were demoted to advisors, Boies stayed on.[188] Not until he and Holmes had a falling out over how to handle federal investigations did he resign and terminate his representation. Theranos and Holmes are now facing both criminal and civil liability for alleged fraud.

In commenting on his role, Boies told a *New York Times* reporter that "greater due diligence" might have led him to decline representation. And in an oblique reference to the role of financial self-interest and his lavish lifestyle, he acknowledged that "I spend a lot of money."[189] But he also defended his hardball tactics. "You don't know all the facts when you take on a client, but once you do, you have a duty of loyalty. You can't represent them halfway."[190] How would you respond?

5. Are there any common threads running through these financial scandals? Can you identify any gerneralizable l correctives?

6. Some financial scandals involve misuse of organizational or taxpayer funds. A case in point was the 2010 disclosure of some $700,000 to renovate the private residence of Mark Yudof, a former law school dean and President of the University of California. At a time when the university was facing massive financial cutbacks, many observers were outraged that large amounts of money and staff time were consumed by the upkeep of a palatial rental home that was not even the official president's house.[191] Similar controversies led to the resignation of Abe Goldstein, another former law school dean and provost at Yale. Cost overruns on redecorations for the provost's house ran to five times the amount budgeted for the project, totaling about $313,000 in current dollars. Those costs included repainting several rooms when Mrs. Goldstein decided she preferred a different color.[192] Are such problems primarily due to inadequate oversight procedures or to lack of ethical sensitivity?

7. Other lawyers have proven similarly insensitive when on the receiving end of illegitimate or excessive payments. Supreme Court Justice Abe Fortas was disgraced by receipt of an exorbitant fee from former business clients for a summer seminar program, and by acceptance of $20,000, intended as the first installment of a lifetime honorarium from the foundation of a former client whom he continued to advise regarding a fraud investigation.[193] Unable to reconcile his salary with his lifestyle, Fortas found the financial aspects of his move to the bench "oppressive and depressing."[194] In resigning under pressure, Fortas continued to deny wrongdoing.[195] Kwame Kilpatrick, while mayor of Detroit, made similar denials when accused of using city funds to lease a car for his family, and charging a city credit card thousands of dollars for spa massages, extravagant dining, and expensive wine.[196] Although Kilpatrick paid back some $9,000, he also denounced ethics-related criticisms as part of a "hate-driven bigoted assault" and "illegal lynch-mob mentality."[197]

Efforts to defend or conceal misconduct can also give rise to financial abuses. A Senate Ethics Panel found that Larry Craig improperly used $213,000 in campaign funds to pay legal fees and public relations costs connected with charges of soliciting sex in an airport restroom. Campaign funds may only be used to pay legal expenses related to a senator's official duties.[198] New York Governor David Patterson was fined by the Commission on Public Integrity for lying about the solicitation of free tickets from the Yankees for the World Series.[199]

8. In some cases of leaders' financial conduct, the ethical issue comes down to symbolism. Consider the criticism of First Lady Michelle Obama in 2010 in response to her heading to a five-star European beach resort with a cavalcade of taxpayer-subsidized staff and security agents, even as most of the country was "pinching pennies" and "sliding into a double-dip depression," and the president was "campaigning against the excesses of the rich." If Obama had wanted an ocean vacation, critics proposed the Gulf coast, where she and her daughters could have "cleaned a few pelicans."[200] Jay Leno quipped that Obama had a new book out: "Spain on $75,000 a day."[201] Is such criticism fair? When asked to comment on the expenditure, which was largely financed by taxpayers, White House advisor David Axelrod responded that "[f]olks in the public eye are also human" and should not have to defer all the opportunities that come with the office.[202] Is that an adequate response?

Consider also the criticism of the Obamas for going on a "date night" in New York City, which required hours of work on the part of their security team and local police, all at taxpayer expense, and considerable inconvenience to New Yorkers caught in traffic diversions and stoppages.[203] If presidents are insensitive to public criticism, is there any realistic remedy? Donald Trump appears unfazed by concerns that he spent an estimated $64 million in trips to his Mar-a-Lago golf resort in the first two years of his presidency.[204]

9. Are some of these examples byproducts of the sense of entitlement and invulnerability that often accompanies power? *Lawyers as Leaders* notes that

leaders sometimes advance by bending rules, and focusing relentlessly on their ascent to the top; by the time they arrive, they have come to believe that they no longer have to sweat the small stuff and that it doesn't much matter what others think. With that mindset, minor misconduct can easily mushroom into a major scandal.[205]

Do you agree? If so, would the moral tripwires that David Luban advocated help keep leaders on track?[206]

MEDIA RESOURCES

A video tour of Rothstein's office and a profile of Marc Dreier are both available on YouTube.[207] Season six of *Veep* features some interesting scenes in which the former president Selena Meyers considers taking a multimillion-dollar contribution to her proposed presidential library in exchange for political favors.[208] In a World Business forum address, former CEO and Harvard lecturer Bill George talks about the need for authentic leadership in the context of the recent financial crisis. Accounts of Bernard Madoff's scandal also provide a window on the dynamics of massive meltdowns.[209] Jon Stewart mocks Charles Rangel's congressional testimony in which he tries to exonerate himself for ethics violations.[210] An interview with Michael Avenatti and commentary on his alleged offenses are also available.[211]

F. SEX

Just about everyone loves a sex scandal, except, of course, the leaders who are experiencing one. In the following excerpt, Ari Adut explores the extent of America's fascination with celebrity sex and some of its causes and consequences.

ARI ADUT, ON SCANDAL:
MORAL DISTURBANCES IN SOCIETY, POLITICS, AND ART

(New York: Cambridge University Press, 2008), pp. 175-183 and 208-222

Sex and the American Public Sphere

The American public sphere was "All Monica, All the time" in 1998. The nation spent an entire year engrossed in a lewd narrative about adulterous sex in the Oval Office between President Clinton and a sprightly White House intern. It was a cheap but very lucrative story for the media, which, to keep the plot moving, fed the public daily with a steady stream of fresh allegations. . . . For most Americans, it was hard not to be interested, not to be amused. The Starr Report, the lurid account of the illicit liaison . . . by the Independent Counsel's office that was investigating the president, was downloaded an estimated nine million times in two days after it hit the Internet.

But the scandal was serious business, too. The revelation of Bill Clinton's affair with Monica Lewinsky and the legal complications that arose thereof plunged the American democracy in a drawn-out constitutional crisis, making the satirical politician, already embattled by a sexual harassment suit, the second impeached president in history and pushed him to the brink of resignation. Recall the generalized outrage among the political and intellectual elite. Conservatives clobbered Clinton for having contaminated the White House; liberals rejoined that it was precisely the unscrupulous Republican onslaught on the office of the presidency that was responsible for the pollution. And the maelstrom soon implicated numerous third parties in a quite direct way [including Robert Livingston who resigned after *Hustler* exposed his own extramarital activity.] . . .

[Public discourse is] still steeped in sex scandals. Just for a small sample, consider all the sleaze that has been alleged or revealed in public in the recent years about [Michael Jackson, Paris Hilton, Arnold Schwarzenegger, former New Jersey governor James McGreevey, the mayor of Detroit Kwame Kilpatrick, television host Bill O'Reilly, and Senator Larry Craig.] . . . Jack Ryan withdrew from the senatorial race in Illinois in 2004, ensuring that the GOP would lose a seat, after the *Chicago Tribune* obtained divorce documents divulging that the Republican politician had propositioned his actress wife to have sex with him in a club. Eliot Spitzer resigned in March 2008 from the office of the governor of New York after a federal investigation caught him contacting an expensive prostitute for an assignation. Allegations of pedophilia by Catholic priests peaked in 2003 and 2004, disgracing the entire Church. The revelation of Mark Foley's off-color Internet communications with Congress pages in October 2006 [and inadequate response by the House speaker] . . . was a factor in the Republican wipeout in the 2006 midterm elections. . . .

Sex scandals luxuriate in settings in which the publicity of sex has lost a good deal of its embarrassing, shameful, discomfiting quality for audiences. I call this declining modesty. The relative attenuation of the puritanism of Americans since the early sixties has dramatically lowered the threshold of shame associated with the publicity of sexuality. . . . A by-product of the relative ease with which contemporary Americans talk about—and especially listen to and read about—sex in public is that the symbolic and emotional costs of public accusations of sexual misconduct both for accusers and audiences have dwindled. . . .

Sex and Scandal

What accounts for the close association, since time immemorial, between sex and scandal? . . . [A] celebrity sex scandal—and contemporary politicians are often celebrities—gratifies on several levels. We are afforded intimate peeks into the lives of important people, whom we often find to be fascinating. We are offered an opportunity to live vicariously through the sexual experiences that are not ordinarily accessible for want of opportunity, moral qualms, lack of imagination, or maybe cowardice. Simultaneously, a sex scandal slakes our all-too-natural resentfulness by giving us a chance to see those, whose better fortunes are frequently unforgivable, to get their comeuppance. And finally, unlike an accounting scandal, a sex scandal is fairly simple and features a cast we can easily identify with or react against. We find it much more natural to adjudicate on sexual matters: the capacity to judge does not call for special expertise because we have all in various ways tackled moral issues regarding our or others' sexual behavior. . . . Sex is not just absorbing. It also lends itself readily to moralizing. . . .

We are now in a better condition to understand the Lewinsky scandal. . . . [In a deposition in the sexual harassment case by Arkansas state employee Paula Jones, Clinton denied that he had sexual relations with Monica Lewinsky. In a later grand jury proceeding brought by Independent Counsel Kenneth Starr, Clinton acknowledged an "improper physical relationship" with Lewinsky but denied having lied in his deposition because he had not consider receiving oral sex to constitute sexual relations. On recommendation by the independent counsel, the House of Representatives impeached Clinton on two grounds: lying under oath and obstructing justice. The Senate lacked the two-thirds votes to convict. An Arkansas judge dismissed Jones's sex harassment case but found the president in contempt for lying to the grand jury and imposed a fine.]

The standard verity about scandals is that cover-ups always backfire. This is patently wrong. Given the first poll figures[, which found that almost half of voters wanted the president out of office if he had engaged in a sexual affair, lied about it, and had asked Lewinsky to lie as well], Clinton was astute to keep the truth from the public; opinion turned soon after. The main reason Americans were mostly with Clinton was the economy, which had been doing swimmingly throughout his second term. . . . As the scandal dragged on and eventually palled on the public, most Americans (60 to 70 percent) blamed Starr. The job approval rating of Clinton actually reached 68 percent while Clinton was being impeached, and the Democrats gained five House seats in the 1998 midterm elections.

For the majority of the public, the scandal was primarily about sex. Clinton perjured himself and obstructed justice, but most Americans were not all that outraged by these legal transgressions and, to the exasperation of the Republicans in Congress, refused to see the matter as something much more than lying about sex. . . .

Clinton's allies also acted strategically. Feminists would have definitely gone after the president had he not been a Democrat who had done much to advance their agenda. So they took his side even though Clinton's lie technically obstructed the course of justice in a sexual harassment case and even though feminists are highly skeptical about the legitimacy of relationships involving power differentials, however consensual they may be. Feminist activists and politicians were more concerned with the political costs of Clinton's demise than with his individual transgression. . . .

In contemporary America, sex norms are not strong enough to make public discussion of sex scandalous, but not weak enough for us to be indifferent to the sexual behavior of others.

NOTES AND QUESTIONS

1. If you had been President Clinton, with his sexual history, what might you have done differently?

2. Before the Lewinsky affair became public through her exposure as a witness in Paula Jones's sexual harassment lawsuit, Clinton offered to settle that suit for $700,000. Although that amount was far in excess of any likely verdict had the case gone to trial, Jones rejected the offer. Prodded by her husband and other politically motivated advisors, she insisted on an apology admitting wrongdoing, which Clinton refused to give, reportedly out of concern that it might encourage other similar suits.[212] If you had been counsel to the president or the White House chief of staff, would you have advised him to make the apology? Alternatively, should you have advised him to refuse to testify and accept a default judgment in the case?

3. As the scandal unfolded, Clinton reported "having to become quite an expert in this business of asking for forgiveness."[213] Compare the following attempts. Which are most and least effective? What would you have said in his place?

   - "I did have a relationship with Miss Lewinsky that was not appropriate. In fact, it was wrong. It constituted a critical lapse in judgment and a personal failure on my part for which I am solely and completely responsible. . . . [However, the Independent Counsel investigation] has gone on too long, cost too much, and hurt too many innocent people. . . . Now this matter is between me, the two people I love most—my wife and our daughter—and our God. It's nobody's business but ours. Even presidents have private lives."[214]

   - "I have acknowledged that I made a mistake, said that I regretted it, asked to be forgiven, spent a lot of very valuable time with my family in the last couple of weeks, and said I was going back to work."[215]

   - "I agree with those who have said that in my first statement after I testified, I was not contrite enough. I don't think there is a fancy way to say that I have sinned. It is important to me that everyone who has been hurt know that the sorrow I feel is genuine: first and most important my family; also my friends; my staff, my Cabinet; Monica Lewinsky and her family; and the American people. I have asked all for their forgiveness. But I believe that to be forgiven, more than sorrow is required, at least two more things. First, genuine repentance; a determination to change, to repair breaches of my own making. I have repented. Second what my Bible calls a "broken spirit": an understanding that I must have God's help to be the person that I want to be. . . ."[216]

According to many experts, the last apology, given at a White House National Prayer Breakfast, was the one "he should have given all along."[217] Do you agree? If so, why do you think it took so long in coming? In 2018, in the wake of #MeToo, Clinton was asked if he should directly apologize to

Monica Lewinsky, which he acknowledged he had never done apart from his public statements. He responded, "No . . . I do not."[218] Should he?

Are you persuaded by Adut's analysis? What are the implications of #MeToo for what the public considers a sexual scandal and an adequate response?

PROBLEM 7-6

In the wake of #MeToo, William Voge, the 61-year-old chair of the global law firm Latham and Watkins, was forced to resign because of sexually explicit texts he exchanged with Andrea Vassell, a married mother of three whom he never met in person.[219] The two met through the New Canaan Society, a national group of Christian businessmen. Voge was a member of its board, which Ms. Vassell contacted to report that its founder had paid to have sex with her. She asked that the group disband and remove the man from its website. Voge intervened to encourage the parties to mediate, and while he was on a business trip his communications with Vassell became flirtatious and then sexually explicit. Ms. Vassell promptly sent copies to the New Canaan Society's chief executive. Voge apologized to Ms. Vassell by phone and text, and told her that he wanted no further contact. She responded that she would neither accept his apology nor remain silent and told him, "You are insane if you think I am not coming after you with everything I have."[220]

Ms. Vassell e-mailed a copy of the letter to two of Latham's partners and general counsel, while making clear that she was not accusing Voge of "sexual misconduct" because both were "consenting adults."[221] She continued sending letters to Voge, his wife, Latham lawyers, New Canaan Society members, and the press. Mr. Voge, for his part, warned Vassell and her husband that she was committing crimes and would go to jail if she didn't stop. She retained a lawyer, who allegedly told Voge's lawyer that her cooperation with a legal trade publication would cease for "at least six figures."[222] Voge finally contacted the police, which opened an investigation into her harassment by electronic means. Latham partners accepted Voge's offer to resign as chair and issued a statement saying that his "lapses in personal judgment made continued service as chair untenable."[223] "I was irrational, I was stupid, and I was reckless," Voge told *Wall Street Journal* reporters.[224] In a subsequent letter to his firm colleagues, Voge wrote, "For those of you who had the courage to tell me of your disappointment, I want you to know that your disappointment in me will never exceed my own disappointment in myself."[225]

Is there anything Voge could have done differently to preserve his position and prevent the scandal from escalating? What lessons do you draw from his experience?

NOTES AND QUESTIONS

1. In her autobiography, Hillary Clinton recalls that most commentators and some of President Clinton's most trusted advisors thought that his initial decision to criticize Independent Counsel Kenneth Starr instead of just apologizing had been a mistake. But, she notes, her husband's "standing in public opinion polls remained high. His standing with me had hit rock bottom."[226]

   Why do you think Clinton's standing remained so high? As information about the affair began to trickle out and Clinton initially denied his involvement, his primary pollster found that 60 percent of voters believed that if he had committed perjury or obstructed justice by asking Lewinsky to lie, he should be removed from office.[227] But by the close of his term, when a court found that he had indeed lied under oath, his approval ratings remained at over 60 percent, although close to that number also denied that he was a "man of character."[228] How do you account for the inconsistency? Was it just about the economy, as Adut suggests? Or are there other lessons for scandal mongers and scandal management?

2. In suggesting that South Carolina governor Mark Sanford was unfit for office because of lies about an extramarital affair, former cabinet member and conservative commentator William Bennett maintained that "[a] cheat in private is going to be a cheat in public. Someone who lies in private is going to lie in public and you can't trust someone who does that."[229] Do you agree? Do comparisons between presidents who were models of marital fidelity (Richard Nixon, Ronald Reagan, Jimmy Carter, and George W. Bush) and those who were not (Franklin Delano Roosevelt, John F. Kennedy, and Bill Clinton) suggest close correlations between honesty about sex and honesty about public affairs or performance in office? What implications follow? Under what circumstances does politicians' personal conduct become a matter of public concern? In addressing that question, commentators have argued that relevant factors include whether the affair involved other illegal conduct, abuse of office, exceptionally poor judgment, or excessively reckless behavior, and also whether the office is one that necessarily entails moral leadership.[230] Under that test, how would you assess the conduct of lawyers recently involved in sexual scandals?

3. Consider the costs of focusing attention on politicians' sexual conduct. Not only does that attention discourage talented individuals from considering public service, it also

   > encourages a kind of Gresham's law of journalism. All it takes is one reporter with a peephole perspective. As soon as a scandal breaks in any major media outlet, it becomes difficult for other members of the press to remain above the fray. The prevailing philosophy of "let the public decide" often encourages the media to pander to our worst instincts, and to divert its attention from more substantive issues. . . .

Details about politicians' sex lives can demean not only politicians but ourselves.[231]

Do you agree? If so, what follows from that fact?

4. Americans have long been divided about the relevance of sexual conduct in evaluating fitness for public office. One of the curiosities of the 2016 presidential campaign was that the Republican candidate was "a self-confessed serial adulterer, yet few conservatives seemed to care. In *The Art of the Comeback*, Donald Trump bragged about his sexual experiences with 'seemingly very happily married and important women.'"[232] But the religious right raised almost no concerns. Does this suggest that public opinion has evolved, or is Trump a unique case? In 2013, half of Americans said they would definitely or probably not vote for a congressman who was unfaithful to his wife.[233] But by 2016, six in ten Americans agreed that elected officials can perform their public duties in an ethical manner even if they have committed immoral personal acts. Seven out of ten white evangelical Protestants agreed, a jump from three in ten who thought so in 2011.[234] What implications do you draw from this trend? Do you think it will persist in the aftermath of #MeToo? 5. Why are almost all of the political leaders embroiled in sesxual scandals men? According to an index of Americans who lost their jobs following allegations of sexual misconduct in the wake of #MeToo, only 3 percent of the alleged perpetrators were women.[235] In another earlier study of some 53 political sex scandals between 1976 and 2009, only one (2 percent) involved a female politician.[236] What accounts for this gender disparity? Is it mainly because fewer women hold positions of leadership? Or are they more risk averse, partly due to lingering double standards of morality, which make promiscuity more costly for women than men (particularly if they are married and have children)? Or, as anthropologist Lionel Tiger argues, is it that women have fewer sexual opportunities because power is not as alluring in women as in men?[237] Or do women have less sense of entitlement to extramarital sex? As the world moves toward greater gender equality in leadership roles, should we expect to see more sex scandals involving women, or fewer involving men? Are wronged husbands likely to play the same role as wronged wives at press events where leaders acknowledge "pain" in their marriages?[238]

6. What enables some leaders to survive sex scandals while others never recover? Consider the following factors. Which are most important? Which should be?

(a) *Hypocrisy.* The greater the disparity between the public image and private conduct, the more judgmental the public is likely to be. Eliot Spitzer, the New York governor who was caught with a high-priced call girl, suffered from having supported increased penalties for patronizing prostitutes and from having cast himself as a moral crusader while attorney general.[239] Mark Foley resigned from the Senate in 2006 after sending sexually suggestive e-mails to male adolescents who had previously worked as

Senate pages. He had a record of support for anti-gay legislation and had criticized Clinton's relationship with a White House intern as "vile."[240] David Vitter, the Louisiana Senator who purchased services from the "D.C. Madam," was pummeled by the press because of his prior stand on "family values," including his condemnation of then-president Bill Clinton as "morally unfit to govern."[241] Many voters agree with the observation of Barney Frank, a lawyer in Congress who survived a scandal involving sex with a gay prostitute because he was out and open about his mistake. As he put it, "Everyone in public life is entitled to privacy but no one in public life is entitled to hypocrisy."[242] Do you agree? Do most Americans? Note that Vitter won reelection in 2010 despite the scandal.

(b) *Deception.* The received wisdom among crisis management professionals is that ineffective attempts to conceal misconduct compound its consequences. A textbook case is Gary Hart, whose extramarital affair aboard a yacht named *Monkey Business* derailed his presidential candidacy. Rather than refusing to discuss charges of extra-marital relationships, Hart flatly denied them and challenged reporters to put a tail on him. "They'll be bored," he predicted.[243] They weren't. In the face of mounting evidence about his frequent contacts with model Donna Rice, Hart claimed that they had no "personal relationship." As a *New York Times* editorial wryly inquired, "[W]ould 'political' or 'business' relationship better describe it?"[244] Hart was forced to permanently suspend his campaign.

So too, presidential candidate John Edwards bungled efforts to evade tabloid reporters and to have his campaign manager falsely assume paternity of Edwards's own illegitimate child, all of which contributed to his political free fall. And Bill Clinton laid the foundations for his impeachment by the House of Representatives when he lied about his affair with Monica Lewinsky.

(c) *Botched Apology.* John Edwards added nails to his coffin by suggesting that a mitigating circumstance during his affair was that his wife's fatal cancer was in remission. As *New York Times* columnist Maureen Dowd noted, this was the "creepiest part of his creepy confession . . . . His infidelity was oncologically correct."[245] Mark Sanford's rambling and detailed public confessional was a textbook case of what not to do. As noted earlier, Clinton's apologies were criticized as too little too late. Can you identify a politician who seemed to have struck the right balance?

(d) *Allies.* One critical factor in surviving a sex scandal is the extent to which others rally around the leader. As Adut notes, Clinton benefitted from the continued support of feminists. However much they deplored his personal sexual history, women's rights activists felt that he had been good on their issues, and that his impeachment would set them back. By contrast, Spitzer's fall was partly attributable to a governing style that had alienated political colleagues.[246] A spouse's clenched-teeth stoicism can often be critical, while a tell-all memoir or interview invites further disaster.[247] Yet although a wife's support can be critical, is having her at a press conference always desirable?. Consider one description of Spitzer's resignation, with his demonstrably mortified wife standing beside him, as reminiscent of "watching someone swallow a hand grenade in real time."[248]

(e) *Related Misconduct.* The misuse of campaign funds or taxpayer dollars to finance an affair can also play a role, as was the case with Edwards and Sanford. Congressman Wayne Hays inflamed voters by employing a secretary whose primary duty was sex; that woman, by her own admission, did not know how to type.

As these examples make clear, multiple factors affect the outcome of sexual scandals. Not all are fatal. But few end happily ever after. And in this world of increasing technological transparency, leaders need to recognize that their sexual footprints will be hard to conceal.[249]

MEDIA RESOURCES

Bill Clinton's grand jury testimony is worth reviewing, as are clips of his various apologies.[250] Other press conferences are also available on YouTube, including Eliot Spitzer's. *Client Nine: The Rise and Fall of Eliot Spitzer*. Mark Sanford provides an excellent example of a failed post-scandal apology. Sanford talks about his soul mate and includes a few comical takes on his infidelity.[251] Jon Stewart's treatment of many of these events can also supply a cautionary tale. The film *The Frontrunner* chronicles Gary Hart's free-fall, and raises interesting questions about media as well as personal ethics. In one scene where reporters are questioning Hart about his sexual conduct, he responds, "[T]his is why people don't like politics . . . this is beneath you." The television series *Scandal* features repeated portraits of sexual misconduct, and *The Good Wife* season one drew inspiration from the Spitzer scandal. A video parody by *The Onion* portrays a politician's press conference in which he apologizes for the sex scandal that he is about to precipitate.[252] Late night comedy hosts mock Anthony Weiner's botched resignation after his sexually explicit self-portrait went viral.[253] Jon Stewart chides Newt Gingrich for his hypocrisy in refusing to answer questions about his marital history.[254] Stephen Colbert satirizes Arnold Schwarzenegger's extramarital affair with his housekeeper and the public's curiosity about it. Film versions of sexual and political scandals include *The American President*, starring Michael Douglas and Richard Dreyfuss, and *Primary Colors*, explored in Chapter 11.

END NOTES

[1] LAURA KIPNIS, HOW TO BECOME A SCANDAL: ADVENTURES IN BAD BEHAVIOR 8, 21 (2010).

[2] KIPNIS, HOW TO BECOME A SCANDAL, 14.

[3] ARI ADUT, ON SCANDAL: MORAL DISTURBANCES IN SOCIETY, POLITICS, AND ART 80 (2008).

[4] LESLIE GAINES-ROSS, CORPORATE REPUTATION: 12 STEPS TO SAFEGUARDING AND RECOVERING REPUTATION 7 (2008), citing Weber Shandwick, *Safeguarding Reputation,* KRC RESEARCH, 2006.

[5] Jacob A. Stein, *Legal Spectator: Who We Are and Who We Want to Be,* WASH. LAWYER, Jan. 2011, at 48 (quoting Maugham).

[6] G.R. Goethals, David W. Messick & S.T. Allison, *The Uniqueness Bias: Studies of Constructive Social Comparison,* in JERRY M. SULS & THOMAS ASHBY WILLS, SOCIAL COMPARISON: CONTEMPORARY THEORY AND RESEARCH 149, 161-62 (1991).

[7] John Schwartz, *Resumes Made for Fibbing,* N.Y. TIMES, May 23, 2010, at WK5.

[8] Piercarlo Valdesolo & David DeSteno, *The Duality of Virtue: Deconstructing the Moral Hypocrite,* 44 J. EXP. SOC. PSYCHOL. 1334 (2008).

[9] Joris Lammers, Diederik A. Stapel & Adam D. Galinsky, *Power Increases Hypocrisy: Moralizing in Reasoning, Immorality in Behavior,* 21 PSYCHOL. SCI. 737 (2010).

[10] See surveys cited in Lammers, Stapel & Galinsky, *Power Increases Hypocrisy,* at 738; Adam D. Galinsky et al., *Power Reduces the Press of the Situation: Implications for Creativity, Conformity, and Dissonance,* 95 J. PERS. SOC. PSYCHOL. 1450 (2008).

[11] Dennis F. Thompson, *Hypocrisy and Democracy,* in DENNIS F. THOMPSON, RESTORING RESPONSIBILITY: ETHICS IN GOVERNMENT, BUSINESS, AND HEALTHCARE 216-17 (2005).

[12] Jillian Jordan, Roseanna Sommers & David Rand, *The Real Problem With Hypocrisy,* N.Y. TIMES, Jan. 15, 2017, at SR 9.

[13] Jordan, Sommers, and Rand, *The Real Problem with Hypocrisy,* SR9.

[14] RUTH W. GRANT, HYPOCRISY AND INTEGRITY: MACHIAVELLI, ROUSSEAU, AND THE ETHICS OF POLITICS 26 (1997). *See also* JUDITH N. SHKLAR, ORDINARY VICES 54 (1984) (arguing that to fail in aspirations is not hypocritical).

[15] GRANT, HYPOCRISY AND INTEGRITY, 178.

[16] GRANT, HYPOCRISY AND INTEGRITY, 53.

[17] GRANT, HYPOCRISY AND INTEGRITY, 181.

[18] SHKLAR, ORDINARY VICES, at 70.

[19] Alan Ehrenhalt, *Hypocrisy Has Its Virtues,* N.Y. TIMES, Feb. 6, 2001, A19.

[20] Marvin Kitman, *Super-source for Scandal: Reporters Are Wasting Time and Money on Politicians' Dirty Secrets. Let's Get It All Organized in a "Sin Bin,"* L.A TIMES, Apr. 6, 2008, at 9.

[21] Peter A. Furia, *Democratic Citizenship and the Hypocrisy of Leaders,* 41 POLITY 114, 123 (2009).

[22] DAVID RUNCIMAN, POLITICAL HYPOCRISY: THE MASK OF POWER, FROM HOBBES TO ORWELL AND BEYOND 53-54 (2008).

[23] ANDREW YOUNG, THE POLITICIAN: AN INSIDER'S ACCOUNT OF JOHN EDWARD'S PURSUIT OF THE PRESIDENCY AND THE SCANDAL THAT BROUGHT HIM DOWN 206-07 (2010).

[24] Maureen Dowd, *Running with Scissors*, N.Y. TIMES, Apr. 21, 2007, at A25.

[25] Some critics faulted Whitman less for hypocrisy than for her callous dismissal of an employee she described as part of her extended family. Susan Estrich, *Meg Whitman's Housekeeper Hypocrisy,* NEWSMAX (Oct. 1, 2010), https://www.newsmax.com/estrich/megwhitmangloriaallred/2010/10/01/id/372216/.

[26] Isabel Macdonald, *Lou Dobbs, American Hypocrite,* THE NATION, Oct. 15, 2010, at 11.

[27] Jonah Lehrer, *The Power Trip,* WALL ST. J., Aug. 14, 2010, at W1.

[28] DACHER KELTNER, THE POWER PARADOX: HOW WE GAIN AND LOSE INFLUENCE 120-29 (2016).

[29] KELTNER, THE POWER PARADOX, 160-61.

[30] Lehrer, *The Power Trip,* at W2.

[31] Carlin McEnroe, *Downsizing the Horse Guard,* FUNNY TIMES, July 2010, at 14.

[32] NICK SMITH, I WAS WRONG: THE MEANING OF APOLOGIES 1 (2004).

[33] Todd S. Purdum, *Washington, We Have a Problem,* VANITY FAIR, Sept. 2010, at 339 (quoting Lauer & Obama).

[34] HARVARD BUSINESS ESSENTIALS, CRISIS MANAGEMENT: MASTER THE SKILLS TO PREVENT DISASTERS 81, 96 (2004).

[35] HARVARD BUSINESS ESSENTIALS, CRISIS MANAGEMENT, 42.

[36] For examples, see KEITH MICHAEL HEARIT, CRISIS MANAGEMENT BY APOLOGY: CORPORATE RESPONSE TO ALLEGATIONS OF WRONGDOING 26-27 (2006). The quote is from Bill Clinton, concerning allegations of his relationship with White House intern Monica Lewinsky. For mistakes made, see CAROL TAVRIS & ELLIOT ARONSON, MISTAKES WERE MADE (BUT NOT BY ME): WHY WE JUSTIFY FOOLISH BELIEFS, BAD DECISIONS, AND HURTFUL ACTS (2007); THE AMERICAN PRESIDENCY PROJECT, https://www.presidency.ucsb.edu; and Charles Baxter, *Dysfunctional Narratives: Or "Mistakes were Made,"* in CHARLES BAXTER ED., BURNING DOWN THE HOUSE: ESSAYS ON FICTION (1997). Lack of knowledge was what Mark Hurd claimed following the Hewlett Packard pretexting scandal described in Chapter 3. Notorious examples of buck passing between corporate entities include the Ford Explorer–Firestone tire recall and the BP Gulf oil spill. Examples of blame placed on consumers involved the Firestone tire and the Toyota "pedal misapplication" accelerator scandal.

[37] HEARIT, CRISIS MANAGEMENT BY APOLOGY, 80.

[38] Brett Kavanaugh, Senate Confirmation Hearing, Sept. 27, 2018, https://www.cnn.com/videos/politics/2018/09/27/kavanaugh-judiciary-calculated-political-hit-sot-vpx.cnn.

[39] Peter H. Kim et al., *Removing the Shadow of Suspicion: The Effects of Apology versus Denial for Repairing Competence-Versus Integrity-Based Trust Violations,* 89 J. APPL. PSYCHOL. 104, 107 (2004).

[40] Donald L. Ferrin et al., *Silence Speaks Volumes: The Effectiveness of Reticence in Comparison to Apology and Denial for Responding to Integrity- and Competence-Based Trust Violations,* 92 J. APPL. PSYCHOL. 893, 894 (2007).

[41] HEARIT, CRISIS MANAGEMENT BY APOLOGY, 207.

[42] HEARIT, CRISIS MANAGEMENT BY APOLOGY, 208; Ferrin et al., *Silence Speaks Volumes,* at 89; HARVARD BUSINESS ESSENTIALS, CRISIS MANAGEMENT, 41: SMITH, I WAS WRONG.

[43] Jessica M. Goldstein, *Terrible Men, Terrible Apologies,* THINK PROGRESS (Nov. 1, 2017), https://thinkprogress.org/sorry-not-sorry-why-are-men-accused-of-sexual-harassment-and-assault-so-bad-at-apologizing-1aeb6d33f926/.

[44] Don Chance, James Cion & Stephen P. Ferris, *Poor Performance and the Value of Corporate Honesty,* 33 J. CORP. FIN. 1 (2015).

[45] Cartoon by David Mankoff, NEW YORKER, Feb. 1, 2010, 70.

[46] Ferrin et al., *Silence Speaks Volumes,* at 906.

[47] Noam Cohen, *Word for Word/Mixed Messages; Swimming with Stock Analysts, or Sell Low and Buy High . . . Enthusiastically,* N.Y. TIMES, May 5, 2002, at 4, 7; Patrick McGeehan, *$100 Million Fine for Merrill Lynch,* N.Y. TIMES, May 22, 2002, at A1.

[48] Steven J. Scher & John M. Darley, *How Effective Are the Things People Say to Apologize? Effects of the Realization of the Apology Speech Act,* 26 J. PSYCHOLINGUISTIC RES. 127, 130 (1997).

[49] Deborah Tannen, *The Power of Talk: Who Gets Heard and Why,* HARV. BUS. REV. 143 (Sept.-Oct. 1995).

[50] Douglas A. Cooper, *CEO Must Weigh Legal and Public Relations Approaches,* 48 PUB. REL. J. 40 (1992).

[51] Jennifer K. Robbennolt, *Apologies and Legal Settlement: An Empirical Examination,* 102 MICH. L. REV. 460, 469, 491-99 (2003).

[52] Jennifer K. Robbennolt, *Attorneys, Apologies, and Settlement Negotiation,* 13 HARV. NEGOT. L. REV. 349, 362 (2008); Ken-ichi Ohbuchi, Masuyo Kameda & Nariyuki Agarie, *Apology as Aggression Control: Its Role in Mediating Appraisal of and Response to Harm,* 56 J. PERS. SOC. PSYCHOL. 219, 224-26 (1989).

[53] Graham G. Dodds, *Political Apologies: Chronological List.*

[54] Lisa Belkin, *Unforgivable,* N.Y. TIMES MAG., July 4, 2010, at 10 (noting that hospitals have found that a disclose and apologize policy has reduced litigation costs); Jennifer K. Robbennolt, *Apologies and Settlement Levers,* 3 J. EMPIRICAL LEGAL STUD. 333 (2006); Robbenalt, *Attorneys, Apologies, and Settlement Negotiation,* at 354-55.

[55] Robbenalt, *Attorneys, Apologies, and Settlement Negotiation,* at 356; Robbennolt, *Apologies and Settlement Levers,* at 336-37.

[56] Robbennolt, *Apologies and Settlement Levers.*

[57] Scher & Darley, *How Effective Are the Things People Say to Apologize*, at 132; HEARIT, CRISIS MANAGEMENT BY APOLOGY, 69; Paul Vitello, *I Apologize. No, Really, I'm Serious, I . . .,* N.Y. TIMES, Febr. 21, 2010, at WK2; David De Cremer & Barbara C. Schouten, *When Apologies for Injustice Matter: The Role of Respect,* 13 EURO. PSYCHOL. 239 (2008).

[58] SMITH, I WAS WRONG, 144.

[59] David D. Kirkpatrick, *In Secretly Taped Conversations, Glimpses of the Future President,* N.Y. TIMES, Feb. 20, 2005, at 1.

[60] Dodds, *Political Apologies.*

[61] MARK D. WEST, SECRETS, SEX, AND SPECTACLE: THE RULES OF SCANDAL IN JAPAN AND THE UNITED STATES 285, 294 (2006), quoting SHOZO SHIBUYA, TECHNIQUES OF APOLOGY 152 (2003).

[62] Hiroko Tabuchi & Bill Vlasic, *Toyota's Top Executive Under Rising Pressure,* N.Y. TIMES, Feb. 6, 2010, at B4 (quoting Tuck School of Business professor Paul Argenti); Micheline Maynard, *The Family Face of Toyota,* N.Y. TIMES, Feb. 24, 2010, B4.

[63] Caroline E. Mayer & Frank Swoboda, *"I Come . . . to Apologize": Firestone CEO Hears Coverup Allegations on Hill,* WASH. POST, Sept. 7, 2000, at A1.

[64] GAINES-ROSS, CORPORATE REPUTATION, 80-82.

[65] GAINES-ROSS, CORPORATE REPUTATION, 119.

[66] Zack Colman, *Two Executives Depart Nature Conservancy After Harassment Probe,* POLITICO (May 29, 2019), https://www.politico.com/story/2019/05/29/the-nature-conservancy-harassment-probe-1488630.

[67] FIRESTEIN, CRISIS OF CHARACTER, 262; GAINES-ROSS, CORPORATE REPUTATION, 85-89.

[68] Linda Klebe Treviño, *Out of Touch: The CEO's Role in Corporate Misbehavior,* 70 BROOK. L. REV. 1195, 1209 (2005); Elizabeth Wolfe Morrison & Frances J. Milliken, *Organizational Silence: A Barrier to Change and Development in a Pluralistic World,* 25 ACAD. MGMT. REV. 706, 707 (2000).

[69] HARVARD BUSINESS ESSENTIALS, CRISIS MANAGEMENT, 115.

[70] William George, *Tragedy at Toyota: How Not to Lead in Crisis,* HARV. BUS. SCH. (Feb. 22, 2010), http://hbswk.hbs.edu/cgi-bin/print?id=6381.

[71] *Presidential Address on Gulf of Mexico Oil Spill,* C-SPAN, June 15, 2010, available at https://www.c-span.org/video/?294074-3/presidential-address-gulf-mexico-oil-spill.

[72] Peter Robison & James Gunsalus, *Boeing Chief Tackles Ethics, All-New Jet,* SEATTLE POST-INTELLIGENCER, May 29, 2006, at 4.

[73] See the discussion of Chip Heath and Dan Heath, *Made to Stick,* in Chapter 4.

[74] Jackie Wattles, *Volkswagen CEO Sorry for "Broken Trust,"* CNN (Sept. 20, 2015), http://money.cnn.com/2015/09/20/autos/volkswagen-ceo-apology/.

[75] Dante D'Orazio, *Volkswagen Apologizes for Emissions Scandal with Full-Page Ad in Dozens of Papers,* THE VERGE (Nov. 15, 2015), http://www.theverge.com/transportation/2015/11/15/9739960/volkswagen-apologizes-with-full-page-ad-in-dozens-of-newspapers.

[76] Belkin, *Unforgivable,* 10 (quoting Hayward).

[77] Peter S. Goodman, *In Case of Emergency: What Not to Do,* N.Y. TIMES, Aug. 22, 2010, at BU1 (quoting Hayward).

[78] STEVEN K. MAY, GEORGE CHENEY & JULIET ROPER, THE DEBATE OVER CORPORATE SOCIAL RESPONSIBILITY 173 (2007).

[79] Alex Altman, *Congress Puts Toyota (and Toyoda) in the Hot Seat,* TIME, Feb. 24, 2010.

[80] Mayer & Swoboda, *"I Come . . . to Apologize"; Firestone CEO Hears Coverup Allegations on Hill,* WASH. POST, Sept. 7, 2000, at A1.

[81] Ben W. Heineman Jr., *GC and CEO Responsibility for GM's Dysfunctional Culture,* CORP. COUNS., June 6, 2014 (quoting Barra). Bill Vlasic & Aaron M. Kessler, *At Hearing on G.M. Recall, Mary Barra Gives Little Ground,* N.Y. TIMES, July 17, 2014.

[82] Dan Merica & Sophie Tatum, *Clinton Expresses Regret for Saying "Half" of Trump Supporters Are Deplorables,* CNN (Sept. 12, 2016), http://www.cnn.com/2016/09/09/politics/hillary-clinton-donald-trump-basket-of-deplorables/.

[83] The President's Address Announcing His Intention to Resign, 10 WEEKLY COMP. PRES. DOC. 1014, 1015 (Aug. 8, 1974).

[84] TAVRIS & ARONSON, MISTAKES WERE MADE, at 1 (quoting Kissinger).

[85] John F. Kennedy, *The President and the Press: Address Before the American Newspaper Publishers Association,* JFKLIBRARY.ORG (Apr. 27, 2017), https://www.jfklibrary.org/Research/Research-Aids/JFK-Speeches/American-Newspaper-Publishers-Association_19610427.aspx.

[86] Id. (quoting Knotts).

[87] Matt Stevens & Sydney Ember, *Nevada Lawmaker Says Biden Kissed Her in 2014,* N.Y. TIMES, Mar. 31, 2019 (quoting Biden).

[88] Ashlee Vance, *H.P. Ousts Chief for Hiding Payments to Friend,* N.Y. TIMES, Aug. 7, 2010, at A1 (quoting Hurd).

[89] Eric Dash, *So Many Ways to Almost Say "I'm Sorry,"* N.Y. TIMES, Apr. 18, 2010, at WK 4 (quoting Prince).

[90] Alexander Burns, Maggie Haberman & Jonathan Martin, *Donald Trump Apology Caps Day of Outrage Over Lewd Tape,* N.Y. TIMES, Oct. 7. 2016 (quoting Trump).

[91] Vanessa Romo, *Joe Biden Offered "Expressions of Affection" But Denies Inappropriate Behavior,* NPR (Mar. 31, 2019), https://www.npr.org/2019/03/31/708537421/joe-biden-offered-expressions-of-affection-but-denies-inappropriate-behavior.

[92] Lisa Lerer, *Biden Jokes About Hugging in a Speech, Then Offers a Mixed Apology,* N.Y. TIMES, Apr. 6, 2019.

[93] Id.

[94] Brett M. Kavanaugh, *I Am an Independent, Impartial Judge,* WALL ST. J., Oct. 4, 2018.

[95] Susan Svrluga, *Berkeley Law School Dean Resigns After Sexual Harassment Complaint,* WASH. POST, Mar. 10, 2016 (quoting Sujit Choudhry).

[96] James V. Grimaldi, *Firestone CEO Says Apology Wasn't Admission of Fault,* WASH. POST, Oct. 10, 2000, at E2.

[97] HEARIT, CRISIS MANAGEMENT BY APOLOGY, 143.

[98] Svrluga, *Berkeley Law School Dean Resigns* (quoting Claude Steele).

[99] Katy Murphy, *Former UC Berkeley Law Dean Accused of Sexual Harassment Sues University,* MERCURY NEWS, Sept. 16, 2016.

[100] Sheryl Gay Stolberg & Jonathan Martin, *Joe Biden Expresses Regret to Anita Hill, but She Says "I'm Sorry" Is Not Enough,* N.Y. TIMES, Apr. 25, 2019 (quoting Hill).

[101] Dahlia Lithwick, *Joe Biden Still Doesn't Understand What He Did to Anita Hill,* SLATE (Apr. 29, 2019), https://slate.com/news-and-politics/2019/04/joe-biden-anita-hill-apology-problem-misunderstand-concern.html; Jane Mayer, *What Joe Biden Hasn't Owned Up To About Anita Hill,* NEW YORKER, Apr. 27, 2019.

[102] Mayer, *Joe Biden* (quoting Biden).

[103] C-SPAN on Twitter, Apr. 2, 2019, @speakerPelosi on allegations against Joe Biden, https://twitter.com/span/status/1113065959361835008?ref.

[104] Richard Hanania, *Does Apologizing Work? An Empirical Test of the Conventional Wisdom,* SSRN (2015), https://papers.ssrn.com/sol3/papers.cfm?abstract_id=2654465.

[105] Sunstein, *Apologies Are for Losers.*

[106] Parul Sehgal, *Sorry, Not Sorry,* N.Y. TIMES MAGAZINE, Dec. 17, 2017.

[107] Sehgal, *Sorry, Not Sorry* (quoting Olivia Munn).

[108] Ben Worthen & Pui-Wing Tam, *H-P Chief Quits in Scandal,* WALL ST. J. Aug. 7, 2010.

[109] Ben W. Heineman Jr., *HP's CEO, Mark Hurd: How Could He Do Something So Stupid?,* ATLANTIC, Aug. 7, 2010.

[110] Joe Nocera, *The Real Reason H.P.'s Board Ousted Its Chief,* N.Y. TIMES, Aug. 14, 2010, at B7.

[111] *Scandal Gets Juicier: Tech Mogul Assails H.P.,* SAN JOSE MERCURY NEWS, Aug. 10, 2010, at A1 (quoting Ellison). Ellison also claimed that "this was the worst personnel decision since the idiots on the Apple board fired Steve Jobs many years ago."

[112] Joe Nocera, *H.P.'s Blundering Board,* N.Y. TIMES, Sept. 11, 2010, at B1, B6.

[113] Richard Waters, *Corporate Ethics: Moral Hazards,* FIN. TIMES, Aug. 15, 2010, at 5 (quoting Coffee).

[114] Heineman, *HP's CEO, Mark Hurd.*

[115] Worthen & Tam, *H-P Chief Quits in Scandal*; Adam Lashinsky with Doris Burke, *What Really Happened Between HP ex-CEO Mark Hurd and Jodie Fisher,* FORTUNE, Nov. 5, 2010.

[116] Eric Dezenhall, *Not All Publicity is Good Publicity,* ETHICAL CORP., July-Aug. 2010, at 42.

[117] Dezenhall, *Not All Publicity Is Good Publicity,* at 43.

[118] Andy Borowitz, *The Borowitz Report,* FUNNY TIMES, July 2010, at 19.

[119] Susan J. Fowler, *Reflecting on One Very, Very Strange Year At Uber,* SUSANJFOWLER.COM (Feb. 19, 2017), https://www.susanjfowler.com/blog/2017/2/19/reflecting-on-one-very-strange-year-at-uber.

[120] Id.

[121] Maya Kosoff, *Mass Firings at Uber as Sexual Harassment Scandal Grows,* VANITY FAIR, June 6, 2017; Barbara Booth, *A Year Later, What Uber Has Done to Revamp its Troubled Image,* CNBC.COM (June 20, 2018), https://www.cnbc.com/2018/06/20/a-year-later-what-uber-has-done-to-revamp-its-troubled-image.html.

[122] Mark Molloy, *Online Shaming: The Dangerous Rise of the Internet Pitchfork Mob,* THE TELEGRAPH, June 25, 2018.

[123] Natalie Proulx, *Does Online Public Shaming Prevent Us From Being Able to Grow and Change?,* N.Y. TIMES, Feb. 20, 2019 (quoting Robin Kanner).

[124] Anne Gearan, *Hillary Clinton Apologizes for E-mail System: "I Take Responsibility,"* WASH. POST, Sept. 8, 2015 (quoting Clinton).

[125] Maggie Haberman & Amy Chozick, *Hillary Clinton's Long Road to "Sorry" Over Email Use,* N.Y. TIMES, Sept. 11, 2015.

[126] Haberman & Chozick, *Hillary Clinton's Long Road* (quoting Clinton).

[127] Haberman & Chozick, *Hillary Clinton's Long Road* (quoting Clinton); Gearan, *Hillary Clinton Apologizes for E-mail System* (quoting Clinton).

[128] Gearan, *Hillary Clinton Apologizes for E-mail System* (quoting Clinton).

[129] Haberman & Chozick, *Hillary Clinton's Long Road* (quoting Axelrod).

[130] Edward Klein, *Hillary Clinton's Legal Adviser Warns Her: Time to Lawyer Up,* N.Y. POST, Oct. 3, 2015.

[131] Biesecker, *Hillary Clinton Has Answered Enough Email Questions*; Michael D. Shear, *FBI Director James Comey Testifies Before Congress,* N.Y. TIMES, July 7, 2016.

[132] Rosalind S. Helderman, *How the FBI Director Systematically Dismantled Hillary Clinton's Email Defense,* WASH. POST, July 5, 2016.

[133] Mark Landler & Eric Lichtblau, *F.B.I. Director James Comey Recommends No Charges for Hillary Clinton on Email,* N.Y. TIMES, July 5, 2016.

[134] Dan Balz, *How Everyone Looks Bad Because Bill Clinton Met With Loretta Lynch,* WASH. POST, July 2, 2016 (quoting Lynch); Chris Cillizza, *Bill Clinton and Loretta Lynch Just Made Hillary's Email Problems Even Worse,* WASH. POST, July 1, 2016 (quoting Lynch).

[135] Balz, *How Everyone Looks Bad* (quoting Lynch).

[136] Balz, *How Everyone Looks Bad.*

[137] Balz. *How Everyone Looks Bad* (quoting Lynch).

[138] Maureen Dowd, *The Clinton Contamination,* N.Y. TIMES, July 10, 2016, SR9.

[139] John M. Broder, *White House Official Resigns after G.O.P. Criticism,* N.Y. TIMES, Sept. 7, 2009, at A1.

[140] Maura Judkis, *Obama Drafts Van Jones as Green Jobs Adviser,* U.S. NEWS & WORLD REP. (Mar. 10, 2009), http://www.usnews.com/money/blogs/fresh-greens/2009/03/10/obama-drafts-van-jones-as-green-jobs-adviser.html.

[141] Sarah Wheaton, *White House Adviser on "Green Jobs" Resigns,* N.Y. TIMES, Sept. 6, 2009, at A17.

[142] Broder, *White House Official Resigns,* at A1. The petition demanded "a call for immediate inquiry into evidence that suggest high-level government officials may have deliberately allowed the September 11th attacks to occur."

[143] Mary Snow, *Obama Did Not Order Van Jones' Resignation, Adviser Says,* CNN, Sept. 6, 2009.

[144] Glenn Beck of Fox News led the campaign. Broder, *White House Official Resigns,* at A1.

[145] Michael Burnham, *Embattled Van Jones Quits, but "Czar" Debates Rage On,* N.Y. TIMES (Sept. 9, 2009), http://www.nytimes.com/gwire/2009/09/08/08greenwire-embattled-van-jones-quits-but-czar-debates-rage-9373.html?scp=1&sq=embattled%20van%20jones%20quits,%20but%20%27czar%27%20debates%20rage%20on&st=cse.

[146] Color of Change, http://colorofchange.org (last visited Aug. 18, 2019). Color of Change is an organization dedicated to strengthening the black political voice and committed to ensuring that all Americans are "represented, served, and protected—regardless of race or class. Van Jones cofounded the organization in 2005. Although criticism of Jones predated the campaign, it accelerated after some of Beck's sponsors withdrew their ads. Border, *White House Official Resigns,* at A1; Burnham, *Embattled Van Jones Quits, but "Czar" Debates Rage On.* The campaign was triggered by Beck's characterization of Obama as a racist. Id.

[147] Burnham, *Embattled Van Jones Quits.*

[148] Broder, *White House Official Resigns,* at A1.

[149] Wheaton, *White House Advisor,* at 17.

[150] Broder, *White House Official Resigns,* at A1.

[151] Broder, *White House Official Resigns,* at A1.

[152] Broder, *White House Official Resigns,* at A1.

[153] *Van Jones: Shirley Sherrod and Me,* NEWSONE, June 25, 2010.

[154] Simon Moya-Smith, *Elizabeth Warren's Native Ancestry Claims Never Compelled an Apology before She Ran for President. So Spare Us Now,* THINK (Feb. 7, 2019), https://www.nbcnews.com/think/opinion/elizabeth-warren-s-native-ancestry-claims-never-compelled-apolygy-sh-ncna968801.

[155] Moya-Smith, *Elizabeth Warren's Native Ancestry Claims*; Chris Cillizza, *Elizabeth Warren's Native American Problem Just Got Even Worse,* CNN (Feb. 6, 2019), https://www.cnn.com/2019/02/06/politics/elizabeth-warren-native-american/index.html.

[156] William Cummings, *"An Apology from the Heart": Senator Elizabeth Warren Sorry for Identifying as Native American,* USA TODAY, Feb. 7, 2019 (quoting Chuck Hoskin Jr.).

[157] Annie Linskey & Amy Gardner, *Elizabeth Warren Apologizes for Calling Herself Native American,* WASH. POST, Feb. 5, 2019; Cummings, *"An Apology from the Heart."*

[158] Alex Shepard, *The Media is Blowing Its Coverage of Warren's Native American Claim,"* NEW REPUBLIC, Feb 8, 2019 (quoting James Robbins).

[159] Shepard, *The Media is Blowing its Coverage.*

[160] IN THE MATTER OF REPRESENTATIVE CHARLES B. RANGEL, ADJUDICATORY SUBCOMMITTEE FROM THE COMMITTEE ON STANDARDS OF OFFICIAL CONDUCT, 111TH CONG. 2D. SESSION, H. REP. NO. 111-661 (2010).

[161] Eric Lipton, *Lawmakers Linked to Centers Endowed by Corporate Money,* N.Y. TIMES, Aug. 6, 2010, at A1.

[162] David Kocieniewski, *Rangel Censured Over Violations of Ethics Rules,* N.Y. TIMES, Dec. 3, 2010, at A1.

[163] David M. Herszenhorn & Carl Hulse, *In House Ethics Battles, A Partywide Threat,* N.Y. TIMES, Aug. 2, 2010, at A11 (quoting McConnell).

[164] Lipton, *Lawmakers Linked to Centers,* at A3 (quoting Ornstein).

[165] DENNIS F. THOMPSON, ETHICS IN CONGRESS: FROM INDIVIDUAL TO INSTITUTIONAL CORRUPTION 135-137 (1995). See also DENNIS ST-MARTIN AND FRED THOMPSON, PUBLIC ETHICS AND GOVERNANCE: STANDARDS AND PRACTICES IN COMPARATIVE PERSPECTIVE (2006).

[166] For Shirley Sherrod's edited speech, see http://www.youtube.com/watch?v=t_xCeItxbQY; For Rangel's press statements, see http://www.cnn.com/2010/POLITICS/07/29/rangel.ethics/; http://www.cnn.com/2010/POLITICS/07/23/rangel.profile/; http://www.cnn.com/2010/POLITICS/07/22/house.rangel.ethics.hearing/index.html. For Fox News's coverage of Van Jones, see http://www.youtube.com /watch?v=tJAz8D14wDQ; http://www.youtube.com/watch?v=VYlx9evcMoA. For Glenn Beck, see http://video.foxnews.com/v/3938743/who-is-van-jones.

[167] The Hayward segment aired June 21, 2010, and one of the Rangel segments aired Nov. 16, 2010.

[168] For Lewis, see The Brian Lehrer Show; for Runciman, with David Willets MP and Executive Editor of the Evening Standard Anne McElvoy, BBC NIGHT WAVES; The Brian Lehrer Show: ACORN Reacts, N.Y. NAT. PUB. RADIO, Sept. 18, 2009.

[169] Paul K. Piff et al., *Higher Social Class Predicts Increased Unethical Behavior,* 109 PROC. NAT. ACAD. SCI. U.S. (PNAS) 4083 (2012).

[170] Alison Leigh Cowan, Charles V. Bagli & William K. Rashbaum, *Lawyer Seen as Bold Enough to Cheat the Best,* N.Y. TIMES, Dec. 13, 2008.

[171] Nathan Koppel & Mike Esterl, *Lawyer Crashes After a Life in the Fast Lane,* WALL ST. J., Nov. 19, 2009, at A16; John Pacenti, *Why Suspicions About Fla. Firm's Alleged Ponzi Scheme Weren't Voiced,* LAW.COM, Dec. 7, 2009.

[172] Jon Burstein et al., *Lawyer Returns as Uproar Grows,* SUNSENTINEL, Nov. 4, 2009, at A1 (quoting Rothstein).

[173] Brittany Wallman, et al., *Life in the Fast and Secret Lane,* SUNSENTINEL, Nov. 6, 2009.

[174] *In re Rothstein Rosenfeldt Adler, P.A.,* 464 B.R. 465, at 5 (S.D. Fla. 2012).

[175] Emily Jane Fox, *Inside the Epic Fall of Michael Avenatti,* VANITY FAIR, Summer, 2019, 109.

[176] Fox, *Inside the Epic Fall,* 108 (quoting Avenatti); Melanie Mason, Michael Finnegan & Nathan Fenno, *Here are Key Takeaways from the Criminal Complaints Against Michael Avenatti,* L.A. TIMES, Mar. 26, 2019.

[177] Rebecca R. Ruiz, *Michael Avenatti Faces New Criminal Charges in Escalated Federal Case,* N.Y. TIMES, Apr. 11, 2019; Roomy Khan, *The Michael Avenatti Saga: What Caused the Meteoric Rise and Precipitous Fall Within A Year?,* FORBES, June 13, 2019.

[178] Khan, *The Michael Avenatti Saga.* See also Fox, *Inside the Epic Fall,* 109.

[179] Fox, *Inside the Epic Fall,* 111.

[180] Fox, *Inside the Epic Fall,* 138.

[181] Erin Griffith, *The Ugly Unethical Underside of Silicon Valley,* FORTUNE, Dec. 28, 2016.

[182] Ken Auletta, *Blood, Simpler,* NEW YORKER, Dec. 15, 2014.

[183] James B. Stewart, *David Boies Pleads Not Guilty,* N.Y. TIMES, Sept. 21, 2018.

[184] Steven Davidoff Solomon, *David Boies's Dual Roles at Theranos Set Up Conflict,* N.Y. TIMES, Feb. 2, 2016. See also Olga V. Mack, *Bad Blood: Even More Red Flags That Were Simply Ignored,* ABOVE THE LAW (Feb. 4, 2019), https://abovethelaw.com/2019/02/bad-blood-even-more-red-flags-that-were-simply-ignored/.

[185] Scott Alan Burroughs, *David Boies's Fall From Grace*, ABOVE THE LAW (Sept. 26. 2018), https://abovethelaw.com/2018/09/david-boiess-fall-from-grace (quoting Carryou); Stewart, *David Boies Pleads Not Guilty* (quoting Carreyrou).

[186] JOHN CARREYROU, BAD BLOOD: SECRETS AND LIES IN A SILICON VALLEY STARTUP (2019), 247.

[187] CARREYROU, BAD BLOOD, 257, 279.

[188] Andrew Pollack, *Theranos, Facing Criticism, Says it Has Changed Board Structure*, N.Y. TIMES, Oct. 28, 2015.

[189] Stewart, *David Boies Pleads Not Guilty* (quoting Boies).

[190] Stewart, *David Boies Pleads Not Guilty* (quoting Boies).

[191] In response to adverse publicity, the university appointed an official charged with oversight of expenditures. Steve Fainaru, *University to Manage Home Costs of President,* N.Y. TIMES, Aug. 27, 2010, at A17. *See also* Steve Fainaru, *University Head's Housing*

Raises Ire, N.Y. TIMES, Aug. 22, 2010, at A23 (quoting official's claim that Yudof had "turned the Office of the President into his personal staff").

[192] *Yale Provost Resigns After Dispute Over Cost of Renovating Home,* N.Y. TIMES, May 2, 1979, at B5; Allison T. Stark, *Yale Provost Quits Over Home Expenses Conflict,* WASH. POST, May 2, 1979, at A14.

[193] This account of Fortas draws on RHODE, LAWYERS AS LEADERS, 118, and LAURA KALMAN, ABE FORTAS: A BIOGRAPHY, 324-326, 352, 377 (1990). See also BRUCE ALLEN MURPHY, FORTAS: THE RISE AND RUIN OF A SUPREME COURT JUSTICE (1988).

[194] KALMAN, ABE FORTAS, at 322, 377 (quoting Fortas and describing his lifestyle).

[195] KALMAN, ABE FORTAS, at 573.

[196] This account of Kilpatrick draws on RHODE, LAWYERS AS LEADERS, 118; D. Kevin McNeir, *Kwame Kilpatrick: The Rise and fall of Detroit's "Hip Hop" Mayor,* MIAMI TIMES, July 12, 2012.

[197] Kwame Kilpatrick, 2008 Detroit State of the City Address (Mar. 11, 2008), https://www.c-span.org/video/?204231-1/detroit-state-city-address.

[198] *Senate Panel to Sen. Craig: You Discredited the Chamber,* CNN, Feb. 13, 2008, available at http://www.cnn.com/2008/POLITICS/02/13/larry.craig/index.html?iref=newssearch.

[199] David M. Halbfinger, *Paterson Fined $62,125 Over World Series Tickets,* N.Y. TIMES, Dec. 20, 2010, A1.

[200] Maureen Dowd, *Feliz Cumpleaños and Adiós,* N.Y. TIMES, Aug. 8, 2010, at WK9.

[201] Jay Leno, *Laugh Lines,* N.Y. TIMES, Aug. 15, 2010, at WK2.

[202] Dowd, *Feliz Cumpleaños,* at WK9 (quoting Axelrod).

[203] MICHELLE OBAMA, BECOMING 327 (2018).

[204] Philip Bump, *Trump's Travel to Mar-a-Lago Alone Probably Cost Taxpayers More than $64 Million,* WASH. POST, Feb. 5, 2019.

[205] RHODE, LAWYERS AS LEADERS, at 119.

[206] David Luban, *Making Sense of Moral Meltdowns,* in MORAL LEADERSHIP: THE THEORY AND PRACTICE OF POWER, JUDGMENT, AND POLICY (Deborah L. Rhode ed., 2007), excerpted in Chapter 6.

[207] *A Video Tour of Scott Roth Rothstein's Office,* MIAMI HERALD (Nov. 6, 2009), http://www.youtube.com/watch?v=9Bmp_4zcrGM. For Dreier, see https://www.youtube.com/watch?v=JEH4fNOqIjM.

[208] Veep, Season 6, Episodes 1 through 4 (2017).

[209] *See* http://www.youtube.com/watch?v=SsSGZezvuSg.

[210] http://www.realestateradiousa.com/2010/11/17/jon-stewart-rips-charlie-rangel-video/.

[211] For Stephen Colbert's commentary see https://www.youtube.com/watch?v=2Mpm3GMUiio. For the interview, see https://www.youtube.com/watch?v=z2iYbRUbMNE.

[212] KEN GORMLEY, THE DEATH OF AMERICAN VIRTUE: CLINTON VS. STARR 257-59 (2011).

[213] WEST, SECRETS, SEX, AND SPECTACLE, at 296 (quoting Clinton).

[214] N.Y. TIMES, *Last Night's Address: In His Own Words,* N.Y. TIMES, Aug. 18, 1998, at A12.

[215] John M. Broder, *Testing of a President: In Moscow; Clinton Defends His TV Admission on Lewinsky Case,* N.Y. TIMES, Sept. 3, 1998, at A1.

[216] N.Y. TIMES, *President Clinton's Address at the National Prayer Breakfast*, N.Y. TIMES, Sept. 12, 1998, at A12.

[217] HEARIT, CRISIS MANAGEMENT BY APOLOGY, 93.

[218] Sarah Quinlan, *Today's Talker: Bill Clinton Hasn't Learned Anything from the #MeToo Movement*, USA TODAY, June 4, 2018 (quoting Clinton).

[219] Sara Randazzo, *The Sexting Scandal That Toppled One of America's Most Powerful Lawyers*, WALL ST. J., July 13, 2018.

[220] Randazzo, *Sexting Scandal* (quoting Vassell).

[221] Randazzo, *Sexting Scandal.*

[222] Randazzo, *Sexting Scandal* (quoting Ekl).

[223] Randazzo, *Sexting Scandal* (quoting Latham and Watkins).

[224] Randazzo, *Sexting Scandal* (quoting Voge).

[225] Randazzo, *Sexting Scandal* (quoting Voge).

[226] HILLARY CLINTON, LIVING HISTORY 468 (2003).

[227] GORMLEY, THE DEATH OF AMERICAN VIRTUE, 413.

[228] See CNN USA Today/gallup poll, Aug 17, 1998; Molly W. Sonner & Clyde Wilcox, *Forging and Forgetting: Public Support for Bill Clinton During the Lewinsky Scandal*, 32 POL. SCI. & POL. 554, 556 (1999). For denial of character, see JAMES DAVISON HUNTER & CARL DESPORTES BOWMAN, THE POLITICS OF CHARACTER 8 (2000).

[229] Gerard Baker, *Sex Americana*, WALL ST. J., June 27-28, 2009, at W1 (quoting Bennett).

[230] DEBORAH L. RHODE, ADULTERY: INFIDELITY AND THE LAW 157 (2016); J. Patrick Dobel, *Judging the Private Lies of Public Officials*, 30 ADMIN. & SOC'Y 115, 129 (1998).

[231] RHODE, ADULTERY, 156-57.

[232] Deborah L. Rhode, *Why Is Adultery Still a Crime*, L.A. TIMES, May 2, 2016.

[233] Quinnipiac University Poll, *U.S. Voters Dislike Politicians Who Cheat Less than Those Who Abuse Power*, QUINNIPIAC U. NAT. POLL FINDS, Apr. 28, 2014.

[234] Robert P. Jones & Daniel Cox, *Clinton Maintains Double Digit Lead Over Trump*, PUB. REL. RES. INS. (PRRI), Oct. 19, 2016.

[235] Email from Davia Temin to Deborah Rhode, Apr. 29, 2019 (referencing Tenan Index data).

[236] Jeanne Zaino, *Where Are the "Bad" Girls?: Why More Female Politicians Engaged in Scandal Might Be a Good Thing*, HUFFINGTON POST (Aug. 13, 2013), https://www.huffpost.com/entry/female-political-sex-scandals_b_3744297.

[237] Rebecca Dana, *Why Women Don't Have Sex Scandals*, THE DAILY BEAST, Dec. 11, 2009 (quoting Tiger's view that "[w]omen tend to prefer males who are more powerful than they [are] and not vice versa").

[238] The reference is to an acknowledgement by Bill Clinton on *60 Minutes* during primaries for the 1992 presidential election. A former nightclub singer accused him of engaging in a 12-year extramarital affair, which Clinton refused to discuss, but later acknowledged having. BILL CLINTON, MY LIFE 385-387 (2004).

[239] RHODE, ADULTERY, 152.

[240] Backpage, NEWSWEEK, June 7, 2010, at 56; Valdesolo & DeSteno, *The Duality of Virtue: Deconstructing the Moral Hypocrite*, 1334, 1337 (quoting Foley).

[241] E.J. Dionne Jr., *Give Him a Break: Sen. Vitter Has Sinned, But It's Time to Stop Nosing Into Our Politicians' Private Lives*, PITT. POST-GAZETTE, July 13, 2007, at B7.

[242] Paul Farhi, *Bad News Travels Fast, and Furiously,* WASH. POST, Mar. 14, 2008 (quoting Frank).

[243] E.J. Dionne Jr., David Johnston, Wayne King & Jon Nordheimer, *Courting Danger: The Fall of Gary Hart,* N.Y. TIMES, May 9, 1987 (quoting Hart).

[244] *Gary Hart's Judgment,* N.Y. TIMES, May 5, 1987, at A34.

[245] Maureen Dowd, *Keeping It Rielle,* N.Y. TIMES, Aug. 9, 2008.

[246] PETER ELKIND, ROUGH JUSTICE: THE RISE AND FALL OF ELIOT SPITZER (2010); LLOYD CONSTANTINE, JOURNAL OF THE PLAGUE YEAR: AN INSIDER'S CHRONICLE OF ELIOT SPITZER'S SHORT AND TRAGIC REIGN (2010); Kristi Keck, *Surviving a Political Sex Scandal,* CNN.COM, July 14, 2009, at 1, available at http://www.cnn.com/2009/POLITICS/07/14/political.sex.scandal.survival/index.html.

[247] JENNY SANFORD, STAYING TRUE (2010); ELIZABETH EDWARDS, RESILIENCE: REFLECTIONS ON THE BURDENS AND GIFTS OF FACING LIFE'S ADVERSITIES (2009).

[248] KIPNIS, HOW TO BECOME A SCANDAL, 5.

[249] Susan Dominus, *Doing Something Sketchy? It's Harder to Cover Up Now,* N.Y. TIMES, Mar. 21, 2008, at B6; Farhi, *Bad News Travels Fast.*

[250] *See, e.g.,* http://www.youtube.com/watch?v=ClfpG2-1Bv4.

[251] http://www.youtube.com/watch?v=DU7eZavVzao&feature=related.

[252] http://www.youtube.com/watch?v=jNX518hfghU. The Huffington Post also posted the video at http://www.huffingtonpost.com/2009/03/04/congressman-offers-preemp_n_172000.html.

[253] http://blogs.wsj.com/speakeasy/2011/06/17/daily-late-night-roundup-anthony-weiner-says-goodbye-edition.

[254] http://www.huffingtonpost.com/2012/01/24/jon-stewart-newt-gingrich-south-carolina-debate-hypocrisy_n_1227547.html.

PART IV

LEADERSHIP CHALLENGES

CHAPTER 8

DIVERSITY IN LEADERSHIP

Prior discussion has focused on what constitutes leadership and what qualities, skills, and organizational dynamics make it effective. This chapter explores who exercises leadership, and how characteristics such as race, ethnicity, gender, and sexual orientation matter in the selection and performance of leaders. Although these are not the only relevant characteristics, are not the only relevant dimensions of diversity, they are the focus of this discussion because but they are the ones that affect most individuals and have generated the most concern, controversy, and research. The materials that follow highlight how different identities intersect to structure the leadership experience.[1] Although constraints of space and research make it necessary to generalize, that should not obscure important differences within and between particular groups.

When commentators first spoke of the "great man" theory of leadership, they were not using the term generically. A comprehensive review of encyclopedia entries published at the turn of the twentieth century identified only about 850 eminent women, famous or infamous, throughout the world over the preceding 2000 years. In rank order, they included queens, politicians, mothers, mistresses, wives, beauties, religious figures, and women of "tragic fate."[2] Most of these women acquired their influence through men. In the United States, until the mid-twentieth century, the vast majority of leadership positions were occupied by white Anglo-Saxon Protestant men.

That began to change in response to broader social, economic, and political dynamics, which the law reflected and reinforced. Presidents Roosevelt, Truman, and Eisenhower made efforts to desegregate the military, and Presidents Kennedy and Johnson promulgated executive orders requiring affirmative action by government contractors. In 1964, Congress passed Title VII of the Civil Rights Act, which prohibited employment discrimination on the basis of race, color, religion, sex, and national origin, and created the Equal Employment Opportunity Commission (EEOC) to pursue complaints and monitor compliance.[3] State and local governments enacted similar legislation and often created their own enforcement agencies.

These mandates, and the broader forces they reflected, prompted significant efforts to level the playing field. Many employers began actively recruiting women and minorities; formalizing hiring, promotion, and compensation criteria; establishing identity-based affinity groups; and creating mentoring and training programs. Government contractors set goals and timetables for the employment and promotion of underrepresented groups. Government agencies reviewed the results, filed discrimination lawsuits, and mediated complaints. Such enforcement action, together with litigation by private parties, resulted in substantial expansion of the pipeline to leadership.

As these efforts evolved, supporters emphasized both the moral and the "business" case for diversity. Equalizing opportunity for women and minorities was not only the right thing to do because it ensured individual fairness and social justice and was necessary for legal compliance; it was also good for the bottom line. Greater inclusiveness, particularly at leadership levels, was said to improve performance, enhance reputation and recruitment, and expand customer and client bases.

Despite continuing diversity efforts, women and racial and ethnic minorities remain significantly underrepresented at leadership levels in law. As this book went to press, while African Americans, Hispanic/Latinx Americans, Asian Americans, and multiracial Americans constituted over a third of the population and over a fifth of law school graduates, they accounted for only 16 percent of the profession and 9 percent of law firm partners.[4] Fewer than 2 percent of partners are black, and fewer than 4 percent are Asian American.[5] Women of color, who account for 14 percent of associates, hold only 3 percent of partnerships.[6] Law is one of the least diverse of the major professions.[7] Women constitute half of law school graduates and a third of the profession, but only 21 percent of equity law firm partners, and 26 percent of Fortune 500 company general counsels, are women.[8] Women are also underrepresented in leadership positions such as firm chairs, members of management and compensation committees, and lead counsel in litigation.[9] Women are much less likely to make partner, even controlling for factors such as law school grades and time spent out of the labor force or on part-time schedules.[10] In the nonprofit sector, people of color occupy only about a fifth of executive director/CEO positions, and an even lower percentage of board member positions.[11] Women of color experience the greatest barriers, despite holding equal qualifications as their white peers.[12]

The readings that follow explore why such underrepresentation might constitute a problem and what should be done to address it. Which arguments appear most and least persuasive? Why have they had only limited success in changing the landscape of leadership? Does it matter? What implications should we draw for future leadership initiatives?

A. THE CASE FOR DIVERSITY

DAVID A. THOMAS AND ROBIN J. ELY, MAKING DIFFERENCES MATTER: A NEW PARADIGM FOR MANAGING DIVERSITY

Harvard Business Review, 74(5) (Sept.-Oct. 1996): 79-90

What will it take for organizations to reap the real and full benefits of a diverse workforce? A radically new understanding of the term, for starters.

Why should companies concern themselves with diversity? Until recently, many managers answered this question with the assertion that discrimination is wrong, both legally and morally. But today managers are voicing a second notion as well. A more diverse workforce, they say, will increase organizational effectiveness. It will lift morale, bring greater access to new segments of the marketplace, and enhance productivity. In short, they claim, diversity will be good for business.

Yet if this is true—and we believe it is—where are the positive impacts of diversity? . . . [Why have] many attempts to increase diversity in the workplace . . . backfired, sometimes even heightening tensions among employees and hindering a company's performance.

This article offers an explanation for why diversity efforts are not fulfilling their promise and presents a new paradigm for understanding—and leveraging— diversity. It is our belief that there is a distinct way to unleash the powerful benefits of a diverse workforce. Although these benefits include increased profitability, they go beyond financial measures to encompass learning, creativity, flexibility, organizational and individual growth, and the ability of a company to adjust rapidly and successfully to market changes. The desired transformation, however, requires a fundamental change in the attitudes and behaviors of an organization's leadership. And that will come only when senior managers abandon an underlying and flawed assumption about diversity and replace it with a broader understanding.

Most people assume that workplace diversity is about increasing racial, national, gender, or class representation—in other words, recruiting and retaining more people from traditionally underrepresented "identity groups." Taking this commonly held assumption as a starting point, we set out six years ago to investigate its link to organizational effectiveness. We soon found that thinking of diversity simply in terms of identity-group representation inhibited effectiveness.

Organizations usually take one of two paths in managing diversity. In the name of equality and fairness, they encourage (and expect) women and people of color to blend in. Or they set them apart in jobs that relate specifically to their backgrounds, assigning them, for example, to areas that require them to interface with clients or customers of the same identity group. African-American M.B.A.'s often find themselves marketing products to inner-city communities; Hispanics frequently market to Hispanics or work for Latin American subsidiaries. In those kinds of cases, companies are operating on the assumption that the main virtue identity groups have to offer is a knowledge of their own people. This assumption is limited—and limiting—and detrimental to diversity efforts.

What we suggest here is that diversity goes beyond increasing the number of different identity-group affiliations on the payroll to recognizing that such an effort is merely the first step in managing a diverse workforce for the organization's utmost benefit. Diversity should be understood as the varied perspectives and approaches to work that members of different identity groups bring.

Women, Hispanics, Asian Americans, African Americans, Native Americans—these groups and others outside the mainstream of corporate America don't bring with them just their "insider information." They bring different, important, and competitively relevant knowledge and perspectives about how to actually do work—how to design processes, reach goals, frame tasks, create effective teams, communicate ideas, and lead. When allowed to, members of these groups can help companies grow and improve by challenging basic assumptions about an organization's functions, strategies, operations, practices, and procedures. And in doing so, they are able to bring more of their whole selves to the workplace and identify more fully with the work they do, setting in motion a virtuous circle. Certainly, individuals can be expected to contribute to a company their firsthand familiarity with niche markets. But only when companies start thinking about diversity more holistically—as providing fresh and meaningful approaches to work—and stop assuming that diversity relates simply to how a person looks or where he or she comes from, will they be able to reap its full rewards. . . .

The Discrimination-and-Fairness Paradigm

Using the discrimination-and-fairness paradigm is perhaps thus far the dominant way of understanding diversity. Leaders who look at diversity through this lens usually focus on equal opportunity, fair treatment, recruitment, and compliance with federal Equal Employment Opportunity requirements. The paradigm's underlying logic can be expressed as follows:

Prejudice has kept members of certain demographic groups out of organizations such as ours. As a matter of fairness and to comply with federal mandates, we need to work toward restructuring the makeup of our organization to let it more closely reflect that of society. We need managerial processes that ensure that all our employees are treated equally and with respect and that some are not given unfair advantage over others.

Although it resembles the thinking behind traditional affirmative-action efforts, the discrimination-and-fairness paradigm does go beyond a simple concern with numbers. Companies that operate with this philosophical orientation often institute mentoring and career-development programs specifically for the women and people of color in their ranks and train other employees to respect cultural differences. Under this paradigm, nevertheless, progress in diversity is measured by how well the company achieves its recruitment and retention goals rather than by the degree to which conditions in the company allow employees to draw on their personal assets and perspectives to do their work more effectively. The staff, one might say, gets diversified, but the work does not. . . .

Without doubt, there are benefits to this paradigm: it does tend to increase demographic diversity in an organization, and it often succeeds in promoting fair treatment. But it also has significant limitations. The first of these is that its color-blind, gender-blind ideal is to some degree built on the implicit assumption that "we are all the same" or "we aspire to being all the same." Under this paradigm, it is not desirable for diversification of the workforce to influence the organization's work or culture. The company should operate as if every person were of the same race, gender, and nationality. It is unlikely that leaders who manage diversity under this paradigm will explore how people's differences generate a potential diversity of effective ways of working, leading, viewing the market, managing people, and learning. . . .

As an illustration of the paradigm's weaknesses, consider the case of Iversen Dunham, an international consulting firm that focuses on foreign and domestic economic-development policy. (Like all the examples in this article, the company is real, but its name is disguised.) Not long ago, the firm's managers asked us to help them understand why race relations had become a divisive issue precisely at a time when Iversen was receiving accolades for its diversity efforts. Indeed, other organizations had even begun to use the firm to benchmark their own diversity programs.

Iversen's diversity efforts had begun in the early 1970s, when senior managers decided to pursue greater racial and gender diversity in the firm's higher ranks. . . . Women and people of color were hired and charted on career paths toward becoming project leaders. High performers among those who had left the firm were persuaded to return in senior roles . . . [and eventually], about 50% of Iversen's project leaders and professionals were women, and 30% were people of color. The 13-member management committee, once exclusively white and male, included five women and four people of color. Additionally, Iversen had developed a strong contingent of foreign nationals.

It was at about this time, however, that tensions began to surface. Senior managers found it hard to believe that, after all the effort to create a fair and mutually respectful work community, some staff members could still be claiming that Iversen had racial discrimination problems. The management invited us to study the firm and deliver an outsider's assessment of its problem.

We had been inside the firm for only a short time when it became clear that Iversen's leaders viewed the dynamics of diversity through the lens of the discrimination-and-fairness paradigm. But where they saw racial discord, we discerned clashing approaches to the actual work of consulting. Why? Our research showed that tensions were strongest among midlevel project leaders. Surveys and interviews indicated that white project leaders welcomed demographic diversity as a general sign of progress but that they also thought the new employees were somehow changing the company, pulling it away from its original culture and its mission. Common criticisms were that . . . women and people of color were undermining one of Iversen's traditional strengths: its hard-core quantitative orientation. For instance, minority project leaders had suggested that Iversen consultants collect information and seek input from others in the client company besides senior managers—that is, from the rank and file and from middle managers. Some had urged Iversen to expand its consulting approach to include the gathering and analysis of qualitative data through interviewing and observation. Indeed, these project leaders had even challenged one of Iversen's long-standing, core assumptions: that the firm's reports were objective. They urged Iversen Dunham to recognize and address the subjective aspect of its analyses; the firm could, for example, include in its reports to clients dissenting Iversen views, if any existed.

For their part, project leaders who were women and people of color felt that they were not accorded the same level of authority to carry out that work as their white male peers. Moreover, they sensed that those peers were skeptical of their opinions, and they resented that doubts were not voiced openly.

. . . Iversen's discrimination-and-fairness paradigm had created a kind of cognitive blind spot; and, as a result, the company's leadership could not frame the problem accurately or solve it effectively. Instead, the company needed a cultural shift—it needed to grasp what to do with its diversity once it had achieved the numbers. If all Iversen Dunham employees were to contribute to the fullest extent, the company would need a paradigm that would encourage open and explicit discussion of what identity-group differences really mean and how they can be used as sources of individual and organizational effectiveness.

Today, mainly because of senior managers' resistance to such a cultural transformation, Iversen continues to struggle with the tensions arising from the diversity of its workforce.

The Access-and-Legitimacy Paradigm

In the competitive climate of the 1980s and 1990s, a new rhetoric and rationale for managing diversity emerged. If the discrimination-and-fairness paradigm can be said to have idealized assimilation and color- and gender-blind conformism, the access-and-legitimacy paradigm was predicated on the acceptance and celebration of differences. The underlying motivation of the access-and-legitimacy paradigm can be expressed this way:

We are living in an increasingly multicultural country, and new ethnic groups are quickly gaining consumer power. Our company needs a demographically more diverse workforce to help us gain access to these differentiated segments. We need employees with multilingual skills in order to understand and serve our customers better and to gain legitimacy with them. Diversity isn't just fair; it makes business sense.

Where this paradigm has taken hold, organizations have pushed for access to— and legitimacy with—a more diverse clientele by matching the demographics of the organization to those of critical consumer or constituent groups. In some cases, the effort has led to substantial increases in organizational diversity. In investment banks, for example, municipal finance departments have long led corporate finance departments in pursuing demographic diversity because of the typical makeup of the administration of city halls and county boards. Many consumer-products companies that have used market segmentation based on gender, racial, and other demographic differences have also frequently created dedicated marketing positions for each segment. The paradigm has therefore led to new professional and managerial opportunities for women and people of color. . . .

Again, the paradigm has its strengths. Its market-based motivation and the potential for competitive advantage that it suggests are often qualities an entire company can understand and therefore support. But the paradigm is perhaps more notable for its limitations. In their pursuit of niche markets, access-and-legitimacy organizations tend to emphasize the role of cultural differences in a company without really analyzing those differences to see how they actually affect the work that is done. Whereas discrimination-and-fairness leaders are too quick to subvert differences in the interest of preserving harmony, access-and-legitimacy leaders are too quick to push staff with niche capabilities into differentiated pigeonholes without trying to understand what those capabilities really are and how they could be integrated into the company's mainstream work. To illustrate our point, we present the case of Access Capital.

Access Capital International is a U.S. investment bank that in the early 1980s launched an aggressive plan to expand into Europe. Initially, however, Access encountered serious problems opening offices in international markets; the people from the United States who were installed abroad lacked credibility, were ignorant of local cultural norms and market conditions, and simply couldn't seem to connect with native clients. Access responded by hiring Europeans who had attended North American business schools and by assigning them in teams to the foreign offices. This strategy was a marked success. Before long, the leaders of Access could take enormous pride in the fact that their European operations were highly profitable and staffed by a truly international corps of professionals. They took to calling the company "the best investment bank in the world."

Several years passed. Access's foreign offices continued to thrive, but some leaders were beginning to sense that the company was not fully benefiting from its diversity efforts. Indeed, some even suspected that the bank had made itself vulnerable because of how it had chosen to manage diversity. A senior executive from the United States explains:

> If the French team all resigned tomorrow, what would we do? I'm not sure what we could do! We've never attempted to learn what these differences and cultural competencies really are, how they change the process of doing business. What is the German country team actually doing? We don't know. We know they're good, but we don't know the subtleties of how they do what they do. We assumed—and I think correctly—that culture makes a difference, but that's about as far as we went. We hired Europeans with American M.B.A.'s because we didn't know why we couldn't do business in Europe—we just assumed there was something cultural about why we couldn't connect. . . . We knew enough to use people's cultural strengths, as it were, but we never seemed to learn from them.

Access's story makes an important point about the main limitation of the access-and-legitimacy paradigm. . . . [O]nce the organization appears to be achieving its goal, the leaders seldom go on to identify and analyze the culturally based skills, beliefs, and practices that worked so well. Nor do they consider how the organization can incorporate and learn from those skills, beliefs, or practices in order to capitalize on diversity in the long run. . . .

Finally, the access-and-legitimacy paradigm can leave some employees feeling exploited. Many organizations using this paradigm have diversified only in those areas in which they interact with particular niche-market segments. In time, many individuals recruited for this function have come to feel devalued and used as they begin to sense that opportunities in other parts of the organization are closed to them. . . .

The Emerging Paradigm: Connecting Diversity to Work Perspectives

Recently, in the course of our research, we have encountered a small number of organizations that, having relied initially on one of the above paradigms to guide their diversity efforts, have come to believe that they are not making the most of their own pluralism. These organizations, like Access Capital, recognize that employees frequently make decisions and choices at work that draw upon their cultural background—choices made because of their identity-group affiliations. The companies have also developed an outlook on diversity that enables them to incorporate employees' perspectives into the main work of the organization and to enhance work by rethinking primary tasks and redefining markets, products, strategies, missions, business practices, and even cultures. Such companies are using the learning-and-effectiveness paradigm for managing diversity and, by doing so, are tapping diversity's true benefits.

A case in point is Dewey & Levin, a small public-interest law firm located in a northeastern U.S. city. Although Dewey & Levin had long been a profitable practice, by the mid-1980s its all-white legal staff had become concerned that the women they represented in employment-related disputes were exclusively white. The firm's attorneys viewed that fact as a deficiency in light of their mandate to advocate on behalf of all women. Using the thinking behind the access-and-legitimacy paradigm, they also saw it as bad for business.

Shortly thereafter, the firm hired a Hispanic female attorney. The partners' hope, simply put, was that she would bring in clients from her own community and also demonstrate the firm's commitment to representing all women. But something even bigger than that happened. The new attorney introduced ideas to Dewey & Levin about what kinds of cases it should take on. Senior managers were open to those ideas and pursued them with great success. More women of color were hired, and they, too, brought fresh perspectives. The firm now pursues cases that its previously all-white legal staff would not have thought relevant or appropriate because the link between the firm's mission and the employment issues involved in the cases would not have been obvious to them. For example, the firm has pursued precedent-setting litigation that challenges English-only policies—an area that it once would have ignored because such policies did not fall under the purview of traditional affirmative-action work. Yet it now sees a link between English-only policies and employment issues for a large group of women—primarily recent immigrants—whom it had previously failed to serve adequately. As one of the white principals explains, the demographic composition of Dewey & Levin "has affected the work in terms of expanding notions of what are [relevant] issues and taking on issues and framing them in creative ways that would have never been done [with an all-white staff]. It's really changed the substance—and in that sense enhanced the quality—of our work."

Dewey & Levin's increased business success has reinforced its commitment to diversity. In addition, people of color at the firm uniformly report feeling respected, not simply "brought along as window dressing." Many of the new attorneys say their perspectives are heard with a kind of openness and interest they have never experienced before in a work setting. Not surprisingly, the firm has had little difficulty attracting and retaining a competent and diverse professional staff. . . .

PROBLEM 8-1

In December 2018, Paul Weiss, one of the nation's most prominent and profitable law firms, posted photos of 12 smiling lawyers on LinkedIn with the message that it was "proud to announce" its new partner class. But as the *New York Times* reported, "what followed was nothing to smile about."[13] It did not escape attention that all the new partners were white and all but one was male. The post, which the firm took down within a week, became a lightening rod for pent-up frustration about the lack of progress on diversity among major firms. As one commentator on *Above the Law* noted, "Biglaw can't solve this problem until it sees it. . . . It's not even that the firms have thoroughly hamstrung efforts to put diverse candidates in a position to succeed; it's that no one can look at an image like this and immediately see the problem."[14]

In a statement on the matter, Brad Karp, Chair of Paul Weiss noted:

> We certainly can—and will—do better. I regret the gender and racial imbalance in our newly elected partnership class (one woman, one Latino, one LGBTQ partner, only 25 percent diverse), which resulted from an idiosyncratic demographic pool and which I can assure you will not be repeated. . . . . There is no more important issue to [this firm's leadership] than diversity and it is critical to me that Paul Weiss maintain its historic leadership role as a firm that champions diversity in terms of race, gender, and sexual orientation.[15]

Karp went on to emphasize the firm's history and current record on diversity, noting that it was the first major firm to hire African-American and female associates and to elect a female partner, and that currently a third of its partners were diverse in terms of race, gender, and sexual orientation. Its record greatly exceeds the average for New York and U.S. law firms and, Karp emphasized, "It would be unfortunate and disappointing if an idiosyncratic demographic pool in one particular year would erase the firm's diversity achievements over the past 75 years."[16] Karp also stated that he expected the firm would shortly hire more minority partners laterally, and that diversity efforts would receive greater attention in compensation decisions.

Follow-up reporting revealed a more mixed picture. Paul Weiss is more diverse at the partnership level than the vast majority of its large firm peers, but that is a fairly low standard. And interviews with current and former lawyers at the firms suggest that many feel that the landscape is far from equal. Some felt that women and lawyers of color were held to more exacting standards, punished more severely for mistakes, and given less professional and client development opportunities.[17] Promotion rates are consistent with those claims. White men account for only about 40 percent of incoming associates, but 70 percent of new partners over the past decade.[18]

Not all Americans are troubled by those disparities, although most who feel this way are reluctant to express their views openly. One exception was the author of a letter to the editor of the *New York Times* in response to its profile of Paul Weiss. He wrote:

> Perhaps I am being naive, but why does diversity have to be the primary yardstick in our society for every decision involving the selection of human beings for elevated positions? There are times when ability should outweigh diversity. . . . In this case, Paul Weiss already had an excellent record when it came to diversity, but it is a law firm in the business of winning cases for its clients. Paul Weiss did not deserve this pubic shaming because in this one instance the two metrics of diversity and ability were not in sync. . . . Clients do not want their attorneys to fight the good fight [on social issues]; they want them to win. Putting diversity ahead of ability can be a self-defeating proposition for the firm—and the client.[19]

What assumptions is the author making about "diversity" and "ability?" How would you respond?

Paul Weiss is clearly not alone in experiencing these problems, and many clients saw its difficulties as emblematic of broader challenges. After its post went viral, the chief legal officers of more than 170 companies signed an open letter to law firms stating:

> We expect the outside law firms we retain to reflect the diversity of the legal community and the companies and the customers we serve. . . . We are disappointed to see that many law firms continue to promote partner classes that in no way reflect the demographic composition of entering associate classes. Partnership classes

remain largely male and largely white. . . . We are left to wonder if you and your partners value diversity enough to put into place programs to develop, promote, and retain talented and diverse attorneys. . . . The reality is that you must consciously and personally invest in diversity and inclusion, and interview, hire, mentor, support, sponsor, and promote talented attorneys who don't always look like you or share your background.

We, as a group, will direct our substantial outside counsel spend to those firms that manifest results with respect to diversity and inclusion, in addition to providing the highest degree of quality representation. We sincerely hope that you and your firm will be among those that demonstrate this commitment.[20]

The *American Lawyer*, which ran a copy of the open letter, also ran a response from a Haitian partner who was skeptical of the effort:

These signatory letters have been more public relations than actual practice. . . . Ask yourselves how many of these same GCs take any real measures to diversify the lawyers they hire on the meaningful matters. Very few do. . . . To be clear, my goal in penning this letter is not to ascribe blame or solicit work from GCs. My goal is to voice the frustration of dozens of racially diverse lawyers like me, who are quite frankly tired of these types of letters and pronouncements leading to no meaningful advancement."[21]

If you were one of the GCs who signed the letter, how would you respond? If you were part of the management committee of Paul Weiss, what steps would you take to make good on the firm's promises to remain a leader on diversity issues? If you were the chair of another Wall Street firm with a similar new partner class, what steps would you take?[22] How would you address and prioritize the different stakeholder interests and expectations that are at issue?

NOTES AND QUESTIONS

The economic case for diversity is not a new argument. Several centuries ago, John Stuart Mill claimed that

[i]t is hardly possible to overrate the value . . . of placing human beings in contact with persons dissimilar to themselves, and with modes of thought and action unlike those with which they are familiar. . . . Such communication has always been, and is peculiarly in the present age, one of the primary sources of progress.[23]

Acceptance of the business case for diversity is important because those who believe that diversity initiatives promote organizational well-being are more committed and effective in implementing them than those who believe they are necessary only to comply with legal requirements or to satisfy moral claims and external stakeholders.[24] Efforts at inclusion that are not linked to organizational self-interest "run the risk of degenerating into half-hearted, symbolic, feel-good gestures."[25]

Research on the business case for diversity generally distinguishes between "cognitive diversity," which refers to differences in information, knowledge, perspectives, and mental models, and "identity diversity," which refers to differences in race, gender, age, ethnicity, religion, physical qualities, and sexual orientation.[26] Although logically distinct, these two forms of diversity are related because "our identities influence what we know, how we perceive events, and how we think."[27] Because of that relationship, identity diversity generally leads to better outcomes involving o non-routine cognitive tasks, such as problem solving, predicting, and innovating. Researchers find that "even if the person who looks 'different' does not bring any new cognitive differences to the table, his or her mere presence has been shown to change the behavior of the group's members. People work harder in identity-diverse environments than they do in homogenous environments."[28]

Insular cultures also have a harder time recognizing the need for change. They tend to resist insights of outsiders and don't learn and adapt.[29] Homogeneity triggers expectations of similarity and less welcoming receptions for different opinions. Diverse groups are more accepting of alternative viewpoints, more willing to reexamine facts and assumptions, and more likely to foster persistent voicing of dissenting perspectives.[30] So too, people anticipating a homogeneous environment prepare less thoroughly than those anticipating a diverse interaction.[31]

Although the business case for diversity is widely accepted in principle, it is often marginalized in practice. Part of the reason may be that findings on its impact are not uniformly favorable. Not all social science research reflects strong, bottom-line benefits from diversity. If poorly managed, it can heighten conflict, discomfort, and communication problems, or cause outsiders to suppress divergent views.[32] The diversity bonus tends not to materialize for tasks where familiarity, trust, and shared understandings are especially critical.[33] Nor do all studies find a correlation between diversity and profitability.[34] In those that do, it is unclear which way causation runs. It may well be that financial success sometimes enhances diversity rather than the converse. Organizations that are on strong financial footing are better able to invest in diversity initiatives or have sound employment practices that promote both diversity and profitability.[35]

Moreover, in skeptics' view, even if diversity has quantifiable advantages in enhancing decision-making, the benefits need to be weighed against the adverse effects of "lowering" standards and provoking backlash based on "identity politics" and "special" treatment."[36] In a study by the Minority Corporate Counsel Association, many white men agreed that "diversity should take a back seat to performance and capability."[37] In their view, too much "reverse discrimination" causes resentment, and "stretch hires of minorities who are not qualified sometimes does much to undermine . . . acceptance of diversity and inclusion."[38] As one participant put it, "Taking opportunities . . . from those with merit and giving [them] . . . to people based upon race, gender, or sexual identity is forcing us apart not bringing us together. . . . I can think of few things worse for an ostensibly color blind and meritocratic society."[39]

By contrast, supporters of diversity initiatives, relying on research summarized in Parts C and D below, argue that they are necessary to counteract the unconscious biases that shape assessments of performance and that limit opportunities for qualified women and minorities to develop leadership capabilities. Pretending that we already live in a strictly meritocratic society will not bring us closer to achieving one. Advocates of diversity also believe that it promotes effective leadership by ensuring difference in backgrounds and perspectives, and by enhancing the quality and legitimacy of decision-making processes.[40] They also note that leaders in today's multicultural society need "cultural competence": the ability to understand differences arising from diverse backgrounds and experiences and to adjust their own actions accordingly.[41]

1. What is your response? How compelling is the business case for diversity? How should it be defined? Are there concerns beyond the "bottom line" of demonstrable financial benefits that deserve equal weight? If so, how should those other concerns be measured?
2. What diversity initiatives have you encountered in employment, education, or other settings? How effective have they been? What might have improved their effectiveness?

B. DIVERSITY CHALLENGES

DEBORAH L. RHODE, LAWYERS AS LEADERS

(Oxford University Press 2013), 138-144

Racial, Ethnic, and Gender Stereotypes

Racial, ethnic, and gender stereotypes play a well-documented role in American culture, and legal workplaces are no exception. The stereotypes vary across groups. For example, blacks and Latinos bump up against assumptions that they are less qualified. Many report that their competence is constantly questioned, and that even if they graduated from an elite law school, they are assumed to be beneficiaries of affirmative action rather than meritocratic selection. Blacks who are assertive risk being viewed as angry or hostile. Asian Americans are saddled with the myths of the "model minority;" they are thought to be smart and hardworking, but also "timid" and insufficiently assertive to command the confidence of clients and legal teams. The result is that talented minorities lack the presumption of competence granted to white male counterparts; up and coming whites may be fast tracked based on promise, while minorities need to demonstrate performance. Even outstanding capabilities of a leader of color may do little to dislodge traditional assumptions. A classic example is the description Senator Joseph Biden offered of Barack Obama during the 2008 presidential campaign, as the "first mainstream African American who is articulate and bright and clean and a nice-looking guy." Psychologists refer to this as the "flower blooming in winter" effect. Although it can provide special recognition for the exceptional leader [of color], it does little to assist those aspiring to such roles.

Gender stereotypes also subject women to double standards and a double bind. Despite recent progress, women, like minorities, often fail to receive the presumption of competence enjoyed by white men. In national surveys, between a third and three-quarters of female lawyers believe that they are held to higher standards than their colleagues. A recent study of performance evaluations finds some support for those perceptions; it reveals that similar descriptions of performance result in lower ratings for women. Mothers, even those working full time, are assumed to be less available and committed, an assumption not made about fathers. In one representative study, almost three-quarters of female lawyers reported that their career commitment had been questioned when they gave birth or adopted a child. Only 9 percent of their white male colleagues, and 15 percent of minority male colleagues, had faced similar challenges. . . .

Women are also rated lower than men on qualities associated with leadership, such as assertiveness, competitiveness, and business development. Even though women are more likely to use effective leadership styles, people more readily credit men with leadership ability and more readily accept men as leaders. An overview of more than a hundred studies confirms that women are rated lower when they adopt authoritative, seemingly masculine styles, particularly when the evaluators are men, or when the role is one typically occupied by men. What is assertive in a man seems abrasive in a woman, and female leaders risk seeming too feminine or not feminine enough. Either they may appear too "soft" or too "strident"—either unable to make tough decisions or too pushy and arrogant to command respect.

Self-promotion that is acceptable in men is viewed as unattractive in women. In a telling Stanford Business School experiment, participants received a case study about a leading venture capitalist with outstanding networking skills. Half the participants were told that the individual was Howard Roizen; the other half were told that she was Heidi Roizen. The participants rated the entrepreneurs as equally competent but found Howard more likeable, genuine and kind, and Heidi more aggressive, self-promoting, and power hungry. Even the most accomplished lawyer leaders can encounter such biases. Brooksley Born, now widely acclaimed for her efforts to regulate high-risk derivatives while chair of the Commodity Futures Commission was dismissed at the time as "abrasive," "strident" and a "lightweight wacko." In commenting on those characterizations, a former aide noted, "She was serious, professional, and she held her ground against those who were not sympathetic to her position. I don't think that the failure to be charming should be translated into a depiction of stridency." Hillary Clinton has been subject to even more vitriolic descriptions: "power-hungry," "castrating," "Hitlerian," and "feminazi." During her presidential campaign[s], she coped with sales of a Clinton nutcracker, charges that she reminded men of a scolding mother or first wife, and hecklers with signs demanding "Iron my shirt."

Other cognitive biases compound the force of traditional stereotypes. People are more likely to notice and recall information that confirms their prior assumptions than information that contradicts those assumptions; the dissonant facts are filtered out. For example, when lawyers assume that a working mother is unlikely to be fully committed to her career, they more easily remember the times when she left early than the times when she stayed late. Such selective recollection may help account for a study finding that where women and men worked similar hours, over a quarter of male lawyers nonetheless thought their female counterparts worked less, and a fifth rated the number of hours of these women as "fair to poor." So too, when female and minority lawyers are assumed to be less effective, their failures will be recalled more readily than their achievements. Both women and minorities also receive less latitude for mistakes. That, in turn, may make lawyers reluctant to seek risky "stretch assignments" that would demonstrate leadership capabilities.

Mentoring, Sponsorship, and Networks

A related set of obstacles involves in-group favoritism. Extensive research documents the preferences that individuals feel for members of their own groups. Loyalty, cooperation, favorable evaluations, mentoring, and the allocation of rewards and opportunities are greater for individuals who are similar in important respects, including gender, race, and ethnicity. As a consequence, outsiders face difficulty developing "social capital:" access to advice, support, sponsorship, desirable assignments, and new business opportunities. In law firms, racial and ethnic minorities often report isolation and marginalization, while many white women similarly experience exclusion from "old boys" networks. In ABA research, 62 percent of women of color and 60 percent of white women, but only 4 percent of white men, felt excluded from formal and informal networking opportunities; most women and minorities would have liked better mentoring.

Part of the problem lies in numbers. Many organizations lack sufficient women and minorities at senior levels who can assist others on the way up. The problem is not lack of commitment. Recent research finds no evidence for the Queen Bee syndrome, in which women reportedly keep others from getting ahead. In a recent Catalyst study, almost three quarters of women who were actively engaged in mentoring were developing female colleagues, compared with 30 percent of men. But the underrepresentation of women in leadership positions, and the time pressures for those juggling family responsibilities, leaves an inadequate pool of potential mentors. Although a growing number of organizations have formal mentoring programs, these do not always supply adequate training, rewards or oversight to ensure effectiveness. And they cannot substitute for relationships that develop naturally and that yield not simply advisors but sponsors—individuals who act as advocates and are in positions to open opportunities. Recent research on the corporate sector finds that men are substantially more likely to have such sponsors than women, and to have their help in promotions. There is no reason to think law is different. As participants in one ABA study noted, female leaders may have "good intentions," but are already pressed with competing work and family obligations or "don't have a lot of power so they can't really help you." Concerns about the appearance of sexual harassment or sexual affairs discourage some men from forming mentoring relationships with junior women, and discomfort concerning issues of race and ethnicity deters some white lawyers from crossing the color divide. In cross-racial mentoring relationships, candid dialogue may be particularly difficult. Minority protégés may be reluctant to raise issues of bias for fear of seeming oversensitive. White mentors may be reluctant to offer candid feedback to minority associates for fear of seeming racist or of encouraging them to leave. The result is that midlevel lawyers of color can find themselves "blindsided by soft evaluations": "your skills aren't what they are supposed to be but you didn't know because no one ever told you."

Assumptions about commitment and capabilities also keep mentors from investing in female or minority subordinates who seem unlikely to stay or to succeed. Such dynamics also put pressure on these lawyers to assimilate to prevailing norms. As one attorney of color put it, the "only way to succeed in a large firm is to make them forget you're Hispanic." If a minority lawyer "just doesn't fit in," the assumption is that the problem lies with the individual not the institution.

In-group favoritism is also apparent in the allocation of work and client development opportunities. Many organizations operate with informal systems that channels seemingly talented junior lawyers, disproportionately white men, to the leadership tracks, while relegating others to "workhorse" positions. In the ABA Commission study, 44 percent of women of color, 39 percent of white women, and 25 percent of minority men reported being passed over for desirable work assignments; only two percent of white men noted similar experiences. Other research similarly finds that women and minorities are often left out of pitches for client business. Lawyers of color are also subject to "race matching"; they receive work because of their identity, not their interests, in order to create the right "look" in courtrooms, client presentations, recruiting, and marketing efforts. Although this strategy sometimes opens helpful opportunities, it can also place lawyers in what they describe as "mascot" or roles in which they are not developing their own professional skills. Linda Mabry, the first minority partner in a San Francisco firm, recounts an example in which she was asked to join a pitch to a shipping company whose general counsel was African-American. "When the firm made the pitch about the firm's relevant expertise, none of which I possessed, it was clear that the only reason I was there was to tout the firm's diversity, which was practically nonexistent. In that moment I wanted to fling myself through the plate-glass window of that well-appointed conference room. . . ."

Workplace Structures and Gender Roles

Escalating workplace demands and inflexible practice structures pose further obstacles to diversity and inclusion. Hourly demands have risen significantly over the last quarter century, and technology that makes it possible for lawyers to work at home make it increasingly impossible not to. Expectations of constant accessibility have become the new norm, particularly for those in leadership positions. Law is the second most sleep-deprived profession, and long hours contribute to lawyers' disproportionate rates of stress, substance abuse, and mental health disorders. These conditions of practice have made leadership positions unattractive to many lawyers, especially those with significant family responsibilities.

Despite some efforts at accommodation, a wide gap persists between formal policies and actual practices concerning work/life conflicts. Although over 90 percent of American law firms report policies permitting part-time work, only about 6 percent of lawyers actually use them. Many lawyers believe, with good reason, that any reduction in hours or availability would jeopardize their leadership opportunities. Stories of the "faster than a speeding bullet" maternity leave like the one that opened this chapter are still common. One woman who drafted discovery responses while timing her contractions saw it as a sensible display of commitment. If you are billing at six-minute intervals, why waste one? Those who opt for a reduced schedule after parental leave often find that it isn't worth the price. Their schedules aren't respected, their hours creep up, the quality of their assignments goes down, their pay is not proportional, and they are stigmatized as "slackers."

These are not only "women's issues," but women bear their greatest impact. Despite a significant increase in men's domestic work over the last two decades, women continue to shoulder the major burden. An MIT study found that only a third of male lawyers, compared with over two thirds of female lawyers, had partners equally or more committed to their careers. Of men with children, 85 percent work over 50 hour weeks, compared with just a third of women. It is still women who are most likely to get the phone call that federal district judge Nancy Gertner received on the first day that she was about to ascend the bench: "Mama, there's no chocolate pudding in my [lunch]." An American Bar Foundation survey reported that women were about seven times more likely than men to be working part-time or to be out of the labor force, primarily due to childcare. Only 2 percent of male lawyers take part time status and many worry that taking significant time off will signal that they are no longer a "player." Their fears are not without foundation. Male lawyers who make such choices suffer even greater financial and promotion costs than female colleagues who do so.

These patterns are deeply rooted in traditional gender roles and cultural norms that give bragging rights to those willing to work sweatshop hours. Particularly in challenging economic times, there are no shortage of lawyers in that category. At large firms, where average billable hours are over 2000, about three quarters of midlevel associates described their workloads as manageable. Of course those who reach such positions are a self-selected group and likely to exclude many of the most talented women that firms can ill afford to lose. The problems are likely to increase. Millennial lawyers, defined as the generation born after [the] 1980s, have expectations inconsistent with prevailing norms. Growing numbers of men as well as women are expressing a desire for better work-life balance, and examples of those who insist on it are in increasingly visible supply at leadership levels. As Governor of California, Earl Warren took no official calls or visitors on business while at home. Bill Clinton while president once put off an important trip to Japan so he could help his daughter, then a high school junior, prepare for her midterms. Barack Obama has refused to "do the social scene" in Washington even though it might have political payoffs because he and his wife "want to be good parents at a time that is vitally important for our kids." A *New York Times* article titled, "He Breaks for Band Recitals," reported that Obama was willing to leave key meetings in order to "get home for dinner by 6 or attend a school function of his 8 and 11 year old daughters." According to senior advisor David Axelrod, certain functions "are sacrosanct on his schedule—kid's recitals, soccer games. . . ." Yet one irony is that President Obama's commitment to a family-friendly schedule in his own life makes it harder for others to do the same. When he adjourns a meeting at 6 and resumes at 8 to allow his dinner break, other high level officials who don't "live over the shop" end up extending their own work day well past their children's bedtimes.

Although bar leaders generally acknowledge the problem of work/life balance, they often place responsibility for addressing it anywhere and everywhere else. In private practice, clients get part of the blame. Law is a service business, and their expectations of instant accessibility reportedly make reduced schedules difficult to accommodate. Resistance from supervisors can be equally problematic. Particularly in a competitive work environment, they have obvious reasons to prefer lawyers at their constant beck and call.

Yet neither are the problems as insurmountable as is often assumed. The evidence available does not find substantial resistance among clients to reduced schedules. They care about responsiveness, and part-time lawyers generally appear able to provide it. In one recent survey of part-time partners, most reported that they did not even inform clients of their status and that their schedules were adapted to fit client needs. Accounting, which is also a service profession, and anything but indifferent to the bottom line, has developed a business model that more than offsets the costs of work/family accommodation by increasing retention. Considerable evidence suggests that law practice could do the same, and reap the benefits in higher morale, lower recruitment and training expenses, and less disruption in client and collegial relationships. Although some leadership positions may be hard to reconcile with substantial family demands, many women could be ready to cycle into those positions as family obligations decrease. The challenge lies in creating workplace structures that make it easier for lawyers of both sexes to have satisfying personal as well as professional lives, and to insure that those who temporarily step out of the workforce or reduce their workload are not permanently derailed by the decision. . . .

Strategies for Aspiring Leaders

Women and minorities who seek leadership positions should be clear about their goals, seek challenging assignments, solicit frequent feedback, develop mentoring relationships, and cultivate a reputation for effectiveness. Succeeding in those tasks also requires attention to unconscious biases and exclusionary networks that can waylay careers.

So, for example, aspiring female leaders need to strike the right balance between "too assertive" and "not assertive enough." Surveys of successful managers and professional consultants underscore the importance of developing a leadership style that fits the organization, and is one that "men are comfortable with." That finding is profoundly irritating to some lawyers. At an ABA Summit on Women's Leadership, many participants railed against asking women to adjust to men's needs. Why was the focus always on fixing the female? But as others pointed out, this is the world that aspiring women leaders inhabit, and it is not just men who find overly authoritative or self–promoting styles off putting. To maximize effectiveness, women need ways of projecting a decisive and forceful manner without seeming arrogant or abrasive. . . . [E]xperts suggest being "relentlessly pleasant" without backing down. Strategies include frequently smiling, expressing appreciation and concern, invoking common interests, emphasizing others' goals as well as their own, and taking a problem-solving rather than critical stance. Successful leaders such as Sandra Day O'Connor have been known for that capacity. In assessing her prospects for success in the Arizona state legislature, one political commentator noted that "Sandy . . . is a sharp gal" with a "steel-trap mind . . . and a large measure of common sense. . . . She [also] has lovely smile and should use it often." She did.

Formal leadership training and coaching can help in developing interpersonal styles, as well as capabilities such as risk-taking, conflict resolution, and strategic vision. Newly emerging leadership programs designed particularly for women or minorities provide particularly supportive settings for addressing their special challenges. Profiles of successful leaders can also provide instructive examples of the personal initiative that opens leadership opportunities. These are not lawyers who waited for the phone to ring. Michele Mayes, one of the nation's most prominent African-American general counsels, recalls that after receiving some encouragement from a woman mentor, she approached the chief legal officer at her company and "told him I wanted his job." After the shock wore off, he worked up a list of the skills and experiences that she needed and recruited her to follow him to his next general counsel job. She never replaced him, but with his assistance she prepared for his role in other Fortune 500 companies. Louise Parent, the general counsel of American Express, describes learning to "raise my hand" for challenging assignments and being willing to take steps down and sideways on the status ladder in order to get the experience she needed. Terry McClure, the General Counsel of United Parcel Service, was told she needed direct exposure to business operations if she wanted to move up at the company. After accepting a position as district manager, she suddenly found herself as a "lawyer, a black woman, [with] no operations experience walking into a . . . [warehouse] with all the truck drivers.

Her success in that role was what helped put her in the candidate pool for general counsel.

Setting priorities and managing time are also critical leadership skills. Establishing boundaries, delegating domestic tasks, and giving up on perfection are essential for those with substantial caretaking commitments. What aspiring leaders should not sacrifice is time spent developing relationships with mentors who can open doors at leadership levels. To forge those strategic relationships, lawyers need to recognize that those from whom they seek assistance are under similar time pressures. The best mentoring generally goes to the best mentees, who are reasonable and focused in their needs and who make sure the relationship is mutually beneficial. Lawyers who step out of the labor force should find ways of keeping professionally active. Volunteer efforts, occasional paying projects, continuing legal education, and reentry programs can all aid the transition back.

Strategies for Organizations and Their Leaders

Supporting aspiring leaders is itself a leadership skill, and one that has received inadequate attention in many legal workplaces. The most important factor in ensuring equal access to leadership opportunities is a commitment to that objective, which is reflected in organizational policies, priorities, and reward structures. That commitment needs to come from the top. An organization's leadership needs to not simply acknowledge the importance of diversity, but also to establish structures for promoting it, and to hold individuals accountable for the results. The most successful approaches tend to involve task forces or committees with diverse and influential members who have credibility with their colleagues and a stake in the results. The mission of that group should be to identify problems, develop responses, and monitor their effectiveness.

As an ABA Presidential Commission on Diversity recognized, self-assessment should be a critical part of all diversity initiatives. Leaders need to know how policies that affect inclusiveness play out in practice. That requires collecting both quantitative and qualitative data on matters such as advancement, retention, assignments, satisfaction, mentoring, and work/family conflicts. Periodic surveys, focus groups, interviews with former and departing employees, and bottom-up evaluations of supervisors can all cast light on problems disproportionately experienced by women and minorities. Monitoring can be important not only in identifying problems and responses, but also in making people aware that their actions are being assessed. Requiring individuals to justify their decisions can help reduce unconscious bias.

Whatever oversight structure an employer chooses, one central priority should be the design of effective systems of evaluation, rewards, and allocation of professional development opportunities. Supervising lawyers and department heads need to be held responsible for their performance on diversity-related issues, and that performance should be part of 360 evaluation structures. Such accountability is, of course, far easier to advocate than to achieve, particularly given the absence of systematic research on what oversight strategies actually work. Our knowledge is mainly about what doesn't. Performance appraisals that include diversity but lack significant rewards or sanctions are unlikely to affect behavior. However, we know little about what has helped firms deal with powerful partners who rate poorly on diversity, or whether incentives like mentoring awards and significant bonuses are effective in changing organizational culture. More experimentation and sharing of information could enable organizations to translate rhetorical commitments into institutional priorities. . . .

The most effective interventions involve mentoring, which directly address the difficulties of women and minorities in obtaining the support necessary for leadership development. Many organizations have formal mentoring programs that match employees or allow individuals to select their own pairings. Well-designed initiatives that evaluate and reward mentoring activities can improve participants' skills, satisfaction, and retention rates. However, most programs do not require evaluation or specify the frequency of meetings and goals for the relationship. Instead, they permit a "call me if you need anything" approach, which leaves too many junior attorneys reluctant to become a burden. Ineffective matching systems compound the problem; lawyers often end up with mentors with whom they have little in common. Formal programs also have difficulty inspiring the kind of sponsorship that is most critical for aspiring leaders. They need advocates, not simply advisors, and that kind of support cannot be mandated.

The lesson for leaders is that they cannot simply rely on formal structures. They need to model, cultivate, and reward sponsorship of women and minorities, and to ensure that diversity is a significant dimension of leadership succession plans. Being proactive in identifying and nurturing high performers should be a high priority. In building cultures of inclusion, it is important to emphasize the mutual benefits that can flow from mentoring relationships. Quite apart from the satisfaction that comes from assisting those in need of assistance, leaders may receive more tangible payoffs from fresh insights and from the loyalty and influence that their efforts secure. They can also take pride in laying the foundations for an organization that is reflective of, and responsive to, the public it serves.

In building that legacy, leaders can also look beyond their own organizations and spearhead pro bono efforts to expand the pool of qualified minorities through scholarships and educational reform initiatives. For example, the law firm Skadden and Arps has pledged $10 million for a ten-year program offering law school preparation to students from disadvantaged backgrounds. As one ABA official notes, "[T]his is the kind of money we need to make a difference. . . . Now we need just 500 other firms to take action." . . .

[T]he most effective leaders are those who are personally invested in building a broad consensus for diversity, and in addressing any sources of inertia or passive resistance. This agenda needs to be seen not as a "women's" or "minority" issue, but as an organizational priority in which women and minorities have a particular stake. As consultants emphasize, "[i]nclusion can be built only through inclusion. . . . Change needs to happen in partnership *with* the people of the organization not *to* them." Leaders are critical in creating that sense of unity and in translating rhetorical commitments into organizational priorities.

NOTES AND QUESTIONS

1. Consider the dilemma of the black woman partner asked to help solicit a black client. What would you have done in her position? What would you have done if you had been the lawyer who asked her to participate? What would you have done if you were the firm's managing partner and heard that she was unhappy about the assignment?

2. Are the strategies the excerpt proposes adequate to deal with the challenges it describes? What stands in their way? Is the letter from GCs reprinted in Problem 8-1 likely to be effective if organizations are not prepared to pull business from non-diverse firms? What little empirical evidence is available suggests that clients rarely do so.[42] A few large corporations have begun insisting on inclusion clauses that enable clients to withhold 10 percent of its fees if its diversity metrics are not met. Other clients have tried bonuses and diversity awards.[43] How would you assess those approaches? What other initiatives would you recommend? Consider that question in light of the issues of gender, race, and ethnicity described in Parts D and E.

3. The difficulties for women in finding mentors have escalated in the wake of recent revelations about sexual misconduct in the workplace. As my overview in an article on #MeToo notes:

> Even before #MeToo, a poll conducted for the *New York Times* found that a majority of women and nearly half of men believed it was unacceptable to have dinner or drinks alone with someone of the opposite sex other than their spouse, and a third of Americans said lunch or car rides alone were also inappropriate. Many male leaders expressed concerns that even innocent conduct could be misinterpreted and cause legal problems. Maureen Sherry, a managing director at a prominent Wall Street firm, heard "more than once . . . that it's just easier to fire a guy or . . . that 'there's just less drama with men.'"
>
> #MeToo has given added force to these concerns. Half of Americans think that the recent increased focus on sexual harassment has made it harder for men to know how to interact with women in the workplace. Most women are very (26 percent) or somewhat (34 percent) concerned that the #MeToo movement is causing women to lose professional opportunities because men are reluctant to work with them. A study of male lawyers found that most (56 percent) were nervous about one-on-one interactions with female coworkers and the charges of impropriety that might result. As a firm leader explained, "One allegation can be a career killer . . . . I will not be alone in the office with any female—whether she is a colleague or support staff member. This is to protect myself."
>
> Diversity consultants and advocacy organizations are finding that more men "are backing away from the role that we try to encourage them to play, which is actively mentoring and sponsoring women in

the workplace. . . . There's apprehension on the part of men that they're going to be falsely accused of sexual harassment." And they "fear what they cannot control." More men are reportedly claiming to follow the "Pence Rule," once known as the "Billy Graham Rule" and now associated with Vice President Mike Pence. Pence says he does not eat alone with women apart from his wife and does not attend events without her that involve alcohol. But if men cannot speak comfortably with women in private, it will increase their exclusion from informal networks of advice and support.[44]

Other research documents similar patterns. [45] How should leaders in legal workplaces respond to this challenge?

C. MANAGING DIVERSITY

Even in organizations that are committed to diversity in leadership, the best path to achieving it is not always clear. In the following article, Dobbin, Kalev, and Kelly explore which strategies are most and least effective in increasing female and minority representation in upper-level positions. Getting more women and lawyers of color into the leadership pipeline is, of course, only the first step toward equity and inclusion. Organizations also need to help them advance and succeed.

FRANK DOBBIN, ALEXANDRA KALEV, AND ERIN KELLY, DIVERSITY MANAGEMENT IN CORPORATE AMERICA

Contexts 6(4) (Fall 2007): 21-27

In the decades since Congress passed the Civil Rights Act of 1964, firms have experimented with dozens of diversity measures. Consultants have been pushing diversity training, diversity performance evaluations for managers, affinity networks, mentoring programs, diversity councils, and diversity managers, to name a few. But some experts question whether diversity programs are counterproductive, raising the hackles of white men who, after all, still do most of the hiring and firing. Certain programs even seem to get firms into trouble— Texaco executives were recorded talking about "black jelly beans" after hearing the term in diversity training seminars.

Until recently, no one had looked systematically at large numbers of companies to assess which kinds of programs work best, on average. Our research shows that certain programs do increase diversity in management jobs—the best test of whether a program works—but that others do little or nothing.

The good news is that companies that give diversity councils, or diversity managers, responsibility for getting more women and minorities into good jobs typically see significant increases in the diversity of managers. So do companies that create formal mentoring programs. Much less effective are diversity training sessions, diversity performance evaluations for managers, and affinity groups for women and minorities. There is no magic bullet for the problem of inequality. Programs that work in one firm may not work in another. Programs that fail on average may be just what the Acme Rocket Co. needs. But we are beginning to understand what works in general and what does not. . . .

The Study

Our challenge was to get accurate data on workforce diversity and on diversity programs for enough companies, over a long enough period of time, so that we could use sophisticated statistical techniques to isolate the effects of, say, diversity training on the percentage of black women in management. . . .

We surveyed 829 of the companies covered in the EEOC's massive data file, putting together a life history of employment practices at each. We asked companies whether they had used dozens of different programs, and when those programs had been in place. Our research question was simple: if a company adopts a particular diversity program, what effect does it have on the share of women and minorities in management? To answer the question, we conducted statistical analyses on the 829 firms over 31 years. . . . Our analyses considered more than 60 workplace characteristics that might affect diversity so as to isolate the effects of diversity taskforces, training, and so on.

Changing Managers' Behavior

One source of gender and racial inequality in the workplace is stereotyping and bias among managers who make hiring and promotion decisions. Research shows that educating people about members of other groups may reduce stereotyping. . . . An industry of diversity trainers emerged in the 1980s to argue that people were unaware of their own racial, ethnic, and gender biases and that sensitivity training would help them to overcome stereotypes. . . .

Some diversity experts dismissed training, arguing that attitudes are difficult to alter but that behavior can be changed with feedback. Instead they supported performance evaluations offering feedback on managers' diversity efforts. Laboratory experiments support this idea, showing that subjects who are told that their decisions will be reviewed are less likely to use stereotypes in assigning people to jobs. . . .

The current enthusiasm for training and evaluations has made them widely popular. Four in ten of the firms we surveyed offered training, and one in five had diversity evaluations. But these programs did not, on average, increase management diversity. . . .

Some psychological research supports our finding that training may be ineffective. Laboratory experiments and field studies show that it is difficult to train away stereotypes, and that white men often respond negatively to training—particularly if they are concerned about their own careers. If training cannot eliminate stereotypes, and if it can elicit backlash, perhaps it is not surprising that, on average, it does not revolutionize the workplace.

We suspect that the potential of diversity performance evaluations is undermined by the complexity of rating systems [and the relative low weight given to diversity performance]. Overall, companies that try to change managers' behavior through training and evaluations have not seen much change. That is disappointing, because training is the single most popular program and, by most accounts, the most costly, and because many companies have put their money on diversity evaluations in recent years.

Creating Social Connections

Another way to view the problem of inequality in management jobs is from the supply side. Do women and minorities have the social resources needed to succeed? Many firms have well-educated white women and minorities in their ranks who fail to move up, and some sociologists suggest this is because they lack the kinds of social connections that ambitious white men develop easily with coworkers and bosses. . . .

Consultants argued that formal programs could help women and minorities develop social networks at work. Company affinity networks became popular. . . . Under these affinity networks, people gather regularly to hear speakers and talk about their experiences.

Many companies also put in formal mentoring programs that match aspiring managers with seasoned higher-ups for regular career-advising sessions. These programs can target women and minorities but are often open to all employees. . . .

When it comes to improving the position of women and minorities in management, network programs do little on average, but mentor programs show strong positive effects. In the average workplace, network programs lead to slight increases for white women and decreases for black men. Perhaps that is not surprising, as studies of these network programs suggest that while they sometimes give people a place to share their experiences, they often bring together people on the lowest rungs of the corporate ladder. They may not put people in touch with what they need to know, or whom they need to know, to move up.

· Mentor programs, by contrast, appear to help women and minorities. . . . Mentor programs put aspiring managers in contact with people who can help them move up, both by offering advice and by finding them jobs. This strategy appears to work.

Making Someone Responsible

Our analyses show that making a person or committee responsible for diversity is very effective. . . . Firms that put in diversity managers see increases for all groups of women, and for black men. In interviews, executives tell us that diversity managers and taskforces are effective because they identify specific problems and remedies. . . . If a company has trouble retaining women, the diversity manager may talk to women at risk of leaving and try to work out arrangements that will keep them on the job. Managers and taskforces feel accountable for change, and they monitor quarterly employment data to see if their efforts are paying off. If not, it is back to the drawing board to sketch new diversity strategies. Taskforces may be so widely effective, some tell us, because they cause managers from different departments to "buy into" the goal of diversity.

Lessons for Executives

What are the most cost-effective strategies for increasing diversity? [Our data show that many] companies were not investing in the strategies that have proven most effective. Three of the four most popular programs—diversity training, evaluations, and network programs—have no positive effects in the average workplace. The two least popular initiatives, mentoring and diversity managers, were among the most effective. . . . Managers might also spend more time assessing programs that don't seem to be working and trying to figure out how to make them effective.

PROBLEM 8-2

"I am one of six people who gather for a meeting to solve a problem: there are three other women and two men. . . . The formal leader begins by explaining that the goal of the meeting is to brainstorm solutions. I offer one. It is quiet as people make notes and think. The next person to talk, a man, repeats my solution. Suddenly people around the table are nodding and endorsing the potential of 'his' idea. I feel myself becoming angry. I fumble for a way to re-claim the idea without sounding like a jerk. I ask: 'What was his idea?' and a woman restates it for me as his face expresses pity for my inability to follow. The situation is not going well, and I wonder whether the time is right to propose implicit bias training. Then I ask myself why I care? My idea . . . will perhaps bring about a positive change.

I care because my understanding is that I do not think I can become a leader without being perceived as bringing something to the proverbial table. . . . My attention snaps back to the meeting when I hear the same individual volunteering to do the work of implementation; having worked with him for quite some time, I know he will not do the work. I then look back to the woman who spoke up, wondering why she did not hear the idea come from my mouth rather than his. . . . This process is not taking advantage of collective wisdom that would allow for quality decision-making. . . . What are my choices? I can disrupt the meeting and risk seeming hostile or difficult. But is there something to be gained by being liked? Is the willingness not to be 'heard' required in order to be perceived as 'nice?'"[46]

NOTES AND QUESTIONS

1. The dynamic profiled in Problem 8-2 is common for women in leadership positions. Christina Romer, who chaired the Council for Economic Advisors in the first Obama administration, reported that male colleagues routinely ignored what she said in meetings or talked over her. But they listened attentively when male council members offered the same ideas.[47] In

commenting on the problem, former Attorney General Loretta Lynch advises aspiring women to "make yourself seen and make yourself heard—this is your idea. . . . Own it, express it, be the voice that people hear."[48] How can women do this without triggering the backlash against women who seem too pushy and self-promoting? Rhode's books, *Women and Leadership* and *Lawyers as Leaders* included below, note that even the most accomplished women lawyers have been subject to such backlash. One of the most prominent recent examples was Donald Trump's characterization of Hillary Clinton as "nasty" during the final 2016 presidential debate.[49] Vendors at Trump rallies sold Hillary Nutcrackers and buttons claiming, "Life's a bitch. Don't vote for one."[50].

How should women respond? In the book from which Problem 8-2 is excerpted, authors offer a number of suggestions. One is for the woman to open a conversation about her experience and ask for guidance from the group about how to ensure a more inclusive culture.[51] Alternatively, she could discuss the problem with her female colleagues, and try to develop strategies, such as bystander intervention by someone other than the person being marginalized. Another option is humor. One commentator proposed language such as: "This idea is great and for some reason sounds a whole lot better the second time it's talked about because when I suggested it just a few minutes ago no one said a word. What's up with that?" The commentator then speculates that someone in the group might respond, "I totally forgot that you had just mentioned it. Thanks for the reminder that the idea originated with you."[52] Does that response seem likely?

How would you advise an aspiring female leader in a highly competitive and aggressive work culture who receives criticism from male supervisors that she has "sharp elbows?" One woman who received such advice initially dismissed it as an example of unconscious bias. Later, when she was about to transition to a high-level government job requiring "significant diplomatic skills," she realized that her "hard charging" style would not serve her well in that new environment. So she began listening more attentively to critical feedback and asking for examples. Her takeaway was that "what I heard might have been sexist and probably was. But now that I needed to change, I found it helpful."[53] How would you evaluate her response? If she had not planned to change jobs, should she have called out the behavior she believed was sexist? If so, how should she have done so? My own research suggests that aspiring women leaders coping with bias remain "relentlessly pleasant" without backing down.[54] What do you see as the relative risks and benefits of the various approaches described above? Are there others that might be more effective?

2. Recent studies find that women are substantially underrepresented as lead trial attorneys.[55] And a survey of some 2,000 senior in-house counsel at large companies around the world found that male clients were one-third less likely than female clients to chose a woman as lead counsel.[56] Much of the problem lies in the double-standard/double-bind dynamic described in the preceding

excerpt from *Lawyers as Leaders*. Women are seen as too aggressive or not aggressive enough, and what is assertive in a man seems abrasive in a woman. How can women respond? Would "relentlessly pleasant" work in a courtroom setting? Under what circumstances should women ever call out judges for bias if it might hurt their client or their own reputation?

3. In a recent McKinsey study, less than half of women, compared with two-thirds of men, believed that law firms were "doing what it takes to improve diversity." And 60 percent of women, compared with 14 percent of men, believed that gender would limit their opportunities.[57] What strategies are most likely to be effective in changing women's perceptions and experience?

4. In a 2016 follow-up article, "Why Diversity Programs Fail," Frank Dobbin and Alexandra Kalev echo the conclusions of the preceding article and add that formal grievance systems do not improve diversity. The reason appears to be that relatively few individuals make formal complaints, and that lulls leaders into assuming that they have no problem.[58] Other research similarly finds that diversity structures create "illusions of fairness" that lead individuals to discount objective evidence of bias.[59] The most effective initiatives, according to Dobbin and Kalev, are ones that spark engagement and promote accountability, such as mentoring and recruiting programs, and diversity task forces and managers.[60] It is particularly important to enlist white men in these efforts because studies suggest that women and men of color who promote diversity are rated lower on competence and performance.[61]

5. The survey of law firm managing partners and general counsel noted earlier revealed that the most common challenge regarding racial and ethnic diversity was the limited pool of candidates and intense competition in recruiting and retaining talented members. The most common difficulties regarding gender involved work/family issues and "getting everybody to buy into the issue" and perceive a serious problem. For both groups, "diversity fatigue" and the difficulty of having an "honest conversation" were ongoing challenges.[62] In terms of strategies, managing partners and general counsel reported mixed success with training programs. Some felt that they "were not solving a problem that we had" and made lawyers feel "preached to and imposed upon." Others thought the programs helped raise awareness of unconscious bias; without them, people "don't know what they don't know."[63] Work/family policies presented difficult challenges because "it's a demanding profession," "we run a 24/7 business," and clients expect constant availability.[64] As one survey participant put it, "It's a real tough [issue]. We do programs on the subject but I'm not sure people have time to attend. I don't think we've done anything really to address that issue."[65]

The best practices that emerged from the survey were similar to those stressed in the preceding excerpts:

- Commitment and Accountability. Diversity needs to be a core value institutionalized in organizational policies, practices, and culture. Women and minorities need to have a critical mass of representation in key positions, supervisors need to be held responsible for their performance on diversity issues, and self-assessment should be a critical priority. "Leaders need to know how policies that affect inclusiveness play out in practice."[66]

- Mentorship and Sponsorship. Organizations should institute and evaluate programs that ensure that women and men of color have not only mentors but sponsors—individuals who will be advocates as well as advisors.[67]
- Work/Life Policies. Organizations should be sure that they have adequate policies and cultural norms regarding family leave, reduced schedules, telecommuting, and emergency childcare.[68]

Other researchers have suggested that organizations reconsider the priority that they place on face time and billable hours, provide training in leadership and business development, and seek to eliminate bias in the distributionn of work.[69] Are there other strategies that you would suggest? What stands in the way? Consider that issue again in the context of law firm challenges discussed in Chapter 9.

6. As Dobbin, Kalev, and Kelly note, and recent research confirms, there is no convincing evidence that the millions of hours and dollars that are invested in diversity training produce measurable reductions in gender biased or abusive behaviors.[70] The investment persists because neither commercial trainers nor the organizations that hire them have sufficient incentive or expertise to objectively evaluate their impact. No one wants to risk a finding that their approach does not demonstrably reduce bias.[71] Although training can increase understanding of what constitutes unacceptable behavior, they do not necessarily change the attitudes and practices that perpetuate it.[72] Poorly designed training can entrench gender stereotypes, encourage male backlash, and reinforce the very biases that it is designed to confront.[73]

That is not to suggest that employers should abandon training. Rather it suggests that they should restructure its approach and evaluate its effectiveness. Based on the limited information available to date, experts have recommended the use of qualified, interactive, and preferably live trainers who adapt their approaches to the type of workplaces involved and include training in bystander intervention.[74] In 2018, Deloitte, the accounting firm, which was well known for its innovative diversity approaches, announced that it was replacing its women employee resource group with outreach to men to teach them to be more inclusive and hold them accountable. The change was prompted by concerns that identity-based affinity groups isolated members from networks of influence that are key to promotions. The firm's leadership reasoned: "Why tell the out-groups they have to figure out how to fit in, instead of teaching the in-groups how to reach out?"[75] Would you support that change? Have you had experience with training programs? What would enhance their effectiveness?

7. Consider an experience that you have had or observed regarding "diversity gone awry." How could it have been handled more effectively? What implications do you draw from the preceding excerpts about how women and

men of color can situate themselves to become leaders? Another increasingly important diversity-related issue is how to prepare leaders to deal with cultural and regional differences. As noted in Chapter 2, nationalities vary across multiple dimensions, including the importance they place on context and relationships in their business dealings. In "low-context" societies, such as the United States, candor and directness are key values; leaders generally want to make the assumptions of transactions explicit and cover contingencies in legal detail. By contrast, in "high-context" societies, including Japan, China, Saudi Arabia, and Spain, leaders tend to rely on personal relationships and shared cultural understandings to provide the backdrop for commercial arrangements.[76] The clash of styles emerges in many settings, in which Americans perceive their counterparts as slow and evasive, and their counterparts see Americans as pushy, distrustful, and overly legalistic. Individuals who are negotiating in a multicultural setting need to be aware of such differences and remember that the "message that ultimately counts is the message that the other person creates in her mind, not the one [they] intended to send."[77]

Have you been in situations in which such differences emerged? How well were they handled? What might have been done differently?

MEDIA RESOURCES

Films, television series, news programs, and training videos offer a wealth of examples of satirical representations of bias and misplaced efforts to combat them. Examples include:

- Stephen Colbert's parody of the role of race and gender in the nomination of Sonia Sotomayor;
- *Saturday Night Live*'s parody of an effort to educate southern legislators about why appearing in blackface is problematic;
- Caricatures of a "diversity day" and a "racial segregation mindset" from *The Office*;
- Will Ferrell's portrayal in *Anchorman* of tensions surrounding diversity; and
- Eddie Murphy's attempt in *Imagine That* to counter a corporate executive's attempts to capitalize on his Native American identity.

Such caricatures offer an opportunity for more serious exploration of why ill-designed diversity training and preferential treatment can provoke backlash, and how such resentment might be avoided. It can also be useful to analyze the effectiveness of promotional videos that corporations and law firms use to showcase their diversity commitment.

D. GENDER AND LEADERSHIP

The materials that follow seek a deeper understanding of the gender dynamics that play out in leadership contexts. As you consider the research summarized below, what seem to be the most significant obstacles confronting women who seek positions of influence? How can they best be addressed? How much does it matter? Why? What role does gender play for male leaders? How might changing the gender composition of leadership influence its effectiveness?

1. WOMEN

ANNE-MARIE SLAUGHTER, 'WHY WOMEN STILL CAN'T HAVE IT ALL,

The Atlantic, July-August 2012

Why Women Still Can't Have It All

It's time to stop fooling ourselves, says a woman who left a position of power: the women who have managed to be both mothers and top professionals are superhuman, rich, or self-employed. If we truly believe in equal opportunity for all women, here's what has to change.

Eighteen months into my job as the first woman director of policy planning at the State Department, a foreign policy dream job . . . , I found myself in New York, at the United Nations' annual assemblage of every foreign minister and head of state in the world. On a Wednesday evening, President and Mrs. Obama hosted a glamorous reception at the American Museum of Natural History. I sipped champagne, greeted foreign dignitaries, and mingled. But I could not stop thinking about my 14-year-old son, who had started eighth grade three weeks earlier and was already resuming what had become his pattern of skipping homework, disrupting classes, failing math, and tuning out any adult who tried to reach him. Over the summer, we had barely spoken to each other—or, more accurately, he had barely spoken to me. And the previous spring I had received several urgent phone calls—invariably on the day of an important meeting—that required me to take the first train from Washington, D.C., where I worked, back to Princeton, New Jersey, where he lived. My husband, who has always done everything possible to support my career, took care of him and his 12-year-old brother during the week; outside of those midweek emergencies, I came home only on weekends.

As the evening wore on, I ran into a colleague who held a senior position in the White House. . . . I told her how difficult I was finding it to be away from my son when he clearly needed me. Then I said, "When this is over, I'm going to write an op-ed titled 'Women Can't Have It All.'"

She was horrified. "You *can't* write that," she said. "You, of all people."

What she meant was that such a statement, coming from a high-profile career woman—a role model—would be a terrible signal to younger generations of women. By the end of the evening, she had talked me out of it, but for the remainder of my stint in Washington, I was increasingly aware that the feminist beliefs on which I had built my entire career were shifting under my feet. I had always assumed that if I could get a foreign-policy job in the State Department or the White House while my party was in power, I would stay the course as long as I had the opportunity to do work I loved. But in January 2011, when my two-year public-service leave from Princeton University was up, I hurried home as fast as I could.

A rude epiphany hit me soon after I got there. When people asked why I had left government, I explained that I'd come home not only because of Princeton's rules (after two years of leave, you lose your tenure), but also because of my desire to be with my family and my conclusion that juggling high-level government work with the needs of two teenage boys was not possible. I have not exactly left the ranks of full-time career women: I teach a full course load; write regular print and online columns on foreign policy; give 40 to 50 speeches a year; appear regularly on TV and radio; and am working on a new academic book. But I routinely got reactions from other women my age or older that ranged from disappointed ("It's such a pity that you had to leave Washington") to condescending ("I wouldn't generalize from your experience. I've never had to compromise, and my kids turned out great.").

The first set of reactions, with the underlying assumption that my choice was somehow sad or unfortunate, was irksome enough. But it was the second set of reactions—those implying that my parenting and/or my commitment to my profession were somehow substandard—that triggered a blind fury. Suddenly, finally, the penny dropped. All my life, I'd been on the other side of this exchange. I'd been the woman smiling the faintly superior smile while another woman told me she had decided to take some time out or pursue a less competitive career track so that she could spend more time with her family. I'd been the woman congratulating herself on her unswerving commitment to the feminist cause, chatting smugly with her dwindling number of college or law-school friends who had reached and maintained their place on the highest rungs of their profession. I'd been the one telling young women at my lectures that you can have it all and do it all, regardless of what field you are in. Which means I'd been part, albeit unwittingly, of making millions of women feel that they are to blame if they cannot manage to rise up the ladder as fast as men and also have a family and an active home life (and be thin and beautiful to boot). . . .

I still strongly believe that women can "have it all" (and that men can too). I believe that we can "have it all at the same time." But not today, not with the way America's economy and society are currently structured. My experiences over the past three years have forced me to confront a number of uncomfortable facts that need to be widely acknowledged—and quickly changed.

Before my service in government, I'd spent my career in academia: as a law professor and then as the dean of Princeton's Woodrow Wilson School of Public and International Affairs. Both were demanding jobs, but I had the ability to set my own schedule most of the time. I could be with my kids when I needed to be, and still get the work done. I had to travel frequently, but I found I could make up for that with an extended period at home or a family vacation.

I knew that I was lucky in my career choice, but I had no idea how lucky until I spent two years in Washington within a rigid bureaucracy, even with bosses as understanding as Hillary Clinton and her chief of staff, Cheryl Mills. My workweek started at 4:20 on Monday morning, when I got up to get the 5:30 train from Trenton to Washington. It ended late on Friday, with the train home. In between, the days were crammed with meetings, and when the meetings stopped, the writing work began—a never-ending stream of memos, reports, and comments on other people's drafts. For two years, I never left the office early enough to go to any stores other than those open 24 hours, which meant that everything from dry cleaning to hair appointments to Christmas shopping had to be done on weekends, amid children's sporting events, music lessons, family meals, and conference calls. I was entitled to four hours of vacation per pay period, which came to one day of vacation a month. And I had it better than many of my peers in D.C. . . .

In short, the minute I found myself in a job that is typical for the vast majority of working women (and men), working long hours on someone else's schedule, I could no longer be both the parent and the professional I wanted to be—at least not with a child experiencing a rocky adolescence. I realized what should have perhaps been obvious: having it all, at least for me, depended almost entirely on what type of job I had. The flip side is the harder truth: having it all was not possible in many types of jobs, including high government office—at least not for very long. . . .

Yet the decision to step down from a position of power—to value family over professional advancement, even for a time—is directly at odds with the prevailing social pressures on career professionals in the United States. One phrase says it all about current attitudes toward work and family, particularly among elites. In Washington, "leaving to spend time with your family" is a euphemism for being fired. . . .

Think about what this "standard Washington excuse" implies: it is so unthinkable that an official would *actually* step down to spend time with his or her family that this must be a cover for something else. How could anyone voluntarily leave the circles of power for the responsibilities of parenthood? Depending on one's vantage point, it is either ironic or maddening that this view abides in the nation's capital, despite the ritual commitments to "family values" that are part of every political campaign. Regardless, this sentiment makes true work-life balance exceptionally difficult. But it cannot change unless top women speak out. . . .

[Consider] Facebook Chief Operating Officer Sheryl Sandberg's widely publicized 2011 commencement speech at Barnard, and her earlier TED Talk, in which she lamented the dismally small number of women at the top and advised young women not to "leave before you leave." When a woman starts thinking about having children, Sandberg said, "she doesn't raise her hand anymore. . . .

She starts leaning back." Although couched in terms of encouragement, Sandberg's exhortation contains more than a note of reproach. We who have made it to the top, or are striving to get there, are essentially saying to the women in the generation behind us: "What's the matter with you?"

They have an answer that we don't want to hear. After the speech I gave in New York, I went to dinner with a group of 30-somethings. I sat across from two vibrant women, one of whom worked at the UN and the other at a big New York law firm. As nearly always happens in these situations, they soon began asking me about work-life balance. When I told them I was writing this article, the lawyer said, "I look for role models and can't find any." She said the women in her firm who had become partners and taken on management positions had made tremendous sacrifices, "many of which they don't even seem to realize. . . . They take two years off when their kids are young but then work like crazy to get back on track professionally, which means that they see their kids when they are toddlers but not teenagers, or really barely at all." Her friend nodded, mentioning the top professional women she knew, all of whom essentially relied on round-the-clock nannies. Both were very clear that they did not want that life, but could not figure out how to combine professional success and satisfaction with a real commitment to family. . . .

I am well aware that the majority of American women face problems far greater than any discussed in this article. I am writing for my demographic—highly educated, well-off women who are privileged enough to have choices in the first place. We may not have choices about whether to do paid work, as dual incomes have become indispensable. But we have choices about the type and tempo of the work we do. We are the women who could be leading, and who should be equally represented in the leadership ranks.

Millions of other working women face much more difficult life circumstances. Some are single mothers; many struggle to find any job; others support husbands who cannot find jobs. Many cope with a work life in which good day care is either unavailable or very expensive; school schedules do not match work schedules; and schools themselves are failing to educate their children. Many of these women are worrying not about having it all, but rather about holding on to what they do have. . . .

The best hope for improving the lot of all women, and for closing what [economists Justin] Wolfers and [Betsey] Stevenson call a "new gender gap"— measured by well-being rather than wages—is to close the leadership gap: to elect a woman president and 50 women senators; to ensure that women are equally represented in the ranks of corporate executives and judicial leaders. Only when women wield power in sufficient numbers will we create a society that genuinely works for all women. That will be a society that works for everyone.

The Half-Truths We Hold Dear

Let's briefly examine the stories we tell ourselves, the clichés that I and many other women typically fall back on when younger women ask us how we have managed to "have it all." They are not necessarily lies, but at best partial truths.

We must clear them out of the way to make room for a more honest and productive discussion about real solutions to the problems faced by professional women.

It's Possible If You Are Just Committed Enough

Our usual starting point, whether we say it explicitly or not, is that having it all depends primarily on the depth and intensity of a woman's commitment to her career. That is precisely the sentiment behind the dismay so many older career women feel about the younger generation. *They are not committed enough*, we say, to make the trade-offs and sacrifices that the women ahead of them made. . . .

These "mundane" issues—the need to travel constantly to succeed, the conflicts between school schedules and work schedules, the insistence that work be done in the office—cannot be solved by exhortations to close the ambition gap. I would hope to see commencement speeches that finger America's social and business policies, rather than women's level of ambition, in explaining the dearth of women at the top. But changing these policies requires much more than speeches. It means fighting the mundane battles—every day, every year—in individual workplaces, in legislatures, and in the media.

It's Possible If You Marry the Right Person

Sandberg's second message in her Barnard commencement address was: "The most important career decision you're going to make is whether or not you have a life partner and who that partner is. . . ."

Still, the proposition that women can have high-powered careers as long as their husbands or partners are willing to share the parenting load equally (or disproportionately) assumes that most women will *feel* as comfortable as men do about being away from their children, as long as their partner is home with them. In my experience, that is simply not the case.

Here I step onto treacherous ground, mined with stereotypes. From years of conversations and observations, however, I've come to believe that men and women respond quite differently when problems at home force them to recognize that their absence is hurting a child, or at least that their presence would likely help. I do not believe fathers love their children any less than mothers do, but men do seem more likely to choose their job at a cost to their family, while women seem more likely to choose their family at a cost to their job. . . .

. . . Male leaders are routinely praised for having sacrificed their personal life on the altar of public or corporate service. That sacrifice, of course, typically involves their family. . . .

It is not clear to me that this ethical framework makes sense for society. Why should we want leaders who fall short on personal responsibilities? Perhaps leaders who invested time in their own families would be more keenly aware of the toll their public choices—on issues from war to welfare—take on private lives. . . . Regardless, it is clear which set of choices society values more today. Workers who put their careers first are typically rewarded; workers who chose their families are overlooked, disbelieved, or accused of unprofessionalism.

In sum, having a supportive mate may well be a necessary condition if women are to have it all, but it is not sufficient. . . .

It's Possible If You Sequence It Right

Young women should be wary of the assertion "You can have it all; you just can't have it all at once." This 21st-century addendum to the original line is now proffered by many senior women to their younger mentees. To the extent that it means, in the words of one working mother, "I'm going to do my best and I'm going to keep the long term in mind and know that it's not always going to be this hard to balance," it is sound advice. But to the extent that it means that women can have it all if they just find the right sequence of career and family, it's cheerfully wrong. . . .

[M]any career women of my generation chose to establish themselves in their careers first and have children in their mid-to-late 30s. But that raises the possibility of spending long, stressful years and a small fortune trying to have a baby. I lived that nightmare: for three years, beginning at age 35, I did everything possible to conceive and was frantic at the thought that I had simply left having a biological child until it was too late.

And when everything does work out? I had my first child at 38 (and counted myself blessed) and my second at 40. That means I will be 58 when both of my children are out of the house. What's more, it means that many peak career opportunities are coinciding precisely with their teenage years, when, experienced parents advise, being available as a parent is just as important as in the first years of a child's life.

Many women of my generation have found themselves, in the prime of their careers, saying no to opportunities they once would have jumped at and hoping those chances come around again later. Many others who have decided to step back for a while, taking on consultant positions or part-time work that lets them spend more time with their children (or aging parents), are worrying about how long they can "stay out" before they lose the competitive edge they worked so hard to acquire.

Given the way our work culture is oriented today, I recommend establishing yourself in your career first but still trying to have kids before you are 35—or else freeze your eggs, whether you are married or not. You may well be a more mature and less frustrated parent in your 30s or 40s; you are also more likely to have found a lasting life partner. But the truth is, neither sequence is optimal, and both involve trade-offs that men do not have to make.

You should be able to have a family if you want one—however and whenever your life circumstances allow—and still have the career you desire. If more women could strike this balance, more women would reach leadership positions. And if more women were in leadership positions, they could make it easier for more women to stay in the workforce. The rest of this essay details how.

Changing the Culture of Face Time

. . . The culture of "time macho"—a relentless competition to work harder, stay later, pull more all-nighters, travel around the world and bill the extra hours that the international date line affords you—remains astonishingly prevalent among professionals today. Nothing captures the belief that more time equals more value better than the cult of billable hours afflicting large law firms across the country and providing exactly the wrong incentives for employees who hope to integrate work and family. Yet even in industries that don't explicitly reward sheer quantity of hours spent on the job, the pressure to arrive early, stay late, and be available, always, for in-person meetings at 11 a.m. on Saturdays can be intense. . . . But more time in the office does not always mean more "value added"—and it does not always add up to a more successful organization. . . .

Long hours are one thing, and realistically, they are often unavoidable. But do they really need to be spent at the office? To be sure, being in the office *some* of the time is beneficial. In-person meetings can be far more efficient than phone or e-mail tag; trust and collegiality are much more easily built up around the same physical table; and spontaneous conversations often generate good ideas and lasting relationships. Still, armed with e-mail, instant messaging, phones, and videoconferencing technology, we should be able to move to a culture where the office is a base of operations more than the required locus of work. . . .

Rediscovering the Pursuit of Happiness

One of the most complicated and surprising parts of my journey out of Washington was coming to grips with what I really wanted. I had opportunities to stay on, and I could have tried to work out an arrangement allowing me to spend more time at home. I might have been able to get my family to join me in Washington for a year; I might have been able to get classified technology installed at my house the way Jim Steinberg did; I might have been able to commute only four days a week instead of five. (While this last change would have still left me very little time at home, given the intensity of my job, it might have made the job doable for another year or two.) But I realized that I didn't just *need* to go home. Deep down, I *wanted* to go home. I wanted to be able to spend time with my children in the last few years that they are likely to live at home, crucial years for their development into responsible, productive, happy, and caring adults. But also irreplaceable years for me to enjoy the simple pleasures of parenting. . . .

Innovation Nation

. . . What is evident, however, is that many firms that recruit and train well-educated professional women are well aware that when a woman leaves because of bad work-family balance, they are losing the money and time they invested in her.

Even the legal industry, built around the billable hour, is taking notice. Deborah Epstein Henry, . . . in her book *Law and Reorder*, . . . describes a legal profession "where the billable hour no longer works"; where attorneys, judges, recruiters, and academics all agree that this system of compensation has perverted the industry, leading to brutal work hours, massive inefficiency, and highly inflated costs. The answer—already being deployed in different corners of the industry—is a combination of alternative fee structures, virtual firms, women-owned firms, and the outsourcing of discrete legal jobs to other jurisdictions. Women, and Generation X and Y lawyers more generally, are pushing for these changes on the supply side; clients determined to reduce legal fees and increase flexible service are pulling on the demand side. Slowly, change is happening.

At the core of all this is self-interest. Losing smart and motivated women not only diminishes a company's talent pool; it also reduces the return on its investment in training and mentoring. In trying to address these issues, some firms are finding out that women's ways of working may just be better ways of working, for employees and clients alike. . . .

Enlisting Men

. . . If women are ever to achieve real equality as leaders, then we have to stop accepting male behavior and male choices as the default and the ideal. We must insist on changing social policies and bending career tracks to accommodate *our* choices, too. We have the power to do it if we decide to, and we have many men standing beside us.

We'll create a better society in the process, for *all* women. We may need to put a woman in the White House before we are able to change the conditions of the women working at Walmart. But when we do, we will stop talking about whether women can have it all. We will properly focus on how we can help all Americans have healthy, happy, productive lives, valuing the people they love as much as the success they seek.

LARA BAZELON, I'VE PICKED MY JOB OVER MY KIDS

New York Times, June 29, 2019

I am a lawyer, a law professor, and a writer. I am also a divorced mother of two young children. I'm often asked some version of: "How do you excel at work and be the best mother you can be?"

Every working mother gets this question, which presupposes that a "work-life balance" is achievable. It's not. The term traps women in an endless cycle of shame and self-recrimination.

Like many women, I often prioritize my job. I do this because, as the head of a single-parent household, I'm the sole breadwinner. My ex-husband, who has joint custody, is an amazing father and my life would be impossible without him. Neither of us pays the other support.

My choice is more than a financial imperative. I prioritize my work because I'm ambitious and because I believe it's important. If I didn't write and teach and litigate, a part of me would feel empty.

In 2013, I was the trial lawyer on a case to free an innocent black man improbably named Kash Register. As a teenager in 1979, because of police and prosecutorial misconduct and witnesses who lied, he was condemned to serve life in prison for a murder he did not commit.

Thirty-four years later, he was still behind bars. Even though we had presented the district attorney's office with what we believed was overwhelming evidence of my client's innocence, it insisted on what was essentially a retrial in front of a judge.

At the time, my son was four and my daughter was two. One month before the retrial started, I moved from San Francisco to a tiny apartment close to the courthouse in Los Angeles. I went long stretches without seeing my children. They were lovingly cared for by their father, their grandmother, my son's preschool teacher, and my daughter's babysitter. When I would fly home, I was often not fully present. My client needed me more than my children did. So he got more of me. A lot more.

During these months, my son had a lot of questions. "Why are you gone so much?" "Why are you always on the phone talking about that guy with the funny name?" I explained what was at stake. The good guys are fighting the bad guys. If we lose, it means racism won and a man's life was destroyed.

"Are you going to win?" he wanted to know.

"That's my job," I said.

I have missed meetings to take my kids to the park or a museum. . . . Recently, I turned down an offer to teach an extra class for a significant amount of money because I didn't want to lose that time with them.

But there is always another client to defend, story to write, or struggling student who just can't wait. Here are things I have missed: my daughter's seventh birthday, my son's tenth birthday party, two family vacations, three Halloweens, every school camping trip. I have never chaperoned, coached, or organized a school event.

Sometimes my choices make me sad. My daughter's seventh birthday was the worst. She cried, and I did everything I could not to. I felt sick to my stomach. But I had a trial starting the next day, six hours away.

I had picked the date, not the judge, because I knew that the other side wasn't ready. Delaying even a few days would have meant losing a crucial advantage. I wasn't going to risk it knowing what was on the line for my client.

Of course, I sometimes feel doubt, shame, and fear. I know I'm not a "normal" mom, because my kids tell me so. I remind myself that this does not make me a "bad mom." I also remind myself that if I were a dad, I would be getting accolades for all the times I scheduled a doctor's appointment or arranged a play date.

I am proud of what I have accomplished. I am prouder that I can support myself and my children. But sometimes I wonder if my choices will damage them.

In 2017, my son's third-grade class had a midday Thanksgiving potluck. Driving back from court, I dashed into the Whole Foods, bought the first thing I saw—a loaf of lemon poppy seed poundcake—and rushed over to school. The room was full of mothers with a smattering of dads. I was the only person in a suit.

I put the lemon poppy seed loaf on a table, next to another mother's homemade stew. My son looked over at me and winced.

After the meal, it was time for presentations. Each child had been given a piece of orange paper shaped like a leaf with prompts to answer: "I appreciate my parents because" and "this helps me to."

One by one, the children stood up and read what they had written. Many of them talked about how much they loved their moms, because they made them delicious food or gave them a safe place to live.

I grew uncomfortable as I listened, my smile frozen on my face. What on earth was my son going to say when it was his turn? That he lived in two different houses and routinely ate boiled hot dogs and chicken fingers while his mother told true crime stories? That he had once told me, politely, as we sat down to dinner, "Mom, I think you forgot the vegetable?"

My son was one of the last children to speak. He stood up and, in a clear voice, said: "I appreciate my parents for being lawyers because they get people out of jail. This really helps me reflect, do the right thing, and have positive role models."

He looked over at me, the barest hint of a smile on his face. I wanted to leap out of my pint-size chair, raise my fists in the air, and yell, "That's my boy." I have his orange leaf on the wall in my office. Sometimes I look over at it when I'm working late at night.

I hope my kids get it. I think they do. I love them beyond all reason, and their existence gives my life profound meaning. And I have the same feelings about my job.

DEBORAH L. RHODE, WOMEN AND LEADERSHIP

(Oxford University Press, 2017), 4-7.

Assumptions about gender differences in leadership styles and effectiveness are widespread, although as Alice Eagly's pathbreaking work notes, the evidence for such assumptions is weaker than commonly supposed. Reviews of more than forty studies on gender in leadership find many more similarities than differences between male and female leaders. Not only are those gender differences small, they are smaller than the differences among women. So too, in the Pew Research Center's recent survey on women and leadership, a large majority of the American public sees men and women as similar on key leadership traits such as intelligence, honesty, ambition, decisiveness, and innovation. The main differences that emerged were compassion and organization, and on those traits women were rated as superior to men. The only gender differences that are consistently supported by evidence on performance are that female leaders are more participatory, democratic, and interpersonally sensitive than male leaders. Eagly notes that women "attend more to the individuals they work with by mentoring them and taking their particular situations into account." Leaders interviewed for this book often spoke of being more collaborative than their male counterparts. . . .

In effect, women are more likely than men to engage in transformational leadership, which stresses inspiring and enabling followers to contribute to their organization. This approach holds advantages over traditional transactional leadership, which focuses on exchanges between leaders and followers that appeal to followers' self-interest. Women tend to use a transformational style because it relies on skills associated with women, and because more autocratic approaches are viewed as less attractive in women than in men. A transformational style has obvious advantages because it enables women to establish a level of trust and cooperation that is essential to effectiveness. Janet Napolitano, former [lawyer], Arizona governor, cabinet secretary, and currently president of the University of California, notes that one critical leadership characteristic is helping others accomplish their mission: "People need to know you are investing yourself in doing what you need to do so they can succeed. It is a big mistake to parachute in with a prepared plan about who will do what. I've seen guys do this all the time." Although transformational leadership is generally viewed as the most effective approach, it does not fit all organizations. Some highly male-dominated settings invite a top-down style, and women who were firsts in those settings, such as Margaret Thatcher, Golda Meir, and Indira Gandhi, led in ways that were as commanding as those of men.

Similar points are applicable to gender differences in leadership priorities. Women are particularly likely to cite assisting and empowering others as leadership objectives, along with promoting gender equality. In a 2015 Pew survey, 71 percent of women believed that having more women in top leadership positions in business and government would improve the quality of life for all women. Of course, not all female leaders are advocates on women's issues. Some are at pains to distance themselves from gender concerns. As Marissa Mayer famously put it, "I'm not a girl at Google, I'm a geek at Google." Other women have internalized the values of the culture in which they have succeeded, and have little interest in promoting opportunities that they never had. They have "gotten there the hard way," and they have "given up a lot"; if they managed, so can everyone else. On the whole, however, women's greater commitment to women's issues emerges in a variety of contexts. For example, most evidence indicates that female judges are more supportive than their male colleagues on gender-related issues. And many women judges, both through individual rulings and collective efforts in women's judicial organizations, have spearheaded responses to women's concerns on matters such as domestic violence, child support, and gender bias training. The same is true of women in management and public office. For some female leaders, their own experiences of discrimination, marginalization, or work-family conflicts leave them with a desire to make life better for their successors. Because these women have bumped up against conventional assumptions and workplace structures, they can more readily question gender roles that men take for granted. Their perspective deserves a hearing in leadership contexts.

As to leadership effectiveness, most research reveals no significant gender differences. Success in leadership generally requires a combination of traditionally masculine and feminine traits, including vision, ethics, interpersonal skills, technical competence, and personal capabilities such as self-awareness and self-control. Contrary to popular assumptions, large-scale surveys generally find that women perform equally with or slightly outperform men on all but a few measures. One recent study found that women scored higher than men on twelve of sixteen leadership competencies. Some evidence also suggests that women are less subject than men to the arrogance and overconfidence that contributes to leadership failures, and are better decision makers under stress. Such differences prompted the quip by the International Monetary Fund's managing director, Christine Lagarde, that the global financial crisis would have played out quite differently "if Lehman Brothers had been Lehman Sisters." However, women cannot be effective unless others accept their leadership—and context matters. One meta-analysis found that men's effectiveness as leaders surpassed women's in roles that were male-dominated, but that women's effectiveness surpassed men's in roles that were less masculine.

Taken as a whole, these findings on gender differences should come as no surprise. Gender socialization and stereotypes play an obvious role; they push women to behave in ways that are consistent with traditional notions of femininity. Yet these differences in leadership contexts are generally small because advancement often requires conformity to accepted images of leadership. And some traditional differences have been blurred by recent trends in leadership development, which have encouraged both sexes to adopt more collaborative, interpersonally sensitive approaches. It is also unsurprising that some studies find superior performance by women leaders, given the hurdles that they have had to surmount to reach upper-level positions and the pressures that they have faced to exceed expectations. To the extent that female leaders gravitate toward a collaborative, interpersonally sensitive approach, it is because that style proves an asset in most leadership settings. Whatever else can be inferred from this research, it is clear that a society can ill afford to exclude so many talented women from its leadership ranks.

PROBLEM 8-3

A recent *New York Times* article profiled two lawyers: they met in college, earned law degrees , went to work for law firms, got married, and had two children. A decade later, she was working 21 hours a week for New York City and caring for the couple's five- and one-year-old children. He was a partner at a midsize firm working at least 60 hours a week, earning four to six times as much as she did. It isn't how they imagined that they would split responsibilities. He acknowledged that he would be happier if he had more time at home and less stress at work, and she regrets going to law school and accumulating so much debt, but both feel that they have made the best choice under the circumstances. Any plausible alternative with more equal parenting would mean far less income and more difficulties juggling responsibilities.[78]

If you were a law firm leader asked to respond to that article, what would you say?

NOTES AND QUESTIONS

1. Experts interviewed for the *New York Times* article noted two trends that have contributed to the dilemma facing Slaughter, Bazelon, and the couple in Problem 8-3. One is the rising income premium for overwork. The other is the rise in "intensive parenting." The number of hours that college-educated parents spend with their children has doubled since the early 1980s, and working mothers today spend as much time on childcare as stay at home mothers did in the 1970s.[79] What has also changed is the number of male workers who want more involvement in family life. But the workplace will not adjust, most researchers believe, until employees demand it. If they do, organizations will have large incentives to redesign the workplace to retain highly qualified professionals. According to one Stanford economist, "[I]t may mean rearranging jobs, but you'd think there'd be a lot of money in it."[80] If he is right, why do you think major law firms have done so little to compete around quality of life issues? What might prompt them to change?

2. Anne-Marie Slaughter's article received considerable attention, as did a book published shortly thereafter by Facebook COO, Sheryl Sandberg, *Lean In: Women, Work, and the Will to Lead.*[81] Sandberg's main argument, which grew out of the TED Talk referenced in Slaughter's article, is that

> [i]n addition to the external barriers erected by society, women are hindered by barriers that exist within ourselves. We hold ourselves back in ways both big and small, by lacking self-confidence, by not raising our hands, and by pulling back when we should be leaning in. We internalize the negative messages we get throughout our lives— the messages that say it's wrong to be outspoken, aggressive, more powerful than men. We lower our expectations of what we can achieve. We continue to do the majority of the housework and child care. We compromise our career goals to make room for partners and children who may not even exist yet. Compared to our male colleagues, fewer of us aspire to senior positions. . . . I have made every mistake on this list. At times I still do.
>
> My argument is that getting rid of these internal barriers is critical to gaining power. Others have argued that women can get to the top only when the institutional barriers are gone. This is the ultimate chicken-and-egg situation. The chicken: Women will tear down the external barriers once we achieve leadership roles. . . . The egg: We need to eliminate the external barriers to get women into those roles in the first place. Both sides are right. So rather than engage in philosophical arguments over which comes first, let's agree to wage battles on both fronts. They are equally important. . . . [These internal obstacles deserve a lot more attention, in part because they are under our own control. We can dismantle the hurdles in ourselves today. We can start at this very moment. . . .

> I know some believe that by focusing on what women can change themselves—pressing them to lean in—it seems like I am letting our institutions off the hook. Or even worse, they accuse me of blaming the victim. Far from blaming the victim, I believe that female leaders are key to the solution.[82]

How would Slaughter respond? How would you? What would you say to Bazelon?

3. What are the greatest barriers to women seeking leadership positions apart from work/family conflicts? Do they vary across practice settings? Have you observed any of the problems that the readings describe? How did the individuals and organizations respond?

4. Recent research that compared a large sample of male and female leaders' performance ratings found further evidence along the lines that the *Women and Leadership* excerpt summarized. Women rated higher than men on 17 of the 19 competencies that were evaluated.[83] Why do you think that those positive evaluations do not translate into greater leadership representation for women? One study that compared women and men who made partners in law firms with those who had not found that among the most successful strategies for women were cultivating friends and mentors at work, forging good relationships with team members, and setting boundaries.[84] Do those findings jive with your sense of what aspiring female attorneys prioritize?

5. In her memoir, former lawyer, now news anchor Megyn Kelly notes that her goal is to

> do the absolute best I can, and don't waste time complaining. The less time talking about our gender the better. . . . Most of my own power has come from excellence, not advocacy. My approach is to say to myself, 'Just *do* better. *Be* better.' That is not to say there's no bias, no sexism. There is and it's not good. It's just that for me, the solution of *doing better* is far more empowering than lamenting one's circumstances. . . . It's not that I reject the idea of demanding a place at the table—quite the contrary. But in my own experience the most effective way to get opportunities is with performance, not persistence.[85]

Is that good advice?

6. When Vice President Joseph Biden asked a former staffer to be his chief legal counsel in the White House, she told him that she was willing if she could have dinner with her young children most nights. He reportedly responded, "Well, you have a phone and I can call you when I need you after dinner time."[86] Would that work in most positions? If Slaughter's family had lived in Washington, D.C., could she have made her position work?

7. Under what circumstances does part-time work address the problem. Does Michelle Obama's experience explain why so few lawyers take advantage of

reduced time schedules? After giving birth to her first daughter, Obama returned to her position at the University of Chicago half-time and recalls:

> [W]hat I didn't realize—and this would also go into my file of things many of us learn too late—is that a part time job, especially when it's meant to be a scaled down version of your previously full-time job, can be something of a trap. Or at least that's how it played out for me. At work, I was still attending all the meetings I always had while also grappling with most of the same responsibilities. The only real difference was that I now made half my original salary and was trying to cram everything into a twenty- hour week. . . . I battled guilt when I had to take work calls at home. I battled a different sort of guilt when I sat at my office distracted by the idea that Malia might be allergic to peanuts. Part-time work was meant to give me more freedom , but mostly it left me feeling as if I were only half doing everything. . . . Meanwhile, it seemed that Barack had hardly missed a stride.[87]

Is there anything that could have been done to make her position manageable? Could more be done to aid lawyers who want to reenter the workforce after time off? Multiple reentry programs have failed due to high costs and low success rates.[88] One that has had at least modest success uses a highly selective screening process to match candidates with organizations willing to take them on for a trial period at salaries well below market rates for first year associates.[89] Even this program is managing to secure permanent positions for only about half of participants. Why do you suppose these initiatives have had such limited success? Is there anything that could be done to improve their effectiveness?

8. One reason apart from work life conflicts that women give for taking themselves off the leadership track is lack of meaning in their work. As one consultant explains women's disproportionate attrition rates, "there are more reasons for women to opt out than there are to opt in."[90] If that is true, what is your response? Is part of the reason for gender disparities that women face less social stigma than men for dialing back their careers. If so, what follows from that fact?

9. In the last few years, women have become more willing to file discrimination suits against law firms for failing to provide equal compensation, promotion, and leadership opportunities.[91] In explaining this trend, Michele Coleman Mayes, Chair of the American Bar Association's Commission on Women in the Profession, noted, "There is more sunlight now. Women are no longer going to be cowed into believing that they have to stay silent or suffer the label that says 'undesirable colleague.'"[92] Such lawsuits often put the plaintiff's female colleagues in a difficult position. In one widely publicized class action lawsuit against Chadbourne & Parke, fourteen female partners publicly

disavowed the suit, and complained that the plaintiff's lawyer did not speak for them and indeed had not even contacted them before filing a suit on their behalf.[93] The plaintiff's lawyer responded that bar rules on solicitation prevented him from making such contact and suggested that people who write such letters on behalf of defendants are often driven by desires to "keep in good standing with the powers that be."[94]

What are the potential costs and benefits to aspiring female leaders in bringing discrimination suits or aligning themselves with those who do? Is it always what one class action lawyer called "a career limiting move"?[95] Under what circumstances can you imagine yourself initiating litigation? What should firm leaders do if they feel that they have been unfairly targeted with such a lawsuit? What should women lawyers do if they feel that they have been fairly treated but that other female colleagues may have legitimate grievances?

10. Many commentators on women and leadership stress the importance of "making your partner a partner" who is equally invested in seeing you succeed. Ruth Bader Ginsburg notes that her husband, a professor of tax law, was the "first reader and critic of articles, speeches[,] and briefs," and that without his lobbying efforts, she "would not have gained a seat on the Supreme Court."[96] Justice Sandra Day O'Connor's husband also lobbied on behalf of her appointment even though, as his son noted, it meant giving up his position as one of the most powerful lawyers in Phoenix to becoming a "second fiddle" in Washington. "He walked away from a firm he loved, a city he loved, a practice he loved, and never gave it a second thought."[97] Consider those observations in light of the following discussion of the gender socialization of men.

2. MEN

NOTES AND QUESTIONS

1. Women are not the only ones who pay a price for gender norms at leadership levels. Men also bear the costs of pressures to be the primary breadwinner, and to conform to the hypermasculine work ethic that characterizes many upper-level positions. In her study of the gender dynamics in high-powered, high-tech work cultures and follow-up research, Marianne Cooper documents men's perception of what is necessary to be a successful "go-to guy." As she notes, a "masculine mystique" or "masculinity contests" dominate the workplace. "The pace is intense. If you stop to take a breath, you may miss out."[98] One man explained, "[G]uys try to out macho each other. . . . There's a lot of 'see how many hours I can work.'" Other comments included: "He's a real man, he works 90 hours a week. He's a slacker; he works 50 hours a week."[99] Another observed that those who "conspicuously overwork are guys and I think it's usually for the benefit of other guys."[100] None of those Cooper interviewed questioned the inevitability of these demands. "I hate to sound like a capitalist," said one man, "but at the end of the day, the company shareholders

aren't holding shares so that we can have flexible lives."[101] Two weeks of paternity leave seemed all that was "capitalistically fair for the company to offer."[102] Another was equally resigned: "I signed up for this life, right . . . and you pay a price if you have a high paying job, or a career you are really fulfilled by. So my price is that I'm exhausted."[103]

Another price is time with family. A vice president who was on the road for a month earned this description: "[H]e doesn't have two kids and a wife, he has people that live in his house."[104] Another described the "emotionally downsized" life of the CEO of his former start-up company:

> [He] had three kids—four, seven, and ten—nice kids but he never ever sees them because he's at work seven days a week. He does triple sevens. He works from 7:00 in the morning until 7:00 in the evening seven days a week. He thought he was a good father because once a year he'd go camping for a week with his kids or one day on a weekend he would take them out . . . for two hours and he'd say it's not the quantity of time, it's the quality of time.[105]

One father who had taken only two days off at the birth of his second child and then gone through a year of seeing his family "almost not at all" finally left his position as vice president. That required renegotiating his identity. He had a new job he liked, decent pay, and an ability to spend time with the family he loved, but he no longer could feel "famous in [my] field."[106]

The trade-off he identified is not one many male leaders feel comfortable making. Derek Bok, former dean of Harvard Law School and president of Harvard University, described a partner in a San Francisco firm who "was always complaining about how hard he worked, so I asked 'Then why don't you just work 3/5 as hard and take 3/5 the salary?' He was tongue tied. But of course the real reason he couldn't is that then he feared he wouldn't be a 'player.'"[107] Those fears are widely shared. In one survey, over three quarters of lawyers who were working part time or on reduced schedules were female.[108] In another study by the American Bar Foundation, female lawyers were about seven times more likely than male lawyers to be working part-time or to be out of the labor force, primarily due to child care.[109] Part of the reason for those disparities is that the small number of fathers who opt to become full-time caretakers suffer even greater financial and promotion costs than female colleagues who make the same choice.[110] Even those who want just minor accommodations for childcare responsibilities encounter resistance, though seldom is it as explicit as the partner who responded, "Don't make it a habit."[111]

These patterns are deeply rooted in traditional gender roles. Time use studies find that women do about 65 percent of the childcare in dual-earner heterosexual marriages, and that when a child is sick, 78 percent of women report that they are the ones who take time off from work.[112] Yet these long-standing norms are also coming under increasing challenge. Growing numbers of men are expressing a desire for better balance between their personal and professional lives, as is clear from the examples cited in *Lawyers as Leaders*. President Obama was frank about the tradeoffs. He acknowledged that when his daughters were young, "while I helped out, it was usually on my schedule and on my terms. The burden disproportionately and unfairly fell on Michelle."[113] After he became president, he noted, "There have been times where I've been constrained by the fact that I had two young daughters who I wanted to spend time with—and that I wasn't in a position to work the social scene in Washington."[114] Yet as noted earlier, Obama's priorities did not necessarily extend to those who worked for him. Obama's first White House chief of staff, Rahm Emanuel, was known for his "Friday-afternoon mantra: 'Only two more workdays until Monday.'"[115]

In the excerpt from her *Atlantic* article, Anne-Marie Slaughter claims that men are not subject to what she labels "the maternal imperative," and seem more likely than women to "choose a job at a cost their family," while women "seem more likely to choose their family at a cost to their job." Do you agree with the implication that this choice may be biologically grounded? Some critics of Slaughter's article argued that she did not see these gender disparities as a problem, rooted in unequal and by no means "imperative" divisions of domestic roles.[116] Is this a fair critique? If so, what should lawyer leaders do to address it, personally and professionally?

Suppose Slaughter and Bazelon had partners or ex-partners who were less supportive and less willing or able to take on a major share of caretaking. Would these men have faced the same degree of criticism as their spouses or ex-spouses if they had put their careers first?

2. Is part of the work/life problem for leaders of their own making? Joe Flomm, the legendary lawyer who built Skadden Arps into a Wall Street powerhouse, was famously unable to take a vacation. As one commentator noted, "[A] part of him was afraid the firm was going to collapse and a part that it wasn't."[117] Flomm is not alone. In many competitive workplaces, "What better way for people to show you just how important they are, how indispensable, than by checking e-mail on the beach."[118] Yet lawyers who prioritize their family can pay a significant price. When Barack Obama was in the state legislature and running for Congress, his daughter got an ear infection while the family was in Hawaii seeing other family over Christmas. His daughter couldn't fly and he chose to remain with his family until she was able to travel. This meant he missed a crucial vote on a crime bill in the legislature, and the *Chicago Tribune* called him one of a "bunch of gutless sheep" who was absent.[119] His main opponent presented him as some kind of high-living lawmaker who'd been on vacation—in Hawaii, no less—and hadn't deigned to come back to vote on something as significant as gun control.[120] Another opponent told a reporter that for him to "use [his] child as an excuse for not going to work shows poorly on the individual's character."[121] If you had been Obama, how would you have handled the issue?

3. Recent research suggests that millennial workers are the most dissatisfied with current policies and that men as well as women say they would take a pay cut, forgo a promotion, or be willing to move jobs to manage work/life demands better. What they most want is flexibility, and its absence is a top reason they change jobs.[122] Yet surveys also find that one in six report negative consequences for adopting a flexible schedule.[123] Legal workplaces do not appear to be an exception.[124] Why? How can their resistance be addressed? Common proposals are to ensure that parental leave policies are gender neutral, to prevent penalties for those who adopt for reduced and flexible schedules, and to make it easier for individuals who temporarily opt off the fast track to opt back on.[125] What other strategies would you propose?

PROBLEM 8-4

You are a lawyer who co-directs the Energy Program for the Natural Resources Defense Council, one of the world's leading environmental public-interest organizations. For much of the last two years, you have been working to secure passage of major energy conservation legislation in California that would serve as a model for the nation and the international community. Negotiations over the bill's content are likely to continue at a frenetic pace during the final weeks of the summer legislative session. You are leading a fragile coalition of consumer and environmental organizations, which is negotiating with industry representatives, state legislators from both parties, and officials from the governor's office.

You also are facing major difficulties on the family front. For years, your elderly and ailing mother-in-law has attempted to arrange a family reunion at her remote summer home in upper Wisconsin. Until now you have resisted, because the home is difficult to reach, and a long weekend requires a day of travel on each end. But your mother-in-law's health—both physical and mental—is declining, and you agreed a year ago to make a trip in mid-August when your sister-in-law could get vacation time.

It now turns out that the weekend you chose is the worst possible one in terms of your work obligations. It coincides with the final days of the legislative session, and no one from your office believes that you are expendable. You are the only one who knows all the major players. Your principal staff on the project—a female attorney and a female scientist—are extremely gifted, but also relatively young and inexperienced, and lack your substantive knowledge, credibility, and contacts. Neither they, nor the female president of the organization, believe that you should take your vacation as planned. Although they are all extremely sensitive to work/family issues, the public's stake in this legislation seems too important to be sacrificed.

Your wife and her family see the issue differently. Your mother-in-law simply does not get it, and her growing dementia makes rational discussion impossible. Your sister-in-law is sympathetic, but she is struggling to cope with her own work and family conflicts and cannot shift the vacation. As a single mother and partner in a major Chicago firm, it is all she can do to carve out a short stint in Wisconsin, and it is too late to reschedule for a different time. Your wife, also a lawyer, is equally empathetic, but equally insistent that you come. She is unwilling to make the trip without you. She believes that the reunion means a great deal to everyone and that her 85-year-old mother might not be physically or mentally able to make the trip next summer. As spouses go, yours has been fairly understanding of your sweatshop work hours in recent years. Now she refuses to believe that the fate of global warming depends on your presence in Sacramento on this particular August weekend.

Your family's summer home does not have good cell phone reception. Nor is it clear that you can effectively oversee negotiations without actually being there or without angering your family. What is clear is that whatever decision you make, you are likely to hear about the fallout for the foreseeable future.

Divide into groups and assign members various roles: the male energy program director, his female staff, his wife, and other members of his coalition. After arguments by all the stakeholders, the director should make a decision and be prepared to defend it.

MEDIA RESOURCES

Alice Eagly, a Northwestern professor and expert on women in leadership, explains why the term "glass ceiling" is misleading.[126] A recent study shows that Supreme Court Justices interrupt their female colleagues three times more often than their male colleagues.[127] A scene from the 2012 Republican debates features Michele Bachman pouring water for the male candidates, unconsciously highlighting gender stereotypes.[128] An interview with Secretary of State Madeleine Albright sexplores the gender barriers she confronted.[129] In "Mansplaining to Hillary Clinton," Jimmy Kimmel offers public speaking advice to Clinton that highlights gender stereotypes.[130] A TED Talk by Sheryl Sandberg, COO of Facebook and author of *Lean In*, highlights hurdles for aspiring female leaders and strategies for addressing them.[131] *Saturday Night Live*'s widely circulated parody of a dialogue between Hillary Clinton and Sarah Palin, featuring Amy Pohler and Tina Fey, exposes some classic gender stereotypes.[132] An episode from Season three of *Scandal* features sex stereotypes in an interview of a presidential candidate and a response of questionable effectiveness.[133] The film, *Equity*, raises a number of issues about ambition and bias for women leaders on Wall Street and in federal prosecutors' offices. An interview with Madeleine Albright on women and leadership, and discussion of Margaret Thatcher's reputation as the "iron lady" highlights gender differences in leadership style.[134]

Examples of gender stereotypes are in ample supply in major films and television series. Scenes of abrasive women and work family conflicts are available in *The Devil Wears Prada, The Proposal, Legally Blonde, Veep, The Good Wife*, and *Madame Secretary*. David Letterman also had an interesting exchange with *Vogue* editor Anna Wintour, about her reputation as an "ice queen," which reportedly inspired Meryl Streep's character in *The Devil Wears Prada*. A scene from *Erin Brockovich* shows the ways in which children punish mothers for working late; and excerpts from *Imagine That* show Eddie Murphy as a divorced executive trying to fit childcare into his overscheduled life. *I Am Sam* features a large firm attorney who botches her work/life balance. A National Public Radio interview of Jon Stewart by Terry Gross also includes a semiserious account of his efforts to balance a demanding job with parenting two small children.[135] In the wake of #MeToo, the second season of *The Good Fight* features a segment, "The One About the Recent Troubles," in which law firm partners consider how to handle revelations that the firm's founder and revered civil rights crusader had sexually assaulted and harassed members of the office staff.

E. RACE, ETHNICITY, AND SEXUAL ORIENTATION

Diversity initiatives targeting race, ethnicity, and sexual orientation are grounded in the case for diversity noted at the outset of the chapter. One objective is to counteract the unconscious biases that restrict equal opportunity in the workplace and to ensure the full utilization of the nation's talent. A second is to expand the effectiveness of leadership by ensuring a broad range of perspectives and experiences among those who exercise it. A third is to ensure the legitimacy and responsiveness of powerful institutions in an increasingly multicultural society. A fourth is to create leaders who can serve as role models and use their influence to combat bias. A fifth is to respond to stakeholders—clients, potential recruits, employees, and the public—who expect legal employers to reflect the diversity of the society they serve. Whether diversity also improves short-term financial performance has been subject to debate.[136] But the growing consensus is that diversity promotes important social and organizational goals regardless of whether they can be readily quantified in terms of immediate economic gain.

The readings below explore the challenges to achieving diversity and inclusion for lawyers of color and LGBTQ attorneys. The materials focus primarily on race and ethnicity because relatively little research is available concerning leadership barriers and initiatives focused on sexual orientation. What the discussion highlights is a central irony: Although lawyers have been at the forefront of this nation's struggle for racial justice, their own workplaces have lagged behind, and typify the problem in many public- and private-sector organizations.

**Vault/MCCA Law Firm Diversity Survey
2018, Executive Summary**

For more than a decade, Vault and the Minority Corporate Counsel Association (MCCA) have worked with law firms across the country to collect information about their diversity and inclusion initiatives, including detailed demographic breakdowns of law firm populations by race/ethnicity, gender, sexual orientation, and disability status.

Key Findings

The latest Vault/MCCA survey results reflect a continuation of many of the trends observed over the last several years:

- Law firms are bringing in more people of color but are less successful at retaining them.[1]

- Despite some gains for minority lawyers as a whole, progress remains uneven among different racial/ethnic groups.

- More women are advancing into partnership and leadership roles, but minority women enjoy fewer of these successes than their white colleagues.

- Even with the progress recorded over the last decade, especially among associates, demographic changes have been slow to trickle upward, as law firm partners remain overwhelmingly white and male.

Minority Representation Continues to Grow

- Nearly 17 percent of law firm attorneys are members of a racial or ethnic minority group. This figure, which is almost a percentage point higher than last year, continues a steady upward trend. Among new attorneys hired in 2017, 26 percent were people of color, and approximately 32 percent of the 2017 summer class were minorities.

- Minority attorneys now represent more than 9 percent of law firm partners, the highest figure to date. Nevertheless, minority lawyers remain significantly underrepresented in law firm partnerships. One in four law firm associates is a member of a racial/ethnic minority group, but only one in ten partners is a person of color.

- Racial minorities also represent a disproportionate share of the lawyers who leave their firms. While we might expect attrition to decline as firms step up efforts to foster more diverse and inclusive environments, the data reveals the opposite. Minority lawyers represented 22 percent of the attorneys who left their firms in 2017. That figure is higher than previous

---

[1] *For the purposes of this report, the terms "minority" and "person of color" refer to individuals identifying with one or more of the following racial/ethnic groups: African American/Black, Hispanic/Latinx, Asian American, Alaska Native/American Indian, Native Hawaiian/Pacific Islander, and Multiracial.*

years, even during the peak of the recession when minorities were hit particularly hard by firm layoffs. . . .

Less Progress for Women of Color

- Roughly one in four women at surveyed law firms is a member of a racial/ethnic minority group. Minority women are being hired in greater numbers than minority men and make up a larger share of the associate population. Women of color represent 14 percent of associates, compared to 11 percent for men.

- But as they progress up the ranks, minority women face both a gender gap and a racial divide: law firm data shows that women of color are far less likely to be partners than either minority men or their white colleagues of either gender. Retention also remains a significant concern. While the number of white women leaving firms has declined over the last several years, departures among minority women continues to climb. In 2010, 10 percent of lawyers who left their firms were minority women; in 2017, that number was closer to 12 percent.

Results Vary among Minority Groups

- Last year's report highlighted some of the differences in progress among individual racial/ethnic minority groups, trends that have largely continued in this year's survey.

- Although Asian Americans represent the single largest racial minority group in law firms, the number of Asians serving as partners or in leadership roles remains disproportionately low. Asian attorneys represent 12 percent of associates but less than 4 percent of partners. Fewer Asians serve on management or executive committees than either African American/Black or Hispanic/Latinx attorneys, even though there are more Asian attorneys than African American/Black and Hispanic/Latinx lawyers combined. That said, the number of Asians promoted or hired into law firm partnerships has steadily grown at a greater rate than other minority groups.

- The number of Hispanic/Latinx attorneys in law firms has slowly but steadily risen over the last decade, and they now represent 5 percent of law firm associates and almost 3 percent of partners. But the latest survey results also show an uptick in the number of Hispanic/Latinx lawyers leaving their firms. Hispanic/Latinx attorneys have generally represented about 4 percent of attorney departures, but in 2017 that number approached 5 percent. Among associates, the figure climbed to 6 percent.

- Progress for African American/Black lawyers has been the most elusive, as their hiring remains below pre-recession levels. African American/Black lawyers have represented about 3 percent of law firm attorneys for nearly a decade. Moreover, departures among African American/Black lawyers continue to outpace those of other minority groups. But one positive sign in the latest results is that almost 8 percent of summer associates at surveyed law firms last year were African American/Black—the highest number to date. And among new attorneys hired, the percentage of African American/Black lawyers limbed over 5 percent for the first time since 2008.

- Among other racial minority groups for which the Vault/MCCA survey collects data, Multiracial lawyers (individuals who identify as two or more races) are the largest, representing just under 2 percent of law firm attorneys. Alaska Natives and American Indians represent less than 0.2 percent of the more than 100,000 attorneys at surveyed law firms, while just 0.08 percent are Native Hawaiians or other Pacific Islanders.

LGBTQ Attorneys...

The numbers reported for openly gay, lesbian, bisexual, and transgender attorneys at law firms continue to grow, as do the number of firms that provide LGBTQ data. The vast majority of law firms surveyed in 2018—94 percent—reported at least some information for LGBTQ attorneys. According to the latest survey results, openly LGBTQ lawyers represent almost 3 percent of law firm attorneys, the highest figure reported to date.

NOTES AND QUESTIONS

A variety of studies suggest that some of the disparities reflected in the Vault/MCCA report reflect unconscious bias. One study involved adult volunteers who evaluated Asian-American and white male attorneys' performance at simulated depositions. All of the volunteers heard the same recording of the deposition, but at the beginning they were shown photographs and names of the fictitious attorneys taking the depositions. Half the volunteers saw a white attorney named William Cole, and half saw an Asian-American attorney named Sung Chang. After listening to the deposition, participants rated the deposition performance. Individuals who claimed that they themselves did not hold racial stereotypes about the ideal litigator but thought that most Americans held those stereotypes, gave lower ratings of competence and likeability to the Asian-American litigator than the ratings given to the white litigator, and individuals were less willing to hire Sung Chang or recommend him to friends and family.[137]

In another study, a consulting firm inserted 22 errors in a legal memo, ranging from minor spelling and grammatical errors, to errors of fact and analysis. Sixty law firm partners received copies of the memos, which they were told was a "writing analysis study." Half the partners were told that the author was an African American named Thomas Meyer; the other half were told that that the writer was a white man named Thomas Meyer. The reviewers gave the memo attributed to the white man a rating of 4.1 on a scale of 5, and a rating to the African American of 3.2. While the white man received praise for his potential and analytical skills, the African American was said to be average at best and in need of "lots of work."[138]

Such unconscious bias may help account for the findings of a third study that followed the career trajectories of black lawyers in law firms. It documented the higher attrition among these lawyers at every stage on the path to partnership and found that among those displaced by law firm dissolutions, white partners had the least difficulty gaining new employment and black associates the most.[139]

Comparable data on barriers for LBTQ lawyers is lacking, but some fragmentary evidence suggests that obstacles persist, particularly outside major metropolitan areas. According to the most recent NALP figures, about 3 percent of lawyers in the U.S. identify as LGBT, a figure slightly lower than in the nation's total adult population, which is estimated at 4.5 percent.[140] As the Deputy Program Officer of the National LGBT Bar Association and Foundation notes, even workplaces "with a culture of inclusivity can have hiring partners on staff who are homophobic or transphobic."[141] Anecdotal accounts suggest that obstacles may be particularly pronounced for transgender attorneys and LGBTQ lawyers of color, and greatest when they are seeking leadership positions.[142]

In 2016, the American Bar Association House of Delegates passed Resolution 113, which urges all providers of legal services "to expand and create opportunities at all levels of responsibility for diverse attorneys." The Resolution further urges corporate clients to support this effort by directing a "greater percentage of the legal services they purchase, both currently and in the future, to diverse attorneys." To support this Resolution, some two dozen general counsel from prominent companies sent a letter to all of the Fortune 1000 general counsel. It asked that they require their outside counsel to complete a standard ABA diversity survey, and that they use the information obtained in deciding which firms to retain or terminate. How much difference this pressure will make is not entirely clear, as reflected in the notes following Problem 8-2.

In 2016, the ABA also adopted a new subsection to Rule 8.4. As amended, Rule 8.4(g) provides that:

> It is professional misconduct for a lawyer to . . . (g) engage in conduct that the lawyer knows or reasonably should know is harassment or discrimination on the basis of race, sex, religion, national origin, ethnicity, disability, age, sexual orientation, gender identity, marital status, or socioeconomic status in conduct related to the practice of law. This paragraph does not limit the ability of a lawyer to accept, decline, or withdraw from a representation.

As this book went to press, only two jurisdictions had adopted that proposed rule, although about half already had some anti-discriminatory language in their rules or comments.[143] The new Rule 8.4(g) has been controversial, and critics claim that it would restrict free expression and "turn ordinary employment disputes into disciplinary matters."[144] Other commentators argue that the proposed provision is likely to have little effect. As they note, disciplinary action is rare in states with professional rules that already prohibit discrimination.[145] One reason, critics suggest, is that the rules do not include prohibitions against retaliation.[146] Another is that most of the barriers to full equality for groups singled out by the Rule have little to do with the kinds of explicit bias that it targets. Rather, the problems involve structural discrimination, unconscious bias, in-group favoritism, and unresponsiveness to work/life conflicts.[147] Some commentators prefer an aspirational provision to Rule 8.4(g) on the theory that this alternative would remove the constitutional problem while serving an "expressive function" that could shame offenders.[148]

To address the broader problems that anti-discrimination provisions target, the American Bar Association's Presidential Initiative Commission on Diversity, the ABA's Commission on Racial and Ethnic Diversity in the Legal Profession, and other experts in the field, have issued a broad set of recommendations. They focus on increasing accountability and racial comfort, and challenging racial bias.[149] For example, employers should intensify their efforts in hiring, retaining, and promoting lawyers of color. In particular, employers should reassess evaluation procedures and criteria that have a disproportionate racial impact. Recruiters should make greater contact with law schools that have substantial minority enrollments, either through on-site interviews or letters to minority student associations and visits to regional minority placement conferences. Hiring standards should avoid excessive reliance on first-year grades, LSAT scores, and law review experience, which disproportionately exclude students of color and do not measure the full range of skills that are necessary for successful practice. Promotion criteria such as collegiality and ability to attract client business need to take into account the special obstacles facing lawyers of color. Evaluations should be evidence-based, and include specific criteria for improvement.[150] Employers should also ensure a favorable working environment for underrepresented groups. Providing adequate mentoring, sponsorship, and opportunities for challenging assignments, supervisory experiences, and client contact should be key priorities.[151]

LGBTQ organizations have proposed a similar agenda aimed to help their members. Their recommendations include mentoring, affinity groups, and training focused on the needs of LGBTQ lawyers, as well as representation of these attorneys at leadership levels, pro bono work around issues of sexual orientation, and monitoring of initiatives to ensure that they are in fact securing an inclusive culture.[152]

National, state, and local bar organizations have also attempted to expand access to the bar by underrepresented groups. Strategies have included increased outreach to minority high school and college students, greater financial assistance for low-income law school applicants, and more educational preparation programs by groups like the Council on Legal Educational Opportunities.

1. Is this agenda sufficient? What stands in its way? What strategies are most critical? Are there others that you would propose?

2. If you were a state Supreme Court Justice, would you support Model Rule 8.4(g) or an aspirational provision?

3. At a reception for law students of color, an African-American woman asked former U.S. Attorney Preet Bharara what minorities could do to overcome discrimination in the legal profession. He responded, "The best way to overcome anything is to work really, really hard. You can overcome prejudice by sheer excellence of work."[153] If you had been present at the event, how would you have responded?

4. Many commentators were critical of then President-elect Donald Trump's choice of Ben Carson for his Secretary of Housing and Urban Development, because the neurosurgeon's only obvious qualifications for the position were that he was black and had once lived in public housing. In commenting on that appointment, and the problem of tokenism more generally, one *New York Times* commentator wrote:

   How do you know when you're being used as an excuse? How can you tell the difference between a new employer who is making earnest steps toward diversity and one who is just trying to cover himself? What about the times when you know it's the latter but want the spot, or need it, or tell yourself that being successful in it will crack the door wider for the next person? How do you prove that you belong? *Can you?*[154]

   How would you respond?

5. Although most discussions of diversity generalize about the "minority" experience, that experience varies significantly within and across racial and ethnic groups, as the Vault/MCCA survey reflects. For example, Asian-American women confront different stereotypes than African-American men. In a recent large-scale study of Asian-American lawyers, half reported that they sometimes or often experienced implicit discrimination, frequently due to stereotypes that they were "worker bees" who lacked "gravitas" and "leadership potential."[155] These stereotypes converge with gender stereotypes, which compounds barriers for Asian American women. So too, even within particular racial or ethnic groups, first-generation immigrants from low-income communities face different challenges than counterparts coming from privileged economic backgrounds. Experiences also vary according to particular sectors of the profession. For example, law firms are a particularly challenging environment for women of color, who have long been the most underrepresented group at partnership levels.[156] And about half of LGBT lawyers in firms are in just four cities: New York, Washington, D.C., Los Angeles, and San Francisco. Outside of those cities, the challenges are

considerably greater. How can diversity initiatives take account of these variations?

6. If you were the general counsel of a large corporation, what role would diversity play in your allocation of business to outside law firms?

7. If you were the managing partner of a prominent law firm, what strategies would you propose to address diversity issues? How would you deal with "diversity fatigue," which experts describe as arising when people "get sick of it because we have to keep saying it because they are not [achieving] it"?[157] How would you respond to situations such as the one described in Problem 8-5 below?

PROBLEM 8-5[158]

Paul Barrett's profile *The Good Black* provides a case history of the profession's difficulties in addressing diversity-related issues. It chronicles the efforts of Lawrence Mungen, an African-American graduate of Harvard College and Harvard Law School, to fit the model that Barrett's title invokes. As a senior associate, Mungen joined the Washington, D.C., branch office of a Chicago law firm, Katten, Muchen and Zavis, and attempted to "play by the rules." After being hired to do complex bankruptcy work in an office that generated too little of it, he fell through the cracks, and landed off the partnership track. But until late in the process, Mungen failed to complain or to raise race-related concerns. He did not want to be typecast as the "angry black." Nor did he take responsibility for supporting or mentoring any of the small number of other minority lawyers at the firm. When his difficulty in obtaining work became clear, some partners made a few well-meaning but ineffectual responses. They slashed his billing rate, which enabled him to take over some routine matters, but also undermined his reputation as someone capable of demanding partnership-caliber work. Although the senior partners eventually offered to relocate him to another office, they did not provide assurances of opportunities that would lead to promotion to partner. He sued for race discrimination and alleged multiple examples, such as the firm's failure to provide formal evaluations, informal mentoring, invitations to client meetings, and help with business development. A largely black District of Columbia jury found in his favor, but a divided appellate panel reversed. Unable to find another comparable position, Mungen made do with temporary, low-level assignments at other firms and, by the end of the book, was contemplating an alternative career.

As many commentators have noted, the case was a kind of "racial Rorschach test" in which observers saw what they expected to see. To lawyers in the firm and sympathizers outside it, including the appellate court, this was a morality play in which no good deed went unpunished. From their perspective, Mungen was treated no worse than white associates, and in some respects considerably better. The slights and oversights that he alleged at trial were "business as usual mismanagement." And the extra efforts that the firm made to keep Mungen were evidence of a commitment to equal opportunity. By contrast, critics, including Barrett, saw this as a textbook case of "reckless indifferent affirmative action."

From their vantage, the firm's efforts were too little, too late. Unsurprisingly, these competing perceptions usually divided along racial lines and typified attitudes within the profession generally. In an ABA survey around the time, only 8 percent of black lawyers, but 41 percent of whites, believed that firms had a genuine commitment to diversity.[159]

Much, of course, depends on what counts as commitment. Katten's management, like that at many firms, undoubtedly did want lawyers of color to succeed. Even from a purely pragmatic standpoint, it helps in recruitment and business development if a firm includes more than the single black lawyer that Katten's Washington office had during Mungen's employment. But while many attorneys want to achieve greater diversity, they do not necessarily want to rethink the structures that get in the way.

1. If you had been managing partner at Katten, what would you have done when Mungen's problems surfaced? Would you have settled his lawsuit? What would you have done after the litigation ended?

2. Psychologist Claude Steele and colleagues have extensively documented a dynamic that they label "stereotype threat." Racial and ethnic minorities underperform in circumstances in which they believe that their performance will be taken as evidence of their abilities and in which members of their group are stereotyped as less proficient.[160] Could this dynamic play out in law firms? How might racial stereotypes have affected Lawrence Mungen's performance?

3. One problem for lawyers of color lies in getting candid critical feedback from mentors who are worried about how it will be received and about seeming racist. This "protective hesitation" often prevents aspiring leaders from developing necessary skills.[161] So too, Robin DiAngelo argues that white Americans' failure to understand systemic racism is often what allows them to perpetuate it. She coins the term "white fragility" to describe the defensive reaction of many white people to suggestions that they hold racial biases or are unintentionally influenced by racial stereotypes.[162] She argues that they need to move beyond surface-level initiatives aimed at being respectful and colorblind: "Niceness will not get racism on the table and will not keep it on the table when everyone wants it off."[163] She advises that people should give candid feedback immediately and privately and ensure that the person on the receiving end feels safe.

    What can organizations do to promote effective feedback? Is training mentors in effective performance evaluations enough?

4. How should leaders respond to concerns of white men who are preempted from certain work because of clients' commitments concerning diversity? In a letter to the editor of the *National Law Journal*, a self-described "young, white straight male attorney who happens to be politically progressive" protested employment-termination decisions attributable to "meeting an important client's newly asserted diversity demands."[164] From his perspective, "surely firing people even partially on the basis of an immutable characteristic is as

unjust when done in the name of increasing diversity as it is when done to maintain homogeneity."[165] Do you agree? If not, how would you respond?

5. In his account of "covering" by sexual, racial, and ethnic minorities, New York University law professor Kenji Yoshino details the pressure that these individuals feel to suppress aspects of their identity to fit in the dominant culture. Some self-help advice to aspiring leaders is to avoid "anything that might be perceived as ethnic,"—everything from Afro hairstyles to clothing that has "Hispanic associations."[166] Yoshino argues that such advice mischaracterizes the problem and the solution. In his view, the answer is for the culture to become more tolerant, not for minorities to become more mainstream. Minority professionals should feel "emboldened" to challenge conformist pressures in the "everyday places where tolerance is made and unmade."[167] Is that the advice you would provide? How would you respond to lawyers of color who feel that that they are "walking into a sea of whiteness" and simply don't want to stand out.[168] What can leaders of organizations do to encourage a more inclusive culture?

6. How can lawyers of color cope with race-related challenges in leadership contexts? For example, Barack Obama and Cory Booker have met with claims that they were "too black" or "not black enough."[169] When Booker first ran for mayor of Newark, he lost to a black opponent who styled himself the "Real Deal" and told Booker, "You have to learn to be an African American, and we don't have time to train you."[170] As politicians of color have learned, minimizing racial identity can maximize leaders' appeal and avoid white backlash, but it can also alienate core supporters and depress voter turnout in communities of color. How can lawyers of color navigate these tradeoffs? One commentator has suggested that these are problems that the public, rather than leaders, needs to solve: There is no "'correct or legitimate way of doing blackness.' Anyone claiming otherwise or handing out honorary Black cards to those who pass muster are part of the problem they claim to want to solve or don't see."[171] Do you agree? If so, what implications does it have for leaders running a political campaign? Preet Bharara, the former U.S. Attorney for the Southern District of New York, has recalled the vitriol he experienced when prosecuting defendants of a similar ethnic background. Dinesh D'Souza, a prominent conservative commentator who pled guilty to campaign finance violations, took every opportunity to accuse Bharara of bias, tweeting, "KARMA IS A BITCH DEPT: @PreetBharara wanted to destroy a fellow Indian American to advance his career."[172] Another case involving prosecution of an Indian diplomat for visa fraud and unfair labor practices unleashed an avalanche of criticism against Bharara by Indian journalists; they claimed he was betraying his roots in order to curry favor with his "white masters." His actual superiors, as Bharara pointed out, were Eric Holder and Barack Obama.[173] When is humor the best response to such slurs? What other strategies are effective?

PROBLEM 8-6[174]

1. Brianna is an African-American managing partner of a midsize, largely white law firm. Her predecessor Jay, one of the firm's founding partners, remains a close advisor, but his "autocratic style rubs Brianna the wrong way." The problem came to a head during a meeting in which Jay told her that she was being "too aggressive" and needed to "'lighten up' on her push to market more vigorously to clients of color." To Brianna, it seemed as if Jay had trouble dealing with the authority of a strong black woman.[175]

   Two friends with whom Brianna discussed Jay's behavior agreed with her interpretation, but didn't have advice about finding a way to work with him. A former professor and mentor suggested that Brianna approach Jay as if he had her best interests at heart, and see whether that seemed correct after their conversation. Pursuing that advice, Brianna found that Jay had doubts about the firm's ability to connect with clients of color, in part because he had doubts about his own ability to do so. He also had never considered that she had "any anxiety about anything. . . . [S]he had always struck him as confidence personified." The candid conversation helped both parties understand each others' concerns and gave Brianna a better sense of how to connect with team members in a way that would avoid inhibiting candid criticism.

   In a *Harvard Business Review* article on which this problem is modeled, professors Robin Ely, Debra Meyerson, and Martin Davidson suggest that Brianna's "investment in being seen as a powerful black woman had gotten in the way of actually being a powerful black woman."[176] Is this a fair way of stating the problem?

2. After a male supervising attorney told a gifted African-American woman lawyer that she had an "attitude problem," she presented him with commentary discussing how often African Americans are subject to that critique. She also said she recognized that she had "room to improve," and requested that he be more specific in his feedback. After that exchange, their relationship improved and he acknowledged that her response had been really helpful. The two leadership coaches who recounted this incident concluded that women and people of color should note that even if a degree of bias is involved in discussions with supervisors, "you are still being given information. It is important to remember that ... key stakeholders' perceptions are real to them. Focusing only or even primarily on what's wrong with whoever gives the feedback is rarely the most effective route for reaching the next level of success. Instead, it can become a subtle form of blaming the messenger, which is a good way to keep yourself unproductively stuck."[177]

   Do you agree? What would you have done in the African-American attorney's place? Would her strategy have worked for the woman described earlier whose supervisors told her that she had "sharp elbows?" What if the response to bias that will most help the individual target is not the one what will produce the most organizational change?

NOTES AND QUESTIONS

1. Ely, Meyerson, and Davidson also describe coping strategies for circumstances such as the one described above. These situations, often termed "identity abrasions," are ones in which individuals believe that they have been targets of bias or unfair accusations of bias. These contexts often breed resentment, conflict, and mistrust. Ely, Meyerson, and Davidson generalize five principles that can guide leaders in navigating such contexts and those involving racial, ethnic, and cultural differences more generally:

   - *Pause* to short-circuit the emotion and reflect.
   - *Connect* with others in ways that affirm the importance of relationships.
   - *Question yourself* to help identify your blind spots and discover what makes you defensive.
   - *Get genuine support* that doesn't necessarily validate your point of view but, rather, helps you gain a broader perspective.
   - *Shift your mind set* from "*You* need to change" to "What can *I* change?"[178]

   Other commentators suggest similar strategies in discussing bias. One strategy is to defuse defensiveness by separating "the act from the actor" and avoiding attributions of conscious racism. It is also helpful to ask for advice in how to address the issue, provide options for responses, and stress the positive consequences of identifying remedies.[179]

   Leaders can also foster a climate for such dynamics by creating safe spaces for dialogue and visibly modeling these strategies in their own behavior. Ely, Meyerson, and Davidson note that

   > the most difficult—and rewarding [principle] is that of questioning oneself. This principle is challenging . . . because it runs counter to the image of the confident, decisive leader. As it turns out, however, leaders who question themselves and learn from others in the service of clear goals do not bespeak a lack of confidence; rather, they demonstrate humility, clarity, and strength. Indeed, the leaders we have observed who exemplify this principle generate fierce respect and loyalty from their followers. They model vulnerability, respond nondefensively to questions and challenges, are aware of their own biases and emotional triggers, demonstrate resilience in the face of identity abrasions, and openly rely on others to test the validity of their perspective. . . .[180]

2. After reflecting on Problem 8-6, the class should break up into teams and construct an "identity abrasion," built on personal experience or a scene from film, literature, or current events. Teams should assign roles and attempt to apply the principles set forth above. Team members should then evaluate their

responses. What challenges did they confront? What might they have done better?

MEDIA RESOURCES

A documentary *What Would You Do?* offers a compelling profile of unconscious bias by onlookers who respond quite differently to a scene of a possible bicycle theft depending on the race and gender of the presumed thief.[181] In a scene from the series *Scandal,* the star crisis management consultant Olivia Pope gets a lecture from her father about how blacks need to work twice as hard to get half as much.[182] For examples of pressures for conformity on professionals of color, see *Hollywood Shuffle,* in which Robert Townsend describes techniques that enable actors to conform to racist stereotypes, and *Strictly Business,* in which a black business executive explains to a black mail room clerk why he needs to act "less black" in order to get a promotion. For an example of "benign" stereotyping, Joe Biden's description of Obama is also available.[183] A scene from *LA Law* portrays the firm's managing partner explaining to a black associate why he has been assigned to help defend a case that will pit him against the black community. The partner points out that the community is not one of the firm's clients. Clips from Barack Obama's 2004 speech at the Democratic National Convention, together with commentary by experts in the field, offer an example of a masterful way of building differences and building alliances across racial, ethnic, and ideological divides.[184]

END NOTES

---

[1] Intersectional approaches start from the premise that different identities overlap or combine to contribute to unique experiences of disadvantage and privilege. *See* Association for Women's Rights in Development (AWID), *Intersectionality: A Tool for Gender and Economic Justice,* 9 WOMEN'S RIGHTS, & ECON. CHANGE 1 (Aug. 2004).

[2] KARIN KLENKE, WOMEN AND LEADERSHIP: A CONTEXTUAL PERSPECTIVE 27 (1996).

[3] 42 U.S.C. §2000. For a history, see Erin Kelly & Frank Dobbin, *How Affirmative Action Became Diversity Management,* 41 AM. BEHAV. SCIENTIST 960, 963-64 (1998).

[4] For law school enrollment, see NALP, CLASS OF 2017 NATIONAL SUMMARY REPORT (2018). For the profession and law firms, see VAULT, MCCA, VAULT-MCCA LAW FIRM DIVERSITY SURVEY REPORT (2018); ABA NATIONAL LAWYER POPULATION SURVEY (2019).

[5] NALP, REPORT ON DIVERSITY IN U.S. LAW FIRMS (Jan. 2019).

[6] VAULT, MCCA, VAULT-MCCA LAW FIRM DIVERSITY SURVEY REPORT (2018).

[7] U.S. BUREAU OF LABOR STATISTICS, LABOR FORCE STATISTICS FROM THE CURRENT POPULATION SURVEY Table 11 (2019).

[8] VAULT, MCCA, VAULT-MCCA LAW FIRM DIVERSITY SURVEY REPORT (2018).

[9] For women in law firm leadership, see Mark A. Cohen, *Why Does the Gender Wage Gap Persist in Law?,* LAW.COM (Apr. 3, 2018), https://www.law.com/2018/04/03/why-

does-the-gender-wage-gap-persist-in-law/; Marc Brodherson, Laura McGee & Mariana Pires dos Reis, *Women in Law Firms,* MCKINSEY & CO. 2 (2017);. See also DEBORAH L. RHODE, WOMEN AND LEADERSHIP 77 (2017); Madeline Shi, *USA: Survey Shows Women Still Underrepresented in Senior Roles in Law Firms,* BUS. INSIDER (FR.) (Oct. 22, 2018); https://www.alm.com/intelligence/who-we-are/ (a business advisory consulting group whose fourteen-person board contains only three women). For women in litigation, see research summarized in Lara Bazelon, *What it Takes to Be a Trial Lawyer If You're Not a Man,* THE ATLANTIC (Sept. 2018) (citing New York Bar Association findings that women accounted for only a quarter of trial lawyers and a fifth of lead counsel in large multiparty cases); Lynne Hermle, *I Defended Kleiner in the Ellen Pao Case—Here's Why We Need More Women Leading Trials,* BUS. INSIDER (Sept. 12, 2017), http://www.businessinsider.com/i-defended-kleiner-in-the-ellen-pao-casde-2017-9_(citing study of federal cases in which only a fifth of lead counsel were female).

[10] RHODE, WOMEN AND LEADERSHIP.

[11] BUILDING MOVEMENT PROJECT, RACE TO LEAD: CONFRONTING THE RACIAL LEADERSHIP GAP (2018); LEADING WITH INTENT: BOARDSOURCE INDEX OF NONPROFIT BOARD PRACTICES (2017).

[12] RACE TO LEAD: WOMEN OF COLOR IN THE NONPROFIT SECTOR, February 6, 2019, https://afpglobal.org/race-lead-women-color-nonprofit-sector.

[13] Noam Scheiber & John Eligon, *Elite Law Firm's All-White Partner Class Stirs Debate on Diversity*, N.Y. TIMES, Jan. 27, 2019.

[14] Joe Patrice, *Paul Weiss Press Release Captures Everything Broken About Biglaw In One Image,* ABOVE THE LAW (Dec. 11, 2018), https://abovethelaw.com/2018/12/paul-weiss-press-release-captures-everything-broken-about-biglaw-in-one-image/.

[15] Christine Simmons, *Paul Weiss Vows to "Do Better" After Partner Promotions Stir Diversity Debate*, LAW.COM, Dec. 18, 2018 (quoting Brad Karp).

[16] Simmons, *Paul Weiss* (quoting Karp).

[17] Scheiber & Eligon, *Elite Law Firm's All-White Partner Class.*

[18] Scheiber & Eligon, *Elite Law Firm's All-White Partner Class.*

[19] Miles E. Kuttler, *Letter to the Editor,* N.Y. TIMES, Jan. 31, 2019.

[20] *An Open Letter to Law Firm Partners*, AM. LAW., Mar. 2019, 42.

[21] Don Prophete, *In Response to GCs/Call for Diversity*, AM. LAW., Mar. 2019, 43, 45.

[22] Joe Patrice, *If a Biglaw Firm Falls In The Woods And No One Issues A Press Release About Its Lack of Diversity…,* ABOVE THE LAW, Feb. 20, 2019 (noting Sullivan and Cromwell's failure to follow a longstanding practice of issuing a press release announcing its new partner class).

[23] JOHN STUART MILL, PRINCIPLES OF POLITICAL ECONOMY, quoted in Katherine W. Phillips, *What is the Real Value of Diversity in Organizations? Questioning Our Assumptions,* in SCOTT E. PAGE, THE DIVERSITY BONUS: HOW GREAT TEAMS PAY OFF IN THE KNOWLEDGE ECONOMY 223 (2017).

[24] Donna Chrobot-Mason, Marian N. Ruderman & Lisa H. Nishii, *Leadership in a Diverse Workplace*, in OXFORD HANDBOOK OF LEADERSHIP AND ORGANIZATIONS 698 (David V. Day ed., 2014).

[25] PAGE, DIVERSITY BONUS, 201.

[26] PAGE, DIVERSITY BONUS, 15, 56-64.

[27] PAGE, DIVERSITY BONUS, 133-134.

[28] Phillips, *What is the Real Value of Diversity in Organizations?*, 230.

[29] ADAM GRANT, ORIGINALS: HOW NON-CONFORMISTS MOVE THE World 180-183 (2016).

[30] Phillips, *What is the Real Value of Diversity in Organizations?*, 231-234; David Rock & Heidi Grant, *Why Diverse Teams Are Smarter*, HARV. BUS. REV. (Nov. 2016).

[31] Denise Lewin Loyd et al., *Social Category Diversity Promotes Premeeting Elaboration: The Role of Relationship Focus*, ORG. SCI. 24 (2013): 757-772.

[32] See studies discussed in David B. Wilkins, *From "Separate Is Inherently Unequal" to "Diversity Is Good for Business": The Rise of Market-Based Diversity Arguments and the Fate of the Black Corporate Bar*, 117 HARV. L. REV. 1548, 1588-90 (2004); Douglas E. Brayley & Eric S. Nguyen, *Good Business: A Market-Based Argument for Law Firm Diversity*, 35 J. LEGAL PROF. 1, 7 (2009); Frank Dobbin & Jiwook Jung, *Corporate Board Gender Diversity and Stock Performance: The Competence Gap or Institutional Investor Bias?*, 89 N.C. L. REV. 809 (2011); Susan E. Jackson & Aparna Joshi, *Diversity in Social Context: A Multi-Attribute, Multi-Level Analysis of Team Diversity and Sales Performance*, 25 J. ORG. BEHAV. 675, 676 (2004); Jonathan S. Leonard, David I. Levine & Aparna Joshi, *Do Birds of a Feather Shop Together? The Effects on Performance of Employees' Similarity with One Another and with Customers*, 25 J. ORG. BEHAV. 731 (2004); Katherine Williams Phillips & Charles A. O'Reilly, *Demography and Diversity in Organizations: A Review of 40 Years of Research*, 20 RES. ORG. BEHAV. 77, 94-95 (1998).

[33] PAGE, DIVERSITY BONUS, 42-48.

[34] See studies discussed in Deborah L. Rhode & Amanda K. Packel, *Diversity on Corporate Boards: How Much Difference Does Difference Make?*, 39 DEL. J. CORP. L. 377 (2014), and RHODE, WOMEN AND LEADERSHIP, 113.

[35] Brayley & Nyugen, *Good Business*, at 34; RHODE, WOMEN AND LEADERSHIP, 113; Rhode & Packel, *Diversity on Corporate Board, s*.

[36] HAZEL ROSE MARKUS & PAULA M. L. MOYA , *Doing Race: An Introduction*, in DOING RACE 1, 6-10 (2010).

[37] MINORITY CORPORATE COUNSEL ASSOCIATION (MCCA), SUSTAINING PATHWAYS TO DIVERSITY 16 (2009).

[38] MINORITY CORPORATE COUNSEL ASSOCIATION (MCCA), SUSTAINING PATHWAYS, at 25.

[39] MINORITY CORPORATE COUNSEL ASSOCIATION (MCCA), SUSTAINING PATHWAYS, at 15.

[40] See sources cited in DEBORAH L. RHODE, THE TROUBLE WITH LAWYERS 77-80 (2015); RHODE, WOMEN AND LEADERSHIP, 3-4; Katherine W. Phillips, *How Diversity Makes Us Smarter*, SCI. AMER., Oct. 2014.

[41] RICHARD D. LEWIS, WHEN CULTURE COLLIDE: LEADING ACROSS CULTURES (3d ed. 2005); Shannon Lloyd & Charmine Härtel, *Intercultural Competencies for Culturally Diverse Work Teams*, 25 J. MGMT. PSYCHOL. 846 (2010).

[42] In one survey of GCs and managing partners, loss of business due to diversity failures was extremely rare. Only one firm reported such a sanction. Deborah L. Rhode & Lucy Buford Ricca, *Diversity in the Legal Profession: Perspectives from Managing Partners and General Counsel*, 83 FORDHAM L. REV. 2483, 2497 (2015).

[43] Meghan Tribe, *Inclusion Clause*, AM. LAW., June 2017, at 58, 61, 63; Rhode & Ricca, *Diversity in the Legal Profession*, 2497.

[44] Deborah L. Rhode, *#MeToo: Why Now? What Next?,* DUKE L. REV. (forthcoming 2019).

[45] Leanne Atwater, *The MeToo Backlash,* HARVARD BUSINESS REV., Sept./Oct. 2019.

[46] Carolyn M. Cunningham, Heather M. Crandall & Alexa M. Dare, *Introduction,* in GENDER, COMMUNICATION, AND THE LEADERSHIP Gap, xiii.-xiv (Carolyn M. Cunningham, Heather M. Crandall & Alexa M. Dare eds., 2017).

[47] Sally Helgesen, *Gender, Communication, and the Leadership Gap,* in GENDER, COMMUNICATION, AND THE LEADERSHIP GAP 4 (Carolyn M. Cunningham, Heather M. Crandall & Alexa M. Dare eds., 2017); RON SUSKIND, CONFIDENCE MEN: WALL STREET, WASHINGTON, AND THE EDUCATION OF A PRESIDENT 1 (2012).

[48] Matt Zapotosky, *Loretta Lynch Says Women Face "Risk of Not Being Seen." She Speaks from Experience,* WASH. POST, Sept. 13, 2017 (quoting Lynch).

[49] Matt Pearce, *Trump Calls Clinton "Such a Nasty Woman,"* L.A. Times, Oct. 19, 2016.

[50] Michelle Cottle, *The Era of "The Bitch" is Coming,* ATLANTIC, (Aug. 17, 2016, https://www.theatlantic.com/politics/archive/2016/08/the-era-of-the-bitch-is-coming /496154/;), https://www.theatlantic.com/politics/archive/2016/08/the-era-of-the-bitch-is-coming/496154/; Adele M. Stan, *Ivanka Trump Is Evidence of Her Father's Misogyny,* AM. PROSPECT, (July 22, 2016,), http://prospect.org/article/ivanka-trump-evidence-her-father%E2%80%99s-misogyny; Jill Filipovic, *What's With Hillary's Woman Problem?,* POLITICO MAG. (Sept./Oct. 2016,), http://www.politico.com/magazine/story/2016/09/hillary-clinton-feminism-white-house-2016-women-214217.

[51] Kelly L. McKenzie & Tammy J. Halstead, *Narrowing the Leadership Gap*, in GENDER, COMMUNICATION, AND THE LEADERSHIP GAP 29, 34, 37-38 (Carolyn M. Cunningham, Heather M. Crandall & Alexa M. Dare eds., 2017).

[52] McKenzie & Halstead, Narrowing the Leadership Gap, 39.

[53] SALLY HELGESSEN & MARSHALL GOLDSMITH, HOW WOMEN RISE 35, 37 (2018).

[54] RHODE, WOMEN AND LEADERSHIP 27.

[55] Bazelon, *What it Takes To Be a Trial Lawyer If You're Not a Man*; New York State Bar Association, *If Not Now, When?: Achieving Equality for Women Attorneys in the Courtrooms and in ADR,* N.Y. ST. B. ASSOC. (Nov. 2017).

[56] Via Chen, *It's Time for the Strong Medicine,* AM. LAW, June 2018, 14.

[57] BRODHERSON, MCGEE & DOS REIS, WOMEN IN LAW FIRMS, 6-7.

[58] Frank Dobbin & Alexandra Kalev, *Why Diversity Programs Fail*, HARV. BUS. REV. (July-Aug. 2016).

[59] Cheryl R. Kaiser et al, *Presumed Fair: Ironic Effects of Organizational Diversity Structures*, 104 J. PERS. & SOC. PSYCHOL. 504 (2013).

[60] Dobbin & Kalev, *Why Diversity Programs Fail.*

[61] Stefanie K. Johnson & David R. Hekman, *Women and Minorities Are Penalized for Promoting Diversity*, HARV. BUS. REV. (Mar. 23, 2016).

[62] Rhode & Ricca, *Diversity in the Legal Profession,* 2492-93.

[63] Rhode & Ricca, Diversity in the Legal Profession, 2495.

[64] Rhode & Ricca, *Diversity in the Legal Profession*, 2500.

[65] Rhode & Ricca, *Diversity in the Legal Profession*, 2500.

[66] Rhode & Ricca, *Diversity in the Legal Profession*, 2502-03.

[67] Rhode & Ricca, *Diversity in the Legal Profession*, 2504.

[68] Rhode & Ricca, *Diversity in the Legal Profession*, 2504-05.

[69] Katherine Earle Yanes & Erin G. Jackson, *Women, Leadership and the Law*, FED. LAW, May 2016, at 52-53.

[70] CHAI FELDBLUM & VICTORIA A. LIPNIC, U.S. EQUAL EMPLOYMENT OPPORTUNITY COMMISSION REPORT OF THE CO-CHAIRS OF THE SELECT TASK FORCE ON THE STUDY OF HARASSMENT IN THE WORKPLACE 8, 46-48 (2016). For a recent large-scale survey finding that diversity training produced no measurable behavioral changes in the target population—groups that were not already strongly supportive of women in the workplace—see Edward H. Chang et al., *The Mixed effects of Online Diversity Training*, 116 PROC. NAT'L. ACAD. SCI U.S.A. (PNAS) 7778 (Apr. 16, 2019).

[71] JENNIFER L. EBERHARDT, BIASED: UNCOVERING THE HIDDEN PREJUDICE THAT SHAPES WHAT WE SEE, THINK, AND DO 280 (2019).

[72] See studies reviewed in FELDBLUM & LIPNIC, U.S. EQUAL OPPORTUNITY COMMISSION REPORT. For an example of research finding men's increased knowledge but also increased belief that both parties contribute to harassment, see Shereen G. Bingham & Lisa L. Scherer, *The Unexpected Effects of a Sexual Harassment Educational Program*, 37 J. APPL. BEHAV. SCI. 125 (2001).

[73] See Joanne Lipman, *How Diversity Training Infuriates Men and Fails Women*, TIME, Jan. 25, 2018; Susan Bisom-Rapp, *An Ounce of Prevention Is a Poor Substitute for a Pound of Cure: Confronting the Developing Jurisprudence of Education and Prevention in Employment Discrimination Law*, 22 BERKELEY J. EMP. & LAB. L. 37-38 (2001).

[74] See Feldblum & Lipnic, 52; Joelle Emerson, *Don't Give Up on Unconscious Bias Training—Make it Better*, HARV. BUS. REV. (Apr. 2017).

[75] Avivah Wittenberg–Cox, *Reframe Diversity by Teaching Inclusivity to All*, in HARV. BUS. REV., HBR GUIDE FOR WOMEN AT WORK 197-199 (2018).

[76] Terry R. Bacon, ADAPTIVE COACHING: THE ART AND PRACTICE OF A CLIENT-CENTERED APPROACH TO PERFORMANCE IMPROVEMENT 240-41 (2003).

[77] Bacon, ADAPTIVE COACHING, at 244.

[78] Claire Cain Miller, *Women Did Everything Right. Then Work Got "Greedy."*, N.Y. TIMES, Apr. 26, 2019.

[79] Miller, *Women Did Everything Right*.

[80] Miller, *Women Did Everything Right (*quoting Nicholas Bloom).

[81] SHERYL SANDBERG WITH NELL SCOVELL, LEAN IN: WOMEN, WORK, AND THE WILL TO LEAD (2013).

[82] SANDBERG WITH SCOVELL, LEAN IN, 8-9.

[83] Jack Zenger & Joseph Folkman, *Research: Women Score Higher than Men In Most Leadership Skills*, HARV. BUS. REV. (June 25, 2019).

[84] Juliet Aiken, Lori Berman & Heather Bock, *Accelerating Lawyer Success: How to Make Partner, Stay Healthy, and Flourish in a Law Firm* (2016), discussed in Lori Berman, Heather Bock & Juliet Aiken, *Data-Driven Answers to Accelerate Success for Women*, 101 WOMEN L. J. 18 (2016).

[85] MEGYN KELLY, SETTLE FOR MORE 211 (2016).

[86] SANDBERG WITH SCOVELL, LEAN IN, 154.

[87] MICHELLE OBAMA, BECOMING, 192-193 (2018).

[88] iRelaunch, *Career Re-entry Programs,* https://www.irelaunch.com/CareerReentry; Jennifer Preston, *Helping Women Get Back in the Game,* N.Y. TIMES, Mar. 18, 2014.

[89] Onramp Fellowship, https://onrampfellowship.com/about/. See *Returnship Program for Female Attys Heads In-House,* LAW360, https://onrampfellowship.com/cteory/press-release/.

[90] Vivia Chen, *Passing on the Brass Ring: High-Performing Women Lawyers Are Finding Partnership Isn't Always For Them,* AM. LAWYER, Mar. 1, 2018, 12.

[91] Stephanie Russell-Kraft & Sanford Heisler, *The Firm Helping Female Lawyers Sue Big Law,* BLOOMBERG LAW, BIGLAWBUSINESS, Apr. 12, 2019, https://biglawbusiness.com/sanford-heisler-the-firm-helping-female-lawyers-sue-big-law.

[92] Olson, *Female Lawyer's Gender-Bias Suit* (quoting Mayes).

[93] Ashby Jones, *Female Partners at Chadbourne Respond to Discrimination Suit,* WALL ST. J., Sept. 12, 2016, http://blogs.wsj.com/law/2016/09/12/female-partners-at-chadbourne-respond-to-discrimination-suit.

[94] Jones, *Female Partners* (quoting David Sanford).

[95] Bronstad, *Bias Class Actions* (quoting Sharon Vinick). For the unflattering portrait of the plaintiff in the Chadbourne class action suit, see Kathryn Rubino, *Chadbourne Swings Back Over Gender Bias Suit,* ABOVE THE LAW, Nov. 7, 2016, http://abovethelaw.com/2016/11/chadbourne-swings-back-over-gender-bias-suit.

[96] Ruth Bader Ginsburg, *Ruth Bader Ginsburg's Advice for Living,* N.Y. TIMES, Oct. 2, 2016, at SR4

[97] EVAN THOMAS, FIRST: SANDRA DAY O'CONNOR 132 (2019).

[98] Marianne Cooper, *Being the "Go-To Guy": Fatherhood, Masculinity, and the Organization of Work in Silicon Valley,* 23 QUALITATIVE SOC. 379 (2000), reprinted in NAOMI GERSTEL, DAN CLAWSON & ROBERT ZUSSMAN, FAMILIES AT WORK: EXPANDING THE BOUNDS 5, 10, 13 (2002). See also Jennifer L. Berdahl, Peter Glick & Marianne Cooper, *How Masculinity Contests Undermine Organizations, and What to Do About It,* HARV. BUS. REV. (Nov. 2, 2018).

[99] Cooper, *Being the "Go-To Guy,"* at 7 (quoting Scott Webster).

[100] Cooper, *Being the "Go-To Guy,"* at 9 (quoting Kirk Sinclair).

[101] Cooper, *Being the "Go-To Guy"* (quoting Chris Baxter).

[102] Cooper, *Being the "Go-To Guy,"* at 24 (quoting Eric Salazar).

[103] Cooper, *Being the "Go-To Guy,"* at 20.

[104] Cooper, *Being the "Go-To Guy,"* at 21 (quoting Rich Kavelin).

[105] Cooper, *Being the "Go-To Guy,"* at 25 (quoting Rich Kavelin).

[106] Cooper, *Being the "Go-To Guy,"* at 26 (quoting Kirk Sinclair).

[107] JOAN C. WILLIAMS, RESHAPING THE WORK-FAMILY DEBATE: WHY MEN AND CLASS MATTER 89 (2010) (quoting Derek Bok).

[108] Aiken & Regan, *Gendered Pathways,* at 314.

[109] RONIT DINOVITZER ET AL., AFTER THE JD II: SECOND RESULTS FROM A NATIONAL STUDY OF LEGAL CAREERS 62 (2009).

[110] NANCY LEVIT & DOUGLAS O. LINDER, THE HAPPY LAWYER: MAKING A GOOD LIFE IN THE LAW 12, 13 (2010); Kenneth G. Dau-Schmidt et al., *Men and Women of the Bar: The Impact of Gender on Legal Careers,* 16 MICH. J. GENDER & L. 49, 112-113 (2009).

[111] R. Lisle Baker, *Designing a Positive Psychology Course for Lawyers,* 51 SUFFOLK L. REV. 207, 241 (2018)

[112] DARCY LOCKMAN, ALL THE RAGE: MOTHERS, FATHERS, AND THE MYTH OF EQUAL PARTNERSHIP 35, 139 (2019).

[113] Irin Carmon, *Low Expectations for Husbands and Presidents*, N.Y. TIMES, Dec. 11, 2016 (quoting Obama).

[114] David Remnick, *Going the Distance*, NEW YORKER, Jan. 19, 2014 (quoting Obama).

[115] Todd S. Purdum, *Washington, We Have a Problem*, VANITY FAIR, Sept. 2010, at 290.

[116] Deborah L. Rhode, *The "Having It All" Debate: We've Heard It All Before*, NAT'L L.J., Aug. 6, 2012.

[117] LINCOLN CAPLAN, SKADDEN: POWER, MONEY, AND THE RISE OF A LEGAL EMPIRE 7 (1993).

[118] Jennifer Close, *Vacation-Taker Denier in Chief*, N.Y. TIMES, Aug. 13, 2017.

[119] OBAMA, BECOMING, 197.

[120] OBAMA, BECOMING, 196.

[121] OBAMA, BECOMING, 197.

[122] Brigid Schulte, *Millennials Want a Work-Life Balance. Their Bosses Just Don't Get Why*, WASH. POST, May 5, 2015.

[123] Schulte, *Millennials Want a Work-Life Balance*.

[124] RHODE, WOMEN AND LEADERSHIP 83-85.

[125] *See, e.g.*, SYLVIA ANN HEWLETT, OFF-RAMPS AND ON-RAMPS: KEEPING TALENTED WOMEN ON THE ROAD TO SUCCESS (2007).

[126] https://youtu.be/tLKQezaz2IA.

[127] https://www.youtube.com/watch?v=lgClR_xr-oM.

[128] https://www.youtube.com/watch?v=My538atyCVY.

[129] https://www.youtube.com/watch?t=17&v=Ar3hJbZuVF8.

[130] Jimmy Kimmel, Mansplaining to Hillary Clinton, https://www.youtube.com/watch?v=j2wBpYT6Zlo.

[131] http:www.ted.com/talks/Sheryl_sandberg_why_we_have_too_few_women_leaders.html.

[132] Palin/Hillary Open, Saturday Night Live (Sept. 23, 2013), https://www.youtube.com/watch?v=vSOLz1YBFG0&t=248s.

[133] https://www.youtube.com/watch?v=Icv1Zxu3qjQ.

[134] For Albright, see WALL ST. J., *Madeleine Albright on Women and Leadership*, YOUTUBE (Nov. 10, 2008), http://www.youtube.com/watch?v=oF-iUTvPRJc.

[135] *Jon Stewart: The Most Trusted Name in Fake News*, FRESH AIR, Oct. 4, 2010, http://www.npr.org/templates/story/story.php?storyId=130321994.

[136] Wilkins, *From "Separate Is Inherently Unequal" to "Diversity Is Good for Business"*; Brayley & Nguyen, *Good Business*, at 7.

[137] Jerry Kang et al., *Are Ideal Litigators White? Measuring the Myth of Colorblindness*, 7 J. EMPIRICAL LEGAL STUD. 886 (2010).

[138] ARIN N. REEVES, WRITTEN IN BLACK & WHITE: EXPLORING CONFIRMATION BIAS IN RACIALIZED PERCEPTIONS OF WRITING SKILLS 3 (2014). *See* Debra Cassens Weiss, *Partners in Study Gave Legal Memo a Lower Rating When Told Author Wasn't White*, ABA J., Apr. 21, 2014.

[139] Christopher I. Rider, Adina D. Sterling & David Tan, *Career Mobility and Racial Diversity in Law Firms*, Second Annual Conference of the Research Group on Diversity, 2016.

[140] Stephanie Russell-Kraft, *LGBTQ Lawyers on Job Hunt Still Fear Facing Firms' Barriers,* BIG LAW BUSINESS, June 27, 2019.

[141] Russell-Kraft, *LGBTQ Lawyers on Job Hunt* (quoting M. Dru Levasseur).

[142] Russell-Kraft, *LGBTQ Lawyers on Job Hunt* (transgender lawyers); Takeia Johnson, *LGBT Attorneys of Color in the Legal Profession: A Discourse on Inclusion,* FED. LAWYER, JAN.-FEB. 2017, 49; Michele Benedetto Neitz, *Pulling Back the Curtain: Implicit Bias in the Law School Dean Search Process,* 49 SETON HALL L. REV. 629,666 (2019).

[143] Debra Cassens Weiss, *Second State Adopts ABA Model Rule Barring Discrimination and Harassment by Lawyers*, ABA J. June 2019.

[144] Eugene Volokh, Letter to the Arizona Supreme Court, In the Matter of: Petition to Amend ER8.4, Rule 42, May 15, 2018.

[145] Alex B. Long, *Employment Discrimination in the Legal Profession: A Question of Ethics?*, 2016 U. ILL. L. REV. 445, 449, 458.

[146] Veronica Root, *Combating Silence in the Profession*, 105 VA. L. REV. 805, 824-833 (2019).

[147] Root, *Combating Silence in the Profession*, 836-40.

[148] Root, *Combating Silence in the Profession*, at 836-837.

[149] AMERICAN BAR ASSOCIATION PRESIDENTIAL INITIATIVE COMMISSION ON DIVERSITY, DIVERSITY IN THE LEGAL PROFESSION: THE NEXT STEPS (2010); ELIZABETH CHAMBLISS, MILES TO GO: PROGRESS OF MINORITIES IN THE LEGAL PROFESSION 97-98 (2004); Devon W. Carbado & Mitu Gulati, *Race to the Top of the Corporate Ladder: What Minorities Do When They Get There*, 61 WASH. & LEE L. REV. 1645, 1662-63 (2004).

[150] EBERHARDT, BIASED, 285; Lori Mackenzie, JoAnne Wehner & Shelley Correll, *Why Most Performance Evaluations Are Biased, and How to Fix Them*, HARV. BUS. REV. (Jan. 2019).

[151] Sam Reeves, *The Carrot Didn't Work So Let's Apply the Stick*, NAT'L L.J., Oct. 23, 2006, at S6, S8; Edgardo Ramos & Lynn Anne Baronas, *What Works: Ways to Increase Diversity at Law Firms*, NAT'L L.J, Jan. 16, 2006, at 13. David B. Wilkins & G. Mitu Gulati, *Why Are There So Few Black Lawyers in Corporate Law Firms? An Institutional Analysis*, 84 CAL. L. REV. 493 (1996).

[152] Russell-Kraft, *LGBTQ Lawyers on Job Hunt;* Johnson, *LGBT Attorneys of Color;* Lateral Link, *LGBTQ in Biglaw: Advice for Law Firms and For Job Seekers,* ABOVETHELAW (Feb. 10, 2017), https://abovethelaw.com/2017/lgbtq-in0-biglaw-advic-for-law-firms-and-for-job-seekers.

[153] Vivia Chen, *It's Not Just About the Work,* AM. LAW., Aug. 7, 2017.

[154] Greg Howard, *Cover Story*, N.Y. TIMES MAG., Jan. 15, 2017, at 17.

[155] Goodwin Liu, *There Are More Asian-American Lawyers than ever—But Not in the Top Ranks*, L.A. TIMES, July 23, 2017.

[156] National Association for Law Placement, *2018 Report on Diversity in U.S. Law Firms* 5, 7 (2019).

[157] SARA AHMED, ON BEING INCLUDED: RACISM AND DIVERSITY IN INSTITUTIONAL LIFE 61 (2012).

[158] This problem is adapted from the discussion in Robin J. Ely, Debra Meyerson & Martin N. Davidson, *Rethinking Political Correctness*, HARV. BUS. REV. 79 (Sept. 2006); DEBORAH L. RHODE, DAVID LUBAN, SCOTT CUMMINGS & NORA FREEMAN ENGSTROM, LEGAL ETHICS 59-60 (7th ed. 2016).

[159] Walter La Grande, *Getting There, Staying There*, ABA J., Feb. 1999, at 54.

[160] For an overview, see Hazel Rose Markus, Claude M. Steele & Dorothy M. Steele, *Colorblindness as a Barrier to Inclusion: Assimilation and Nonimmigrant Minorities*, 29 DAEDELUS 233, 250 (2000).

[161] Shelley Correll & Caroline Simard, *Research: Vague Feedback Is Holding Women Back*, HARV. BUS. REV. (Apr. 29, 2016).

[162] ROBIN DIANGELO, WHITE FRAGILITY: WHY IT'S SO HARD FOR WHITE PEOPLE TO TALK ABOUT RACISM (2018).

[163] R. Haley Riemer, *White Tears*, WOMEN'S REVIEW OF BOOKS, Jan./Feb. 2019, 21 (quoting DeAngelo).

[164] Ben Martin, *Letter to the Editor*, NAT'L L.J., Nov. 6, 2006, at 23.

[165] Martin, *Letter to the Editor*, at 23.

[166] AHMED, ON BEING INCLUDED, at 41; Kenji Yoshino, *The Pressure to Cover*, N.Y. TIMES MAG., Jan. 15, 2006.

[167] AHMED, ON BEING INCLUDED.

[168] The phrase comes from AHMED, ON BEING INCLUDED, at 35.

[169] *See* Jonathan Capehart, *Ben Carson and Cornel West Actually Agree: Obama's "Not Black Enough"*, WASH. POST, Feb. 23, 2016; David A. Graham, *A Short History of Whether Obama is Black Enough, Featuring Rupert Murdoch*, ATLANTIC, Oct. 8, 2015; Ta-Nehisi Paul Coates, *Is Obama Black Enough*, TIME, Feb. 1, 2007; ADIA HARVEY-WINGFIELD & JOE R. FEAGIN, YES WE CAN? WHITE RACIAL FRAMING AND THE OBAMA PRESIDENCY 42 (2013); ANDREA GILLESPIE, THE NEW BLACK POLITICIAN: CORY BOOKER, NEWARK, AND POST-RACIAL AMERICA 56-64 (2012).

[170] Peter J. Boyer, *The Color of Politics*, NEW YORKER, Feb. 4, 2008.

[171] Capehart, *Ben Carson and Cornel West Actually Agree* (quoting Toure).

[172] PREET BHARARA, DOING JUSTICE: A PROSECUTOR'S THOUGHTS ON CRIME, PUNISHMENT, AND THE RULE OF LAW 195 (2019).

[173] BHARARA, DOING JUSTICE, 207.

[174] Part 1 of this problem is adapted from a discussion in Robin J. Ely, Debra Meyerson & Martin N. Davidson, *Rethinking Political Correctness*, HARV. BUS. REV. 79 (Sept. 2006). Part 2 comes from HELGESSEN & GOLDSMITH, HOW WOMEN RISE, 36.

[175] Ely, Meyerson & Davidson, *Rethinking Political Correctness*, at 84.

[176] Ely, Meyerson & Davidson, *Rethinking Political Correctness*, at 84.

[177] HELGESSEN & GOLDSMITH, HOW WOMEN RISE, 36.

[178] Ely, Meyerson & Davidson, *Rethinking Political Correctness*, at 80.

[179] Steve Mortenson, *Confronting Implicit and Benevolent Bias in Teams*, in GENDER, COMMUNICATION, AND THE LEADERSHIP GAP 47, 53, 56, 62 (Carolyn M. Cunningham, Heather M. Crandall & Alexa M. Dare eds., 2017).

[180] Ely, Meyerson & Davidson, *Rethinking Political Correctness*, at 87.

[181] https://youtu.be/ge7i60GuNRg.

[182] https://www.youtube.com/watch?v=zgpq2Rqjg4c.

[183] For Joe Biden's comments, see Jason Horowitz, *Biden Unbound: Lays into Clinton, Obama, Edwards*, N.Y. OBSERVER (Feb. 4, 2007), http://observer.com /2007/02/biden-unbound-lays-into-clinton-obama-edwards/.

[184] https://www.youtube.com/watch?v=OFPwDe22CoY.

CHAPTER 9

LEADERSHIP IN LAW FIRMS AND IN-HOUSE LEGAL DEPARTMENTS

A. LAW FIRMS

Does leadership in law firms require different qualities or styles than leadership in other contexts? What distinctive challenges confront managing partners? How can they best be addressed? The materials that follow explore those issues. Although their focus is on managing partners, similar points apply to law firm lawyers who lead in other positions, such as heads of departments, client engagement teams, and multiparty litigation.[1] The topic is of critical importance given findings that that "the single most important determinant of law firm success and profitability is the leadership skills and practices of partners."[2] The most successful firms are those that value and support leadership development.[3]

Lawyers who lead law firms face particular challenges arising from flat demand, heightened client expectations, and increased competition for both business and legal talent.[4] To prosper in this environment, firms need to focus more on business development, client responsiveness, technological sophistication, and cost-effective delivery of services.[5] To that end, firm leaders "must understand their markets and their firm's place in them," and must be able to forge consensus around appropriate responses.[6] As one report by the Center on Creative Leadership put it, "agreeing on the key challenges is another challenge."[7]

A survey of leaders of professional service firms (including law firms) found that the most important leadership qualities involved interpersonal skills and personal qualities such as empathy, integrity, courage, humility, and respect for others. Only one quality, understanding of the business, involved technical analytical skill. Particularly in times of stress, a key capacity was the ability of leaders to engage colleagues around a vision that was compelling and attainable.[8] Such research is consistent with other published surveys of law firm managing partners, who also emphasize the importance of emotional intelligence and interpersonal skills.[9] These skills include awareness and management of their own emotions as well as understanding and responsiveness concerning the emotions of others.[10] To that end, leaders need to engage in active listening, in which they ask probing questions and pay attention to what is, but also what is not, being said.[11] According to managing partners, leaders also need to convey through words and example, the "inclusive, collegial, respectful interactions" they want in their workplaces.[12] Modeling integrity, accountability, collaboration, fairness, and innovation is critical.[13]

In terms of strategy, a study of professional service firms (including law firms) by Harvard Business School professors found that the qualities most essential to effective leadership were charting a direction; gaining commitment to that direction; following through on goals; and setting personal examples.[14] Commentary from law firm managing partners and consultants echoes those views and also stresses the need to encourage teamwork, enforce standards, and confront problems directly.[15] Leaders need deep knowledge about the firm, its market, and its members. They need to understand the organization's strengths, weaknesses, core competencies, and competitive position, as well as its lawyers' values, perceptions, and aspirations.[16] Self-knowledge is equally critical. Leaders should delegate tasks to others who are strong in areas where the leaders themselves are weak, and should encourage these individuals to develop their own capabilities.[17]

Lawyers aspiring to leadership positions should also proactively seek positions where they can exercise influence and learn from experience. They should also equip themselves with the marketing, accounting, and administrative skills that are necessary for law firm management. In the absence of internal candidates with those traits, a growing number of firms are appointing nonlawyers to top positions.[18]

Casey Stengel, the longtime manager of the New York Yankees, famously noted that "getting good players is one thing. The harder part is getting them to play together."[19] Law firm leaders say the same thing. The following excerpt explores some of the challenges that they face in an increasingly competitive climate.

DEBORAH L. RHODE, LAWYERS AS LEADERS

(Oxford University Press, 2013), pp. 167-175

As the title of a recent *Economist* article noted, American law firms confront "A Less Gilded Future." There are no universally successful responses to these challenges, but some leadership strategies are more effective than others. Strategic planning is among the most critical. Although many lawyers tend to be skeptical of the process, researchers and consultants underscore its importance. Its point is to identify the firm's central mission and direction, to specify the steps necessary for achieving its goals, and to establish governance structures that advance those goals and ensure accountability for the results. When done well, the process requires leaders to face tough questions, consult widely, and forge consensus on a definition of success and measures to achieve it. A realistic assessment of the firm's strengths, limitations, and market position, together with concrete initiatives and buy-in from stakeholders, are essential to such strategic planning. Leaders who try to achieve agreement by papering over differences generally find that "vague ambiguous mandates . . . result in vague ambiguous responses."

Although the conventional assumption is that profit maximization will always be central to a firm's mission, its relative importance varies in light of other values. As a presiding partner of Cravath once put it, "there has to be a lot more than money to hold a group of very smart Type A partners together." Growth, reputation, public service, collegiality, quality of life, intellectual challenge, and diversity are among the other objectives that assume different priorities in different firms. Some law firms thrive through a tradition of client and public service and a reward structure that is not narrowly focused on revenue production. Paradoxically, leaders who focus most intensely on increasing profitability sometimes have most difficulty achieving it. Research on corporate financial performance over a sustained period finds that companies that have made maximizing shareholder wealth the dominant concern do less well financially than businesses that have broader visions and goals.

Developing and implementing a successful strategic plan generally depends on leaders' ability to "herd . . . factions" and forge agreement. In one survey of firm leaders, almost twice as many described themselves as leading by consensus as by decree, and other research similarly finds that the characteristic they rate most highly is "builder of coalitions." How leaders achieve agreement varies in light of their styles and their firms' size, culture, governance structure, and financial circumstances. Some partners receive deference because of their founding role and economic importance to the firm. "He built it. He made it. I may disagree with him but I trust his judgment" is a common view. A *California Lawyer* magazine profile, *The Great Sonsini,* leaves no doubt that [the Silicon valley firm] Wilson Sonsini operates on this principle. Other leaders earn respect through their understanding of the culture and politics of the firm, and their willingness to consult widely, admit mistakes, and respond to others' concerns. Particularly during their "honeymoon phase," leaders should listen to everyone, from clients to the mailroom staff, about what is working and what is not. In that process, leaders need to be perceived as having not "a personal agenda," but a rather a desire to do "what is best for the firm."

Firms vary in how they allocate governance authority. Everything from benign dictatorships to direct democracy can work if adapted to meet evolving needs. Whatever the structure, leaders should ensure that potentially divisive issues, such as compensation, promotion, or controversial clients, should be resolved through processes that are transparent, widely accepted, and responsive to competing concerns. Research on organizational culture underscores the importance of making individuals feel that they are treated with fairness and respect. As one chair noted, "It's much more important that your partners believe that what you're going to do is the product of an open inclusive discussion [than that] . . . they believe it is the right thing to do." Soliciting and addressing associates' concerns can also be crucial for recruitment, retention, and engagement.

Personal example is equally important. . . . [For example], two founding partners of the Howrey firm helped it weather the collapse of its antitrust practice by convincing the ten most highly compensated partners to take a steep pay cut. As one attorney recalled, "that bought a decade and a half of loyalty from junior partners," and enabled the firm to broaden its scope of practice. When he was editing *The American Lawyer*, Steven Brill observed that the "leaders . . . of almost every successful firm that I have seen, have 'bought' their leadership role in part by sacrificing personal income for the sake of building the institution.". . .

Leaders can also take innovative approaches in addressing a greying workforce. One is to better integrate senior lawyers into firm pro bono programs. Most surveyed lawyers report wanting to work after they reach retirement age, but income is not their primary motivation. Many seek opportunities for meaningful service, and pro bono activities are an ideal way to give back to the community and to strengthen firms' charitable initiatives. Senior lawyers can provide valuable training and mentoring and help develop signature projects, including joint ventures with clients. Providing such opportunities can also encourage older lawyers to transition clients' paid work to younger colleagues. To that end, leaders can more actively encourage pro bono efforts by accommodating retired attorneys' substantive interests and ensuring adequate administrative support and malpractice coverage.

A final, frequently neglected strategy involves cultivating future leaders and providing for orderly transfers of authority. Surveys find that only about a quarter of firms have succession plans, and only a fifth have formal leadership development programs. A common assumption is that leaders will just "emerge naturally. Yet . . . this view understates the extent to which leadership skills can be consciously cultivated, and the value of formal programs in assisting that process. Not all lawyers who rise through the ranks "naturally" have the full range of necessary skills, and other lawyers with significant potential will not put themselves forward without direct encouragement. In recognition of that fact, a growing number of firms are creating structures to identify potential leaders and to provide the training, responsibilities, and mentoring that will support their professional development. Leaders need to be proactive in grooming their own successors and in stepping aside when a transition would serve firm interests, if not necessarily their own. Organizations that have the most sustained financial performance have leaders with "ambition not for themselves but for their [organizations]."

Leadership Failures

The breakdowns of prominent firms during the early 21st century provide further insights into leadership strategies, particularly those unlikely to be effective. . . . A Hildebrandt Institute study of some 80 failed law firms found that about half had "fundamental flaws . . . [stemming] from a lack of clear strategies, of clearly articulated and compatible goals among their partners, and of strong leadership to achieve their mutually shared strategic visions." Problems fell into three main categories. The first was inadequate financial performance, typically involving unproductive partners, excessive borrowing to fuel growth or sustain profits, and poor "financial hygiene," such as failing to control partners' discounts on fees. A second category of problems involved internal dynamics, including the absence of a realistic strategic focus, loss of trust, and poorly conceived compensation structures. A third group of difficulties involved external competitive pressures, and leaders' failure to respond to market trends as well as to manage partner expectations in light of those dynamics. Enough details are publicly available about some breakdowns to suggest more specific leadership lessons.

At its height, Brobeck, Phleger & Harrison LLP [Brobeck] was one of the nation's most respected firms. It had over 1,000 attorneys in offices across the nation and represented prominent global corporations such as Apple, Bank of America, and Chevron. When the firm dissolved in 2003, some outsiders blamed it on the recession and the high-tech boom and bust cycle. However, insiders also faulted leaders who were unable to forge consensus in an exceptionally competitive, combative, and Balkanized workplace. Longstanding differences over growth and compensation came to a head as the economy worsened. Some senior lawyers, including the firm's chair, Tower Snow, believed that the partners should take pay cuts during the downturn. To Snow, it seemed "only fair that the people who had benefited the most from the boom should absorb the shock of the bust. A partner who earned hundreds of thousands of bucks a year instead of $1.17 million would still be rich. A laid-off secretary or associate was in danger of losing everything." As he put it to colleagues, "Do you really want to fire 100 people to put $10,000 in your pocket, $5000 of which will go to Uncle Sam?" Many of his colleagues were put off by the implicit accusations of greed. In their view, "Partners are owners and [major dips in their] income are disconcerting and undesirable." They circulated a no-confidence petition that triggered Snow's resignation as chair.

His replacements immediately began dismantling the firm's previous management team and many day-to-day operations fell to inexperienced attorneys who were ill-equipped to handle them. Without strong central leadership, branch offices began running themselves and key partners began jumping ship with entire practice groups in tow. When the firm leadership heard that Snow and thirty colleagues were talking with British-based Clifford Chance, it summarily expelled him. By the end of 2002, some 70 partners had left and the firm had trouble paying bills, funding retirement accounts, and renegotiating leases. To avoid reducing partner income, the firm also began drawing down its line of credit. The situation worsened when Citibank demanded repayment of the debt. Partners then agreed to compensation cuts, but another group of defections caused negotiations over leases and a potential merger to collapse, and the firm filed for bankruptcy.

Another prominent meltdown involved Wolf Block, a distinguished Philadelphia-based firm with nine offices. The precipitating cause of its 2009 collapse was the recession, particularly the downturn in the real estate market, which accounted for about 40 percent of the firm's revenues. Deeper problems reflected failures of leadership. For a decade, the firm was chaired by a "Troika" that reportedly "ruled by fear" and secrecy. Its approach led to hoarding of clients, defections of partners, and a failure to diversify into profitable specialties. The chair who replaced the Troika was a pleasant and talented attorney, but an indecisive leader who was unwilling to make tough choices or pressure colleagues to do so. When the firm faced difficulties in obtaining a necessary line of credit, many partners were reluctant to accept the loan out of fear that others would leave and those remaining would be stuck with the debt. The chair's equivocation about his own plan was the final straw.

After the antitrust and intellectual property powerhouse Howrey disbanded in 2011, its Chair Robert Ruyak blamed market factors and partners' willingness to offer flat, discounted, and contingent fee arrangements that yielded insufficient and irregular profits. His colleagues identified a range of leadership failures: overly optimistic financial projections, excessive emphasis on growth, high risk investments in contingent fee cases, lack of disclosure and consultation concerning the firm's financial difficulties, and an unwillingness to prune unproductive partners or to rein in problematic billing practices. With the rapid acquisition of laterals and branch offices, the firm lost much of its "cultural glue;" new hires were not well integrated into the organizational culture, and the governance structure was not designed to encourage collaboration and consensus. Ruyak's focus on establishing new European offices diverted attention from other managerial concerns, and the process for acquisition lacked due diligence; no one was studying the factors likely to influence profitability, and the results were often disappointing. Financial problems were increasing by the time of a 2008 partner's retreat, where Ruyak provided a pamphlet with an unintentionally prescient title: "Our Iceberg is Melting." Although his point was to underscore partners' need to pay attention to their market surroundings, Ruyak gave an unduly rosy account of the firm's overall position. "Howrey: Succeeding Against All Odds" was the title of his accompanying report. In fact, it wasn't and members of the executive committee were playing a passive role. Ruyak's style was to present them with "prepackaged" plans and say "This is what I'm doing. Does anyone disagree?" The deaths of two high earning partners, unprofitable branches, and four straight years of declines in demand took their toll on compensation, and jeopardized a credit agreement with Citibank. No other partner was willing or able to replace Ruyak, and heads of profitable practice groups began to depart rather than do the "heavy lifting" necessary to keep the firm together. In a comment that speaks volumes about the lack of insight that led to the failure, Ruyak looked back on his own performance and concluded "I have no regrets."

Coudert Brothers, an international pioneer with a 150 year legacy and 28 offices around the world, confronted similar difficulties. It declared bankruptcy in 2005 and years of infighting followed about who owed what to whom. By all accounts, the firm's demise was attributable to overly ambitious expansion. Coudert prided itself on being the first American firm in distant locations like Singapore and Moscow, whether or not they were profitable. As one former partner noted, its overseas offices were based on "opportunity and impulse, rather than thorough analysis of business potential. . . ." Faced with growing global competition and an inadequate domestic client base to feed its international offices, the firm began to curtail compensation and lose partners. Rivals "cherry picked" the highest earners who could sometimes double their incomes by leaving. In summarizing the problem, the great grandson of one of the founders noted, "You have to have a strategy. I don't think we ever did."

Jenkins and Gilchrest, by contrast, had a clear strategy, but one based on excessive risk and ambition. This pillar of the Dallas legal establishment, and at one point the fastest growing firm in the United States, disbanded in 2007 to avoid prosecution for tax fraud. The firm also paid a $76 million penalty, settled a client class action suit for $81.5 million, and publicly acknowledged that it had "marketed fraudulent tax shelters and failed to exercise effective oversight and control over the firm's tax shelter practice." Underlying the debacle was the desire of a regional firm for a national presence and reputation. Beginning in the late 1990s, Jenkins launched a plan of rapid expansion. To staff eight new offices, leaders looked for lateral acquisitions with premium business. To lure those high earners, the firm needed to boost its profits per partner. Accordingly, in 1998, leaders recruited Paul Daugerdas, a partner with a highly lucrative tax shelter practice. It was a controversial decision. Some partners questioned the legality of his shelter plans and the potential malpractice exposure that they created. Concerns also surfaced about his "difficult" personality and the compensation structure that he demanded, which gave him an above average percentage of the revenue that his shelter practice generated, rather than the customary arrangement of a share of the firm's overall profits, with adjustments for revenue generation. The effect was to give him a large stake in growing his practice but not in the firm's overall well being. Moreover, he would be working from a new branch office in Chicago, which lessened opportunities for informal oversight and integration into the firm culture. On balance, however, firm leaders thought that his practice would be worth the price. No lawyer had ever been sued, much less prosecuted, for giving a shelter opinion and the IRS was not then much concerned with policing abuses. According to William Durbin, the principle champion of Daugerdas and the firm's later chair, his recruitment promised a highly profitable and "not a terribly risky" way to give the firm a presence in another major metropolitan area.

Firm leaders were right about the profits and wrong about the risks, and grossly underestimated both. Daugerdas had initially projected that his practice would generate $6 million in its first year. In fact, by 2000 it was accounting for fifteen times that amount, almost a third of Jenkins' total revenues. In four years, his shelter practice reportedly generated $267 million in revenue for the firm and $95 million for himself. That profit level could not help but raise ethical questions. How could his work be so much more lucrative than that of other top tier firms if it was perfectly legal? Although his practice did dramatically boost profits per partner, he proved difficult in other respects. He failed to disclose side business arrangements, continually complained about compensation, and fought with the Texas partner whom the firm had designated to provide a second opinion on the legality of his shelter opinions. That lawyer, not a shelter expert, was suddenly deluged with an overwhelming volume of fact-sensitive transactions and could scarcely provide close oversight. As Georgetown law professor Milton Regan notes, anyone in that position would face "powerful pressures to sign off on opinions generating such a huge stream of revenue."

In 2001, the problems with Daugerdas had become sufficiently apparent that the firm's governing board agreed in a straw vote to ask him to leave. However, it delayed taking formal action in an effort to close the year in a strong financial position. Then Durbin took over as chair, and was, by his own account, "bottom-line oriented." No ouster occurred. Lawsuits by clients and a competitor, and an investigation by the IRS, forced the end of Daugerdas' shelter practice in 2002, but not his departure. As one former Jenkins partner explained, "You don't want to be at war with someone who is a primary witness in defending yourself." To compensate for the lost tax revenue, Durbin proposed de-equitizing some lower earning partners, a highly divisive strategy.

By 2004, internal acrimony and external lawsuits were taking their toll. Durbin was forced to resign, Daugerdas left under pressure, and other lawyers began to depart. Jenkins' new leaders began merger discussions, but found no firm willing to commit until the civil and criminal liability issues were resolved. By the time that happened, it was too late. Departures had escalated and a no-prosecution agreement with the government was conditional on the firm's dissolution. A further posthumous blow to the firm's reputation came with felony convictions of Daugerdas and two other Jenkins tax partners. Looking back on the debacle, Durbin issued a strong statement of regret about his preoccupation with profits and failure to close down the shelter work when problems surfaced. "I wish I could have been more courageous. I played a very large part in bringing about the demise of a firm . . . that I loved."

In 2012, a stunned legal profession watched as one of New York's largest and most distinguished firms, Dewey & LeBoeuf, imploded. No one doubted that leadership failures were partly responsible. Following a merger in 2007, the firm negotiated lavish pay arrangements with key partners and lured laterals with multimillion dollar, multiyear guarantees. The result was gross inequality in compensation; partners' incomes ranged from $300,000 to $7,000,000. To finance expansion, the firm took on massive debt, and when the economic slowdown hit and revenues shrank, the firm kept expanding. Its leader, Steve Davis, was described as a "vision guy, not an execution guy," and the management committee failed to compensate for his weaknesses. It also failed to demand transparency concerning compensation packages, and partners were not aware that about a third of the partners had guaranteed incomes not tied to performance. Nor did they learn that the firm's obligations in current and deferred compensation exceeded profits by $250 million until the firm was on the edge of bankruptcy. As it became unable to meet its financial obligations, layoffs and an exodus of partners followed. As one expert summed up widely held views, "This absolutely falls into the category: What were they thinking? This was Mismanagement 101 across the board."

The distinctiveness of Dewey's plight has been subject to debate. Certainly some of its problems seem attributable to its own mistakes: the size and duration of compensation guarantees, the amount of long-term debt, and the possible financial irregularities by its chair, which triggered a criminal investigation and civil claim for fraud. But some of its problems are widely shared. Representative articles ran under titles such as "Dewey's Fall Underscores Law Firms' New Reality," and "Dewey & LeBoeuf Crisis Mirrors the Legal Industry's Woes." Intense competition for clients and for partners who seem able to deliver them are endemic to the legal market. Many firms have relied on compensation guarantees in order to hire laterally and found that they are "extremely corrosive culturally because they are divorced from individual or firm performance. . . ." As Michael Trotter summarized the situation, "Dewey's problems are [not] just a matter of a management mistake here or there but instead reflect a change in the fundamental competitive environment in the legal services industry." Dewey could not "generate enough legal business at high enough prices to meet the income expectations of its partners." Dewey's woes are widely shared, and in Trotter's views, other firms may well suffer a similar fate.

Lessons for Leaders

"Every unhappy law firm is unhappy in its own way," notes Regan. But some pathologies are more common than others and underscore the leadership lessons noted earlier. One is the importance of a strategic vision that is both inspirational and realistic. As Chapter 4 indicated, cognitive biases toward optimism and over-confidence are particularly problematic in leadership settings. To prevent defections, rally the troops, and burnish their own image, leaders are often prone to emphasize the positive. Without a culture and governance structure that encourages transparency, divisive issues and discomfiting trends may get buried. In many of the failed firms, influential partners failed to keep leaders honest, ask tough questions, and demand corrective actions. According to Howrey's consultant Peter Zeughauser, no one on the executive committee "ever put their foot down to ask for more and earlier information." Some Jenkins and Dewey partners similarly "turned a blind eye." Although these tendencies can never be wholly avoided, they can be mitigated by formal checks and balances in decision-making authority, and by informal norms requiring candor and accountability.

A second set of insights fall under the category "be careful what you wish for." A fixation on growth or profits per partner comes at a price. Particularly when leaders see size as measure of status, rather than a rational economic strategy, they are setting themselves up for problems. Steven Kumble helped guide Finley and Kumble to bankruptcy by aspiring to be the biggest law firm in America and to enable lawyers to "make as much money as they could as fast as they could." Why don't we concentrate on being the best?, asked one irate colleague. "Then we can think about becoming the biggest." "When [we're] the biggest," Kumble responded, "everyone will think we're the best." Everyone didn't. Firms that expand quickly through mergers, lateral acquisitions, and branch offices have difficulty sustaining a common culture and pursuing core values apart from profits. Insuring a good fit requires considerable due diligence at the outset. Gaining consensus can be a daunting task when lawyers are spread across "different economic environments with different risks" and different practice norms. Yet focusing single mindedly on the one concern that everyone shares—money—raises problems as its own, as several of the preceding examples demonstrate. "Greed is definitely not good" is the lesson that some commentators drew from the demise of Jenkins. But such clichés are beside the point in the world that leaders inhabit. Greed is rampant, and needs to be managed, not simply lamented.

There are no all-purpose prescriptions. One of leaders' greatest challenges lies in balancing concerns of partners whose productivity suffers from factors beyond their control and the reluctance of high earners to subsidize those colleagues. "We are the only industry that carries their wounded," noted one managing partner, and many see this as a luxury their firms cannot afford. "De-equitize the couch potatoes," "clean out . . . the weak links" and "deadwood," is their prescription. By contrast, others believe that assisting partners who are victims of market swings or temporary personal problems is part of what distinguishes professional firms from businesses. An excessive focus on rainmaking or billable hours can erode collegiality and cooperation, and devalue other contributions to law firm performance, such as mentoring, recruitment, management, and pro bono service. A central leadership priority should be establishing widely accepted processes for resolving these issues before tensions and departures escalate.

A related priority should be cultivating the sense of group identity and institutional loyalty that tends to reduce self-interested behavior. As law professors Ronald Gilson and Robert Mnookin famously argued, a strong firm culture and firm-specific capital are the best ways to prevent lawyers from "shirking, grabbing, and leaving." To that end, leaders should focus on cultivating the firm's internal and external reputation, treating all lawyers with concern and respect, and modeling institutional commitment.

A related leadership lesson is to beware of quick fixes to long-term difficulties. The financial crises that can precipitate firm failures are often symptomatic of deeper productivity problems and conflicting organizational priorities. Short-term strategies such as additional borrowing or layoffs are no solution to these deeper difficulties. Such strategies may temporarily sustain profits and prevent defections, but they do not increase productivity or efficiency, and they may paper over conflicts that will ultimately prove fatal. Leaders need realistic initiatives to boost performance, such as developing more profitable specialties, and improving staff utilization, client satisfaction, and marketing strategies. For example, one firm that helped its real estate practice rebound from a slump in the market by focusing on "premium work for premium clients" and by providing attorneys with personalized development plans and candid feedback. Other firms have begun to develop quality management programs that stress continuous self- assessment through standardization of routine tasks, performance measures, and peer review. To promote more effective governance, a growing number of firms have also instituted in-house leadership initiatives. These programs typically offer specially tailored workshops and projects, and provide participants with mentors who design individualized professional development plans and monitor performance.

Finally, the challenges that leaders encounter in their own firms should encourage involvement in broader debates over practice structures. Other nations and other professions have outpaced American law firms in innovations concerning governance, lay investment, and service delivery. The merits of these initiatives deserve consideration. It is, as Richard Susskind notes, "hard to convince a room full of millionaires that they have their business model wrong." But American firm leaders need to be open to that possibility. In an increasingly globalized practice setting, they need to learn from their competition and to develop professional conduct rules that permit cost-effective innovations. Lawyers with personal leadership experience have much to contribute in wider dialogues about how best to meet the structural challenges facing contemporary law firms.

PROBLEM 9-1

You are the chair of a major San Francisco firm. During a national economic downturn, your firm's profits have taken a substantial dip. Rather than cut compensation for equity partners, the firm's leading rainmakers prefer deferred offers, layoffs of associates and staff, and pay cuts for underemployed non-equity partners, which will encourage their departures. None of these options is appealing. If the firm decreases compensation for equity partners, it risks losing some of its highest-billing attorneys. If it downsizes the workforce, it will impose undeserved hardships on those least able to bear them, reduce the ranks of experienced employees necessary when the economy rebounds, and adversely affect morale, recruiting, and reputation.

If the firm decides that reductions are necessary, you are not sure whether to freeze all new hiring, layoff associates and non-equity partners who are underemployed, and/or furlough new recruits with partial pay. Nor are you sure of what criteria to use in targeting cuts. Should layoffs and deferred hiring be based on the work available in individuals' specialty areas? Should you encourage high-performing associates to retool in a different field? You also face questions about whether to ask laid-off employees to leave immediately, or whether to allow them a period of transition in which they can look for another position. The latter is more humane, but it also imposes more salary and support costs for the firm, risks retaliation, and jeopardizes workplace morale.

A further difficulty is how forthcoming to be about the firm's financial position and the likelihood of further reductions. Full candor could damage the firm's reputation with clients and potential recruits, thus compounding its financial problems. Lack of transparency could also jeopardize the firm's standing and further sour workplace relationships.

If you were the managing partner of the firm, how would you handle these challenges?

NOTES AND QUESTIONS

Issues involving profitability pose challenges for leaders in any employment context, but law firms raise some distinctive concerns. Underlying these problems are the characteristics of individuals who choose legal careers, the qualities reinforced in legal practice, and the structures of legal workplaces.

One cluster of difficulties involves autonomy, skepticism, and distrust. Partners value their independence and are often wary of governance structures based on shared credit, collaboration, and subordination of personal interests to the greater good.[20] The result is a low-trust environment, which is exacerbated by lateral movement, mergers, and branch offices. Particularly during times of stress, partners are reluctant to make sacrifices that they are not confident will be reciprocated. A related set of problems involves decision-making styles. Most lawyers take a highly analytic view of management, which focuses on financial scorecards and devalues soft skills. Lawyers often rise to leadership positions because of their skills as lawyers, not as leaders. They are hampered by colleagues whose tendency in evaluating proposals is to look for loopholes, counterexamples, exceptions, and risks; the result can be strategic paralysis. According to consultant David Maister, the main reason many lawyers do so well financially is that they "compete only with other lawyers." But they fail to realize their organizational potential by behaving as "bands of warlords, each with his or her followers . . . acting in temporary alliance—until a better opportunity comes along."[21]

These problems came to a head as the economy worsened in the early twenty-first century. Many law firms found themselves confronting some variation of the facts described in Problem 9-1. The legal system lost 15,000 jobs between 2008 and 2010, and a number of leading firms dissolved while others imposed layoffs and salary freezes, ceased recruiting, deferred associate start dates, and/or instituted structural changes in hiring and promotion practices (such as more contract and counsel positions, and longer tracks to partnership).[22] Even after the economy rebounded, many firms struggled as increased competition was not matched with increased demand for services.

1. As the preceding materials indicate, a key leadership strategy is aligning individual and organizational objectives and uniting stakeholders around a common vision. Could leaders in the firms discussed above have done anything differently to achieve such unity and prevent their firms' dissolution? Break into small groups and consider what you would have done in Problem 9-1 and in one of the examples described in the preceding excerpt.

2. In *How the Mighty Fall*, Jim Collins analyzes major corporate failures over the last several decades and identifies five stages leading to decline or demise.

   • Stage 1. Hubris Born of Success. "Stage 1 kicks in when people become arrogant, regarding success virtually as an entitlement, and [when] they lose sight of the true underlying factors that created success in the first place."[23]

   • Stage 2. Undisciplined Pursuit of More. "Companies in Stage 2 stray from the disciplined creativity that led them to greatness in the first place, making undisciplined leaps into areas where they cannot be great or growing faster than they can achieve with excellence, or both."[24]

- Stage 3. The Denial of Risk and Peril. "In Stage 3, leaders discount negative data, amplify positive data, and put a positive spin on ambiguous data. Those in power start to blame external factors for setbacks rather than accept responsibility . . . [and engage in] rigorous fact-based dialogue."[25]
- Stage 4. Grasping for Salvation. In Stage 4, instead of addressing underlying problems, leaders look for "a charismatic visionary leader, a bold but untested strategy, a radical transformation . . . a 'game-changing' acquisition, or any number of other silver-bullet solutions. Initial results from taking dramatic action may appear positive, but they do not last."[26]
- Stage 5. Capitulation to Irrelevance or Death. "In Stage 5, accumulated setbacks and expensive false starts erode financial strength and individual spirit to such an extent that leaders abandon all hope. . . . In some cases, their leaders just sell out; in other cases, the institution atrophies into utter insignificance . . . [or simply dies outright]."[27]

Collins notes that some companies skip a stage and move through them at varying paces. And some manage to pull themselves out by realistically addressing their root problems. Do these stages shed light on the law firm failures described above? Collins description of Stage 2 seems particularly apt:

> [S]uccess creates pressure for more growth, setting up a vicious cycle of expectations; this strains people, the culture and systems to the breaking point. . . . People in power allocate more for themselves or their constituents—more money, more privileges, more fame, more of the pols of success—seeking to capitalize as much as possible in the short term, rather than in investing primarily in building for greatness. . . .[28]

If you were a leader in a Stage 2 law firm, what strategies might be most promising?

3. When and how to conduct layoffs in the workforce has attracted increasing attention since the 2008 recession. Many experts note that the downsides of downsizing are often underestimated. Historically, the average economic recession lasts only about 11 months, and companies that must rehire shortly after cutbacks generally do worse than those that ride out the downturn, given the costs of recruitment and retraining, and the morale, stress, and defections that accompany layoffs.[29] When downsizing is necessary, mistakes to avoid include inadequate information, unfulfilled promises of consultation and assistance, or increased compensation for those responsible for the layoff decision.[30] Law firm consultants emphasize that treating displaced workers with respect and compassion is critical.[31]

4. Other experts similarly advocate "downsizing with dignity." Such approaches demand honesty and fairness, realistic appraisals of the organization's economic circumstances, and distribution of hardships in as even-handed a way as possible. Leaders should avoid "death by a thousand cuts," which

triggers defection by the most marketable employees and demoralization and anxiety among the others.[32] Would any of these approaches be feasible for law firms under circumstances such as those in Problem 9-1?

5. As the preceding expert notes, financial difficulties are often symptomatic of deeper problems involving productivity and clashes in organizational priorities. Short-term strategies such as additional borrowing, layoffs, and expenditure freezes may be only temporary solutions to long-term concerns, particularly if they do not increase cost-effective services and paper over conflicts.[33] In firms with low-trust environments, the "best and the brightest lawyers [often] jump quickly to a less risky platform" rather than help stabilize a difficult situation.[34]

Some experts see law firm failures as occasions for the profession to rethink traditional organizational models. They recommend more flexibility in ownership and compensation structures, more involvement of the entire firm in designing cost-saving strategies, and more implementation of professional development programs that enlist leaders in addressing concrete challenges.[35] Many commentators also argue that the selection process for leaders needs modification. Currently, the main criteria are outstanding legal work and client development. To retain their credibility, leaders often feel that they must maintain their reputation for excellence and control over a large book of business. These criteria are highly imperfect indicators of leadership ability and may leave leaders with insufficient time for management.[36] Accordingly, leadership selection and organizational reward structures should focus less on individual achievement and more on contributions to the firm. Partner compensation should give more weight to activities such as mentoring, cross selling, and collaborative marketing.[37] What other alternatives are available to firms facing difficulties of the sort described above?

6. In a widely discussed op-ed., Ben Heineman and William Lee argue that

> [l]aw firms must be run in a businesslike manner. But they should not be run for the greatest possible profit. . . . [T]he historic concept of what it means to be a legal professional . . . has generally meant that private lawyers have public responsibilities beyond their immediate self-interest and beyond the needs of their immediate clients. . . . The partnership must regain a sense of common community, with shared values and aspirations, instead of existing as balkanized practitioners, practice groups or geographies intent on their own narrow self-advancement. Creating a common culture based on professional values of service, collegiality, loyalty, quality, integration, and cooperation is probably the greatest challenge for today's law firm leader.[38]

Do you agree? If so, how should the leaders in Problem 9-1 have met that challenge?

PROBLEM 9-2

You are the managing partner of a midsize firm. Several years ago, your firm recruited a partner who had a quarter century's experience at two other firms where she had headed their consumer product safety department. She has since developed a substantial practice for the firm, and in the past year, she generated over $5 million in revenue. However, she has now complained to you that although her billings placed her among the firm's leading earners, her income placed her in the bottom third of partner pay. She has also complained that the management committee that makes compensation decision is all male, and that process lacks transparency and clear metrics.

When you raise her concerns with the committee, the members are not inclined to revisit their decision. It resulted from a system of awarding points based on anticipated revenues attributable to the partner's efforts. Committee members believe that the complaining partner's recent billings are a fluke, and that her practice is not a good "fit" for the firm. They propose reducing her compensation in order to encourage her to find another position.

How do you respond? What considerations would guide your view? What other information might you need going forward?[39]

NOTES AND QUESTIONS

As Chapter 8 notes, gender bias suits against law firms are increasing, and many involve disparities in compensation. A 2016 survey by Major, Lindsey & Africa found a 44 percent difference in pay between female and male partners at large American firms, largely because men bring in more high paying matters, or are better at getting credit for doing so.[40] Other problems are that: men pass down their clients to other men without formal succession planning; women are pressured into remaining as service partners, who do the work but don't receive the financial recognition; or that they are used as "eye candy" to show diversity at pitches without receiving work or credit if the pitches are successful.[41] One recent study found that gender is a strong predictor of the origination credit gap even when controlling for relevant factors including the hours worked and number of clients for whom the lawyer was the lead partner; the primary explanation seemed to be men's tendency to pass on clients to junior lawyers who are "just like me."[42] Many lawyers complain about the system for allocating credit for originating business on the ground that the process lacks transparency, clear criteria, and a way to challenge decisions. Some believe that it encourages a "silo mentality."[43] Others argue more broadly that "eat what you kill" compensation systems provide too little incentive for collaboration and shared efforts, and too little reward for activities like mentoring and recruiting that advance collective interests.[44]

In response to these concerns, some leaders have attempted to move to a shared origination system. In one firm, the managing partner began his effort by interviewing all stakeholders individually and then commissioning an analysis of the firm's competitive position. It showed that the firm didn't function well enough as a team, and that this weakness impaired its profitability. The managing partner then created a strategic planning committee and hired an experienced consultant to share best practices and advise the members. The next step was to bring the issue before the entire partnership. Opponents of change objected that without the "eat what you kill" system, lawyers would have less incentive to work hard. Supporters of change claimed that lawyers would be more willing to pool their efforts and work as teams. After months of debate, the firm adopted a shared origination plan in which anyone in the firm, including associates and staff, could be rewarded for attracting or enlarging business. Each practice group would decide how to distribute credit. Only if the group could not reach agreement would a central committee step in to resolve the issue. The result was that more individuals engaged in seeking clients and cross selling services.[45]

Would such an initiative be appropriate on the facts of Problem 9-2? What other strategies might be necessary? Should the firm create a special forum to resolve disputes or establish clear rules about sharing credit and passing on clients?[46] As the firm's managing partner, how would you try to enlist support?

MEDIA RESOURCES

Layoffs are the subjects of many excellent media portraits.[47] In *Margin Call*, the leader of an investment firm attempts to persuade employees that recent layoffs are beneficial because they will reduce competition for promotion among those who are left.[48] The film *Up in the Air* features George Clooney as a consultant who makes his living by firing workers whose managers do not want to do it themselves. The film involves a difficult ethical issue when Clooney is asked about a termination that his subordinate orchestrated, in which the employee threatened suicide and later made good on her threat. An honest answer to the question could derail the subordinate's career. *The Company Men* chronicles the effect of downsizing on the lives of three executives at a fictional Boston corporation. *Roger and Me*, one of Michael Moore's first documentaries, is about the economic conditions that ravaged Detroit and the leaders who did not want to deal with the consequences. Season three, episode 13 ("Shut the Door. Have a Seat") of the television series *Mad Men* explores challenges facing the central characters as they orchestrate a secret defection from their advertising agency, which is being absorbed in a merger.

Law firm dynamics figure in a number of television series, including *LA Law*, *The Good Wife*, *The Practice*, and *The Good Fight*. The opening episodes of the first season of *The Good Fight* portray the difficulties that a prominent firm leader has in finding an alternative position after her early retirement plans fall through and her firm declines to take her back. The first season of *The West Wing* has an evocative scene in which a senior Wall Street associate up for partner tries to convince a client at the last minute to pull out of deal involving oil tankers that might leak, and is chastised by a senior partner.[49] *How I Met Your Mother* features a partner's lack of emotional intelligence and interpersonal skills when he yells at an associate during Take Your Daughter to Work Day.[50] The film *Equity* raises issues surrounding greed, turf battles, and gender bias in investment banking that have obvious parallels in law firms.

U.S. District Judge Rakoff describes how competition between firms leads firms to engage in risky, potentially unethical behavior along the lines shown in some of the fictional portraits.[51] MSNBC describes King and Spaulding's controversial decision to defend and then drop its defense of the Defense of Marriage Act.[52]

B. IN-HOUSE COUNSEL

The role of the general counsel, or chief legal officer in American corporations, has evolved over time. Between the late nineteenth century and the late 1930s, the position had prestige and influence.[53] Then, between the 1940s and 1970s, the role diminished in stature and scope, only to remerge in the late twentieth century with steadily increasing power and status.[54] Growth in regulation, globalization, stakeholder activism, and scrutiny by media and nonprofit organizations all expanded the responsibilities of in-house counsel. Corporations increased the size and quality of their legal departments to handle complex risk management and corporate governance, as well as more routine matters.[55] Because inside lawyers were familiar with the corporation's business, and had no economic incentives to inflate hours, they could often handle such work more efficiently and cheaply than outside counsel. Ben Heineman, the general counsel of General Electric and a leading architect of the trend, ended up supervising a global department of 1,400 lawyers.

In the course of this development, general counsel became part of the strategic management team. Hillary Krane, general counsel of Nike and formerly of Levi Strauss, notes that the role is not just legal and "not just about fire prevention and fire fighting—it is part of a team that is trying to run and grow a . . . business . . . . [The GC is a] senior executive jointly charged with creating, nurturing, and projecting a sustainable future."[56] He or she is expected to give business as well as legal advice and to anticipate and help remove obstacles that impede business growth and profitability.[57] In a survey of some 1,200 chief legal officers by the Association of Corporate Counsel, the most common advice to aspiring in-house lawyers was to "learn the business"; they should also develop relationships and a broad skill set.[58]

Not only have general counsel grown in power and influence within the corporation, they have also grown in similar ways in their relations with outside counsel. They have brought more work inside and exercised greater control over the law firms that they retain in order to enhance predictability, efficiency, and cost effectiveness.[59] Tensions have arisen because inside counsel are under constant pressure to decrease legal costs, while law firms that bill by the hour have incentives to increase them. This creates what Ben Heineman terms the "productivity disconnect.[60] To address this tension, general counsel have increasingly moved to competitive bidding, alternative fee arrangements that reward efficiency, and preferred provider or strategic partnerships with selected firms. About three-quarters of corporations report using alternative fees for some of their matters, but commentators often argue that these arrangements are still dramatically underutilized.[61]

Many non-hourly arrangements are a form of value billing that seeks more equitable allocation of risks and rewards between the client and outside firm and that incorporates incentives for attaining mutually defined objectives. Strategic alliances typically involve a flat fee for all of the company's work in a particular area.[62] Like law firms, corporations are also outsourcing more of their work to temporary and offshore providers and nonlegal vendors.[63] Managing costs is, as Heineman notes, one of general counsel's most "difficult and uninspiring tasks."[64] But it has had some upsides. As relations with outside lawyers have become more short term and transactional, general counsel have increasingly stepped into the role of trusted advisor once occupied by firm attorneys.

This role presents some unique challenges as well as opportunities. Geoffrey Hazard, the Reporter for the ABA Model Rules of Professional Conduct, believes that the position of general counsel "is among the most complex and difficult" of any position occupied by lawyers.[65] Part of the difficulty is the multiplicity of roles that GCs play: advisor, manager, mediator, problem solver, and advocate.[66] As one study found, inside counsel are "cops, counsel, and entrepreneurs," and those roles can sometimes be in tension, particularly if the compliance function thwarts business objectives of non-lawyer colleagues.[67] In the book excerpted below, Ben Heineman refers to this as the "partner-guardian tension."

Another difficulty is that, as the Model Rules make clear, in-house counsel represents the "organization acting through its duly authorized constituents," but does not represent those constituents.[68] Obvious problems arise when those constituents, typically management and the board of directors, disagree or when their interests conflict with those of the organization.[69] In some cases, "the CEO may want and expect an enabler; the board may want and expect a guardian."[70] These problems are compounded by the general counsel's own interests in job security, in maintaining an effective working relationship with the corporate leadership, and in receiving the bonuses and other rewards that may depend on that relationship.[71] GCs' close personal ties with management may lead to unconscious self-serving biases along the lines discussed in Chapter 3; the result will be to compromise their objectivity in determining the entity's best interest.[72]

At the same time, however, those ties may assist inside counsel in gaining the knowledge, credibility, and authority necessary to assure legal compliance.[73] Compared with outside lawyers, general counsel typically have more access to back channel information and are harder to circumvent if they become knowledgeable about misconduct.[74] It is widely accepted that general counsel are at least one, and for some purposes, the primary, "conscience of the corporation."[75] They are, after all, responsible for detection and deterrence of corporate wrongdoing.[76] Yet according to some commentators, general counsel also have both "economic incentives and cognitive biases that systematically incline them to stay on the good side of the corporations' managers and . . . [absent] the proverbial smoking gun . . . to turn a blind eye to indicia of misconduct."[77]

By contrast, many general counsel believe that other forces push in the opposite direction. Compared with outside lawyers, in-house counsel are often harder to fire for giving unwelcome advice because they are embedded in the organization and usually have supportive constituencies.[78] So too, as Krane notes, general counsel appreciate that "making money is only good if you keep the money" and moral myopia can have disastrous financial consequences for companies; the examples in previous chapters made that abundantly clear.[79] Moreover, general counsel are now facing heightened risk of personal legal liability for acquiescing in misconduct.[80] An example is the general counsel of Google, David Drummond, who accepted a cease and desist order based on his failure to ensure appropriate treatment of stock options for management, and failure to inform the board of directors concerning the issues they raised.[81]

Accordingly, many believe that the general counsel is, "most importantly, the 'guardian of the corporate integrity.'"[82] As a "lawyer statesman," the GC tries to "lead the client to 'do the right thing' from a moral, ethical, and sensible business perspective."[83] To perform adequately in that role, the general counsel needs: (a) technical legal and financial skills, (b) wisdom, tact, and judgment as a counselor, (c) strong leadership ability, (d) independence, and (e) an "unwavering moral compass."[84] The failures of some general counsel to prevent corporate misconduct appear attributable to a lack of these traits.[85] And the stronger the general counsel's reputation along those dimensions, the greater the credibility he or she will have with management and the board.

In the excerpt that follows, Ben Heineman elaborates the ideal role of the general counsel and the challenges it poses in ethical contexts.

BEN W. HEINEMAN, JR., THE INSIDE COUNSEL REVOLUTION: RESOLVING THE PARTNER-GUARDIAN TENSION

(Chicago: American Bar Association, 2016), pp. 3, 15-16, 25-26, 184, 193-196

The core mission of the global corporation is the fusion of high performance with high integrity and sound risk management. The ideal of the modern general counsel is a lawyer-statesman who is an outstanding technical expert, a wise counselor, and an accountable leader . . . For the lawyer statesman, the first question is: "Is it legal?" But the ultimate question is: "Is it right?" . . .

High performance means strong sustained economic growth . . . which in turn provides durable benefits for shareholders and other stakeholders upon whom the company's health depends. . . . High integrity means robust adherence to the spirit and letter of *formal rules*, both legal and financial; voluntary adoption of binding *global ethical standards* that go beyond existing rules . . . and employee commitment to *core values* of honesty, candor, fairness, trustworthiness and reliability. . . . Achieving high integrity obviously involves resources and cost.

Sometimes, business leaders will face a trade-off between integrity and performance, between ethics and financials. But, the fusion of performance with integrity and sound risk management ultimate creates value in a wide variety of ways; attracting, motivating, and retaining superb talent; increasing productivity; enhancing customer loyalty; mitigating or eliminating far more expensive risks; increasing brand value; allowing premium pricing; creating operational efficiencies; and enhancing reputation with stakeholders both inside and outside the corporation. . . .

As a global General Counsel . . . recently said, the conception of the lawyer-statesman focusing ultimately on what is right "initially struck me as aspirational, unattainably so," but it "is actually a basic requirement for a senior in-house lawyer in a global, highly regulated corporation. And, as Ken Frazier, CEO of Merck, said in a speech to the American Law Institute: "Sophisticated clients don't want 'pure' legal advice, they want workable solutions to their problems—problems that they understand to be situated at the intersection of law, business, technology, politics and moral judgment. Smart clients expect their lawyer to help them find these integrated solutions to their most vexing problems." . . .

[Q]uestions about ethical positions occur in four broad areas:

- Duties to the corporation and its employees.
- Duties to all other stakeholders.
- Duties to the rule of law and administration of justice.
- Duties to help secure public goods that are vital to societal well-being but that cannot be realized through market mechanisms.

The General Counsel should play an important, often central, role in *organizing the processes* by which the corporation makes ethical determinations, in *generating options* about voluntary standards for addressing specific issues, and in *offering considered substantive views* about what is the "right" approach. . . .

Two useful [frameworks] are the Caux Round Table *Principles for Business* and an analysis of corporate codes around the world conducted by a team at the Harvard Business School (HBS) that identified eight core ethical principles recognized in global businesses. The HBS study covered the following subjects: fiduciary duties of care and loyalty, respect for property, reliability, transparency, respecting individual dignity, fairness, being a responsible community citizen, and being responsive to the legitimate claims of others. And, in both the Caux Principles and the HBS study, there more detailed issues under these ethical subjects. For example, under the dignity principle alone there are these issues: respect for individuals, promoting health and safety, protecting privacy and confidentiality, abjuring use of force, respecting freedom of association and expression, and providing learning and development. And to go one step further, under "health and safety" there is enumeration of these ethical subjects: ensure that products and services sustain or enhance customer health and safety, protect employees from avoidable injury and illness in the workplace, provide a work environment that is free from substance abuse, and prefer suppliers and partners whose work practices respect international labor standards and health and safety. Importantly, in a follow-up study, the authors of the HBS article on ethical principles found that a high percentage of employees they surveyed said the broad principles identified in the first study should be adopted by their companies, but a smaller percentage said that their companies had actually adopted them. . . .

In assessing the 'economics' of voluntarily accepting global standards, it is important to keep several perspectives in mind. First, the outlays for such changes are not just costs, but are *investments* in improving the company. Second, the *benefits* of such investments cannot always have financial precision and cannot always be expressed as having an internal rate of return (IRR). Whether the global stand will enhance the corporation's reputation—and perhaps increase its brand's value—will often turn *as much (or more) on judgment as on financial analysis.* What is the value of taking an action that will avoid public embarrassment from an action perceived as inappropriate, even if not illegal, and the associated costs of making an effective public response . . . ? Third, decision makers should take a long view of the relevant *accounting period.* The benefits that may result from an investment in a binding ethical standard may not occur in the next quarter or the next year but may occur over a number of years. The full benefits of making a special effort to hire highly educated and talented women in China and Japan, for example, may be realized over time, not just in a few quarters or even a few years. Fourth, as indicated earlier, there may be *moral choices a corporation makes that, regardless of cost, are the right thing to do.* A corporate policy against discrimination may fit into the flexible "good judgment" framework of investors and "soft" benefits over a long period of time outlined here. But it may also be justified simply and directly on its own terms. There are certain acts of corporations—no bribes—that, in the view of its leaders, are appropriate because they are simply the ethical thing to do. . . .

NOTES AND QUESTIONS

1. Not all general counsel are comfortable with the role of "conscience of the company." In commenting on that description, Matt Fawcett, General Counsel of NetApp, maintained that "if you are perceived as the corporate conscience, you have lost the ability to play that role." And if you try, "it lets the rest of the organization off the hook." To be effective, general counsel need to be seen as "enablers, not simply enforcers."[86]

   Other commentators raise further concerns. Some echo the warning given to CEOs, that when "aspirational rhetoric is paired with middling financial performance, there is rarely a happy ending."[87] Others suggest that asking a general counsel to be the conscience of the corporation places a "target on her back" in lawsuits alleging corporate misconduct.[88] Another objection, as IBM General Counsel Robert Weber put it, is that "there is nothing in my training that makes me better or worse suited on matters of conscience than any other senior leader at my company."[89] Weber also is uncomfortable with the idea of being "'guardian of corporate integrity' primarily because I have no idea what that means."[90]

2. Heineman responds, "Really, no idea?" He emphasizes that his claim is not that in-house counsel is "the" guardian but only that he is one of them—one with valuable training in law, ethics, and policy.[91] Are you persuaded? If not, how would you respond?

3. Geoffrey Hazard claims that "[c]orporate lawyers cannot be distinctly more virtuous than the corporate management by which they are employed, and many corporate managements are not distinctly virtuous. Hence, sometimes a corporate lawyer will fail, more or less consciously, to see what there is to be seen."[92] Is he right? Robert Gordon similarly notes that the "most favorable conditions for public-minded lawyering have arisen, not surprisingly, when the clienteles themselves promoted a broad vision of the national interest."[93] And in commenting on Heineman's book, Gordon describes a number of ethical scandals under Heineman's tenure at General Electric, and points out that his advocacy of the lawyer-statesman role occurred after, not during, his time as general counsel.[94] Recall some of the ethical scandals noted in preceding chapters, such as fraud at Enron and General Motors, and pretexting at Hewlett-Packard. What might have prevented the ethical failures of general counsel?

4. In the FTC's recent antitrust case against chipmaker Qualcomm, the federal trial judge singled out in-house lawyers for choosing to continue licensing practices that unlawfully suppressed competition.[95] The company's former legal counsel reportedly received tens of millions of dollars for his contributions to Qualcomm's licensing strategies.[96] Should such compensation arrangements trigger greater scrutiny by the board, and insistence on an independent assessment by outside counsel? What other strategies might be useful?

5. An increasing number of in-house lawyers have faced criminal prosecutions because, as a Securities and Exchange Commission official put it, they "twisted themselves into pretzels to accommodate the wishes of company management."[97] How can general counsel avoid such complicity? What strategies other than resignation might be effective?

6. Consider the conduct of in-house lawyers at Wells Fargo and Volkswagen during the fraud and safety scandals discussed in Chapter 5. In the case of Wells Fargo, the general counsel's office seemed at best "willfully ignorant" of the extent of the problem once a widespread pattern emerged of accounts opened and fees charged without consumers' consent.[98] In the Volkswagen scandal, a plea agreement by the company indicates that some of these lawyers tipped off employees about an oncoming litigation and one attorney indicated that emissions-related data should be kept "only if necessary." As a consequence, thousands of documents were deleted, but later recovered. At least one attorney was subject to criminal investigation, and the general counsel was moved into a new position.[99] Similar advice by an in-house lawyer for the Arthur Andersen accounting firm during the Enron scandal led to

widespread document destruction, a congressional investigation, criminal proceedings, and the implosion of the firm.[100] What might counteract the pressures to be a "team player" in these circumstances?

7. Another widely publicized scandal involving in-house lawyers involved Uber General Counsel Salle Yoo, who approved the company's use of a controversial "Greyball" program to evade regulators. In essence, the program allows the company to identify law enforcement officials by looking at their credit card information and tracking destinations, and then telling them that no cars are available or providing a fake app, populated with ghost cars.[101] According to one consultant, the difficulties for general counsel to be both partners with company managers but objective about legal risks is particularly great in entrepreneurial companies. Businesses like Uber, which disrupt industries "when pursuing new business models . . . could put pressure on legal departments to approve things that are in grey areas."[102] In these contexts, experts emphasize the need for General Counsel to document their recommendations, consider their internal and external reporting obligations, explore other ways to achieve the company's business objectives, and if in doubt, consult outside counsel.[103]

What is your view? If a technique like "Greyballing" is designed to thwart law enforcement but is not clearly illegal, is it enough for general counsel to advise CEOs of the risks and let them make the call? Or should GCs decline to give their legal blessing to such measures?

Michael Callahan, former general counsel at LinkedIn and Yahoo, suggests that for issues that are in ethical grey areas, it is often useful to ask executives to consider the reputational standard discussed in Chapter 7; how would we feel if the New York Times ran a front-page story on this issue? In Callahan's experience, broadening the focus beyond a purely regulatory or liability concern "can be effective because every [leader] knows or should know the power of reputation and how quickly it can be lost." [104]

Consider Facebook's recent reputational damage for pushing the envelope in apparent disregard of users' privacy concerns. If regulatory efforts haven't kept pace with public needs, when should in-house lawyers push for self-regulation?

8. In commenting on Heineman's book, Stanford Professor Robert Gordon notes that

> the lawyer may not perhaps himself be blessed with a superior moral disposition or instincts but is something of an expert in anticipating moral reactions in others . . . [And because of their position outside the organizational culture] lawyers, or some lawyers anyway, may bring to the corporation a . . . less parochial viewpoint, more aware of the institutional and cultural infrastructures in which the company must operate. . . . [And] because of their connection with public institutions and values of the legal system, lawyers may have some influence over the ways their business clients voluntarily comply with,

resist, defy, or try to nullify taxi and regulatory regimes and how they seek through judicial, legislative, or agency action to change those regimes. . . . Even under pressures of competition and financial markets, it seems that managements have considerable leeway in setting business strategies—[such as labor policies], environmental policies, and political causes. Heineman's book [is], for all [its] limitations, [a] sign pointing in the right direction.[105]

How would Hazard respond? How would you?

9. One strategy that Heineman proposes, and Gordon endorses, is for general counsel to help recruit other companies into "coalitions of the willing" to pressure for policies such as strengthening the Foreign Corrupt Practices Act, and passage of the U.S. Climate Action Partnership. Another example is the amicus briefs that consortiums of corporations have filed in important Supreme Court cases in defense of universities' affirmative action programs.

In a 2017 article on the general counsel's policy role "in an age of upheaval," Heineman argues that these lawyers should help:

- Develop fairer, clearer facts in policy disputes;
- Balance values in conflict such as short-term costs and long-term benefits in environmental regulation;
- Build coalitions and promote bipartisanship and compromise; and
- Take ethical action in the absence of regulation.[106]

What influence could, and should, general counsel exercise in the current political climate concerning social and regulatory policies? Give an example.

10. How can general counsel position themselves to play the role that Heineman envisions? Common strategies include:

- Coming to a clear understanding up front with the CEO and other leaders about the general counsel's ethical and compliance role;
- Creating processes for identifying ethical issues (e.g., employee surveys, ombudspersons, anonymous hotlines);
- Communicating that the GC's door is open for confidential concerns;
- Meeting regularly with the board;
- Ensuring that the board has a role in the GC's hiring, firing, and compensation;
- Hiring outside counsel when necessary to ensure independent and credible investigations;
- Establishing early warning systems for identifying future legal risks (e.g., canvassing legal and legislative developments, news stories, NGO activism).

- Fostering a culture of open candid communication that encourages lawyers to surface views and information that they might worry will be unwelcome.[107]

What other strategies would you propose? What would help general counsel respond in the problems below?

PROBLEM 9-3

In 2003, a shift in power in the Chinese government brought a new crackdown on freedom of expression, including peaceful political comment on the Internet. Despite such repression, Google in 2006 launched a Chinese search engine. After much internal debate, Google's leaders concluded that "the benefits of increased access to information for people in China" outweighed the costs of complicity in censorship.[108] As required by the government, the search machine filtered coverage of matters such as the 1989 Tiananmen Square massacre, Human Rights Watch, and the Dalai Lama. Other American companies, including Microsoft and Yahoo, made similar decisions, all of which received substantial criticism from the civil liberties community. As Harvard professor Jonathan Zittrain noted, these actions offered a "near-textbook case study on the deep question of how much assistance, if any, companies chartered in free societies should render to regimes that censor political and cultural expression."[109]

The issue sparked congressional hearings and a heated public debate. In House Subcommittee Hearings, Representative James Leach of Iowa accused Google of serving as a "functionary of the Chinese government," and added that if "we want to learn how to censor, we'll go to you."[110] Google's CEO Eric Schmidt responded, "I think it's arrogant for us to walk into a country where we are just beginning operations and tell that country how to run itself."[111] Rather, the company announced to users that its China service did not "accord fully with its principles," and it disclosed when search results were censored.[112] Reaction within the human rights community was mixed. According to Human Rights Watch, the Chinese system of electronic surveillance had become the most advanced in the world, and it had been significantly aided by American corporations.[113] Others took the view expressed by Harvard researcher Rebecca Mackinnon: "Bottom line, it's good they're in China. . . . But there's a lot more they can do" to protect users, such as publicizing sites that were delisted and collaborating with other U.S. Internet firms to lobby for more "transparency and accountability" in Chinese government practices.[114]

The issue arose again in 2010 when Google discovered that Chinese hackers had illegally breached its security, along with that of some twenty other companies, and had accessed the accounts of American, Chinese, and European advocates of human rights in China. In response, the company refused to continue filtering censored material from its Chinese language search engine, and began rerouting Chinese users to an uncensored Hong Kong site. The Chinese government then used its Internet filter to block banned material.[115]

If you were the general counsel of Google, what recommendations would you make about continuing to do business in China or other countries that censor Internet use? The stakes are substantial, given the huge potential market at issue. China has 400 million Internet users, more than any other nation, and a fifth of the global market, and Google provides the second-largest search engine for those individuals.[116] However, its profit levels from the Chinese market are relatively small, only about 1 percent of its total revenues.[117]

China is not, however, the only country that routinely engages in such censorship. About 40 other nations do as well, and more than 25 have blocked Google service over the last decade.[118] Some experts argue that toleration of censorship poses a far greater financial risk than the loss of a single market because the company's "entire business model [depends on] a free and open Internet."[119] Others argue that some censorship is an acceptable price to pay for giving millions of individuals access to information that helps lead to a freer society.

What would you propose if you were the company's general counsel; how would you handle concerns about doing business with nations that censor?

NOTES AND QUESTIONS

1. Google identifies three principles that inform its decisions to operate in new markets:

   - Access: maximizing information flow;
   - Transparency: informing users when information has been removed at government demand; and
   - Trust: protecting users' privacy and security.[120]

   As the general counsel of Google, how would you assess the trade-offs between those principles in China? If the government threatens to oust Google entirely if it will not continue filtering information, what would you recommend?

2. Google is not the only Internet service provider that is subject to Chinese censorship. Microsoft's Bing search engine and LinkedIn's professional network have also operated in China.[121] If you had been the GC advising those companies, what would you have proposed?

PROBLEM 9-4

You are the general counsel for a North American corporation that sells inexpensive home furnishings. One of your profitable product lines is carpets woven in India and Nepal. Rugmark Foundation has recently launched a "Most Beautiful Rug" campaign in major metropolitan areas to raise awareness about child labor in the industry.[122] The Foundation certifies hand-knotted rugs in India, Pakistan, and Nepal that are produced only by adults who are paid a minimum wage. To finance inspections and rehabilitate illegally employed children, the foundation collects a license fee from exporters, who pay .25 percent of the value of the product, and importers, who pay 1.75 percent.[123] An increasing number of customers have asked why all your carpets do not carry the Rugmark label. You have been unwilling to impose this requirement because you do not believe that the label can in fact ensure the absence of underage workers. Nor are you confident that children banned from looms in some of the poorest areas of your supply chain are better off as a consequence; reports by NGOs suggest that many former child rug workers end up in more hazardous occupations, including prostitution. However, the negative publicity resulting from the Rugmark campaign has raised questions about whether you should reconsider that decision or drop the product line altogether. That latter course of action would minimize the risk of media exposés, but it would hardly be an optimal solution for impoverished workers in Nepal and India.

You are preparing a report with recommendations on this issue. How should you proceed? What options might you consider? What further information would you need to make the decision? Is there anything that you could do to make consumers more aware of the complexity of the issues?

NOTES AND QUESTIONS

Child labor poses increasing challenges for American companies that rely on global supply chains. Since 1919, the International Labor Organization (ILO) has adopted ten conventions regarding minimum ages for work in different sectors.[124] The vast majority of nations have signed treaties committing them to the abolition of child labor. The Convention concerning the Prohibition and Immediate Action for the Elimination of the Worst Forms of Child Labour (ILO No. 182) (1990) has been ratified by 169 nations, including the United States. It obligates signatories to take "immediate and effective measures to secure the prohibition and elimination of the worst forms of child labor, such as work involving coercion, bondage, sexual exploitation and hazardous conditions." Despite such governmental commitments, the ILO estimates that about one out of seven children in the world today is involved in child labor.[125] Much of that work, particularly when combined with domestic tasks within the family, can severely compromise children's educational opportunities, as well as psychological development.[126] For transnational corporations, the most publicized abuses have occurred in the garment, shoe, carpet, and cocoa trades. In the Indian hand-knotted rug industry alone, estimates suggest that over a fifth of the workforce is underage, and in the country as a whole, an estimated 13 million children work.[127] Contributing causes include poverty, inadequate education, gender and caste discrimination, and long-standing cultural norms.

Although India has not ratified the Convention on the Worst Forms of Child Labour, it has both constitutional and statutory prohibitions on the employment of children in hazardous occupations, which include the carpet industry. Widespread violations of these prohibitions in India, along with related abuses in surrounding nations, prompted the formation of the South Asian Coalition on Child Servitude. This Coalition, which now has over 400 organizational members, joined with various human rights groups and trade unions to pressure consumers and retailers to demand carpets made without child labor. In 1995, the Rugmark Foundation was established to certify hand-knotted rugs made by only adult workers. The effectiveness of the labeling program is subject to dispute. One study estimated that the incidence of child labor in looms not covered by social labeling was about 24 percent, compared to 7 to 18 percent in looms subject to labeling requirements.[128] But the high incidence of abuse has made many retailers wary of a label promising "no child labor." For example, IKEA, a Scandinavia-based home furnishing company, declined to join Rugmark's consortium because it was skeptical that the foundation could effectively monitor such a fragmented production process. IKEA estimated that there were some 175,000 looms alone in one Indian carpet belt, each accommodating two or three workers, and many located in small workshops or homes. Moreover, the company worried that a strategy focused solely on prohibition could have unwelcome by-products. For example, a crackdown on child labor in the Bangladeshi garment industry in the 1990s led to the ouster of an estimated 50,000 underage factory workers, who were then pushed into more hazardous and lower-paying occupations, including prostitution.[129] An ILO initiative to eliminate child labor in stitching soccer balls had similarly unintended consequences; home labor was eliminated to facilitate monitoring, and because cultural norms prevented women from working outside the home, some 20,000 adult female employees lost their livelihood.[130]

To address the issue, IKEA developed its own auditing system, along with a community development initiative aimed at addressing the root causes of the problem. Partnering with UNICEF, the company set up alternative learning centers for the 24,000 children in the heart of India's carpet belt who were unable to attend government-run schools. Because illness and debt were often responsible for forcing children into paid labor, the initiative also provided vaccinations and supported microenterprise.[131]

Despite the program's substantial success concerning education, health, and financial security, the company faced continued criticism for child labor. At a time when annual audits revealed between nine and thirteen cases of underage workers among some 1500 suppliers, and resulted in at least ten terminations of suppliers for ethical reasons, a British survey of trade practices gave IKEA only a half-star rating in its five-star scale. The study also encouraged consumers to consider boycotting the worst-performing stores.[132]

Other companies have faced similar criticisms for labor abuses. Among the most publicized are Apple's safety, wage and hour, and child worker violations.[133] The company has over 200 global suppliers, and although it conducts over 450 audits annually, and has made substantial improvements, chronic problems remain.[134] One of the most troubling exposes was Amnesty International's report on human rights abuses in cobalt mines in the Democratic Republic of Congo. The mines, which supply Apple, Samsung, and Microsoft electronics, employed children as young as seven, for as many as 12 hours, and exposed workers to permanent lung disease.[135]

1.   Ben Heineman writes:

> Corporations must ask whether in banning child labor they are protecting their reputation but harming children. Yet, corporations are not social welfare agencies and have limited capacity to effect broad economic and social change in emerging market communities. . . . Global corporations cannot employ "underage" children, but forcing third-party suppliers to stop child labor, without health and education alternatives for the children, is a morally ambiguous choice. I felt that GE could not employ child labor but that the company was not competent to conduct social welfare programs in emerging markets.[136]

Do you agree? If he is right, what is the "right" course of action for the general counsel on the facts of Problem 9-4?

2.   In order to reduce supplier's incentives to rely on child labor, Apple adopted a plan designed by a social responsibility firm that operates in China, India, and Bangladesh. Under that plan, any supplier guilty of employing underage workers must not only pay for their education but also must pay them lost wages until they graduate (thereby removing any incentive to stay out of school). Yet surprisingly, only about a third of the children eligible for the program actually take advantage of it. Many prefer to continue working at higher wages than those available under the school-plus-stipend program.[137] If you were Apple's general counsel, how would you respond to these labor violations? How would you weigh the costs of auditing and complying with labor standards against the reputational damage the violations exact? Are independent monitor reports needed at all suppliers? Does the answer depend on how much American consumers are willing to pay for decent working conditions abroad? What other concerns are relevant? In commenting on Apple's challenge, one commentator noted that the company is playing a "game of whack-a-mole that no other company even attempts with such transparency."[138] Other commentators have been less charitable. Mark Dummett, a human rights researcher at Amnesty International, argues that "[c]ompanies whose global profits total $125 billion cannot credibly claim that they are unable to check" on labor conditions. If you were the Apple GC, how would you respond?

3.   In a landmark 2018 decision, the Ninth Circuit Court of Appeals permitted a suit to proceed under the Alien Tort Statute by former child slaves from the Ivory Coast against large American manufacturers, purchasers, and retail sellers of cocoa beans. According to the complaint, the plaintiffs were forced to work long hours without pay and suffered severe abuse by those guarding them. The defendants allegedly sought to keep their labor costs low by knowingly providing financial, technical, and other support to farmers dependent on child labor.[139] Studies backed by the U.S. Labor Department revealed that despite the industry's professed efforts to combat underage labor, the number of children working in Ghana and the Ivory Coast has been

increasing. The area's cocoa industry now involves more than 2 million children, aged 5 to 17, who work under hazardous conditions.[140] Nestle claims that it has built or renovated over 40 schools in the area, helped support families keep their children in school, and created monitoring systems to identify at-risk youth. Such efforts cost the company about $5.5 million annually, against sales of about $90 billion.[141] According to Tulane Professor William Bertrand, a researcher who co-authored the Labor Department studies, chocolate manufacturers "talk a lot about the money spent on various activities related to child labor, but when we did the calculations, a fair proportion of that money was spent on sitting around and talking about it in London and Geneva."[142]

If you were the general counsel of Nestle, how would you respond? How much responsibility do American companies have for addressing known labor abuses in their supply chain? What can the cocoa industry learn from the carpet industry? What strategies will be most effective for NGOs that seek to challenge slave labor?

MEDIA RESOURCES

Apple CEO Bruce Sewell's testimony before Congress about why the company would not comply with the FBI's request for an iPhone key offers a window into complex issues surrounding privacy.[143] Many excellent movies and documentaries are available concerning transnational corporations and human rights. Documentaries on child labor include:

- *Slavery, a Global Investigation*, which profiles child labor in Ivory Coast cocoa farms;
- *A Kind of Childhood*, which documents six years in the lives of working children in Bangladesh;
- *Stolen Childhoods*, which chronicles child labor in Brazil, India, the United States, Mexico, Indonesia, Kenya, and Nepal;
- *India: The Little Serfs*, which explores bonded child labor in the rug, jewelry, and mining trades;
- *Tomorrow We'll Finish*, which follows the lives of three girls in the Nepal rug trade;
- *The Day My God Died,* which portrays child sex trafficking in Nepal and India; and
- *Slavery: A Global Investigation*, which examines bonded labor in rug-making sectors of India, in cocoa plantations in the Ivory Coast, and at the homes of World Bank officials in Washington, D.C.[144]
- Other recent documentaries on child labor and sex trafficking include *The Price of Free, Frontline: Trafficked in America, Invisible Hands, The Rescue List, Toni, Tuk Tuk,* and *Mass e Bhat.*

- Documentaries about U.S. companies with global supply chains that have problematic labor practices include *Complicity*, *The True Cost*, and *The Dark Side of Chocolate.*

C. PRO BONO SERVICE

The bar's tradition of providing unpaid legal assistance *pro bono publico* (for the good of the public) has extended historical roots, reaching back to classical Rome and medieval ecclesiastical courts.[145] How often it occurred, and who benefited, is not entirely clear. What is clear is that recent decades have brought a substantial increase in pro bono commitments, particularly for those most in need. According to the most recent ABA survey, only a fifth of lawyers report doing no public service. However, only about a third of the lawyers reported meeting the aspirational standard of the Model Rules of Professional Conduct: over 50 hours of service to persons of limited means (or organizations that support them) per year.[146] Given that the response rate for the survey was under one percent and probably overrepresented those who made some contribution, the actual national figures are doubtless lower.[147] A recent survey by the American Bar Foundation found that about half of lawyers reported doing pro bono work, with an average of 25 hours per year.[148] These modest rates of service are in part a response to organizational values and priorities. In a national survey of some 24,000 lawyers that asked about what was necessary to succeed in a legal career, only about a quarter saw pro bono work as necessary; slightly under half thought it was advantageous; and another quarter thought it was irrelevant.[149] So too, in the American Corporate Counsel survey, only a third of chief legal officers reported actively encouraging staff to engage in pro bono work, mainly because their departments were already stretched too thin.[150]

Leaders can make a difference in several respects. The first is by personal example. As with other ethical issues, the "tone at the top" is critical, and when a general counsel or managing partner of a law firm makes time for public service, it is harder for others to say they cannot do the same. A second form of influence involves setting policy and reward structures. As discussion below indicates, legal workplaces vary in how much they value and in how effectively they select and facilitate pro bono work. A third context in which leadership matters involves the rules and incentives that the profession collectively establishes for public service.

On all of these dimensions, progress remains to be made. While applauding the dedication of many pro bono lawyers, commentators raise concerns about both the quantity and quality of service. The following excerpt explores the challenges facing the bar in ensuring that its charitable work best serves the public's, and not just the profession's, interests.

DEBORAH L. RHODE,
RETHINKING THE PUBLIC IN LAWYERS' PUBLIC SERVICE:
PRO BONO, STRATEGIC PHILANTHROPY, AND THE BOTTOM LINE

77 Fordham Law Review 1435 (2009)

Introduction

Law firms . . . do not support pro bono unless there is a business reason
to do so. The bottom line on this question is the bottom line.

—Chicago law firm partner

The preamble to the American Bar Association's (ABA) Model Rules of
Professional Conduct declares, "A lawyer, as a member of the legal profession, . . .
[is] a public citizen having special responsibility for the quality of justice." One of
those responsibilities is the commitment to provide unpaid service "pro bono
publico"—for the good of the public. But in practice, pro bono has never been only
about what is good for the public; it has also been about what is good for lawyers.
What will enhance their reputation, experience, contacts, and relationships? The
occasional disjuncture between public and professional interests in charitable work
is the focus of this essay. In particular, the concern is that lawyers' own pragmatic
interests have marginalized more socially responsible considerations and resulted
in inadequate evaluation, strategic planning, and accountability.

That is not to discount the extraordinary contributions of time and talent that
thousands of lawyers make. Nor is it to overlook the equally impressive increase
in pro bono contributions over the last decade. But it is to argue against
complacency. It is a shameful irony that the country with the world's highest
concentration of lawyers has done so little to make legal assistance available to
low-income individuals who need it most. Equal justice is what we put on
courthouse doors; it does not describe what goes on behind them. Lawyers, both
individually and collectively, have a responsibility for the quality of justice that
implies a responsibility for effective pro bono assistance. This obligation is too
often overlooked in contemporary practice.

I. The Role of Self-Interest

Whether self-interest matters in public service is part of a long-standing debate
about the meaning of altruism. Some branches of philosophy and economics deny
the possibility of wholly disinterested behavior. Their assumption is that all
reasoned action is motivated by some self-interest—after all, why else would
someone act? According to this view, when people attempt to benefit another, it is
because they derive personal satisfaction from doing so. And from a societal
standpoint, why should their motivation matter? To borrow philosopher Bernard
Williams's example, when a man gives money to famine relief, why should we
care whether his objective is to enhance his standing with the Rotary Club? So too,

what difference does it make if law firms volunteer time less out of concern for social justice than a desire to improve their recruitment, reputation, training, and media rankings. The point is to get their contributions.

Yet, to view public service solely in terms of professional interests is troubling on both moral and pragmatic grounds. As a matter of principle, an action taken because benefiting others feels intrinsically rewarding stands on different ethical footing than an action taken because it will bring extrinsic rewards. Part of what individuals find fulfilling about charitable work is a sense that they are expressing moral values and serving broader social objectives. A wide array of evidence suggests that selfless action is good for the self; it enhances satisfaction, health, and self-esteem. Moreover, as a practical matter, encouraging individuals to engage in public service for intrinsic reasons rather than extrinsic rewards serves societal objectives. It is generally less expensive and more effective to rely on internal motivations than on external incentives and sanctions to ensure quality assistance. That is particularly true in contexts like pro bono legal work, where most clients are not in a position to evaluate or challenge the adequacy of aid. Those who provide legal services based on deeply felt values are more likely to do their best than those who are merely fulfilling a firm's hourly quota or improving their legal skills. Some evidence also suggests that lawyers motivated by internalized commitments are the most likely to engage in substantial and sustained service.

Of course, intrinsic and extrinsic motivations are not mutually exclusive; they are often mutually reinforcing. Billable hours credit can ensure that individuals have the time to offer assistance that they are internally motivated to provide. The point is simply that encouraging individuals and employers to view pro bono contributions in terms of their social impact is likely to enhance their performance. A strategic philanthropic orientation also encourages the kind of public service that most benefits the public.

Yet this ethical focus is too often eclipsed by the "business case" for pro bono service. This essay explores the way that lawyers' own pragmatic interests can marginalize more socially responsible considerations. It also chronicles the inadequacies in program design, evaluation, and reporting and accountability standards that have compromised the effectiveness of even the best-intentioned public service initiatives. The full potential of pro bono work is more likely to emerge under a framework grounded in strategic philanthropy. In essence, that framework demands clarity in goals and specific measurements of achievement. Its premise is that those who make philanthropic contributions want the maximum social return on their investment. For lawyers' pro bono programs, that will require a more reflective process for establishing priorities and evaluating progress. . . .

III. Pro Bono for Whom? The Profession's Interest in Public Service

[What exactly should count as pro bono work is a matter of long-standing dispute. Should any unpaid work qualify, including favors for family, friends, and paying clients; service on nonprofit boards; or cases involving deadbeat clients or court-awarded fees?] The lack of consensus about what constitutes pro bono work is partly attributable to the lack of consensus about why lawyers should do it. Attorneys' public service reflects the same mix of motives that underpins other charitable work. People contribute out of a sense of empathy and obligation, and out of a desire for rewards and recognition. Giving makes givers feel good and translates into tangible personal and professional benefits. Lawyers are no exception. When asked about motivating factors for pro bono work, lawyers most often cite personal satisfaction, and then a sense of professional obligation, followed by employer policies and encouragement, and career advancement. For many attorneys, public service offers their most rewarding experiences; it is a way to feel that they are making a difference and to express the values that sent them to law school in the first instance. Work for racial, ethnic, or other disadvantaged groups can also be an important form of "giving back" and affirming identity. So too, for attorneys phasing into retirement, volunteer service is a way to continue making productive use of their skills on a less demanding schedule. Other lawyers cite practical payoffs. Public service can bring recognition, contacts, trial experience, direct client relationships, and expertise in a field in which they would like to obtain paid work. . . .

As bar leaders have also recognized, the profession has a strong self-interest in seeing that its members voluntarily assume such obligations. In a society in which over four-fifths of the legal needs of the poor, and two- to three-fifths of the needs of moderate-income individuals remain unmet, bar pro bono assistance can help relieve pressure for more systemic reforms that would reduce the need for attorneys. . . . In one representative [public opinion] survey, which asked what could improve the image of lawyers, the response most often chosen was "provision of free legal services to the needy"; two-thirds of Americans indicated that it would favorably influence their opinion.

Legal employers, for their part, have comparable interests in supporting pro bono work. Those interests vary somewhat across practice settings. Particularly for junior attorneys in large firms, nonpaying cases can offer training, litigation experience, client contact, intellectual challenge, and responsibility far beyond what is available in their other work. . . .

Such work can also enhance a firm's reputation and visibility in the community. The benefits are particularly great for the largest firms. They have the resources to attract and underwrite high-profile cases, and their pro bono performance is ranked by the *American Lawyer* based on the number of hours per lawyer and the percentage of lawyers who contribute more than twenty hours. A firm's pro bono rating also accounts for a third of its score in the competition for membership on the *American Lawyer*'s coveted "A-List" of the nation's top twenty firms. A low score also risks relegating the firm to the magazine's occasional profiles of cellar dwellers. Interviews with senior managers leave no doubt that many firms have responded to these rankings by substantially improving their pro bono programs.

IV. Limitations of Existing Programs

These bottom-line concerns have led many bar leaders to stress the business case for pro bono initiatives. As one veteran repeatedly emphasized to American Bar Foundation researchers—"often pounding the table—self-interest, self-interest, self-interest." The risk, however, is that the public interest may become an unintended casualty. Problems arise in several forms: the quality of service, the need for recognition, and the criteria for selection.

One chronic difficulty stems from the inadequacy of oversight and accountability. Law firms and media ranking systems compile information on the quantity, not quality, of pro bono work, and clients often lack the knowledge or leverage to raise concerns. . . . In my own recent survey of leading public interest legal organizations, almost half reported extensive or moderate problems with quality in the pro bono work they obtained from outside firms. . . .

A related problem involves lawyers who "want to do pro bono work in theory but in practice, don't want to make the commitment." Although many firms go to considerable lengths to ensure that public service clients are not treated as second class citizens, others let bottom-line considerations prevail. These employers look for "training and opportunities for bored associates, but don't want to give them the time . . . when other paid work comes up."

In some cases, the difficulty lies with the associates who are disenchanted with their pro bono options, often because the programs do not provide sufficient choice or credit. Here again, *American Lawyer* rankings may have perverse results if firms pressure attorneys to participate without providing a range of satisfying opportunities. Almost half the lawyers in my pro bono study expressed dissatisfaction with the kind of work their firms permitted. Favors for clients, other lawyers, and their relatives, or partners' "pet organizations" struck many associates as "not truly" pro bono. . . .

A [further] problem involves the lack of strategic focus in formulating selection standards. Despite all the discussion about the business case for pro bono, most firms are strikingly unbusinesslike in the way that they structure their programs. The result is missed opportunities for both the profession and the public. Research on strategic philanthropy in general and public interest legal efforts in particular suggests that the most effective approach is to be systematic in identifying goals, designing cost-effective strategies to address them, and developing criteria to measure their achievement. By this standard, most lawyers' pro bono work falls short. Relatively few firms engage in any systematic assessment of community needs or of the most cost-effective use of resources. Seldom do they even survey their own membership about giving priorities or attempt to monitor the satisfaction of clients or the social impact of particular initiatives. When asked about how effectiveness is measured, one Wall Street partner expressed a common view with uncommon candor: "'We are not able to answer this question as it is posed. . . . [W]e cannot opine as to which of our pro bono projects most effectively contributes to the community.'" The result is often a mismatch between public needs, partner priorities, and associate satisfaction. . .

V. A Strategic Approach to Pro Bono Service

Paul Brest, former Stanford law professor, and now president of the Hewlett Foundation, likes to remind nonprofit organizations that "if you don't know where you are going, any road will take you there." Pro bono decision-making often lacks that sense of direction. Many lawyers have not thought deeply about their objectives or have no principled way of resolving conflicts among them. The result is often a "spray and pray" approach, which spreads assistance widely in the hope that somehow something good will come of it. Something usually does, but the result is not necessarily the most cost-effective use of resources. . . .

[A well-designed] approach should have at least four critical dimensions:

- A process for identifying objectives and establishing priorities among them;
- A process for selecting projects that will best advance those objectives;
- Policies that encourage widespread participation; and
- A system for overseeing performance and evaluating how well objectives are being met.

In essence, those who make substantial pro bono contributions need to become more strategic in setting goals and monitoring progress in achieving them. . . .

Research on philanthropy in general and pro bono programs in particular leaves no doubt about the strategies most likely to promote involvement. First, organizations need to demonstrate a commitment to public service that is affirmed by their leadership and institutionalized in their policies. According to surveyed lawyers, the reforms most likely to encourage volunteer work included crediting it toward billable hour requirements and valuing it in promotion and compensation decisions. . . .

Enlisting students, clients, and the legal media in efforts to pressure legal employers also makes sense. . . . If a significant number of students [make clear their desire for pro bono opportunities] . . . many employers will respond accordingly. So too, some government and corporate counsel's offices here and abroad have begun considering pro bono records in allocating legal work. If more clients joined a coordinated campaign, involving a broad spectrum of the legal market, the result might be a significant difference in law firm priorities. And if more legal publications published pro bono rankings of more legal employers, the heightened visibility might help improve performance. . . .

A final group of strategies should focus on evaluation. Employers need to know not simply who contributes and how much, but also how satisfied stakeholders are with their contributions. The ABA Standards for Programs Providing Civil Legal Services to Persons of Limited Means identifies strategies for assessing effectiveness, which include collecting evaluations from participants, clients, referring organizations, and peer review teams.

More effort should also address social impact. It is, of course, true, as Albert Einstein reportedly observed, that "'[n]ot everything that counts can be counted, and not everything that can be counted counts.'" In many charitable contexts, the social return on investment is hard to quantify and evaluate. . . . But that is no reason to avoid the effort, and there are better and worse ways of making such evaluations. As research on philanthropy demonstrates, donors who want to make a difference cannot afford to conflate good intentions with good results. Yet lawyers have a tendency to do just that. They often assume that anything given pro bono is pro bono; representation is taken as a good in and of itself, regardless of cost-effectiveness.

A more strategic approach would incorporate criteria similar to those that public interest legal organizations often use in allocating resources and evaluating their efforts. For example, are they meeting needs that experts or client groups consider most compelling? How many individuals are they assisting? If the matter involves policy or work or impact litigation, what are the chances of a long-term legal or political payoff? Will the work help to raise public understanding or empower clients? Is the assistance filling gaps in coverage or bringing some special expertise to the table? What are the other uses of lawyers' time? Might they find better ways to address the sources rather than symptoms of the problems? . . .

Conclusion: Beyond the Bottom Line

In today's increasingly competitive legal market, it comes as no surprise that pro bono is increasingly presented as a bottom-line issue. Nor is that strategy entirely misplaced. Convincing lawyers that they will do well by doing good is a key strategy in sustaining charitable commitments. But to present public service purely in those terms is to compromise altruistic impulses and societal objectives. When attorneys talk about pro bono, they generally speak in shorthand. "Publico" has dropped out of the discourse. We can afford to lose the Latin, but not the concept.

PROBLEM 9-5

If you were a general counsel or chair of a law firm pro bono committee, what process would you establish to determine the amount and distribution of your organization's charitable contributions? How would you establish priorities? How much freedom would you give to individuals to choose where to commit time or money? Would you require a minimum commitment from all attorneys? Would you cap the amount of pro bono work that could count toward billable hour quotas? How would you measure cost effectiveness?

NOTES AND QUESTIONS

1. One advantage of relying on "bottom-line" justifications for pro bono work is that they make it less vulnerable to cutbacks when the economy goes south. During the 2008 recession, large firms' charitable work went up 15 percent even as other economic indicators went down.[151] Rather than treating pro bono programs as an unaffordable luxury, firms generally relied on them to provide training and professional development for attorneys lacking sufficient paid work. Media ranking systems have also focused firms' attention on pro bono

involvement as an important measure of reputation, which matters in recruitment and retention. Yet as the preceding excerpt notes, that bottom-line focus has not come without costs. One is the absence of incentives for lawyers to focus on measures of performance apart from the number of hours contributed. My survey with Scott Cummings of pro bono counsel at large law firms found that none attempted any systematic analysis of the cost-effectiveness or social impact of their efforts. Nor did any have formal mechanisms for gauging satisfaction among clients and nonprofit organizations that referred or co-counseled pro bono cases.[152] Many pro bono programs seemed to operate on the assumption that any unpaid service is a good in itself, and that its value need not be questioned unless someone actually complains. This reactive approach is particularly ill suited to pro bono contexts. Unlike paying clients, who can vote with their feet if dissatisfied with performance, recipients of aid may lack alternatives or the sense of entitlement to express concerns.

How should lawyers and law firms be held accountable for the quality and impact of their contributions? What could you do as a general counsel, a managing partner of a firm, or a bar association president to promote greater accountability?

2. What might a strategic approach to pro bono involve for a law firm or an in-house counsel office? ABA reports emphasize the need for committed leadership, formal structures and policies, substantive training and support, and identification of opportunities.[153] A growing number of firms are attempting to partner with clients in order to build relationships and expand capacity. For example, Baker McKenzie has collaborated with in-house lawyers and other corporate employees at companies including Google, Accenture, and Merck to tackle issues in Nepal involving exploitation of women, discrimination, education, and labor abuses.[154] McGuire Woods has partnered with Bank of America and other corporations to provide triage programs that offer key services that local legal aid offices are unable to provide.[155] Coca Cola's legal department has worked with its outside firm King and Spaulding to create a Wills on Wheels program that provided assistance to individuals who couldn't afford services.[156] What interests do these collaborations serve? What other approaches might you recommend?

3. Mark Pulliam criticizes pro bono litigation on the ground that it often

> masks a distinct political agenda that undermines representative self government while simultaneously increasing the grip of an insular and out-of-touch ruling class. . . . Enshrining the LGBT agenda in the Constitution by judicial edict is a prime example. . . . And so on, not just in the Supreme Court, but in federal courts across the country, with litigation challenging President Trump's rescission of DACA, seeking to overturn Texas's enactment of laws regulating abortion, and seeking to restore voting rights for convicted felons. Law firm pro bono programs mirror the latest

progressive fashions, unfailingly promoting policy goals favored by the Left—what is sometimes referred to euphemistically as "social justice."[157]

Pulliam is particularly incensed by subsidies for pro bono work by publicly traded corporations, which he claims "owe their shareholders their full devotion to maximizing profits and increasing share value," which is inconsistent with "meddling" in social policy.[158] If you were a law firm or corporate leader responsible for your organization's pro bono policy, how would you respond? Would you authorize organizational support for an individual lawyer's pro bono work that other members of the organization find objectionable? If not, what process would you recommend to screen pro bono matters?

4. Should firms or in-house counsel offices require a minimum contribution in time (or a financial equivalent) from all lawyers? Should courts or bar associations? Or should they require reporting of contributions in an effort to shame lawyers into greater participation? Would it be possible to ensure reasonable levels of competence and compliance under a mandatory pro bono system? Esther Lardent, the former president of the Pro Bono Institute, warned that mandatory systems make a "very small dent in a very large problem." In her view, the costs of training participants, administering referrals, and monitoring performance are likely to exceed the benefits:

> Unfortunately, the end product of a successful campaign for a mandatory pro bono program probably will fail to meet the original goals of the program's proponents. Experience demonstrates that the political compromises involved in securing approval of such a program will result in a definition of pro bono service so broad that it encompasses activities already undertaken by virtually all lawyers. All lawyers will be in compliance, yet no additional services to address unmet legal needs will be provided. . . . Mandatory pro bono will not increase services, enhance professionalism, or improve the performance of existing pro bono programs.[159]

Supporters of pro bono requirements respond that even if they were imperfectly administered and enforced, their existence would at least support lawyers who would like to provide more pro bono assistance but whose employers have other priorities. A mandatory program that restricted the definition of qualifying pro bono programs, offered training and support services, and provided a financial buyout alternative, could also respond to lawyers who lack expertise or interest in addressing unmet legal needs.[160]

What is your view? Should lawyers be subject to pro bono requirements by the bar or their employer? What about law students? Have you participated in organized volunteer work? Did it provide significant personal or professional benefits? How might public service enhance lawyers' performance in leadership positions?

MEDIA RESOURCES

Many law firms include material on their pro bono efforts on their websites. Some legal aid and public interest organizations also have promotional videos.[161] The American Bar Association's Center on Professional Responsibility compiles profiles of the winners of its annual Pro Bono Award. The film *I Am Sam* reflects the problems of ensuring quality assistance by pro bono attorneys through a scene in which a child welfare lawyer criticizes a volunteer attorney for her shallow commitment. For that attorney, the pro bono case "is an award for you at some luncheon. You win, you're out the door!"[162]

END NOTES

[1] ROBERT W. CULLEN, THE LEADING LAWYER: A GUIDE TO PRACTICING LAW AND LEADERSHIP 18 (2010); Stuart Levine, *The Power of Leading an Engagement Effectively*, LAW PRAC. MAG., Sept./Oct. 2015, at 44; Jessicca Erickson, *The Market for Leadership in Corporate Litigation*, 2015 U. ILL. L REV. 1479 (2015).

[2] Laurie Bassi & Daniel McMurrer, *Leadership and Law Firm Success: A Statistical Analysis*, MCBASSI & CO., Mar. 2008, at 9, http://www.leadershipforattorneys.org/articles/WhitePaper-LeadershipAndLawFirmSuccess%20Feb%208.pdf.

[3] Bassi & McMurrer, *Leadership and Law Firm Success*, at 9.

[4] CENTER FOR THE STUDY OF THE LEGAL PROFESSION AT GEORGETOWN UNIVERSITY LAW CENTER AND THOMSON REUTERS LEGAL EXECUTIVE INSTITUTE AND PEER MONITOR, 2018 REPORT ON THE STATE OF THE LEGAL MARKET 4-6 (2018); HILDEBRANDT CONSULTING LLC, 2016 CLIENT ADVISORY 12 (2016).

[5] HILDEBRANDT CONSULTING LLC, 2016 CLIENT ADVISORY, at 9-11.

[6] Michael J. Moore, *Succession Planning: Where Will Your Firm's New Leaders Come From?*, 87 WISC. LAWYER 28 (Feb. 2014).

[7] ROLAND B. SMITH & PAUL BENNETT MARROW, THE CHANGING NATURE OF LEADERSHIP IN LAW FIRMS 5 (2009).

[8] MAUREEN BRODERICK, THE ART OF MANAGING PROFESSIONAL SERVICES: INSIGHTS FROM LEADERS OF THE WORLD'S TOP FIRMS 267 (2010), as excerpted in Maureen Broderick, *Leading Gently*, AM. LAW., Dec. 2010, at 63, 64.

[9] KENNETH VAN WINKLE JR., *The Managing Partner's Role in Today's World*, in MANAGING A LAW FIRM: LEADING LAWYERS ON UNDERSTANDING THE IMPACT OF THE ECONOMIC CRISIS, IDENTIFYING AND DEVELOPING GROWTH OBJECTIVES, AND RECRUITING AND RETAINING TOP TALENT (INSIDE THE MINDS) 46, 47 (Rich Meneghello et. al. eds., 2010); Abraham C. Reich & Mark L. Silow, *Democracy, Transparency and Rotation: Keys to Running a Successful Law Firm*, in MANAGING A LAW FIRM 71, 81 (Rich Meneghello et. al. eds., 2010).

[10] Carol Schiro Greenwald, *Successful Managing Partners Practice EL-Based Leadership*, 88 N.Y. ST. B. J. 28 (Sept. 2016).

[11] Levine, *The Power of Leading an Engagement Effectively*, at 45.

[12] Levine, *The Power of Leading an Engagement Effectively*, at 45 (quoting Jeff Citron).

[13] Levine, *The Power of Leading an Engagement Effectively*, at 45 (quoting Dan Hollis); Greenwald, *Successful Managing Partners*; ROLAND B. SMITH & PAUL BENNETT MARROW, LEADING IN TIMES OF COMPLEXITY AND UNCERTAINTY: THE CHANGING NATURE OF LEADERSHIP IN LAW FIRMS (2008); ROBERT W. CULLEN, THE LEADING LAWYER: A GUIDE TO PRACTICING LAW AND LEADERSHIP 10-11 (2010)

[14] THOMAS J. DELONG, JOHN J. GABARRO & ROBERT J. LEES, WHEN PROFESSIONALS HAVE TO LEAD: A NEW MODEL FOR HIGH PERFORMANCE (2007), as reprinted in AM. LAW., Dec. 2007, at 125-29.

[15] PATRICK J. MCKENNA & DAVID H. MAISTER, FIRST AMONG EQUALS: HOW TO MANAGE A GROUP OF PROFESSIONALS 6 (2002); Linda Chiem, *7 Habits of Highly Effective Firm Leaders*, LAW360, Mar. 10, 2015.

[16] THOMAS C. GRELLA, LESSONS IN LEADERSHIP: ESSENTIAL SKILLS FOR LAWYERS 56-57 (2013).

[17] Thomas C. Grella, *Mountains and Molehills: The Challenge of Law Firm Leadership*, 41 LAW PRACT., 60 May/June 2015.

[18] Anna Stolley Persky, *Who's Running the Business of Law?*, WASH. LAW., July/Aug. 2016, at 21.

[19] MCKENNA & MAISTER, FIRST AMONG EQUALS, 5 (quoting Stengel).

[20] David Maister, *The Trouble with Lawyers*, AM. LAW., Apr. 2006, at 100; Larry Richard, *Herding Cats: The Lawyer Personality Revealed*, LAWPRO MAG., Winter 2008, at 1, 3; JEFF FOSTER, LARRY RICHARD, LISA ROHRER & MARK SIRKIN, UNDERSTANDING LAWYERS: THE PERSONALITY TRAITS OF SUCCESSFUL PRACTITIONERS (Hildebrandt White Paper, 2010).

[21] Maister, *The Trouble with Lawyers*, 100.

[22] David Segal, *Is Law School a Losing Game?*, N.Y. TIMES, Jan. 8, 2011, at B1; Eli Wald, *Foreword: The Great Recession and the Legal Profession*, 78 FORDHAM L. REV. 2051 (2010); Nathan Koppel, *Recession Batters Law Firms, Triggering Layoffs, Closings*, WALL ST. J., Jan. 26, 2009, at A1, A11; Joan Indiana Rigdon, *Cost Effect*, WASH. LAW., Apr. 2010, at 17.

[23] JIM COLLINS, HOW THE MIGHTY FALL: AND WHY SOME COMPANIES NEVER GIVE IN 21 (2009).

[24] COLLINS, HOW THE MIGHTY FALL, 21.

[25] COLLINS, HOW THE MIGHTY FALL, 22.

[26] COLLINS, HOW THE MIGHTY FALL, 22.

[27] COLLINS, HOW THE MIGHTY FALL, 22-23.

[28] COLLINS, HOW THE MIGHTY FALL, 63-64.

[29] Darrell K. Rigby, *Look Before You Lay Off*, HARV. BUS. REV. 3 (Apr. 2002); Robert Sutton, *Layoffs: Are They Ever the Answer?*, in *Doing Layoffs Right*, HARV. BUS. REV. COLLECTION (June 2009).

[30] LEE BOLMAN & TERENCE E. DEAL, UNCOMMON JOURNEY 93-95 (2001); Anthony J. Nyberg & Charile O. Trevor, *After Layoffs, Help Survivors Be More Effective*, HARV. BUS. REV. 15 (June 2009) (describing costs in productivity from anticipation of layoffs and role of inadequate information); LESLIE GAINES-ROSS, CORPORATE REPUTATION: 12 STEPS TO

SAFEGUARDING AND RECOVERING REPUTATION 108 (2008) (describing AT&T's ill-timed grant of $10 million in stock options to its CEO following layoffs).

[31] PATRICK J. MCKENNA & DAVID H. MAISTER, FIRST AMONG EQUALS: HOW TO MANAGE A GROUP OF PROFESSIONALS 215 (2002).

[32] JOHN DALLA COSTA, THE ETHICAL IMPERATIVE: WHY MORAL LEADERSHIP IS GOOD BUSINESS 274-75 (1990).

[33] Pfeffer, *The Real Keys to High Performance* (quoting Richard Kovacevich); RONALD A. HEIFETZ & MARTY LINSKY, LEADERSHIP ON THE LINE: STAYING ALIVE THROUGH THE DANGERS OF LEADING 59 (2002).

[34] Koppel, *Recession Batters Law Firms*, at A11 (quoting consultant Brennan).

[35] HILDEBRANDT, THE ANATOMY OF LAW FIRM FAILURES.

[36] Susan L. White, *Leadership: Do We Have It All Wrong?*, ABA LAW PRACT. TODAY, Oct. 12, 2017. https://www.lawpracticetoday.org/article/leadership-do-we-have-it-wrong/.

[37] White, *Leadership*; Timothy B. Corcoron, *Legal Marketing*, AM. LAW., Mar. 1, 2018.

[38] Ben W. Heineman Jr. & William F. Lee, *Noblesse Oblige*, AM. LAW., May 2010, at 49, 50.

[39] The facts in this problem are modeled on a 2016 lawsuit against Chadbourne & Parke. *See* Elizabeth Olson, *Female Lawyer's Gender-Bias Suit Challenges Law Firm Pay Practices*, N.Y. TIMES, Aug. 31, 2016.

[40] Elizabeth Olson, *A 44 % Divide for Female and Male Law Partners, Survey Says*, N.Y. TIMES, Oct. 12, 2016; JEFFREY LOWE, MAJOR, LINDSEY & AFRICA 2016 PARTNER COMPENSATION SURVEY (2016).

[41] Joan C. Williams & Marina Multhaup, *What the Partner Pay Gap Tells Us About Bias*, NAT'L L.J., Oct. 24, 2016.

[42] Heidi Gardner, *Harvard Study: On Gender and Origination in the Legal Profession*, BLOOMBERG LAW (2016).

[43] Greenwald, *Successful Managing Partners*.

[44] GRELLA, LESSONS IN LEADERSHIP, at 33.

[45] Greenwald, *Successful Managing Partners*.

[46] Williams & Maulthaup, *What the Partner Pay Gap Tells Us*.

[47] For a CBS report on *Lemonade*, a film about layoffs and a silver lining, see https://www.cbsnews.com/news/making-lemonade-after-losing-livelihood/.

[48] http://www.youtube.com/watch?v=0rqofLr9HE0.

[49] West Wing, Second Season 2, Episode2, "In the Shadow of Two Gunmen Part II."

[50] "The Chain of Screaming," Season 3, Episode 15, available on Netflix Instant.

[51] Jed Rakoff, "'Fierce' Competition Has Changed Law Firms For the Worse," https://player.fm/series/big-law-business/judge-rakoff-fierce-competition-has-changed-law-firms-for-the-worse.

[52] http://www.youtube.com/watch?v=jZCcrSrgqEE.

[53] Carl D. Liggio Sr., *A Look at the Role of Corporate Counsel: Back to the Future— Or Is It the Past?*, 44 ARIZ. L. REV. 621 (2002).

[54] Liggio, *A Look at the Role of Corporate Counsel*, 621; Deborah A. DeMott, *The Discrete Roles of General Counsel*, 74 FORDHAM L. REV. 955, 958-60 (2005); PRASHANT DUBEY & EVA KRIPALANI, THE GENERALIST COUNSEL: HOW LEADING GENERAL COUNSEL

ARE SHAPING TOMORROW'S COMPANIES 1-4 (2013); Steven L. Schwarcz, *To Make or to Buy: In-House Lawyering and Value Creation*, 33 J. CORP. LAW 497 (2008).

[55] DUBEY & KRIPALANI, THE GENERALIST COUNSEL, at 4-5.

[56] DUBEY & KRIPALANI, THE GENERALIST COUNSEL, at xiv (quoting Hilary Krane).

[57] DUBEY & KRIPALANI, THE GENERALIST COUNSEL, at 153.

[58] ASSOCIATION OF CORPORATE COUNSEL, ACC CHIEF LEGAL OFFICER (CLO) 2015 SURVEY 13 (2015).

[59] BEN W. HEINEMAN JR., THE INSIDE COUNSEL REVOLUTION: RESOLVING THE PARTNER GUARDIAN TENSION 10 (2016); CENTER FOR THE STUDY OF THE LEGAL PROFESSION & THOMSON REUTERS LEGAL EXECUTIVE INSTITUTE AND PEER MONITOR, 2018 REPORT ON THE STATE OF THE LEGAL MARKET, 15- 17.

[60] HEINEMAN, THE INSIDE COUNSEL REVOLUTION, 404-05; Ben W. Heineman, Jr., *How GC's Decide Who Gets the Work*, AM. LAW., May 2016, at 29.

[61] Melissa Masleske & Lauren Williamson, *Budget Blues: Law Departments Tighten Up*, INSIDE COUNSEL, Mar. 2009, at 68. For a critique of current corporate billing practices, see Matt Fawcett, *BigLaw Profits: Who's Footing the Bill?* (May 20, 2019), https://linkedin.com/pulse/biglaw-profits-whos-footing-bill-matt-fawcett/; Matt Fawctt, *Don't Blame Big Law*, May 21, 2019, https://www.linkedin.com/pulse/innovation-change-up-us-matt-fawcett/.

[62] HEINEMAN, THE INSIDE COUNSEL REVOLUTION, 409.

[63] E. NORMAN VEASEY & CHRISTINE T. DI GUGLIELMO, INDISPENSABLE COUNSEL: THE CHIEF LEGAL OFFICER IN THE NEW REALITY 182-83 (2011); Heineman, *How GC's Decide,* at 29.

[64] HEINEMAN, THE INSIDE COUNSEL REVOLUTION, 415.

[65] Geoffrey C. Hazard, Jr., *Ethical Dilemmas of Corporate Counsel*, 46 EMORY L.J. 1011 (1997).

[66] VEASEY & GUGLIELMO, INDISPENSABLE COUNSEL, 40-45.

[67] Robert L. Nelson & Laura Beth Nielsen, *Cops, Counsel, and Entrepreneurs: Constructing the Role of Inside Counsel in Large Corporations*, 34 LAW & SOC'Y REV. 457, 474 (2000).

[68] MODEL RULES OF PROF'L CONDUCT r. 1.13 (AM. BAR ASS'N 1983).

[69] DUBEY & KRIPALANI, THE GENERALIST COUNSEL, 163; VEASEY & GUGLIELMO, INDISPENSABLE COUNSEL, 39.

[70] VEASEY & GUGLIELMO, INDISPENSABLE COUNSEL, 34.

[71] Sung Hui Kim, *The Banality of Fraud: Re-Situating the Inside Counsel as Gatekeeper*, 74 FORDHAM L. REV. 983, 1005-07 (2005); Sung Hui Kim, *Gatekeepers Inside Out*, 21 GEO. J. LEGAL ETHICS 411, 439-41 (2008).

[72] DeMott, *Discrete Roles*, at 969; SUSAN P. SHAPIRO, TANGLED LOYALTIES: CONFLICT OF INTEREST IN LEGAL PRACTICE 32, 104-05 (2002); Sung Hui Kim, *Inside Lawyers: Friends or Gatekeepers?*, 84 FORDHAM L. REV. 1867 (2014); Kim, *The Banality of Fraud*, at 1026-34.

[73] Geoffrey C. Hazard Jr., *Ethical Dilemmas of Corporate Counsel*, 46 EMORY L.J. 1011, 1018-19 (1997); VEASEY & GUGLIELMO, INDISPENSIBLE COUNSEL, 61.

[74] Kim, *Gatekeepers Inside Out*, 454-56, 460; Schwarcz, *To Make or to Buy*.

[75] VEASEY & GUGLIELMO, INDISPENSABLE COUNSEL, 100 (quoting Dan Cooperman).

[76] Steven Andersen, *Greasy Palms*, INSIDE COUNSEL, Jan. 2009, at 34.

---

[77] STEPHEN M. BAINBRIDGE, CORPORATE GOVERNANCE AFTER THE FINANCIAL CRISIS 293 (2012). *See also* Kim, *The Banality of Fraud*; and Kim, *Inside Lawyers*.

[78] A. Douglas Melamed, Personal Correspondence, Nov. 2016.

[79] DUBEY & KRIPALANI, THE GENERALIST COUNSEL, 72 (quoting Hilary Krane).

[80] Association of Corporate Counsel, *In-House Counsel in the Liability Crosshairs* (Sept. 2007); VEASEY & GUGLIELMO, INDISPENSABLE COUNSEL, 204-09; DeMott, *Discrete Roles*, at 956.

[81] DUBEY & KRIPALANI, THE GENERALIST COUNSEL, 157-58; *In the Matter of Google, Inc. and David Drummond*, SEC. ACT RELEASE NO 8523 (Jan. 13, 2005).

[82] VEASEY & GUGLIELMO, INDISPENSABLE COUNSEL, 4.

[83] Ben W. Heineman, Jr., *Forward, in*, INDISPENSABLE COUNSEL: THE CHIEF LEGAL OFFICER IN THE NEW REALITY xvii (E. Norman Veasey & Christine T. Di Guglielmo eds., 2012); VEASEY & GUGLIELMO, INDISPENSABLE COUNSEL, 5.

[84] VEASEY & GUGLIELMO, INDISPENSABLE COUNSEL, 3; HEINEMAN, THE INSIDE COUNSEL REVOLUTION, 69-70. For the importance of financial skills, see DUBEY & KRIPALINI, THE GENERALIST COUNSEL, 108; HEINEMAN, THE INSIDE COUNSEL REVOLUTION, 387.

[85] DeMott, *Discrete Roles*, at 979 (noting failures of Enron's general counsel to grasp the nature of the company's financial transactions); HEINEMAN, INSIDE COUNSEL REVOLUTION, at 101, 117 (faulting Enron's lawyers for succumbing to pressures and "craven non-investigation" of whistleblower complaints); David Barstow, *Wal-Mart Hushed Up a Vast Mexican Bribery Case*, N.Y. TIMES, Apr. 21, 2012 (describing complicity of Wal-Mart Mexico's general counsel in bribery of local officials).

[86] Matt Fawcett, *Comments at Stanford Law School Panel*, May 21, 2019.

[87] David Gelles, *The Week the C.E.O.s Got Smacked*, ,N.Y. TIMES, Sept. 29, 2019.

[88] Kim, *The Banality of Fraud*, at 983.

[89] Robert C. Weber, *Is the GC the Conscience of the Company? Maybe Not*, CORP. COUNSEL, Feb., 2013.

[90] Weber, *Is the GC the Conscience of the Company?*

[91] Ben Heineman Jr., *General Counsel Are One Conscience of the Company: A Response to IBM's Robert Weber*, CORP. COUNSEL, Jan. 2013.

[92] Hazard, *Ethical Dilemmas of Corporate Counsel*, at 1017.

[93] Robert W. Gordon, *The Citizen Lawyer: A Brief Informal History of a Myth with Some Basis in Reality*, 50 WM. & MARY L. REV. 1169, 1188 (2009).

[94] Robert W. Gordon, *The Return of the Lawyer-Statesman?*, 69 STAN. L. REV. 1731, 1759-1760 (2017).

[95] *Federal Trade Commission (FTC) v. Qualcomm Inc.*, __F. Supp. __ (N.D. Cal. 2019).

[96] Jenna Greene, *Ouch. Judge Koh Names and Shames Qualcomm In-House Lawyers*, RECORDER, May 23, 2019.

[97] Richard M. Strassberg, David B. Pitofsky & Samantha L. Schreiber, *Lawyers on Trial*, N.Y. L. J., July 18, 2005 (quoting Steven M. Cutler).

[98] ANTHONY C. THOMPSON, DANGEROUS LEADERS: HOW & WHY LAWYERS MUST BE TAUGHT TO LEAD 131 (2018).

[99] Sue Reisinger, *Bad Advice From "Attorney A,": A VW In-House Lawyer is Implicated in Obstruction of Justice Charges*, AM. LAW., Mar. 2017, at 10.

[100] See DEBORAH L. RHODE, DAVID LUBAN, SCOTT L. CUMMINGS & NORA FREEMAN ENGSTROM, LEGAL ETHICS 420-422 (7th ed. 2016).

[101] Mike Isaac, *How Uber Deceives the Authorities Worldwide*, N.Y. TIMES, Mar. 3, 2017; Jennifer Williams-Alvarez, Uber's "Greyball" Scandal Drives at Legal Department Challenges, LAW.COM (Mar. 7, 2017), http://www.corpcounsel.com /id=1202780727037/Ubers-Greyball-Scandal-Drives-at-Legal-Department-Challenges.

[102] Williams-Alvarez, *Uber's "Greyball" Scandal* (quoting Jason Winmill).

[103] Williams-Alvarez, *Uber's "Greyball" Scandal*.

[104] Michael Callahan, email to Deborah Rhode, Sept. 30, 2019.

[105] Gordon, *Return of the Lawyer Statesman?*, 1758-64.

[106] Ben W. Heineman Jr., *GC's Critical Public Policy Role in an Age of Upheaval*, ACC DOCKET (Mar. 22, 2017), http://www.accdocket.com/articles/gc-s-public-policy-role-in-an-age-of-upheaval.cfm.

[107] John C. Coffee Jr., *Preserving the Corporate Superego in a Time of Stress: An Essay on Ethics and Economics*, 33 OXFORD REV. ECON. POL'Y (2017) (recommending regular reports to board); HEINEMAN, INSIDE COUNSEL REVOLUTION, 78-79, 119, 157, 186 (recommending at least two private meetings annually with the board, creating process for identifying issues and identifying risk); Chad R. Brown, *In-House Counsel Responsibilities in the Post-Enron Environment*, 21 ACCA DOCKET 92, 96 (2003) (reporting view of in-house counsel about the need for access to the board); Hazard, *Ethical Dilemmas of Corporate Counsel*, at 1021 (recommending open door policy); VEASEY & GUGLIELMO, INDISPENSABLE COUNSEL, 50, 61 (recommending hiring outside counsel and board role in hiring, firing and compensation of GC); Callahan, email correspondence (recommending culture of communication encouraging candor).

[108] *Hearing on Global Internet Freedom and the Rule of Law, Part II,* before the U.S. Senate Judiciary Committee Subcommittee on Human Rights and the Law (Mar. 2, 2010) (Testimony of Nicole Wong, Vice President and Deputy General Counsel, Google, Inc.).

[109] Michael Bazeley, *Google's New Frontier: Firm Says Some Information Is Better than None at All*, SAN JOSE MERCURY NEWS, Jan. 25, 2006, at 2C (quoting Zittrain).

[110] Tom Zeller Jr., *Web Firms Are Grilled on Dealings in China*, N.Y. TIMES, Feb. 16, 2006, at C1; Joseph Nocera, *Enough Shame to Go Around on China*, N.Y. TIMES, Feb. 18, 2006, at B1, B13.

[111] Jim Yardley, *Google Chief Rejects Putting Pressure on China*, N.Y. TIMES, Apr. 13, 2006, at C7.

[112] Mure Dickie, *Internet Groups "Shirk Human Rights Duties in China,"* FIN. TIMES (LONDON), July 20, 2006, at 10.

[113] HUMAN RIGHTS WATCH, RACE TO THE BOTTOM: CORPORATE COMPLICITY IN CHINESE INTERNET CENSORSHIP (2006).

[114] Philip P. Pan, *U.S. Firms Balance Morality, Commerce; Critics Say Companies Overlook Human Rights*, WASH. POST, Feb. 19, 2006, at A17; HUMAN RIGHTS WATCH, RACE TO THE BOTTOM.

[115] James Glanz & John Markoff, States's Secrets Day 7; *Vast Hacking by a China Fearful of the Web*, N.Y. TIMES, Dec. 5, 2010, at A1; Jessica E. Vascellaro, *Brin Drove Google Pull Back in China*, WALL ST. J., Mar. 24, 2010, at A18.

[116] David M. Dickson, *Google Weighs Leaving China Over Attacks and Censorship*, WASH. TIMES, Jan. 25, 2010, at 1.

[117] Miguel Helft, *Google Tries to Salvage Chinese Activities; Despite Censorship Rift, Company Hopes Lucrative Business Units Can Stay*, INT'L HERALD TRIB., Jan. 21, 2010, at 17. *See* Ben Worthen & Siobhan Gorman, *Google Prepares to Stop Censoring in China*, WALL ST. J., Mar. 12, 2010 (discussing plans to leave some business in China).

[118] Wong, Testimony.

[119] Dickson, *Google Weighs Leaving China* (quoting Rebecca MacKinnon, of the Open Society Institute).

[120] Wong, Testimony.

[121] HEINEMAN, INSIDE COUNSEL REVOLUTION, 51.

[122] For discussion of one such campaign, see Jennifer Hollett, *Magic Carpets: Canadian Designers Are Pulling Rug Out from under Child Labour*, THE GLOBE AND MAIL (CANADA), June 14, 2008, at 19.

[123] Sayan Chakrabarty & Ulrike Grote, *Child Labor in Carpet Weaving: Impact of Social Labeling in India and Nepal*, 37 WORLD DEV. 1683, 1684 (2009).

[124] Geeta Chowdhry & Mark Beeman, *Challenging Child Labor: Transnational Activism and India's Carpet Industry*, 575 ANNALS AM. ACAD. POL. & SOC. SCI. 158 (2001).

[125] INTERNATIONAL LABOR ORGANIZATION, FACTS ON CHILD LABOR (2008), http://www.ilo.org/ipecinfo/product/viewProduct.do?productId=8213.

[126] FEDERICO BLANCO ALLAIS, ASSESSING THE GENDER GAP; EVIDENCE FROM SIMPOC SURVEYS (2009).

[127] Chakrabarty & Grote, *Child Labor in Carpet Weaving*; *India: Ban on Child Labor in Homes, Hotels*, N.Y. TIMES, Aug. 3, 2006, at 6.

[128] Alakh N. Sharma, *Impact of Social Labeling on Child Labour in Carpet Industry*, 73 ECON. & POL. WKLY. 5202 (Dec. 28, 2002-Jan. 3, 2003).

[129] Christopher A. Bartlett, Vincent Dessain & Anders Sjoman, *IKEA's Global Sourcing Challenge: Indian Rugs and Child Labor (A)*, HARV. BUS. REV .CASE STUDY 3 (May 2006).

[130] Bartlett, Dessain & Sjoman, *IKEA's Global Sourcing Challenge*, at 3.

[131] Bartlett, Dessain & Sjoman, *IKEA's Global Sourcing Challenge*, at 4.

[132] Bartlett, Dessain & Sjoman, *IKEA's Global Sourcing Challenge*, at 35; Severin Carrell, *Shops Score Poorly in Fair Trade Survey; Trade Ethics: Environmentalist Urges Consumers to Use Spending Power on the High Street to Stop Exploitation*, THE INDEPENDENT (LONDON), June 16, 2002, at 4.

[133] Neil Gough & Brian X. Chen, *Groups Accuse Apple Supplier in China of Labor Violations*, N.Y. TIMES, Sept. 4, 2014; Gabriel Madway, *Apple's Annual Audit Finds Some Violations from Suppliers*, REUTERS (Mar. 1, 1010), http://blogs.reuters.com /mediafile/2010/03/01/apples-annual-audit-find-some-violations-from-suppliers; HEINEMAN, INSIDE COUNSEL REVOLUTION, 206; Ben W. Heineman Jr., *Apple is about to Discover the Price of Fair Labor*, ATLANTIC, Mar. 30, 2012.

[134] Gough & Chen, *Groups Accuse Apple Suppliers*; James Vincent, *Despite Successes, Labor Violations Still Haunt Apple*, THE VERGE (Feb. 12, 2015), http://www.theverge.com/2015/2/12/8024895/apple-slave-labor-working-conditions-2015.

[135] AMNESTY INTERNATIONAL, THIS IS WHAT WE DIE FOR (2015); Anthony Cuthbertson, *Apple, Samsung and Microsoft Accused of "worst Forms" of Child Labor*

Abuse, NEWSWEEK (Jan. 19, 2016), http://www.newsweek.com/apple-samsung-and-microsoft-linked-child-labor-abuse-claims-417313.

[136] HEINEMAN, INSIDE COUNSEL REVOLUTION, 204-05.

[137] Tim Fernholz, *What Happens When Apple Finds a Child Making Your iPhone*, QUARTZ (Mar. 7, 2014), http://qz.com/183563/what-happens-when-apple-finds-a-child-making-your-IPhone.

[138] Vincent, *Despite Successes*.

[139] *Doe v. Nestle*, 906 F.3d 1120 (9th Cir. 2018).

[140] Rosa Furneaux, *Your Halloween Candy's Hidden Ingredient: Child Slave Labor*, MOTHER JONES, Oct. 31, 2018.

[141] Furneaux, *Your Halloween Candy's Hidden Ingredient*.

[142] Furneaux, *Your Halloween Candy's Hidden Ingredient* (quoting William Bertrand).

[143] Apple vs. FBI Encryption Opening Statements (C-SPAN), https://www.youtube.com/watch?v=RwqggNnP_sM.

[144] *A Kind of Childhood* (2002) is distributed by Direct Cinema Ltd., Santa Monica, CA; *Stolen Childhoods* (2003) is distributed by Galen Films, Vineyard Haven, MA; *India: The Little Serfs* (2003) is distributed by Films for the Humanities and Sciences, Princeton, NJ; *Tomorrow We'll Finish* (1994) is distributed by UNICEF (Division of Communications); and *Slavery: A Global Investigation* (2000) is distributed by Free the Slaves, Washington, D.C.

[145] *See* DEBORAH L. RHODE, PRO BONO IN PRINCIPLE AND IN PRACTICE 3-4 (2005).

[146] ABA STANDING COMM. ON PRO BONO & PUBLIC SERVICE, SUPPORTING JUSTICE III: A REPORT ON THE PRO BONO WORK OF AMERICA'S LAWYERS VI (2013); MODEL RULES OF PROF'L CONDUCT r. 6.1 (AM BAR ASS'N 1983).

[147] ABA STANDING COMM., SUPPORTING JUSTICE III, at 13.

[148] Rebecca L. Sandefur, *What AJD3 Lawyers Do*, in AFTER THE JD III: THIRD RESULTS OF A NATIONAL STUDY OF LEGAL CAREERS 37 (GABRIELE PLICKERT ed. 2017).

[149] ALLI GERKMAN, FOUNDATIONS FOR PRACTICE: THE WHOLE LAWYER AND THE CHARACTER QUOTIENT 10 (Institute for the Advancement of the American Legal System, 2016).

[150] AMERICAN CORPORATE COUNSEL ASSOCIATION, ACC CHIEF LEGAL OFFICERS SURVEY, 11.

[151] David Bario, *Has Pro Bono Become Recession-Proof?*, AM. LAW., July 2, 2009.

[152] Scott L. Cummings & Deborah L. Rhode, *Managing Pro Bono: Doing Well by Doing Better*, 78 FORDHAM L. REV. 2357 (2010).

[153] For an in-house department, see ABA STANDING COMMITTEE ON PRO BONO AND PUBLIC SERVICE AND THE CENTER FOR PRO BONO, CORPORATE COUNSEL (2011).

[154] *The Gift of Giving*, FIN. TIMES, Dec. 1, 2010.

[155] Emma Cueto, *McGuire Woods Harnesses In-House Talent For Legal Aid*, LAW 360 (Nov. 18, 2018), https://www.law360.com/access-to-justice/articles/1100703/mcguirewoods-harnesses-in-house-talent-for-legal-aid?nl_pk=1504fb36-b465-44a-994e.

[156] Cathleen Flahardy, *Refreshing Communities*, INSIDE COUNSEL, May 2011, at 91.

[157] Mark Pulliam, *White Shoe Social Justice Warriors: The Pro Bono Racket* (Oct. 16, 2018), https://misruleoflaw.com/2018/10/16/white-shoe-social-justice-warriors-the-pro-bono-racket/.

[158] Pulliam, *White Shoe Social Justice Warriors*.

[159] Esther F. Lardent, *Mandatory Pro Bono in Civil Cases: The Wrong Answer to the Right Question*, 49 MD. L. REV. 78, 100, 101 (1990).

[160] RHODE, PRO BONO IN PRINCIPLE AND IN PRACTICE, 29-46.

[161] For a documentary by the Legal Aid Foundation of Los Angeles, see https://www.youtube.com/channel/UCnIrfkLkZ8gNCsOcyDRfqzA.

[162] *I Am Sam,* Scene 11, "Free Lucy Dawson!".

CHAPTER 10

LEADERSHIP FOR SOCIAL CHANGE

A. INTRODUCTION

Lawyers are at the forefront of social change. As government, nonprofit, and social movement leaders, they play a critical role in cultural transformation. Their formal positions vary considerably. Nelson Mandela led anti-apartheid activism from a South African prison cell, and Barack Obama issued executive orders from the Oval Office. Yet whatever their position, leaders who seek social change confront some common challenges in defining goals, forging coalitions, mobilizing followers, formulating policy, attracting resources, and engaging public attention.

Social movements are key drivers of change, and despite the importance of leadership in such movements, its role has only recently received systematic analysis.[1] This chapter draws on that emerging research, as well as on other historical and contemporary portraits of lawyers and cultural transformation.[2] The discussion below begins with an overview of the conditions that are likely to yield social movements and the role of leaders in creating or capitalizing on such conditions. More in-depth analysis then explores two American civil rights campaigns in which lawyers have played crucial leadership roles—campaigns challenging discrimination based on race and on sexual orientation.

1. THE CONDITIONS OF SOCIAL CHANGE AND THE ROLE OF LEADERS

Social movements result from a complex interrelationship of factors whose relative importance is subject to debate. Clearly leaders both influence and are influenced by external conditions. Yet how much leadership matters relative to other structural conditions is difficult to assess. Research on the same social movements often comes to different conclusions. For example, some accounts of Martin Luther King's role in the American civil rights campaign insist that "the movement made Martin; Martin did not make the movement."[3] According to Clayborn Carson, director of Stanford University's Martin Luther King Papers Project, even without King "the black struggle would have followed a course of development similar to the one it did."[4] King himself famously suggested as much before a mass meeting during the 1955 Montgomery bus boycott: "If M. L. King had never been born, this movement would have taken place. I just happened to be here. You know there comes a time when time itself is ready for change."[5] Yet others believe that the skills King brought to the movement were critical in shaping its early successes; the "times were ready for King," but so also "King was ready for the times."[6] Cross-cultural research similarly underscores the importance of leadership capabilities. Similar public policy initiatives in similar circumstances have different outcomes depending on leaders' skills and strategies.[7]

In any event, whatever the relative importance of social circumstances or personal abilities in accounting for particular social changes, there is no doubt that one of the key characteristics of successful leaders is their skill in creating or capitalizing on conditions conducive to progress. From a vast body of literature exploring such conditions, a few overarching themes bear emphasis.

The first involves the importance of the climate for change—its social, economic, and political dynamics—and leaders who take advantage of them.[8] For example, the contemporary American women's movement arose at a time when traditional gender roles had become increasingly out of step with social realities. Increasing longevity and access to birth control meant that women in the 1960s could anticipate spending about two-thirds of their lives without children under eighteen. These changes in family patterns, together with the economy's rising demand for trained workers, propelled growing numbers of women into the workforce. The prejudice they encountered there, as well as in civil rights and other political activities, became catalysts for change.[9] A related factor was President Kennedy's appointment of a Commission on Women with the official mandate of recommending changes to further the "full realization of women's rights." An unofficial purpose of the commission was to discharge political debts to his female campaign workers, none of whom obtained other significant administration posts. Leaders of the commission took full advantage of their opportunity. Not only did they recommend legislation such as the Equal Pay Act, they also created task forces and a Citizen's Advisory Council that began documenting problems of discrimination and placing them on the political agenda.[10] A growing cadre of women's rights lawyers and activists then coordinated legal challenges and public protests that laid the foundations for broader change.

Other catalysts for social change are disaster, crisis, violence, or some equally pivotal event that captures widespread attention. For example, media coverage of southern police brutalizing peaceful civil rights protesters in the early 1960s helped build the necessary coalitions for antidiscrimination statutes.[11] Contemporary coverage of police shootings of unarmed black victims has similarly launched the Black Lives Matter movement and its calls for major reforms in law enforcement.[12] Coastal oil spills, accidents at Fukushima, Three Mile Island, and Chernobyl nuclear reactors, and natural disasters exacerbated by climate change have raised the public's environmental consciousness and laid foundations for policy responses.[13] The 1991 televised hearings at which Anita Hill made claims of sexual harassment by Supreme Court nominee Clarence Thomas before an almost entirely male Senate Judiciary Committee galvanized the women's movement and advanced its agenda.[14] A police raid on a New York gay bar, the Stonewall Inn, and employers' public refusal to hire workers lacking "normal heterosexual values" both raised awareness of homophobia, and prompted gay rights activism.[15] The mounting evidence of sexual abuse triggered by #MeToo toppled the careers of hundreds of male leaders and sparked significant organizational and legislative reforms.[16] The election of Donald Trump energized many progressive constituencies. In his first 15 months in office, membership to the ACLU tripled and online donations increased from $5 to $120 million.[17]

A further impetus for social change comes from widespread recognition of injustice and some general consensus about causes and potentially effective responses.[18] Those perceptions of grievances typically arise less from objective circumstances than from a sense of relative deprivation—peoples' conviction either that their circumstances have fallen short of expectations or that they are disadvantaged relative to another relevant reference group.[19] The American Tea Party and Alt Right movements are a case in point. Social movements often draw on this indignation as well as a sense of collective identity based on shared characteristics, experiences, or ideology.[20] To inspire activism as well as sympathy, movements also need foundations of group solidarity. Participants must see that their own status and interests are connected to those of a broader group.[21]

2. LEADERSHIP CHARACTERISTICS

Cultural Capital

As Chapter 1 suggested and studies of social change confirm, what makes for successful leadership depends on context. Movements have different needs at different times, stages, and levels. Typically, they benefit from a combination of what sociologists label universal cultural capital, local cultural capital, and symbolic cultural capital.[22] Universal cultural capital, as French theorist Pierre Bourdieu famously described it, refers to individuals' general knowledge, capabilities, and social networks: education, background, analytic and communication abilities, ties to government, media, funders, and so forth. Leaders need to understand the values of the broader constituencies they seek to engage, and to work effectively in multiple settings with widely varying audiences. Local cultural capital refers to individuals' knowledge of the particular groups they are seeking to lead and their relationships with members. A personal history that is shared with the group can be invaluable. Symbolic cultural capital refers to the legitimacy conferred by particular affiliations or positions, such as being a pastor of a church, an elected head of an organization, a member of another respected leader's family, or a target of government repression.

No single individual may be strong on all these dimensions, but social change generally needs leadership that combines them. Large social movement organizations often have several tiers of leaders: those who hold the top position, those who advise that individual, and those who lead local groups.[23] As Harvard professor Marshall Ganz notes, developing leadership all the way down needs to be a central priority. For example, the Sierra Club pursues its environmental agenda through 750,000 members and 380 local groups with 12,500 leadership positions, all of which need individuals adept at mobilizing resources and public support.[24] Many of the most effective anti-poverty and community development movements here and abroad have made building leadership capacity among the disempowered a priority as both a means and an end. "Social innovation" activism relies on community members to guide the process and serve as advocates and representatives on boards, in hearings, in media outreach, and in other public settings.[25]

Some of America's most successful lawyer leaders have been rich in general or local cultural capital. Louis Brandeis' legendary analytic and organizational abilities helped him orchestrate a broad range of progressive social campaigns. His rebuilding of a moribund American Zionist movement after World War II transformed a federation with a $12,000 budget into a multi-million-dollar organization with considerable political power.[26] Building on a vision of Israel as a home for displaced and persecuted European Jews, he tapped into Jewish Americans' sense of cultural heritage and religious identity. So too, a lawyer who earned a *New York Times Magazine* profile for building local capital is John Rosenberg, the head of the Appalachian Research and Defense Fund. When Rosenberg arrived in Western Kentucky, the local residents saw him as a radical and communist, and refused to rent him office space.[27] Two decades later, he was inducted into the County Chamber of Commerce Hall of Fame. What makes that honor particularly impressive is that he had spent the intervening years suing the establishment on behalf of the poor. But he had also won broad-based support for his work in local charities and community organizations. Over time, as the executive director of the Kentucky Bar Association put it, "familiarity bred respect."[28] At age 29, Bryan Stevenson, a respected African-American civil rights lawyer, founded the Equal Justice Initiative, which focuses on defending indigents in death penalty and juvenile cases and on promoting criminal justice reform. The project has saved more than one hundred defendants from execution and also helped establish a national memorial to honor victims of lynching.[29]

Symbolic capital has come to lawyers from multiple sources. Some achieve it through family relationships. Hillary Clinton launched her political career on her status as first lady and on public sympathy for a "woman wronged" by her husband's infidelity. When naming his brother, Robert Kennedy, as Attorney General at the age of 34, John Kennedy famously quipped that "I just wanted to give him a little legal practice before he becomes a lawyer."[30] Other leaders earn legitimacy through personal sacrifice. Steve Bright, when Director of the Southern Center for Human Rights, took no salary and worked the kind of hours that made others embarrassed ever to refuse his requests by saying "I'm too busy. You'll have to do it yourself."[31] Ralph Nader won similar respect for his Spartan lifestyle and sweatshop schedule. He also achieved martyr status when his publication of *Unsafe at Any Speed* prompted General Motors's notoriously unsuccessful effort to have private investigators dig up damaging personal information.[32] Nader sued the corporation for invasion of privacy and used proceeds from the settlement to establish the Center for the Study of Responsive Law.

Personal Qualities

Leaders of social change also need the personal qualities identified in Chapter 1, particularly those concerning vision, values, and interpersonal skills. Part of what attracts employees, donors, and volunteers is a compelling public purpose. Those at the helm need to communicate an inspiring mission and to exemplify the personal integrity that builds widespread trust and commitment. They also need the inner resolve and resilience that will enable them to stay the course over the sustained period generally necessary for significant progress. Equally important is interpersonal sensitivity and influence.[33] Leaders of high-impact organizations tend to share internal leadership and nurture external networks.[34]

Leadership Development

The less established the organizational structure, the more critical the leader's capabilities, particularly those that involve enhancing the capabilities of others. Ronald Heifitz and Marty Linsky note that

> for transformative change to be sustainable, it not only has to take root in its own culture, but also has to successfully engage its changing environment. . . . Therefore, leadership needs to start with listening and learning, finding out where people are . . . and build from there. It's dangerous to lead with only a change idea in mind. You need both a healthy respect for the values, competence, and history of people [affected,] as well as the changing environment, to build the capacity to respond to new challenges and take advantage of new openings.[35]

That is not to say that transformative leaders are always bound by the initial views of those whom they seek to lead. Elizabeth Cady Stanton, one of the founders of the 19th-century American women's rights movement, recalled that after the first convention that set forth a Declaration of Sentiments, "so pronounced was the popular voice against us, in the parlor, press, and pulpit, that most of the ladies who had attended the convention and signed the declaration, one by one, withdrew their names and influence, and joined our persecutors."[36] It took decades of grassroots organizing to persuade women to risk the public denigration and ridicule that accompanied campaigns for suffrage and other legal rights. Part of what enabled leaders including Stanton to stay the course was that they learned, as Hiefitz and Linsky counsel, not to "take 'personal' attacks personally," and not to allow themselves to become the issue.[37]

Collaborative Capacities

Lawyers who are most successful in achieving social impact generally focus on developing collaborative capacities.[38] Commentators such as Lani Guinier and Gerald Torres describe lawyering for social movements as a "participatory, power sharing process," in which counsel are accountable to mobilized clients.[39] Because movement lawyering aims to help marginalized groups gain power to change the conditions of their inequality and alter social attitudes, it depends on such accountability. Kathleen Kelly Janus's work on social entrepreneurship describes this as "reversing the pyramid": decisions are made by the people who will be affected by them.[40] The best leaders are often those who, in Nelson Mandela's phrase, "lead from behind." [41] Marshall Ganz, a former United Farm Workers organizer turned Harvard professor, describes the task as working to "deepen peoples' understanding of who they are, what they want, and why they want it," and then inspire them to collaborate on behalf of shared values and interests.[42] That is the model for the Nebraska Appleseed Center for Law in the Public Interest, which focuses on empowering low-income individuals to represent their own interests in community and legal forums.[43] So too, the lawyers at Mississippi Center for Justice help communities identify their own social justice goals and collaborate with other grassroots and national organizations to achieve them.[44]

For movement lawyers, leadership involves a "collaborative and collective engagement."[45] Struggles such as the school desegregation battles of the 1950s and 1960s involved partnerships among multiple leaders: lawyers, community activists, parents, judges, and students.[46] The most effective leaders are willing to sacrifice personal credit and control to achieve the necessary alliances.[47] The focus of these leaders is on creating the conditions that enable and empower others.[48] Sustained change requires movement-centered leaders, not leader-centered movements.[49] As Chapter 2 noted, Lao Tse put it this way centuries ago: A leader is most effective when people barely know he exists; when his work is done, "[t]he people all remark, 'we have done it ourselves.'"[50]

That is not to imply that all lawyers who lead social change efforts manage to avoid self-aggrandizing behaviors. There are, as one commentator observed, some "colossal egos" in public interest law, and "everyone wants their fiefdom."[51] But the most effective leaders are those able to subordinate their own interests to those of a broader movement.

3. LEADERSHIP CHALLENGES AND STRATEGIES

Shared Power and Diffusion of Responsibility

Leaders seeking to secure major social change confront many of the same obstacles, and need many of the same strategies concerning influence and innovation described in Chapter 4. However, leaders in this context also face certain distinctive challenges. One involves the diffusion of authority. In *Leadership for the Common Good*, Barbara Crosby and John Bryson note that "anyone who tries to tackle a public problem . . . sooner or later comes face to face with the dynamics of a shared power world."[52] Leaders of social movements typically lack coercive authority. Even heads of state or government agencies with social change objectives cannot rely simply on command and control styles of leadership. American presidents who have achieved major policy victories have succeeded only by persuading key constituencies of the necessity of change and of their own stake in achieving it. In confronting major social issues where "no one is in charge," leaders need to rely on soft power and collaborative networks, often involving both governmental and nongovernmental organizations.[53]

Timing: Windows of Opportunity for Big Wins or Incremental Change

Leaders also need a sense of timing and the ability to focus resources strategically in light of "windows of opportunity."[54] Effective policy entrepreneurs know when to assume the risks of seeking "big wins" and when to settle for incremental "small wins" that can build confidence, test solutions, and lay foundations for broader change.[55] A case in point involves the effort by Families Against Mandatory Minimums (FAMM) to achieve national legislation that would give federal judges discretion to reduce sentences for non-violent first-time drug offenders. To achieve passage, leaders had to drop their insistence on making the bill retroactive. That meant excluding from coverage the incarcerated relatives of FAMM members who had worked so hard to make the bill possible. Painful though that compromise was, the end result was that one in four persons entering federal prison have had their sentences reduced by as much as three years compared to what the earlier mandatory minimum would have required.[56]

Another issue of to timing involves finding the right moment for action. The issue is frequently complicated by competition within a social movement. For example, lawyers heading public interest organizations have an obvious interest in arriving first at courthouse doors. They benefit from the influence, public attention, and donor support that come from litigating a landmark case. Politicians gain similar rewards from sponsoring major legislative or policy initiatives. Yet moving too early on an issue can entrench opposition, as then President Clinton learned in his early unsuccessful efforts to secure universal health care and end sexual orientation discrimination by the military. Premature escalation of conflict can also demoralize supporters; it deprives them of the small victories that sustain hope and make the ends of activism seem worth its price.[57]

The challenges are compounded by leaders' frequent lack of control over key events, and the need to respond quickly in the face of unforeseen opportunities. Representative examples involve bus boycotts and sit-ins during the early civil rights campaigns. Some of the precipitating incidents arose without advance planning. Rosa Parks' refusal to move to the back of a segregated Montgomery bus was not the product of a coordinated strategy. Nor was a similar decision by two black Tallahassee college students; unlike Parks, they did not even have a history of prior involvement with any civil rights organizations. But once these events occurred, leaders saw the need to seize the momentum and to organize boycotts. In some cases, involvement in protests led to an unanticipated broadening of their agendas. In Montgomery, many organizers initially had been wary of being too far out in front of public opinion, and of asking for more than a fairer system of allocating seats on public transit.[58] But resistance stiffened their resolve, and like other activists, they quickly saw the need to challenge segregation head-on. That, in turn, required seeking support beyond the local communities involved and developing coordinated protest strategies against a broad range of public accommodations. In addition to bus boycotts, leaders organized sit-ins at restaurants, sleep-ins at motels, wade-ins at beaches, and knee-ins at churches that excluded blacks.[59]

Group Differences

The issue becomes more complicated when activists are deeply divided about timing, and the costs and benefits of incremental change. One example involves immigration, where activists during the Obama Administration were divided over whether to hold out for comprehensive reform or accept a separate bill for "DREAMERS," undocumented individuals brought to the country as children.[60] Another case in point involves the contemporary animal rights movement. Activists are united in their desire to achieve recognition of animals as sentient beings with rights analogous to human rights, who should not be treated merely as a means to human ends.[61] But the movement divides over whether to push for modest improvements in animal welfare, which some believe undercut broader efforts, or to insist on comprehensive reform. According to Gary Fancione, the founder of the first law school animal rights clinic, incrementalism "sends a powerful message that exploitation is acceptable" and legitimates consuming animals and animal products. In his view, advocates should argue for "empty cages, not bigger cages."[62] By contrast, Norm Phelps, another animal rights advocate, argues,

> [S]ince we cannot liberate all animals in the immediate—or even foreseeable—future, I believe that we have a moral obligation to relieve their suffering to whatever extent we can, in whatever way we can. We cannot deliberately allow real animals to suffer in the present for the sake of a future utopia that they will never live to see. And finally, I am convinced that rather than undercut the animal rights message, "welfarist" reforms can reinforce it by forcing people to think of animals as sentient, sensitive individuals whose well-being matters. This paves the way for more far-reaching reforms.[63]

How should leaders resolve these differences over strategies, particularly where some major stakeholders are by definition unable to speak for themselves? John Gardner famously noted that one view of leadership

> is that leaders do not lead the parade, but find out where it is going and get out ahead of it. For most leaders today, however, the single parade moving on an identifiable path is an anachronism. There are groups of constituents scurrying in every direction.[64]

How should movement lawyers decide which of these groups to represent, and how should they attempt to ensure some measure of accountability to stakeholders?

Complexity

A further leadership challenge involves the complexity of many social problems and the political and financial constraints in addressing them. Leaders of a wide array of public interest organizations have noted the difficulties in dealing with more complicated issues than those facing their predecessors. As the head of the Sierra Club noted, the initial focus of their legal staff was to identify polluters and "just say no. Shut it down. Clean it up."[65] Global climate change presents far greater challenges. So too, the underpinnings of many current gender inequalities are, as the then-president of Legal Momentum pointed out, "more complex and less susceptible to legal solutions" than the overt sexism of earlier eras.[66]

Even relatively narrow issues, such as police shootings of unarmed black men, are, as Bryan Stevenson notes, "symptoms of a larger disease. Our society applies a presumption of dangerousness and guilt to young black men, and that's what leads to wrongful arrests and wrongful convictions and wrongful death sentences, not just wrongful shootings."[67] Pursuit of racial justice requires attention to the structural causes of inequality. The same is true for women's rights organizations.

Social and Political Climate

Leaders are also facing these problems in a social, political, and fiscal climate that is less hospitable than the one in which most public interest legal organizations were founded. On some issues, the public has become more complacent; on others, it is more skeptical of the ability of government and advocacy organizations to achieve major social change. Some groups, as one public interest organization president put it, are, "victims of our own success."[68] Many original supporters believe that the major battles have been won. Other organizations, such as those representing poor communities, confront a public "exhausted by their plight" and resistant to initiatives requiring additional resources.[69]

So too, the growth in number of social change organizations has increased competition for public attention and donor support. In earlier eras, a small group of organizations did almost all the "heavy lifting."[70] Now, as the president of Public Advocates put it, "there is somebody for every issue."[71]

Multiple Arenas

Leaders also face challenges in working simultaneously in multiple arenas. Lawyers have learned that overreliance on a single lever of change can be disabling. Leaders need what law professor Scott Cummings calls "integrated advocacy," which means "venue shopping" in multiple legislative, administrative, legal, media, business, funding, and grassroots arenas. For example, focusing too much on litigation can result in "victory in the courts but . . . not victory in practice."[72] Judges may lack the legitimacy, expertise, and enforcement resources necessary for meaningful social reform.[73] Framing complex problems in forms susceptible to legal remedies can narrow issues, individualize grievances, and undercut momentum for collective action.[74] Leaders of public-interest legal organizations such as the American Civil Liberties Union, the NAACP Legal Defense Fund, the Natural Resources Defense Council, the Western Center on Law and Poverty, and the National Women's Law Center all have ample experience with legal rights gone wrong.[75] Judicial decisions without a political base to support them are vulnerable to chronic noncompliance, public backlash, and statutory or doctrinal reversal.[76] Litigation is most successful when used in tandem with other strategies to gain public attention, mobilize group support, impose costs, attract resources, and increase policy leverage. As Ralph Nader once summed it up, "You have to deal with the adversary on all the fronts on which the adversary deals with you."[77]

That requires resources—both time and money. The ability to mobilize support quickly in response to opportunities is often a key strategy in building social movements. Part of the success of the civil rights movement came from the capacity to frame the struggle in ways that resonated both with racial minorities and with the broader public. Martin Luther King was particularly gifted in combining appeals based on black experiences and spiritual traditions with invocations of broader American ideals of liberty and justice.[78] As Chapter 4 notes, his "I Have a Dream" speech and "Letter from a Birmingham Jail" were effective in mobilizing support across a broad range of audiences. Such appeals, together with strategies offering credible responses to injustice, gave meaning to the promise that "we shall overcome."

Cesar Chavez had similar success in framing the struggle to organize farm workers in ways that built group solidarity and attracted widespread public support. Prior organizing efforts by the predominantly white leaders of national labor organizations had been unsuccessful. Intransigence by growers, intimidation by police, and recruitment of immigrant replacements had doomed initial strike efforts.[79] Chavez, who had deep knowledge of the local community as well as ties to potential support groups outside it, reframed the struggle to appeal to both constituencies. He stressed racial injustice, recruited clergy and college students, and organized dramatic protests. One of the most celebrated examples was a pilgrim-like march through farm worker communities timed to arrive on Easter at the California governor's mansion. The national union affiliate declined to join; its leaders insisted that the struggle was a "labor union dispute, not a civil rights movement or a religious crusade."[80] Chavez and his advisors cast the campaign as all three and recognized the expressive value of social activism. Although they had far fewer financial and organizational resources than the nationally affiliated union, they had wider aspirations, more inspiring strategies, and more enduring successes.

Decision-Making

As that example illustrates, organizations differ in their "strategic capacity," and leaders can help lay the institutional foundations for success.[81] That requires striking the right balance in decision-making processes. Either too much or too little structure can be disabling.[82] Movements can be stifled by what social theorist Robert Michels termed the "iron law of oligarchy," that is, the tendency of leaders to resist challenges to their power, and to close off channels for diverse views and grassroots engagement.[83] But movements can also suffer from the "tyranny of structurelessness," in which the absence of authoritative decision-making leads to schisms and prevents coherent coordinated actions.[84] To avoid these pathologies, effective leaders need to create open but authoritative deliberative processes that draw on resources from diverse constituencies and that ensure accountability for results.[85] Because many public interest organizations have relatively flat decision-making structures, leaders who want to retain talented staff need to look for ways of sharing power and providing opportunities for professional growth.[86]

A more pragmatic problem arises from the lack of management skills among movement leaders. Researchers find that many nonprofits are "strongly led but under-managed," and the lack of financial discipline and metrics for progress diminish social impact.[87] Some visionary leaders are uninterested or unskilled in organizational efficiency or suffer from "mission creep," an aspiration for change that exceeds capacity. To avoid these difficulties, experts recommend strategic clarity and balanced leadership teams. Organizations first need to determine, "What impact are we prepared to be held accountable for?" and "What do we need to do—and not do—in order to achieve this impact?"[88] Organizations then must establish clear metrics and ensure that some high-level staff have the necessary management expertise. That may sometimes require decisions that public interest leaders find particularly difficult: "letting go of employees who may be passionately dedicated to the organization, but who are not able to contribute to the level they should."[89]

Technological Innovation and Social Media

Recent technological innovations, particularly those involving social media, have created new opportunities and new challenges. They have democratized leadership by giving anyone the "ability to start a movement . . . and gain a following."[90] Online organizing can increase participation in social movements and accelerate responsiveness by lessening the efforts that it requires. Within days after the mass shooting at Stoneman Douglas High School in Parkland, Florida, students had organized a movement, defined policy objectives, and planned a national protest.[91]

Yet although people can become armchair activists by pushing a few buttons, building deep and sustained support remains difficult. At one point, the Save Darfur Coalition had 1.2 million members, but they contributed only an average of nine cents.[92] So too, because online organizing networks tend to lack strong centralized leadership, they have difficulty reaching consensus and developing coherent long-term strategies:

> Technology makes it possible to organize mass protests quickly and effectively but has limitations in sustaining a social movement. The value of large protests is that they energize and connect participants and signal power—if participants can do this, what else can they do? But because they have no means of collective decision-making, they may have difficulty generating a united message and long-term strategy. Participants may be caught in a tactical freeze, in which they keep repeating the same tactic after it has outlived its usefulness, and the country may suffer from protest fatigue.[93]

As Malcolm Gladwell sums it up, new technologies "make it easier for activists to express themselves and harder for that expression to have any impact."[94]

When used strategically, however, social media represents an extraordinarily efficient way of achieving what Jennifer Aaker and Andy Smith describe as the "dragonfly effect."[95] The dragonfly is the only insect able to propel itself in any direction when its four wings act in concert. Aaker and Smith use the term to symbolize the importance of integrated efforts in achieving a ripple effect. The method "relies on four essential skills or wings: 1) *focus*: identify a single concrete and measurable goal; 2) *grab attention*: cut through the noise of social media with something authentic and memorable; 3) *engage*: create a personal connection, accessing higher emotions such as compassion and empathy; and 4) *take action*: enable and empower others to take action."[96] A master in these techniques has been Bryan Stevenson. His TED Talk, "We Need to Talk About Injustice," has been viewed more than 5 million times and has raised over a million dollars for his Equal Justice Initiative.[97] His memoir, *Just Mercy: A Story of Justice and Redemption*, spent years on bestseller lists, and his efforts to create a national memorial to victims of lynching have made him a national celebrity. So too, leaders in organizations such as Families Against Mandatory Minimums have been adept at putting a human face on social problems; a poster child for their efforts was a woman who was imprisoned for life after being caught with her boyfriend when he was arrested for drug trafficking, even though he insisted that she had nothing to do with his illicit activities.[98]

Scaling Small Success

Another strategy for attempting to leverage modest resources is to scale small successes. Psychologists Chip Heath and Dan Heath describe this approach as "looking for bright spots"; other experts describe it as searching for "positive deviants."[99] An example is Jerry Sternin's campaign to fight child malnutrition in Vietnam during the 1990s. At the root of the problem was poverty and the resulting inadequacies in food, sanitation, and clean water. Sternin found such explanations TBU, "true but useless."[100] His organization, Save the Children, lacked the capacity to make significant inroads on poverty. However, in touring rural villages, he noticed that some children managed to fare reasonably well despite their circumstances, and he began searching for reasons why. He found that the mothers of these children fed them more frequently in smaller amounts than was customary, and they also provided a more varied diet. His strategy then was to organize local cooking classes for mothers, which could be replicated throughout the country. The result was to improve the life chances of some 2.2 million children. Similar "bright spot" strategies have brought significant social change in a wide variety of contexts.[101] Generalizing from these examples, Heath and Heath conclude that leaders facing seemingly intractable social problems may sometimes do best by focusing less on underlying causes and more on scaling modest successes.[102]

It may also be important to appeal to people's sense of identity as well as interests. A case in point is that of Paul Butler, who pioneered efforts to save an endangered species of parrot, found only on the Caribbean island of St. Lucia. Hunters, pet seekers, and environmental degradation had put this bird on a path to extinction. The only solutions—steep criminal penalties and creation of a parrot sanctuary—would require a groundswell of public support that was notably lacking. Butler, "fresh out of college, working with the forestry department, and armed with a budget in [only] the hundreds of dollars, had to figure out a way to rally the people of St. Lucia behind a parrot that most of them took for granted (and some of them ate)."[103] His answer was an appeal to national pride through "made to stick" messages. He organized parrot puppet shows, distributed parrot tee shirts, enlisted local businesses in printing bumper stickers and calling cards, and convinced ministers to preach environmental stewardship. One card featured a gorgeous parrot next to a homely American bald eagle, making it obvious whose bird looked better. The message was clear: "This parrot is ours. Nobody else has this but us. We need to cherish it and look after it." The people agreed. They passed tough laws, established a sanctuary, virtually ended illicit trade, and preserved the parrots. The conservation organization Rare has now replicated that strategy in about 120 campaigns to save endangered species.[104]

Common Action Problems

That example points out the challenges in securing change on issues that involve "common action" problems on which no individual has a significant personal stake. The problems are compounded in many environmental contexts, such as climate change, in which many responses seem technical and hard to assess, consequences are long-term and intergenerational, and actions by any single person or political entity are unlikely to have significant impact. To motivate change in these circumstances, it is helpful to

- build a sense of urgency through vivid, dramatic messages that appeal to core values and concerns (devastating storms and wildfires, polar bears stranded on melting ice caps, financial savings from energy conservation);
- harness peer pressure to create social norms of responsibility (telling people that their neighbors have reduced energy consumption); and
- appeal to people's self-image as socially responsible individuals (link consumer choices to environmental stewardship).[105]

Once leaders get a "foot in the door" and convince people to take small steps toward social responsibility, their commitment is likely to escalate.[106]

Collaboration and Collective Impact

In seeking large-scale social change, leaders also must build collaborations among a broad range of nonprofit, private, and government organizations. As the president of the National Women's Law Center noted, "Almost never will a single organization have the capacity to achieve major policy change." In a survey of 50 leading public interest organizations, close to 90 percent reported collaboration with grassroots organizations, an even higher percent reported coalitions with other public interest legal organizations, and nearly half were in partnerships with government or private sector organizations.[107] Although such alliances can pose problems of control and credit, they can also reduce costs, increase influence, expand a political base, and prevent duplicative or inconsistent strategies. But to insure that such collaborations can work effectively, leaders often need to subordinate their own desires for recognition and to accept compromises in pursuit of common ends. Often, progress is most readily achieved through unlikely alliances. For example, the Nebraska Appleseed Center fought against caps on benefits for welfare mothers who have additional children by enlisting both the American Civil Liberties Union and the Catholic Church.[108]

Such "collective impact" coalitions generally need centralized staff and decision-making structures, shared evaluation systems, continuous communication, and mutually reinforcing activities.[109] For example, Strive, a nonprofit subsidiary of Knowledge Works, achieved dramatic improvements in Cincinnati students' educational performance through such collaboration. Organizers coordinated a collective effort by 300 leaders of local organizations, including heads of influential private and corporate foundations, city government officials, school district representatives, university presidents, and executive directors of hundreds of education-related nonprofit groups.[110] Of course, the broader the coalition, the more problems can arise in developing consensus on key strategies and priorities. And some collective impact proposals have been subject to criticism for not being realistic about resource constraints and not giving those most affected a significant role in the decision-making process.[111]

In principle, all of these strategies seem straightforward. In practice, the challenge lies in knowing how best to pursue them, and in determining which will be most cost effective in particular contexts. Politicians, activists, and lawyers involved in social movements often agree on goals but divide sharply on strategies. What litigation, legislation, or policy initiatives make most sense? When should leaders wait for greater public, political, or judicial support? How can they prevent ill-conceived lawsuits or precipitous government action from derailing a coherent national strategy? Those issues are the subject of the excerpt and case studies that follow.

Consider Scott Cumming's description of "movement lawyers." In what sense are they leaders of social change? Does that role ever conflict with traditional advocacy for their clients?

SCOTT L. CUMMINGS, MOVEMENT LAWYERING

2017 University of Illinois Law Review 1645 (2017)

The movement lawyer's focus on representing mobilized clients spotlights three familiar, yet significant, issues in progressive lawyering. One is client selection. In a context of limited legal resources, movement lawyers must make choices among competing demands for their assistance. Because social movements, by definition, have conflicting interests and opposing claims to leadership and agenda-setting authority, how lawyers make client selection decisions invariably involves choosing sides in internal movement debates— implicating the very questions about accountability to broader movement constituencies that the movement lawyering model seeks to minimize.

Accordingly, a movement lawyer's choice of client is a decision freighted with political significance. It therefore puts the onus on lawyers to exercise discretion to choose which movement organizations to support based on a careful evaluation of the degree to which such organizations do, in fact, represent a constituency's discernible point of view—so that the choice of client does not become simply become a choice of representing the most established or well-funded social movement organization simply by virtue of their power or visibility in the field.

The second issue, also implicating political discretion, is the movement lawyer's approach both to organizational counseling and to managing conflicts that might arise when representing individuals in the context of a broader movement campaign. Although traditional legal ethics treats the representation of organizations as a straightforward exercise in following the clearly defined instructions of an organization's "duly authorized constituents," scholars have persuasively shown how this view rests on the unhelpful fiction of organizational personhood that obscures underlying governance complexity and potential conflicts of interest. Particularly in a more fluid environment of grassroots organizations with nascent or more decentralized governance structures, deferring to "authorized constituents" may risk accepting the views of the more empowered voices within movement conversations. In these contexts, movement lawyers must make choices about whether to take a more or less activist approach to advising organizational decision makers on how to articulate movement goals, define remedies, or shape strategy.

Scholars have also focused on the potential for conflicts that arise when movement lawyers represent individuals in order to advance broader movement objectives. The potential for conflict between client interests and commitment to the cause—what David Luban has termed the "double agent problem" in cause lawyering—occurs when the lawyer's commitment runs simultaneously to individual clients and social movement organizations with whom the lawyer is collaborating to support the campaign. This type of conflict may occur, for example, when low-wage workers wish to settle claims of labor violations [but] when organizers seek to keep up the pressure on an employer in order to advance an organizing campaign. Individual clients may theoretically waive such a conflict in advance—effectively agreeing to settle only on terms acceptable to the movement organization—but such waivers have been viewed skeptically by courts particularly when they are made by less sophisticated clients who are not independently represented by counsel.

Finally, the movement lawyering model's emphasis on mobilized clients begs the question of what to do in situations of weak or even nonexistent organizational leadership. Some scholars suggest that, where movements are not already mobilized, lawyers may help spark them by partnering with "community-based organizations and . . . utiliz[ing] the law to assist with community-building as a step toward fortifying sustainable movements." In the absence of existing organizational structure, movement lawyers may also take the initiative to conduct research and initiate lawsuits challenging institutional inequality with the goal of building publicity and hence generating grassroots attention and organizational investments. The ACLU's recent challenge to solitary confinement in New York State is a case in point. Prisoners in solitary are an unorganized and underrepresented group by virtue of their incarceration and isolation. After issuing a report in 2012 detailing the extensive and arbitrary use of extreme isolation as punishment for violation of prison rules—with more than 68,000 extreme isolation sentences issued against prisoners from 2007 to 2011—the ACLU's New York affiliate filed a class action lawsuit against the state department of corrections. In conjunction with the lawsuit, the ACLU supported a letter writing campaign to pressure the governor to support changing prison practice, while also testifying in front of the Inter-American Commission on Human Rights and collaborating with criminal justice reformers to start a new reform organization, the New York Campaign for Alternatives to Confinement. Against the backdrop of this legal and political work, the state agreed to a sweeping 2015 settlement, which required it to mandate a massive reduction in the number of prisoners in solitary, a reduction in the length of solitary confinement sentences, and enhanced rehabilitative services. The lawsuit stimulated resources for ongoing implementation and transitional support upon reentry. Although mirroring the classic lawyer-led reform campaign of legal liberalism, the ACLU's challenge to solitary confinement suggests how such campaigns may be thoughtfully connected to movement-building activities to create opportunities for sustained political engagement by affected constituents and other stakeholders. In short, it suggests how a lawsuit might help spark a movement.

B. Integrated Advocacy

Whereas the representation of mobilized clients is at bottom a choice by the movement lawyer to advance substantive ends, integrated advocacy is about the most effective means to achieve those ends. The essential thrust of integrated advocacy is to break down divisions associated with legal liberalism—between lawyers and nonlawyers, litigation and other forms of advocacy, and courts and other spaces of law making and norm generation—toward the end of producing more democratic and sustainable social change.

This section discusses three central features of integrated advocacy, which build on the concepts of *organizational*, *tactical*, and *institutional* integration. Organizationally, integrated advocacy emphasizes horizontal relations: building partnerships with social movement organizations in order to strengthen constituent control over the design and implementation of campaigns. In doing so, it seeks to create networks of lawyers and other problem-solvers—across the public and private sectors—who contribute different types of expertise and support to campaign goals. Tactically, the model stresses the contribution of legal advocacy to a comprehensive political strategy; it thus seeks to break down what proponents view as artificial distinctions between law and politics. Toward this end, lawyers combine modes of advocacy—litigation, policy reform, transactional work, organizing support, media relations, and community education—in order to maximize political pressure and transform public opinion. The utility of litigation is judged relative to campaign goals. It is neither privileged nor discounted, but rather evaluated for its pragmatic impact. Finally, integrated advocacy pursues reform across institutional domains. Depending on the dictates of specific campaigns, lawyers focus efforts in and across plural lawmaking and norm-generating institutions (courts, legislatures, agencies, community) and at multiple scales (local, state, federal, international).

In addition to representing mobilized clients, movement lawyers seek to further build and deepen relationships with social movement organizations outside of direct representation in order to strengthen claims to constituent accountability. In this organizational dimension of integrated advocacy, the impulse is to push away from the legal liberal model of the heroic lawyer, toiling in isolation to craft legal theory that persuades appellate judges of a novel legal position. Instead, examples of integrated advocacy show lawyers embedded in thicker movement contexts, connected by different types of organizational relationships.

There are two main categories of organizational integration. One connects lawyers to nonlawyer activists and community members through horizontal relationships arrayed along a spectrum: from short-term, issue-specific campaign *coalitions* to long-term, multi-issue political *partnerships*. The other type of integration connects lawyers across organizational settings (nonprofit, private, government, educational), linking together those with different types of expertise and commitments to the underlying cause. In each case, the move is to decentralize (but not abandon) professional expertise—strengthening its ultimate impact by integrating other forms of organizational knowledge and power.

Cross-disciplinary collaboration between lawyers and nonlawyers is a foundation of integrated advocacy. In this approach, lawyers build relations with nonlegal organizations to amplify their legal claims, connect to organizing campaigns, promote monitoring and compliance over time, and shift public opinion. Building upon the movement lawyer's commitment to representing mobilized clients—and similarly responding to the legal liberal critiques of lawyer accountability and legal efficacy—these collaborations seek to deepen the *participation* of marginalized communities in movement activities and the *impact* of those activities over time.

. . . Many of the "new" public interest lawyers of the 1960s and 1970s rejected a go-at-it-alone strategy focused exclusively on court-based reform. For instance, Marian Wright Edelman, reflecting on her early career at the NAACP in Mississippi, concluded: "The thing I understood after six months there was that you could file all the suits you wanted to, but unless you had a community base you weren't going to get anywhere."

Contemporary examples of movement lawyering pick up on the theme of connecting litigation to base-building and organizing, but also move beyond it in ways that suggest a broader conception of how multifaceted advocacy tactics might fit together and be mutually reinforcing in social movement campaigns. In contrast to earlier stories, new movement lawyering reflects a self-conscious and often explicit commitment to a social change methodology built upon sophisticated insights from social movement theory and practice. By using contextualized analyses of legal advocacy embedded within broader social movement activism, the new stories of movement lawyering illuminate *the interconnected use of tactics outside of court, as well as efforts to synchronize litigation with a comprehensive movement strategy....*

[A representative] strategy was used by advocates at the National Day Labor Organizing Network (NDLON) and the Mexican American Legal Defense and Education Fund (MALDEF), who developed an advocacy blueprint for challenging antisolicitation laws banning day laborers—mostly recently arrived immigrant men—from seeking work in public spaces like street corners. By the early 2000s; roughly forty cities in the greater Los Angeles area had passed such laws. To challenge them, NDLON organized day laborers at key hiring sites into committees, on whose behalf MALDEF filed lawsuits arguing that the laws violated day laborers' First Amendment right to seek employment. When the lawsuits were filed, NDLON and MALDEF would "stage a public event, marching from the day labor site to city hall." This was done to jointly advance the legal strategy—by pressuring city officials to negotiate—and the organizing strategy—by promoting worker participation. In the words of the main MALDEF lawyer in the campaign: "Working together we could accomplish the legal policy goal and NDLON could organize groups around California." Using this model, the campaign succeeded in winning a dramatic legal victory in the Ninth Circuit Court of Appeals invalidating most of the day labor antisolicitation laws around the region. In addition to coordinating the litigation, organizing, and media efforts in specific legal challenges, movement lawyers supported the campaign by playing a range of other roles: organizing students to pose as day laborers and getting local news media to film their arrest, coordinating favorable news editorials and other media coverage, negotiating with construction retailers to set up day labor sites, testifying at city council hearings against proposed ordinances, drafting legislation, and briefing public defenders charged with representing day laborers prosecuted under the antisolicitation laws on the larger campaign stakes.

... [A]lthough some version of movement lawyering has long existed within the legal profession, shaped by shifting opportunities and resources for political mobilization by marginalized groups, the contemporary idea of movement lawyering has taken on a particular meaning in the current political context. Thus, on the one hand, what is "new" about movement lawyering is really "old": drawing upon models of progressive legal practice that have long existed, albeit under different names. Yet, on the other, the movement turn in progressive lawyering has responded to elements of real change: a change in progressive politics that has refocused attention on the transformative potential of social movements and a change in the professional self-conception of progressive lawyers that has made them receptive to movement-centered practice.

QUESTIONS

1. Consider a social movement with which you are familiar. What were the major challenges facing its leaders? What strategies did they most effectively pursue? What could they have done differently? How would Cummings' "movement lawyers" have responded?

2. In a follow-up article, Cummings and Susan Carle note the challenges for movement lawyers who intervene in

> complex environments, in which decision making is diffuse and contested. . . . [C]oalitions comprised of multiple organizations with different levels of power and resources can submerge internal schism and sometimes may even give an air of legitimacy to groups that do not genuinely reflect the range of constituent interests.[112]

Carle and Cummings argue that in these contexts, lawyers cannot remain neutral. They need to make principled decisions about which groups to represent or which interests within complex organizations or coalitions to support. If that is correct, what criteria should guide lawyers' decision-making?

3. Compare the websites and public outreach strategies of three different social-change organizations that focus on a similar issue. What seem to be the most and least effective approaches? If you were the leader of one of these organizations, what changes would you make?

4. Barack Obama claimed that the three years he spent as a grassroots organizer was "seared into my brain," and the "best education I ever had, better than anything I got at the Harvard Law School."[113] What can law schools do to better prepare lawyers who want to be leaders of social change?

PROBLEM 10-1

Divide into teams and select an issue on which you would like to see major social change. Identify the fundamental challenges and devise a strategy for overcoming them. What allies do you need to enlist? Where and how will you obtain resources and political support? What communication initiatives will you pursue? What external opposition and internal conflicts do you anticipate? How will you address them?

PROBLEM 10-2[114]

You are a lawyer holding a leadership position in a major public interest environmental organization based in the United States. One focus of your work is fostering sustainable development in countries where key ecosystems are at risk. You have recently been advising the Coastal Zone Management Authority and Institute of Belize, a small Central American country rich in natural resources and a number of endangered species. In 2009, its reef system was listed as a UNESCO

World Heritage Site in Danger due to excessive development and tourism in the region.

The country, with only 380,000 residents, hosts over a million tourists annually, and tourism-related activities directly or indirectly account for over a third of its employment and GDP. However, many of those activities are jeopardizing the ecosystems on which tourism, and other valued industries, depend. For example, oceanfront hotels often remove mangroves along the shoreline in order to enhance views and guest access to swimming and boating. Coastal zones are also threatened by climate change, overfishing, and pollution from agricultural pesticides and other industry byproducts.

Efforts to promote sustainable development and protect ecosystems have been stymied by a government oversight structure that has traditionally operated through separate agencies for tourism, fisheries, forestry, transportation, and agriculture. Under this structure, agencies have pursued different, often conflicting objectives and priorities. To address the problems of natural resource degradation and conflicting human uses of the coastal zone, the government established a Coastal Zone Management Authority that in turn created nine Coastal Advisory Committees responsible for spearheading regional planning. Each committee is to include business interests, NGO and government representatives, academic experts, and community members whose livelihoods and cultural beliefs give them a special stake in sustainable use of the region's coastal resources.

Your role is to advise these committees. What processes would you suggest for selecting members, engaging and informing stakeholders, adopting and enforcing regional plans, and resolving competing interests over short- and long-term interests?

B. CIVIL RIGHTS IN SOCIAL CONTEXT

The readings that follow explore leadership challenges in two phases of the American struggle for racial justice. They begin with dilemmas facing the NAACP Legal Defense Fund in orchestrating litigation challenges to racial discrimination in the mid-twentieth century. Discussion then turns to lawyer leaders in the Kennedy administration in responding to racial injustice.

Starting in the 1930s, NAACP lawyers launched a plan to end state-sponsored segregation, which gradually moved from bringing isolated lawsuits to "treat[ing] each case in a context of jurisprudential development."[115] That strategy required assessing any particular challenge in light of multiple factors, such as whether the facts were sufficiently favorable, resources were available to develop the case, courts were ready to rule favorably on the issue, lead lawyers were effective advocates, and so forth. The excerpt from *Simple Justice* describes that process in the context of litigating one of the major school desegregation cases leading to the Supreme Court's landmark decision in *Brown v. Board of Education.* How far to push the Supreme Court was one of the key considerations. Conventional wisdom is that the Court is never too far ahead of public opinion, particularly on volatile social issues.[116] Surveys at the time indicated that slightly over half of Americans favored segregated public facilities, but 89 percent thought that blacks should have equal opportunities to get a good education.[117] Consider how public attitudes shaped the strategies of early civil rights leaders. What assumptions did different leaders make about the best way to influence opinion? How did differences of class complicate the struggle for racial justice and what strategies were most effective in bridging them? What lessons can be drawn for contemporary struggles?

RICHARD KLUGER, SIMPLE JUSTICE: THE HISTORY OF BROWN V. BOARD OF EDUCATION AND BLACK AMERICA'S STRUGGLE FOR EQUALITY

(New York: Vintage Books, 1977), pp. 511, 513-518, 521, 530, 535-536, and 580

Nowhere in the pleadings of *Bolling v. Sharpe*, which [Attorney James] Nabrit filed in early 1951 in U.S. District Court [to challenge racial discrimination in Washington, D.C. schools], was any claim made that young Bolling and the other plaintiffs were attending schools unequal to those provided white children. [One school had a science lab consisting of a single Bunsen burner and a bowl of goldfish.] Their plainly inferior facilities were entirely beside the point, as Nabrit framed the case. He based it entirely upon the fact of segregation itself. The burden of proof, he argued, was not upon the black plaintiffs but upon the District government to show that there was any reasonable basis for or public purpose in racial restrictions on school admission. . . .

[However, advisors to the NAACP, such as Columbia law professor Herbert Wechsler, raised troubling issues about a frontal assault on segregation rather than an easily provable claim that schools for children of color were clearly inferior to schools for white children.] [W]as it so plain, Wechsler countered, that a Negro child attending a segregated school was worse off than a Negro child attending a non-segregated school where he might feel the full brunt of white prejudice? . . .

A cautionary tale was told as well by one of Thurgood Marshall's newer and most astute outside advisors, John P. Frank, then an associate professor at Yale Law School. . . . [After noting at an NAACP Strategy Conference that] "[a] judge cannot be blamed if he shrinks from precipitating a race riot," John Frank told the Howard crowd it was plain that the Supreme Court was stalling on both *Briggs* and *Brown* and he wondered if the Justices were not likely to delay a good deal longer in a presidential election year. Unquestionably, the NAACP "should not hesitate in its just demands for fear of reaping the whirlwind" because "judicial victories will not be won without asking for them." But "Vigor is not recklessness," Frank asserted. "The most daring army guards its lines of retreat. So should a litigation strategist." It would be a mistake to push the attack on segregation itself to the exclusion of victories won on lesser grounds (that is, equalization). For if the Court were pushed "inescapably" to a decision on the validity of school segregation where no other element of discrimination is present, "it may decide in behalf of segregation; and the morale and prestige loss to the anti-segregation forces from such a decision would be incalculable.". . . .

[James Nabrit responded with passion.] Of those who said blood would run in the streets if the segregation fight was waged in the face of intransigent white-supremacists, Nabrit demanded, "Suppose it does? Shall the Negro child be required to wait for his constitutional rights until the white South is educated, industrialized, and ready to confer these rights on his children's children?" "No," he thundered. . . .

NOTES AND QUESTIONS

Robert Carter, another of the lead attorneys in *Brown v. Board of Education* and the general counsel of the NAACP after Brown, was also willing to risk pushing the Court out of its comfort zone in segregation cases. In his view, "[I]f we win, we make some progress. And if we lose, we've lost nothing. Our children are in terrible schools, so if we lose we are where we started out. We'll come back and try again."[118] Does that fully respond to Frank's concern about the costs of an adverse precedent? Notice that none of these lawyers seemed particularly concerned about what the black community and litigants wanted. Should they have been?

Similar issues continue to arise in various civil rights contexts. Some widely publicized examples involved large school desegregation lawsuits filed by the NAACP Legal Defense Fund in Boston and other major cities. As certified, the classes included all black children who were then attending or who would be attending public schools. Conflicts arose between the parents who favored integration through busing and those who preferred improvements in their de facto segregated neighborhood schools. Derrick Bell, then a prominent litigator for the NAACP, published a landmark law review article criticizing NAACP lawyers for "serving two masters," and placing their own integration ideals over the desires of class members for quality local education. "Idealism," he maintained, "though perhaps rarer than greed, is harder to control."[119] A similar dispute surfaced around the same time when MALDEF attorneys reported opposition to integration efforts that would dilute minority control and undermine barrio solidarity.[120]

Nathanial Jones, NAACP General Counsel, defended the organization's position. The courts, he pointed out, had recognized a right to integration, not to educational quality.[121] In his view, pursuit of integration made sense from a practical as well as doctrinal standpoint. As Jones put it, "green follows white"; the best way to attract dollars for minority schools was to increase their white enrollment.[122]

Yet over the next two decades, as doctrinal and practical realities shifted, leadership priorities also needed to change. A series of Supreme Court decisions restricting remedies in school desegregation cases, together with growing residential housing segregation, made further integration impossible. Declining inner-city financial resources forced the civil rights community to seek new responses to persistent inequalities. Today's debates focus less on racial balance and more on issues such as equitable financing, accountability for student performance, and the role of choice and charter schools. If there are lessons to be learned from prior leadership struggles that could inform these debates, they are the importance of humility and diverse perspectives. Predicting long-term social change is an inherently inexact business. Leaders of wisdom and integrity can be utterly wrong about the consequences of events they set in motion.

Such disputes pose difficult issues for civil rights organizations. How much risk of an adverse ruling should leaders assume? How much involvement should class members have in deciding remedial priorities? How can or should class preferences be assessed when members are constantly changing and often poorly informed over the long duration of a lawsuit?

In the following excerpt, Harvard professor Ronald Heifetz explores a related question: when should leaders take a principled stand on civil rights, when should they compromise, and when should they stay their hand in the hope of forcing others to act responsibly? Consider Lyndon Johnson's efforts to reshape and respond to public opinion in the context of the Selma protest discussed below. If you had been Johnson's Attorney General, what would you have advised him to do?

RONALD A. HEIFETZ, LEADERSHIP WITHOUT EASY ANSWERS

(Cambridge, MA: Belknap Press of Harvard
University Press, 1994), pp. 129-149

Prelude: The Ripening of the Issue

. . . Of his many initiatives, perhaps Johnson's most successful were in civil rights. At his best, Lyndon Johnson built for himself the opportunity for leadership by listening intently to the nation, identifying its internal contradictions, and transforming the dialogue of competing interests into legislation and programs. . . . Progress would be made by pushing people to engage with one another to adjust their views or reach compromises. The parties would be made to do the work.

Indeed, in his legislative program Johnson routinely put the pressure on the people who asked him for help. Thus, Johnson put the pressure on black leaders to persuade reluctant conservatives. The key to success on civil rights, in Johnson's opinion, lay in the hands of the minority party, the Republicans headed by Senator Everett Dirksen. Without their support, no new legislation could get past Senator Richard Russell and the block of Southern Democratic senators committed to its defeat. They would filibuster it to death, as they had done with nearly every civil rights bill for nearly a century. Yet Johnson was not going to do the lobbying work alone. To win the Republicans over, Johnson called on Roy Wilkins, head of the National Association for the Advancement of Colored People (NAACP), as prelude to introducing the Civil Rights Act of that year. He placed the call on January 6, 1964, six weeks after assuming the presidency.

Johnson: ". . . I think you are going to have to sit down with Dirksen and persuade him this is in the interest of the Republican party, and you think that if the Republicans go along with you on cloture, why you'll go along with them at elections. And let them know that you're going with the presidential candidate that offers you the best hope and the best chance of dignity and decency in this country, and you're going with a senatorial man who does the same thing. *I'm no magician.* Now I want to be with you, and I'm going to help you any way I can. But you're going to have to get these folks in here, and the quicker you get them the better. If we lose this fight we're going back ten years."

Indeed, the Senate went through seventy-five days of filibuster over the Civil Rights bill—the longest in its history. But on June 10, 1964, it was ready to vote on cloture. The key, as Johnson had said, was Dirksen. . . . Declaring "civil rights is an idea whose time has come . . . we are confronted with a moral issue," he had turned around. Dirksen's priorities had shifted in the course of his conversations with Wilkins and others. The issue had been made to ripen. As Johnson later described the problem to his biographer Doris Kearns: "The challenge was to learn what it was that mattered to each of these men, understand which issues were critical to whom and why. Without that understanding nothing is possible. Knowing the leaders and understanding their organizational needs let me shape my legislative program to fit both their needs and mine." In pursuing domestic policies in general, Johnson sought to induce the relevant parties—business leaders, educators, labor, the media—to get involved with one another. Some authorities might concentrate on getting people to acquiesce to their commands. Johnson sought to educate people to cooperate with one another, respecting one another's goals. He corralled people into collaborative work. As he described it, "I wanted each of these men to participate in my administration in a dozen different ways. The key was to get men from different groups so involved with each other on so many committees and delegations covering so many issues that no one could afford to be uncompromising on any one issue alone."

Johnson intended to mobilize the nation as a whole to work on issues that had been avoided for nearly two hundred years. Yet mobilizing the society to tackle hard problems and learn new ways required far more than fashioning deals in the legislature; it required public leadership. Johnson had to identify the adaptive challenges facing the nation, regulate the level of distress, counteract work-avoiding distractions, place responsibility where it belonged, and protect voices of leadership in the community. Nowhere did he illustrate this strategy of leadership better than during events in Selma, Alabama.

Selma—Eight Days in 1965

On Sunday, March 7, 1965, black Americans set out to march from Selma to the state capital at Montgomery in an all-out drive for voting rights. Selma, a city of about 29,000, had slightly more black people than white, but only 3 percent of the people on its voting rolls were black. Out of 15,000 black citizens, 325 were registered to vote. The county had used time-worn methods to prevent black citizens from registering to vote, including lengthy written examinations and tricky oral questions like: Recite the Thirteenth Amendment to the Constitution, and what two rights does a citizen have after indictment by a grand jury? Governor Wallace of Alabama had declared during his campaign in 1962: "From this cradle of the Confederacy, this very heart of the great Anglo-Saxon Southland . . . , segregation now! Segregation tomorrow! Segregation forever!"

In response to the voting rights march, Governor Wallace sent the state police against the 600 unarmed black people as they reached the city limits. Americans throughout the country witnessed with shock and fury the televised scenes of black men, women, and children being beaten with billy clubs, stricken with tear gas, and bull-whipped by troopers on horseback. As loud as the screaming was the yelling of white onlookers, "Git 'em! Git 'em!" In reaction, spontaneous demonstrations sprang up across the land as massive pressure focused on President Johnson to mobilize the national guard.

Johnson, however, refused to move. In fact, he faced contrary pressures from Sunday's bloodshed, each with its own long history. On one hand, the outraged public called on the President to act forcefully at once to protect the marchers in Selma. People marched and sat-in at the White House; they marched and sat-in at the Justice Department; they berated him in the press nationwide. Dr. Martin Luther King Jr., "dismayed and discouraged," accused the federal government of "timidity." On the other hand, many others wanted Johnson to keep out of the matter. They expressed great fear of federal interference in their own state affairs. White Southerners, among others in the nation, were tired of federal government intervention into their way of life and wanted to maintain local norms and control. Johnson was faced with a conflict between two different constituencies with two opposing values: states' rights, which represented white supremacy, and voting rights. . . .

This conflict was nothing new. . . . The country had spent years deliberating and testing the issue and, by and large, had come down on the side of protecting civil rights against local transgression. But not fully. The previous year, Congress had been unable to agree on a voting rights provision for the 1964 Civil Rights Act. Johnson had floated the idea, but Congress rejected it. Too many white people found it hard enough to integrate restaurants and schools. They refused to give blacks political power. The Congressional stalemate on voting rights indicated that the country as a whole was not yet ready to enfranchise minorities. Urgency over the issue was far from widespread; voting rights had not yet fastened in people's minds. The steps taken in 1964 toward guaranteeing civil rights were as large as the public seemed able to take at that moment. . . .

In private meetings in early 1965, Johnson, knowing the constraints of his role, encouraged King in his plans to ripen the voting rights issue. Although he hoped there would be no violence, he thought public pressure might set the stage for legislative action. As did King. By generating nationwide urgency, the civil rights movement aimed to change the public's priorities and throw Congress into motion. King and his strategists had learned through decades of effort that the federal government would protect the rights of black Americans when public pressure forced it to. So the civil rights movement would turn up the heat. Through the carefully scripted presence of television reporters, the brutality of racism would be transmitted into living rooms throughout the land. Demonstrations would force the nation to pay attention. On Sunday, March 7, after the televised beatings in Selma, Dr. King announced:

> In the vicious maltreatment of defenseless citizens of Selma, where old women and young children were gassed and clubbed at random, we have witnessed an eruption of the disease of racism which seeks to destroy all of America. . . . The people of Selma will struggle for the soul of the Nation, but it is fitting that all Americans help to bear the burden. I call, therefore, on clergy of all faiths, representative of every part of the country to join me in Selma for a minister's march on Montgomery Tuesday morning.

In anticipation of Tuesday's march, the pressure on Johnson grew enormously. Marches and demonstrations proliferated across the country. Busloads and planeloads of priests, ministers, rabbis, nuns, and lay people descended on Selma. In Washington, D.C., sit-ins at the Justice Department continued to block Attorney General Katzenbach's office. The White House was deluged with telegrams and calls to take action. A group of demonstrators sat-in during a White House tour, yelling angry epithets at whoever passed by. Clearly, the public did not relish the prospect of more televised beatings, this time with King and the nation's clergy at the forefront. The public looked to President Johnson to restore order. As he described it, "Everywhere I looked I was being denounced for my 'unbelievable lack of action.'"

On Monday afternoon, King's lawyers appealed to the federal court in Montgomery for an injunction forbidding local and state authorities from interfering with Tuesday's march. Instead, Judge Frank Johnson issued a restraining order to delay the march entirely for a few days until proper safety precautions could be made. In light of this order, President Johnson felt compelled to step in. He quietly sent LeRoy Collins from the Justice Department aboard Air Force One to negotiate a middle path with King that would keep the public pressure on without going farther than any President could legally allow. At the very last minute, on Tuesday morning as the march itself was moving, they made a deal. King avoided clashing with local and State police, and with the federal court, and turned the march back after a dramatic moment of prayer at the site of Sunday's violence. The nation held its breath as it lived through the encounter on television. And though momentarily relieved, the acute level of tension remained very high. Dr. King insisted that the full three-day march to Montgomery still lay ahead.

Johnson continued to hold steady. He neither quelled nor inflamed the situation. Rather than take dramatic public action or a clear stand, Johnson issued a lukewarm statement Tuesday afternoon deploring the brutality in Selma and urging leaders on all sides to "approach this tense situation with calmness, reasonableness, and respect for law and order." He added that he would be sending a voting rights bill to Congress by the weekend. Privately, however, after seeing the televised beatings and judging their public impact, he called in the Justice Department and asked them to draft the strongest bill that would have any chance of surviving a constitutional challenge.

On Tuesday night, Reverend James J. Reeb, a white Unitarian minister from Boston, was beaten badly by a group of white people in Selma; he died two days later. His was the second death. Jimmy Lee Jackson, a seventeen-year-old black man, had been shot by state troopers two weeks before while marching in nearby Marion, Alabama. Reverend Reeb's fatal beating added more fuel to the demonstrations and the urgency. "But," as Kearns described it, "Johnson refused to be pushed. Pickets surrounded the White House, carrying placards calculated to shame him into action: 'LBJ, open your eyes, see the sickness of the South, see the horrors of your homeland.' Telegrams and letters demanding action streamed into the President's office." Still, Johnson held steady through Tuesday night, Wednesday, Thursday, and Friday. At one point, a presidential aide interjected, "We have to do something." Johnson replied, "We will. Keep the pressure on. Make it clear we're not going to give an inch. Now that Wallace . . . it's his ox that's in the ditch, let's see how he gets him out."

Finally, on Friday, Wallace asked to meet with the President, and Johnson granted the request at once. As Johnson understood the situation, Wallace had national aspirations. He had run briefly for President in 1964. He could ill afford more bloodshed broadcast nationwide from his state. As much as he hated to give in on civil rights, Wallace also had to maintain law and order. Thus, Johnson had something Wallace needed. He could help Wallace back out of his corner because he, Johnson, had refused to back into one himself. "On Saturday, in the Oval Office, they discussed the question of troops. Johnson appealed to the large ambition and the populist strain that he perceived in Wallace: How could there be any fixed limits, he suggested, to the political career of the first Southern governor to combine economic and social reform with racial harmony? Why not Wallace?"

The meeting resulted in an arrangement. Johnson would rescue Wallace from his obligations to maintain the law and protect innocent black people, for which he would have paid dearly with his own white constituents, but Wallace would have to ask Johnson publicly to mobilize the national guard. Following the meeting, Johnson took Wallace into a prearranged press conference where he made sure that Wallace was still publicly on the hook, that is, accountable for protecting all citizens, black and white. Johnson announced: "If local authorities are unable to function, the federal government will completely meet its responsibilities."

The next day, Sunday, while 15,000 demonstrators outside the White House sang "We shall overcome," and chanted: "LBJ, just you wait, See what happens in '68," Johnson solicited an invitation to appear before a joint session of Congress the next evening, Monday, March 15, and he began to prepare for his now historic speech.

Principles of Leadership

. . . *Identifying the Adaptive Challenge* . . . No authoritative presidential decision would "fix" this kind of problem. This problem existed in the minds and hearts of citizens, and only adjustments *there* would resolve the value conflict. What the President could do was animate and prod people across the nation to address the internal contradiction between the values of freedom and equality they espoused and the mode of suppression they lived or permitted. Although laws, political stands, and programs could not mandate adaptive change, they could fix attention on the need for adjustment. They could begin to change institutions to create new norms and set new limits on behavior. As Johnson commented after passage the previous year of the Civil Rights Act, "I understand that a law doesn't change people's feeling. But it's a beginning. It shows the way."

. . . Johnson did not have the final answers. But his responses to Selma illustrate at least four conditions for stimulating adaptive change after the challenge has been identified: *managed stress*, disciplined by *attention to the issues*, with *pressure* on those who need to take responsibility for the changes in their midst, and *protective cover* for threatened leadership voices.

Regulating Distress. In the midst of crisis, the first priority is to evaluate the level of social distress, and, if it is too high, take action to bring it into a productive range. Confronted by overwhelming distress, a society and its factions may fall back on extreme measures to restore direction, protection, and order: authoritarian rule, suppression of dissent, fragmentation into smaller identity groups (ethnic, religious, regional), and war (civil and otherwise). Thus, Johnson had to assess the level of disequilibrium in the society in order to determine whether or not emergency actions were called for, like sending in the National Guard. Could the nation sustain the storm without breaking apart? . . .

King and his organizers turned up the heat, but Johnson let the stew simmer. By his calm demeanor and lukewarm statements, Johnson communicated that the crisis was no emergency. But by inaction, Johnson raised the level of tension so that people could no longer ignore their own responsibility for the harsh reality of black people being beaten for requesting an equal right to vote.

Directing Disciplined Attention to the Issues. By having waited over a week to make a move, Johnson allowed television images of racial brutality to settle into the public consciousness. He prevented premature closure. When he finally announced during his press conference with Wallace that, if necessary, he would take decisive action, he merely relieved the immediate source of distress. The underlying issue had now fastened in people's minds, where it would continue to generate dissonance. Dissonance would call for more action. The issue would ripen: people would come to see the issue as a public priority. And therein lay the opportunity. Johnson waited to seize that moment when he could address the issue of racial justice rather than merely diffuse the dissonance. He took the event and gave it meaning that would have been lost before.

Had Johnson intervened as the nation demanded, by mobilizing the National Guard, he would surely have reduced the public's distress over police brutality against black Americans. Johnson's action would have directed the nation's attention to a side issue: protecting the marchers' right to express their demands. Yet as Johnson unbundled the issues, the point was not the right to march; the point was the right to vote. Had Johnson intervened immediately, the issue might have been understood the wrong way—the easy way.

Worse, his intervention would also have diverted the nation's attention from the issue of racism to the issue of states' rights. Johnson, the Southern politician, knew better than to let that happen.

> If I just send in federal troops with their big black boots and rifles, it'll look like Reconstruction all over again. I'll lose every moderate, and not just in Alabama but all over the South. Most southern people don't like this violence; they know, deep in their hearts, that things are going to change. And they'll accommodate. They may not like it, but they'll accommodate. But not if it looks like the Civil War all over again. That'll force them right into the arms of extremists, and make a martyr out of Wallace. And that's not going to help the Negroes. . . . I may have to send in troops. But not until I have to, not until everyone can see I had no other choice.

Had he intervened immediately, Johnson would probably have survived quite well, personally. As a Southerner intervening with federal troops to protect innocent black people, he would likely have gained considerable popularity throughout much of the nation. There were good precedents for federal interference into racial disturbances: Kennedy in Mississippi, Eisenhower in Arkansas. And *they* were Northerners.

Stepping in decisively to resolve the crisis, however, would have interrupted the work being done in the polity. By letting the distress persist for over a week, Johnson provided the nation with no choice but to face the issue of racism itself. The appalled public would not permit Southern whites to frame the issue as states' rights. Furthermore, voters throughout the nation had witnessed from their own living rooms that the marchers longed for the right to vote, not the right to march. The issue would not be mistaken as states' rights or the right of black people to march. By refusing to be pushed by the public, Johnson pushed people to face the internal contradictions of *their* society, embodied in the sights they could not avoid watching on television.

Giving the Work Back to People. Johnson's long experience taught him to be wary of the trap that Wallace had set—shifting all responsibility to the highest authority. By stepping in with troops, Johnson would have presented himself and his office as a receptacle for blame or credit. Either would be a diversion from working on the problem of equality. The solution to the crisis would have become "Johnson's solution," framed as federal interference in states' affairs, or federal protection of the right to march. Instead, Johnson did nothing to divert responsibility until the public's will had crystallized. He let the people with the problem bear weight. He let blacks carry the major responsibility for provoking change. He waited for Wallace to request federal troops. And he waited until voters across the nation had done enough work to reveal to themselves, and to him, the outlines of a solution—their solution. As Kearns described it, "When Johnson finally sent troops to Alabama [two weeks after the crisis began], the act was generally regarded, not as an imperious imposition of federal power, but as a necessary measure to prevent further violence. By waiting out his critics and letting the TV clips make their own impression on the country, he had succeeded in persuading most of the country that he had acted reluctantly and out of necessity, not because he was anxious to use federal power against a guilty South."

The civil rights movement had focused attention and ripened the issue. Johnson's task was to restrain himself from absorbing the attention and responsibility. The tactic of holding steady shifted the feeling of necessity to the public so that it would face the issue with its costs and its gains. The public and its representatives were made to do the work of changing their attitudes and priorities about justice.

Thus, by keeping the spotlight on the persons embodying the issues, Johnson gave the work of adjustment back to the people with the problem: the civil rights activists, George Wallace, Congress, and the general public. For example, he encouraged King in private meetings to arouse public attention. Animated constituents would generate the political will and leeway for legislative action. . . . Moreover, he let Wallace stew for awhile, appealing to him at the White House in his moment of distress to adjust his own view of himself. . . . When Wallace finally asked for federal assistance (on the grounds that Alabama could not afford the cost of protecting the marchers), Johnson let everyone know that he was acting on Wallace's initiative. He made sure that the debate remained focused on civil rights and not on states' rights, and that Wallace had borne the burden. . . .

Protecting Voices of Leadership in the Community. Johnson provided protection to King and his colleagues in the form of encouragement, guidance, and warning. . . . To avoid a confrontation between King and the federal government, Johnson tried to dissuade King from marching that day; King insisted, however, and they reached a compromise. In essence, Johnson made clear to King the limits of the cover he could provide. The march went on in truncated form, and Johnson held steady through it. . . .

The Speech

By waiting, Johnson raised the stakes, not only for the nation but for himself. If, as President, he failed to act decisively after what seemed so prolonged a time of crisis, the public would hold him accountable. Public expectations constrained him. As with any person in a position of senior authority, a President eventually has to provide a clear focal point to restore a sense of direction and order. Johnson did that eight days after the crisis in Selma had begun. By that time, the nation looked to Johnson with ever heightened anticipation. But by that time, the nation was ready to hear what it needed to hear, and not just what it wanted to hear. Johnson spoke before a joint session of Congress during prime evening television. The speech, excerpted at length, captures Johnson's strategy.

I speak tonight for the dignity of man and the destiny of democracy. . . .
There is no cause for pride in what has happened in Selma. There is no cause

for self-satisfaction in the long denial of equal rights of millions of Americans. But there is cause for hope and for faith in our democracy in what is happening here tonight. . . .

Last time a President sent a civil rights bill to Congress it contained a provision to protect voting rights. That bill was passed after eight long months of debate. And when that bill came to my desk for signature, the heart of the voting provision had been eliminated. This time, on this issue, there must be no delay, no hesitation, no compromise with our purpose. . . .

But even if we pass this bill, the battle will not be over. What happened in Selma is part of a far larger movement which reaches into every section and state of America. It is the effort of American Negroes to secure for themselves the full blessings of American life. Their cause must be our cause too. It is not just Negroes, but all of us, who must overcome the crippling legacy of bigotry and injustice. *And we shall overcome.* As a man whose roots go into Southern soil I know how agonizing racial feelings are. I know how difficult it is to reshape attitudes and the structure of society. . . . I say to all of you here and to all in the Nation tonight, that those who ask you to hold on to the past do so at the cost of denying you your future.

This great, rich, restless country can offer opportunity and education to all—black and white, North and South, sharecropper and city dweller. These are the enemies—poverty and ignorance—and not our fellow man. And these too shall be overcome. Let no one, in any section, look with prideful righteousness on the troubles of his neighbors. There is no part of America where the promise of equality has been fully kept. In Buffalo as well as Birmingham, in Philadelphia as well as Selma, Americans are struggling for the fruits of freedom. This is one nation. What happens in Selma or in Cincinnati is a matter of legitimate concern to every citizen. But let each of us look within our own communities and our own hearts, and root out injustice there. . . .

The real hero of this struggle is the American Negro. His actions and protests—his courage to risk safety and even life—have awakened the conscience of the Nation. His demonstrations have been designed to call attention to injustice, to provoke change and stir reform. He has called upon us to make good the promise of America. And who among us can say we would have made the same progress were it not for his persistent bravery, and his faith in American democracy. For at the heart of battle for equality is a belief in the democratic process.

Historic in its sweep and claim, this speech inspired much of the country. It also demonstrates and helps summarize our principles of leadership. First, Johnson spoke clearly to the orienting values of the nation, the values that had made it one nation: freedom, equality, and democracy. The issue of civil rights was to be seen in that context. He identified the adaptive challenge by identifying the discrepancy between our values and behavior. Indeed, he identified the next adaptive challenge as well: poverty.

Second, by speaking in so dramatic a fashion—before a joint session of Congress—Johnson tried to maintain the level of urgency at the same time that he addressed its causes. Taking charge might have reduced the pressure had Johnson not demanded immediate Congressional action. Moreover, Johnson pointed out that Congress had failed to complete its work on voting rights in the earlier civil rights legislation. These acts kept the pressure on.

Finally, Johnson exercised leadership in one of the few ways that authority figures can—by protecting the voices of those who lead with little authority, even though such voices often will be both deviant and annoying. He credited the civil rights movement for provoking the nation to face the large gap between what we stood for and the way we lived.

In exercising leadership on civil rights, was Johnson advancing his own vision for the country? Not really. As a Southern congressman since 1937 and senator since 1949, Johnson came out in favor of civil rights only in 1956 when he saw the issue ripening and saw himself as a national contender. For nearly twenty years he had voted against every civil rights bill before Congress—laws to end the poll tax, segregation in the armed services, and lynching. . . .

It seems then that the civil rights movement and the events in Selma had their impact on Johnson's conscience, as well as that of the nation. As he described in his memoirs, "Nothing makes a man come to grips more directly with his conscience than the Presidency . . . ."

We often think that leadership means having a clear vision and the capacity to persuade people to make it real. In this case, Johnson had authored no vision. Events acted on him to shape the vision to which he then gave powerful articulation. He *identified the nation's vision* and put it into words. . . .

Johnson signed the Voting Rights Act into law on August 6, 1965. Within one week, federal registrars set up shop; six months later, 9,000 black people were registered to vote in Selma.

QUESTIONS

1. With the benefit of hindsight, Johnson's decision to delay sending federal troops to Selma seems clearly justified. But at the time that he made it, was that outcome clear? What risks was he assuming? Suppose Judge Johnson had not delayed the march, violence had broken out, and hundreds of protestors had been injured. Suppose Wallace had refused to ask for federal help and Johnson had been forced to respond belatedly. How would you have advised Johnson if you had been Attorney General?

2. Compare Johnson's address on civil rights legislation with Barack Obama's historic speech on race, discussed in Chapter 4. What rhetorical strategies do they share that make them effective? Obama faced criticism, particularly during his first term as president, for failing to take more decisive action on race-related issues. Was he motivated by some of the same considerations that delayed Johnson's response to Selma? Was there anything Obama should have done differently?

3. One lesson from the Selma decision is the importance of a leader's understanding of the motives and constraints of other key players, and his or

her willingness to accept criticisms and risks of short-term costs in pursuit of larger goals. How might this lesson inform the contemporary struggle for racial justice? Are there other lessons from the early civil rights strategies that are generalizable to contemporary public interest contexts?

PROBLEM 10-3

Consider a contemporary social issue on which leaders are divided. What accounts for their conflict? Have they created appropriate structures for handling it? What lessons do the readings suggest about how you might respond to these challenges?

MEDIA RESOURCES

Many documentaries on civil rights movements are available; among the best are *Eyes on the Prize* and *Freedom Riders*.[123] Footage of antidiscrimination protests, an interview with Martin Luther King, and his last speech can also give context to the campaign for social justice.[124] The movie *Selma* paints a portrait of the Selma march somewhat different from Heifetz's. Nelson Mandela's account of bringing factions together to abolish racial apartheid in South Africa suggests useful leadership parallels to the American experience.[125] The film *Invictus* provides a moving fictional account of those efforts. For contemporary struggles, Marbre Stahly-Butts, executive director of Law for Black Lives, discusses how she became a social movement lawyer.[126] Bryan Stevenson's celebrated TED Talk reviews the relationship of racial injustice and mass incarceration in the United States.[127]

There are a wide array of documentaries, TED Talks, and media accounts of many other social movements facing leadership challenges similar to those described above. An account of the quest for Native American rights appears in *Modern Day Warriors, We Shall Remain*, and *Alcatraz Is Not an Island*.[128] For a historical overview of farm workers' rights, see *Dolores*, a CBS News Special on Dolores Huerta, as well as *The Fight in the Fields, Chicano! History of the Mexican American Civil Rights Movement*, and *Harvest of Shame*.[129] For the history of the U.S. environmental rights movement, see American Experience's *Earth Days, Disruption*, or *A Fierce Green Fire*.[130] Al Gore's *An Inconvenient Truth* shows the power of images in conveying the urgency of climate change.[131] For the contemporary use of civil disobedience in that movement, see a discussion of the Climate Defense Project, which provides legal representation to environmental activists.[132] For a history of women's rights, see *A History of Women's Achievement in America, Sisters of 77*, and *One Woman One Vote*.[133] For the disability rights movement, consult *Beyond Affliction: The Disability History Project* and *Lives Worth Living*.[134]

C. CONFLICTING VIEWS OF COMMON INTERESTS

The following materials explore a recurring question in civil rights movements: when should activists force an issue into the courts and when should they pursue broader political strategies while waiting for a more favorable case or judicial climate? In the excerpt below, Harvard Law School professor William Rubenstein addresses that question in the context of racial discrimination and gay marriage litigation. To resolve disputes over that question, Rubenstein proposes a model of collective decision-making. In principle, his framework has much to recommend it. In practice, what complications arise when any litigant who takes a different view holds keys to a courthouse door? Consider those difficulties in light of the following readings and problem on the California same-sex marriage case.

WILLIAM B. RUBENSTEIN, DIVIDED WE LITIGATE: ADDRESSING DISPUTES AMONG GROUP MEMBERS AND LAWYERS IN CIVIL RIGHTS CAMPAIGNS

106 Yale L.J. 1623 (April 1997)

Should political processes control the kinds of litigation a private attorney general can institute? Groups are messy. They are, by definition, comprised of many individuals and thus encompass a range of desires and agendas. Any group must generate ways to reach decisions among these competing possibilities. Typically, groups develop formal and informal mechanisms to define their goals and strategies. . . .

But consider litigation. . . . [T]wo questions [] lie at the heart of more informal groups' decisionmaking about litigation: Why is any individual group member able to step forward in the litigation arena and unilaterally claim to represent, and indeed bind, all similarly situated group members to a particular legal position? Further, why can any single attorney litigating one of many cases brought on behalf of a group decide alone what tactics and strategies to employ in pursuing that case? There is one immediate answer to both of these questions: Group decisions about litigation are structured by the rules of litigation, that is, by the rules of civil procedure and professional ethics, and those rules currently adhere to an individualist model. . . .

I. The Problem: Disputes among Group Members and among Lawyers in Civil Rights Campaigns

A. The Story of *Shelley v. Kraemer*

In the spring of 1947, Thurgood Marshall was annoyed. The source of his frustration was an attorney from St. Louis named George Vaughn. Vaughn had just done something Marshall did not want him to do: He had filed a petition for certiorari with the United States Supreme Court in a case called *Shelley v. Kraemer*, one of the many cases pending throughout the country in which the constitutionality of racially restrictive housing covenants was at issue. Marshall did not want Vaughn to file this petition because he did not think that the black community's legal position in the many restrictive covenant cases was sufficiently developed to be heard by the Supreme Court; Marshall and his NAACP colleagues had been working on developing that position for many years. Marshall also did not believe Vaughn's factual record in the *Shelley* case was the best that could be brought before the Court; he and the NAACP attorneys had been working closely with social scientists to generate a compelling policy analysis of the effects of these covenants.

Marshall was also worried about Vaughn's legal abilities. Vaughn was not a constitutional scholar. He was an able municipal court lawyer in St. Louis, and, in part because of his political influence within the Democratic party, had prevailed in the Shelley case in municipal court. But Vaughn's 1945 victory was shortlived; by the end of 1946, the Missouri Supreme Court had overturned it. . . .

Vaughn's filing of the petition that spring forced Marshall's hand. He and other NAACP staff took over the appeal of a case pending in Michigan, which Marshall had [previously] deemed not the right test case. . . . Better to argue a less than perfect Michigan case than to have Vaughn argue the issue alone in the Supreme Court. . . .

The restrictive covenant cases were argued for seven hours in the Supreme Court. Philip Elman, an attorney in the Solicitor General's office who helped produce the government's brief in *Shelley v. Kraemer*—and who would write the government's brief in *Brown v. Board of Education*—was present for the argument. He tells this story of George Vaughn's argument:

> [H]e made an argument that as a professional piece of advocacy was not particularly distinguished. You might even say it was poor. He mainly argued the thirteenth amendment, which wasn't before the Court. He tried to distinguish cases when it was clear that the cases were indistinguishable and the only way to deal with them was to ignore or overrule them. He didn't cut through all the underbrush; he got caught in it. And the Justices didn't ask many questions. It was a dull argument until he came to the very end. He concluded his argument by saying . . . "Now I've finished my legal argument, but I want to say this before I sit down. In this Court, this house of law, the Negro today stands outside, and he knocks on the door, over and over again, he knocks on the door

and cries out, 'Let me in, let me in, for I too have helped build this house.'"

All of a sudden there was drama in the courtroom, a sense of what the case was really all about rather than the technical legal arguments. . . . [It was] the most moving plea in the Court I've ever heard.

Vaughn's speech was so compelling that he was invited to repeat it at the 1948 Democratic National Convention.

In May 1948, the Supreme Court ruled in the black litigants' favor, holding in *Shelley v. Kraemer* that court enforcement of racially restrictive covenants would violate the Equal Protection Clause of the Constitution. Legend has it that Thurgood Marshall argued Shelley. Legend does not say much about George Vaughn.

B. The Lessons of *Shelley v. Kraemer*

The story of the litigation campaign that culminated with *Shelley* exemplifies the central concerns that motivate this Article: the difficulty the NAACP attorneys had "controlling" civil rights litigation even at a time when so few lawyers were involved that control seemed plausible, and, more importantly, the intriguing question of what values are furthered by such control. Before turning to the exploration of these themes, it is necessary to state several key premises, each of which also flows from the *Shelley* story. First, this Article talks of "communities" pursuing "goals," despite the fact that civil rights campaigns are not waged by easily identifiable "communities" pursuing settled, concrete goals. The restrictive covenant cases reflected the interests of a particular segment of the African-American community, the black middle-class home-buyers, and the extent to which such cases represented an important element of the civil rights struggle was contested among the various factions struggling to define that movement. Similarly, there is not a fixed "lesbian and gay 'community.'" Indeed, if anything, the fact that lesbians, gay men, and bisexuals are generally not visually identifiable makes the boundaries of this "community" especially amorphous. . . .

C. Disputes about Goals: Lessons from the Same-Sex Marriage Debate

In the fall of 1989, a lesbian/gay intellectual journal called Out/Look published a debate concerning same-sex marriage. On one side of the debate was Tom Stoddard, then the executive director of Lambda; on the other side of the debate was Paula Ettelbrick, then Lambda's legal director. Stoddard's contribution, entitled *Why Gay People Should Seek the Right to Marry*, set forth a practical, political, and philosophical argument for gay marriage and urged the gay community to give marriage priority as an issue: "I believe very strongly," Stoddard wrote, "that every lesbian and gay man should have the right to marry the same-sex partner of his or her choice, and that the gay rights movement should aggressively seek full legal recognition for same-sex marriages." Ettelbrick dissented. In her article, entitled *Since When Is Marriage a Path to Liberation?*, Ettelbrick stated that:

> [M]arriage will not liberate us as lesbians and gay men. In fact, it will constrain us, make us more invisible, force our assimilation into the mainstream and undermine the goals of gay liberation. . . . Marriage runs contrary to two of the primary goals of the lesbian and gay movement: the affirmation of gay identity and culture; and the validation of many forms of relationships. . . .
>
> The moment we argue, as some among us insist on doing, that we should be treated as equals because we are really just like married couples and hold the same values to be true, we undermine the very purpose of our movement and begin the dangerous process of silencing our different voices. . . .
>
> We will be liberated only when we are respected and accepted for our differences and the diversity we provide to this society. Marriage is not a path to that liberation.

The Stoddard/Ettelbrick exchange was a "marriage announcement" of sorts, a declaration that the issue of marriage was moving from the margin to the center of the lesbian/gay movement. Yet from the moment of its reintroduction, the marriage issue produced controversy among community members. The Stoddard/Ettelbrick debate exposed one fissure, whether the community ought to prioritize and pursue marriage at all, and reflected a discussion within Lambda about how the organization should respond to increasing demands that it file a same-sex marriage case. This was not the only contentious issue. The community also disputed when such cases ought to be filed, where such filings might be made, and on whose behalf. The community generally, and the lawyers at Lambda specifically, were confronted by a significant conundrum: What constituted a satisfactory response to these divisions?

Stoddard and Ettelbrick's response was to air their debate publicly, first in the pages of Out/Look and then "on the road." The two leaders traveled around the United States to debate in front of community audiences. By taking their debate to the community, Stoddard and Ettelbrick apparently envisioned that some resolution of their disagreement would emerge from the community discussion, perhaps that some consensus would evolve to guide their actions.

A similar attempt to gauge community consensus occurred at the outset of a marriage challenge in Hawaii. In 1990, some individuals in Hawaii approached the ACLU affiliate in that state, asking the organization to file a challenge to Hawaii's marriage laws on their behalf. The local ACLU affiliate contacted the ACLU's National Lesbian and Gay Rights Project in New York seeking guidance. Nan Hunter, then Director of the Project, suggested that the Hawaii affiliate measure support for the case within the lesbian and gay community in Hawaii before pursuing the issue. The ACLU's Hawaii affiliate translated Hunter's advice into an informal poll of gay community leaders. By letter, the Hawaii affiliate attorney sought input from the community about whether there was "broadly based support for such litigation" in Hawaii, writing that the "ACLU would not want to act in a manner inconsistent with the opinion of a substantial number of gays and gay rights activists." The ACLU was attacked for taking this approach: A community activist in Hawaii wrote that "[i]ndividuals or civil rights should never be construed as a popular opinion issue, but rather a right of each human being."

The internal community debate largely subsided after lesbians and gay men, without support from the legal experts, proceeded with their own legal actions. In late 1990, Craig Dean, a gay lawyer, filed his own case challenging the District of Columbia's marriage law on behalf of himself and his lover. In May 1991, three lesbian and gay male couples in Hawaii filed an action in Hawaii state court without the support of the ACLU; they were represented by a former staff attorney at the ACLU of Hawaii. After the cases were filed, the community legal organizations ultimately provided support for them, thus quelling the internal community drama. All of the actors had different perspectives on how this resolution was accomplished: The professionals viewed it as a rebuke of their expertise, or of some community consensus, by rogue individuals; the individuals defended their actions either as in the best tradition of courageous individuals, or as capturing a community consensus while their leaders fiddled. . . .

III. The Democratic Model

Group members and attorneys could address disputes concerning the conduct of impact litigation by employing more democratic means of decisionmaking. Democratic values would lend significant legitimacy to goal-based decisions, but would have less applicability to the more technical decisions about legal strategies. . . . Under such a regime, individuals would not be authorized to litigate the group's rights on their own; instead, their role would be to participate in the group's decisionmaking about its litigation options. The question of whether to file a marriage case would be decided by the group collectively. Such a group decision could be achieved either through a formal vote or according to a more informal democratic process, and could be practically implemented by any number of possible procedural innovations. . . . [One value of democratic decisionmaking is that it would involve] the community more closely in the decisions affecting its life. If the community members actually controlled the filing and pursuit of litigation, they would be forced into a more active engagement with one another about these issues. This obligation could counter the alienation that results from dependence on lawyer-experts, increase the individuals' sense of belonging to the community, and could further the civic republican's much-idealized community discourse. . . .

Limited to a strict voting approach, however, the democracy model confronts several significant hurdles. Given the ambiguous contours of the "communities" at issue and the often complicated and fluid nature of litigation decisionmaking, it would be nearly impossible to identify a meaningful voting constituency and to conduct a worthwhile vote. Moreover, only an insignificant percentage of the "electorate" may be interested or informed enough to involve itself in the "election." Permitting filing only after a community vote also limits some individuals' autonomy and threatens to disenfranchise permanent minorities within the community. These types of problems with voting mechanisms have largely constrained their application to problem-solving in the related context of complex class action jurisprudence. In determining whether a proposed representative will adequately represent the interests of a class, courts generally have not relied on community sentiment in support of or against certification, but have engaged in an independent (albeit cursory) analysis of the quality of the proposed representative. Similarly, in determining whether to approve a proposed settlement, courts rarely rely on voting devices like surveys of class members, nor weigh majority sentiment heavily. Relatively few class members respond to court mailings and those who do are not representative. Even more disturbing, few class members attend meetings convened by their attorneys in civil rights cases. Those who do respond or attend are often neither knowledgeable nor unbiased observers, and their views are typically shaped by the attorneys presenting the issues to them. . . .

[Yet in many contexts, the issues at stake in filing a lawsuit] are neither complicated nor beyond intelligent community discourse. . . . [If we ask members generally] whether they believe gay people should file lawsuits seeking the right to marry, or blacks to integrate their local schools, or women to enter the Citadel [military academy], . . . chances are they will have opinions. Most importantly, democratic values can be embodied in procedural rules without requiring reliance on formal voting mechanisms. For instance, rules that enhance community dialogue, increase individual participation, or "rectify the antidemocratic exclusion of chronically disadvantaged groups from the theatre of politics," serve democratic values. Rules of procedure could be constructed around these values of democracy without requiring formal voting processes. Rules that required individuals or experts filing group-based cases to demonstrate that some level of community dialogue preceded the decision to file, or to show some level of community participation in the filing, or to establish approval for their filings from democratically elected representatives, could capture some of the benefits of democracy without falling prey to the unworkability of elections about litigation. . . .

NOTES AND QUESTIONS

1. Following the disputes over gay marriage described above, controversy continued within the gay rights community and the broader public. Although the Hawaii litigation resulted in recognition of gay marriage, the victory was short lived. Voters passed an initiative reserving the definition of marriage to the legislature, which reversed the court.[135] Other states similarly passed statutes or constitutional amendments preventing gay marriage, a move encouraged by the federal Defense of Marriage Act. It outlawed the provision of federal benefits to same-sex partners and allowed states to refuse recognition of out-of-state gay marriages. Within a decade, 45 states had such bans.[136]

Controversy also persisted within the gay rights movement. One issue was how much priority to place on marriage equality, relative to other pressing issues such as hate crimes, AIDs, and discrimination in employment and housing.[137] How should leaders of social movements make and implement priority decisions?

Another controversy existed over whether to pursue marriage rights through litigation or legislation. A major victory for marriage equality in the Massachusetts Supreme Court in 2003 set the stage for a major controversy in California.[138] In 2004, after San Francisco Mayor Gavin Newsom invoked the Massachusetts precedent to authorize the city's issuance of marriage licenses to same-sex couples, lawsuits by Christian Right groups challenged those unions. The dispute ended up before the California Supreme Court, which grounded a right to gay marriage in the state constitution.[139] The voters then passed Proposition 8, which reserved marriage to a man and a woman. In their comprehensive overview of the marriage-law controversy, law professors Scott Cummings and Douglas NeJaime note that Newsom did not involve LGBT leaders in his decision, and that many questioned his motives. In their view, Newsom was using the issue to shore up his political base, which had been put at risk by a progressive challenger in the mayoral election. He also may have been hoping to be perceived as the "Rosa Parks" of a movement that voters ultimately would support.[140] However, his famous prediction that gay marriage was coming "whether you like it or not" also galvanized opposition, especially when it was replayed in Proposition 8 campaign adds. How would you evaluate Newsom's leadership on this issue? What would you have done in his place?

2. In 2005, a coalition of gay rights groups issued a statement titled "Winning Marriage: What We Need to Do," which charted a state-by-state political strategy for winning marriage equality. At the time, only five states and the District of Columbia recognized same-sex marriage. The statement discouraged federal lawsuits because the odds of winning in the U.S. Supreme Court weren't good. The groups reasoned that the Court "typically does not get too far ahead of either public opinion or the law in the majority of states. . . . A loss now may make it harder to go to court later. It will take us a lot longer to get a good Supreme Court decision if the Court has to overrule itself." Speaking to the California experience, the statement concluded, "We lost the right to marry in California at the ballot box. That's where we need to win it back."[141]

That statement met widespread support among LGBTQ activists and constitutional law experts. Experts noted that Supreme Court Justices are leaders with enormous power, but that power comes not from the "sword or the purse" but from the credibility of the Court as an institution. That credibility depends in part on keeping judicial interpretations of the law within bounds that the public will perceive as legitimate. On issues of constitutional rights, the Court can sometimes effectively prod the nation to live up to its own aspirations, as it did in cases involving interracial marriage and racially segregated schools. But when the Justices push too far too fast, legislators and government officials often push back, and that backlash may derail the progress that the original decision was designed to secure. Many, though not all, commentators view the *Roe v. Wade* decision recognizing women's right to an abortion as an example.

However, not all activists agreed about the need for prioritizing legislative over litigation strategies. In 2009, conservative lawyer Ted Olson and liberal lawyer David Boies brought a challenge to Proposition 8 on behalf of the American Foundation for Equal Rights.[142] California gay rights groups, which were not consulted in the decision to sue, were largely opposed, but once the lawsuit was filed, sought to intervene. Olson and Boies opposed the motion, and the trial court agreed.

PROBLEM 10-4

1. Assume that you are the leader of a national gay/lesbian rights organization. You learn from a confidential source that Theodore Olson and David Boies are planning to bring a federal lawsuit challenging Proposition 8, California's ban on same-sex marriage. You discuss the matter with the directors of two other gay rights organizations whose confidentiality you trust. They are both incensed. What infuriates them is not only the substance of the decision but the fact that two "publicity-hungry" straight men have decided to undermine the carefully planned strategy that the gay/lesbian community has struggled for a decade to develop. One director proposes that your organizations beat Olson to the courthouse door by filing a similar suit first. How do you respond?

2. Assume that you are one of the leading lawyers working with Olson and Boies in the Proposition 8 challenge. After the suit is filed, gay rights organizations that had opposed the litigation want to intervene. Olson opposes sharing control and publicity. Other members of your litigation team disagree. They believe that it would be a politically constructive gesture that would also generate additional support and expertise. Olson responds that the expertise will be available in any case; the groups will have no choice but to cooperate. What is your view?

NOTES AND QUESTIONS

1. The trial court held that Proposition 8 violated the plaintiff's constitutional rights and California officials declined to appeal. Rather, sponsors of the proposition pursued the appellate litigation. The court of appeals affirmed the trial court's ruling, but on narrower grounds than Olson and Boies had argued. Rather than finding that gay and lesbian couples had a right to marriage under the Federal Constitution, the court reasoned that couples already granted that right under the state constitution could not have the right taken away without a legitimate non-discriminatory reason, which was absent in the ratification of Proposition 8. The Supreme Court granted certiorari, but declined to review

the constitutionality of Proposition 8. Rather, it held that the ballot sponsors lacked standing to appeal on behalf of the state.[143] However, that same term, the Court struck down the federal Defense of Marriage Act, which defined marriage for purposes of federal law as a legal union between one man and one woman.[144] Two years later, in 2015, the Court held, by a five-four majority, that the state's refusal to recognize same-sex marriages violated the Fourteenth Amendment.[145] Does that result alter your views of Olson and Boies's decision to sue?

2. A *New York Times* account of the Olson and Boies suit describes the consensus of the gay community that the litigation was "the wrong claim in the wrong court in the wrong state at the wrong time."[146] In commenting on the decision to sue without consulting gay rights groups before the filing of the California lawsuit, one of the plaintiff's lawyers, Thomas Boutros, explained, "We did not want to have a big debate about what we felt was the right strategy."[147] Why not? What would have been the advantages and disadvantages of involving the coalition of gay rights groups that had been active on the issue? If you had been in Boutros's place, what would you have done?

3. In defending the decision to bring the California lawsuit, Olson reasoned that millions of gay couples would like to be married, and one was bound to file a constitutional challenge. "So if there's going to be a case, let it be us . . . because we have the resources [and experience] to do it."[148] Are you persuaded? Given Olson's own self-interest, was he in a good position to assess who would have been the best lawyers to lead the charge? What cognitive biases might have influenced his judgment? One difference between the early civil rights cases and the contemporary gay-marriage dispute involves the number of litigants willing and able to bring constitutional challenges. In the 1940s and 1950s, filing a racial discrimination lawsuit often exposed parties and attorneys to substantial physical and financial risks, and brought little favorable public recognition. By contrast, today's litigants have more to gain and less to lose. In the contemporary climate, how can national strategies be forged? Would Rubenstein's proposal of community involvement in decision-making have helped in the California gay-marriage dispute?

4. One difficulty for leaders of social change is that, as Howard Zinn noted in an article titled *The Optimism of Uncertainty*, history is full of examples of unexpected victories of the relatively powerless. "Revolutionary change," he noted, "does not come as one cataclysmic moment . . . but as an endless succession of surprises, moving zigzag toward a more decent society."[149] What few predicted at the time Olson and Boies filed suit was how rapidly public opinion was evolving on gay marriage. By the time the issue reached the Supreme Court, 37 states permitted same-sex unions, 60 percent of Americans supported them, and the majority of Justices who found constitutional protection for that right were squarely within the mainstream.[150] What do you think accounts for the rapid evolution of views, and what lessons does the marriage equality struggle hold for other cause lawyers and social change activists?

In responding to that question, one commentator noted, what changed in the space of a generation "wasn't the Constitution—it was the country. And what changed the country was a movement."[151] In explaining the success of the movement, and the litigation campaigns that helped propel it, Scott Cummings notes that supporters met with less powerful opposition than other social activists.

> This is in part because of the nature of the right to marry, which removes state barriers to private action rather than requiring significant state resources to enforce. In addition, permitting marriage by same-sex couples does not impose zero-sum costs on opponents, who object to the impact of including same-sex couples on marriage as an institution but adduce no evidence that marriage, or society, suffers as a result.[152]

By contrast, other legal efforts to promote social change demand power or resource redistributions, or other initiatives that more directly and adversely affect opponents.

After assessing the value of litigation in various contemporary social movements, Cummings concludes:

> Litigation is often given less centrality, in part owing to the composition of the Supreme Court but also because of the commitment of advocates to sustainable reform through political and cultural change. A key point is that the way that litigation is used in campaigns depends on the strength of political alternatives to legal action, which changes over time.
>
> Litigation is important when campaigns are getting off the ground and the resources and opportunities for political change are relatively weak. For example, in the antisweatshop campaign, litigation was initially used to spotlight egregious conduct—the enslavement of trafficked garment workers—and gain redress for the victims. Movement lawyers then deployed litigation over time for its direct and indirect movement effects. Lawsuits targeted high-profile garment companies to build public attention, send messages to bad actors to promote compliance, and create the template for statewide legislative change that strengthened joint employer liability [that made manufacturers accountable for unpaid wages by contractors]. Specifically, litigation set legal precedent and stimulated policy advocacy resulting in statewide codification of the joint employer standard. . . .
>
> In the absence of a political movement, litigation becomes a central tool to check government power, even though it is ultimately limited in what it can accomplish. This was evident in the War on Terror campaign, in which advocates were operating from a position

of political weakness owing to public support for punitive government policy and executive control of law enforcement and military power. This campaign was [among] the most traditionally legalized, but not because lawyers believed courts could halt preventative detention and torture, but rather because courts were the only leverage to push back against the government and galvanize public attention.[153]

Do you agree? If so, what implications do you draw for the value of litigation for other contemporary social movements such as immigration, reproductive justice, or racial bias in law enforcement?[154]

AMNA A. AKBAR, TOWARD A RADICAL IMAGINATION OF LAW

93 New York University Law Review 405, 407-414
(2018)

[In a recent seminar on law and social movements, racial justice organizer] James Hayes praised the technical chops and procedural expertise lawyers bring to the table. But that is not enough, he said. "Most lawyers see a problem and think, 'How can I fix this law?'" This view is too narrow: it obscures the stakes and concedes to status quo arrangements. "The role of the law is to protect the state," Hayes reasoned. "Lawyers must work with movements to imagine with us the kind of state we want to live in. Only from there can we work together to think about the laws we need."

In conversations with intellectuals and organizers around the country, I realized the Movement for Black Lives (M4BL or Move- ment)—the larger movement configuration in which the chapter-based Black Lives Matter network functions—was having a far richer and more imaginative conversation about law reform than lawyers and law faculty. The Movement for Black Lives was situating their critique in Black history and intellectual traditions, and their imagination of alternate futures in Black freedom movements. Their critique was more expansive at the same time that it was more grounded, and their imagination more radical.

Legal scholars often assume the movement's fight is over policing: indictments for police killings, independent prosecutors to investigate police shootings, better training and supervision for police, more diverse police forces, and so on. But, as Hayes suggested, the most imaginative voices within contemporary racial justice movements are fighting for much more than body cameras and police convictions.

The movement is focused on shifting power into Black and other marginalized communities; shrinking the space of governance now reserved for policing, surveillance, and mass incarceration; and fundamentally transforming the relationship among state, market, and society. Movement actors have made policy proposals and engaged in law reform campaigns at the same time that they have prominently contested law and politics as usual.

In the few years after Ferguson police officer Darren Wilson's killing of Michael Brown, there were shut-downs of bridges and highways; die-ins at courthouses and state-houses; occupations of police stations, police unions, and universities; arrests and curfews; tear gas and riot gear. But the movement's high-profile campaigns have not been waged by lawyers or via litigation. Indeed, the movement has largely refrained from fighting to strengthen preexisting rights or demanding legal recognition of new ones. The focus is not on investing even-handedness to law or the police, not on restoring criminal justice to some imaginary constitutional or pre-raced status quo, and not on increasing resources for community policing. But it would be wrong to think the movement has given up on law. The movement is not attempting to operate outside of law, but rather to reimagine its possibilities within a broader attempt to reimagine the state. Law is fundamental to what movement actors are fighting against and for.

To illustrate how the movement approach reorients traditional criminal law reform conversations, I examine the 2016 policy platform of the Movement for Black Lives, "A Vision for Black Lives: Policy Demands for Black Power, Freedom, and Justice" (the Vision). I put the Vision in conversation with the Ferguson and Baltimore reports by the Department of Justice, which represent more traditional liberal approaches to criminal law reform. The Vision and the DOJ reports offer some of the most damning critiques of policing in recent memory, but differ fundamentally in their analysis and conclusions. The contrast reflects the limitations of liberal law reform at the same time that it opens up a more imaginative set of possibilities about reorganizing the very structure of our society. . . .

The Vision and DOJ reports offer alternate conceptualizations of the problem of policing and the appropriate approach to law reform. Reflective of liberal law reform projects on police, the DOJ reports identify policing as a fundamental tool of law and order that serves the collective interests of society, and locate the problems of police in a failure to adhere to constitutional law. As a corrective, the DOJ reports advocate for investing more resources in police: more trainings, better supervision, and community policing. In contrast, the Vision identifies policing as a historical and violent force in Black communities, underpinning a system of racial capitalism and limiting the possibilities of Black life. As such, policing as we now know it cannot be fixed. Thus, the Vision's reimagination of policing—rooted in Black history and Black intellectual traditions—transforms mainstream approaches to reform. In forwarding a decarceral agenda rooted in an abolitionist imagination, the Vision demands shrinking the large footprint of policing, surveillance, and incarceration, and shifting resources into social programs in Black communities: housing, health care, jobs, and schools. The Vision focuses on building power in Black communities, and fundamentally transforming the relationships among state, market, and society. In so doing, the movement offers transformative, affirmative visions for change designed to address the structures of inequality—something legal scholarship has lacked for far too long.

The DOJ reports document the problems endemic to policing. While presenting a critical view of Ferguson's and Baltimore's police departments, the reports are committed to the legal status quo, to a mode of governance that relies on criminal law enforcement to deal with a broad set of deep-seated social problems, and to rules and authorities that are historically and functionally oppressive. As a result, the reports double down on traditional reforms that reinvest in law and police. This approach cedes more legitimacy—not to mention more resources—to the police and the legal frameworks in which they operate without a meaningful consideration of alternatives. . . .

Imagining with social movements acknowledges how social change occurs beyond the courts. Social change happens on the streets and in formal and informal domains where power and legitimacy circulate. Most law scholarship is invested in centering rationality and reason as the terrain for decision-making, and courts, executives, and legislatures as the places where reform happens. Law scholarship generates a world that relies on law-making and enforcing bodies as the repositories of understanding law's functioning and meaning, and as the central targets for change. The way to reform law, law scholarship suggests, in form and substance, is to convince these legal institutions through superior argumentation and appeals to rationality. This comports with the predominant marketplace-of-ideas metaphor, which in turn borrows from capitalism's ideological commitments to the superiority of the market in producing optimal results: The best arguments will rise to the top. In this way, law scholarship minimizes the relationship between power and the ideas that govern; erases how power circulates through and benefits from formal law-making and law-executing channels; and ignores the disconnect between legal institutions and the public, from which power and legitimacy should flow in a democratic society.

NOTES AND QUESTIONS

The "Vision for Black Lives" that Akbar describes was a collaboration of 50 organizations, and was endorsed by 500 more. It sets forth a vision of change well beyond traditional police and criminal justice reforms. Its agenda includes a strategy to invest and divest—spend more on education, health, and safety in black communities and less on criminal law enforcement and incarceration. It also calls for economic justice, political power for racial minorities, and community control of institutions including the police. In support of that agenda, it quotes from a report by the Center for Popular Democracy, Law for Black Lives, and BYP100: Freedom to Thrive: Reimagining Safety & Security in Our Communities. That report notes:

> Over the last 30 years, the U.S. has dramatically increased its investment in policing and incarceration, while drastically cutting investments in basic infrastructure and slowing investment in social safety net programs. Elected officials have stripped funds from mental

health services, housing subsidies, youth programs, and food benefits programs, while pouring money into police forces, military grade weapons, high-tech surveillance, jails, and prisons. These investment choices have devastated Black and brown low-income communities. . . . Moreover, the choice to invest in *punitive* systems instead of stabilizing and nourishing ones does not make our communities safer. Study after study shows that a living wage, access to holistic health services and treatment, educational opportunity, and stable housing are more successful in reducing crime than more police or prisons.[155]

Akbar and the Vision for Black Lives statement call for an end to jails, prisons, and deportations as we know them, and a radical redistribution of resources. Without those reforms, proponents argue, the law-oriented solutions of the Department of Justice and related liberal groups are unlikely to fundamentally alter the racial violence, inequality, and injustice that gave rise to Black Lives Matter.

Do you agree? If so, how would you create support in the white community and make that agenda politically possible? If not, what reforms would you propose as an alternative? If you were the lawyer in the Justice Department responsible for the reports that Akbar criticizes, how would you respond?

MEDIA RESOURCES

Many documentaries on the gay-marriage struggle are available, as are advertisements from the Proposition 8 campaign.[156] Olson and Boies justify their strategy in an interview with Rachel Maddow.[157] Clips from Harvey Milk's speeches and the film *Milk* also can provide interesting historical context.[158] In the film, Sean Penn portrays Milk, the San Francisco assemblyman who led a statewide movement to oppose a ban on gay schoolteachers. A documentary, *The Times of Harvey Milk*, is also available. It includes a powerful recording of him reading part of his will shortly before his murder, acknowledging the risk of assassination, and his sense of his role less as a "candidate" than as a "cause."[159] A poem raising concerns about the inadequacy of race and class consciousness in the LGBTQ movement underscores the need to take account of different experiences and priorities.[160]

For material on Black Lives Matter, see:

- *Unapologetically Black: The Movie Documentary*:
  https://www.youtube.com/watch?v=myrbHEsND38
- A promotion video for MB4L's Electoral Justice Project:
  https://www.youtube.com/watch?v=8z8einKu6Z4
- A clip of a CNN town hall where an audience member asked if the Black Lives Matter movement is racist:
  https://www.youtube.com/watch?v=IuASG9C7Jb4
- A short interview with Alicia Garza, co-founder of Black Lives Matter, about the impact of the movement:

https://www.youtube.com/watch?v=7UnBykVezRI. Alternatively, the three founders of BLM were interviewed at a TED event together: https://www.youtube.com/watch?v=tbicAmaXYtM

END NOTES

[1] For inattention, see Sharon Erickson Nepstad & Clifford Bob, *When Do Leaders Matter? Hypotheses on Leadership Dynamics in Social Movements*, 11 MOBILIZATION: INT'L J. 1 (2006); Aldon D. Morris & Suzanne Staggenborg, *Leadership in Social Movements*, in THE BLACKWELL COMPANION TO SOCIAL MOVEMENTS 171 (David A Snow, Sarah A. Soule & Hanspieter Kriesi eds., 2004); COLIN BARKER, ALAN JOHNSON & MICHAEL LAVALETTE, *Leadership Matters: An Introduction*, in LEADERSHIP AND SOCIAL MOVEMENTS 1 (2001).

[2] THOMAS R. ROCHON, CULTURE MOVES: IDEAS, ACTIVISM, AND CHANGING VALUES 7 (1998); GARY T. MARX & DOUGLAS MCADAM, *Collective Behavior in Oppositional Settings: The Emerging Social Movement*, in COLLECTIVE BEHAVIOR AND SOCIAL MOVEMENTS (1993); Doug McAdam, *Political Opportunities: Conceptual Origins, Current Problems, and Future Directions*, in COMPARATIVE PERSPECTIVES ON SOCIAL MOVEMENTS: POLITICAL OPPORTUNITIES, MOBILIZING STRUCTURES, AND CULTURAL FRAMINGS (Doug McAdam, John D. McCarthy & Mayer N. Zald eds., 1996); ENRIQUE LARANA, HANK JOHNSTON & JOSEPH R. GUSFIELD, NEW SOCIAL MOVEMENTS: FROM IDEOLOGY TO IDENTITY (1994); John D. McCarthy & Mayer N. Zald, *Resource Mobilization and Social Movements: A Partial Theory*, in COLLECTIVE BEHAVIOR AND SOCIAL MOVEMENTS 40, 43 (Russell L. Curtis & Benigno A. Aguirre eds., 1993).

[3] Alan Johnson, *Self-Emancipation and Leadership: The Cases of Martin Luther King*, in LEADERSHIP AND SOCIAL MOVEMENTS 96, 99 (Colin Barker, Alan Johnson & Michael Lavalette eds., 2001) (quoting civil rights activist Ella Baker).

[4] Clayborne Carson, *Reconstructing the King Legacy: Scholars and National Myths*, in WE SHALL OVERCOME: MARTIN LUTHER KING, JR., AND THE BLACK FREEDOM STRUGGLE 243, 246 (Peter J. Albert & Robert Hoffman eds., 1993).

[5] DAVID J. GARROW, BEARING THE CROSS: MARTIN LUTHER KING, JR., AND THE SOUTHERN CHRISTIAN LEADERSHIP CONFERENCE 56 (1st Perennial Classics ed. 2004) (quoting King).

[6] Aldon Morris, *A Man Prepared for the Times: A Sociological Analysis of the Leadership of Martin Luther King, Jr.*, in WE SHALL OVERCOME, Albert & Hoffman, 36.

[7] JOE WALLLIS & BRIAN DOLLERY, MARKET FAILURE, GOVERNMENT FAILURE, LEADERSHIP AND PUBLIC POLICY 119 (1999).

[8] Gill Robinson Hickman & Ricahrd A. Couto, *Causality, Change, and Leadership*, in LEADING CHANGE IN MULTIPLE CONTEXTS 18 (Gill Robinson Hickman ed., 2010).

[9] DEBORAH L. RHODE, JUSTICE AND GENDER: SEX DISCRIMINATION AND THE LAW 54-55 (1989).

[10] RHODE, JUSTICE AND GENDER, at 56; ROCHON, CULTURE MOVES, 207.

[11] Douglas McAdam, *Culture and Social Movements*, in NEW SOCIAL MOVEMENTS: FROM IDEOLOGY TO IDENTITY 40 (Enrique Larana, Hank Johnston & Joseph R. Gusfield eds., 1994).

[12] *About the Black Lives Matter Network*, Black Lives Matter (2017), http://blacklivesmatter.com/about/.

[13] ROCHON, CULTURE MOVES, at 8; McAdam, *Culture and Social Movements*, 40.

[14] ROCHON, CULTURE MOVES, 190-98; Deborah L. Rhode, *Sexual Harassment*, 65 S. CAL. L. REV. 1459 (1992).

[15] Nicole C. Raeburn, *Working It Out: The Emergence and Diffusion of the Workplace Movement for Lesbian, Gay, and Bisexual Rights*, in AUTHORITY IN CONTENTION: RESEARCH IN SOCIAL MOVEMENTS, CONFLICTS AND CHANGE 187 (Daniel J. Myers & Daniel M. Cress eds., 2004).

[16] Deborah L. Rhode, *#MeToo: Why Now? What Next?*, DUKE L. REV. (2019).

[17] Joel Lovell, *A.C.L.U. v Trump*, N.Y. TIMES MAG., Jul. 8, 2018, at 33-34.

[18] Bert Klandermans, *The Demand and Supply of Participation: Social-Psychological Correlates of Participation in Social Movements*, in THE BLACKWELL COMPANION, Snow, Soule & Kriese eds., 360, 362; Marshall Ganz, *Leading Change: Leadership Organization, and Social Movements*, in HANDBOOK OF LEADERSHIP THEORY AND PRACTICE 527, 533 (Nitin Nohria & Rakesh Khurana eds., 2010); McCarthy & Zald, *Resource Mobilization and Social Movements*, at 40.

[19] Joan Neff Gurney & Kathleen J. Tierney, *Relative Deprivation and Social Movements: A Critical Look at Twenty Years of Theory and Research*, in COLLECTIVE BEHAVIOR AND SOCIAL MOVEMENTS, Curtis and Aguirre eds., 141. *See also* Herbert Buner, *Social Problems as Collective Behavior*, in COLLECTIVE BEHAVIOR AND SOCIAL MOVEMENTS, Curtis & Aguirre, eds., 54 (noting that harmful conditions are not sufficient to mobilize a movement; they need to be legitimated as a problem that can be addressed by social action).

[20] Scott A. Hund & Robert D. Benford, *Collective Identity, Solidarity, and Commitment*, in THE BLACKWELL COMPANION, Snow, Soule & Kriese eds., 433, 439; ROCHON, CULTURE MOVES, at 124-61.

[21] ROCHON, CULTURE MOVES, 104.

[22] Morris & Staggenborg, *Leadership in Social Movements*, 174-75; Sharon Erickson Nepstad & Clifford Bob, *When Do Leaders Matter? Hypotheses on Leadership Dynamics in Social Movements*, 11 MOBILIZATION: INT'L J.1 (2006).

[23] BARKER, JOHNSON & LAVALETTE, *Leadership Matters*, 3.

[24] Ganz, *Leading Change*, at 527-28.

[25] MARC PARES, SONIA M. OSPINA & JOAN SUBIRATS, SOCIAL INNOVATION AND DEMOCRATIC LEADERSHIP: COMMUNITIES AND SOCIAL CHANGE FROM BELOW 88 (2017)

[26] MELVIN L UROFSKY, LOUIS D. BRANDEIS: A LIFE 399-419 (2009).

[27] Michael Winerip, *What's a Nice Jewish Lawyer Like John Rosenberg Doing in Appalachia*, N.Y. TIMES MAG., June 29, 1997, at 26.

[28] Winerip, *What's a Nice Jewish Lawyer*, at 27 (quoting Bruce Davis).

[29] Jeffrey Toobin, *The Legacy of Lynching, On Death Row*, NEW YORKER, Aug. 22, 2016.

[30] EVAN THOMAS, ROBERT KENNEDY: HIS LIFE 110-11 (2000).

[31] Cynthia Cotts, *Trumpeting the Cause of Civil, Human Rights*, NAT'L L. J., Aug. 24, 1998, at C15.

[32] See the discussion of Nader's personal life in Chapter and the General Motors suit in CHARLES MCCARRY, CITIZEN NADER 25-27 (1972).

[33] Darren C. Treadway et al., *The Skills to Lead: The Role of Political Skill in Leadership Dynamics*, in THE OXFORD HANDBOOK OF LEADERSHIP AND ORGANIZATIONS 505, 510 (David V. Day ed., 2014).

[34] Leslie R. Crutchfield & Heather McLeod-Grant, *Local Forces for Good*, STAN. SOC. INNOV. REV., Summer 2012, at 36.

[35] RONALD HEIFETZ & MARTY LINSKY, LEADERSHIP ON THE LINE: STAYING ALIVE THROUGH THE DANGERS OF CHANGE xiv (2017).

[36] ELIZABETH CADY STANTON, EIGHTY YEARS AND MORE: REMINISCENCES 1815-1897 149 (1970).

[37] HEIFITZ & LINSKY, LEADERSHIP ON THE LINE, 191.

[38] Sonia Ospina & Erica G. Foldy, *Toward a Framework of Social Change Leadership*, NYU WAGNER RES. PAPER (2005), http://ssrn.com/abstract=1532332.

[39] Lani Guinier & Gerald Torres, *Changing the Wind: Notes Toward a Demosprudence of Law and Social Movements*, 123 YALE L.J. 2574 (2014), discussed in Scott L. Cummings, *Movement Lawyering*, 2017 U. ILL. L. REV. 1645 (2017).

[40] KATHLEEN KELLY JANUS, BREAKTHROUGH: HOW THE BEST SOCIAL STARTUPS SCALE TO CHANGE THE WORLD (2019).

[41] Mandela, recalling a lesson he learned from a tribal leader, stated "a leader . . . is like shepherd. He stays behind the flock, letting the most nimble go out ahead, whereupon the others follow; not realizing that all along they are being directed from behind." NELSON MANDELA, LONG WALK TO FREEDOM: THE AUTOBIOGRAPHY OF NELSON MANDELA 19 (1994).

[42] PAUL SCHMITZ, EVERYONE LEADS: BUILDING LEADERSHIP FROM THE COMMUNITY UP 76 (2012) (quoting Marshall Gantz).

[43] NYU/Wagner, Research Center for Leadership in Action, *Using Sensible Legal Strategies and Unlikely Alliances to Achieve Fairness for Immigrants in Nebraska* 3-4 (Sept. 2003).

[44] ARTIKA R. TYNER, THE LAWYER AS LEADER: HOW TO PLANT PEOPLE AND GROW JUSTICE 112 (2014).

[45] TYNER, LAWYER AS LEADER, 146.

[46] Hickman & Coutro, *Causality, Change, and Leadership*, at 3-31.

[47] For discussion of the structures conducive to social impact, see John Kania & Mark Kramer, *Collective Impact*, STAN. SOC. INNOV. REV. (Winter 2011).

[48] Ganz, *Leading Change*, 509.

[49] The distinction was used to criticize Martin Luther King. *See* Johnson, *Self-Emancipation and Leadership*, 106; STEPHEN B. OATES, LET THE TRUMPET SOUND: A LIFE OF MARTIN LUTHER KING, JR. 122-23 (1982).

[50] LAO-TZU & STEPHEN MITCHELL, TAO TE CHING: A NEW ENGLISH VERSION 21 (1988).

[51] ANN SOUTHWORTH, LAWYERS OF THE RIGHT: PROFESSIONALIZING THE CONSERVATIVE COALITION 31 (2008).

[52] BARBARA C. CROSBY & JOHN M. BRYSON, LEADERSHIP FOR THE COMMON GOOD: TACKLING PUBLIC PROBLEMS IN A SHARED-POWER WORLD 3 (2005).

[53] Ricardo S. Morse, *Integrative Public Leadership: Catalyzing Collaboration to Create Public Value*, 21 LEADERSHIP Q. 231, 243 (2010); PARES, OSPINA & SUBIRATS, SOCIAL INNOVATION, 226-228.

[54] WALLLIS & DOLLERY, MARKET FAILURE, GOVERNMENT FAILURE, LEADERSHIP AND PUBLIC POLICY, 145.

[55] CROSBY & BRYSON, LEADERSHIP FOR THE COMMON GOOD, 275-78.

[56] NYU Wagner Research Center for Leadership in Action, *Changing Mandatory Drug Sentencing Laws on the Federal and State Levels: Putting a Human Face on Injustice Reversing a Political Juggernaut, Families Against Mandatory Minimums (FAMM)* 6 (2009).

[57] CROSBY & BRYSON, LEADERSHIP FOR THE COMMON GOOD, 122.

[58] GAIL COLLINS, WHEN EVERYTHING CHANGED: THE AMAZING JOURNEY OF AMERICAN WOMEN FROM 1960 TO THE PRESENT 110 (2009).

[59] ROCHON, CULTURE MOVES.

[60] Sameer M. Ashar, *Movement Lawyers in the Fight for Immigrant Rights,* 64 UCLA L. REV. 4 (2017); Scott L. Cummings, *Law and Social Movements: Reimagining the Progressive Canon,* 2018 WIS. L. REV 441, 499 (2018).

[61] GARY L. FANCIONE, RAIN WITHOUT THUNDER: THE IDEOLOGY OF THE ANIMAL RIGHTS MOVEMENT 2 (1996).

[62] FANCIONE, RAIN WITHOUT THUNDER.

[63] NORM PHELPS, THE LONGEST STRUGGLE: ANIMAL ADVOCACY FROM PYTHAGORAS TO PETA 285-286 (2007). FRANCIONE, RAIN WITHOUT THUNDER.

[64] JOHN W. GARDNER, LIVING, LEADING, AND THE AMERICAN DREAM 151 (Francesca Gardner ed., 2003).

[65] Deborah L. Rhode, *Public Interest Law: The Movement at Midlife,* 60 STAN. L. REV. 2027, 2035 (2008) (quoting Carl Pope).

[66] Rhode, *Public Interest Law,* at 2035 (quoting Kathy Rogers).

[67] Toobin, *The Legacy of Lynching* (quoting Bryan Stevenson).

[68] Rhode, *Public Interest Law,* at 2040 (quoting Ted Shaw).

[69] Rhode, *Public Interest Law,* at 2045 (quoting Bryan Stevenson).

[70] Rhode, *Public Interest Law,* at 2033 (quoting Jon Davison, Lambda Legal).

[71] Rhode, *Public Interest Law,* at 2033 (quoting Jamienne Studley).

[72] Rhode, *Public Interest Law,* at 2027, 2043 (quoting Barbara Olshansky, Center for Constitutional Rights and citing sources).

[73] GERALD N. ROSENBERG, THE HOLLOW HOPE: CAN COURTS BRING ABOUT SOCIAL CHANGE? (1991); ROSS SANDLER & DAVID SCHOENBROD, DEMOCRACY BY DECREE: WHAT HAPPENS WHEN COURTS RUN GOVERNMENT (2003); Kenneth Lee, *Where Legal Activists Come From,* AM. ENTERPRISE, June 2001, at 50; Gerald Rosenberg, *Courting Disaster: Looking for Change in All the Wrong Places,* 54 DRAKE L. REV. 795 (2006).

[74] Catherine Albiston, *The Dark Side of Litigation as a Social Movement Strategy,* 96 IOWA L. REV. BULL. 61, 63 (2011).

[75] Rhode, *Public Interest Law,* at 2043.

[76] STUART A. SCHEINGOLD, THE POLITICS OF RIGHTS: LAWYERS, PUBLIC POLICY, AND POLITICAL CHANGE xxiv (2004); Kevin R. Den Dulk, *In Legal Culture, but Not of It: The Role of Cause Lawyers* in *Evangelical Legal Mobilization,* in CAUSE LAWYERS AND SOCIAL MOVEMENTS 199-200 (Austin Sarat & Stuart Scheingold eds., 2006); Ann Southworth, *Lawyers and the "Myth of Rights,"* in *Civil Rights and Poverty Practice,* 8 B.U. PUB. INT. L.J. 469 (1999).

[77] NAN ARON, LIBERTY AND JUSTICE FOR ALL: PUBLIC INTEREST LAW IN THE 1980S AND BEYOND 90 (1989) (quoting Nader).

[78] McAdam, *Culture and Social Movements*, at 36, 38. *See generally* Johnston, Laranna & Gusfield, *Identities, Grievances, and New Social Movements* in Larrana, Johnston & Gusfield eds., NEW SOCIAL MOVEMENTS, 10, 189-190.

[79] J. Craig Jenkins & Charles Perrow, *Insurgency of the Powerless: Farm Worker Movements (1946-1972)*, in COLLECTIVE BEHAVIOR AND SOCIAL MOVEMENTS, Curtis & Aguirre eds., 341, 351-52; Mashall Ganz, *Resources and Resourcefulness: Strategic Capacity in the Unionization of California Agriculture, 1959-1966*, 105 AM. J. SOC. 1003, 1033-43 (2000).

[80] Ganz, *Resources and Resourcefulness*, at 1039.

[81] Ganz, *Resources and Resourcefulness*, at 101-14.

[82] Morris & Staggenborg, *Leadership in Social Movements*, at 189-90.

[83] Colin Barker, *Robert Michels and the "Cruel Game,"* in LEADERSHIP AND SOCIAL MOVEMENTS, Barker, Johnson & Lavelette eds., 24.

[84] BARKER, JOHNSON & LAVALETTE, *Leadership Matters*, at 12-14.

[85] Ganz, *Resources and Resourcefulness*, at 1014-16.

[86] JANUS, BREAKTHROUGH.

[87] DANIEL STID & JEFF BRADACH, STRONGLY LED, UNDER-MANAGED: HOW CAN VISIONARY NONPROFITS MAKE THE CRITICAL TRANSITION TO STRONGER MANAGEMENT? 2 (Bridgespan Group, July 2008).

[88] STID & BRADACH, STRONGLY LED, 4.

[89] STID & BRADACH, STRONGLY LED, 8.

[90] MARTIN DEMPSEY & ORI BRAFMAN, RADICAL INCLUSION: WHAT THE POST 9/11 WORLD SHOULD HAVE TAUGHT US ABOUT LEADERSHIP 73 (2018).

[91] Emily Witt, *How the Survivors of Parkland Began the Never Again Movement,* NEW YORKER, Feb. 19, 2018.

[92] Malcolm Gladwell, *Snatch*, NEW YORKER, Oct. 4, 2010, at 42. *See* JENNIFER AAKER & ANDY SMITH, THE DRAGONFLY EFFECT: QUICK, EFFECTIVE, AND POWERFUL WAYS TO USE SOCIAL MEDIA TO DRIVE SOCIAL CHANGE (2010).

[93] Zeynep Tufekci, *Twitter and Tear Gas: The Power and Fragility of Networked Protest*, TWITTERANDTEARGAS.ORG (2017).

[94] Gladwell, *Snatch*, at 42.

[95] Jennifer Aaker & Andy Smith, *The Dragonfly Effect*, STAN. SOC. INNOV. REV. (Winter 2011).

[96] Aaker & Smith, *The Dragonfly Effect*, at 31, 32.

[97] Toobin, *The Legacy of Lynching*.

[98] NYU Wagner, Research Center for Leadership in Action, *Changing Mandatory Drug Sentencing*.

[99] CHIP HEATH & DAN HEATH, SWITCH: HOW TO CHANGE THINGS WHEN CHANGE IS HARD 28 (2010).

[100] HEATH & HEATH, SWITCH, 28 (quoting Sternin).

[101] See the work summarized by The Positive Deviance Initiative at Tufts, *About the Positive Deviance Initiative (PDI)*, http://www.positivedeviance.org/about_pdi/.

[102] HEATH & HEATH, SWITCH, 29-39, 40.

[103] HEATH & HEATH, SWITCH, 150.

[104] HEATH & HEATH, SWITCH, 151.

[105] Deborah L. Rhode & Lee D. Ross, *Environmental Values and Behaviors: Strategies to Encourage Public Support for Initiatives to Combat Global Warming*, 26 VA. ENVTL L. J. 161, 167-87 (2008).

[106] For examples, see HEATH & HEATH, SWITCH, 159-161; Rhode & Ross, *Environmental Values*, at 181.

[107] Rhode, *Public Interest Law*, at 2064, 2067.

[108] NYU Wagner Research Center for Leadership in Action, *Using Sensible Legal Strategies and Unlikely Alliances.*

[109] Kania & Kramer, *Collective Impact*, at 36, 38.

[110] Kania & Kramer, *Collective Impact*, at 36.

[111] Tom Wolff, *Ten Places Where Collective Impact Gets It Wrong*, 7 GLOBAL J. COMMUNITY PSYCHOL. PRAC. 1 (Mar. 15, 216).

[112] Susan D. Carle & Scott L. Cummings, *A Reflection on the Ethics of Movement Lawyering*, 31 GEO. J. LEGAL ETHICS 447, 462 (2018).

[113] Serge Kovalweski, *Obama's Organizing Years, Guiding Others and Finding Himself*, N.Y. TIMES, July 7, 2008 (quoting Obama).

[114] This problem draws on SHELLEY RATAY & JULIA NOVY-HILDESLEY, COASTAL PLANNING IN BELIZE: SYSTEMS THINKING AND STAKEHOLDER ENGAGEMENT ON A NATIONAL SCALE, Case: Change X 1801, STAN. SCH. EARTH, ENERGY & ENVTL. SCI. (May 4, 2018).

[115] Derrick A. Bell Jr., *Serving Two Masters: Integration Ideals and Client Interests in School Desegregation Litigation*, 85 YALE L.J. 470, 473 (1976).

[116] *See generally* BARRY FRIEDMAN, THE WILL OF THE PEOPLE: HOW PUBLIC OPINION HAS INFLUENCED THE SUPREME COURT AND SHAPED THE MEANING OF THE CONSTITUTION (2009).

[117] Michael Murakami, *Desegregation*, in PUBLIC OPINION AND CONSTITUTIONAL CONTROVERSY 18-20 (Nathaniel Persily, Jack Citrin & Patrick J. Egan eds., 2008). Eighty-five percent of Americans thought that "Negros who lived in their town [did] have the same chance as whites to get a good education." Murakami, *Desegregation*, at 20.

[118] LEWIS M. STEEL WITH BEAU FRIEDLANDER, THE BUTLER'S CHILD: AN Autobiography 103 (2016).

[119] Bell, *Serving Two Masters*, at 470, 504.

[120] GARY ORFIELD, MUST WE BUS? 212 (1978).

[121] Nathaniel R. Jones, *Correspondence: School Desegregation*, 86 YALE L.J. 378, 379 (1976).

[122] Jones, *Correspondence*, at 380.

[123] *Eyes on the Prize: America's Civil Rights Years 1954-1965* (PBS Video, 2006); *Freedom Riders*, http://www.pbs.org/wgbh/americanexperience/films/freedomriders/; *Freedom Riders (PBS)*, YOUTUBE (Nov. 3, 2012), https://www.youtube.com /watch?v=DcvsWXrS2PI.

[124] For a 1957 interview with King discussing strategies, see *first interview with Martin Luther King from 1957 part 1*, YOUTUBE (July 14, 2007), http://www.youtube.com/watch?v=-Ll4QmvnGcU and *first interview with Martin Luther King from 1957, part 2*, YOUTUBE (July 14, 2007), https://www.youtube.com/watch?v=HXlfeeh_Wqg&list=PLAF57E5EB76BB5B64&inde

x=3&t=0s. For King's last speech, see *Martin Luther King's last speech*, YOUTUBE (Apr. 27, 2007), http://www.youtube.com/watch?v=o0FiCxZKuv8.

[125] https://www.youtube.com/watch?v=6VvFwGGF8QY.

[126] https://www.ebony.com/news/race-culture/freeblackmamas-campaign-aims-reunite-families-mothers-day/.

[127]

https://www.ted.com/talks/bryan_stevenson_we_need_to_talk_about_an_injustice?language=en#t-1256814.

[128] *Modern Day Warriors* (Native American Rights Fund, 2008); *Alcatraz Is Not An Island (PBS)*, YOUTUBE (May 15, 2013), https://www.youtube.com/watch?v=pBtWknpytvg&t=183s.

[129] *The Fight in the Fields: Cesar Chavez and the Farmworkers' Struggle* (Paradigm Productions, 1997); *Chicano! History of the Mexican American Civil Rights Movement (PBS)*, YOUTUBE (Sep. 8, 2010), https://www.youtube.com/watch?v=rRixnONgH54; *Harvest of Shame* (Columbia Broadcasting System, 1960). For the CBS special on Dolores Huerta, http://www.cbsnews.com/news/dolores-huertas-50-years-of-civil-rights-activism/.

[130] *American Experience: Earth Days* (PBS Distribution 2010); *A Fierce Green Fire*, YOUTUBE (Dec. 6, 2016), https://www.youtube.com/watch?v=ZpPTn4VG41s.

[131] For the trailer, see https://www.youtube.com/watch?v=Bu6SE5TYrCM.

[132] https://www.echoinggreen.org/fellows/kelsey-skaggs.

[133] *A History of Women's Achievement in America*, (Ambrose Video Pub., 2006); *Sisters of "77 (Trailer)*, YOUTUBE (Jul. 9, 2008), https://www.youtube.com/watch?v=FzcyqWxsR6g; *One Woman One Vote* (PBS Home Video 2005).

[134] *Beyond Affliction: The Disability History Project*, NATIONAL PUBLIC RADIO (Straight Ahead Pictures, 1998), https://www.npr.org/programs/disability/ba_shows.dir/index_sh.html.

[135] *Baehr v. Lewin*, 852 P.2d 44 (Haw.1993).

[136] Cummings, *Law and Social Movements*, 473.

[137] Sandra R. Levitsky, *To Lead with Law: Reassessing the Influence of Legal Advocacy Organizations in Social Movements*, in CAUSE LAWYERS AND SOCIAL MOVEMENTS 145-165 (Austin Sarat & Stuart Scheingold eds., 2006).

[138] *Goodridge v. Department of Public Health*, 798 N.E.2d 941 (Mass. 2003).

[139] *In re Marriage Cases*, 183 P.3d 384 (Cal. 2008).

[140] Scott L. Cummings & Douglas NeJaime, *Lawyering for Marriage Equality*, 57 CAL. L. REV. 1235, 1276 (2010) (quoting anonymous member of the San Francisco Board of Supervisors).

[141] WINNING MARRIAGE: WHAT WE NEED TO DO, quoted in Margaret Talbot, *A Risky Proposal: Is It Too Soon to Petition the Supreme Court on Gay Marriage*, NEW YORKER, Jan. 18, 2010.

[142] DAVID BOIES & THEODORE B. OLSON, REDEEMING THE DREAM: THE CASE FOR MARRIAGE EQUALITY (2014).

[143] *Hollingsworth v. Perry*, 133 S. Ct. 2652 (2013).

[144] *United States v. Windsor*, 133 S. Ct. 2675 (2013).

[145] *Obergefell v. Hodges*, 135 S. Ct. 2584 (2015).

[146] Adam Liptak, *In Battle over Gay Marriage, The Timing May Be Key*, N.Y. TIMES, Oct. 27, 2009, at A14.

[147] Chuleenan Svetvilas, *Anatomy of a Complaint: How Hollywood Activists Seized Control of the Fight for Gay Marriage,* CAL. LAWYER, Jan. 20, 2010 (quoting Boutros).

[148] Talbot, *A Risky Proposal* (quoting Olson).

[149] Howard Zinn, *The Optimism of Uncertainty,* THE NATION, Sept. 20, 2004.

[150] Adam Liptak, *Supreme Court Makes Same-Sex Marriage a Right Nationwide,* N.Y. TIMES, June 26, 2015; Justin McCarthy, *Record High 60% of Americans Support Same-Sex Marriage,* GALLUP, May 19, 2015.

[151] Molly Ball, *How Gay Marriage Became a Constitutional Right,* ATLANTIC, July 1, 2015.

[152] Cummings, *Law and Social Movements,* 477.

[153] Cummings, *Law and Social Movements,* 495.

[154] Cummings, *Law and Social Movements,* 477-496; Amna Akbar, *Toward a Radical Imagination of Law,* 93 NYU L. REV. (2018).

[155] CTR. FOR POPULAR DEMOCRACY ET AL., *Freedom To Thrive: Reimagining Safety & Security In Our Communities* (2017), https://populardemocracy.org/news/publications/freedom-thrive-reimagining-safety-security-our-communities.

[156] For a parody of an antigay marriage advertisement see *Vote NO on Prop 8,* YOUTUBE (Oct. 16, 2008), http://www.youtube.com/watch?v=exPoH1JX0Q8&feature=related.

[157] *The Rachel Maddow Show: Ted Olson and David Boies, The Case for Gay Marriage* (MSNBC television broadcast, Jan. 12, 2010).

[158] MILK (Universal Studios 2009). For a Harvey Milk speech on hope, see https://www.youtube.com/watch?v=X9vol-8HYEc.

[159] THE TIMES OF HARVEY MILK (New Yorker Films 1984).

[160] https://www.youtube.com/watch?v=9dYBpj4VaBo.

CHAPTER 11

LEADERSHIP IN LITERATURE AND FILM

Courses on leadership can be taught entirely through literature or film, and although that is obviously not the approach of this book, much can be gained from approaching leadership issues through a narrative lens.[1] For that reason, prior chapters have included references to relevant literary and media materials. In this chapter, we identify books and movies that would be worth discussing in their entirety, but that also could be excerpted in connection with topics addressed earlier.

We begin with a rationale for studying leadership through narrative, focusing on fiction, and then anchor discussion around one novel, Leo Tolstoy's *The Death of Ivan Ilych*. The remaining discussion is organized around different settings in which lawyers lead. Most of the literature surveyed has corresponding film adaptations. By exploring common challenges through diverse narrative forms, this chapter seeks to deepen understanding of themes that have figured throughout the book and that will arise in any leadership position.

A. LEADERSHIP THROUGH THE LENS OF NARRATIVE

Why analyze leadership through narrative? One reason is that the arts "interpret and amplify experience." In the words of the organizers of the Edinburgh International Festival, artistic works "engage the mind, touch the heart, feed the soul."[2] Because stories speak to our emotion as well as intellect, they give us a broader, sharper, and more intense understanding than what is available through other experiences. As philosophy professor Martha Nussbaum notes, "much of actual life goes by without that heightened awareness that comes through narrative."[3] Stories are, in the metaphor explored in Chapter 4, "made to stick" in ways that other knowledge is not. Social science research makes clear that narratives often shape the moral intuitions that guide decisions, particularly in high-pressure situations.[4]

A related reason for exploring leadership through literature and film is their capacity to engage our moral imagination. Anton Chekov's *Gooseberries* notes that in ordinary life:

> Everything is peaceful and quiet and only mute statistics protest: so many people gone out of their mind . . . so many children dead from malnutrition—and such a state of things is evidently necessary; obviously the happy man is at ease only because the unhappy ones bear their burdens in silence. . . . Behind the door of every contented happy man there ought to be someone standing with a little hammer and continually reminding him with a knock that there are unhappy people, that however happy he may be, life will sooner or later show him its claws, and trouble will come to him—illness, poverty, losses, and then no one will see or hear him, just as he now neither sees nor hears others. But there is no man with a hammer. The happy man lives at his ease, faintly fluttered by small daily cares, like an aspen in the wind—and all is well.[5]

Fiction supplies a hammer. Psychiatrist Robert Cole, who taught a celebrated Harvard Business School course on moral leadership through literature, sees fiction as a corrective to our tendency to "shrug off, shake off . . . close our eyes to the world of unhappiness." A "compelling narrative is a gift of grace." It can "prick our conscience," and remind us of the moral imperatives that should guide our relationships. Heeding the "call of stories" is, "[a]ll in all, not a bad start for someone trying to find a good way to live this life."[6]

A final justification for looking at leadership through a fictional lens is that it supplies a foundation for lifelong learning. In the final analysis, the best that any single book or course can offer its audience is a greater capacity for continuing professional development. An ability to gain leadership insights from literature and film is an acquired skill that will pay dividends over an entire career. Central to that skill is self-reflection, and here narrative can help. As Harvard professor Sandra Sucher notes, understanding not only why fictional characters act the way they do but also how and why we respond to their actions, sheds light on our own values, aspirations, and moral blind spots.[7]

B. LOST OPPORTUNITIES: *THE DEATH OF IVAN ILYCH*

1. HISTORICAL BACKGROUND

Count Lev Nikolayevich Tolstoy was born in 1828, the son of an aristocratic landowning family. Both parents died during his childhood, and he was raised by a devout aunt. During his childhood, he was at best an indifferent student. In describing his aptitude for learning, a tutor remarked, "Leo neither wishes nor can," a description Tolstoy himself echoed.[8] At a provincial university, he studied law and oriental languages but left without a degree. After several years of a dissolute life in Moscow, he joined an artillery regiment that saw service in the Crimean War. He then began writing and established his reputation in fashionable circles in St. Petersburg. Disillusioned by that life, in his early thirties he returned to his family estate, became a magistrate, and built a school for peasant children. In 1862, he married and for the next fifteen years had a relatively happy life. He wrote two great novels, *War and Peace* and *Anna Karenina*, fathered thirteen children, and achieved considerable fame and fortune.

In his early fifties, he underwent a spiritual crisis. As he later explained in *The Confession*,

> [t]he question, which in my fiftieth year had brought me very close to suicide, was the simplest of all questions—one to make itself heard in the heart of every man from undeveloped childhood to wisest old age: a question without which, as I had myself experienced, life became impossible.
>
> That question was as follows: "What result will there be from what I am doing now, and may do to-morrow? What will be the issue of my life?" Otherwise expressed, it may run: "Why should I live? Why should I wish for anything? Why should I do anything?" Again, in other words it is: "Is there any meaning in my life which can overcome the inevitable death awaiting me?"[9]

In attempting to answer that question, Tolstoy came to realize that he had not been living by God's values, or even by his own, but by society's. In his social circle, "ambition, love of power, covetousness, lasciviousness, pride, anger and revenge were all respected." But when confronting the notion of death, he doubted the validity of such goals. "Well, I have now six thousand 'desatins' in the government of Samara, and three hundred horses—what then? . . . 'Well, what if I should be more famous than Gogol, Poushkin or Shakespeare, Moliere—than all the writers in the world—well, and what then?' I could find no reply."[10]

Neither his readings of the great philosophers nor the teachings of organized religion offered an answer. In Tolstoy's view, conventional Christian doctrine of damnation and salvation had robbed people of their ability to make moral choices on their own.[11] The only way that he could ultimately make sense of the meaning of life was through a personal belief in the existence of God. Over the next decade, he wrote a series of pamphlets denouncing war, violence, private property, the church, the courts, and the desires of the flesh. By the close of his life he was also indicting his prior fiction, along with *King Lear* and other classic Shakespearean works.[12] His alternative worldview was an "instinctive," "unmediated sense of religious and moral truth," rooted in love and compassion.[13] In 1901, the Russian Holy Synod excommunicated him, and he died nine years later en route to a monastery.

2. NOTES ON THE NOVEL

Ivan Ilych was Tolstoy's first work of fiction after his spiritual conversion, and it is regarded by many, including Vladimirovich Nabokov, as "Tolstoy's most artistic, most perfect, and most sophisticated achievement."[14] The inspiration was not his own experience, although he did at one point suffer from a painful leg ulcer, which left him bedridden for nine weeks, tended by his wife.[15] Rather, the model was the sudden and painful death of Ivan Ilych Mechnikov, a 45-year-old prosecutor in a regional court near Tolstoy's estate.[16] According to the memoir of Tolstoy's sister-in-law, she had told him what she had learned from Mechnikov's wife: that the dying man's thoughts had been of the "uselessness of the life he had lived."[17]

In a letter just before the novel's publication, Tolstoy indicated that he had wanted to write a "description of the simple death of a simple man from his point of view."[18] For millions of readers, however, *The Death of Ivan Ilych* has been much more than that.

From the standpoint of leadership, Ilych's life is a cautionary tale. He occupies a leadership position; he is a judge with opportunities to do justice for those who come before him. But the role offers few such satisfactions. As the narrator notes, "[t]he pleasures Ivan Ilych derived from his work were those of pride; the pleasures he derived from society were those of vanity; but it was genuine pleasure that he derived from playing whist."[19] For today's professionals, the functional equivalent might be golf, shopping, or a summer home. Yet, in the face of an agonizing death, these pleasures seldom add up. For Ivan Ilych, the physical pain of his illness is amplified by psychological anguish at the banality of his existence. As he recognizes:

> That what had appeared perfectly impossible before, namely that he had not spent his life as should have done, might after all be true. It occurred to him that his scarcely perceptible attempts to struggle against what was considered good by the most highly placed people, those scarcely noticeable impulses which he had immediately suppressed, might have been the real thing, and all the rest false. And his professional duties and the whole arrangement of his life and of his family, and all his social and official interests, might all have been false. He tried to defend all those things to himself and suddenly felt the weakness of what he was defending. There was nothing to defend.

"What is it all for?" Ivan Ilych asks, which invites readers to do the same. The novel prods us to think about what really matters in life and why, before it is too late.

QUESTIONS

1. In the novel's opening chapter, Ivan Ilych's servant Gerasim makes a common sense point about death: "We all come to it one day." Yet one of Tolstoy's

powerful points is the extent to which we generally manage to avoid that fact. At one point in the story, Ivan Ilych recalls Kieswetter's syllogism: "Caius is a man: men are mortal; therefore Caius is mortal." Yet he cannot accept that this logic might apply to him personally. "I Vania, Ivan Ilych, with all my feelings and thoughts" cannot be mortal in the same way as Caius is mortal: that is "how he felt." When you read the syllogism, did you share that emotional response? How might coming to terms with death affect how leaders choose to lead?

2. The author of a distinguished biography of Tolstoy writes of *The Death of Ivan Ilych* that "there are, in fact, few stories whose intended meaning is so abundantly clear."[20] Is it? What meaning do you take from the novel?

3. If you were in Ivan Ilych's place, how would you evaluate your own life to date? What would you most want said at your memorial service? Are you living your day-to-day life with your fundamental values clearly in view?

BIBLIOGRAPHIC AND MEDIA RESOURCES

Many biographies of Tolstoy are readily available, as are books and articles on *Ivan Ilych*.[21] A comprehensive website with pictures and biographical material appears at www.ltolstoy.com. A text of *The Confession* and audio of Tolstoy speaking are also available online. Interesting background material appears in the documentary *Alexander II and His Times: A Narrative History of Russia in the Age of Alexander II, Tolstoy, and Dostoevesky*.[22]

C. LAW

1. HARPER LEE, *TO KILL A MOCKINGBIRD* (1960)

Harper Lee was born in 1926 in Monrocville, Alabama, the daughter of a prominent lawyer. She studied law for several years at the University of Alabama, and then as an exchange student at Oxford University, but never earned a degree. Instead, she went to New York to become a writer, and after a brief stint working as an airline reservation clerk, managed to produce the novel that would become her legacy. *To Kill a Mockingbird* is an undisguised portrait of her father, and the racial dynamics of the community in which he practiced. It won a Pulitzer Prize, sold over 12 million copies, and inspired a movie that earned several Academy Awards, including one to Gregory Peck in the starring role.[23]

The book has also generated considerable debate within the legal community. A key dispute is whether the novel's main character, Atticus Finch, is a moral hero. Should the bar honor a lawyer who acted as he did?

The conventional view has been that Finch represents the highest ideals of the profession. Some loyalists have viewed any criticism of his conduct as tantamount to attacks on "God, Moses, Jesus, Gandhi, and Mother Theresa."[24] From his defenders' perspective, Finch does his utmost to provide effective representation in a court-assigned case involving the most unpopular kind of defendant in Jim Crow Alabama: a black man accused of raping a white woman. Finch risks his life to save his client from a lynch mob, treats blacks with respect, and treats his opponents with civility and empathy. As his neighbor concludes, "we trust him to do right. It's that simple."[25]

By contrast, critics fault Finch on multiple grounds. The first is his brutal cross-examination of the rape complainant, his exploitation of sexist stereotypes, and his indifference to her own victimization. He assumes she is lying, which some law professors have found less self-evident than conventional readings suggest.[26] But even if that assumption is correct, commentators note that his defense builds on class and gender prejudices in ways that are gratuitously demeaning and that reinforce her status as a social pariah. He presents her as white "trash," a woman whose uncontrolled sexual desires have led her to violate the community's ultimate moral code. As he sums it up for the jury, "[s]he was white and she tempted a Negro. . . . No code mattered to her before she broke it, but it came crashing down on her afterward," causing her to falsely claim rape.[27] To further impugn her character, Finch elicits testimony suggesting that she had previously been raped by her father. Neither this possibility nor her serious injuries following that sexual encounter elicits any sympathy from Finch or the town's citizens; no one even offered medical treatment.[28] Indeed, Finch's nine-year-old daughter seems to have greater empathy for the complainant than any of the community's respected citizens do. Only she recognized that the woman "must have been the loneliest person in the world. . . . [W]hite people wouldn't have anything to do with her because she lived among pigs; negroes wouldn't have anything to do with her because she was white."[29] As Malcolm Gladwell noted in a *New Yorker* review, Finch did not "challenge the foundations of [race or class] . . . privilege. Instead Finch does what lawyers for black men did in those days. He encourages [white male jurors] . . . to swap one of their prejudices for another."[30]

Worse still, according to law professor Monroe Freedman, is Finch's complicity in racism. He tells his children that the leader of a lynch mob "is basically a good man" who "just has his blind spots along with the rest of us."[31] Finch did not volunteer for the case, although he believed his client innocent of a capital charge, and he also acknowledges that he had "hoped to get through life without a case of this kind . . . ."[32] As far as we know, never does Finch once "in his professional life voluntarily tak[e] a case in an effort to ameliorate the evil . . . [of] apartheid . . . ." Neither as a lawyer nor a state legislator did he "voluntarily use his legal training and skills . . . to make the slightest change in the social injustice of his own town."[33]

Finally, and to some critics even more disturbingly, Finch betrays his own professional responsibilities after his children are threatened by the father of the disgraced complainant. A reclusive neighbor saves the children but kills the would-be assailant. Finch and the town sheriff agree to avoid public inquiry by pretending that the assailant died by his own hand, and Finch tells his children to lie about what happened. The result may be rough justice, but the means are not what legal ethics experts expect from a moral icon.[34]

QUESTIONS

1. What is your view? Was Atticus Finch a hero for his times? Deeply flawed? Or, for a white man in small-town Alabama in the 1930s, "probably ahead of the curve?"[35]

2. In 2015, *Go Set a Watchman, a* "new" novel by Harper Lee was published. It was actually an early manuscript containing themes and characters that appeared in *To Kill a Mockingbird*. After comments from her editor, Lee revised the manuscript significantly to turn it into *To Kill a Mockingbird*, refocusing it on the rape trial, and setting it in the 1930s Depression era told from the perspective of young Scout.[36] The biggest shock of *Go Set a Watchman* was that

> Atticus Finch—the crusading lawyer of "To Kill a Mockingbird," whose principled fight against racism and inequality inspired generations of readers—is depicted in "Watchman" as an aging racist who has attended a Ku Klux Klan meeting, holds negative views about African-Americans and denounces desegregation efforts. "Do you want Negroes by the carload in our schools and churches and theaters? Do you want them in our world?" Atticus asks his daughter, Jean Louise (the adult Scout), in "Watchman."[37]

   Does this version change your view of the morality of Atticus Finch?

3. Could Finch have effectively defended his client without playing to race and class privilege? What did moral leadership require in his situation?

2. ROBERT BOLT, *A MAN FOR ALL SEASONS* (1960)

Robert Bolt (1924-1995) was born in Manchester, England, the son of a small shopkeeper. After attending Manchester University, serving briefly in the military, and doing postgraduate work at Exeter, he became a schoolmaster in English literature. In his mid-thirties, he started writing full time, and was best known for *A Man for All Seasons*. The play won a Drama Critics award and two Tony awards, and the film adaptation earned Academy Awards for Bolt for the screenplay and Paul Scofield for best actor. Bolt also achieved recognition as a scriptwriter for *Lawrence of Arabia*, and notoriety during its production when he was arrested in a nuclear arms protest. He initially refused to sign a pledge to keep the peace, which would secure his release from jail. However, after pressure from the studio, he agreed to the condition in order to prevent costly delays in the filming schedule. That decision reportedly left him with a deep sense of guilt, in part because his capitulation compared unfavorably to the resistance of Sir Thomas More (1477-1535), the hero of *A Man for All Seasons*.[38]

More was a lawyer and scholar who became Lord Chancellor of England during the reign of Henry VIII. His conflict with the King over the role of the

Roman Catholic Church and the validity of Henry's marriage cost More his life. The conflict unfolded against the backdrop of the Reformation, which responded to doctrinal cleavages and corruption in the Church hierarchy. During that period, popes often were embroiled in scandal, religious offices went to the highest bidder, sinners could purchase indulgences, and taxes were levied for seemingly excessive expenses. Calls for reform intensified with Martin Luther's famous *Ninety-Five Theses* (1517). They supplied the foundation for a Protestant movement, which stressed the individual's direct relationship to God, and made salvation dependent on faith rather than rituals mediated by the Church hierarchy.

In England, this reform movement played out against a complicated and contested split of authority between king and pope. At the turn of the sixteenth century, estimates suggested that the Church controlled as much as a third of all the land in England. However, the Crown exercised authority over taxation and the appointment of high Church officers who were also civil servants. But Rome controlled matrimonial law, which for Henry VIII proved highly inconvenient. He gained the throne in 1509, and soon after married Catherine of Aragon, the daughter of the King of Spain. Although she had formerly been married to Henry's deceased brother, she claimed that the union had never been consummated. But given biblical prohibitions against marrying a brother's widow, a papal dispensation was arranged to safeguard the legitimacy of her marriage with Henry.

By the 1520s, Catherine had failed to produce a male heir, which Henry interpreted as divine retribution for contradicting bans against incest. Although divorces were not then available, he asked for an annulment, a practice common where royalty was involved. In this case, however, the annulment was problematic, both doctrinally (because of the prior dispensation) and politically (because the Pope was under the control of the Holy Roman Emperor, Catherine's nephew). Henry's impatience with the annulment process increased as a result of his infatuation with reformist-leaning Ann Boleyn. To secure his right to remarriage, he appointed a new Archbishop of Canterbury, Thomas Cranmer, who granted an annulment. Henry also installed a new chief advisor, Thomas Cromwell, who helped secure Parliament's passage of the 1534 Act of Supremacy. The Act established Henry as the new head of the English church, and he demanded that leading church and political figures swear an oath acknowledging his supremacy.[39] More, a devout Catholic, refused. After a year of solitary confinement in the Tower of London, he was convicted of treason through perjured testimony and beheaded.

As Bolt describes him in the Preface and portrays him in the play, More had all the qualities of a great leader. Born to a merchant, not noble, family, he earned distinction first as a scholar, then as a lawyer and politician of great wisdom and integrity. He "corresponded with the greatest minds of Europe" and published an important tract, *Utopia*. As Bolt sums it up, More "parted with more than most men when he parted with his life."[40]

In the play, when More asks why he has been chosen as Lord Chancellor, Henry replies:

Because you are honest. What's more to the purpose, you're known to be honest. . . . There are those like [the Duke of] Norfolk who follow me because I wear the crown, and there are those like Master Cromwell who follow me because they are jackals with sharp teeth and I am their lion, and there is a mass that follows me because they follow anything that moves—and there is you.[41]

Yet the choice turns out to be disastrous for both men: for Henry, because he ultimately values loyalty more than integrity, and for More, because his prominence draws attention to his silence regarding the king's supremacy. As Cromwell puts it at trial, that silence is "booming throughout Europe."[42]

What makes More's decision so illuminating from the standpoint of leadership is not just the personal price he is willing to pay for principle, but also the political costs that he is willing to impose on the nation. The price becomes apparent in a dialogue with Cardinal Wolsey, who argues that More should not let his own religious convictions take precedence over the safety of the country. More responds: "I believe that when statesmen forsake their own private conscience for the sake of their public duties . . . they lead their country by a short route to chaos." Wolsey is not persuaded and reminds More of the consequences if Henry is unable to remarry. "Do you remember the Yorkist Wars? Let him die without an heir and we'll have them back again. Let him die without an heir and this 'peace' you think so much of will go out like that," Wolsey predicts, extinguishing a candle.[43]

Aware of the risk to the country, as well as to himself and his family, More attempts to avoid confrontation with the King. He does not seek martyrdom by openly asserting his principles, and he studiously avoids commenting on the king's plans for remarriage. At one point when More and Wolsey look out a window and see the King returning to the castle, presumably after an evening with Ann Boleyn, Wolsey says to More, "The King wants a son; what are you going to do about it?" More deflects rather than answers the question: "I'm sure the King needs no advice from me on what to do about it." When Wolsey persists, and again asks More how he will help Henry obtain an heir, More responds that he prays for it daily.[44]

But when silence will no longer suffice, More cannot sacrifice principle to pragmatism. After the Duke of Norfolk shows More a list of all the government and Church leaders who have pledged to support the King and entreats More to "do what I did and come with us for fellowship," More resists: "And when we stand before God, and you are sent to paradise for doing according to your conscience, and I am damned for not doing according to mine, will you come with me, for fellowship?"[45]

More's adherence to principle stands in sharp relief to others in the play, who are motivated primarily by their own interests. The clearest example is Richard Rich, an academic who seeks a position in the government and ultimately gives false testimony against More to secure it. More has clues of Rich's possible betrayal, and More's wife Alice, daughter Margaret, and son-in-law William Roper all urge that Rich be arrested. More declines in what is one of the play's most celebrated exchanges:

Margaret: "That man's bad."

More: "There is no law against that."

Roper: "There is, God's law."

More: "Then God can arrest him. . . . The law, Roper, the law. I know what's legal, not what's right. And I'll stick to what's legal."

Roper: "Then you set man's law above God's!"

More: "No, far below; but let me draw your attention to a fact—I'm not God. The current and eddies of right and wrong, which you find such plain sailing, I can't navigate. . . ."

Alice (exasperated, pointing after Rich): "While you talk, he's gone!"

More: "And go he should, if he was the Devil himself, until he broke the law."

Roper: "So now you'd give the Devil benefit of law?"

More: "Yes. What would you do? Cut a great road through the law to get after the Devil?"

Roper: "I'd cut down every law in England to do that!"

More (roused and excited): "Oh?" (advancing on Roper) "And when the last law was down, and the Devil turned round on you—where would you hide, Roper, the laws all being flat." (He leaves him.) "This country's planted thick with laws from coast to coast—man's laws, not God's—and if you cut them down—and you're just the man to do it—d'you really think you could stand upright in the winds that would blow then?" (quietly) "Yes, I'd give the devil benefit of law, for my own safety's sake."[46]

More clearly has the best of the argument, even though it turns out that giving Rich the benefit of the law ultimately undermines More's safety. But Rich's betrayal also brings home one of the enduring lessons of the drama. It underscores the contrasting values that earn More sainthood, and leave Rich one of the most detested figures of the English stage. Rich is rewarded for his perjury condemning More by the position of Attorney General of Wales. After observing Rich lie at trial with the Attorney General's chain around his neck, More invokes scripture to drive home his point: "For Wales? Why, Richard, it profits a man nothing to give his soul for the whole world. . . . But for Wales?"[47]

QUESTIONS

1. Could More have done anything that would have avoided the conflict between personal principle and political loyalty that cost him his life?

2. If More was willing to elevate his view of "God's law" over the Supremacy Act, why was he reluctant to invoke God's law to arrest Rich and prevent his betrayal?

3. Does motive matter? If More's objective was to secure glory in the next life rather than this one, does that make him a moral hero? Is that the same motive that impels suicide bombers? Consider T. S. Eliot's analysis of that issue for Thomas Becket in *Murder in the Cathedral*: "The last temptation is the greatest

treason: to do the right deed for the wrong reason."[48]

4. Are there any contemporary leaders who have exemplified More's courage and commitment to principle? What happens when they encounter leaders such as Henry VIII, who value loyalty over the rule of law? What, if anything, can they do to avoid consequences like the ones that More confronted?

D. POLITICS

1. ROBERT PENN WARREN, *ALL THE KING'S MEN* (1953)

Robert Penn Warren was born in Kentucky in 1905, and earned a graduate degree in literature as a Rhodes scholar. He wrote both poetry and prose, and was named the first Poet Laureate of the United States. *All the King's Men* is his most famous work. It is also one of the nation's most celebrated political novels, although Warren famously claimed that it was "never intended to be a book about politics."[49] Modeled on the regime of Louisiana Governor and Senator Huey Long (1893-1935), it was a national bestseller, winner of a Pulitzer Prize, and the basis for two movies, the second starring Sean Penn and Jude Law in the lead roles.

The story centers on Willie Stark, who begins as an idealistic lawyer and evolves into a populist demagogue, shedding most of his principles along the way. He loses his initial position as a county treasurer by supporting the low bid on a school-contracting case. A higher bidder gets the contract, cuts corners, and causes a tragic accident, which makes Stark a local hero. He is then duped into running for governor by an aide to the corrupt incumbent, who needs to split the rural vote. When Stark discovers the truth, he drops out of the race and learns some lessons that enable him to win the next election. His story is told by Jack Burden, a political reporter who becomes an aide and similarly loses much of his initial idealism. In analyzing Stark's first failed race, Burden concludes: "[T]oo much talk about principles, and not enough about promises."[50]

That ceases to be a problem as Stark's career evolves. Although he retains concern for the masses, he becomes increasingly ruthless toward any individual who stands in his way. When told that no dirt was available about an opponent, he responds, "There's always something." He is diligent about finding it, and develops a flexible view of ethics. As he observes, "You've got to make good out of bad. That's all you've got to make it with." Moreover, the very concepts of good and bad come to seem less and less like fixed principles in his political world. From his vantage,

[w]hat folks claim is right is always just a couple of jumps short of what they need to do business. Now an individual . . . he will stop doing business because he's got a notion of what is right, and he is a hero. But folks in general, which is society, . . . is never going to stop doing business. Society

is just going to cook up a new notion of what is right."[51]

Law suffers from the same deficiency, as it is "always too short and too tight for growing humankind. The best you can do is do something and then make up some law to fit and by the time that law gets on the books you would have done something different."[52]

As Stark's aide, Burden initially comes to a similar view. Unlike journalism, where his goal was to learn the truth, in politics, "the world was full of things that I [Burden] didn't want to know."[53] "Maybe," he notes at one point, "a man has to sell his soul to get the power to do good."[54] But by the end of the novel, that is not the conclusion that Burden ultimately embraces. And even Stark himself, as he dies from an assassin's bullet, insists that "it might have been different. You got to believe that."[55]

The extent to which *All the King's Men* captured a realistic view of politics has been subject to considerable debate. Clearly, many events in the novel are modeled on Long's career, including his initial failed political campaigns and his impeachment and assassination.[56] But Warren himself rejected interpretations that reduced the narrative to political commentary. As he put it in an Introduction to a Modern Library edition,

> [o]n one hand, there were those who took the thing to be a not-so-covert biography of, and apologia for, Senator Long. . . . There is really nothing to reply to this innocent boneheadedness or gospel-bit hysteria. As Louis Armstrong is reported to have said, there's some folks that, if they don't know, you can't tell 'em. . . . But on the other hand, there were those who took the thing to be a rousing declaration of democratic principles and a tract for the assassination of dictators. This view, though somewhat more congenial to my personal political views, was almost as wide of the mark. For better or worse, Willie Stark was not Huey Long. Willie [Stark] was only himself. . . .
>
> [His career suggests] the kind of doom that democracy may invite upon itself. The book, however, was never intended to be a book about politics. Politics merely provided the framework in which the deeper concerns, whatever their final significance, might work themselves out.[57]

QUESTIONS

1. If *All the King's Men* is taken not simply as a book about politics in a given era but as an exploration of leadership, what insights does it suggest?
2. What might have made things different in Stark's career?
3. What would be modern examples of the "dirty hands" dilemmas that "all the king's men" confront?[58]

2. KAZUO ISHIGURO, *THE REMAINS OF THE DAY* (1989)

Kazuo Ishiguro was born in 1954 in Nagasaki, Japan. When he was five, his family moved to Great Britain, where his father, an oceanographer, began work on a North Sea research project. Despite his Japanese heritage, Ishiguro had what he described as a "very typical middle-class southern English upbringing."[59] After working briefly as a grouse beater for the Queen Mother at a Scottish castle, Ishiguro studied English and philosophy at the University of Kent. He then spent a year working on behalf of London's homeless, and another year obtaining a master's degree in creative writing. His first novels were set in Japan, but his first critical success was *The Remains of the Day*, the story of a British butler between the 1930s and 1950s. It won the prestigious Booker Prize and was adapted for an award-winning film produced by Merchant Ivory, with Anthony Hopkins and Emma Thompson in the lead roles.

The story is told through the eyes of Stevens, the butler, in a series of flashbacks. It opens in 1956, after the "great house" in which he served Lord Darlington for most of his life has been sold to an American. To rebuild Britain after World War II, the government imposed such high inheritance taxes that most large ancestral homes were donated to the National Trust, opened to tourists, or put up for sale to developers and foreign investors. The declining appeal of domestic service also created enormous problems in staffing country manors, and Stevens is now faced with the task of running a household with 4, rather than 28, retainers.[60] In all his years of service, Stevens has never taken a vacation. When his new employer gives him the opportunity, Stevens adds a business purpose. He takes Darlington Hall's car to visit its former housekeeper, Miss Kenton. She has married and resettled in the West Country, but a recent letter suggests that she may be open to leaving her husband and returning to service.

Over the course of the trip, Stevens reflects on his professional life and is not entirely happy with how it has played out. His work as a butler provides an ideal way to explore the complexities of leader-follower relationships, because that position puts its occupants in both roles simultaneously. In his relations with his employer, the butler must display unqualified subservience. In his relations with the household staff, he exacts the same obedience from others.

For Stevens, both dimensions of this role held moral significance:

The question was not simply one of how well one practiced one's skills, but to what end one did so; each of us harboured the desire to make our small contribution to the creation of a better world, and saw that, as professionals, the surest means of doing so would be to serve the great gentlemen of our times in whose hands civilization had been entrusted. . . .
A "great" butler can only be, surely, one who can point to his years of service and say that he has applied his talents to serving a great gentleman—and through the latter, to serving humanity.[61]

Ishiguro sees a nobility in this role, and one that is a model not just for butlers. As he explained in an interview, "I chose the figure [of a butler] deliberately, because that is what I think most of us are. . . . For most of us, the best we can hope for is to use our rather small skills in serving people and organizations that really do matter."[62]

The central difficulty for Stevens is that Lord Darlington matters in the wrong way, and from a historical standpoint, does not figure as a "great gentleman" worthy of his staff's unqualified loyalty. He is a Nazi sympathizer who arranges several secret meetings with the German ambassador and British leaders in the hope of forestalling conflict. His appeasement sympathies earn him a warm reception from the Third Reich and a despised status in postwar Britain. Even before the war begins, Stevens sees some evidence of his employer's misplaced moral compass when Darlington demands the dismissal of two German Jewish housemaids. Despite their excellent service and the difficulties that they will face in gaining other work, Darlington explains: "It's regrettable . . . but we have no choice. There's the safety and the well being of my guests to consider. Let me assure you, I've looked into this matter and thought it through thoroughly. It's in our best interests."[63] Stevens conveys this decision to Miss Kenton, who is outraged, and threatens to quit. He responds by reminding her that

> our professional duty is not to our own foibles and sentiments, but to the wishes of our employer. . . . You are hardly well placed to be passing judgments of such a high and mighty nature. The fact is, the world of today is a very complicated and treacherous place. There are many things you and I are simply not in a position to understand concerning, say, the nature of Jewry. Whereas his lordship, I might venture, is somewhat better placed to judge what is best.[64]

Looking back on the incident, Stevens recalls: "[M]y every instinct opposed the idea of their dismissal. Nevertheless, my duty in this instance was quite clear, and as I saw it, there was nothing to be gained at all in irresponsibly displaying such personal doubts. It was a difficult task, but as such, one that demanded to be carried out with dignity."[65]

Miss Kenton recalls the incident differently. The topic arises a year after the maids' dismissal, when Lord Darlington acknowledges to Stevens that "it was wrong what happened," and that he "would like to recompense them somehow."[66] Stevens raises the issue with Miss Kenton in the vain hopes of finding the maids' addresses. She then confesses her shame at her "cowardice" in not resigning. "Whenever I thought of leaving, I just saw myself going out there and finding nobody who knew or cared about me. There, that's all my high principles amount to. I feel so ashamed of myself. . . . But I just couldn't bring myself to leave."[67] When Stevens then shares his own "distress" and "concern" about the episode, she asks: "[Why] did [you] not tell me so at the time? . . . Do you realize how much it would have helped me? Why, Mr. Stevens, why, why, why do you always have to pretend?"[68]

The same question arises in another scene that captures the ethical dilemmas of the follower's role. At one of Lord Darlington's dinner parties, some guests decide to make a point about the follies of universal suffrage at Stevens's expense. To expose the ignorance of the common voter, they begin grilling Stevens on the nuances of monetary and foreign policies. This forces him repeatedly to acknowledge that he can give no "satisfaction." The film is especially effective in conveying Stevens's repressed anger and humiliation, and in exposing yet another of Darlington's leadership failures in tolerating the abusive exchange.

The personal costs of Stevens's professional role are measured not only in such indignities but also in his total absorption in work. As his father lies dying upstairs, Stevens feels obligated to continue supervising a dinner party. In their final exchange, his father (himself a butler) tells his son: I'm proud of you. . . . I hope I've been a good father to you. I suppose I haven't." Rather than provide reassurance, Stevens replies simply, "I'm afraid we're extremely busy now, but we can talk again in the morning,"[69] which, of course, they cannot. Another forgone opportunity is presented by Miss Kenton, who clearly signals a desire for a deeper relationship.

At the close of the novel, Stevens realizes his loss, and sums it up for another butler that he meets on his travels:

> [Lord Darlington] wasn't a bad man. . . . And at least he had the privilege of being able to say at the end of his life that he made his own mistakes. . . . He chose a certain path in life, it proved to be a misguided one, but there, he chose it, he can say that at least. As for myself, I cannot even claim that. You see, I *trusted.* I trusted in his lordship's wisdom. All those years I served him, I trusted I was doing something worthwhile. I can't even say I made my own mistakes. What dignity is there in that?[70]

QUESTIONS

1. Is there dignity in that? Is it possible to take moral satisfaction from effectively discharging a professional role, independent of the ends that those efforts serve? Is that what many lawyers do?

2. Was Lord Darlington "not a bad man?" Would he have been better served by less servility? Could actions by Stevens or Kenton have changed his mind about the maids' dismissal? Could either or both have enlisted allies among other staff, or were the risks to their livelihoods too great? What would you have done in their place?

3. Whose conduct seems most ethically problematic in connection with that incident? Is it that of Miss Kenton, who believes that Lord Darlington is wrong and that she should resign, but who lacks courage to do so? Or is it the conduct of Stevens, who is distressed by Darlington's decision but refuses to second-guess his moral judgment?

4. Many commentators have drawn parallels between the role of the butler and the role of the lawyer.[71] What are the similarities and differences? To what

extent should either be held accountable for the morality of their employer's actions? If a lawyer had been asked to dismiss Jewish employees, would his responsibility have been different than a butler's if the dismissals were "within the limits imposed by law" as provided by the American Bar Association's Model Rules of Professional Conduct?[72]

3. *INVICTUS* (2009)

Invictus is a film adaptation of John Carlin's *Playing the Enemy*. It describes Nelson Mandela's early years as South Africa's president, and his relationship with François Pienaar, captain of the nation's rugby team. The movie, produced by Clint Eastwood, stars Morgan Freeman as Mandela and Matt Damon as Pienaar. It begins in 1994, just after Mandela's election as president. Although the formal trappings of apartheid have been dismantled, its legacy of hatred and mistrust remains. Mandela's central leadership challenge is to bridge this racial divide and create a unified South Africa.

During the 1950s and early 1960s, Mandela had been an anti-apartheid activist working with the African National Congress. In 1962, he was sentenced to life imprisonment for sabotage and treason. He spent the next 27 years in brutal prison conditions. Eventually, international pressure as well as domestic protest forced the white South African government to release Mandela and negotiate terms for a peaceful transition to a democratic society. Mandela shared a Nobel Peace Prize with the white Afrikaner leader for managing that transfer of power, and shortly thereafter he won election as the nation's first black president.[73] After the inauguration, the new black commander of the presidential bodyguard resists Mandela's suggestion that the guard include white officers who may have abused blacks under the apartheid regime. Mandela, however, refuses to perpetuate racial segregation in his own administration. "Reconciliation and forgiveness begin here," he reminds the commander.

Mandela sees another opportunity to build bridges through rugby, a previously Afrikaner sport. The South African team, the Springboks, had a poor record and was seen by lacks as a symbol of apartheid. When the national rugby association comes under Black control, its members want to change the team's name. Mandela believes that the change would alienate the white community. At a meeting of the association, he convinces its members to retain the name. He then reaches out to Pienaar, the team's captain, to involve him in repositioning the team, both in its athletic performance and its symbolic impact. By the time South Africa hosts the 1995 Rugby World Cup finals, Mandela wants the Springboks to be source of national pride and unity. With Mandela's assistance, Pienaar helps make that happen. To build players' understanding of the legacy of apartheid, he takes them to the prison where Mandela was incarcerated for almost three decades, and has them provide rugby workshops for impoverished Black youths. As the team comes to see its symbolic role in the nation's reconciliation, its performance rises to the occasion. The film ends with scenes of how effective leadership can help bridge the deepest cleavages of class and race: lack street urchins join white police officers to hear a radio broadcast of the final match, and a white family brings its lack maid to attend the game. The ultimate message is that of the poem by William Ernest Henley, from which the movie title is drawn, and which reportedly sustained Mandela during his incarceration.

> Out of the night that covers me
> Black as the Pit from pole to pole;
> I thank whatever gods may be
> For my unconquerable soul.
> It matters not how strait the fate
> How charged with punishments the scroll,
> I am the master of my fate,
> I am the captain of my soul.[74]

QUESTIONS

1. How does Mandela help Pienaar become an effective leader without ever suggesting what to do? What generalizations can you draw from their joint effort?
2. Consider the qualities of Mandela's leadership as portrayed in the film and book. What makes him so effective? What strategies of influence convince the rugby association to retain the name Springbok?
3. What risks was Mandela taking in allowing the team to keep its name, and in investing so much of his own personal capital in the team's support? Would you have made the same decisions?

4. ANONYMOUS [JOE KLEIN], *PRIMARY COLORS* (1996)

Primary Colors, a best-selling novel by *Newsweek* columnist Joe Klein and an acclaimed film directed by Mike Nichols, views political leadership through a contemporary lens. The story centers on the presidential election campaign of Jack Stanton, and the narrative draws on Bill Clinton's 1992 victory. The narrator is Henry Burton, an idealistic African-American campaign worker modeled on George Stephanopoulos. Although key facts have been altered, both the novel and film capture much of the reality of current political life. As Richard Cohen put it in a *Washington Post* review, sometimes only "fiction can do justice to the truth."[75]

From a leadership standpoint, several themes bear emphasis. One involves the qualities of leaders discussed in Chapters 1 and 2. Stanton, played by John Travolta, projects the magnetism that enabled Bill Clinton to connect to voters, despite his many personal failings. The movie opens with an exploration of the Stanton handshake. The scene then moves to a campaign event at an adult literacy class where Stanton exudes empathy (and follows it up by having a quick fling in a hotel room with the class teacher). This link between Stanton's sexual and political charm also comes through in the novel's portrayal of a conversation between Burton and a woman who had had an affair with Stanton during college. In recalling his two-timing behavior, she notes:

> He loved her. He loved me. He loved every stray cat in the quad. That boy is not deficient in the love zone—he's got more than enough to go around and it's all legit. He's never faking it. . . . I knew I'd never really have him. He was too needy and it wasn't the usual male kind of needy."[76]

Cohen's review observes the same quality, apparent in Clinton as well, and draws connections between these leaders' political strengths and personal weaknesses: "The fictional Stanton is the most indefatigable campaigner of our times, a man whose keenest sexual fantasy is to reach out and hug the American people—touch them all, love them, and have them love him back. If he can't love them that way, he'll just have to love them one at a time."[77] By contrast, Susan Stanton, portrayed by Emma Thompson, captures Hillary Clinton's harder edges but more disciplined strategies. As one reviewer notes, it is the "wronged and humiliated" wife who puts the "steel back in the election effort. Both 'Susan' and Jack Stanton have their eyes on the prize, but Susan/Hillary is the one who keeps her gaze from wandering."[78]

A second theme involves the role of honesty in politics: when and why it sometimes appears expendable. At one campaign event, Stanton tells his audience: "I'm gonna do something really outrageous—tell the truth." The irony of that statement is not lost on Henry Burton, part of the cleanup team for Stanton's indiscretions and deceptions, or on American audiences who hear it through the filter of Clinton's famous falsehoods discussed in Chapter 7.

A third theme involves the role of followers, and the extent to which a leader's "dirty hands" inevitably soil those around them. Henry Burton faces difficult ethical trade-offs, including those that place his loyalty to the black community at issue.

An illuminating sidebar involves the dilemma for Joe Klein, who wrote the novel under the pen name "Anonymous," not expecting either that the book would become "A VERY BIG DEAL" or that his initial denials of authorship would be believed.[79] When they were, both Klein and his publisher saw advantages to retaining anonymity, even though it forced Klein into ever more public lies to colleagues and friends. When the truth finally came out, Klein wrote a rueful half apology in which he acknowledged being "sorry and horrified that [his] actions caused pain for people at *Newsweek*." But he also insisted that the "world didn't really need to know who 'Anonymous' was." And most importantly, he learned

> what it's like to live as a politician. . . . It's impossible to think straight. It's very easy to screw up, and it is unrelenting. But [political candidates] do it every day and that is no way for a civilized nation to choose its leaders. Of course, this was one the themes of "Primary Colors"—but I was just imagining what it was like on the other side of the press conference. Now that I've lived it, I hope I'll show a little more mercy on

this [*Newsweek*] page for the brave, frail fools and heroes who live our public lives. I hope you will too.[80]

QUESTIONS

1. If voters followed Klein's advice, how might that change political campaigns?
2. Consider the discussion of the Clinton-Lewinsky scandal in Chapter 7, as well as the Gennifer Flowers's affair portrayed in the book through the character of Cashmere McCloud. Does the fictional account give you greater understanding of what drives sexual indiscretions, or their relevance to leadership capabilities?
3. Under what circumstances should private sexual affairs ever become matters of public debate? Under what, if any, circumstances, should lies about those affairs be viewed as disqualifying? How do you evaluate Donald Trump's behavior during the 2016 presidential campaign concerning his prior sexual activities? How would you have handled the issue in *Primary Colors* if you had been Jack or Susan Stanton?
4. What "dirty hands" dilemmas did the Stantons face? What would you have done in their place?
5. Was Henry Burton a good follower? Did he make trade-offs that you would not?
6. Another film that explores the relevance of a politician's sexual conduct in determining fitness for public office is *The Frontrunner*. The movie is based on a biography of Gary Hart, a former lawyer and Colorado senator who withdrew from the 1988 presidential race after disclosures that he had lied about his serial infidelity.[81] When reporters questioned him about an extramarital affair, Hart not only denied the adultery, but invited the media to prove him wrong: "Follow me around. I'm serious. If anybody wants to put a tail on me, go ahead. They'll be bored."[82]

   They weren't. And many commentators who were not particularly bothered by Hart's infidelity were troubled by his dishonesty, recklessness, and callous treatment of his wife and mistress. Would such conduct be disqualifying today? Have Trump's extramarital relationships normalized womanizing? How has the activism of the #MeToo movement changed the terms of the debate?

END NOTES

[1] For example, Robert Coles taught a famous course on moral leadership through novels at Harvard that he discusses in THE CALL OF STORIES: TEACHING AND THE MORAL IMAGINATION (1989); Sandra J. Sucher has taught a Harvard course that served as the foundation for her book, THE MORAL LEADER: CHALLENGES, TOOLS AND INSIGHTS (2008); and Scott McClellan has taught leadership through literature at Harvard and Stanford.

[2] ROGER GILL, THEORY AND PRACTICE OF LEADERSHIP 6 (2006) (quoting Hart Leaders Program, Leadership in the Arts, and Edinburgh Festival). For a bibliography on the teaching through fiction, see *Pedagogy of Narrative: A Symposium* 40 J. LEGAL EDUC. (1990). For its value in teaching law, see Kim L. Scheppele, *Forward: Telling Stories,* 87 MICH. L. REV. 2073 (1989); Kathryn Abrams, *Hearing the Call of Stories,* 79 CAL. L. REV. 971 (1991).

[3] MARTHA C. NUSSBAUM, LOVE'S KNOWLEDGE: ESSAYS ON PHILOSOPHY AND LITERATURE 47-48 (1990).

[4] GARY A. KLEIN, SOURCES OF POWER: HOW PEOPLE MAKE DECISIONS 177-96 (1998).

[5] Anton Chekhov, *Gooseberries,* in THE RUSSIAN MASTER AND OTHER STORIES, TRANS., RONALD HINGLEY 132-33 (1984).

[6] COLES, THE CALL OF STORIES, 191, 205.

[7] SUCHER, THE MORAL LEADER, 12.

[8] AYLMER MAUDE, THE LIFE OF TOLSTOY, VOL. 1, 29 (1987).

[9] COUNT LYOF N. TOLSTOI, MY CONFESSION: AND, THE SPIRIT OF CHRIST'S TEACHING 40 (1887).

[10] TOLSTOI, MY CONFESSION, 27.

[11] George J. Gutsche, *Moral Fiction: Tolstoy's Death of Ivan Il'ich,* in GARY R. JAHN, ED., TOLSTOY'S THE DEATH OF IVAN IL'ICH: A CRITICAL COMPANION 55, 57 (1999).

[12] LEO TOLSTOY, TOLSTOY ON SHAKESPEARE: A CRITICAL ESSAY ON SHAKESPEARE, TRANS., VLADIMIR TCHERTKOFF & ISABELLA FYVIE MAYO (1907).

[13] Gutsche, *Moral Fiction,* 61.

[14] VLADIMIR NABOKOV, LECTURES ON RUSSIAN LITERATURE 238 (1981).

[15] A. N. WILSON, TOLSTOY 368 (1988).

[16] Richard Pevear, *Introduction,* in TOLSTOY, THE DEATH OF IVAN ILYCH AND OTHER STORIES, TRANS., RICHARD PEVEAR & LARISSA VOLOKHONSKY (2009).

[17] Gary R. Jahn, *Introduction,* in GARY R. JAHN, ED., TOLSTOY'S THE DEATH OF IVAN IL'ICH 22 (1999).

[18] Robert Russell, *From Individual to Universal: Tolstoy's "Smert" Ivana Il'icha,* 76 MOD. LANG. REV. 629, 639 (1981) (quoting Tolstoy's 1885 letter).

[19] LEO TOLSTOY, THE DEATH OF IVAN ILYCH 22 (1886).

[20] Gary R. Jahn, *The Role of the Ending in Lev Tolstoi's The Death of Ivan Il'ich,* CANADIAN SLAVONIC PAPERS 24, 229, 237 (1982).

[21] *See* DONNA T. ORWIN, THE CAMBRIDGE COMPANION TO TOLSTOY (2002); ROMAIN ROLLAND, THE LIFE OF TOLSTOY, TRANS., B. BIAL (1911); JAHN, TOLSTOY'S THE DEATH OF IVAN IL'ICH; NABOKOV, LECTURES ON RUSSIAN LITERATURE.

[22] http://people.emich.edu/wmoss/publications/.

[23] Timothy Hoff, *Influences on Harper Lee: An Introduction to the Symposium,* 45 ALA. L. REV. 389, 390-401, n.7545 (1994).

[24] Monroe H. Freedman, *Finch: The Lawyer Mythologized,* LEGAL TIMES, May 18, 1992, at 25.

[25] HARPER LEE, TO KILL A MOCKINGBIRD 216 (1960).

[26] Steven Lubet, *Reconstructing Atticus Finch,* 97 MICH. L. REV. 1339, 1345-50 (1999).

[27] LEE, TO KILL A MOCKINGBIRD, 216.

[28] During Finch's cross-examination of Sheriff, Finch asks, "Did anybody call a doctor?" The sheriff responds, "It wasn't necessary," while also acknowledging that "[s]he was mighty banged up." LEE, TO KILL A MOCKINGBIRD, 169-70.

[29] LEE, TO KILL A MOCKINGBIRD, 185.

[30] Malcolm Gladwell, *The Courthouse Ring: Atticus Finch and the Limits of Southern Liberalism,* NEW YORKER, Aug. 10, 2009.

[31] LEE, TO KILL A MOCKINGBIRD, 168. *See* Monroe H. Freedman, *Atticus Finch—Right and Wrong,* 45 ALA. L. REV. 473, 476 (1993).

[32] LEE, TO KILL A MOCKINGBIRD, 62.

[33] Freedman, *Atticus Finch,* at 481.

[34] William H. Simon, *Moral Icons: A Comment on Steven Lubet's Reconstructing Atticus Finch,* 97 MICH. L. REV. 1376, 1377 (1999).

[35] Randolph N. Stone, *Atticus Finch, In Context,* 97 MICH. L. REV. 1378, 1381 (1999).

[36] Randall Kennedy, *Harper Lee's 'Go Set A Watchman,'* N.Y. TIMES (Jul. 14, 2015), http://www.nytimes.com/2015/07/14/books/review/harper-lees-go-set-a-watchman.html.

[37] Alexandra Alter, *While Some Are Shocked by 'Go Set a Watchman,' Others Find Nuance in a Bigoted Atticus Finch,* N.Y. TIMES (Jul. 11, 2015), http://www.nytimes.com/2015/07/12/books/racism-of-atticus-finch-in-go-set-a-watchman-could-alter-harper-lees-legacy.html?.

[38] *See* SUCHER, THE MORAL LEADER, 117-118. *See* Sarah Lyall, *Robert Bolt Is Dead at 70; Oscar-Winning Screenwriter,* N.Y. TIMES, Feb. 23, 1995, at 10.

[39] For overviews, see SUCHER, THE MORAL LEADER, at 111-19; PETER ACKROYD, THE LIFE OF THOMAS MORE (1998); SUSAN BRIGDEN, NEW WORLDS, LOST WORLDS: THE RULE OF THE TUDORS, 1485-1603 (2000).

[40] ROBERT BOLT, PREFACE, A MAN FOR ALL SEASONS: A PLAY IN TWO ACTS xv (1990).

[41] BOLT, PREFACE, 55.

[42] BOLT, PREFACE, 115.

[43] BOLT, PREFACE, 22.

[44] BOLT, PREFACE, 20.

[45] BOLT, PREFACE, 132. For an overview of the conflict, see JOSEPH L. BADARACCO JR., QUESTIONS OF CHARACTER: ILLUMINATING THE HEART OF LEADERSHIP THROUGH LITERATURE 141-50 (2006).

[46] BOLT, A MAN FOR ALL SEASONS, 65-66. For a review of the exchange and its importance, see Patrick J. Whiteley & Robert Bolt, *Natural Law and the Problem of Certainty: Robert Bolt's "A Man for all Seasons,"* CONTEMP. LIT. XLIII 760 (2002).

[47] BOLT, A MAN FOR ALL SEASONS, 158.

[48] T.S. ELIOT, MURDER IN THE CATHEDRAL (1935).

[49] ROBERT PENN WARREN, INTRODUCTION, ALL THE KING'S MEN vi (Modern Library ed. 1953).

[50] WARREN, ALL THE KING'S MEN 75.

[51] WARREN, ALL THE KING'S MEN, 257-58.

[52] WARREN, ALL THE KING'S MEN, 136.

[53] WARREN, ALL THE KING'S MEN, 142.

[54] WARREN, ALL THE KING'S MEN, 418.

[55] WARREN, ALL THE KING'S MEN, 400.

---

[56] Warren began the novel as a verse play in the 1930s, when Long was in his prime. *See* KEITH PERRY, THE KINGFISH IN FICTION: HUEY P. LONG AND THE MODERN AMERICAN NOVEL (2004); Ladell Payne, *Willie Stark and Huey Long: Atmosphere, Myth or Suggestion,* 20 AM. Q. 580 (1968). There are also important differences between Stark's and Long's careers, including the circumstances of their assassinations. For Stark, the cause was an affair; for Long, it was politics.

[57] WARREN, INTRODUCTION, vi.

[58] For a critical commentary, see Joyce Carol Oates, *'All the King's Men'—A Case of Misreading?,* NEW YORK REV. OF BOOKS (NYRB), Mar. 28, 2002; Steven P. Ealy, *Corruption and Innocence in Robert Penn Warren's Fiction,* 47 MOD. AGE 139 (2005); John Blair, *"The Lie We Must Learn to Live By": Honor and Tradition in "All the King's Men,"* 25 STUD. IN THE NOVEL 457 (1993).

[59] Bill Bryson, *Between Two Worlds,* N.Y. TIMES, Aug. 29, 1990 (quoting Ishiguro). For other bibliographic information, see sources cited in SUCHER, THE MORAL LEADER, 103-05.

[60] For women, domestic service was one of the largest categories of work available during the early twentieth century, and the time-intensive work connected with heating, cooking, laundry, and cleaning made servants a necessity for a comfortable middle- or upper-class life. The opening up of job opportunities during the war and postwar periods, coupled with the development of labor saving technologies, led to a dramatic decline in domestic work. *See generally* FRANK DAWES, NOT IN FRONT OF THE SERVANTS: A TRUE PORTRAIT OF UPSTAIRS DOWNSTAIRS LIFE (1989); SUCHER, THE MORAL LEADER, 101-05.

[61] KAZUO ISHIGURO, THE REMAINS OF THE DAY 115-17 (1989).

[62] Patricia Highsmith, *Reminiscences of a Gentleman's Gentleman: The Remains of the Day by Kazuo Ishiguro,* L.A. TIMES, Oct. 1, 1989 (quoting Ishiguro).

[63] ISHIGURO, THE REMAINS OF THE DAY, 147.

[64] ISHIGURO, THE REMAINS OF THE DAY, 149.

[65] ISHIGURO, THE REMAINS OF THE DAY, 148.

[66] ISHIGURO, THE REMAINS OF THE DAY, 151.

[67] ISHIGURO, THE REMAINS OF THE DAY, 153.

[68] ISHIGURO, THE REMAINS OF THE DAY, 153-54.

[69] ISHIGURO, THE REMAINS OF THE DAY, 97.

[70] ISHIGURO, THE REMAINS OF THE DAY, 243.

[71] Rob Atkinson, *How the Butler Was Made to Do It: The Perverted Professionalism of The Remains of the Day,* 105 YALE L.J. 177 (1995-1996).

[72] The comment to Model Rule 1.2 notes that the Rule "confers upon the client the ultimate authority to determine the purposes to be served legal representation, with the limits imposed by law and the lawyer's professional obligations." ABA Model Rules of Professional Conduct (2003).

[73] For discussion of Mandela's leadership, see DEBORAH L. RHODE, CHARACTER: WHAT IT MEANS AND WHY IT MATTERS 186-199 (2019).

[74] WILLIAM ERNEST HENLEY, *Invictus,* in BOOK OF VERSES (1888).

[75] Richard Cohen, *Who Wrote This Book?,* WASH. POST, Jan. 30, 1996, at A15. For some of the differences between fact and fiction, see Robert Stam, *Primary Colors: Adapting the President,* http://www.girlsaresmarter.com/laura/papers/PrimaryColors.html.

[76] Kerry Dougherty, *Washington's Mystery Novel: The Nation's Leaders Are Buzzing about a Clinton Book by an Unnamed Author,* VIRGINIAN-PILOT, Feb. 18, 1996, at 12 (quoting Primary Colors).

[77] Cohen, *Who Wrote this Book?,* at A15.

[78] Alex Beam, *Anonymous' Bedtime Reading Fits the Bill; Book Review: Primary Colors,* B. GLOBE, Feb. 6, 1996, at 53.

[79] Joe Klein, *A Brush with Anonymity,* NEWSWEEK, Jul. 29, 1996.

[80] Klein, *A Brush with Anonymity.*

[81] MATT BAI, ALL THE TRUTH IS OUT: THE WEEK POLITICS WENT TABLOID (2014). For an account of the relationship between Hart's personal conduct and fitness for political office, see DEBORAH L. RHODE, ADULTERY: INFIDELITY AND THE LAW 135-138 (2016).

[82] E. J. Dionne Jr., David Johnston, Wayne King & Jon Nordheimer, *Courting Danger: The Fall of Gary Hart,* N.Y. TIMES, May 9, 1987.

CHAPTER 12

CONCLUSION

"We have all occasionally encountered top persons who couldn't lead a squad of seven year olds to the ice cream counter," noted John Gardiner.[1] This book has attempted to keep you from becoming one of those persons. In that spirit, we close with a review of key insights and thoughts on the legacy that your skills make possible.

A. THE NATURE OF LEADERSHIP

Our discussion began in Chapter 1 with the meaning of leadership and the importance of seeing it as a process, not a position, and as a relationship, not a status. A title may give someone subordinates, but not necessarily followers. To borrow Joseph Nye's metaphor, having a fishing license does not mean you will catch fish.[2] Leadership has to be earned.

The qualities and styles necessary to the task vary somewhat across circumstances. Yet although research reveals no uniform profile of the ideal leader, certain characteristics do appear effective for most leadership situations.[3] They cluster in five categories:

- Values (integrity, honesty, trust, service);
- Personal skills (self-awareness, self-control, and self-direction);
- Interpersonal skills (social intelligence, empathy, persuasion, and collaboration);
- Vision (forward looking, inspirational);
- Technical competence (knowledge, preparation, and judgment).[4]

The need for such qualities has never been greater. Contemporary leaders confront a landscape of increasing competition, complexity, scale, pace, and diversity. Many decisions play out on a wider stage, with less time for informed deliberation. What further complicates these challenges is the "leadership paradox": the frequent disconnect between the qualities that enable individuals to attain positions of power and the qualities that are necessary to perform effectively once they get there. Successful leadership requires subordinating interests in personal achievement to creating the conditions for achievement by others. The best uses of power generally involve empowering followers.

The leaders we most admire generally are able to "gain some degree of freedom from ego," which is often a struggle because those who have achieved positions of influence "have more reason than most to lack humility. . . . But even moderate success in that struggle can be a powerful force for keeping their . . . lives and their work on a positive track."[5]

How then do leaders develop the necessary strategies and skills? Experience is critical, as is reflection on experience—both their own and that of others. As Aldous Huxley put it, "[E]xperience is not what happens to a man. It is what a man does with what happens to him."[6] Aspiring leaders need to seek opportunities for exercising influence, obtaining candid feedback, and learning from research and educational initiatives. Those who have obtained positions of power can assist the process by creating "learning organizations" that will effectively generate, transfer, and incorporate knowledge, as well as develop new leaders.[7] Those who are most effective in enlisting others are generally able to recognize their own limitations, and who invite and respond to constructive criticism.[8]

B. LEADERSHIP SKILLS

What are the key skills that leaders need to learn? One involves decision-making. To be effective, lawyers should engage in conscious deliberation before and after they act. Rather than simply reacting to events, successful leaders consider what they most want to achieve and anticipate what might stand in the way. After they act, these leaders reflect on what worked and what did not, and what they might do differently in the future.[9] Skilled decision makers also recognize that even the most thoughtful processes are subject to biases in perception, memory, and problem solving. Sound judgment depends on recognizing bounded rationality and building in appropriate correctives. Information that is vivid or consistent with stereotypes and self-interest will be disproportionately "available" to skew decision-making unless leaders make conscious adjustments. Cost-benefit calculations can go awry due to psychic numbing and the salience of individual victims and immediate consequences; these dynamics can lead to overinvestment in short-term remedial responses and underinvestment in long-term preventative strategies. Groupthink and social pressure can also sabotage judgment. Creating processes that will ensure independent and diverse points of view is an essential leadership skill.

Mastering strategies of influence is equally critical. Power comes in multiple currencies, and often the most obvious rewards and sanctions are less available or effective than other persuasive approaches, such as reciprocity, peer pressure, or association. These techniques are essential in building relationships in a world in which boundaries separating leaders and followers are increasingly blurred. Leaders also need strategies for innovation and conflict management. To be successful, they have to overcome inertia, chart a path for change, and create environments that will sustain it. In dealing with conflict, avoidance is generally to be avoided. In most cases, the preferable approach is collaborative problem solving, in which parties build on shared concerns and respect in search of mutual gain. Leaders can facilitate the process, not only by assisting individual dispute resolution, but also by creating "conflict competent" organizations that can do the same.

Finally, leaders need effective communication skills. They should know their objectives, their audience, their occasion, and their substance. To create messages "made to stick," speakers should look for material that is succinct, unexpected, credible, emotional, and that tells a story. They should avoid the curse of knowledge; less may be more, and visual images may be the most powerful persuasive strategy.

C. VALUES IN LEADERSHIP

Effective leadership depends not only on skills but also on values. Challenges often arise when ethical commitments are in conflict or in tension with situational pressures. Leaders face trade-offs between immoral means and moral ends; adherence to principles often comes at a cost.

Dilemmas of "dirty hands" are particularly common in political life, and those that Machiavelli described five centuries ago play out in similar forms in contemporary settings. Although many of these dilemmas lack clear answers, leaders need to be accountable for their responses, and their choices need to serve public, not just personal interests. Lawyers who lead must find ways of reinforcing ethical behavior. That, in turn, requires addressing the peer pressures, cognitive biases, individual self-interests, and diffusion of responsibility that compromise moral judgment. Research on the banality of evil makes clear how readily minor missteps or social conformity can entrap individuals in major misconduct. To maintain their moral compass, leaders as well as followers should consult widely, enlist allies, observe bright-line rules, and cultivate self-doubt. Those in leadership positions can also foster ethical conduct by setting the tone at the top, establishing appropriate reward structures, and ensuring adequate oversight.

Leaders also need private lives that are consistent with professional responsibilities. Power both imposes special obligations and creates special temptations. Leaders have more than the customary opportunities for abuse; they are surrounded by subordinates reluctant to challenge it. Self-serving biases can further reinforce leaders' sense of entitlement and invulnerability. The result is a steady stream of scandal, fed by media eager to fill a continuous news cycle, and equipped with technological resources to make it possible. In this climate, crisis management has become a critical part of the leadership tool kit, and the art of apology is an essential skill. So too is the capacity to use scandals as catalysts for constructive change. Market meltdowns, environmental disasters, or product defects can supply the urgency needed for organizational and regulatory reform. Where personal conduct is at issue, leaders need to be attentive to even the appearance of impropriety. In an era of increasing transparency and instant notoriety, those in positions of power need to consider how private conduct would play in public settings, before it is too late to change.

D. LEADERSHIP CHALLENGES

Contemporary leaders face a host of challenges, and diversity is high among them. Appropriate responses require understanding how characteristics such as race, ethnicity, and gender matter in the selection and performance of leaders. Despite considerable progress over the last half century, lawyers of color and women of all races and ethnicities are underrepresented in positions of influence. Unconscious stereotypes, in-group biases, and inflexible workplace structures remain substantial obstacles. There are strong reasons to address them. Women and men of color together constitute the majority of today's legal talent, and effective performance in an increasingly multicultural environment demands a level playing field. When managed well, diversity can also enhance the quality and legitimacy of decision-making. To that end, leadership strategies should proceed on three levels: helping underrepresented groups develop leadership skills, qualifications, and sponsors; promoting diversity and inclusion initiatives; and increasing accountability for progress.

For lawyers in private practice, other challenges arise from market pressures and governance structures. Leaders of law firms are coping with increased competition for client business and legal talent. To be effective, they need deep understanding of their firm's mission, market, strengths, and limitations. They also need the interpersonal skills that can forge consensus around a shared vision, compatible goals, and strategic plan. General counsel need to juggle multiple roles and loyalties. Their client is an organization that speaks through management and a board that may have competing objectives. Effectively responding to those concerns requires both legal and business skills as well as an independent moral compass. Lawyers in private practice also have unique opportunities and obligations to give back through pro bono service. Leaders can create the conditions that encourage these contributions and ensure their quality and cost effectiveness.

Lawyers who spearhead movements for social change also face complex challenges. These leaders play a pivotal role in creating or capitalizing on conditions for progress. Their ability to inspire hope, enlist allies, attract public support, and reinforce shared identities can provide the foundations for social transformation. However, the best path forward is seldom self-evident. Conflicts often arise about timing or strategies, such as when to litigate, which cases to bring, and who should decide. A distinguishing feature of great leaders is the ability to mediate such disputes and build a coherent unifying strategy in pursuit of social justice.

E. THE LEGACY OF LEADERSHIP

Leadership not only poses special challenges and special obligations, it can also bring exceptional rewards. Those that are most fulfilling are generally not, however, the extrinsic perks that accompany positions of power. A wide array of psychological research suggests that satisfaction with work depends on feeling effective, exercising strengths and virtues, and contributing to socially valued ends that bring meaning and purpose.[10] Goals that transcend the self have the greatest impact on people's sense of fulfillment.[11] As one British military leader put it, "You make a living by what you get; you make a life by what you give."[12] Individuals who are motivated by "intrinsic aspirations," such as personal growth, interpersonal relationships, and social contributions, tend to be more satisfied than those motivated primarily by extrinsic aspirations, such as wealth or fame.[13] Part of the reason is that desires, expectations, and standards of comparison tend to increase as rapidly as they are satisfied. Leaders can become trapped on a "hedonic treadmill": the more they have the more they need to have.[14] So too, money and status are positional goods; individuals' satisfaction depends on how they compare relative to others, and increases in wealth or position are readily offset by changes in reference groups.[15] Leaders who look hard enough can always find someone getting more.

How then can individuals with high needs for achievement and recognition find greatest fulfillment? Positive psychology research points to the importance of strong relationships and a sense of meaning and accomplishment, which generally involve contributing to a legacy that transcends self-interest.[16] Similar findings came from a study by Laura Nash and Howard Stevenson of the Harvard Business School, which focused on leaders who by conventional standards had achieved "success that lasts":

> Our research uncovered four irreducible components of enduring success: happiness (feelings of pleasure and contentment); achievement (accomplishments that compare favorably against similar goals others have strived for); significance (the sense that you've made a positive impact on people you care about); and legacy (a way to establish your values or accomplishments . . .).[17]

The challenge for leaders is how to set priorities that strike a balance among all four domains. Many believe that the primary goal in life is to be happy. Yet research indicates that happiness is most often a byproduct of participating in worthwhile activities that do not have happiness as their primary goal.[18] Well-being generally requires both pleasure and meaning: the experience of positive emotions in the present, and the pursuit of goals that will have meaning over time. The philosopher William James insisted that the greatest use of life is to spend it on something that outlasts it, and contemporary social science research points in a similar direction.[19]

Leaders should not, however, confuse fame with legacy.[20] As Chapter 1 noted, a focus on ensuring recognition of one's legacy can get in the way of achieving it; leaders can be tempted to hoard power, status, and credit. It is important to distinguish between "making a difference" and "making 'my' difference and making sure everyone knows it."[21] As English essayist Charles Montague noted, "there is no limit to what a man can do so long as he does not care a straw who gets the credit for it."[22] Leaders can never control how others will ultimately interpret their contributions; pigeons may nest on unvisited monuments. Thinking about legacy is helpful only if it directs attention to ultimate goals and values, not if it diverts energy into futile quests for lasting glory.

It is never too soon for leaders to be thinking about what they want said at their eulogies. Marion Wright Edelman, head of the Children's Defense Fund, recalled an entry in her journal at the beginning of her work in civil rights: "The time has come for you, Marion, to have a frank talk with yourself. Where are you headed? . . . Get a hold of yourself and then forget yourself. What do you really want. . . ?"[23] Columnist David Brooks suggests focusing less on "resume virtues" and more on "eulogy virtues."[24] To that end, leaders should focus on several key issues.

- Who am I? What are my character strengths and deficiencies today?
- Who am I becoming? What is . . . my character likely to be tomorrow if I carry on with the way I'm doing things now?
- What do I want to be? What is it about my character that I'd like to change . . . ?
- What am I going to do to become what I want to be? What actions will I take . . . ? How will I know that I've got there?[25]

Disaffected leaders have often stopped asking those questions. These are individuals who feel that "something is missing" and that "somewhere along the way they got off track. They're working harder than ever, but they're not sure why and they've lost touch with what's important in life."[26] Some "successful" leaders who have focused on the external trappings of success have been sustained by the assumption that once they reached the pinnacle, they would be happy:

> And then they get there, and the 'there' that they expected is nowhere to be found. Having been stripped of the illusion that most people live under—that material prosperity can provide lasting happiness—they are struck by the 'what now?' syndrome."[27]

When that happens, leaders need to ask hard questions about what they truly value and how they can make a difference. Michael Lewis reminds aspiring professionals that "when you start your career, you might think you are going to change the world, but the world is far more likely to change you. So watch yourself, because no one else will."[28]

Abraham Lincoln was a lawyer legendary for setting aside his own concerns in the service of broader ends. He put rivals in his cabinet and appointed Salmon Chase, who had frequently campaigned against him, as Chief Justice of the Supreme Court.[29] As Lincoln told a colleague at the time, he "would rather have swallowed his buckhorn chair than to have nominated Chase," but the decision was right for the country.[30] Such priorities began early. When Lincoln was 23 years old and running for office the first time, he said, "Every man is said to have his peculiar ambition. I have no other so great as that of being truly esteemed of my fellow men, by rendering myself worthy of their esteem."[31]

In commenting on that quote, Barack Obama, at the end of his second presidential term, offered a "friendly amendment." He believed that youthful ambition "has very much to do with making your mark in the world." But after leaders have achieved some notoriety, "there's a point when the vanity burns away. . . . And then you are really focused on: What am I going to get done with this strange privilege that's been granted to me? How do I make myself worthy of it? And if you don't go through that, then you start getting into trouble, because then you're just . . . clinging to the prerogatives and the power and the attention."[32] In Obama's view, "if you're going to grow up as a politician or as a person, then at a certain point the vanity has to fade away. Then you have to be doing these things for something bigger than yourself."[33] For him, the longer he had been in politics, the more that "striving for power and rank and fame seems to betray a poverty of ambition, and that I am answerable to the steady gaze of my own conscience."[34]

When asked how he wished to be remembered, Supreme Court Justice Thurgood Marshall responded: "He did what he could with what he had."[35] Leaders have many ways to leave a legacy. For most lawyers, it is less through grand triumphs of historical importance than through smaller acts that, taken together, improve the lives and institutions around them. Our hope is that this book will aid your leadership, and prompt deeper reflection about what your own legacy will be.

END NOTES

[1] JOHN W. GARDNER, ON LEADERSHIP 2 (1990).

[2] JOSEPH S. NYE JR., THE POWERS TO LEAD 19 (2008).

[3] *See* Robert Goffee & Gareth Jones, *Why Should Anyone Be Led by You?*, HARV. BUS. REV. 63, 64 (Sept.-Oct. 2000); Jay W. Lorsch, *A Contingency Theory of Leadership,* in NITIN NOHRIA & RAKESH KHURANA, HANDBOOK OF LEADERSHIP THEORY AND PRACTICE 411-424 (2010).

[4] For values, see WARREN BENNIS, ON BECOMING A LEADER 32-33 (2d ed. 1994) (citing integrity, trust); MONTGOMERY VAN WART, DYNAMICS OF LEADERSHIP IN PUBLIC SERVICE: THEORY AND PRACTICE 16, 92-119 (2005) (citing integrity and an ethic of public service); JAMES M. KOUZES & BARRY Z. POSNER, THE LEADERSHIP CHALLENGE: HOW TO

MAKE EXTRAORDINARY THINGS HAPPEN IN ORGANIZATIONS 21 (4th ed. 1995) (citing honesty). For personal skills, see DANIEL GOLEMAN, RICHARD BOYATZIS & ANNIE MCKEE, PRIMAL LEADERSHIP: REALIZING THE POWER OF EMOTIONAL INTELLIGENCE 253-56 (2002) (citing self-awareness, self-management); VAN WART, DYNAMICS, 16 (citing self-direction). For interpersonal skills, see GOLEMAN, BOYATZIS & MCKEE, PRIMAL LEADERSHIP, 253-56 (citing social awareness, empathy, persuasion, and conflict management). For vision, see BENNIS, ON BECOMING A LEADER 33 (citing vision); KOUZES & POSNER, LEADERSHIP CHALLENGE, 21 (citing foresight, the ability to inspire). For competence, see KOUZES & POSNER, LEADERSHIP CHALLENGE, 21; LORSCH, A CONTINGENCY THEORY, 417. For judgment, see NOEL M. TICHY & WARREN G. BENNIS, JUDGMENT: HOW WINNING LEADERS MAKE GREAT CALLS (2007).

[5] WILLIAM DAMON & ANNE COLBY, THE POWER OF IDEALS: THE REAL STORY OF MORAL CHOICE 150 (2015).

[6] Aldous Huxley, *The Perennial Philosophy*, quoted in WARREN G. BENNIS & ROBERT J. THOMAS, LEADING FOR A LIFETIME: HOW DEFINING MOMENTS SHAPE LEADERS OF TODAY AND TOMORROW 94 (2007).

[7] David A. Gavin, *Building a Learning Organization*, HARV. BUS. REV. 78-79 (July-Aug. 1993).

[8] DAMON & COLBY, THE POWER OF IDEALS, 148.

[9] LINDA A. HILL & KENT LINEBECK, BEING THE BOSS: THE 3 IMPERATIVES FOR BECOMING A GREAT LEADER 215 (2011).

[10] DAVID G. MYERS, THE PURSUIT OF HAPPINESS: WHO IS HAPPY, AND WHY? 32-38 (1992); David G. Myers & Ed Diener, *Who Is Happy,* 6 PSYCHOL. SCI. 10, 17 (1995); CHRISTOPHER PETERSON & MARTIN E.P. SELIGMAN, CHARACTER STRENGTHS AND VIRTUES: A HANDBOOK AND CLASSIFICATION (2004); WILLIAM C. COMPTON, AN INTRODUCTION TO POSITIVE PSYCHOLOGY 48-49, 53-54 (2004); Ed Diener et al., *Subjective Well-Being: Three Decades of Progress,* 125 PSYCHOL. BULL. 276 (1999).

[11] JONATHAN HAIDT, THE HAPPINESS HYPOTHESIS: FINDING MODERN TRUTH IN ANCIENT WISDOM 88, 170 (2006); THOMAS J. DELONG, FLYING WITHOUT A NET: TURN FEAR OF CHANGE INTO FUEL FOR SUCCESS 47-48 (2011).

[12] This quote has been attributed to Air Vice-Marshal Sir Norman Duckworth Kerr MacEwen, but its definitive origin is unknown.

[13] Christopher P. Niemiec, Richard M. Ryan & Edward L. Dei, *The Path Taken: Consequences of Attaining Intrinsic and Extrinsic Aspirations in Post-College Life,* 43 J. RES. PERS. 291 (2009); Robert A. Emmons, *Personal Goals, Life Meaning, and Virtue: Well Springs of a Positive Life,* in FLOURISHING: POSITIVE PSYCHOLOGY AND THE LIFE WELL-LIVED (Corey L. M. Keyes & Jonathan Haidt eds., 2003); Tim Kasser & Richard M. Ryan, *Further Examining the American Dream: Differential Correlates of Intrinsic and Extrinsic Goals,* 22 PERS. & SOC. PSYCHOL. BULL. 280 (1996); Kennon M. Sheldon and Andrew J. Elliot, *Goal Striving, Need Satisfaction and Longitudinal Well-Being: The Self-Concordance Model,* 76 J. PERS. & SOC, PSYCHOL. 482 (1999).

[14] MARTIN E.P. SELIGMAN, AUTHENTIC HAPPINESS: USING THE NEW POSITIVE PSYCHOLOGY TO REALIZE YOUR POTENTIAL FOR LASTING FULFILLMENT 49 (2002); Ed Diener, Richard E. Lucas & Christie Napa Scollon, *Beyond the Hedonic Treadmill: Revising the Adaptation Theory of Well-Being,* 61 AM. PSYCHOL. 305 (2006).

[15] Robert H. Frank, *How Not to Buy Happiness,* 133 DAEDALUS 69, 69-71 (2004); MYERS, THE PURSUIT OF HAPPINESS, 39.

[16] Martin E. P. Seligman, Flourish: A Visionary New Understanding of Happiness and Well-Being 16 (2011); Joo Yeon Shin & Michael F. Steger, *Promoting Meaning and Purpose in Life*, in The Wiley Blackwell Handbook of Positive Psychological Interventions 95 (Acacia C. Parks & Steven M. Schueller eds., 2014); Robert A. Emmons, *Personal Goals, Life Meaning, and Virtue: Well Springs of a Positive Life*, in Flourishing: Positive Psychology and the Life Well-Lived 108 (Corey L. M. Keyes & Jonathan Haidt eds., 2003); Emmons, *Personal Goals*, 108.

[17] Laura Nash & Howard H. Stevenson, *Success That Lasts*, 102 Harv. Bus. Rev. 104 (Feb. 2004).

[18] Emmons, *Personal Goals*, 105-106.

[19] Shin & Steger, *Promoting Meaning and Purpose in Life*, 95; Patrick McKnight & Todd B. Kashdan, *Purpose in Life as a System That Creates and Sustains Health and Well-Being: An Integrative, Testable Theory*, 13 Rev. Gen. Psychol. 242 (2009).

[20] J. Patrick Dobel, *Managerial Leadership and the Ethical Importance of Legacy*, in Denis Saint-Martin & Fred Thompson, Public Ethics and Governance: Standards and Practices in Comparative Perspective 195, 200-203 (2006).

[21] Dobel, *Managerial Leadership*, 201.

[22] Fred R. Shapiro, The Yale Book of Quotations 532 (2006) (quoting Montague).

[23] Marion Wright Edelman, Lanterns: A Memoir of Mentors 61 (1999).

[24] David Brooks, The Road to Character (2015). Brooks's TED Talk is available at https://www.ted.com/talks/david_brooks_should_you_live_for_your_resume_or_your_eulogy/discussion#t-1427.

[25] Mary Crossan, Gerard Seijts & Jeffrey Gandz, Developing Leadership Character 184 (2016).

[26] Lee G. Bolman & Terrence E. Deal, Leading With Soul: An Uncommon Journey of Spirit 5 (2011).

[27] Tal Ben-Shahar, Happier: Learn the Secrets to Daily Joy and Lasting Fulfillment 57 (2007).

[28] Michael Lewis, *Occupational Hazards of Working on Wall Street,* Bloomberg View (Sept. 24, 2014), https://www.bloomberg.com/opinion/articles/2014-09-24/occupational-hazards-of-working-on-wall-street.

[29] Archie Brown, The Myth of the Strong Leader: Political Leadership in the Modern Age 346-47 (2014); Doris Kearns Goodwin, Team of Rivals: The Political Genius of Abraham Lincoln (2006).

[30] Brown, The Myth of the Strong Leader, 347 (quoting Lincoln).

[31] Doris Kearns Goodwin, *Barack Obama and Doris Kearns Goodwin: The Ultimate Exit Interview*, Vanity Fair, Nov. 2016, at 158 (quoting Lincoln).

[32] Goodwin, *Barack Obama and Doris Kearns Goodwin*, at 159 (quoting Obama).

[33] Jessica Curry, *Barack Obama: Under the Lights*, Chi. Life, Aug. 1, 2004.

[34] Barack Obama, The Audacity of Hope: Thoughts on Reclaiming the American Dream 134 (2006).

[35] Ruth Marcus, *Plain-Spoken Marshall Spars with Reporters,* Wash. Post, June 29, 1991, at A1, A10.

INDEX